The Routledge Handbook of Metaphor and Language

The Routledge Handbook of Metaphor and Language provides a comprehensive overview of state-of-the-art interdisciplinary research on metaphor and language. Featuring 35 chapters, written by leading scholars from around the world, the volume takes a broad view of the field of metaphor and language, and brings together diverse and distinct theoretical and applied perspectives to cover six key areas:

- Theoretical approaches to metaphor and language, covering Conceptual Metaphor Theory, Relevance Theory, Blending Theory and Dynamical Systems Theory;
- Methodological approaches to metaphor and language, discussing ways of identifying metaphors in verbal texts, images and gestures, as well as the use of corpus linguistics;
- Formal variation in patterns of metaphor use across text types, historical periods and languages;
- Functional variation of metaphor, in contexts including educational, commercial, scientific and political discourse, as well as online trolling;
- The applications of metaphor for problem solving, in business, education, healthcare and conflict situations;
- Language, metaphor, and cognitive development, examining the processing and comprehension of metaphors.

The Routledge Handbook of Metaphor and Language is a must-have survey of this key field, and is essential reading for those interested in language and metaphor.

Elena Semino is Professor of Linguistics and Verbal Art and Head of the Department of Linguistics and English Language at Lancaster University, UK. She also holds a Visiting Professorship at Fuzhou University in China.

Zsófia Demjén is Senior Lecturer in Applied Linguistics at UCL Institute of Education, University College London, UK.

Routledge Handbooks in Linguistics
Routledge Handbooks in Linguistics provide overviews of a whole subject area or subdiscipline in linguistics, and survey the state of the discipline including emerging and cutting edge areas. Edited by leading scholars, these volumes include contributions from key academics from around the world and are essential reading for both advanced undergraduate and postgraduate students.

The Routledge Handbook of Syntax
Edited by Andrew Carnie, Yosuke Sato and Daniel Siddiqi

The Routledge Handbook of Historical Linguistics
Edited by Claire Bowern and Bethwyn Evans

The Routledge Handbook of Language and Culture
Edited by Farzad Sharifian

The Routledge Handbook of Semantics
Edited by Nick Riemer

The Routledge Handbook of Linguistics
Edited by Keith Allan

The Routledge Handbook of the English Writing System
Edited by Vivian Cook and Des Ryan

The Routledge Handbook of Metaphor and Language
Edited by Elena Semino and Zsófia Demjén

The Routledge Handbook of Language and Media
Edited by Daniel Perrin and Colleen Cotter

The Routledge Handbook of Phonological Theory
Edited by S.J. Hannahs and Anna Bosch

The Routledge Handbook of Theoretical and Experimental Sign Language Research
Edited by Annika Hermann, Roland Pfau and Josep Quer

The Routledge Handbook of Linguistic Anthropology
Edited by Nancy Bonvillain

The Routledge Handbook of Metaphor and Language

*Edited by Elena Semino and
Zsófia Demjén*

Routledge
Taylor & Francis Group

LONDON AND NEW YORK

First published 2017
by Routledge
2 Park Square, Milton Park, Abingdon, Oxon OX14 4RN

and by Routledge
52 Vanderbilt Avenue, New York, NY 10017

First issued in paperback 2020

Routledge is an imprint of the Taylor & Francis Group, an informa business

© 2017 selection and editorial matter, Elena Semino and Zsófia Demjén; individual chapters, the contributors

The right of the editors to be identified as the authors of the editorial material, and of the authors for their individual chapters, has been asserted in accordance with sections 77 and 78 of the Copyright, Designs and Patents Act 1988.

All rights reserved. No part of this book may be reprinted or reproduced or utilized in any form or by any electronic, mechanical, or other means, now known or hereafter invented, including photocopying and recording, or in any information storage or retrieval system, without permission in writing from the publishers.

Trademark notice: Product or corporate names may be trademarks or registered trademarks, and are used only for identification and explanation without intent to infringe.

British Library Cataloguing-in-Publication Data
A catalogue record for this book is available from the British Library.

Library of Congress Cataloging-in-Publication Data
A catalog record for this title has been requested

ISBN 13: 978-0-367-58142-8 (pbk)
ISBN 13: 978-1-138-77536-7 (hbk)

Typeset in Times New Roman
by Swales & Willis Ltd, Exeter, Devon, UK

Contents

List of figures ix
List of tables x
Acknowledgements xi
Contributors xii

Introduction: metaphor and language 1
Zsófia Demjén and Elena Semino

PART I
Theoretical approaches to metaphor and language **11**

1 Conceptual metaphor theory 13
   Zoltán Kövecses

2 Figurativeness, conceptual metaphor, and blending 28
   Barbara Dancygier

3 Relevance theory and metaphor 42
   Robyn Carston

4 Metaphor, language, and dynamical systems 56
   Raymond W. Gibbs, Jr.

PART II
Methodological approaches to metaphor and language **71**

5 Identifying metaphors in language 73
   Gerard Steen

6	Finding systematic metaphors *Robert Maslen*	88
7	From linguistic to conceptual metaphors *Alice Deignan*	102
8	Corpus-linguistic approaches to metaphor analysis *Heli Tissari*	117
9	Analysing metaphor in gesture: a set of metaphor identification guidelines for gesture (MIG-G) *Alan Cienki*	131
10	Analysing metaphors in multimodal texts *Elisabeth El Refaie*	148

PART III
Formal variation of metaphor in language — **163**

11	Metaphor and parts-of-speech *Tina Krennmayr*	165
12	Textual patterning of metaphor *Aletta G. Dorst*	178
13	Genre and metaphor: use and variation across usage events *Rosario Caballero*	193
14	Creative metaphor in literature *Marco Caracciolo*	206
15	Conventional and novel metaphors in language *Gill Philip*	219
16	Metaphor and diachronic variation *Wendy Anderson*	233
17	Metaphor in translation *Christina Schäffner*	247
18	Metaphor in sign language *Michiko Kaneko and Rachel Sutton-Spence*	263

PART IV
Functional variation of metaphor in language — 281

19 Metaphor use in educational contexts: functions and variations — 283
    Jeannette Littlemore

20 Metaphor and the representation of scientific issues: climate change in print and online media — 296
    Nelya Koteyko and Dimitrinka Atanasova

21 Metaphor and persuasion in politics — 309
    Andreas Musolff

22 Metaphor and persuasion in commercial advertising — 323
    Laura Hidalgo-Downing and Blanca Kraljevic-Mujic

23 Metaphor and story-telling — 337
    L. David Ritchie

24 Metaphor, impoliteness, and offence in online communication — 353
    Zsófia Demjén and Claire Hardaker

PART V
Applications and interventions: using metaphor for problem solving — 369

25 Using metaphor in healthcare: mental health — 371
    Dennis Tay

26 Using metaphor in healthcare: physical health — 385
    Zsófia Demjén and Elena Semino

27 Using metaphor as a management tool — 400
    Linda Greve

28 Using metaphor in the teaching of second/foreign languages — 413
    Fiona MacArthur

29 Using metaphor for peace-building, empathy, and reconciliation — 426
    Lynne Cameron

30 Using metaphor to influence public perceptions and policy: how metaphors can save the world — 443
    Joseph Grady

PART VI
Language, metaphor, and cognitive development   **455**

31 Metaphor processing   457
Herbert L. Colston and Raymond W. Gibbs, Jr.

32 Psycholinguistic approaches to metaphor acquisition and use   472
Albert N. Katz

33 Metaphor acquisition and use in individuals with neurodevelopmental disorders   486
Gabriella Rundblad

34 Metaphor comprehension and production in a second language   503
Susan Nacey

Epilogue: metaphors for language and communication   517
Philip Eubanks

Index   *529*

Figures

2.1	ARGUMENT IS WAR: the conceptual metaphor	30
2.2	ARGUMENT IS WAR: the blend	33
9.1	Gesture produced when saying 'draw your line'	132
9.2	Preparation phase (2a), stroke phase (2b), retraction phase (2c)	138
10.1	Forney's *Marbles* (2012), p. 59	156
10.2	Forney's *Marbles* (2012), p. 49	158
10.3	Forney's *Marbles* (2012), p. 77	159
15.1	Definition of 'banana' (Sinclair 2001). Cobuild	223
15.2	Output from @MetaphorMagnet	230
18.1	The BSL sign WHAT	265
18.2	(a) an established sign for dog in BSL; (b) productive sign showing the dog enthusiastically wagging its tail at a human beside it; (c) productive sign showing the dog running	266
18.3	The sign TREE	271
18.4	Metaphorical and iconic mappings for the sign EAT	273
18.5	Metaphorical and iconic mappings for the sign MAINSTREAM	273
18.6	The sign REINDEER	274
18.7	The signs with bent fingers in Wim Emmerik's *Garden of Eden*	276
18.8	Handshapes used in this chapter	279
22.1	Huawei ad	332
25.1	Enhancing therapeutic protocols which use metaphor	377
27.1	Two buildings from the dataset, showing two different representations of knowledge	409
29.1	Discourse dynamics model of empathy–dyspathy	438

Tables

6.1	Sample vehicle groups in PCTR research	94
6.2	Metaphors of government responses to terrorism as violent physical action	95
6.3	Data from analysis of *Evangelii Gaudium*	97
7.1	Using the five steps to analyse war metaphors	106
7.2	Most significant collocates of 'horse' and 'galloping'	111
8.1	Metaphors of hope in the corpora per 10,000 words	125
10.1	Possible distribution of roles in verbo-pictorial metaphors	151
11.1	Absolute numbers and percentages of metaphorically used words in four different registers in the VU Amsterdam Metaphor Corpus	174
13.1	Rhetorical structure of architectural reviews	200
16.1	Senses of *inflame* in the *Historical Thesaurus of English* with corresponding Mapping Metaphor category headings	240
16.2	Connections between 'Illumination' and categories in the area of life and movement	242
16.3	Connections between 'Illumination' and categories in the area of the mind and thought	243
21.1	Range and size of the whole corpus	315
26.1	MELC corpus composition	394
34.1	Translations of *karakteristisk for hans kjerringa-mot-strømmen-holdning*	512

Acknowledgements

First and foremost, we wish to thank the authors of the 34 chapters and Epilogue of this handbook for their hard work and patience as we assembled this volume. The handbook, quite literally, would not have been possible without them. We are also grateful to Veronika Koller for her contribution to the early stages of this project, and to John Heywood for his advice and attention to detail in proofreading a number of the chapters.

We are grateful to Nadia Seemungal, Helen Tredget and Rachel Daw at Routledge for their support throughout the editing process and to Lizzie Kent for her wonderful attention to detail.

The editors and publisher are grateful to the following for permission to reproduce copyrighted materials: Equinox Publishing for the tables from Cameron and Maslen's (2010) *Metaphor Analysis* in Chapter 6; CTS Publishing for extracts from the English translation of the papal exhortation *Evangelii Gaudium* in Chapter 6; Gotham Books, an imprint of Penguin Publishing Group, a division of Penguin Random House LLC, for extracts from *Marbles: Mania, Depression, Michelangelo, and Me: A Graphic Memoir* by Ellen Forney, copyright 2012 by Ellen Forney, in Chapter 10; Paul Scott, Richard Carter and Tim Northam for their kind permission to use their images in Chapter 18; Huawei for the advertisement in Chapter 22; and the *Journal of Cognitive Linguistics* (periodically published by the Japanese Cognitive Linguistics Association; publisher: Kaitakusha, Tokyo) for the article on which Chapter 30 is based: Grady, J. (2015) 'Metaphor and the public interest: how metaphors can save the world', *Journal of Cognitive Linguistics*, 1: 99–112.

Contributors

Wendy Anderson is Reader in English Language and Linguistics at the University of Glasgow. She is Principal Investigator of the 'Mapping Metaphor with the *Historical Thesaurus*' project (www.gla.ac.uk/metaphor) and of the follow-on project 'Metaphor in the Curriculum'. Her broader research and teaching interests lie in semantics, corpus linguistics and intercultural language education.

Dimitrinka Atanasova is Research Assistant at Queen Mary University of London. She is interested in health and science communication, framing and discourse analysis and metaphors. Her work has appeared in *Obesity Reviews*, *Environmental Communication* and *Public Understanding of Science* among others. Prior to her PhD, she was a media consultant.

Rosario Caballero is Associate Professor in the Universidad de Castilla-La Mancha. Her research interests include professional genres, the role of metaphor in genre, and sensory language. She is the author of *Re-viewing Space: Figurative Language in Architects' Assessment of Built Space* (2006, Mouton), the co-editor of *Sensuous Cognition. Explorations into Human Sentience: Imagination, (E)motion and Perception* (2013, Mouton) and the author of journal papers on metaphor in several discourse genres.

Lynne Cameron is currently Senior Fellow and Artist-in-Residence at the Cinépoetics project, Freie Universität, Berlin. She is also Professor Emerita at The Open University, UK, having left the university in 2014 to work as full-time artist. In metaphor studies, she spent many years researching metaphor in talk and developing the Discourse Dynamics approach. She co-founded the Researching and Applying Metaphor (RaAM) Association and the journal *Metaphor and the Social World*. Her books include *Metaphor in Educational Discourse* (2003), *Researching and Applying Metaphor* (1999, co-edited with Graham Low), *Metaphor Analysis* (2010, co-edited with Robert Maslen) and *Metaphor and Reconciliation* (2011).

Marco Caracciolo is a Postdoctoral Researcher at the English Department of the University of Freiburg (Germany) and at the Freiburg Institute for Advanced Studies. He is interested mainly in phenomenological approaches to literature and cognitive narrative theory. He is the author of *The Experientiality of Narrative: An Enactivist Approach* (De Gruyter, 2014) and *A Passion for Specificity: Confronting Inner Experience in Literature and Science* (co-authored with psychologist Russell Hurlburt; Ohio State University Press, 2016).

Robyn Carston is Professor of Linguistics at University College London and Senior Researcher at the CSMN, Oslo. Her work on language and communication is strongly interdisciplinary, integrating ideas from linguistics, philosophy of language and cognitive science. Her research areas include the semantics/pragmatics distinction, explicit and implicit communication, relevance theory, non-literal uses of language, and the nature of word meaning. Her publications include the widely cited monograph *Thoughts and Utterances* (2002, Blackwell); she is currently working on a collection of papers, *Pragmatics and Semantic Content*, to be published by Oxford University Press.

Alan Cienki is Professor of Language Use and Cognition at the Vrije Universiteit, Amsterdam, the Netherlands, and Director of the Multimodal Communication and Cognition Lab at Moscow State Linguistic University, Russia. He co-edited the book *Metaphor and Gesture* (Benjamins, 2008) and the two-volume handbook *Body–Language–Communication* (De Gruyter, 2013, 2014). He has served as Chair of the Association for Researching and Applying Metaphor and as Vice President of the International Society for Gesture Studies.

Herbert L. Colston is Professor and Chair of the Department of Linguistics at the University of Alberta, Canada. His research addresses comprehension, usage and production of a variety of figurative language forms, as well as how social, psychological, multimodal and other processes contribute to figurative and other language processing proper to affect meaning and pragmatic effects. He has published four books – most recently, *Using Figurative Language* with Cambridge University Press (2015).

Barbara Dancygier is Professor in the Department of English, University of British Columbia, Canada. Her interdisciplinary work combines interests in language, cognition, figuration and multimodal forms of communication. Her publications in cognitive linguistics, cognitive narratology and cognitive poetics bring together the study of language and work on literature, visual artifacts, materiality, embodiment and performance. She has published three monographs, a textbook and three edited volumes (see http://faculty.arts.ubc.ca/bdancygier/index.html).

Alice Deignan is Professor of Applied Linguistics in the School of Education, University of Leeds, UK. She has previously worked as a teacher of ESL/EFL and as a lexicographer. In her research she uses large corpora to investigate lexical meaning, especially focusing on metaphor and metonymy. She is also interested in comparisons across genres and registers and the implications for non-expert language users such as young people and language learners.

Zsófia Demjén is Senior Lecturer in Applied Linguistics at UCL Institute of Education, University College London, UK. Her research interests include discourse analysis, metaphor, medical humanities and health communication. She is author of *Sylvia Plath and the Language of Affective States: Written Discourse and the Experience of Depression* (2015, Bloomsbury), and her work has appeared in the *Journal of Pragmatics*, *Metaphor and the Social World*, *Communication & Medicine* and the BMJ's *Medical Humanities* among others.

Aletta (Lettie) G. Dorst is an Assistant Professor in English Linguistics and Translation Studies at Leiden University, the Netherlands. Lettie was part of the team that developed MIPVU and applied the procedure to analyse the forms and functions of metaphor in fiction. Her current research interests lie in metaphor and translation, metaphor and stylistics, metaphor and religion, and metaphor in health communication.

Contributors

Elisabeth (Lisa) El Refaie is a Senior Lecturer at the Centre for Language and Communication Research, Cardiff University, UK. The focus of her research is on (verbo-)visual forms of metaphor and narrative. She is the author of *Autobiographical Comics: Life Writing in Pictures* (2012), and her articles have appeared in a wide range of journals and edited volumes. For the past three years she has been working on a project with an NGO in Africa, using comics-drawing workshops to encourage teenagers to express their thoughts and feelings about HIV and Ebola and to share important health messages with their peers.

Philip Eubanks is Professor of English at Northern Illinois University, USA, where he teaches courses in professional writing and theories of rhetoric and composition. He is the author of three books on metaphor and rhetoric, including *The Troubled Rhetoric and Communication of Climate Change: The Argumentative Situation* (Routledge, 2015).

Raymond W. Gibbs, Jr. is Distinguished Professor of Psychology at the University of California, Santa Cruz, USA. His research interests focus on embodied cognition, pragmatics and figurative language. He is the author of several books, including *The Poetics of Mind: Figurative Thought, Language and Understanding* (1994), *Intentions in the Experience of Meaning* (1999), *Embodiment and Cognitive Science* (2006) and (with Herb Colston) *Interpreting Figurative Meaning* (2012), all published by Cambridge University Press. He is also editor of *The Cambridge Handbook of Metaphor and Thought* (2008, CUP) and editor of the journal *Metaphor and Symbol*.

Joseph Grady, PhD, is a cognitive linguist and public interest communications strategist. For more than 15 years, he and his colleagues in Cultural Logic and the Topos Partnership (strategic communications firms he co-founded) have conducted research for non-profit organizations, helping them find more effective ways of explaining important issues. Grady has taught linguistics at the University of Maryland and Georgetown University and is former Senior Fellow for Public Policy at the Pell Center (Salve Regina University, USA).

Linda Greve is Master of Theology and Rhetorics and holds a PhD in Business Communication. Her research is centred around metaphors in knowledge communication. She has authored a book on metaphors as a tool for change in Danish (*Forandrende Ledelseskommunikation*, 2012) and has worked as a consultant in both the private and the public sectors. She is currently employed as lecturer and educational developer at the Centre for Teaching and Learning at Aarhus BSS, Aarhus University, Denmark.

Claire Hardaker is a Lecturer in Forensic Corpus Linguistics at Lancaster University, UK. Her research focuses on online deception, aggression and manipulation. She is currently working on a European Union project investigating the role of the Internet in human trafficking, and she was Principal Investigator on the recently completed ESRC-funded project 'Twitter Rape Threats and the Discourse of Online Misogyny' (ES/L008874/1). She is currently writing a book titled *The Antisocial Network*.

Laura Hidalgo-Downing is Associate Professor at the Universidad Autónoma of Madrid, Spain. Her research interests include discourse analysis, metaphor, persuasion, multimodal media discourse, stylistics and cognitive poetics. She is the author of *Negation, Text Worlds and Discourse: The Pragmatics of Fiction* (Ablex, 2000). She is the co-editor, together with Blanca Kraljevic, of a special issue on 'Metaphorical Creativity across Modes' (*Metaphor* *in the Social World* 13: 2, 2013) and the co-author, together with Robert Cockroft, Susan Cockroft and Craig Hamilton, of the third revised edition of *Persuading People: An Introduction to Rhetoric* (Palgrave Macmillan, 2014).

Michiko Kaneko is a Lecturer in the Department of South African Sign Language, the School of Literature, Language and Media, at the University of the Witwatersrand, Johannesburg, South Africa, where she teaches and researches in the areas of sign linguistics and sign language literature.

Albert N. Katz is a Canadian cognitive psychologist with active research programmes in psycholinguistic investigations of non-literal language (especially metaphor, sarcasm and proverb) and in the study of human autobiographical memory. He received his undergraduate education at McGill University in Montreal (BSc, Anthropology) and at the University of Western Ontario (PhD, 1976), where he was subsequently hired, becoming a Full Professor in 1991 and serving as Departmental Chair from 2007 to 2014. His most recent interests lie in testing implications arising from embodied cognition in the comprehension of sarcasm, metaphor and musical cognition.

Nelya Koteyko is a Reader in Applied Linguistics at Queen Mary University of London. Her research is focused on the discursive framing of developments in science, technology and medicine in print and digital media.

Zoltán Kövecses is Professor of Linguistics in the School of English and American Studies, Eötvös Loránd University, Budapest, Hungary, where he is head of the Cultural Linguistics doctoral programme. His research interests include metaphor, metonymy, emotion language, American English and culture, and the relationship between metaphoric conceptualization and context. His major publications include *Metaphor and Emotion* (2000, Cambridge UP), *American English: An Introduction* (2000, Broadview Press), *Metaphor: A Practical Introduction* (2002/2010, Oxford UP), *Metaphor in Culture* (2005, Cambridge UP), *Language, Mind, and Culture* (2006, Oxford UP) and *Where Metaphors Come From* (2015, Oxford UP).

Blanca Kraljevic-Mujic is Senior Lecturer at the Universidad Rey Juan Carlos, Madrid, Spain. Her research interests focus on multimodal metaphor and metonymy in advertising and narrative discourse. She is a guest co-editor with Laura Hidalgo-Downing of the *Metaphor and the Social World* (2013) special issue on 'Metaphorical Creativity across Modes' and a co-author of 'Multimodal Metonymy and Metaphor as Complex Discourse Resources for Creativity in ICT Advertising Discourse' (*Annual Review of Cognitive Linguistics*, 2011) among other publications.

Tina Krennmayr is Assistant Professor at Vrije Universiteit Amsterdam, the Netherlands. She does corpus research on metaphor variation in discourse and develops methods for metaphor identification. She has also published on ESP teaching and the development of figurative language proficiency in non-native speakers of English.

Jeannette Littlemore is Professor of English Language and Applied Linguistics at the University of Birmimgham (UK) and a Distinguished Professor of Applied Linguistics at the Open University, Hong Kong. She has published widely on metaphor, metonymy, cognitive linguistics and applied linguistics. Recent monographs include: *Metonymy: Hidden Shortcuts in Language, Thought and Communication* (2015, CUP) and *Figurative Language, Genre and Register* (2013, CUP, with Alice Deignan and Elena Semino).

Fiona MacArthur is a Senior Lecturer in English with over 30 years' experience of teaching English as a foreign language at the University of Extremadura, Spain. Her main research interest is in metaphor, particularly as it affects intercultural communication. Her major publications have focused on describing the subtle but important differences between similar metaphor themes in English and Spanish and how these may affect communication between speakers of these two languages.

Robert Maslen did his doctoral research at the Max Planck Child Study Centre, University of Manchester, UK. He has held research fellowships at Leeds University Business School's Centre for Decision Research and the Open University.

Andreas Musolff is Professor of Intercultural Communication at the University of East Anglia in Norwich, UK. His research interests include the pragmatics of intercultural and multicultural communication, metaphor studies and public discourse. His publications include *Metaphor and Political Discourse* (2004), *Metaphor, Nation and the Holocaust* (2010), *Metaphor and Intercultural Communication* (2014, co-edited) and *Political Metaphor Analysis. Discourse and Scenarios* (2016).

Susan Nacey is Professor of English as a Second/Foreign Language at Hedmark University of Applied Sciences in Norway, where she is the Vice Dean for Research. She is a corpus linguist and the author of *Metaphors in Learner English* (John Benjamins, 2013).

Gill Philip is Associate Professor of English Language and Translation at the University of Macerata, Italy, where she teaches undergraduate and Master's courses in corpus linguistics, translation, cognitive linguistics and TEFL. Most of her research investigates aspects of the interplay between cognition and linguistic communication, particularly with respect to phraseology and figurative language.

L. David Ritchie is Professor of Communication at Portland State University in Portland, Oregon, USA. His primary research focus is metaphor use, storytelling and humour in naturally occurring discourse, including conversation, political speeches and environmental communication. He is the author of two books on metaphor, *Context and Connection in Metaphor* (Palgrave Macmillan, 2006) and *Metaphor* (CUP, 2013), and has another book forthcoming, *Metaphorical Stories in Discourse* (CUP).

Gabriella Rundblad is Reader in Applied Linguistics at King's College London, UK. Her expertise lies in language, cognition and behaviour, with special emphasis on semantics and pragmatics in typical/atypical language development. She has also managed a number of research projects in the area of semantics and pragmatics in health communication.

Christina Schäffner is Professor Emerita at Aston University, Birmingham, UK. Until her retirement in September 2015, she was the Head of Translation Studies, teaching courses on translation theory and practice and supervising Master's dissertations and PhD students. Her main research interests are political discourse in translation, news translation, metaphor and translation, and translation didactics, and she has published widely on these topics. From 2011 to 2014, she was a member of the TIME project (Translation Research Training: An Integrated and Intersectoral Model for Europe), an initial training network (ITN) funded under the European Commission's FP7-PEOPLE.

Elena Semino is Professor of Linguistics and Verbal Art in the Department of Linguistics and English Language at Lancaster University, UK. She holds a Visiting Professorship at the University of Fuzhou in China. Her interests are in stylistics, medical humanities, health communication, corpus linguistics, narratology and metaphor theory and analysis. She has (co-)authored four monographs, including *Metaphor in Discourse* (Cambridge University Press, 2008) and *Figurative Language, Genre and Register* (Cambridge University Press, 2013, with Alice Deignan and Jeannette Littlemore).

Gerard Steen is Professor of Language and Communication at the University of Amsterdam, the Netherlands, and Director of the Metaphor Lab Amsterdam. He has published over 100 articles and book chapters and over 15 monographs, edited books and special issues in linguistics and poetics. His special interest is metaphor in discourse.

Rachel Sutton-Spence is a Lecturer in the Department of Arts and Sign Language Studies (DALi) at the Federal University of Santa Catarina, Brazil, with a specialist interest in sign language literature and folklore.

Dennis Tay is Assistant Professor in the Department of English at the Hong Kong Polytechnic University, China. His research interests include cognitive linguistics, metaphor theory and the discourse analysis of healthcare communication, with a particular emphasis on psychotherapy in English and Chinese speaking contexts.

Heli Tissari currently teaches in the Department of English at Stockholm University, Sweden. While writing for this volume, she worked as a senior lecturer at the University of Eastern Finland. She is also a Docent at the University of Helsinki, Finland, where she finished her PhD thesis on words and metaphors for love in the English language in 2003. Her research has mainly focused on English words for emotions and their histories since the Late Middle English period. She is also interested in the relationship between concrete and abstract meaning.

Introduction
Metaphor and language

Zsófia Demjén and Elena Semino

Why a handbook of *metaphor* and language?

It is difficult to overstate the importance of metaphor in human language(s), thought and experience. Over centuries of scholarship and a period of particularly intense focus in the last four decades, metaphor has been defined, theorized and applied in many different and sometimes mutually incompatible ways. Nonetheless, a fairly broad consensus exists that metaphor involves the perception of similarities or correspondences between unlike entities and processes, so that we can see, experience, think and communicate about one thing in terms of another – our lives as journeys, our minds as machines, our emotions as external forces, people as animals, inanimate objects as people, and so on. This expands our ability to feel, reason and communicate in ways that are characteristically human.

Since at least classical antiquity – and particularly the work of Aristotle – there has been a steady interest in metaphor from different perspectives, including rhetoric, philosophy, ethics, politics, philology, linguistics, literary and cultural criticism, psychology and cognitive science. These perspectives not only involved different questions, definitions and sources of evidence, but also generated debates about the status of metaphor as something special or ordinary, good or bad, illuminating or obfuscating, and as separate from or connected with other aspects of language and thought. The debates intensified, and developed a particular focus in the late 1970s and early 1980s with the publication and subsequent influence of two books: Andrew Ortony's edited collection *Metaphor and Thought* (1979, with a second edition in 1993) and George Lakoff and Mark Johnson's *Metaphors We Live By* (1980, with a second edition in 2003). Both books focused on metaphor primarily as a cognitive phenomenon, and presented it as central to thought. Lakoff and Johnson, in particular, famously introduced a theory that came to be known as Conceptual Metaphor Theory (CMT). Within this theory, metaphor is first and foremost a matter of cognition. Much of our thinking, it is claimed, relies on conventional conceptual metaphors – systematic sets of correspondences between, typically, concrete 'source' domains such as JOURNEY and abstract 'target' domains such as LIFE. Within this view, metaphors in language, such as 'I'm at a crossroads in my life', are seen as linguistic realizations of the conceptual metaphors we think by.

Although its central ideas were not in fact new (e.g. Black 1962, and Jäkel 1999 for an overview), Conceptual Metaphor Theory arguably caused a paradigm shift in research on metaphor, and (re)asserted metaphor as an important phenomenon within many disciplines, including areas as diverse as chemistry and music (e.g. Brown 2003, Zbikowski 2008). At the time of writing, the search engine Google Scholar identifies over 38,000 citations of Lakoff and Johnson's book (including the 2003 second edition), and since 1980 the theory has been developed (e.g. Grady 1997, Kövecses 2015), tested (e.g. Gibbs 1994, Thibodeau and Boroditsky 2011), critiqued (e.g. Murphy 1996, Vervaeke and Kennedy 1996) and applied in a variety of ways (e.g. Charteris-Black 2004, Tay 2013). At the same time, other theoretical accounts of metaphors were developed (e.g. Sperber and Wilson 1986, Glucksberg 2001, Fauconnier and Turner 2002, Cameron 2011), resulting both in fierce debates and in accounts that reconcile different perspectives, especially in the last two decades (e.g. Grady et al. 1999, Bowdle and Gentner 2005, Tendahl and Gibbs 2008). There are now two international journals dedicated specifically to metaphor – *Metaphor and Symbol* (originally *Metaphor and Symbolic Activity*) from 1986 and *Metaphor and the Social World* from 2011; a book series – Metaphor in Language, Cognition, and Communication, launched by John Benjamins in 2013; an international professional association – Researching and Applying Metaphor, founded in 2006; and numerous conferences and events every year. There is also already a handbook dedicated to metaphor, albeit with a focus on thought: *The Cambridge Handbook of Metaphor and Thought*, edited by Gibbs (2008). Metaphor is now used as a 'tool' in different areas of professional practice (e.g. Stewart 2015 on pain management in physiotherapy) and regularly receives media attention, particularly from a critical perspective (e.g. Granger 2014).

With so much attention already being focused on metaphor, one might wonder why it is worth publishing a new handbook dedicated to the topic.

Referring back to the second edition of Ortony's collection (Ortony 1993), Gibbs pointed out in the introduction to *The Cambridge Handbook of Metaphor and Thought* that 'much has changed in the world of metaphor since 1993' (Gibbs 2008: 3). In the same way, *The Routledge Handbook of Metaphor and Language* is a response to developments in the fast-growing field of metaphor research since 2008 and before. The sheer quantity, extraordinary variety and richness of recent work on metaphor means that the field can appear fragmented and overwhelming. This is true not only for newcomers trying to get to grips with the basics and potentials of the phenomenon, but also for experienced metaphor researchers who may need to keep up with developments in areas beyond their own specialisms. In this volume we aim to address the needs of both types of readers and, we hope, anyone in between. The handbook presents the background as well as the state of the art in research on metaphor from a number of key perspectives, and maps out future directions in both research and practice in a variety of contexts. It brings together theoretical, methodological, applied and practical contributions, and shows both the diversity of the field and the threads that link together different types of research. Each chapter aims to be both accessible and up-to-date and includes one or more concrete examples of current research alongside overviews of the literature and of critical issues, debates and future directions. In this way, the handbook not only reflects the current state of the field but also aims to contribute to its future development.

Why a handbook of metaphor and *language*?

Given the influence of Lakoff and Johnson's (1980) notion of 'conceptual metaphor', one might also wonder why a handbook should be dedicated to *language* and metaphor. As we pointed out above, much has changed in metaphor research since 1980, and one of the most important changes has been a reappraisal of the value of language and discourse in developing our understanding of the role of metaphor in our lives.

This reappraisal is consistent with a long-standing tradition in the study of metaphor in language, not just in the twentieth century (e.g. Richards 1936, Black 1962, Ricoeur 1977, Kittay 1987) but also earlier, such as in the work of Aristotle, Locke, Vico and Kant (see Jäkel 1999, Mahon 1999). Some of this work, of course, also recognized and theorized the relationship between conventional metaphors in language and metaphors in thought, as Mahon (1999) shows for Aristotle's *Poetics* and *Rhetoric*, and as Jäkel (1999) shows in relation to the works of Kant, Blumenberg and Weinrich.

Language, broadly conceived, is the human faculty and behaviour in which metaphor has been observed most extensively, and the main source of questions, hypotheses or evidence for any theory of metaphor. In this respect, Conceptual Metaphor Theory is no exception: Lakoff and Johnson (1980) based their claims mostly on linguistic data, and much of the work they inspired did the same. Both Ortony's (1979 and 1993) and Gibbs's (2008) volumes on metaphor and thought recognize the centrality of metaphor in language by devoting a section to that topic. Nonetheless, there had not yet been an entire handbook with specific emphasis on metaphor in language until this one.

While relying overwhelmingly on linguistic examples as evidence for their claim that metaphor is central to cognition, Lakoff and Johnson (1980) still presented metaphor in language as secondary to metaphor in thought. They did not regard the different linguistic forms metaphor can take and the different functions it can perform in discourse as worthy of attention in their own right. They cited decontextualized lists of sentences as data, and treated a 'language' such as English as a homogeneous whole, with no consideration for differences and variation depending on medium, register or genre. These aspects of Lakoff and Johnson's approach cast a long shadow on subsequent work on metaphor, often depriving theoretical work of sufficient empirical grounding, and encouraging a cavalier approach to methods and data.

Over the last two decades, there has been increasing recognition of the need for and value of investigating metaphor in language, from the lexicon to authentic discourse from many sources. This refocusing on language has resulted in major advances in our understanding of metaphor in communication, cognition and culture: it has inspired the development of new theoretical approaches; it has led to improved and more reliable methods of investigation; it has highlighted how metaphor varies in different registers and genres; it has shown the importance of considering how verbal metaphors interact with metaphors in other modes; it has enabled new ways of assessing attitudes and ideologies embedded in different types of communication; it has led to new insights into language development (both phylogenetic and ontogenetic) and into second/foreign language learning; and it has illuminated some of the ways and circumstances in which metaphors can be helpful or harmful.

It is these developments, insights and threads that this new handbook draws together.

The structure of this handbook

The chapters in *The Routledge Handbook of Metaphor and Language* are divided into six parts:

I. Theoretical approaches to metaphor and language
II. Methodological approaches to metaphor and language

III. Formal variation of metaphor in language
IV. Functional variation of metaphor in language
V. Applications and interventions: using metaphor for problem solving
VI. Language, metaphor, and cognitive development.

The handbook is then rounded off by a (self-)reflexive epilogue on metaphors *for* language and communication.

This structure reflects the developments and refocusing that have taken place in recent years, and particularly since Gibbs's (2008) handbook. There is also, however, continuity with previous collections on metaphor. This is particularly apparent in the reappearance in the present volume of a number of the contributors to Gibbs's handbook (Cameron, Cienki, Deignan, Kövecses, Semino and Steen, as well as Gibbs himself). There is also a continuing interest in a number of topics and types of metaphor research, notably, the role of metaphor in literature, metaphor as a tool in psychotherapy and education, metaphor as manifest in gesture and imagery, and various theoretical and empirical views on metaphor processing. The chapters are all organized in such a way as to provide an overview and contextualization for a particular area of metaphor study, showing continuity in the field, before highlighting key debates and current research developments. Depending on the part of the handbook, these developments might be theoretical, methodological, applied or a combination of these.

The chapters in the first part cannot of course do justice to centuries of scholarship, but capture the main current theoretical approaches to metaphor. In acknowledgement of the continued significance of CMT, Kövecses opens Part I by outlining the theory, including a consideration of some of its critiques, and providing an overview of the latest developments (e.g. the ways in which conceptual metaphors are not independent of each other, but may be organized in various hierarchical systems). This chapter is followed by two similarly significant but different cognitive theories – Blending Theory and Relevance Theory – that both see metaphor as 'unremarkable' in cognitive or communicative terms (see also Fauconnier and Turner 2002 and Sperber and Wilson 1986). In Chapter 2, Dancygier shows how metaphor can be seen as one type of blend among others, while, in Chapter 3, Carston describes it as one type of loose use among others. Dancygier explicitly compares and contrasts CMT with Fauconnier and Turner's (2002) Blending Theory, and argues that looking at conceptual underpinnings of various figurative forms offers a better explanation of the discourse effects of metaphor and other tropes. Carston not only introduces the Relevance Theory approach to metaphor, but also develops it to allow for different routes of metaphor understanding, in this way accounting for a larger variety of linguistic manifestations. In Chapter 4, Gibbs draws from Dynamical Systems Theory to present the newest theoretical approach to metaphor. Gibbs argues that the main strength of the dynamical systems view of metaphor lies in its ability to capture the complexity of the phenomenon and to integrate a number of other accounts, both cognitive and discursive.

The six chapters in Part II of the handbook cover different methods for capturing and accounting for metaphor in language. In some ways, the chapters in this part represent the most needed and most obvious new developments of recent years, motivated primarily by a focus on real data, often in large quantities. These data involve not just verbal communication, but also other modes, thereby requiring methods for analysing metaphor in images, gestures and sign languages. Part II begins with Steen in Chapter 5 outlining the Pragglejaz Group's (2007) Metaphor Identification Procedure (MIP) and its more recent developments in MIPVU (Steen et al. 2010) as ways of identifying metaphors in verbal language. In Chapter 6, Maslen also considers the identification of metaphor vehicles in language, but focuses more specifically on how to analyse what has been identified as metaphor in language. This results in the formulation of 'systematic metaphors' as bottom-up generalizations from metaphor use in particular discourse contexts. While Maslen's chapter remains at the level of metaphor patterns in language, in Chapter 7 Deignan tackles the controversial move from linguistic to conceptual metaphors and considers ways of making this analytical move more transparent, rigorous and replicable. This step in metaphor analysis, for those who wish to take it, remains problematic, but Deignan argues that it can lead to valuable insights as long as it is approached rigorously. While the methods of Corpus Linguistics are discussed by Deignan as just one way of taking this particular analytical step, they are the whole focus of Tissari's Chapter 8. Tissari argues that corpus methods add value to metaphor research in the same way that they add value to any linguistic research: by speeding up the analysis of large datasets, by making research replicable and by providing quantitative information about linguistic patterns. She demonstrates this by using a diachronic corpus approach to investigate the metaphors for the emotion 'hope' in English. Chapters 9 and 10 outline methods for capturing metaphor in different modes. Cienki tackles the methodological challenge of identifying metaphor in gesture and proposes 'MIG-G' – a new set of Metaphor Identification Guidelines for Gesture. MIG-G aims for the kind of transparency and replicability that has led to the success of MIP and MIPVU for metaphor in verbal data. El Refaie turns to metaphor in multimodal texts and shows how such metaphors can be identified and analysed on the basis of their formal qualities or of the thought patterns they evoke. She also discusses experiments, surveys, interviews and focus groups that have been used to investigate the comprehension of multimodal metaphors.

The next two parts of the handbook involve a separation between 'form' and 'function' that is, of course, not at all clear-cut. Nevertheless, the eight chapters in Part III emphasize how metaphors vary in their linguistic and textual manifestations, while the six chapters in Part IV emphasize how metaphors vary depending on the role they play in discourse. In Chapter 11, Krennmayr starts off Part III by discussing how metaphors vary – both in their manifestations and in their interpretation – depending on the parts of speech they belong to. Krennmayr draws on both corpus linguistics and experimental evidence, and discusses parts-of-speech variation in different registers and genres. Genre and register continue to be themes in Dorst's Chapter 12, but here the focus is on the types of patterns that metaphors (and similes) create within and across texts. Dorst also reports on experimental studies of how such patterns affect the reception of metaphors. In Chapter 13, Caballero then focuses more specifically on formal variation in metaphor by genre, looking at a variety of genres, but zooming in on the peculiarities of metaphor in architectural reviews. Caballero's chapter is followed by two chapters looking at conventionality and novelty in metaphor use, with Caracciolo focusing on literature and Philip exploring novelty in language generally, using corpus methods. In Chapter 14, Caracciolo takes a measured look at the so-called 'literary metaphor' and the different uses of metaphors that can be found in literature. He discusses recent research on how specific stylistic and narrative strategies in metaphor use may shape readers' interpretations. Philip begins Chapter 15 with a discussion of the ways in which the novelty/conventionality of particular metaphors can be established, and then explores potential constraints on novelty, particularly in idiomatic expressions. The final three chapters in Part III move on to variation across time and languages. In Chapter 16, Anderson outlines the literature on metaphor variation across historical periods, arguing that developments in metaphor use indicate not only semantic changes in language but also broader changes in society. She then presents some of the findings from an innovative study that exploits the

Historical Thesaurus of English to map metaphorical connections across semantic domains over the history of English. Schäffner considers metaphor variation across languages in Chapter 17, and shows how this variation impacts on translators and translations. She specifically contrasts metaphors in English, German and French in the context of politics, taking into account the practices of translators themselves. Finally, in Chapter 18, Kaneko and Sutton-Spence discuss metaphor in sign language, partially in contrast with metaphor in verbal languages. They discuss the particular significance of iconicity and metaphor at sublexical levels, but also focus on more recent work on metaphor in sign language at the level of narrative.

Given the interrelatedness of form and function, some of the chapters in Part III already discuss the functions of different types of formal variation in metaphor use (e.g. Chapters 12, 13 and 14), and therefore anticipate the focus of Part IV. In Part IV, however, centre stage is given to some of the key functions that metaphors can perform in discourse, or the different purposes to which they can be put. Littlemore begins Chapter 19 with a discussion of the different functions of metaphor (and its potential shortcomings) in educational contexts. Here metaphor is often used to explain complex ideas, but it can also fill terminological gaps or be employed to check students' understanding. In Chapter 20, Koteyko and Atanasova discuss related functions of metaphor (to understand and explain) in the context of scientific communication. They focus on public communication about the environment and climate change, pointing in particular to the ways in which metaphor can 'frame' debates about these controversial topics. Chapter 21 by Musolff is the first of two focusing on the persuasive power of metaphor. Musolff's interest is in persuasive metaphor in political discourse. He describes how this particular role of the trope has been recognized (and taught) since the rhetorical traditions of antiquity, and applies both long-standing and recent approaches to metaphor to data concerning the European Union and immigration. Hidalgo-Downing and Kraljevic-Mujic return to metaphor in different modes again in Chapter 22, discussing its role in persuasion within commercial advertising. They consider, among other things, the ethical implications of using metaphor for this purpose. In Chapter 23, Ritchie reflects on how metaphor can be used to tell stories. In particular, he makes a distinction between stories that are told with metaphorical intent (akin to allegory) and metaphors that themselves have the potential to suggest stories. In Chapter 24, Demjén and Hardaker explore a less-researched function of metaphor: causing offence. They look in detail at offensive, misogynistic tweets and reflect on how the vividness and concision that metaphor can achieve might make it particularly appropriate to be used for maximum effect in a medium/genre with tight space constraints.

Part V of the handbook deals with an area that has some history but seems to have increased in significance over the last 15 years: the ways in which metaphors can be used as tools for solving communicative, organizational or societal problems. The six chapters in this part of the handbook focus on different domains of activity. Chapter 25 and 26 both focus on the application of metaphor to the context of health and illness, but deal respectively with mental and physical illness. In Chapter 25, Tay argues that the use of metaphor as a tool in counselling could be improved by closer working relationships between therapists and discourse analysts. He suggests that these closer relationships would facilitate interventions that make more sensitive and effective use of the spontaneous, creative and emergent qualities of metaphor. Demjén and Semino in Chapter 26 recognize that metaphors can be both harmful and helpful in healthcare contexts, but use recent research to warn against the uncritical rejection or promotion of particular metaphors. Instead, they argue that healthcare professionals need a keen understanding of communication, as well as a sensitivity to and tolerance of the language of the individuals they are caring for, including metaphorical uses of language. Chapter 27 moves from healthcare to the context of business: Greve looks at metaphor as a practical tool in management. In particular, she discusses how metaphor, both verbal and multimodal, can be used effectively to facilitate organizational change and manage knowledge. In Chapter 28, MacArthur returns to the context of education, and specifically foreign language teaching and learning. She argues that teachers should foster learners' deep engagement with the metaphorical senses of words and phrases in the target language in order to facilitate comprehension and recall. Chapters 29 and 30 look at the uses of metaphor in more public domains of activity. In the former chapter, Cameron discusses the role that metaphor can play in peace-building and reconciliation, both as an indicator of progress (if the metaphor use of opposing parties begins to converge) and as a way of identifying and surfacing underlying assumptions. In Chapter 30, Grady outlines the role of metaphor in making public communication about complex issues more effective. He warns, however, that there are multiple ways for metaphors to fail in their communicative intent, meaning that success can be ensured only by testing potential metaphors with members of the public.

Similarly to the chapters in Part I of this handbook, the chapters in the final part recognize the importance of the interaction/relationship between language and cognition, but also emphasize how the nature of this relationship is far from clear. In Chapter 31, Colston and Gibbs attempt to make sense of the large and contradictory literature on metaphor processing by suggesting that metaphors are likely to be processed differently depending on variables such as form, text, context, text producers and receivers, and experimental design and setting. In Chapter 32, Katz similarly explores metaphor understanding, but through the psycholinguistic lenses of acquisition and use. In this approach, the focus is much more on the individuals using and/or interpreting metaphors, and how/why they are doing so (e.g. to create a sense of intimacy or express aspects of identity), than on the possible entailments of the specific metaphors. Rundblad continues the discussion of metaphor understanding and use, but looks at evidence from non-neurotypical individuals in Chapter 33. She focuses on people with specific language impairment, Down's syndrome, Williams syndrome, autism spectrum disorders and schizophrenia, and explores how Theory of Mind, executive function and weak central coherence might explain any differences in metaphor acquisition and use between them and neurotypical individuals. Rundblad points out how this also leads to insights about metaphor processing in general. At the end of Part VI, in Chapter 34, Nacey returns to second language learning and explores metaphor comprehension and use in people learning a second language. She introduces the concept of 'metaphoric competence', and considers its problematic assessment via metaphor understanding and production. She finishes by presenting a recent study that used translation activities to measure and encourage metaphor use in a second language.

Finally, after Part VI, an epilogue rounds off the volume by taking a reflexive and reflective perspective on the topic of metaphor and language. Rather than focusing on metaphors in language, Eubanks considers 'language' itself as the topic or target of metaphoricity. He discusses the variety of metaphors that are used in English to talk about language and communication, and reflects on the ideological implications of these metaphors in terms of what we understand language to be and do.

Although the chapters are broadly similar in structure and style, there is of course also some variation. This is a result of one of the key strengths of this handbook, that it draws together contributions from a variety of theoretical perspectives, disciplines, contexts and understandings of 'language'. What unites all contributions is their central concern with metaphor in 'real' language use.

Other themes within the handbook

While a handbook such as the present one needs to have a clear-cut structure, the division of the chapters into the parts we have just described inevitably backgrounds some of the common threads and themes that run across the volume.

As far as theory is concerned, most chapters outside the 'Theoretical approaches' part of the handbook take Conceptual Metaphor Theory as their main theoretical point of reference, and assume some connection between metaphors in linguistic data and conceptual metaphors. Out of this group of chapters, a few aim to make a contribution to Conceptual Metaphor Theory itself (e.g. Chapter 16 by Anderson, Chapter 21 by Musolff, Chapter 25 by Tay). Others broadly adopt Conceptual Metaphor Theory but also critique it, particularly for its methodological failings and its inability to account satisfactorily for the varied manifestations of metaphor in discourse (e.g. Chapter 4 by Gibbs, Chapter 7 by Deignan, Chapter 15 by Philip). In contrast, a number of chapters locate themselves, wholly or in part, within other theories of metaphor. Several chapters draw in different ways from the insights into metaphor provided by Aristotle (e.g. Chapter 14 by Caracciolo, Chapter 21 by Musolff, Chapter 22 by Hidalgo-Downing and Kraljevic-Mujic, Chapter 32 by Katz). Chapters 6 and 29, by Maslen and Cameron respectively, adopt the methodological approach known as 'Metaphor-Led Discourse Analysis' (Cameron et al. 2009), which is consistent with the theoretical account of metaphor proposed within Dynamics Systems Theory (see Chapter 4 by Gibbs). Other chapters make reference more eclectically to different theoretical approaches to metaphor, drawing from areas such as pragmatics and critical discourse analysis on the one hand (e.g. Chapter 21 by Musolff, Chapter 22 by Hidalgo-Downing and Kraljevic-Mujic), and, on the other hand, different theories of metaphor and cognition (e.g. Chapter 32 by Katz, Chapter 33 by Rundblad). Finally, as we have mentioned, Chapter 31 by Colston and Gibbs explicitly argues that different theories are best suited to account for the processing of different types and uses of metaphor in different settings.

Methods in research on metaphor also receive explicit attention in many chapters outside the 'Methodological approaches' part of the handbook. Issues of identification are addressed in many chapters, particularly with reference to the MIP method first proposed in Pragglejaz Group (2007) and then developed as MIPVU in Steen et al. (2010). A number of chapters consider the relationship between metaphor and other tropes, discussing metonymy and/or simile in contrast or interaction with metaphor (e.g. Chapter 2 by Dancygier, Chapter 11 by Krennmayr, Chapter 12 by Dorst, Chapter 18 by Kaneko and Sutton-Spence, Chapter 24 by Demjén and Hardaker, the epilogue by Eubanks). Corpus linguistic methods are referred to and/or demonstrated in several chapters beyond Tissari's, which is devoted to them (e.g. Chapter 11 by Krennmayr, Chapter 15 by Philip, Chapter 24 by Demjén and Hardaker, Chapter 26 by Demjén and Semino, Chapter 34 by Nacey), while the example of current research in Chapter 16 by Anderson involves an innovative use of a digital historical thesaurus of English. Kaneko and Sutton-Spence's contribution (Chapter 18) on metaphor in sign language includes an explicit methodology for analysing signs, as well as metaphorical signs, in sign language. And the chapters in Part VI provide detailed accounts of different experimental methods in psychology and psycholinguistics and of what can be learnt from them.

A number of chapters in the handbook also show how the analysis of metaphor in authentic discourse data has theoretical and/or methodological implications for fields of research beyond metaphor. Cienki discusses implications for gesture studies in Chapter 9, Caballero for genre studies in Chapter 13, Anderson for historical linguistics in Chapter 16 and Rundblad for language acquisition in Chapter 33. In Chapters 19, 28 and 34 respectively, Littlemore, MacArthur and Nacey consider implications for second language teaching and learning. In Chapter 24, Demjén and Hardaker reflect on how metaphor can inform theories of (im)politeness, while in Chapter 29 Cameron uses metaphor to propose a new theory of empathy. In other words, these and other chapters show that, in spite of the advances already achieved through interdisciplinary approaches to metaphor over the last 40 years, metaphor scholars still have much to contribute to research and applications across many fields.

While most chapters in the handbook focus on English, the applicability of the relevant theories/methods/findings is usually broader. A number of chapters, however, explicitly discuss metaphor in other languages. Schäffner's chapter on translation (Chapter 17), for instance, discusses examples from Arabic and Chinese, as well as from several European languages. Chinese is also the language of Tay's data in Chapter 25, while European languages are also considered by Tissari in Chapter 8 (Spanish and French), Philip in Chapter 15 (Italian) and Koteyko and Atanasova in Chapter 20 (Swedish and Russian). In Chapter 18, Kaneko and Sutton-Spence additionally deal with research on different sign languages, while several chapters deal with the learning and use of metaphors by second-language learners of English with a range of mother tongues (e.g. Chapter 19 by Littlemore, Chapter 28 by MacArthur, and Chapter 34 by Nacey).

The chapters in this volume also give a sense of the different types of data that are considered in metaphor research. While most chapters focus primarily on written language, several chapters deal with spoken data (e.g. Chapter 19 by Littlemore, Chapter 25 by Tay, Chapter 27 by Greve, Chapter 29 by Cameron), and other chapters consider multimodal data (e.g. Chapter 9 by Cienki, Chapter 10 by El Refaie, Chapter 22 by Hidalgo-Downing and Kraljevic-Mujic, and Chapter 27 by Greve). Communication mediated by computers is discussed in Chapter 24 by Demjén and Hardaker and Chapter 26 by Demjén and Semino, while in Chapter 15 Philip deals with language generated by computers. The kinds of data discussed in different chapters also vary along other dimensions, such as formality (e.g. the papal encyclical in Chapter 6 by Maslen vs. the Twitter data in Chapter 24 by Demjén and Hardaker) and context specificity (e.g. architectural reviews in Chapter 13 by Caballero vs. literature in Chapter 14 by Caracciolo).

Despite this variation, one theme emerges again and again: the ability of metaphors to 'frame' topics and ideas in particular ways. Framing in relation to metaphor is not a new idea: two of the most influential chapters in Ortony (1979) (those by Schön and Reddy) shared a view of metaphors as 'framing' devices: ways of thinking and talking about entities, phenomena and experiences that involve particular perspectives and facilitate different inferences and evaluations. However, recent empirical work (e.g. Thibodeau and Boroditsky 2011) has rekindled an interest in understanding in what circumstances and in what ways metaphors have framing effects. While framing is not the specific focus of any one chapter, it is discussed explicitly by Koteyko and Atanasova in Chapter 20, Musolff in Chapter 21, Tay in Chapter 25, Demjén and Semino in Chapter 26, Cameron in Chapter 29, Grady in Chapter 30 and Eubanks in the Epilogue. This potential effect of metaphor is likely to be a key area of future development.

References

Black, M. (1962) *Models and Metaphors: Structure in Language and Philosophy*, Ithaca, NY: Cornell University Press.
Bowdle, B. F. and Gentner, D. (2005) 'The career of metaphor', *Psychological Review* 112(1): 193–216.
Brown, T. L. (2003) *Making Truth: Metaphor in Science*, Urbana, IL: University of Illinois Press.
Cameron, L. (2011) *Metaphor and Reconciliation*, New York: Routledge.
Cameron, L., Maslen, R., Todd, Z., Maule, J., Stratton, P. and Stanley, N. (2009) 'The Discourse Dynamics approach to metaphor and metaphor-led discourse analysis', *Metaphor and Symbol* 24(2): 63–89.

Charteris-Black, J. (2004) *Corpus Approaches to Critical Metaphor Analysis*, Basingstoke, UK: Palgrave Macmillan.

Fauconnier, G. and Turner, M. (2002) *The Way We Think: Conceptual Blending and the Mind's Hidden Complexities*, New York: Basic Books.

Gibbs, R. W., Jr. (1994) *The Poetics of Mind*, Cambridge and New York: Cambridge University Press.

—— (ed.) (2008) *The Cambridge Handbook of Metaphor and Thought*, Cambridge, UK: Cambridge University Press.

Glucksberg, S. (2001). *Understanding Figurative Language: From Metaphors to Idioms*, Oxford, UK: Oxford University Press.

Grady, J. (1997) 'Foundations of meaning: primary metaphors and primary scenes', unpublished Ph.D. diss., Department of Linguistics, University of California at Berkeley.

Grady, J., Oakley, T. and Coulson, S. (1999) 'Blending and metaphor', in R. W. Gibbs, Jr. and G. Steen (eds), *Metaphor in Cognitive Linguistics*, pp. 101–24, Amsterdam, The Netherlands: John Benjamins.

Granger, K. (2014) 'Having cancer is not a fight or a battle', *The Guardian*. http://www.theguardian.com/society/2014/apr/25/having-cancer-not-fight-or-battle.

Jäkel, O. (1999) 'Kant, Blumenberg, Weinrich: Some forgotten contributions to the Cognitive Theory of Metaphor', in R. W. Gibbs, Jr. and G. J. Steen (eds), *Metaphor in Cognitive Linguistics*, pp. 9–27, Amsterdam, The Netherlands: John Benjamins.

Kittay, E. F. (1987) *Metaphor: Its Cognitive Force and Linguistic Structure*, Oxford, UK: Clarendon.

Kövecses, Z. (2015) *Where Metaphors Come From: Reconsidering Context in Metaphor*, Oxford and New York: Oxford University Press.

Lakoff, G. and Johnson, M. (1980/2003) *Metaphors We Live By*, Chicago, IL: University of Chicago Press.

Mahon, J. E. (1999) 'Getting your sources right: What Aristotle didn't say', in L. Cameron and G. Low (eds), *Researching and Applying Metaphor*, pp. 69–80, Cambridge, UK: Cambridge University Press.

Murphy, G. L. (1996) 'On metaphoric representation', *Cognition* 60: 173–204.

Ortony, A. (ed.) (1979/1993) *Metaphor and Thought*, Cambridge and New York: Cambridge University Press.

Pragglejaz Group (2007) 'MIP: A method for identifying metaphorically used words in discourse', *Metaphor and Symbol* 22: 1–39.

Richards, I. A. (1936) *The Philosophy of Rhetoric*, Oxford, UK: Oxford University Press.

Ricoeur, P. (1977) *The Rule of Metaphor: Multi-disciplinary Studies of the Creation of Meaning in Language*, Toronto, Ontario: University of Toronto Press.

Sperber, D. and Wilson, D. (1986) *Relevance: Communication and Cognition*, Oxford, UK: Blackwell.

Steen, G. J., Dorst, A. G., Herrmann, J. B., Kaal, A. A., Krennmayr, T. and Pasma, T. (2010) *A Method for Linguistic Metaphor Identification: From MIP to MIPVU*, Amsterdam, The Netherlands: John Benjamins.

Stewart, M. (2015) 'The hidden influence of metaphor within rehabilitation', *In Touch*, 153: 8–13.

Tay, D. (2013) *Metaphor in Psychotherapy. A Descriptive and Prescriptive Analysis*, Amsterdam, The Netherlands and Philadelphia, PA: John Benjamins.

Tendahl, M. and Gibbs, R. W., Jr. (2008). 'Complementary perspectives on metaphor: Cognitive linguistics and relevance theory', *Journal of Pragmatics* 40: 1823–64.

Thibodeau, P. H. and Boroditsky, L. (2011) 'Metaphors we think with: The role of metaphor in reasoning', *PLoS ONE* 6(2): e16782. http://journals.plos.org/plosone/article?id=10.1371/journal.pone.0016782.

Vervaeke, J. and Kennedy, J. (1996) 'Metaphor in language and thought: Falsification and multiple meanings', *Metaphor and Symbol* 11: 273–84.

Zbikowski, L. (2008) 'Metaphor and music', in R. W. Gibbs, Jr. (ed.) *The Cambridge Handbook of Metaphor and Thought*, pp. 502–24, Cambridge, UK: Cambridge University Press.

Part I
Theoretical approaches to metaphor and language

1
Conceptual metaphor theory

Zoltán Kövecses

Introduction and a definition

Conceptual metaphor theory (CMT) started with George Lakoff and Mark Johnson's book *Metaphors We Live By* (1980). The theory goes back a long way and builds on centuries of scholarship that takes metaphor not simply as an ornamental device in language but as a conceptual tool for structuring, restructuring and even creating reality. Notable philosophers in this history include, for instance, Friedrich Nietzsche and, more recently, Max Black. A recent overview of theories of metaphor can be found in Gibbs (2008), and one of CMT in particular in Kövecses (2010a).

Since the publication of Lakoff and Johnson's (1980) work, a large amount of research has been conducted that has confirmed, added to and also modified their original ideas. Often, the sources of the new ideas were Lakoff and Johnson themselves. Given this situation, it is obvious that what we know as conceptual metaphor theory today is not equivalent to the theory of metaphor proposed in *Metaphors We Live By*. Many of the critics of CMT assume, incorrectly, that CMT equals *Metaphors We Live By*. For this reason, I will not deal with this kind of criticism in this introduction to CMT.

The standard definition of conceptual metaphors is this: *A conceptual metaphor is understanding one domain of experience (that is typically abstract) in terms of another (that is typically concrete)*. This definition captures conceptual metaphors both as a process and as a product. The cognitive process of understanding a domain is the process aspect of metaphor, while the resulting conceptual pattern is the product aspect. In this survey of the theory, I will not distinguish between the two aspects.

Overview of main concepts and development of CMT

In this section, I attempt to spell out the main features of CMT, as I see them. Other researchers might emphasize different properties of the theory. At the same time, I try to select those features on which there is some agreement among practitioners of CMT.

Metaphors are all-pervasive

In *Metaphors We Live By*, Lakoff and Johnson (1980) suggested that metaphors are pervasive not only in certain genres striving to create some artistic effect (such as literature) but also in the most neutral, i.e., most non-deliberately used, forms of language. CMT researchers, especially in the early stages of work on conceptual metaphors, collected linguistic metaphors from a variety of different sources: TV and radio broadcasts, dictionaries, newspapers and magazines, conversations, their own linguistic repertoires and several others. They found an abundance of metaphorical examples, such as "*defending* an argument", "*exploding* with anger", "*building* a theory", "*fire* in someone's eyes", "*foundering* relationship", "a *cold* personality", "a *step-by-step* process", "*digesting* an idea", "people *passing away*", "*wandering aimlessly* in life" and literally thousands of others. Most, if not all, of such linguistic metaphors are part of native speakers' mental lexicon. They derive from more basic senses of words and reflect a high degree of polysemy and idiomaticity in the structure of the mental lexicon. The magnitude of such cases of polysemy and idiomaticity in the lexicon was taken to be evidence of the pervasiveness of metaphor. Based on such examples, Lakoff and Johnson proposed what came to be known as "conceptual metaphors". However, CMT does not claim that each and every metaphor we find in discourse belongs to a particular conceptual metaphor.

Other researchers, however, find the presence of metaphor in real discourse less pervasive. As noted by Gibbs (2009), different methods produce different results in frequency counts of metaphors.

Systematic mappings between two conceptual domains

The standard definition of conceptual metaphors we saw earlier can be reformulated somewhat more technically as follows: *A conceptual metaphor is a systematic set of correspondences between two domains of experience*. This is what "understanding one domain in terms of another" means. Another term that is frequently used in the literature for "correspondence" is "mapping". This is because certain elements and the relations between them are said to be mapped from one domain, the "source domain", onto the other domain, the "target". Let us illustrate how the correspondences, or mappings, work with the conceptual metaphor ANGER IS FIRE. Before I provide the systematic conceptual mappings that constitute this metaphor, let us see some *linguistic metaphors*, as derived by the lexical method, that make the conceptual metaphor manifest in English:

> That *kindled* my ire.
> Those were *inflammatory* remarks.
> *Smoke* was *coming out* of his ears.
> She was *burning* with anger.
> He was *spitting fire*.
> The incident *set* the people *ablaze* with anger.

Given such examples, the following set of correspondences, or mappings, can be proposed:

> the cause of fire → the cause of anger
> causing the fire → causing the anger
> the thing on fire → the angry person

the fire → the anger

the intensity of fire → the intensity of anger

With the help of these mappings, we can explain why the metaphorical expressions listed above mean what they do: why, for instance, *kindle* and *inflammatory* mean causing anger, and why *burning, spitting fire*, and being *ablaze* with anger indicate a high intensity of anger, with probably fine distinctions of intensity between them.

This set of mappings is systematic in the sense that it captures a coherent view of fire that is mapped onto anger: There is a thing that is not burning. An event happens (cause of fire) that causes the fire to come into existence. Now the thing is burning. The fire can burn at various degrees of intensity.

Similarly for anger: There is a person who is not angry. An event happens that causes the person to become angry. The person is now in the state of anger. The intensity of the anger is variable.

The mappings bring into correspondence the elements and the relations between the elements in the FIRE domain (source) with the elements and the relations between the elements in the ANGER domain (target). Indeed, it seems reasonable to suggest that, in a sense, the mappings from the FIRE domain actually bring about or create a particular conception of anger relative to the view of fire we have just seen. This is what it means that a particular source domain is used to conceptualize a particular target domain. (I will come back to this issue later.)

In many cases, however, the two-domain account does not work and must be supplemented by a model of explanation that relies on four domains, or spaces (see Chapter 2 on conceptual integration and metaphor).

Given the metaphorically used set of elements in a domain, we can derive further knowledge about these elements, and can also map this additional knowledge onto the target. This additional kind of source-domain knowledge is often called "metaphorical inference", or "metaphorical entailment". For example, to stay with the metaphor above, in somewhat formal and old-fashioned English we can find sentences like "He took revenge, and that *quenched* his anger". Quenching anger can be regarded as a metaphorical inference, given the ANGER IS FIRE metaphor. If anger is metaphorically viewed as fire, then we can make use of our further knowledge of anger-as-fire; namely, that the fire can be quenched. CMT provides an elegant explanation of such cases of extending conceptual metaphors.

At this point, an important question may arise: Can everything be mapped from one domain to another? Obviously not. Given a particular conceptual metaphor, there are many things that cannot be mapped, or carried over, from the source to the target. For example, given that THEORIES ARE BUILDINGS, the number of rooms or whether the building has a cellar or an attic is not mapped. Several explanations have been offered to delimit the amount of knowledge that can be transferred from the source. One of them is the "invariance hypothesis" developed by Lakoff (1990). It suggests that everything from the source can be mapped onto the target that does not conflict with the image-schematic structure of the target. Another is proposed by Grady (1997a, 1997b), who claims, in essence, that those parts of the source domain can be mapped that are based on "primary metaphors" (see below). Finally, Kövecses (2000a, 2002) proposed that the source maps conceptual materials that belong to its main meaning focus or foci. It should be noted that the three suggestions differ with respect to which part of a conceptual metaphor they rely on in their predictions concerning what is mapped. The first relies primarily on the target, the second on the connection between source and target, and the third on properties of the source. None of these is entirely satisfactory.

From concrete domain to abstract domain

As we just saw, CMT makes a distinction between a "source domain" and a "target domain". The source domain is a concrete domain, while the target is an abstract one. In the example conceptual metaphor LIFE IS A JOURNEY, the domain of JOURNEY is much more concrete than the target domain of LIFE (which is much more abstract); hence, JOURNEY is the source (domain). In general, CMT proposes that more-physical domains typically serve as source domains for more-abstract targets, as in the LIFE IS A JOURNEY metaphor.

This observation is based on the examination of hundreds of conceptual metaphors that have been discovered and analysed in the literature so far (such as LIFE IS A JOURNEY, ANGER IS FIRE, THEORIES ARE BUILDINGS). The assumption that most conceptual metaphors involve more-physical domains as sources and more-abstract domains as targets makes a lot of intuitive sense. For example, the notion of life is hard to pin down because of its complexity; that of anger is an internal feeling that remains largely hidden from us; that of theory is a sophisticated mental construct; and so on for other cases. In all of them, a less tangible and thus less easily accessible target concept is conceptualized as and from the perspective of a more tangible and thus a more easily accessible source concept.

In our effort to understand the world, it makes a lot more sense to move conceptually in this particular direction: that is, to conceptualize the cognitively less easily accessible domains in terms of the more easily accessible ones. Notice how odd and unintuitive it would be to attempt to conceptualize journeys metaphorically as life, fire as anger or buildings as theories. We would not find this way of understanding journey, fire or building helpful or revealing, simply because we know a lot more about them than about such concepts as life, anger and theory. This is not to say that the reverse direction of conceptualization never occurs. It may occur, but when it does, there is always some special poetic, stylistic, aesthetic or similar purpose or effect involved. The default direction of metaphorical conceptualization from more tangible to less tangible applies to the everyday and unmarked cases.

Metaphors occur primarily in thought

According to CMT, metaphor resides not only in language but also in thought. We use metaphors not only to speak about certain aspects of the world but also to think about them. As we saw above, CMT makes a distinction between linguistic metaphors, i.e. linguistic expressions used metaphorically, and conceptual metaphors, i.e. certain conceptual patterns we rely on in our daily living to think about aspects of the world. For example, metaphors such as LIFE IS A JOURNEY can actually govern the way we think about life: We can set goals we want to reach, we do our best to reach those goals, we can make careful plans for the journey, we can prepare ourselves for facing obstacles along the way, we can draw up alternative plans in the form of choosing a variety of different paths, we can prefer certain paths to others and so on. When we entertain such and similar ideas, we actually think about life in terms of the LIFE IS A JOURNEY conceptual metaphor. And, consequently, we can use the language of journeys to also *talk* about life.

The idea that we think about a domain in terms of another can actually mean several different things. In one sense, as above, people may be guided by a particular conceptual metaphor in how they conceive of a domain, such as LIFE. In another, given a conceptual metaphor, they may utilize some of the implications of a particular domain they rely on (such as JOURNEY) in a conceptual metaphor and apply those implications to the other domain (such as LIFE) in their reasoning about it (see below for an example). Finally, it can also mean that in the course of the online process of producing and understanding a linguistic metaphor, the metaphor activates both the source and the target concept. (This issue is discussed in Chapter 31 on metaphor processing.)

A major consequence of the idea that metaphors are conceptual in nature, i.e. that we conceive of certain things in metaphorical ways, is that, since our conceptual system governs how we act in the world, we often act metaphorically.

When we conceptualize an intangible or less tangible domain metaphorically as, and from the perspective of, a more tangible domain, we create a certain metaphorical reality. We imagine life one way when we think of it as a journey (see above), and in another way when we think of it as a theatre play, as reflected in Shakespeare's famous lines "All the world is a stage / and all men and women are merely players". The two source domains result in very different views on life, and in this sense they create very different realities.

Whenever a new source domain is applied to a particular target, we see the target domain differently than we saw it before. The limiting case of this situation is the one where a particular target domain does not exist at all, but by the application of one (or several) source domain(s), it actually gets created. Very often, the etymologies of words for abstract concepts reflect this early conceptualization. For example, COMPREHENSION ("understanding") is clearly an abstract concept. Given the UNDERSTANDING IS GRASPING conceptual metaphor (as in "I did not *grasp* what he said", "He is slow on the *uptake*"), it makes sense that the English word *comprehend* derives from the word that means "grasp" in Latin.

This kind of "reality construction" is very common in advertising, where, often, interesting or amusing cases of metaphorical reality get created. When advertisements for, say, deodorants promise "24-hour protection", they make us see a deodorant as our helper or ally in a fight or war against an enemy. The enemy is none other than our own body odour. So if we did not think of our body odour as our enemy before, i.e. as something we have to be protected against, the advertisements can easily make us view it as such. In this manner, the metaphors used in advertisements and elsewhere can create new realities for us. Such realities are of course metaphorically defined. But this does not make them unimportant for the way we live. If we think of our body odour as something we need to be protected against and as a result go and buy a deodorant to overcome the enemy, we are clearly thinking and acting according to a metaphorically defined reality. This is a further example of how the implications of a source domain for a particular target can be utilized (in a process I called metaphorical inference or entailment above).

Finally, if metaphor is part of the conceptual system, it follows that conceptual metaphors will also occur in any mode of expression of that system. Research indicates that the conceptual metaphors identified in language also occur in gestures, visual representations (such as cartoons), visual arts (such as painting) and so forth. This does not mean that the metaphors found in these modes of expression are exactly the same as those found in everyday language and thought, but that a large number of them are (see, e.g. work by Forceville 2008; Cienki and Müller 2008).

Conceptual metaphors are grounded

Why is a particular source domain paired with a particular target domain? The most traditional answer to this question is to say that there is a similarity, or resemblance, between two things or events. Several different types of similarity are recognized in the literature: objectively real similarity (as in the *roses* on one's cheeks), perceived similarity and similarity in generic-level structure. An example for perceived similarity would be a case where certain actions in life and their consequences are seen as gambles in a gambling game with a win-or-lose outcome; cf. LIFE IS A GAMBLING GAME. We can take as an example for the last type of similarity the conceptual metaphor HUMAN LIFE CYCLE IS THE LIFE CYCLE OF A PLANT. The two domains share a generic-level structure that can be given as follows: In both domains, there is an entity that comes into existence; it begins to grow, and reaches a point in its development when it is strongest; then it begins to decline; and finally it goes out of existence. Based on this shared structure, the plant domain can function as a source domain for the human domain. In other words, the similarity explains the pairing of this particular source with this particular target; that is, the metaphor is grounded in similarity – though of a very abstract kind.

In many other cases, however, this explanation does not work: The source cannot be viewed as similar in any way to the target. CMT offers another explanation or justification for the emergence of these metaphors as well. Let us take the conceptual metaphor in one of the metaphor systems we examined in the previous section: INTENSITY IS HEAT. This metaphor is a generic-level version of a number of conceptual metaphors like ANGER IS FIRE, ENTHUSIASM IS FIRE, CONFLICT IS FIRE, and so on. The specific concepts share an intensity dimension that is metaphorically conceptualized as heat. The concept of HEAT bears no resemblance to that of INTENSITY whatsoever. Heat is a physical property of things that we experience with our bodies, while intensity is a highly abstract subjective notion (on a par with *purpose*, *difficulty*, or as a matter of fact, *similarity*). What, then, allows the use of HEAT as a source domain for INTENSITY? CMT suggests that there is a correlation in experience between intensity and heat. Often, when we engage in activities at a high intensity (be it physical or emotional), our body develops body heat. In this sense, intensity is correlated with heat, and this provides the motivation for the use of HEAT as a source domain for INTENSITY as a target. The generic-level conceptual metaphor INTENSITY IS HEAT can then be regarded as grounded in a correlation between a sensorimotor experience and an abstract subjective one.

Conceptual metaphors of this kind are called "primary metaphors" by Lakoff and Johnson (see, e.g. 1999), who borrowed the term from Joe Grady (1997a, b). Grady proposed a number of such metaphors in his dissertation (1997a), including SIMILARITY IS CLOSENESS and PERSISTENCE IS BEING ERECT, and reanalysed several of the conceptual metaphors in Lakoff and Johnson's early (1980) work along the same lines (e.g. MORE IS UP, PURPOSES ARE DESTINATIONS). He suggested furthermore that several primary metaphors can be put together to form "compound metaphors". For example, the PURPOSEFUL LIFE IS A JOURNEY metaphor is based on the primary metaphors PURPOSES ARE DESTINATIONS, DIFFICULTIES ARE IMPEDIMENTS and others.

Many conceptual metaphors (both the similarity-based ones and the primary metaphors) are based on "image schemas". These are abstract, preconceptual structures that emerge from our recurrent experiences of the world (Johnson 1987; Lakoff 1987). Such skeletal preconceptual structures include CONTAINER, SOURCE-PATH-GOAL, FORCE, VERTICALITY and several others. For example, the STATES ARE CONTAINERS primary metaphor derives from the CONTAINER image schema, the LIFE IS A JOURNEY metaphor from the SOURCE-PATH-GOAL schema, the EMOTIONS ARE FORCES metaphor from the FORCE schema and so on.

The research on primary metaphors has intensified the study of metaphors in the brain. Lakoff (2008) suggested a "neural theory of metaphor". In it, individual neurons in the brain form neuronal groups, called "nodes". There can be different types of neural circuits between the nodes. In the "mapping circuit" that characterizes metaphor, there are two groups of nodes corresponding to the source and target domains. The circuitry between the two groups of nodes will correspond to the mappings, or correspondences. In primary metaphors, one group of nodes represents a sensorimotor experience in the brain, while the other represents an abstract, subjective experience.

Provenance of source domains

Since the human body and the brain are predominantly universal, the metaphorical structures that are based on them will also be predominantly universal. This explains why many conceptual metaphors, such as KNOWING IS SEEING, can be found in a large number of genetically unrelated languages. This does not mean, however, that *all* conceptual metaphors that are based on primary metaphors will be the same from language/culture to language/culture. It was recognized early on that the particular culture in which a metaphor develops is just as significant in shaping the form of the conceptual metaphors in different languages/cultures as the universal bodily experiences themselves (see, e.g. Taylor and MacLaury 1995; Yu 1998, 2002; Musolff 2004). Furthermore, several researchers pointed out that variation in metaphor can also be found within the same language/culture (for a survey of this research, see, e.g. Kövecses 2005).

As the latest development in this trend, scholars have recognized that it is not only culture that functions as an important kind of context in shaping the metaphors that emerge. More and more researchers in this area take into account the tight connection between metaphorical aspects of our cognitive activities and the varied set of contextual factors that influence the emergence of metaphors (see, e.g. Cameron 2003; Semino 2008; Goatly 2007; Gibbs and Cameron 2008; Kövecses 2010b). The overall result is a much richer account of metaphor. First, it has become possible to account for metaphors that may be completely everyday but at the same time do not fit any pre-established conceptual metaphors (see, e.g. Musolff 2004; Semino 2008). Second, by taking into account the role of context, we are now in a much better position to see a fuller picture of metaphorical creativity than before. Indeed, it can be suggested that contextual factors can actually create novel metaphors that can be referred to as "context-induced" ones (Kövecses 2010b, 2015). Third, these context-induced metaphors are not limited to the kinds of basic correlations in experience that form the bases of primary metaphors. Thus, we seem to have a cline of metaphors, ranging from universal primary metaphors to non-universal context-induced ones. In other words, metaphors can derive from the body, cultural specificities and also the more general context.

An example of current research in CMT: interlocking metaphor hierarchies

As we have seen above, the source domains of conceptual metaphors constitute coherent organizations of experience, and the mappings from the source onto the target domains create equally systematically organized target domains. But the question is whether such systematic source-to-target mappings are isolated from each other. I suggest that they are likely to belong to larger, hierarchically organized systems of metaphors.

The principles for the organization of such metaphor systems can be of several distinct kinds. In one (a), the metaphors are organized in a straightforward hierarchy such that both the source and the target are specific cases of higher generic-level concepts. In another (b), different aspects of a given generic-level concept can be differentially conceptualized by means of conceptual metaphors. In still other cases (c), a single aspect of several different abstract concepts may organize a large number of subordinated specific-level conceptual metaphors into a hierarchy. In a fourth (d), the conceptual metaphors form a system because the target domains are part of an independently existing hierarchy of concepts. In a fifth (e), what connects the conceptual metaphors and makes them form a system is the fact that a particular specific-level target concept is a special case of a number of different higher-level concepts that have their own characteristic conceptual metaphors. There are probably additional ways in which metaphor systems are formed, but for the present purposes it is sufficient to take these five possibilities into account and briefly describe them.

Straightforward hierarchies

In this case, both the source and the target are specific-level concepts of generic-level conceptual metaphors. This is the simplest and most straightforward type of hierarchy, and it involves a large number of cases. Let us take the well-known ANGER IS A HOT FLUID metaphor. This is an instance of the generic-level metaphor EMOTIONS ARE FORCES. Actually, the HOT FLUID source can be further specified, yielding, for example, the concept of STEW as a potential source domain. We can represent this as follows:

EMOTIONS ARE FORCES
    ANGER IS A HOT FLUID IN A CONTAINER (He was *boiling* with anger.)
    ANGER IS A STEW (He was *stewing*.)

We can find the same situation for love:

EMOTIONS ARE FORCES
    LOVE IS A NATURAL FORCE (I was *overcome* with love.)
    LOVE IS THE WIND (It was a *whirlwind* romance.)

Different aspects of a single generic concept

What is known as the Event Structure Metaphor system presents a more complicated situation (see Lakoff 1993). Events in general (i.e. the generic-level concept of event) can be actions and occurrences, and they both involve states, causes and changes. Actions also include long-term activities, where progress is an issue. Actions are characterized by purposes, potential difficulty in execution, and manner of performance. These various aspects of events (EVENT 1) are conceptualized in different ways:

Events: EVENTS ARE MOVEMENTS
    Occurrences: OCCURRENCES ARE MOVEMENTS (What's *going on* here?)
    Actions: ACTIONS ARE SELF-PROPELLED MOVEMENTS (What's going to be the next *step*?)
        Cause: CAUSES ARE FORCES (You're *driving* me nuts.)
        State: STATES ARE LOCATIONS / BOUNDED REGIONS (She's *in* love.)
        Change: CHANGE IS MOTION (FROM ONE LOCATION TO ANOTHER) (I almost *went* crazy.)
    Actions: ACTIONS ARE SELF-PROPELLED MOVEMENTS
        Purpose: PURPOSES ARE DESTINATIONS (I want to *reach* my goals.)

Difficulty: DIFFICULTIES ARE IMPEDIMENTS (TO MOTION) (Let's *get around* this problem.)

Manner: MANNER IS PATH (OF MOTION) (We'll do it another *way*.)

Activity: LONG-TERM PURPOSEFUL ACTIVITIES ARE JOURNEYS (We have a *long way to go* with this project.)

Progress: EXPECTED PROGRESS IS A TRAVEL SCHEDULE (I am way *behind* schedule.)

As we can see, the highest-level metaphor here is related to the overarching category of events: EVENTS ARE MOVEMENTS. Events come in several forms, and they are characterized by a variety of different aspects. The various forms and aspects of events are in turn metaphorically viewed in terms of the source domains of movement, location and force. These can of course be further elaborated at still more specific levels of concepts.

A single aspect of several different specific-level concepts

Several conceptual metaphors may belong together by virtue of the fact that they share a particular aspect that is conceptualized metaphorically by means of the same source domain. The target domains to which a single source domain is applied are the "scope of a source domain" (Kövecses 2000a, 2010a). Thus, the scope of a source can be narrow or wide. Consider the following conceptual metaphors:

ANGER IS FIRE (He was *smouldering* with anger.)

LOVE IS FIRE (The *fire* was gone from their relationship.)

DESIRE IS FIRE (It was his *burning* ambition to become a lawyer.)

IMAGINATION IS FIRE (The scene *set fire to* his imagination.)

ENTHUSIASM IS FIRE (He lost the *fire*.)

CONFLICT IS FIRE (The *fire* of war *burnt down* Europe several times in the course of its history.[1])

ENERGY IS FIRE (She's *burning the candle* at both ends.)

All of these target domains share the aspect of (degrees of) intensity through the application of a single source (HEAT OF FIRE). We can suggest that the FIRE source domain has the "main meaning focus" of intensity (Kövecses 2000a, 2010a). Thus, one way of metaphorically understanding intensity is in terms of the heat of fire. This yields the generic metaphor INTENSITY IS HEAT. Consequently, the specific metaphors above are instances of this generic-level metaphor. This is a further way in which conceptual metaphors may form a hierarchical system. As a matter of fact, primary metaphors (see below) can be seen as forming such systems in a natural way, since their target domains represent shared aspects (like intensity) of several different concepts.

Several different aspects of a single specific-level concept

A specific-level abstract concept may inherit conceptual metaphors from several different generic-level metaphor systems by virtue of the fact that its prototypical cognitive-cultural model consists of elements that belong to the different metaphor systems. We can exemplify this with the specific-level abstract concept of friendship (Kövecses 1995). The model of friendship conceptually partakes of a number of different metaphor systems. Since according to the cognitive-cultural model of friendship,

    it is a state that two people attribute to each other,
    it involves communication between the friends,
    it implies mutual interaction with each other,
    it consists of the friends and their interactions as a complex system,
    it includes participants that feel certain emotions towards each other,
    and some other aspects,

the conceptual metaphors that characterize friendship include the following:

    State metaphor system:

        STATES ARE OBJECTS
        ATTRIBUTED STATES ARE POSSESSED OBJECTS (Lakoff 1993)

    Communication metaphor system:

        THE MIND IS A CONTAINER
        LINGUISTIC EXPRESSIONS ARE CONTAINERS
        MEANINGS ARE OBJECTS
        COMMUNICATION IS SENDING (Reddy 1979)

    Interaction metaphor system:

        INTERACTIONS ARE ECONOMIC EXCHANGES (Kövecses 1995)

    Complex system metaphor system:

        ABSTRACT COMPLEX SYSTEMS ARE COMPLEX PHYSICAL SYSTEMS (Kövecses 1995, 2010a)

    Emotion metaphor system:

        EMOTION IS DISTANCE
        EMOTION IS TEMPERATURE (Kövecses 1990, 2000b)

The conceptual metaphors for friendship emerge from these various metaphor systems. Specifically, we find metaphors such as the following in the descriptions of friendship:

    State metaphor system:

        FRIENDSHIP IS A POSSESSED OBJECT (*My* friendship with her did not last long.)

    Communication metaphor system:

        SHARING (COMMUNICATING) EXPERIENCES IS SHARING OBJECTS (We *share* intimate things with each other.) (Kövecses 1995, 2000b)

The metaphor arises because communication between friends often involves sharing ideas and feelings.

Interaction metaphor system:

> INTERACTIONS IN FRIENDSHIP ARE ECONOMIC EXCHANGES (There is a lot of *give and take* in our friendship.) (Kövecses 1995)

The interactions are conceptualized as "economic" exchanges because people often mention a *fifty–fifty basis* in their friendship interactions, which indicates not just a physical exchange of objects.

Complex system metaphor system:

> FRIENDSHIP IS A COMPLEX PHYSICAL SYSTEM (BUILDING, MACHINE, PLANT) (We have *built* a strong friendship over the years.) (Kövecses 1995, 2010a)

Emotion metaphor system:

> AN EMOTIONAL RELATIONSHIP IS A DISTANCE (They have a *close* friendship.)
>
> EMOTION IS TEMPERATURE (They have a *warm* friendship.) (Kövecses 1990, 2000b)

The last two conceptual metaphors have to do with the notion of intimacy that characterizes several emotions, yielding the metaphors INTIMACY IS CLOSENESS and INTIMACY IS WARMTH (both of which are primary metaphors).

More generally, since aspects of friendship constitute a part of these metaphor systems, the hybrid concept of friendship will share with them the specific metaphors.

The target concepts form a hierarchical system of concepts

The best example for this kind of metaphor system is what is called the Great Chain of Being (Lakoff and Turner 1989). This is a hierarchical system of concepts corresponding to objects and entities in the world, such as humans, animals, physical things, and so on. The extended version of this hierarchy consists of the following (Lakoff and Turner 1989; Kövecses 2010a):

God

Complex systems (universe, society, mind, theories, company, friendship, etc.)

Humans

Animals

Plants

Complex physical objects

Inanimate objects

The hierarchy becomes a metaphor system when things on a particular level are conceptualized as things on another level. Notice that this can happen in both directions. Lower-level concepts can function as source domains for higher-level ones as target (e.g. PEOPLE ARE ANIMALS), and higher-level ones can function as source domains for lower-level ones as target (e.g. ANIMALS ARE PEOPLE). Furthermore, the HUMAN, ANIMAL and PLANT categories are often graded internally – a conceptualization that can lead to racist language (e.g. an "*inferior* race").

In summary, conceptual metaphors are not isolated conceptual patterns in the mind but seem to cluster together to form a variety of interlocking hierarchical relationships with each other.

Debates and critiques of CMT

In the world of academia, CMT is in a curious situation: Despite its many undeniable achievements and its obvious usefulness in and popularity across several disciplines, each and every aspect of it has come under criticism in the past thirty years. Indeed, several scholars have expressed their skepticism regarding the very existence of conceptual metaphors (e.g. Cameron and Maslen 2010).

A further curious aspect of the situation is that a considerable body of the criticism is based on Lakoff and Johnson's (1980) work exclusively, which represents only the initial stage of CMT, ignoring much of the later work in CMT. Since this chapter has described, or at least briefly mentioned, some of that work subsequent to *Metaphors We Live By*, I will not take up the criticisms that relate to these features of CMT. I will not discuss issues regarding the processing of conceptual metaphors either, since these are described in another chapter of the present volume (see Chapter 31).

A charge sometimes levelled at CMT is that it works with the concept of domain (as in the idea that conceptual metaphors involve two domains) and that it is itself not a well-defined concept and probably cannot be defined precisely at all. But, as a matter of fact, CMT works with a fairly clear definition of a domain that goes back to Fillmore's definition of a frame: A domain, or frame, is a coherent organization of human experience. This definition makes do in most cases.

Another criticism maintains that CMT is based on circular reasoning. Here the claim is that on the one hand scholars in CMT use linguistic metaphors to identify conceptual metaphors, and that on the other hand, at the same time they suggest that the linguistic metaphors exist because of the already present conceptual ones. One cannot base the existence of conceptual metaphors on linguistic metaphors and at the same time explain the presence of linguistic metaphors on the basis of conceptual metaphors. However, this criticism ceased to be valid after several experiments that did not involve language or linguistic metaphors (beginning with Gibbs's work in the early 1990s) unambiguously confirmed the existence of conceptual metaphors. If conceptual metaphors have been proven to have psychological reality by psycholinguistic experiments, linguists should not deny their existence; they should work to see how they appear and function in language (and other modalities). (For summaries of these experiments, see Gibbs 1994, 2006; Gibbs and Colston 2012.)

But the most commonly and strongly expressed criticism concerns methodological issues; namely, how to identify metaphors in discourse, how the study of metaphor should be based on real data (rather than just lexical or intuitive data) and so forth (see, e.g. Deignan 2005; Pragglejaz Group 2007). As I indicated above, we should now take these developments as an integral part of CMT. However, the need to use real data for metaphor analysis reveals an apparently real weakness of CMT: that CMT researchers do not pay sufficient attention to the discourse and social-pragmatic functions of metaphor in real discourse. This sounds like a valid point. However, I do not think that CMT should be thought of as a view of metaphor whose only job is to collect metaphorical expressions, set up conceptual metaphors based on the expressions, lay out the mappings that constitute those conceptual metaphors and see how the particular conceptual metaphors form larger systematic groups. A large further part of the mission of CMT is to describe the particular syntactic, discursive, social, pragmatic, rhetorical, aesthetic, etc. behaviour and function of the metaphors in real data. And this is precisely something that is currently being conducted by a great number of researchers (e.g. Low et al. 2010). But, to my mind, these researchers are not competing with more "traditional" CMT scholars; instead, they are working out an aspect of CMT that was "neglected" by CMT scholars. The addition is necessary and more than welcome. This kind of work is just as much part of CMT as other aspects of the theory. In other words, I find that the "neglect" was not really neglect. The lack of sufficient attention to the syntactic, pragmatic, etc. features of metaphors resulted from CMT scholars' effort to add a cognitive dimension to metaphor that was mostly lacking in previous work. This was, and still is, the mission of CMT, in collaboration with other metaphor researchers. Without pursuing that mission, we would know much less about metaphor today.

The present state and future directions of CMT

In my view, CMT is a complex and coherent theory of metaphor. As even the sketchy picture above reveals, CMT is a theory of metaphor that is capable of explaining a variety of issues concerning metaphor. In particular, it can explain:

- why we use language from one domain of experience systematically to talk about another domain of experience;
- why the polysemy of words in the lexicon follows the patterns it does;
- why the senses of words are extended in the concrete-to-abstract direction;
- why children acquire metaphors in the sequence they do;
- why the meanings of words emerge historically in the sequence they do;
- why many conceptual metaphors are near-universal or potentially universal;
- why many other conceptual metaphors are variable cross-culturally and intraculturally;
- why many conceptual metaphors are shared in a variety of different modes of expression (verbal and visual);
- why many metaphor-based folk and expert theories of a particular subject matter are often based on the same conceptual metaphors;
- why so many conceptual metaphors are shared between everyday language and literature (and other forms of non-everyday uses of language);
- why and how novel metaphors can, and do, constantly emerge;
- etc.

No other theory of metaphor is capable of explaining all of these issues. This does not mean, however, that CMT has achieved a "state of perfection", and that it has no room to develop further. I have pointed out several issues where CMT scholars need to do much more to explain the facts. One such issue is the discrepancy resulting from making use of different methodologies in establishing the frequency of metaphors in discourse. Another outstanding issue that was mentioned is which conceptual materials are carried over from one domain to another. These are just some of the difficult questions that await answers, but there are additional ones that need to be answered in the future.

On a more positive note, there are also several new research directions that promise an even better understanding of metaphor than what we have today. Lakoff and his colleagues' work on the neural theory of metaphor is one of them (see, e.g. Lakoff 2008). What complicates research on the neural aspects of metaphor, which is itself extremely complex, is that metaphor use is taking place in a variety of different contexts that are constantly monitored by the brain in the course of metaphorical conceptualization. These contextual factors can be regarded as actually priming the use of particular linguistic metaphors that may or may not belong to conventional primary or compound conceptual metaphors (see Kövecses 2015). The result is an extremely complex situation that challenges, and calls for the cooperation of, researchers from a variety of different disciplines, such as neuroscience, metaphor theory and pragmatics, just to mention a few. This is a research project that will surely take several years to complete.

Finally, we have seen that conceptual metaphors occur not in isolation but in a variety of different and interlocking hierarchical structures. This poses several challenges to researchers. First, how do such metaphorical hierarchies emerge in social cognition? And more specifically, how do they emerge and how are they represented in the brain? Second, how and on what basis do the users of metaphors select the appropriate level at which they formulate their metaphors in discourse? Third, how can "context-induced" metaphors be integrated into such hierarchical systems? Or, possibly, should we suppose a larger system that would accommodate both the body-based and the non-body-based metaphors? These are just some of the research issues for the future study of the hierarchical organization of metaphors.

Even more generally, it can be suggested that CMT will continue to play a key role in the development of cognitive linguistics as a general study of language (as well as several other disciplines outside linguistics), as we keep discovering its extensive presence at all levels of linguistic description and its important contribution to connecting the mind with the body, language with culture, the body with culture, and language with the brain.

Note

1 It might be worth mentioning in connection with this example that it has both a literal and a metaphorical interpretation. Clearly, it is the latter that is intended here.

Further reading

Barcelona, A. (ed.) (2000) *Metaphor and Metonymy at the Crossroads*, Berlin, Germany: Mouton.
Cameron, L. and Low, G. (eds) (1999) *Researching and Applying Metaphor*, Cambridge, UK: Cambridge University Press.
Gibbs, R. W., Jr. (ed.) (2008) *The Cambridge Handbook of Metaphor and Thought*, Cambridge and New York: Cambridge University Press.
Gibbs, R. W., Jr. and Steen, G. (eds) (1999) *Metaphor in Cognitive Linguistics*, Amsterdam, The Netherlands: John Benjamins.
Katz, A. N., Cacciari, C., Gibbs, R. W., Jr. and Turner, M. (1998) *Figurative Language and Thought*, New York and Oxford, UK: Oxford University Press.

References

Cameron, L. (2003) *Metaphor in Educational Discourse*, London: Continuum.
Cameron, L. and Maslen, R. (eds) (2010) *Research Practice in Applied Linguistics, Social Sciences and the Humanities*, London: Equinox.
Cienki, A. and Müller, C. (2008) 'Metaphor, gesture, and thought', in R. W. Gibbs, Jr. (ed.), *The Cambridge Handbook of Metaphor and Thought*, pp. 483–501, Cambridge, UK: Cambridge University Press.
Deignan, A. (2005) *Metaphor and Corpus Linguistics*, Amsterdam, The Netherlands: John Benjamins.
Forceville, C. (2008) 'Metaphors in pictures and multimodal representations', in R. W. Gibbs, Jr. (ed.), *The Cambridge Handbook of Metaphor and Thought*, pp. 462–82, Cambridge, UK: Cambridge University Press.
Gibbs, R. W., Jr. (1994) *The Poetics of Mind*, Cambridge and New York: Cambridge University Press.
—— (2006) *Embodiment and Cognitive Science*, Cambridge and New York: Cambridge University Press.
—— (ed.) (2008) *The Cambridge Handbook of Metaphor and Thought*, Cambridge and New York: Cambridge University Press.

—— (2009) 'Why do some people dislike conceptual metaphor theory?', *Journal of Cognitive Semiotics* 1–2: 14–36.
Gibbs, R. W., Jr. and Cameron, L. (2008) 'Social-cognitive dynamics of metaphor performance', *Cognitive Systems Research* 9: 64–75.
Gibbs, R. W., Jr. and Colston, H. (2012) *Interpreting Figurative Meaning*, Cambridge and New York: Cambridge University Press.
Goatly, A. (2007) *Washing the Brain: Metaphor and Hidden Ideology*, Amsterdam, The Netherlands: John Benjamins.
Grady, J. (1997a) 'Foundations of meaning: Primary metaphors and primary scenes', unpublished Ph.D. diss., Department of Linguistics, University of California at Berkeley.
—— (1997b) 'THEORIES ARE BUILDINGS revisited', *Cognitive Linguistics* 8: 267–90.
Johnson, M. (1987) *The Body in the Mind*, Chicago, IL: University of Chicago Press.
Kövecses, Z. (1990) *Emotion Concepts*, Berlin, Germany, and New York: Springer-Verlag.
—— (1995) 'American friendship and the scope of metaphor', *Cognitive Linguistics* 6: 315–46.
—— (2000a) 'The scope of metaphor', in A. Barcelona (ed.), *Metaphor and Metonymy at the Crossroads*, pp. 79–92, Berlin, Germany: Mouton.
—— (2000b) *Metaphor and Emotion*, Cambridge and New York: Cambridge University Press.
—— (2002) *Metaphor: A Practical Introduction*, Oxford and New York: Oxford University Press.
—— (2005) *Metaphor in Culture: Universality and Variation*, Cambridge and New York: Cambridge University Press.
—— (2010a) *Metaphor: A Practical Introduction*, 2nd edn, Oxford and New York: Oxford University Press.
—— (2010b) 'A new look at metaphorical creativity in cognitive linguistics', *Cognitive Linguistics* 21(4): 663–97.
—— (2015) *Where Metaphors Come From: Reconsidering Context in Metaphor*, Oxford and New York: Oxford University Press.
Lakoff, G. (1987) *Women, Fire, and Dangerous Things*, Chicago, IL: University of Chicago Press.
—— (1990) 'The invariance hypothesis: Is abstract reason based on image schemas?', *Cognitive Linguistics* 1(1): 39–74.
—— (1993) 'The contemporary theory of metaphor', in A. Ortony (ed.), *Metaphor and Thought*, 2nd edn, pp. 202–51, Cambridge and New York: Cambridge University Press.
—— (2008) 'The neural theory of metaphor', in R. W. Gibbs, Jr. (ed.), *The Cambridge Handbook of Metaphor and Thought*, pp. 17–38, Cambridge and New York: Cambridge University Press.
Lakoff, G. and Johnson, M. (1980) *Metaphors We Live By*, Chicago, IL: University of Chicago Press.
—— (1999) *Philosophy in the Flesh*, New York: Basic Books.
Lakoff, G. and Turner, M. (1989) *More Than Cool Reason: A Field Guide to Poetic Metaphor*, Chicago, IL: University of Chicago Press.
Low, G., Todd, Z., Deignan, A. and Cameron, L. (eds) (2010) *Researching and Applying Metaphor in the Real World*, Amsterdam, The Netherlands: John Benjamins.
Musolff, A. (2004) *Metaphor and Political Discourse: Analogical Reasoning in Debates about Europe*, Basingstoke, UK: Palgrave Macmillan.
Pragglejaz Group (2007) 'MIP: A method for identifying metaphorically used words in discourse', *Metaphor and Symbol* 22: 1–39.
Reddy, M. (1979) 'The conduit metaphor', in A. Ortony (ed.), *Metaphor and Thought*, pp. 284–324, Cambridge, UK: Cambridge University Press.
Semino, E. (2008) *Metaphor in Discourse*, New York: Cambridge University Press.
Taylor, J. R. and MacLaury, R. (eds) (1995) *Language and the Cognitive Construal of the World*, Berlin, Germany: Mouton de Gruyter.
Yu, N. (1998) *The Contemporary Theory of Metaphor: A Perspective from Chinese*, Amsterdam, The Netherlands: John Benjamins.
—— (2002) 'Body and emotion: Body parts in Chinese expression of emotion', *Pragmatics & Cognition* 10(1): 341–67.

2
Figurativeness, conceptual metaphor, and blending

Barbara Dancygier

Figurative language has interested stylisticians, literary scholars, and linguists for a long time. The last thirty years of scholarship have brought about an interest in figurative language which also includes a study of the conceptualizations underlying figuration. One of the first, and most broadly discussed, figures in this context is *conceptual metaphor* (see Chapter 1).[1] The conceptual approach now also includes a different mapping, known as *conceptual integration* (or *blending*). Both concepts have been used in general studies of linguistic meaning, but have also increasingly appeared in discussions of other aspects of language, and have become popular in cognitive discussions of visual artifacts, discourse genres, and also non-linguistic disciplines. Much of the extant literature does not make clear distinctions between the two conceptual explanations of meaning; also, analysts and students are often not sure how the two concepts are similar and different. An explanation is clearly needed. In what follows, I will outline some major features of Conceptual Metaphor Theory (CMT) and Conceptual Integration/Blending Theory (CBT), often referred to simply as Blending Theory. I will also suggest practical ways in which the central concepts of a conceptual metaphor and a blend can be used in text analysis, and draw comparisons between them, also in the context of other forms of figurative language.

Introduction

Both CMT and CBT build on a well-known fact that words often become polysemous, but also argue that mechanisms of polysemy in such cases are dictated by the nature of thought. The assumption is that figurative meaning is not a special case, where new senses emerge for poetic or rhetorical reasons, but an inherent feature of how words and other linguistic devices are used.

The concept of metaphor outside of CMT has been used in the rhetorical study of figurative language (in poetic or other non-literal contexts), alongside other tropes, such as metonymy, simile, or irony, but metaphor clearly holds a privileged position (starting from Aristotle 1960 all the way through Burke 1969). Since the 1980 seminal book by Lakoff and Johnson (see also Lakoff and Johnson 1999 and Chapter 1), metaphor has been discussed as a conceptual mapping, connecting two conceptual domains, and allowing speakers to talk about abstract phenomena or emotions in terms of more concrete experiences. Once metaphor was established as a conceptual mapping, other tropes started to be redefined in conceptual terms (for an overview, see Littlemore 2015 on metonymy; Moder 2008, 2010 on simile; or Tobin and Israel 2012 on irony). CBT, for comparison, has never been used to discuss tropes. It was first introduced in the 1990s, primarily describing blending as a broad conceptual process. CBT supports the treatment of meaning in terms of conceptual domains, but does not limit the possible combinations to two such domains (source and target); instead, it postulates that a new concept is formed, called a blend. The CBT approach, just like CMT, has been applied in various areas of conceptualization and expression (see Fauconnier and Turner 1996, 1998, 2002; Grady, Oakley and Coulson 1999; Coulson 2001).

Descriptions of metaphors and blends[2] often highlight their similarities rather than their different general goals. Both concepts rely on the idea of conceptual structure being projected into another conceptual structure; the nature and number of these structures and the scope of the projection can be seen differently (see below), but the very idea of a conceptual structure as a representation of meaning and the possibility of taking meaning from one such structure to project it into another is shared by both concepts. As a result, some scholars present conceptual metaphor as a sufficient term, others assume the same about blending, and still others reserve one or the other term for a specific range of interpretations. Very few attempt to clearly connect or distinguish the concepts (Fauconnier and Turner 2008).

In this chapter, I will go over the major claims of CMT and CBT, showing the similarities but also the differences. The chapter will also include a discussion of some examples, putting CMT and CBT in the context of analyzing how language is used in discourse.

Overview: conceptual metaphor and blending

In this section, I will give basic examples of the kinds of mappings CMT and CBT discuss, and outline the primary mechanisms of meaning emergence.

Definitions of mappings cannot quite be formulated without reliance on other, underlying concepts. One such concept is a *domain* (typically used in CMT). Chronologically, the concept of the domain was originally proposed in Lakoff and Johnson's first explanation of conceptual metaphor (1980). It refers to a conceptual package including a range of connected elements, and is potentially referred to by a shared term. For example, a domain such as War[3] includes a number of components such as opponents, weapons, attack and defense, victory and defeat. These components can be used as the basis for a range of metaphoric expressions representing, generally speaking, the domain of an Argument (an exchange of thoughts assuming some initial disagreement, and various procedures and results of those procedures). In talking about an argument in terms of war (<u>attack someone's position, win the dispute</u>, etc.), the War domain is the *source* of structure, while Argument is the *target*. Based on this, a metaphoric mapping can be defined as a relation between two conceptual domains (the source domain and the target domain) which sets up links (mappings) between specific elements of the two domains' structures.[4]

In CMT, the assumption is that the source domain is rich in conceptual structure, and that that structure is basically concrete in nature, so that the domain evokes real life knowledge or experience. This means that the domain of War is filled with information we can think of to describe specific events and we are able to tell the difference between a war and a

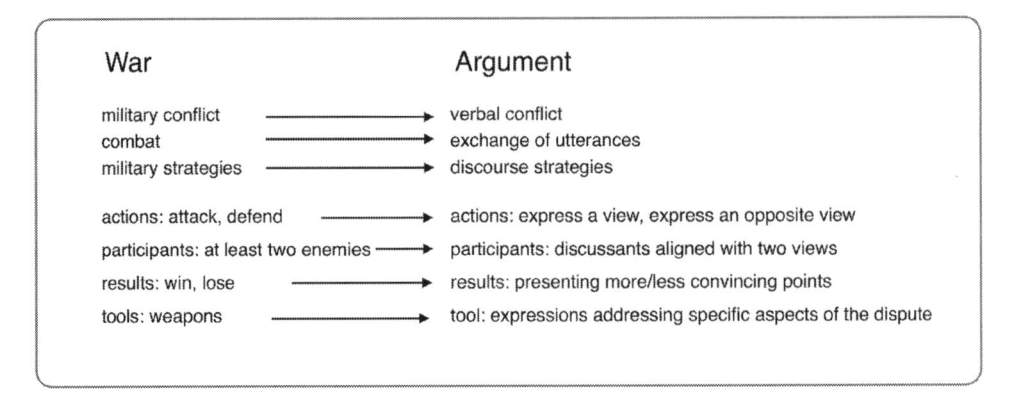

```
War                                    Argument

military conflict          ──────▶    verbal conflict
combat                     ──────▶    exchange of utterances
military strategies        ──────▶    discourse strategies

actions: attack, defend              ──────▶  actions: express a view, express an opposite view
participants: at least two enemies   ──────▶  participants: discussants aligned with two views
results: win, lose                   ──────▶  results: presenting more/less convincing points
tools: weapons                       ──────▶  tool: expressions addressing specific aspects of the dispute
```

Figure 2.1 ARGUMENT IS WAR: the conceptual metaphor.

peaceful negotiation between opposing parties. As regards the target domain, it has very little concrete structure, and may in fact be quite abstract. This is the case of the domain of Argument, which we understand as a specific type of verbal exchange, where opposing views are expressed. Using War as the source domain allows us to describe the progress of the argument beyond simply saying 'and then A said something, and then B disagreed, and then A said something again ... ', etc. The target domain is enriched with conceptual structure from the source domain, such that the arguing parties will eventually be seen as winners or losers. The above description assumes that the projection of conceptual structure goes one way only—from source to target—and as a result of the projection the target can be talked about in more specific terms. That is, the result is a range of metaphoric expressions made possible by the mapping (as in <u>designing a new line of attack, bringing out the heavy guns, withdrawing from one's position</u>, etc.) The metaphorical mapping is schematically represented in Figure 2.1.

Blending considers a broader range of possibilities of projection, and it also explains the nature of the projection differently. For example, the media have been referring to the increasing number of retiring seniors and their potential impact on the economy as <u>the silver tsunami</u>. The expression relies on two domains (in blending terms, they are called 'inputs'),[5] Seniors and Tsunami, but also makes a reference to the Economy. Here is how we might briefly describe the blend:

a. The concept relies on the *generic space*, based primarily on a cause-and-effect pattern, such as 'inevitable change through time which brings catastrophic results'.
b. *Input 1* is the domain of Seniors (an element in the domain of Age), which includes knowledge about the fact that as people age, their lifestyle changes as well.
c. *Input 2* is the domain of Tsunami (an element in the domain of Natural Events), including knowledge about their consequences for people.
d. Both inputs contain a number of elements, but, in agreement with the causal pattern in the generic space, only some elements are chosen for projection. Because of its limited scope, it is called *selective projection*. In the Seniors domain, the blend represents seniors by their grey, or silver, hair (a metonymic reference to age) and their common lifestyle (no longer employed). In the Tsunami domain, the blend selects features of a catastrophic wave which wipes out everything in its path.

e. The selection focuses on the image of an increasing number (of seniors) *cross-mapped* with the increased height, weight, and power of a tsunami wave. Also, the changes in the number of seniors over time are described as increasing along a trajectory—based on the trajectory of the tsunami wave moving forward. When the blend is *run*, the motion and destructive power of the wave is projected into the changes in the Seniors domain, giving them speed and profiling a specific result.
f. The expression uses the term tsunami to signify a catastrophic change, but the results of that change will be felt in the domain of economic stability. To represent this, we need another domain, *Input 3*, that of the Economy, profiled as the domain of destruction caused by the wave.
g. The selected elements are projected into a new construct, called the *blend*. In the blend, we now have a new configuration of concepts, with seniors and their life changes (from *Input 1*) profiled as the cause, and economic change (from *Input 3*) profiled as the result; finally, the nature of that change would be seen as catastrophic (*Input 2*). This new conceptual structure is called the *emergent structure*.
h. The final stage is *backwards projection*, from the blend back to one of the inputs. The causal chain presenting retirement as a potential cause of economic hardship is projected back to the Seniors input, where we now gain the specific view of the effects of the number of seniors growing. This might not change the general concept of aging, but it adds another way of seeing it.

Crucially, the effect is that in the blend thus set up, we are now seeing the growing number of seniors as a negative phenomenon. Outside of the blend, retirement can still be seen as a desirable situation, where people who have worked hard all their lives are now given a chance to relax. In the blend, this is presented as undesirable, because of potential effects on other people. This is the crucial aspect of blending—the point of view constructed by the blend is only valid in that blend, not as a general change in meaning. It is not surprising that the whole concept of the silver tsunami is causing a lot of controversy—not everyone wants to see retirement as harmful.

The blend in this case relies on a number of implicit conceptualizations specific to the inputs. For example, using a (rather formulaic) description of old age by referring to hair color is a case of metonymy. Also, the concept of a wave relies on simpler images of the power of a wave being proportional to its size (the higher the wave, the more destructive it can be), of the wave moving forward (and thus removing obstacles in its way), of the motion of the wave being impossible to stop, etc. All these elements contribute to the impact of the blended image.

The process described above is rather complex, since the blend analyzed belongs to the most powerful (and most complex) category of blends, called double-scope blends.[6] The primary explanation of how three very different domains can be fused into a new concept is the idea of *compression*. The differences across various elements of the three inputs are compressed into a tight and easily manageable structure in the blend. The primary axes along which compression happens in this blend (in CBT, such axes are referred to as *vital relations*) are Causation and Analogy. Outside the blend, old age may be a Change, but in the blend it is a Cause; also, the complex nature of a rising wave (based on the amount of water) provides an analogy to the increase in retirements (where the number of seniors is what causes the problems). Further discussion of vital relations is beyond the scope of this chapter, but it is good to keep in mind that they guide the kinds of changes that elements of inputs undergo as a result of being projected into the blend.

Can conceptual metaphors be interpreted as blends?

There are several kinds of blends described in CBT. They all postulate the independent structure called the blend, and one sub-type, called a single-scope blend, represents conceptual metaphors. Returning now to the ARGUMENT IS WAR metaphor outlined above, in a blending interpretation the nature of conceptual relations between the domains of War and Argument is described in somewhat different terms; the steps are discussed here and the resulting blend is represented in Figure 2.2.

a. As in the example above, the domains are referred to as *input spaces*; thus the domain of War would constitute *Input 1*, and the domain of Argument would constitute *Input 2*.
b. They are matched in terms of a more general domain, called *generic space*. This would contain the idea of opposing options, participants representing those options, actions these participants would undertake (such as trying to affect the opponent's stance), etc. These concepts are applicable both to wars and to arguments, and thus the integration of War and Argument would rely on an abstract frame of oppositional behavior.

    The way in which such knowledge is represented is an important issue in comparing metaphorical analyses with blending analyses. In blending, the generic space needs to be formulated independently of the inputs, for the purposes of the emerging meaning. In metaphorical mappings, there is no dedicated construct justifying the connection between the source and the target; rather, it is assumed that the oppositional behavior characteristic of war is projected into the frame of the argument, thus representing it as an example of oppositional behavior.
c. Metaphor analysis would focus on the effect of the projection—how the target is changed as a result (Kövecses 2002 discusses the effect of *highlighting* the relevant aspects of the target; see also Chapter 1). That is, a metaphor analysis maintains its interest in the relationship between the source domain and the target domain. Blending, for comparison, proposes that the projection does not flow directly from (the source) input to (the target) input, but that both inputs project into another structure, called the *blend*.
d. There are several steps leading to the full fusion in the blend. First, elements in the inputs are connected through *cross-mapping*. Crucially, the participants in a debate are cross-mapped with the warring parties. An argument, like war, is a series of events, where both participants alternate performing similar actions (physical actions such as attack and defense versus verbal events, such as formulating a new thought intended to prove the opponent wrong or serve as a rebuttal).
e. The final stages are like the ones outlined for the silver tsunami example above: conceptual content is selectively projected into the blend, where the new emergent structure is set up, allowing for further inferences or new expressions. The effects of all these processes are represented in Figure 2.2.

If we compare the two blends described above ('Argument is War' and the silver tsunami), the steps in the emergence of the blend are the same. But differences arise on the basis of the number and type of inputs and the scope and complexity of projections into the blend.

These stages of the blending process do not represent the actual sequence of events developing in time, of course. They show the way in which we can represent in some detail what it is for one concept to start structuring another. There are guiding principles that make the connections possible (the generic space), there is contribution from all inputs, but there is

Figurativeness, metaphor, blending

```
┌─────────────────────────────────────────────────────────────┐
│                    Generic space                            │
│                     Opposing                                │
│  two opposed options; alignment; actions; participants;     │
│                    results: tools                           │
└─────────────────────────────────────────────────────────────┘
```

Input 1 — War
- military conflict
- combat
- military strategies
- actions: attack, defend
- participants: at least two enemies
- results: win, lose
- tools: weapons

Input 2 — Argument
- verbal conflict
- exchange of utterances
- discourse strategies
- actions: express a view, express an opposite view
- participants: discussants aligned with two views
- results: presenting more/less convincing points
- tools: expressions addressing specific aspects of the dispute

cross-mapping

The blend — Argument understood as War
- verbal / military conflict
- exchange of utterances / combat moves
- discourse / military strategies
- actions: express a view, express an opposite view / attack, defend
- participants: discussants aligned with two views / enemies
- results: presenting more/less convincing points / winning, losing
- tool: expressions addressing specific aspects of the dispute / weapons

selective projection

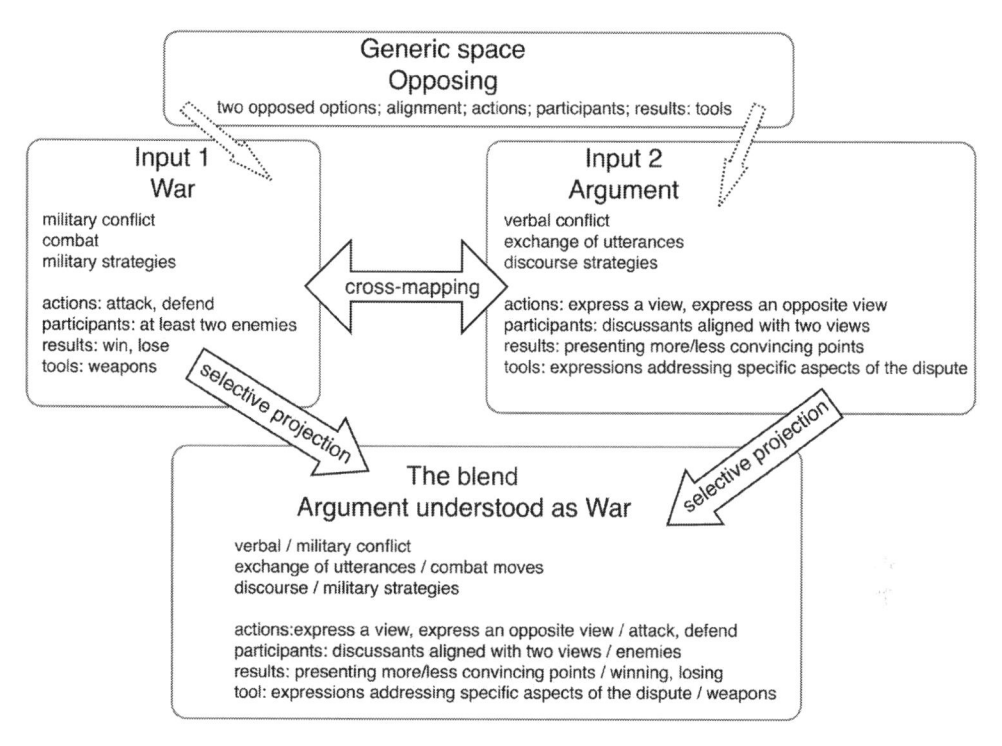

Figure 2.2 ARGUMENT IS WAR: the blend.

also a new concept, one which does not exist in any of the inputs alone, but instead is an independent conceptual structure with its own dynamic.

As the discussion above shows, much of the CMT work would focus on the productive emergence of more and more expressions based on one metaphorical mapping (so that much of the discourse on Argument can rely on War). CBT is less interested in the effect of one mapping, and centers its attention on the online spontaneous communicative effects of giving a tight and unique form to a complex set of various issues and attitudes (so that one aspect of the complex issue of the number of seniors is given a compact and easily manageable label). Fauconnier and Turner (2002) talk about the result of blending as achieving 'global insight' and 'human scale'—indeed, the image of a dangerous tsunami is simple and triggers immediate responses of fear, creating attitudes to seniors which may not make sense outside the blend.

As was noted above, conceptual metaphors can be represented as single-scope blends. Thus, whether we describe the construal of arguments as wars in terms of conceptual metaphor or blending, basically the same facts are accounted for.

Both CMT and CBT use similar operations to describe new meanings. They both postulate that meanings need to be represented as complex structures (whether they are called domains or inputs), and they both propose that projecting aspects of meaning from one such structure to another is the core of the process. But there are important differences as well. Metaphor is more specific about the nature of the changes in the target domain, while blending describes these kinds of changes as resulting from a more general process.

Because of the different goals of the two approaches, one or the other might be chosen with respect to the kind of data under analysis. Blending analysts intend to represent emergence of meaning beyond conceptual metaphor, and so focus on the variety of possibilities serving different discourse goals. The result is that in considering applications of blending, we need to look at a variety of unrelated examples. They may come from any area of language use and structure. There are examples in the formation of new words, as in a <u>webinar</u>—a seminar held online, or the verb to <u>guestimate</u>—estimate by guessing. There are also important examples of complex blending even in the simplest adjectival modification. If someone wishes you <u>Happy travels!</u> as you are boarding a train, they are attributing the future state of happiness to you as a traveller, and not to the actual motion from one location to the next which travel may represent. In this blend, the expression connects the emotional state to the participant in the travel event, not to the event as a whole, creating a complex image of a person pleased with the experience of travel. The meaning does not arise by a simple sum total of the adjective *happy* and the noun *travel*: it is a blend using the full complexity of the *travel* input and the idea that wishing someone something typically relates to a type of experience an event may evoke.

Examples of how various language forms prompt blending structures are numerous, and so CBT covers a broad range of phenomena where new meanings emerge, but not for purposes typically assigned to conceptual metaphor. In comparing CMT and CBT, we need to keep in mind that there is a limited range of examples where both theories can be equally explanatory.

Critical issues

The most important question that arises out of the comparison of the two theories is the analytical benefits of choosing one or the other. Indeed, the practices of various scholars are quite different.

The first strategy is to use the concept of metaphor quite broadly, with some reference to its conceptual nature, but without distinguishing it from blending as a related, but different, conceptual mapping. This is a common practice in many contexts where the specific details of meaning construction of a particular expression are less important to the general points being made. For instance, we will find metaphor being discussed as a broad analytical tool in discussions of discourse (Semino 2008; Chilton 2004; Charteris-Black and Hart 2010; Musolff and Zinken 2009; Deignan, Littlemore and Semino 2013). What these analysts typically aim at is a broad understanding of how a figurative thought pattern affects ways to discuss an issue, construe a problem, draw inferences, etc., especially in a specific discourse genre. It is often the case then that the metaphors postulated have rich domains as sources—the discussion typically focuses on the domains of Journey, War, or similarly salient and productive concepts.

These analyses often uncover important discourse phenomena. For example, in analyses of the discourse of cancer, much discussion is devoted to the Battle (or War) metaphor. The cancer sufferer is portrayed as fighting the illness. Importantly, the motivational nature of such discourse has recently come under much criticism from the medical profession, as too much responsibility for the results of the treatment is placed on the patient's shoulders, and dying of cancer is then implied to be some sort of failure on the part of the sufferer. The discourse can thus be actually harmful to the patient's morale (cf. Chapter 26). In such discussions, the metaphor is viewed as a mindset embedded in the choice of discourse. In many cases, then, the term 'metaphor' is used quite broadly, as a most general pattern of figurative language and thought.

Blending, for comparison, is often chosen to discuss meaning emergence in selected complex expressions. To remain within the discourse of cancer, interesting examples can be found in some of the writing on the subject of cancer by Christopher Hitchens. When first diagnosed with cancer, Hitchens describes his experience as a gentle deportation—he refers in this way to being abruptly removed from his daily professional routines and taken to a new and unfamiliar place where only sick people reside. This is clearly a metaphorical usage. But when later in the article Hitchens talks about the medical discourse of cancer as Tumorville tongue (which he then describes in terms that make it sound like a foreign language), CBT seems to be a better choice in explaining the name of Tumorville. It is a non-existent name of a non-existent town, using the ending -ville, a component of many real city names (such as Louisville, Charlotteville), but also made-up names of film and sit-com locations (Pleasantville, Psychoville, or Smallville, all with predictable local character). So the -ville part is suggesting an invented location, and the Tumor part evokes the actual disease, thus creating an imaginary location of cancer sufferers, though with a charming tone to it. CBT seems a much more effective way of describing the combination of the City Names input with the Tumor input, to create the concept of not just a location for cancer patients, but a whole city-like environment, with its own local flavour, tongue, and rules. Tumorville is not a basis of a reasoning pattern or broader discourse; on the contrary, it is a jocular one-off implementation of the word formation process and a broader idea of pockets of life that healthy people do not know about. Roughly speaking, then, we might say that CMT is a more common tool when one broad concept is talked about in terms of a pattern borrowed from another, while CBT is a natural choice when a creative term is used to encapsulate a rich and complex combination of meanings for the purposes of current expression. Crucially, though, it would be hard to argue that only one of the approaches is appropriate.

This becomes a bit more complex when visual artifacts are involved. Just like the Tumorville expression, visual advertisements often rely on some visual combination of two independent concepts (Forceville 1996; Forceville and Urios-Aparisi 2009). For example, one of many anti-smoking ads shows a hospital bed, neatly made up and empty, with the colors of the bedding resembling a cigarette—three quarters white and one quarter yellow-brown, like a cigarette filter. The bed input clearly suggests illness, serious enough to warrant hospitalization, while the empty and desolate look of the bed suggests that it has just been emptied by a terminally ill smoker-patient, or that it has been reserved for a smoker who will become a patient soon. The cause of the serious illness is only suggested by the colors of the bedding—we understand that the patient was/will be a smoker based only on that. The crucial aspect of such an image is that the warning against the health dangers of smoking is implied through a clever combination of two images, each evoking one of the aspects of the situation. CMT would not help here, because we cannot claim that the knowledge of hospital beds is projected into the concept of a cigarette, or vice versa. Rather, the image depends on metonymy, such that the bed evokes serious illness, warranting hospital treatment and potentially ending badly, while the colors evoke cigarette smoking. The threatening meaning of the image does not arise as a result of projection from one domain to the other, but rather from evocation of two concepts and connecting them into a causal chain: smoking is the cause, illness is the result. Imposing causality is what creates the emergent structure, held together by the so-called vital relation of cause and effect (similarly to the silver tsunami example above). Importantly, then, the causal structure and the resulting warning do not exist in any of the inputs alone—they exist only in the blend the viewer creates by extending and elaborating the two domains into a cohesive structure.

Blending theorists incorporate metaphors into blending and postulate a very broadly applicable mechanism (which is useful in explaining not only language forms or visual artifacts, but also forms in other arts, mathematics, film, theater, etc.). Conceptual metaphor theorists focus on one type of projection while building out other types of figurative meaning from that basis. As this suggests, relying on one framework or the other is largely a matter of a selective approach to what will get covered as a central case. For metaphor theorists, consistent lexical usage and its discourse consequences are central, while for blending theorists, spontaneous emergence of various communicative forms is the primary interest.

This seems to lead to a practical division (though no theorist would likely accept it as his or her own). The conceptual theory of metaphor has made strong claims about metaphors being conceptual in nature and relying on correlations which yield a broad range of conceptually related uses. This makes metaphor theory ideal for discourse work, where the full potential of underlying mappings is clearly seen. Blending focuses on mechanisms of creativity and emergence of new forms expressing new meanings, and it is quite naturally more graceful in explaining the packaging of complex meanings into visual or linguistic chunks, thus allowing for efficient reference and discourse manipulation.

These goals in either case are quite broad, and it is often the case that analysts choose to discuss data in terms of conceptual metaphor or in terms of blending for reasons not clearly connected to the nature of the data under discussion. Some analysts talk exclusively about blends, and others talk exclusively about conceptual metaphor, without trying to distinguish the two. The readers may not be given any justification for the choice of term the analyst makes, and thus may assume that only one way of describing mappings is the correct way. As I show above, there are differences. But also, as I will show below, what is in fact needed is a more flexible and multi-faceted approach to discourse. What should matter more is the accuracy of interpretation, not the preferences in the choice of terminology.

An example of current research

As even our cursory presentation above shows, both metaphors and blends build on simpler structures and various underlying processes. The nature of that hidden structure seems to be more important than a (partly arbitrary) choice of a label. This issue was recently discussed in detail in Dancygier and Sweetser (2014) under the rubric of 'levels of schematicity'. The approach assumes that more complex conceptual structures, such as domains or inputs, build on lower-level structures.

The view of how these structures are connected relies on broadly conceived theories of embodiment, which argue (based on language evidence but also a range of experimental data) that concepts, even many abstract ones, are built on the basis of embodied experience. There are numerous versions of the theories, some very radical and some more partial, but they all see basic embodied experience as the groundwork on which conceptualization is built. For example, all humans mature in the environment in which they desire to move, see objects, or reach for them, but are often blocked by barriers and obstacles. Thus, early on we develop very schematic concepts, called *image schemas*, such as 'path', 'move', 'occlusion', etc. (Johnson 1987; Lakoff and Johnson 1999). These very essential spatial concepts provide a foundation for the development of further concepts. Image schemas are not mappings; rather, they are basic spatial or force-dynamic structures used in understanding other, more complex experiences. Furthermore, recent studies suggest that we should distinguish more than one level of conceptualization to account for what has been discussed as image schemas so far (Mandler and Cánovas 2014), which gives more importance to their role in the emergence of complex meanings.

The next stage of conceptual development, where we can talk about mappings as connections between concepts, is the stage of *primary metaphors* (Grady 1997; Lakoff and

Johnson 1999). For example, the schema of occlusion, and the resulting understanding that one has to have visual access to objects to know what they are, yields one of the very basic metaphors built on actual experience: KNOWING IS SEEING. (Think of the fun a small child has playing 'peekaboo'). Primary metaphors are directly rooted in basic experience and provide a background to more complex, socially motivated and culturally specific metaphors.

There is much research to be reported on the subject. Here, I will assume only what seems necessary—namely, that image schematic structure is used in the emergence of more complex concepts, that primary metaphors underlie the use of complex metaphors, and that broad, lower-level mappings linking embodied activity to abstract activity are often at the core of more complex expressions. All these concepts are illustrated in the examples below.

To consider other conceptual mappings, we can approach the issue of *simile* in an analogous way. Most high school and college textbooks present simile as similar to metaphor except for the additional use of words such as 'like' or 'as' (She was singing like a canary; She was as pretty as a rose). However, recent work shows that simile is a more complex case. First, the presence of 'like' or 'as' is not a sufficient description of simile—the main point is that simile is explicitly comparing two things (e.g., a person's voice and bird song) and choosing a specific focus for the comparison. Setting up a simile relation is not as productive as setting up a conceptual metaphor, because simile typically ends with just one dimension of comparison (pretty as a rose does not imply also smelling like a rose, or having rosy cheeks).[7] Simile is thus to be seen alongside metaphor and blending, but as different from them.

In his inaugural 2013 speeches, Pope Francis explained his concept of the role of the church, relying very heavily on many figurative language forms. Some of the expressions he used are as follows:

(1) "We have to find a new balance; otherwise even the moral edifice of the church is likely to fall like a house of cards [. . .]."
(2) "This Church with which we should be thinking is the home of all, not a small chapel that can hold only a small group of selected people."

In these fragments, the pope talks about the institution of the church in terms of buildings, but he also evokes simpler underlying concepts (through expressions like balance, fall, and hold). He uses several image schemas—balance, up/down, and containment. Humans generally have a very basic concept of balance; they know instinctively that balancing your body or other erect structures (here the up/down schema plays a role too) gives them stability and shape and allows various forms of interaction. In the earliest experience, a well-balanced structure made of wooden blocks will have the desired shape and make play possible. If it loses its balance, it falls down and disintegrates, and using it in pretend play as a castle or a mountain will not be possible. Because remaining in an upright position affords more possibilities for action, it is generally considered a positive situation. Containment is another such schema, imposing boundaries and deciding not only on size but also access. Being inside or outside the playpen affords different possibilities for action and, again, could affect us in a positive way (protection) or negative way (restriction of movement).

The schemas described underlie a range of primary metaphors: GOOD IS UP, PERSISTING IS REMAINING ERECT, ABSTRACT STRUCTURE IS PHYSICAL STRUCTURE, and IMPORTANT IS BIG (cf. Grady 1997; Lakoff and Johnson 1999). Even before the reader can appreciate the concept of the church that is being proposed, it is already clear that the speaker's intention is to ring a note of alarm against lack of stability, limited importance, exclusivity, and potential cracks in the structure. It can then be easily appreciated that the speaker wants to remove all of these symptoms of weakness and dangers of potential collapse.

Quite a lot of the impact of the discourse depends on those lowest levels of schematic structure. From there, much additional complexity is added, but not at all through consistent use of any of the forms of figurative language. Rather, the combination of a variety of means is what gives the fragment its full impact:

a. Complex metaphor: COMPLEX ORGANIZATIONS ARE BUILDINGS
   Expressions such as <u>edifice</u>, <u>chapel</u>, and <u>house of cards</u> refer to types of buildings (see Grady 1997 for an in-depth discussion of the metaphors connected to the Building domain) to describe various possible views of the social importance of the church—from an imposing edifice to a modest chapel to a shaky house of cards, destined to fall down at the slightest provocation.
b. Simile: *like a house of cards*
   This expression evokes the least stable kind of structure, to present the dangers facing the church unless changes are made. Let us note too that this common simile, almost a cliché, relies on the same image schemas and primary metaphors as the complex metaphor in a., using Buildings as the source domain.
c. Metonymy: BUILDING FOR INSTITUTION
   A church is literally a building, but it metonymically represents the religious institution, as most believers interact with the religious organization through the activities and events located in or around the church building. <u>A small chapel</u> further instantiates the metaphor IMPORTANT IS BIG, as it represents the image of the religious institution which has only limited impact on people. But it also belongs to the same part of the frame the Church Building belongs to, as it represents the way in which church-goers interact with the institution. Importantly, though essentially metonymic, the expressions also participate in the Building domain, and so represent the primary and complex metaphors referring to stability, persistence, etc.
d. Blending: *moral edifice of the church*
   This blend is realized through a combination of lexical and syntactic choices.

There is a common type of a blend which uses adjectives derived from nouns to modify other nouns. For example, the expression <u>an economic tsunami</u> (a simpler version of <u>the silver tsunami</u> above) uses the term <u>tsunami</u> to apply it to a situation in the domain of the Economy. Various patterns of adjectival modification have been described as blends (cf. Sweetser 1999), in which an adjective as a modifier does not simply add new information, but may in fact change the meaning of the noun—which is what the adjective <u>moral</u> does here. The prepositional phrase <u>of the church</u> also represents a figurative construction, explicitly identifying the institution and the building as related (rather than metonymically having one stand for the other).

The adjective <u>moral</u> as a modifier thus prompts a blend where aspects of the meaning of <u>edifice</u> (its imposing, serious nature) are related to the domain of morality. Overall, the blend suggests a moral construct of specific importance and power. However, the addition of the prepositional phrase <u>of the church</u> further supports the construal under which the selective projection does not include the Building part of the domain of Edifice, and applies the solidity and significance of the building to the institution of the church.

To sum up, the figurative expressions used in this short fragment are primarily driven by image schemas, and primary metaphors such as: GOOD IS UP, PERSISTING IS REMAINING ERECT,

ABSTRACT STRUCTURE IS PHYSICAL STRUCTURE, and IMPORTANT IS BIG. However, they are also used in combination with complex metaphors, metonymy, simile, and blending, each of which supports some aspect of the main idea—that the church is in danger as an institution and as a moral authority, and so changes are needed to avert the threats. Discourse like this makes it clear that approaches insisting on just one way of dealing with figurative expressions are bound to miss important aspects of the interpretation. It is equally ineffective to insist on a traditional approach relying on narrow definitions of tropes as decorative stylistic choices, or on conceptual metaphor as the only tool, or on blending as the best solution. Each of the conceptual forms mentioned above (schemas, primary metaphors, complex metaphors, metonymy, simile, and blending) participates in the message offered by Pope Francis in its own way. Each of these 'tropes' functions at a different level of conceptual schematicity and grammatical form, and thus contributes to the overall message. They represent a range of types of figurative conceptualizations.

Future directions

In the above analysis, I outlined the contribution of various figurative forms to the overall message of a short fragment. What is certainly worth studying further, though, is how the complex clusters of conceptual mappings work together. In the example described above, primary metaphors provide connecting tissue on which the complex message is built—hence, probably, the immediate appeal and clarity of the discourse. The Building domain connection is effective precisely because of its embeddedness in basic schemas of uprightness and strength and its simultaneous realization of various conceptual mappings. In the end, each conceptual figure contributes to a different aspect of meaning.

What an attempt to compare conceptual metaphor and blending also shows is that it is crucial not to be led entirely by terminological differences. You can call a structure a 'domain' or an 'input', but it is possibly best to keep in mind that we cannot effectively describe any of the central figures without making it clear first what the nature of these basic conceptual structures is. In the end, it is the nature of figurative language that allows us to talk about metaphor and blending as same or different, and it should remain the core of the question we are investigating.

Given that both CMT and CBT are now increasingly applied in various discourse contexts, including multimodal contexts such as advertising or comics (Forceville 1996; Forceville and Urios-Aparisi 2009) or new achievements in technology (Harrel 2013), one can expect more work on clarifying the nature of the two concepts and their most natural contexts of application. But at the same time, we can expect more interest in redefining figurative language overall (Dancygier and Sweetser 2014; Gibbs and Colston 2012) in terms of conceptual patterns and interpretive strategies. This is exciting work, which might eventually shake the artificial divide between literal and figurative language. Figuration might soon be considered a norm rather than an exception.

Notes

1 Dancygier and Sweetser (2014), for example, propose a conceptual interpretation of figurative meaning overall, including metaphor, metonymy, simile, and other tropes.
2 In the discussion below, I will use the term 'metaphor' to refer to a conceptual mapping, and the term 'blending' or 'blend' to discuss the processes and structures postulated in CBT.
3 Throughout the chapter, words with their first letter capitalized stand for domains or inputs.

4 In literature on conceptual metaphor, one may also find domains defined in terms of 'frames.' See Sullivan (2013).
5 The term 'input' is specific to CBT, but in most cases it is equivalent to CMT's definition of a domain. I use 'domain' here as a generic term, applicable in both theoretical frameworks.
6 In Fauconnier and Turner (2002) blends are claimed to be of four kinds, with respect to the type of relation between the inputs. Full discussion of all these types is beyond the scope of this chapter, and I focus only on two types—double-scope and single-scope. A single-scope blend is heavily dependent on the conceptual structure in one of the inputs, and thus CBT argues that most metaphorical expressions can be described as single-scope blends. A double-scope blend, for comparison, draws from both inputs in complex and often unpredictable ways; it is thus better suited to the description of new, one-off expressions.
7 Dancygier and Sweetser (2014) describe simile as a construction setting up a *limited-scope blend* (following the observations about the scope of simile made in Moder 2008, 2010). For the purposes of this discussion, though, I will treat simile as an independent trope.

Further reading

Dancygier, B. and Sweetser, E. (2014) *Figurative Language*. New York: Cambridge University Press.
Sullivan, K. (2013) *Frames and Constructions in Metaphoric Language*. Amsterdam, The Netherlands: John Benjamins.
Fauconnier, G. and Turner, M. (2008) 'Rethinking metaphor'. In R. W. Gibbs, Jr. (ed.), *Cambridge Handbook of Metaphor and Thought*, pp. 53–66. New York: Cambridge University Press.
Grady, J. (1997) 'THEORIES ARE BUILDINGS revisited.' *Cognitive Linguistics* 8: 267–90.

References

Aristotle. (1960) *The Rhetoric of Aristotle*. Trans. Lane Cooper. Upper Saddle River, NJ: Prentice Hall.
Burke, K. (1969) *A Grammar of Motives*. Berkeley, CA: University of California Press.
Charteris-Black, J. (2004) *Corpus Approaches to Critical Metaphor Analysis*. Basingstoke, UK: Palgrave-MacMillan.
Chilton, P. A. (2004) *Analysing Political Discourse: Theory and Practice*. London: Routledge Chapman & Hall.
Coulson, S. (2001) *Semantic Leaps: Frame Shifting and Conceptual Blending in Meaning Construction*. New York: Cambridge University Press.
Dancygier, B. and Sweetser, E. (2014) *Figurative Language*. New York: Cambridge University Press.
Deignan, A., Littlemore, J. and Semino, E. (2013) *Figurative Language, Genre and Register*. Cambridge, UK: Cambridge University Press.
Fauconnier, G. and Turner, M. (1996) 'Blending as a central process of grammar.' In A. Goldberg (ed.), *Conceptual Structure, Discourse, and Language*, pp. 113–30. Stanford, CA: CSLI Publications.
—— (1998) 'Conceptual integration networks'. *Cognitive Science* 2(22): 133–87.
—— (2002) *The Way We Think: Conceptual Blending and the Mind's Hidden Complexities*. New York: Basic Books.
—— (2008) 'Rethinking metaphor.' In R. W. Gibbs, Jr. (ed.), *Cambridge Handbook of Metaphor and Thought*, pp. 53–66. New York: Cambridge University Press.
Forceville, C. (1996) *Pictorial Mapping in Advertising*. London: Routledge.
Forceville, C. and Urios-Aparisi, E. (2009) *Multimodal Metaphor*. Berlin, Germany: Mouton de Gruyter.
Gibbs, R. W., Jr. and Colston, H. L. (2012) *Interpreting Figurative Meaning*. New York: Cambridge University Press.
Grady, J. (1997) 'THEORIES ARE BUILDINGS revisited.' *Cognitive Linguistics* 8: 267–90.
Grady, J., Oakley, T. and Coulson, S. (1999) 'Blending and metaphor.' In G. Steen and R. W. Gibbs, Jr. (eds.), *Metaphor in Cognitive Linguistics*. Philadelphia, PA: John Benjamins.

Harrell, D. F. (2013) *Phantasmal Media: An Approach to Imagination, Computation, and Expression*. Cambridge, MA: MIT Press.

Hart, C. (2010) *Critical Discourse Analysis and Cognitive Science: New Perspectives on Immigration Discourse*. Basingstoke, UK: Palgrave Macmillan.

Johnson, M. (1987) *The Body in the Mind: The Bodily Basis of Meaning, Imagination, and Reason*. Chicago, IL: Chicago University Press.

Kövecses, Z. (2002) *Metaphor: A Practical Introduction*. Oxford, UK: Oxford University Press.

Lakoff, G. and Johnson, M. (1980) *Metaphors We Live By*. University of Chicago Press.

—— (1999) *Philosophy in the Flesh: The Embodied Mind and Its Challenge to Western Thought*. New York: Basic Books.

Littlemore, J. (2015) *Metonymy: Hidden Shortcuts in Language, Thought and Communication*. Cambridge, UK: Cambridge University Press.

Mandler, J. and Cánovas, C. P. (2014) 'On defining image schemas.' *Language and Cognition* 6(4): 510–32.

Moder, C. (2008) 'It's like making a soup: Metaphors and similes in spoken news discourse.' In A. Tyler, Y. Kim and M. Takada (eds.), *Language in the Context of Use: Discourse and Cognitive Approaches to Language*, pp. 301–20. Berlin, Germany: Mouton de Gruyter.

—— (2010) 'Two puzzle pieces: Fitting discourse context and constructions into Cognitive Metaphor Theory.' *English Text Construction* 3(2): 294–320.

Musolff, A. and Zinken, J. (eds.) (2009) *Metaphor and Discourse*. Basingstoke, UK: Palgrave Macmillan.

Semino, E. (2008) *Metaphor in Discourse*. New York: Cambridge University Press.

Sullivan, K. (2013) *Frames and Constructions in Metaphoric Language*. Amsterdam, The Netherlands: John Benjamins.

Sweetser, E. (1999) 'Compositionality and blending: Semantic composition in a cognitively realistic framework.' In T. Janssen and G. Redeker (eds.), *Cognitive Linguistics: Foundations, Scope, and Methodology*, pp. 129–62. Berlin, Germany: Mouton de Gruyter.

Tobin, V. and Israel, M. (2012) 'Irony as a viewpoint phenomenon.' In B. Dancygier and E. Sweetser (eds.), *Viewpoint in Language: A Multimodal Perspective*, pp. 25–46. New York: Cambridge University Press.

3
Relevance theory and metaphor

Robyn Carston

Introduction: metaphorical language as a pragmatic phenomenon

Metaphor is without doubt a phenomenon of language. It may also be a phenomenon of thought, but that is less obvious and needs to be argued for. In this chapter, the starting position is that metaphors arise from linguistic communication, that they are the result of speakers and writers employing words to achieve particular effects on hearers and readers, and that they thus fall within the discipline of pragmatics. The questions to be addressed are why speakers use metaphors, how addressees grasp the meanings thus expressed, what cognitive processes or mechanisms are involved, and what cognitive effects or benefits arise from using language in this way. The particular approach to pragmatics which is the focus of this chapter is that developed within the framework of Relevance Theory (RT) (Sperber and Wilson 1986a/1995; Carston 2002; Wilson and Sperber 2004).

The range of metaphorical language to be discussed runs from highly conventionalised single-word uses, such as those in (1), through cases employing familiar metaphorical schemes, whether lexical or extended, such as those in (2), to novel, creative, perhaps poetic/literary uses, whether lexical or (much more) extended, such as those in (3):[1]

(1) a. Jane is an *angel*.
    b. Her boyfriend is a *pig*.
    c. I must *fly*.
(2) a. It was daily *warfare* between my parents when I was a kid.
    b. Life is a *journey*, with *mountains to climb*, *rivers to navigate* and other *travellers* to *walk with* or *flee from*.
(3) a. 'The gold standard performance comes from McDiarmid. Vocally, he is spellbinding, giving lines *dexterous topspin* and unexpected bursts of power.'
                                      Theatre critic David Jays, reviewing a play,
                                            The Sunday Times, 4 September 2011

b. Life's but a walking shadow, a poor player
That struts and frets his hour upon the stage
And then is heard no more: it is a tale
Told by an idiot, full of sound and fury,
Signifying nothing.

Shakespeare: Macbeth V.v. 24–30

Fundamental to the relevance-theoretic (RT) approach to metaphor is the view that it is a pervasive feature of everyday linguistic communication and one that does not differ in kind from other instances of loose use (that is, cases where the speaker is not strictly literal in her use, as demonstrated below). According to the theory, there are no mechanisms or processes specific to the recognition and comprehension of metaphor, which is understood in essentially the same way as literal and loose uses. There are essentially three periods in the development of the RT account of metaphor, which can be characterised by the following moves: (a) the claim that metaphorical use of language is a kind of loose use (mid 1980s); (b) the assimilation of metaphorical uses of words into 'lexical pragmatics', a sub-theory within RT pragmatics, according to which words are frequently used to communicate a different concept from the one they linguistically encode (mid 1990s); and (c) the proposal that there are two distinct relevance-driven routes to metaphor understanding, depending on a range of factors including degree of familiarity, complexity, and creativity of the metaphor (late 2000s). An interesting issue that cross-cuts all of these stages is that of the role and status of such non-propositional (experiential) effects of metaphor as imagery, sensation, and affect.[2]

Before addressing these matters in some detail, I briefly set out some essential components of the general relevance-based approach to pragmatics in the next section. Then I discuss the two key components of the orthodox RT account of metaphor, that is, loose use and ad hoc concepts. This is followed by a brief overview of some issues/objections to the account, and then a discussion of current research within the framework which goes some way towards addressing the issue of imagistic effects. I conclude with a short review of directions for future research.

Overview: linguistic underspecification and relevance-theoretic pragmatics

It is widely recognised that the linguistic expressions that speakers utter standardly do not encode the thoughts (or propositions) that they are used to communicate. This applies not only to the obvious case of the thoughts that speakers (merely) implicate but also to those that are more closely associated with the linguistic meaning of their utterances and can be thought of as explicitly communicated (explicatures, in RT).[3] Consider the following rather ordinary exchange between two university lecturers, focusing on what Amy means by her utterance:

(4) Bill: Did the staff-student meeting go well?
    Amy: We gave up – the students wouldn't engage.

Clearly, what Bill takes Amy to be communicating depends on a rich background of assumptions that Amy assumes are accessible to him, but we all have access to some of these assumptions (based on general and cultural knowledge) and can surmise that she has communicated at least the following two propositions (or very similar ones):

(5) a. Amy and the other staff members at the meeting gave up on their attempt to discuss certain issues with the students who were at the meeting because those students would not engage with these issues.
b. The meeting did not go well (from the point of view of Amy).

There is a considerable gap between the meaning of the sentence types used by Amy ('We gave up', 'The students wouldn't engage') and the meaning she conveyed. Not only does Amy implicate a thought, (5b), that is entirely distinct in content from the sentences she uttered, but her explicature, (5a), although incorporating the meaning of the sentence uttered, involves considerable pragmatic inferential development. This gap is a perfectly general phenomenon of linguistic communication and it is the business of a pragmatic theory to explain how it is bridged, that is, how hearers are able to recover rich specific messages on the basis of utterances of linguistic expressions that radically underspecify those messages. There are many different manifestations of this linguistic underspecification of what the speaker meant (or communicatively intended): ambiguities (lexical and structural), referential indeterminacies such as 'we' and 'the students' in Amy's utterance above, unspecified quantifier domains as in '*Everyone* left early', incomplete expressions as in 'The students didn't *engage*' *[with what?]* or 'Mary is *ready*' *[for what?]*, vague expressions like 'He is *young*' or 'They live *nearby*', implicit clausal connections like the sequential and cause–consequence relation between the two parts of Amy's utterance above.

An interesting subset of cases of this phenomenon of speaker meaning being underspecified by encoded linguistic meaning consists of those in which the concept expressed/communicated is different from the concept encoded: it may be more specific (narrower in its denotation); more general (broader in its denotation); both of these (that is, more specific in some respects and broader in others, so that its denotation merely overlaps with that of the encoded concept); or a case of what is sometimes called 'transfer' (so there is no overlap in denotation between the encoded and the communicated concepts, although the two concepts may be closely associated). Here are plausible examples of each of these possibilities:

(6) a. It's not *open* yet.
b. The children formed a *circle*.
c. My husband is a *bachelor*.
d. *The Ford Capri* is deliberately cutting in front of us.

In the case of (6a), there are many possible specific concepts that could be communicated by the use of the very general (literal) concept OPEN encoded by the adjective 'open'; for instance, there are quite distinct kinds of opening stereotypically associated with a door, a book, a lap-top, a shop, a tomb, a washing-machine, etc., any one of which could be being referred to by the use of 'it' here; each of these concepts is a narrowing (or specification) of the encoded lexical concept.

The use of 'circle' in (6b) is an approximation, allowing for quite a degree of irregularity in the shape the children formed, hence the concept communicated is broader than the encoded lexical concept. In (6c), the concept communicated can be roughly paraphrased as 'man who behaves in irresponsible, uncommitted ways', and its denotation includes some married men (hence is a broadening of the encoded concept) and excludes some actual bachelors (hence is also a narrowing). Finally, the referent of 'The Ford Capri' in (6d) is not a car but the driver of that car – this sort of metonymic use of a word is neither a narrowing nor a broadening of denotation but works in some other way. As we will see below, on the RT account, metaphorical uses of words and phrases are taken to fall into this lexical modulation process, specifically involving a denotational broadening, as in (6b) and (6c).

According to the relevance-theoretic approach, the processes responsible for recovering all the various pragmatic components of meaning are constrained by addressees' context-specific expectations of relevance. More fundamentally, all our cognitive processing is seen as relevance-driven, that is, it is geared towards deriving as many cognitive benefits as possible (increasing the accuracy, richness, and well-organisedness of our representation of the world) for as little processing cost as possible. Among the stimuli we process, verbal utterances, along with other communicative gestures, have a special status, in that they are 'ostensive': they overtly demand the addressee's attention (hence effort) and encourage him[4] to explore the communicator's intentions in producing them, with the expectation that particular cognitive benefits will be derived and there will be no gratuitous processing effort involved in their derivation. Thus, what licenses an addressee's expectations of relevance (of cognitive effects to be gained and effort to be expended) on any particular occasion of utterance is a completely general presumption of 'optimal relevance' conveyed by all utterances (ostensive stimuli). This is the presumption that it is relevant enough to be worth processing, and as relevant as the communicator is able and willing to make it.[5] On this basis, the comprehension heuristic standardly employed by addressees in processing an utterance is to follow a path of least effort in constructing an interpretation of the utterance (including such processes as resolving ambiguities and referential indeterminacies, enriching and adjusting lexical meaning, and computing implicatures) up to the point at which their expectations of relevance are satisfied. How this works in practice will be demonstrated below for cases of metaphorical use.

Metaphor as a kind of loose use

The foundational claim of the RT account of metaphor is that it is a kind of 'loose use' of language (Sperber and Wilson 1986a/1995, 1986b). This remains a central component of the RT account to this day, although, as will be discussed in subsequent sections, the way in which this loosening (or broadening) of linguistic content is taken to manifest itself has changed over the past 25 years.

Obvious instances of loose use include approximations like 'Oxford is *sixty miles* from London'; 'The children formed a *circle*'; cases where absolute terms that denote the absence of some property, like 'raw', 'painless', 'silent', or 'bald', are relaxed so as to include a low level of the property (e.g. 'The house was *silent*' uttered when, strictly speaking, there were various sounds of creaking and dripping); the use of brand names for the more generic object or activity, such as 'I need a *kleenex*' or 'Please *xerox* 50 copies'; and hyperbolic uses like 'The queue for tickets is 100 miles long'. The radical claim made by Sperber and Wilson was that 'there is no discontinuity between those loose uses and a variety of "figurative" examples which include the most characteristic examples of poetic metaphor' (Sperber and Wilson 1986a/1995: 235).

In this early RT work on loose use (including metaphorical use), the idea was that speakers express propositions that they do not endorse and that they do not expect their addressees to believe; that is, they don't *communicate* the proposition expressed, but rather employ it as a vehicle for the communication of a range of implicatures. For example, an utterance of the sentence in (7a) might express the proposition given in (7b), but this is not a component of the speaker's meaning, which consists of a set of implicatures such as those in (7c). The utterance has no explicitly communicated content (other than the higher level proposition THE SPEAKER HAS SAID THAT THE STEAK$_x$ IS RAW; note: the subscript 'x' indicates that a specific member of the category of steaks has been picked out).

(7) a. This is raw.
    b. THE STEAK$_x$ IS RAW.
    c. THE STEAK$_x$ IS VERY UNDERCOOKED.
       THE SPEAKER REGARDS THE STEAK$_x$ AS INEDIBLE.
       THE STEAK$_x$ SHOULD BE RETURNED TO THE KITCHEN FOR FURTHER COOKING.

An essential ingredient of the account was the idea that one propositional form can be used to represent another one, where the relation between the two forms is one of 'interpretive resemblance', that is, of resemblances in the logico-semantic content of the two propositions. On a literal use, a speaker employs an utterance whose propositional form is identical to the propositional form of the thought whose content she wants to communicate, so that the two forms share all their logical and semantic properties (entailments, contextual implications). In fact, rather few utterances are wholly literal, but the following is a possible case: 'Some oak trees are deciduous'. On a loose use, the propositional form of the utterance shares some, but not all, of its logical properties with the propositional form of the thought it is being used to represent. In (7), for instance, the proposition expressed shares with the speaker's thought the implications in (7c), which are communicated, but it also carries the implication that the steak in question has received no cooking at all (the literal meaning of 'raw'), which is not shared with the thought the speaker has in mind and is not communicated. For this to work, it is crucial that addressees have the ability to sort out those implications of the utterance's propositional form which are meant by the speaker from those which are not. That they can and do achieve this sorting follows directly from the precepts of relevance theory: addressees follow a path of least effort in deriving contextual implications from the utterance, using the most accessible items of encyclopaedic information associated with lexically encoded concepts, and the inferential process ends when their expectations of relevance are satisfied. In the case of (7), as uttered in a typical restaurant scenario, the implications most easily derived concern the edibility of the steak and its qualities as a satisfactory meal. It is unlikely that the implication that it totally lacked any cooking would be accessed, and, if it were, it would be immediately discarded as incompatible with what we know about the standard practices of restaurants.

More generally, the idea is that quite often a literal interpretation of an utterance is not intended and would not satisfy the presumption of optimal relevance because it would require unnecessary effort to derive the intended cognitive effects when those effects could be derived more economically from a loose use. This is especially evident in cases involving numbers, so telling someone that I earn £2,000 a month (rather than £1,983, which, let us suppose, is in fact the case) will enable him to derive the intended implications about my living standard, my status, and my purchasing power with less effort than processing the strictly correct amount. In the case of the loose use of 'raw' in (7), this is a more economical and effective way of conveying the speaker's thought(s) about the steak than any attempt at literal encoding, such as 'This steak is undercooked to the extent that I find it repellent to contemplate eating it'.

In other cases, there may simply be no linguistic encoding of the thought(s) the speaker wants to convey, not even a long or complex one, so she has no option but to choose an expression whose loose use will enable the addressee to infer the content of the thought(s).

This may be the case for quite a few metaphors, in particular those that are felt to be especially evocative or poetic. Consider, in this regard, two of the more novel and creative metaphors given above in (3) and repeated here as (8a) and (8b):

(8) a. Vocally, he is spell-binding, giving lines *dexterous topspin* and unexpected bursts of power.
b. Life's but a walking shadow, a poor player
That struts and frets his hour upon the stage
And then is heard no more: it is a tale
Told by an idiot, full of sound and fury,
Signifying nothing.

Taking (8a) first, the phrase 'dexterous topspin' is typically used to describe a particularly skilful hitting or throwing of a ball in tennis or cricket, a technique that makes the ball rotate forwards as it moves through the air, so that it falls earlier and faster than normal and is consequently hard for the opponent to return. As used here, to describe the way an actor spoke his lines, the literal meaning drops away and what is communicated is an array of implications concerning the skill with which the actor used his voice, its compelling effect on the audience, and, perhaps, the difficulty the other actors had in matching it. Doubtless, this description does not do justice to the cognitive (and perhaps sensory) effects of this metaphor, but it suffices to indicate not only the relevant semantic resemblances between the speaker's intended meaning and the proposition expressed by his utterance, but also the lack of any literal language by means of which that intended meaning could have been expressed. Turning to (8b), this unparaphraseability is all the more apparent: what is communicated are implications about the brevity and pointlessness of life, the self-important delusions that drive us, how little real value there is in our frantic efforts to achieve, etc. Again, this characterisation of the meaning conveyed is no more than an indication, as there simply is no fully adequate way to express it literally.

Not only is it not possible to give literal expression to the implicatures of the examples in (8), there is a degree of indeterminacy about them, especially in the case of (8b): while one member of the audience might derive implications about the meaninglessness of human existence, another might focus more on implications concerning the high ambitions and terrible compromises one makes only for it all to come to nothing in the end. These facts about the variability of equally good interpretations are usually ignored by pragmatic theories, but they are explained in the RT framework by its account of communication as occurring with different degrees of strength. The strength with which a proposition is communicated is a matter of the degree to which the communicator makes evident her intention to make that particular proposition manifest to the addressee. The implicature of Amy's utterance in (4) is strongly communicated, in the sense that she can be taken to have specifically intended it, while those conveyed by (8a) and (8b) are considerably weaker, in the sense that the speaker/author need not specifically intend that particular propositions are recovered, but rather that the audience infer some of the propositions that fall within a wide range made manifest to some degree by the utterance, enough of them to satisfy their expectations of relevance. Metaphorical utterances, like all other uses, literal or non-literal, may communicate some implicatures strongly and others relatively more weakly, so, for instance, the author of (8a) strongly communicates that the actor delivered his lines skilfully and effectively, but weakly communicates other propositions concerning the pitch changes of his voice, his interaction with his fellow actors on stage, the effects of his speeches on the audience, etc. Different readers will derive different subsets of these weak implicatures. When an utterance or piece of text achieves most of its relevance through a wide array of weak implicatures, as in the case of (8b), the resulting effect is what Sperber and Wilson (1986a/1995: 222) term a 'poetic effect'. Despite the 'weakness' of the implicatures in such a case, the effect on the audience is often very powerful, due both to the density of the array of propositions made weakly manifest, and to the responsibility, hence the personal engagement, of the audience in recovering particular propositions from the wide range the speaker/writer has encouraged him to explore.[6]

Metaphor, lexical pragmatics, and ad hoc concepts

The development of a subfield of 'lexical pragmatics' in the mid-1990s brought with it a change to the way in which metaphor and (other) loose uses of language have been explained in RT. As mentioned earlier, the modulation of encoded word meaning in context may result in a concept that has a narrower and/or broader denotation than the concept encoded by the word. The claim is that there is a single process of accessing items of encyclopaedic information and using them as contextual assumptions to derive contextual implications. These, in turn, lead to adjustments of the concept which made those encyclopaedic assumptions accessible. Whether the resulting concept is narrower or broader (or both) in denotation than the encoded lexical concept is entirely a function of the encyclopaedic information deployed in the given case. The following example should make the process clear.

Consider an utterance of (9), where the speaker is the mother of a 5-year-old boy, Billy, and the addressee is the boy's father, who is angry with him for breaking a toy:

(9) He's just a child.

Plausible implications of the mother's utterance, derived via highly accessible background information associated with the concept CHILD, are that Billy's behaviour is due to him being very young and inexperienced and is, therefore, understandable and forgivable. Arguably, this results in a concept, CHILD*, which is somewhat narrower than the lexically encoded concept CHILD, roughly paraphraseable as 'child who is not yet physically and psychologically developed'. Now consider a different scenario, in which (9) is uttered by a woman who is referring to her husband, Mike, who avoids household chores and spends many hours a day playing computer games. Here, the implications communicated are that he is not fulfilling normal adult responsibilities, assumes he can play while others work, is morally underdeveloped, etc., which, by backwards inference, results in a concept, CHILD**, which is broader than the lexically encoded concept CHILD, including in its denotation not only actual children but also adults who behave in certain childish ways.

In both cases, we talk of the pragmatically inferred word meaning as an ad hoc concept (indicated by asterisks to distinguish it from the linguistically encoded concept), and it is a component of the explicature of the utterance. So, for the case of concept broadening, that is, the loose use of 'child' in the second scenario, the resulting interpretation looks like the following:

(10) Explicature: MIKE_x IS JUST A CHILD**
     Implicatures: MIKE_x IS IRRESPONSIBLE
                    MIKE_x SPENDS HIS TIME PLAYING RATHER THAN DOING USEFUL WORK
                    MIKE_x HAS THE PSYCHOLOGICAL DEVELOPMENT OF A BOY RATHER THAN A MAN

An important mechanism involved here is that of 'mutual parallel adjustment' of explicature, contextual assumptions, and contextual implications (or implicatures): the lexical concept CHILD has associated with it an encyclopaedic entry of items of information (general and cultural knowledge about children, specific episodic memories of children), with fluctuating degrees of accessibility of the component items, strongly influenced on any occasion of use by the specifics of the context of utterance. In the current case, information about the lack of responsibilities of children, their dependence on others, and their freedom to play would be highly accessible and would be recruited as contextual assumptions, leading, by deductive inference, to the contextual implications about Mike suggested above. Then, by a process of backwards inference, the lexically encoded concept CHILD is adjusted to the ad hoc concept CHILD**, which warrants just these context-specific implications. There may be several iterations of these processes of mutual parallel adjustment of explicature, contextual assumptions, and contextual implications, until the overall interpretation meets the addressee's specific expectations of relevance, based on the general presumption of 'optimal relevance'.

The RT claim about metaphorical use is that it works in exactly the same way, as do all the other cases of loose use discussed above (approximations, category extensions, hyperboles, and so on), which vary only with regard to the specific items of encyclopaedic information accessed and thus the implications inferred (that is, the particular way in which the utterance achieves relevance on the particular occasion). A clear case of a metaphorical use of 'child' is given in (11), in discussing Mary, who, after 15 years of dedicated work, has finally finished her treatise on the yin-yang duality in British politics:

(11)   I wonder how she'll cope now that her big project is finished. It's been central to her life for so long. It was her child.

Again, certain encyclopaedic assumptions, accessed via the concept CHILD, are more accessible than others, in particular those whose activation is increased by their connection with concepts made available by the earlier part of the discourse and the wider context. The ad hoc concept communicated here, CHILD***, is inferred from such contextual implications as that the project was of great importance to Mary, that she lavished much care and attention on it over a long period of time, that she will miss it badly now that it is no longer part of her daily life, etc. Note that the variable degree of strength/weakness of implicatures (and hence their indeterminacy), as discussed in the previous section, carries over to the lexical pragmatic account and, in fact, extends to the ad hoc concept communicated, hence to the explicature. It is likely that the speaker of 'It was her child' in (11) does not specifically intend particular individual implicatures but rather leaves it to the hearer to derive some subset within a range of activated assumptions concerning Mary's relation to her cherished project, her 'child'. Given that the ad hoc concept the hearer forms is, to a large extent, driven by the relevance of these contextual implications, the characteristic of indeterminacy must carry over from them to that concept and so to the explicature of which it is a constituent.

Most people judge (11) to be a clear case of a metaphor, probably because the use of 'child' here involves shifting from one domain or category (human beings), to which its literal denotation pertains, to another entirely distinct domain (intellectual endeavours or areas of study). However, some might also think that the use of 'child' in (10) to describe a grown man is metaphorical, since it can be argued that children and men belong to distinct categories (or subcategories within the category of human beings). It is unclear what constitutes a sufficiently distinct or distant domain/category for a word use to count as metaphorical. Others might think that (10) is a hyperbolic use of 'child' (a blatantly exaggerated way of characterising Mike's behaviour), or that it is both hyperbolic and metaphorical to some extent. These variable judgements are just what Sperber and Wilson's view would predict: 'we see metaphors as a range of cases at one end of a continuum that includes literal, loose, and hyperbolic interpretations' (2008: 84); 'the absence of any criterion for distinguishing literal, loose, and metaphorical utterances [is] evidence [. . .] that there are no genuinely distinct categories,' (2008: 95). Most importantly, as demonstrated with the 'child' examples, one and the same relevance-based inferential process is used in interpreting all these different cases (literal/encoded, literal enriched, loose, hyperbolic, metaphorical). Thus, the RT view of metaphor is very 'deflationary': 'There is no mechanism specific to metaphors, no interesting generalisation that applies only to them' (Sperber and Wilson 2008: 84).

Critical issues and an example of current research

There are several issues that have been raised for the RT account of metaphor, both by people working within the framework and by those pursuing alternative approaches. I will briefly mention some of these before focusing on one in particular.

First, within the 'cognitive linguistics' framework, metaphor is viewed as originating in thought, and many of the abstract concepts we employ are taken to be inherently metaphorical, their use and understanding being dependent on mappings to other more concrete concepts (see Chapter 1). Often cited cases of such 'conceptual metaphors' are LIFE IS A JOURNEY, TIME IS SPACE, ARGUMENT IS WAR, and there are many more (Lakoff and Johnson 1980). A key source of evidence cited in support of this cognitive/conceptual view of metaphor is the systematic nature of much of our metaphorical language. For example, we talk of ourselves (our lives) as 'reaching a cross-roads', 'forging ahead', 'taking a new direction', 'being derailed', 'getting back on course', and so on, all of which can be seen as surface manifestations of the mapping between the abstract conceptual domain LIFE and the more concrete conceptual domain JOURNEY. This raises several questions for the RT account, which takes metaphor to arise not in cognition but in linguistic communication, as a result of speakers using language loosely in an attempt to convey complex thoughts, which need not themselves be metaphorical. One question is whether or not the two approaches can be reconciled, perhaps with a role for conceptual metaphors in the pragmatic processes of understanding metaphorical language (see Tendahl and Gibbs 2008 for positive suggestions). Another question is whether the RT account can explain the existence of families of related metaphorical uses, such as the various aspects of life described as aspects of a journey in the examples just mentioned. In response to this, Wilson (2011) has set out an account of how repeated encounters with linguistic metaphors linking two conceptual domains (e.g. the domains of life and journeys, or time and space) could lead to this kind of systematicity of metaphorical use.

A second set of issues concerns the phenomenon of so-called 'emergent properties' and whether and how the RT account can explain these (see Chapter 2). These are properties which are understood as being attributed to the topic of the metaphor but which are not part of our representation of the metaphor vehicle. Consider the following two examples, the first fairly conventionalised, the other relatively novel (adapted from (3a) above):

(12) a. I'm afraid to ask my line-manager. He is such a *bulldozer*.
  b. The actor gave his lines *dexterous topspin* and unexpected bursts of power.

Among the properties we might plausibly take the speaker of (12a) to be attributing to her line-manager are: insensitivity, strong and simplistic views, refusal to take account of other people's opinions. For (12b), properties attributed to the actor's delivery of his lines may include skilful variations in pitch and startling acoustic effects. These properties are not part of our information store about bulldozers (heavy machinery) or topspin (a motion of a ball), respectively, that is, they are not directly recoverable from the encyclopaedic entries associated with the literal encoded concepts BULLDOZER and TOPSPIN. This issue has been confronted to some extent within the RT framework: see Wilson and Carston (2006) and Vega Moreno (2007) for discussion of more conventionalised cases such as (12a), and Wearing (2014a) for discussion of the more novel case in (12b), with regard to which she suggests that an element of analogical processing may be required in deriving implicatures and thus constructing the ad hoc concept TOPSPIN*.

A third area of contention for the RT account concerns the phenomenology of metaphor understanding, an issue which is a focus of my current research. What people often find most striking about a metaphor are what seem to be sensory, imagistic, or affective effects, making for a qualitative experience, which is not obviously captured by the amodal propositional representations (explicatures and implicatures) that, according to the theory, comprise the communicated content. Although Sperber and Wilson's approach is notable for its engagement with the rich open-endedness of the effects that many metaphors (and other evocative uses of language) can have, their account remains resolutely propositional: 'What look like non-propositional effects associated with the expression of attitudes, feelings and states of mind can be approached in terms of weak implicature' (1986a/1995: 222), and 'if you look at these apparently affective effects through the microscope of relevance theory, you see a wide array of minute cognitive effects' (ibid.: 224). Whether or not this is true of apparently affective effects of particular uses of language,[7] I do not think it can be true of the mental imagery that seems to be characteristic of many metaphors and which I will focus on here.

The following is a strikingly clear case of a metaphor which requires us to actively visualise what is described by the literal content of the metaphorical language, and to use that mental imagery in imagining the taking off and flight of the bird:

(13)   ... a heron launched itself from low ground to our south, a foldaway construction of struts and canvas, snapping and locking itself into shape just in time to keep airborne, ...

From: R. Macfarlane, The Old Ways: A Journey on Foot, *p. 298*

A famous 'image' theory of metaphor is that of Davidson (1978), who maintains that metaphors do not communicate cognitive contents, neither implicatures nor ad hoc concepts, but rather prompt us to notice a wide range of non-propositional aspects of the topic just as pictures and photographs do. In his view, the literal content of a metaphor (which is its only 'meaning') evokes an image or images, and the result is that we see one thing as another (the boss as a bulldozer, Mary's thesis as her child, the heron as a foldaway construction, etc.).

However, while the example in (13) seems to support Davidson's view, in that any attempt to say what propositions it implicates or what ad hoc concepts are communicated by 'foldaway construction', 'struts', 'canvas', etc., seems misplaced, this is less obvious for some of our earlier examples. A speaker who says 'I must fly now' seems to be expressing a proposition, one which can be embedded in the scope of operators like the conditional or negation (e.g. 'If you have to fly now, we can defer our discussion to tomorrow'), and, in fact, to be making a statement, one that the addressee might question or disagree with ('No, you have plenty of time'). Of course, this is a fairly conventionalised case, and it might be supposed that Davidson's 'image' account applies only to novel metaphors while propositional accounts, such as the RT ad hoc concept account, apply only to established cases whose imagery potential is much reduced.[8] My approach is conciliatory. Taking aspects of both the RT propositional account and Davidson's image theory, I have argued that there are propositional and imagistic components across the whole range of metaphors, but that these components differ greatly in their relative weightings in different cases. My proposal is not that there are two distinct classes of metaphor, but that there are two different routes to the understanding of metaphors – the quick, local, on-line meaning-adjustment process, as discussed earlier, and a slower, more global appraisal of the literal meaning of the metaphorical language from which inferences about the speaker's meaning are made (Carston 2010). This latter route is especially likely to be taken when the addressee is processing a new, creative, and/or extended metaphorical use of language, that is, when the metaphor places such demands on the interpretive process that it is diverted from its standard quick mode of meaning adjustment. As regards mental imagery, while it may be evoked even for familiar cases like 'I must fly', 'Life is a long hard journey', 'John is a pig', etc., that is, those for which the ad hoc concept account works well, it will generally be more attended to by hearers/readers (more noticed/experienced by them) on the literal meaning route. This is at least partly because this route involves a delay in deriving any communicatively intended propositional meaning, as the literal meaning is processed in a more reflective mode than is typical of the process of ad hoc concept construction.[9]

To illustrate the second 'literal' route, consider again the moderately extended and creative metaphor in (3b), repeated here:

(14) Life's but a walking shadow, a poor player
That struts and frets his hour upon the stage
And then is heard no more: it is a tale
Told by an idiot, full of sound and fury,
Signifying nothing.

Shakespeare: Macbeth V.v. 24–30

After the introduction of the topic, 'Life', virtually every word here is used metaphorically. According to the ad hoc concept account, there would be constant lexical adjustments, with the derived concepts WALKING-SHADOW*, POOR-PLAYER*, STRUTS*, FRETS*, HOUR*, STAGE*, etc., replacing each of the literal lexical meanings in the developing interpretation. According to my alternative account, what happens here is that the literal meaning is highly activated while processes of ad hoc concept formation are overly demanding, so that the literal meaning stays in play until a later stage of the understanding process. That is because, in this extended metaphor, the linguistically encoded concepts are sufficiently closely related that they semantically prime and reinforce each other, to the extent that their activation levels are so high that a literal interpretation unfolds – a description of an indifferent theatre performance, with accompanying mental imagery of the inadequate entertainer briefly moving about on the stage, performing his prescribed script, and then exiting. Of course, this is not what is communicated by the speaker, since she obviously does not endorse any of the literal representations as factual. Rather, this set of literal representations is framed or metarepresented as an imaginary or fictional world, which is subject, as a whole, to further reflective inferential processing. This process effectively extracts implications about life that are relevantly and plausibly attributable to Macbeth at this stage of the play (when all his grand ambitions have come to nought) – concerning its brevity and pointlessness, the deluded self-importance of each of us, how little our best efforts are valued by anyone else, and so on. It is these that are taken to have been (weakly) implicated and which, therefore, constitute the meaning of Macbeth's soliloquy. For further examples and discussion of why and when the processing of a metaphor is tipped into this second processing mode, see Carston (2010) and Carston and Wearing (2011).

Future directions

While the ad hoc concept account of metaphor understanding is well developed and quite widely accepted, the alternative literal meaning (or 'metaphorical world') account is fairly new and needs much more development, both with regard to the factors that trigger it and the nature of the 'reflective' pragmatic processes that operate on it to derive the intended propositional meaning. These processes are just as much driven by the goal of finding an optimally relevant interpretation as any other pragmatic process, but the claim is that something about the metaphorical use in these cases induces a change of gear: processing is slowed down and extra attentive effort is expended, so, as predicted by RT, extra effects are achieved, which, in many instances, will include an array of weak implicatures. An important question concerns the status of the non-propositional imagistic effects that many hearers/readers experience, whether they are to be construed as components of the intended effects (along with implicatures) or as just a by-product, albeit a pleasing one, of the greater attention given to the literal meaning of the metaphor.

As well as further work needed on the theoretical side, future research must focus on spelling out precise predictions of the RT accounts where possible and testing them experimentally. This has already begun with experimental investigations of the orthodox RT 'loose use continuum' view of metaphor, testing whether or not there is any clear interpretive distinction between what are pre-theoretically taken to be two distinct tropes, hyperboles and metaphors (Rubio-Fernández, Wearing and Carston 2015). And there is experimental work now underway to test the idea that there are two routes to metaphor understanding, one of which proceeds via ad hoc concept construction and the other of which employs the literal meaning of the metaphors to build a metaphorical world, from which the implicatures of the utterance are inferred.

Finally, it will be worth investigating what some of the current intensive work on embodied cognition and processes of sensory-motor simulation in language comprehension (Dove 2011) might contribute to the RT account of metaphor. In this respect, fMRI experiments by Desai et al. (2011) are encouraging in that they report that, while sensory-motor areas of the cortex are activated to some extent for all action metaphors (e.g. 'grab life by the throat'), they are considerably more active for unfamiliar cases than for familiar cases. Based on the observed areas of brain activation, Desai et al. also report that 'metaphor understanding is not completely based on sensory-motor simulations but relies also on abstract lexical semantic codes' (ibid.: 2376). I take this to be at least consistent with the position in Carston (2010) that there are both propositional and imagistic components involved in metaphor understanding and that their relative weightings vary depending on a range of factors, including novelty/familiarity.

Notes

1 What exactly falls under the label 'metaphor' is, of course, an open question and far from being resolved; for instance, are 'extended metaphors' such as (3b) metaphors properly speaking or more like allegories, and in what ways do allegories differ from clear cases of metaphor? Terms like

'metaphor', 'hyperbole', 'simile', allegory', etc. are pre-theoretic folk labels, and an account of the cognitive processes/mechanisms employed in understanding/interpreting them may end up distinguishing cases quite differently from these intuitive categorisations.
2 It is assumed in relevance theory that we communicate propositions (or thoughts), that is, descriptions of the world that can be evaluated as true or false. What is not so clear is whether we also communicate non-propositional effects, like images and feelings, which are not truth-evaluable.
3 In a sense, talk of propositions being 'explicitly communicated' is paradoxical, since virtually no 'explicature' is fully explicit, but is a hybrid of linguistically encoded and pragmatically inferred content. The point, though, is that this is in the very nature of linguistic communication so that the propositions pragmatically developed from linguistic meaning are as explicit as it gets (Carston 2002).
4 I follow the standard practice in relevance theory of treating the speaker as female and the addressee as male.
5 This is the RT approach to pragmatics in a nutshell. For a more detailed summary, see Wearing (2014b), and, for the full account, see Sperber and Wilson (1986a/1995), Wilson and Sperber (2004).
6 The explanation of communication as varying in degree of strength is an important feature of RT and unique to it, as far as I know. For a fuller and more technical account of strong/weak implicatures and poetic effects, see Sperber and Wilson (1986a/1995, 2008), and for their application to creative and/or literary metaphors, see Pilkington (2000).
7 Pilkington (2000) emphasises the centrality of the qualitative, non-propositional effects of metaphor and a need for more attention to them within the RT framework.
8 However, it is clear that this is not what Sperber and Wilson intend with regard to the ad hoc concept account; see, for instance, their discussion of 'The fog comes on little cat feet' from the poem by Carl Sandburg (Sperber and Wilson 2008).
9 Note that the same point holds for literally used language. There is evidence that in processing quite banal utterances, like 'The ranger saw an eagle in the sky', we automatically token visual imagery (Zwaan and Pecher 2012), and that for more evocative literal descriptions we are consciously aware of and attend to mental imagery.

Further reading

Carston, R. (2010) 'Metaphor: Ad hoc concepts, literal meaning and mental images', *Proceedings of the Aristotelian Society* 110: 297–323.
—— (2012) 'Metaphor and the literal–nonliteral distinction', in K. Allan and K. Jaszczolt (eds) *Cambridge Handbook of Pragmatics*, Cambridge: Cambridge University Press.
Sperber, D. and Wilson, D. (1986) 'Loose talk', *Proceedings of the Aristotelian Society* 86: 153–71. Reprinted in S. Davis (ed.) (1991) *Pragmatics: A Reader*, Oxford, UK: Oxford University Press.
—— (2008) 'A deflationary account of metaphors', in R. W. Gibbs, Jr. (ed.) *The Cambridge Handbook of Metaphor and Thought*, New York: Cambridge University Press.
Wilson, D. and Carston, R. (2007) 'A unitary approach to lexical pragmatics: Relevance, inference and ad hoc concepts', in N. Burton-Roberts (ed.) *Pragmatics*, Basingstoke, UK: Palgrave Macmillan.

References

Carston, R. (2002) *Thoughts and Utterances: The Pragmatics of Explicit Communication*, Oxford, UK: Blackwell.
—— (2010) 'Metaphor: *Ad hoc* concepts, literal meaning and mental images', *Proceedings of the Aristotelian Society* 110: 297–323.
Carston, R. and Wearing, C. (2011) 'Metaphor, hyperbole and simile: A pragmatic approach', *Language and Cognition* 3: 283–312.
Davidson, D. (1978) 'What metaphors mean', *Critical Inquiry* 5: 31–47. Reprinted in D. Davidson (1984) *Inquiries into Truth and Interpretation*, Oxford, UK: Oxford University Press.

Desai, R., Binder, J., Conant, L., Mano, Q. and Seidenberg, M. (2011) 'The neural career of sensory-motor metaphors', *Journal of Cognitive Neuroscience* 23: 2376–386.

Dove, G. (2011) 'On the need for embodied and dis-embodied cognition', *Frontiers in Psychology* 1: 1–13.

Lakoff, G. and Johnson, M. (1980) *Metaphors We Live By*, Chicago, IL: University of Chicago Press.

Pilkington, A. (2000) *Poetic Effects: A Relevance Theory Perspective*, Amsterdam, The Netherlands: John Benjamins.

Rubio-Fernández, P., Wearing, C. and Carston, R. (2015) 'Metaphor and hyperbole: Testing the continuity hypothesis', *Metaphor and Symbol* 30: 24–40.

Sperber, D. and Wilson, D. (1986a/1995) *Relevance: Communication and Cognition*, 2nd edn, Oxford, UK: Blackwell.

—— (1986b) 'Loose talk', *Proceedings of the Aristotelian Society* 86: 153–71.

—— (2008) 'A deflationary account of metaphors', in R. W. Gibbs, Jr. (ed.) *The Cambridge Handbook of Metaphor and Thought*, New York: Cambridge University Press.

Tendahl, M. and Gibbs, R. W., Jr. (2008) 'Complementary perspectives on metaphor: Cognitive linguistics and relevance theory', *Journal of Pragmatics* 40: 1823–64.

Vega Moreno, R. (2007) *Creativity and Convention: The Pragmatics of Everyday Figurative Speech*, Amsterdam, The Netherlands: John Benjamins.

Wearing, C. (2014a) 'Interpreting novel metaphors', *International Review of Pragmatics* 6: 78–102.

—— (2014b) 'Relevance theory: Pragmatics and cognition', *WIREs Cognitive Science*. doi: 10.1002/wcs.1331.

Wilson, D. (2011) 'Parallels and differences in the treatment of metaphor in relevance theory and cognitive linguistics', *Intercultural Pragmatics* 8: 177–96.

Wilson, D. and Carston, R. (2006) 'Metaphor, relevance and the "emergent property" issue', *Mind and Language* 21: 404–33.

Wilson, D. and Sperber, D. (2004) 'Relevance theory', in L. Horn and G. Ward (eds) *Handbook of Pragmatics*, Oxford, UK: Blackwell.

Zwaan, R. and Pecher, D. (2012) 'Revisiting mental simulation in language comprehension: Six replication attempts', *PLoS ONE* 7(12): e51382. doi:10.1371/journal.pone.0051382.

4

Metaphor, language, and dynamical systems

Raymond W. Gibbs, Jr.

Introduction

Consider the following excerpt of a conversation, from the Santa Barbara Corpus of Spoken American English, between an American man and woman, lying in bed, discussing, at this point, the woman's prior marriage. Pay attention to the participants' different verbal metaphors (some candidate phrases containing metaphorically used words are presented in boldface) (Du Bois & Englebretson, 2004):

Pamela: I used to have this . . . sort of, **standard line**, . . . that, there **were two things I got out of . . . my marriage.** One was a name that was easy to spell, and one was . . . a child. . . . That . . . **really got me grounded.** But, the fact of the matter is, . . . that the marriage itself, I mean as **hellish as it was** . . . it's like **it pulled me under, like a giant octopus, or a giant,** . . . **giant shark.** And **it pulled me all the way under.** And then, . . . and there I was, it was **like the silent scream** and then, . . . then I found that . . . **I was on my own two feet again.** And it really was . . . .what was **hell in that** . . . **that marriage** became, . . . **became a way out for me.** . . . It was the flip side . . . It's like sometimes you go through things, . . . and you come out the other side of them, you . . . come out so much better. . . . And if I hadn't had that, if I hadn't had . . .
Darryl: It's not the way with food.
Pamela: . . . What do you mean.
Darryl: . . . What goes in one way, doesn't come out.
Pamela: Okay, comes out very **hellish**.
Darryl: Yeah.
Pamela: Very **hellish**.
Darryl: . . . So what did that have to do . . .
Pamela: But it's so good . . . so good going down. I mean
Darryl: What did
Pamela: there's there's [*sic.*] **the opposites** again.
Darryl: It's
Pamela: The food is like, all unique

Darryl: Hey
Pamela: and wonderful
Darryl: it's **major league ... Yin and Yang**.
Pamela: and **heavenly** ... (tsk) **major league**.

This conversation has several notable features that are typical of the ways people use metaphor in discourse. First, both speakers produced a variety of metaphors to talk about different aspects of the same idea. For instance, Pamela, in one extended turn, described her previous marriage in several metaphorical ways. These metaphors, and their different conceptual metaphorical foundations (e.g., all related to EVENT STRUCTURE metaphors such as MARRIAGE AS A LOCATION, CONTAINER, or JOURNEY; see Chapter 1), illustrate that speakers often talk of abstract concepts, such as marriage, in multiple metaphorical ways. What explains how and why people use different metaphorical ideas to talk about the same topic?

Second, speakers typically employ some combination of conventional and novel metaphorical phrases as they express their thoughts about abstract topics. For instance, Pamela characterized her previous marriage using conventional phrases, such as 'I got out of my marriage' and 'It's like sometimes you go through things ... ,' and novel ones, including mixed metaphors and similes, such as 'it pulled me under, like a giant octopus, or a giant, giant shark.' This flexibility in metaphorical language use highlights people's abilities to rely on both entrenched linguistic conventions and more innovative metaphorical conceptions when describing their experiences. What linguistic and psychological processes enable this kind of adaptive metaphor use in context?

Third, the two speakers sometimes used different metaphors, perhaps reflecting their alternative ways of thinking about some idea. For example, Darryl took the conversation in a new direction by offering a contrasting way of interpreting Pamela's use of a particular metaphor (i.e., a case of 'metaphor recontextualization'—see Semino, Deignan, & Littlemore, 2013). Thus, after Pamela mentioned that she originally entered her marriage 'journey' in one way, and later came out the other side 'so much better,' Darryl complained that the analogy did not work when applied to a real physical process, such as when one ingests and digests food. People often wrestle for control of the metaphors in discourse and offer their own, personal, views of specific metaphorical concepts (e.g., MARRIAGE IS A JOURNEY). How can we best explain the ways speakers collaborate and coordinate via their different metaphorical expressions?

Looking in detail at how metaphorical language unfolds in speech and writing reveals significant insights into people's real-time adaptive behaviors. My purpose in this chapter is to consider some of the complexities of metaphorical discourse in terms of how verbal metaphors are produced, understood, and have communicative impact. Many of the ongoing theoretical debates in the interdisciplinary world of metaphor scholarship are natural outcomes of different attempts to explain the ways metaphor works in language, thought, and communication. I specifically advance a dynamical perspective on metaphor because it offers the possibility of greater convergence among metaphor theories. This theoretical approach is not about metaphor per se, as it stems from research in the physical and biological sciences. Nevertheless, a dynamical view provides a broader framework for thinking about human behavior that has important implications for theories of metaphorical language use. The main highlight of the dynamical view is its acknowledgment of multiple causes for metaphorical behaviors, such as seen in Darryl and Pamela's conversation, which demands understanding something about the probabilistic and self-organizing character of human performance.

Overview of theoretical and empirical background

A dynamical approach seeks to explain both the regularities and context-sensitive variations in human metaphor performance, such as those seen in Darryl and Pamela's conversation, as part of a single, comprehensive theory. Within the dynamical perspective, adaptive linguistic behaviors are self-organizing and are not solely caused by specific biological, psychological, or linguistic mechanisms (Bak, 1997). Any system can be said to self-organize whose structure is not imposed from outside forces or from internal blueprints alone (e.g., internal mental rules or representations). Self-organizing systems are capable of creating new structures because of their components' interacting dynamics rather than by the activity of isolated components alone (e.g., the activation of a conceptual metaphor; see Chapter 1). Different cognitive and linguistic behaviors, such as a person uttering a verbal metaphor, are temporary, or 'soft-assembled,' because they go away when the dynamic interaction between components changes sufficiently (Gibbs & Van Orden, 2010). Soft-assembly operates in a highly context-sensitive fashion, within particular environmental niches, to create the very specific physical patterns and overt behaviors of living systems.

A wide variety of physical, biological, and human behaviors have now been described as emergent products of self-organizational processes, including the formation of galaxies, termite nests, snowflakes, the foraging patterns of bees and ants, the dynamic shapes of flocks of birds, the symmetrical patterns on butterfly wings, the regular spots on a leopard's skin, the formation of whirlpools in rivers, the formation of bacterial cultures, the dynamics of traffic jams on freeways, the performance of stock markets, and neuronal activity in the human brain (Gibbs, 2012). The field of dynamic systems theory, as it is called, seeks to discover the general rules under which self-organized structures appear, the forms that they can take, and the methods of predicting the changes to the structure that will result from changes to the underlying system.

Consider first the example of traffic patterns on freeways. These patterns are not imposed by some external agent or force (i.e., they are autonomously given); they exhibit moments where traffic flows easily and then bottles up into traffic jams (i.e., they exhibit non-linear stabilities and instabilities over time); they are influenced by roundabouts, traffic signs, and weather patterns (i.e., basins of 'attractors' or stable patterns within the system); they comprise fast-occurring local interactions among several cars as well as slower-developing large-scale patterns of traffic flow over an entire city (i.e., they comprise several hierarchical levels each operating on its own time-scale). Moreover, larger-scale freeway paralysis emerges from very few smaller interactions among just a few individual cars (i.e., global patterns emerge from local, bottom-up interactions among individual components). Finally, the emergent structure of a traffic jam influences when individual cars must stop and go (i.e., demonstrating top-down constraints on the behaviors of component processes, in this case individual drivers).

Similar to explaining the patterns of traffic jams, a self-organizational approach to human behavior maintains that different regularities and instabilities unfold over time according to particular dynamical constraints. Consider one example of a human action that may be understood as emergent products of self-organizing processes. Imagine that you are taking a tennis swing when engaged in a match against another player. If you are a beginner, you may find yourself making an effort to adequately track the ball, keep your racket perpendicular to the court, hit the ball squarely, etc. But an expert, who is absorbed in the game, experiences something quite different. The expert's focus is on the opponent and the oncoming ball. All the expert feels is their arm being drawn to the appropriate position, the racket forming the optimal angle with the court. The cumulative experience is one of satisfying these different constraints. The expert's actions are brought forth by perceived circumstances in such a way as to bring about some satisfactory result (e.g., hitting the ball so that it is difficult for your opponent to return).

Your expert tennis shot simultaneously satisfies a stack of goals. The same tennis swing keeps you physically active, furthers your enjoyment of tennis, wins the match, wins the set, breaks an opponent's serve, wins the rally, and makes the shot, for example. All these aspects of the swing are intentional, but the various intentions are sustained on different time-scales, some of which are longer than the motor coordination required to produce any one swing. Coordinative structures on shorter time-scales, closer to real time, are expressed in the specific swing at a particular tennis ball, which comes on a specific trajectory, requiring an exact return force to reach the opponent's baseline (but not an inch further!). The actual swing produced is never explicitly 'represented' in a player's mind, nor are the goals that a specific swing satisfied. A player's exact swing unfolds in ways that satisfy various circumstantial constraints.

This analysis of skilled tennis swings illustrates how we act in the world without first representing our actions as single causes. Adaptive behavior does not require the explicit mental representation of goals or the bodily movements that would achieve those goals. Instead, intelligent behavior simply requires constraints that circumscribe the possibilities for action. Cognitive scientists have applied this idea to explain how many simple and complex human behaviors are higher-order products of self-organizational processes (Gibbs & Van Orden, 2010; Spivey, 2007). A major thrust of this research is to show how many factors simultaneously shape human cognition and action.

For instance, individual cognition can be explained as a self-organizing process. When making real-life decisions, both big and small, people often experience the sense of being pulled in different directions at once. McKinstry, Dale, and Spivey (2008) have demonstrated that this impression has some literal truth to it. Participants in one experiment were asked questions like 'Is murder sometimes justified?' and moved a computer mouse to click on their chosen response box as quickly and accurately as possible (i.e., 'yes' or 'no'). Even though people always gave a specific response, an analysis of their mouse trajectories revealed the simultaneous 'pull' from different response alternatives in their thinking about whether murder is sometimes justified. This finding suggests that decision-making need not necessarily be complete, in some specialized cognitive subsystem or module, before the output is shared with other subsystems, including the periphery of the body's actual motor response. Instead, similar to all cognitive activities, decision-making may self-organize in-the-moment according to dynamical principles, constrained within the ongoing interactions among brain, body, and world.

Self-organization does not only occur within individual minds and bodies, but also shapes group behaviors. For example, one study looked closely at this using two people sitting next to one another in rocking chairs. Intrinsic rocking frequencies of the chairs were manipulated by positioning weights at the base of the chairs (Richardson, Marsh, Isenhower, Goodman, & Schmidt, 2007). Participants observed each other's chairs or looked away from one another. Most interestingly, when participants looked at each other, they soon settled into a dynamic of rocking synchronously, even when the natural frequencies of their chairs differed. People unknowingly rocked against the natural frequencies of their chairs in order to reach synchrony with the other person. This finding offers an example of self-organization resulting in an emergent temporal structure across two individuals (e.g., their joint rocking together).

Similar dynamical principles explain social behaviors where simple local interactions over time tend to promote the emergence of group level (e.g., cultural and social) properties. Various research in dynamical social psychology has demonstrated the utility of a self-organizational theory to explain social interactions, close relationships, conformity, social judgments, attitude change, group dynamics, and persuasion, to name just a few of the many studies conducted (Vallacher, Read, & Nowak, 2002). People spontaneously organize into effective problem-solving groups, for example, without one person necessarily having to take centralized control of the process. Individuals participate in collective interactions in ways that they sometimes neither understand nor perceive, with social organizations both affecting and being shaped by individual behaviors. This conclusion illustrates how individual behaviors shape the emergence of group norms at the same time that ongoing collective actions influence what people individually do, exactly like what happens when understanding traffic patterns.

Most generally, self-organization in behavior, both for individuals and groups, arises from the complex interplay of brain, body, and environment as a single 'context-sensitive' system. My major claim is that metaphorical language also emerges from the interplay of the brain, bodies, and world, and must be ultimately explained as the product of an entire context-sensitive dynamical system. Producing and understanding metaphor has many similarities to what happens when one is swinging at a tennis ball or when two people are rocking in chairs next to one another. Metaphorical utterances may be enacted in an intentional way without there being an underlying intention (i.e., a conscious intention to use metaphor) driving the action. Speakers' metaphorical words (and accompanying paralinguistic and bodily actions) are produced to simultaneously achieve a stack of goals, including coordinating with others in the moment, making a specific comment in light of what else has just been said or occurred, relieving a sense of incompatibility between what you expected and what occurred, and perhaps reestablishing some equilibrium with others in context. These different goals act as constraints on what words are uttered, what bodily acts are undertaken, and how linguistic utterances are interpreted, with each of these activities being sustained on different time-scales. Producing and understanding metaphors are constrained by the combination of different forces, which offers new insights into several enduring debates in the metaphor literature (see Gibbs & Cameron, 2007; Larsen-Freeman & Cameron, 2008).

A new approach to the study of metaphor

The dynamical view of human action will now be applied to addressing four enduring problems in the empirical study of metaphor: (1) What causes people to use metaphor in the diverse ways they do? (2) How do people coordinate their varying metaphorical perspectives when speaking about a particular topic in discourse? (3) How much effort is required to interpret a verbal metaphor? Finally, (4) do embodied conceptual metaphors play a role in the production and interpretation of metaphorical actions? A dynamical approach offers unique answers to each of these important issues and sets the stage for future research and theories on metaphor.

What causes people to use metaphor?

Recall Darryl and Pamela's conversation in which Pamela stated a series of metaphors regarding her prior marriage, including 'a standard line,' 'two things I got out of my marriage,' 'really got me grounded,' 'it's, like it pulled me under, like a giant octopus' and so forth. What explains why Pamela used metaphors to communicate her ideas in this conversational turn?

Answering this question is extremely difficult, and metaphor scholars have offered a number of proposals on how to do so. A traditional view assumes that people produce certain metaphors only for special rhetorical purposes, such as to be vivid, polite, or memorable (Ortony, 1975). One contemporary view of this perspective maintains that only a few, specific instances of language really convey metaphorical meanings (Steen, 2011). These 'deliberate' metaphors stand in contrast to 'non-deliberate' metaphors that originated as metaphors but no longer convey metaphorical messages for contemporary speakers. Under this view, only some of Pamela's metaphors were 'deliberate' (e.g., 'it pulled me under like a giant octopus'), with most others being automatically produced with little thought given to any underlying cross-domain mapping.

In contrast to the traditional approach, the cognitive revolution in metaphor studies, starting with Lakoff and Johnson (1980), claimed that metaphors in language are primarily surface manifestations of enduring metaphorical thoughts (i.e., conceptual metaphors; see Chapter 1). People produce linguistic metaphors because they ordinarily think about abstract concepts in concrete, mostly embodied, ways. In this respect, the continued existence of certain patterns of metaphorical language, both conventional and novel, is motivated by the persistence of embodied metaphorical thoughts (Gibbs, 1994, 2006; Lakoff & Johnson, 1999).

Many critics of the conceptual metaphor theory (CMT) suggest, however, that metaphoricity in language is driven by non-cognitive factors. For instance, many conventional metaphors arise not simply because individual speakers just so happen to think in particular metaphorical ways, but because of important ideological, cultural, and contextual factors (Koller, 2004; Kövecses, 2015; Semino, 2008; Quinn, 1992). Another approach claims that the specific linguistic forms of metaphor emerge from local social forces, such as those that operate when very specific topics are discussed in particular social contexts, or when particular speakers interact in a variety of idiosyncratic contexts (Zinken & Musolff, 2009). These observations have led scholars to argue that metaphor is inherently a discourse phenomenon, and must not be reductively characterized in terms of cognitive or bodily/embodied factors. Finally, other scholars have criticized the cognitive focus on metaphor by exploring the idiosyncratic historical and linguistic factors that shape metaphorical language use. The analysis of specific lexical items and particular grammatical forms in contemporary discourse suggests that these non-cognitive, non-embodied forces have an important role in shaping many specific metaphorical word choices (Svanlund, 2007).

The above arguments, and accompanying evidence, highlight the relevance of many levels of analysis for constructing a comprehensive theory of metaphor. Still, there is a strong tendency for metaphor scholars to highlight their own preferred level of analysis and downplay or ignore others when making theoretical claims. Too many of the current debates in the multidisciplinary world of metaphor scholarship are structured around the assumption that there really is a single dimension of metaphor that best captures what influences people to talk and write metaphorically in the ways they do. My view is that these scholarly debates about what shapes metaphorical language use are overly simplistic and ignore the possibility that many levels of experience actively constrain why and how people use verbal metaphors. A dynamical perspective offers a major corrective to past debates by highlighting the ways metaphor emerges in the moment from the interaction of many factors via self-organizational processes.

Consider some of the different forces, and their respective time-scales, that likely constrain Darryl and Pamela's conversation:

- evolutionary forces to maintain cooperation with in-group individuals to enhance individual and group welfare, including survival;
- culturally specific ideas about appropriate forms of discourse with one's romantic partner, including when and how to discuss potentially problematic issues, such as prior marriages, or cultural beliefs related to the understanding of 'hell,' a term Pamela used to describe her earlier marriage;
- historical forces related to Darryl and Pamela's past experiences of speaking with one another, including those regarding intimate matters such as previous romantic relationships;
- social forces related to beliefs about when it is appropriate for Darryl and Pamela to talk about certain topics at certain times (e.g., 'pillow talk');
- linguistic factors related to conventions of use, such as when Pamela says 'silent scream' to describe one aspect of her emotional response to being married earlier;
- present bodily experience, such as Darryl and Pamela's specific positions in bed, their degree of fatigue, their desire for intimate contact with one another, and so on;
- immediate communicative motivations to respond appropriately in the conversation given the touchy subject of prior marriages;
- previously stated words, and non-linguistic behaviors, that primed each speaker's use of certain terms (e.g., 'really got me grounded,' 'it's, like it pulled me under, like a giant octopus,' and sequences of verbal affirmation and rejection);
- brain and neural activity, including that which emerges as brain systems become coupled during particular interpersonal interaction.

These are just a few of the forces that constrain Darryl and Pamela's ongoing conversational behaviors. Each force operates along a different time-scale, with some of these crawling along at very slow speeds, such as evolutionary and cultural forces, while others zip along at very fast speeds, such as immediate linguistic processes and the firing of neurons in human brains. The various time-scales are not independent, but are hierarchically organized, and are nested within one another so that different forces affecting language experience are coupled in complex, non-linear ways.

As with all discourse, Darryl and Pamela's talk stems from a hierarchy of constraints, and not just from the intentional mental states of each speaker. Take, for example, Pamela's utterance that her marriage 'pulled me under.' A cognitive linguistic analysis would suggest that this utterance was motivated by a single conceptual metaphor, namely, MARRIAGE RELATIONSHIPS ARE PHYSICAL FORCES. However, a dynamical view maintains that the specific words uttered are affected by multiple constraints. Thus, Pamela's specific comment is related to her previous remark about her marriage being 'hell,' which places the discourse focus on a particular embodied, conceptual metaphor (i.e., BAD IS DOWN), but one that is imbued with cultural meaning (e.g., cultural beliefs and imagery about hell). The participants' present bodily position in bed reinforces this downward interpretation. Pamela could have said other things to convey a negative impression about her prior marriage, such as describing it as being dirty, stained, or poisoned (i.e., DIRTY IS BAD). Nonetheless, Pamela's subsequent choice of the metaphorically used words 'pulled me under' reflected her exact brain, body, and world contingencies at the very moment of her speaking about different, abstract topics. In some cases, very local contextual cues shape metaphor production, yet these too always combine with other dynamical forces (Koller, 2004; Kövecses, 2015; Semino, 2008). We can offer a model of how those possible contingencies arise, and interact, according to the principles of self-organization, to explain metaphorical speech behavior without postulating the existence of any specific component of mind, such as a conceptual metaphor or deliberate metaphor mechanism, as the *sole* driving force in the metaphor production process.

Consider another example of how a metaphor may be produced, this time in the context of written discourse. Imagine the time and place when William Shakespeare created his famous metaphor 'Juliet is the sun' in his play *Romeo and Juliet*. Some of the forces that possibly served as the context for Shakespeare's production of 'Juliet is the sun' in the very moment he wrote these words include the following:

- cultural models active at that time about love, sex roles, and astrology;
- evolutionary history of 'sun' as metaphor;
- contemporary uses of 'sun,' including Shakespeare's own in life and in his prior plays;
- Shakespeare's in-the-moment imaginings/simulations of Romeo's predicament;
- Shakespeare's present physical context and bodily positions/movements;
- Shakespeare's just-written statement alluding to the sun rising, namely, 'It is the East';
- Shakespeare's immediately preceding speech and plans for future plays;
- Shakespeare's entrenched neural bindings for people and physical objects.

Shakespeare's writing of 'Juliet is the sun' was not simplistically caused by some full-blown intentional mental state, or some deliberate thought about what to say, nor was it motivated only by a conceptual metaphor. However, Shakespeare's choice of words was 'decided' or 'determined' by the interaction between his immediate dynamics and the environment as his writing behavior unfolded over time. A soft-assembled, self-organized process took care of the fine-grained details of Shakespeare's real-world linguistic behavior, including whether he communicated his thoughts in terms of a specific verbal metaphor as he worked on different drafts of the play.

A dynamical approach sees the context for metaphor performance as a whole system activity and again as emerging from the dynamic interaction of forces operating along many different time-scales. These forces are tightly coupled so that it makes no sense to focus exclusively on one time-scale (e.g., cultural or historical forces) and ignore others (e.g., faster-acting cognitive and neural forces) in a theory of what causes metaphor production. Metaphor scholars may focus on particular time-scales in their studies, but they should always be aware that these do not function autonomously in the production of particular metaphorical expressions.

How do people collaborate and coordinate using metaphors?

How do speakers, such as Darryl and Pamela, understand each other's metaphors as part of their attempts to successfully communicate? Most theories of conversational coordination presume that different speakers must align their separate mental representations about particular topics and that they do so by referring to common-ground knowledge (i.e., community co-membership, linguistic co-presence, and physical co-presence). The accrual of common ground enables speakers and listeners to more readily coordinate their intentional meanings in discourse. In fact, many experimental studies show that the criteria by which listeners judge that they have understood an utterance are a joint product requiring coordination and cooperation between listeners and speakers (Clark, 1996). However, other studies indicate that speakers and listeners sometimes act more egocentrically and fail to automatically keep people's communicative intentions forefront in mind. For instance, listeners do not consistently consider common ground in their comprehension of speakers' messages (Barr & Keysar, 2005).

Must Darryl and Pamela explicitly share particular common-ground knowledge and beliefs to understand each other's verbal metaphors? Metaphor theorists face two problems in responding to this question. First, the coordination seen in many conversations is often viewed as arising only from a mental alignment between speakers. Darryl understands Pamela's metaphors only if he correctly infers the implied cross-domain mappings, or conceptual metaphors, that motivate the meanings of her utterances. This characterization of the metaphor in talk process appears to require a rather sophisticated, highly rational, degree of common-ground assessment. Are people really able to successfully create these mind-to-mind linkages? Many linguists and philosophers voice skepticism about this possibility (Sperber & Wilson, 1995; see Chapter 3).

The second problem with explaining metaphor coordination and collaboration is that metaphor theories rarely acknowledge the full, embodied actions that speakers engage in during talk. For example, a closer analysis of the audiotape of Darryl and Pamela's conversation suggests tremendous complexity as they manage their turn-taking using a variety of linguistic and non-linguistic devices. Darryl and Pamela's discourse exhibited coordination on many different levels, including their use of certain words, syntax, intonation, prosody, response cries (e.g., 'tsk'), and topics touched on. But how do different levels of linguistic and physiological activity become coordinated to produce coherent, meaningful behavior? How might lower-level aspects of speech rhythm and body sway, for instance, shape higher-level aspects of word choice, syntax, and particular thoughts, and how do these high-level factors influence what happens with lower-level behaviors?

Metaphor scholars now recognize important relations between metaphorical language and metaphorical gesture (Müller & Cienki, 2009). Still, much cognitive science research demonstrates the emergent, implicit coordination between people in terms of their speech, prosody, gaze, posture, gestures, and body positioning during conversation (Shockley, Richardson, & Dale, 2009). For example, studies show that people tend to engage in synchronous bodily behaviors, along many dimensions, when they are discussing a topic in which both speakers agree, compared to cases in which they diverge in their opinions (Paxton & Dale, 2013). Even people's brain activities become coordinated during talk (Stephens, Silbert, & Hasson, 2010). These findings, along with many others, are compatible with dynamical system models that explicitly acknowledge the ways that people *implicitly* coordinate in their interactions to form their own coupled systems.

The coordination between two people using metaphorical language is an emergent product of self-organization. Speakers do not understand verbal metaphors because of some mental matching up of their different conceptual metaphorical representations or simply via the recognition that some metaphor was stated deliberately. Darryl and Pamela's 'common ground' is neither all or none, and certainly not just a sharing of similar thoughts, but a matter of degree and must always be characterized in fully embodied, dynamical terms. Metaphorical meanings, and even embodied metaphorical concepts, are not properties of individual minds, but are higher-order products of the coupling among two or more individuals as they interact. Just as two people may be unaware of their rocking in harmony when sitting in rocking chairs, conversational participants automatically self-organize in ways where their coordination of metaphors, and what they contextually imply, can occur without deliberation or awareness.

How much effort does it take to interpret a verbal metaphor?

One of the longest debates in metaphor studies concerns the effort needed to interpret what any figure of speech implies in context. A traditional view assumes that metaphorical meaning is pragmatically inferred only after some literal analysis of a statement has been interpreted and rejected (Grice, 1975). However, many psycholinguistic studies have shown that people can interpret metaphorical statements quite quickly in discourse and in some cases faster than literal paraphrases (Gibbs, 1994, Gibbs & Colston, 2012). These experimental findings suggest that context plays an immediate role in linguistic interpretation such that literal meanings are not obligatorily analyzed in a bottom-up manner before top-down contextual processes work to create metaphorical interpretations. Nonetheless, other research shows that there are still instances in which metaphorical meanings require more effort to interpret (Giora, 2003; Romero & Soria, 2013). These different empirical findings support very strongly contrasting visions of when context is presumed to influence the online processing of linguistic metaphor.

Is it possible to reconcile these different empirical findings and theoretical accounts? Once again, a dynamical approach to metaphor understanding is most capable of explaining what are now viewed as divergent findings within experimental psycholinguistics. Rather than assuming that metaphors must always, or never, be easy to understand, the cognitive effort needed to interpret metaphor in context will always depend on a host of interacting factors. In some cases, the contextual constraints and the metaphor employed will enable people to easily infer metaphorical meaning, but will create a more difficult understanding task in other situations, as seen in various psycholinguistic studies (see Gibbs & Colston, 2012).

One of the great advantages of a dynamical approach is that it forces researchers to articulate the different levels of metaphor processing and products, and not assume that 'metaphor' is always one sort of meaning that listeners and readers must necessarily interpret in each and every situation. Gibbs and Colston (2012) reviewed the vast literature on metaphor understanding and showed that the data one obtains in psycholinguistic experiments can be influenced by four broad, interacting factors: (1) the people, (2) the specific language and utterance encountered in context, (3) the specific understanding task, and (4) the method by which the data are analyzed to assess language comprehension. It is simply impossible to control for all these factors in any single experiment in order to create some 'neutral' or 'normative' theory of metaphor understanding. This reality makes it impossible to simply predict whether metaphors are easy or difficult to process without detailed knowledge of the dynamics involved in each case.

Furthermore, a dynamical approach maintains that metaphorical meaning is not a final, static product (e.g., a blended space; see Chapter 2), but an ongoing process that emerges and dissipates in continuous time. Indeed, there are many instances when people infer only partial metaphorical meanings, or a complex of meanings that involve both present and recently understood metaphorical ideas. In this way, the goal of processing time studies should not be to explain how people, on average, come to infer a single, specific metaphorical meaning, because people will comprehend indeterminate meanings depending on a host of personal and situational factors. This observation is rarely acknowledged in metaphor studies across all academic disciplines, which too often aim to characterize metaphor as a specific kind of linguistic meaning, one that contrasts with a literal meaning. However, scholars, from whatever discipline, can explore in detail how any of the above variables push around the time-course of metaphor processing and the meaning products people infer when they encounter metaphor in speech or writing.

Do embodied, conceptual metaphors shape metaphor understanding?

The same dynamical principles that influence the time-course of verbal metaphor understanding can also be applied to debates over whether conceptual metaphors shape verbal metaphor use. Cognitive linguistic research has long argued that recurring conceptual metaphors motivate the meanings of many verbal metaphors (Lakoff & Johnson, 1980, 1999; see Chapter 1). Cognitive linguistic studies have also proposed that many of the source domains within conceptual metaphors (e.g., JOURNEY in LIFE IS A JOURNEY) are grounded in recurring patterns of bodily activity and experience.

Many psycholinguistic and neuroscience studies provide evidence that is consistent with cognitive linguistic claims about the embodied foundations of many forms of metaphorical meaning (Gibbs, 1994, 2006; Gibbs & Colston, 2012). For example, people's bodily experiences of anger give rise to the conceptual metaphor ANGER IS HEATED FLUID IN THE BODILY CONTAINER that is recruited when understanding conventional metaphorical phrases, such as 'blow your stack' and 'flip your lid' (Gibbs, 1992). People's immediate bodily actions prime their use and understanding of different metaphorical expressions. Thus, people's grasping movements facilitate their subsequent understanding of the verbal metaphor 'grasp the concept' (Wilson & Gibbs, 2007), while their coughing actions prime their mental imagining of the phrase 'cough up a secret' (Gibbs, Gould, & Andric, 2006). Furthermore, studies show that people imagine themselves taking a physical journey when hearing the metaphorical phrase 'Our relationship was moving along in a good direction,' which affects their subsequent real-world walking behavior (Gibbs, 2013). Cognitive neuroscience research also adds empirical support for the embodied basis of metaphorical understanding. Thus, some metaphor processing for statements like 'Sam had a rough day' activates selective sensory areas in the brain that are associated with the source domain (i.e., the feeling 'rough' is related to touch or texture).

All these studies, along with dozens of others, support the idea that embodied conceptual metaphors are a significant constraint on verbal metaphor interpretation. Still, there are heated debates over embodiment in language use, including metaphorical talk and understanding, which have led some scholars to be skeptical about claims for the psychological reality of embodied conceptual metaphors (Haser, 2005).

A dynamical perspective maintains that resolution of the debate over embodied conceptual metaphors is not either a 'yes, embodied conceptual metaphors are always inferred' or a 'no, embodied conceptual metaphors are never inferred' during verbal metaphor understanding. Instead, the degree to which embodied conceptual metaphors are instantiated depends on the precise dynamics in each instance of verbal metaphor use. Contrary to CMT's simple claim, when people hear a verbal metaphor, they do not always activate a fully encoded conceptual metaphor from memory in order to interpret that linguistic metaphor. For example, understanding Pamela's metaphor 'something you go through' may recruit aspects of the underlying conceptual metaphor without necessarily activating a fully composed structure that includes the cross-domain mapping (e.g., LIFE IS A JOURNEY) and all of its most relevant metaphorical entailments. What role an embodied metaphor plays in any act of verbal metaphor understanding depends on the context and many other factors, as described earlier.

Furthermore, when Pamela produces several verbal metaphors in her one extended turn, our understanding of each phrase does not start afresh at the beginning of each utterance. Some remnants of previously understood verbal metaphors, including those conceptual metaphors which were previously inferred, may continue to have some influence on the dynamics of how each new verbal metaphor is comprehended (Gibbs & Santa Cruz, 2012).

In addition, other metaphorical information, such as the presence of specific hand gestures or facial displays (e.g., metaphorical disgust when one disagrees with what was just stated), also provides part of the context shaping people's immediate understanding of verbal metaphors. Thus, combinations of factors interact, in probabilistic ways, to allow verbal metaphor understanding to dynamically unfold over time. As each situation changes, embodied conceptual metaphors will have more or less influence on verbal metaphor interpretation.

Implications and future directions

A dynamical view of metaphor claims that multiple, nested hierarchies of constraints, operating along different time-scales, interact in non-linear ways to produce metaphorical behaviors. Of course, many of the factors, ranging from cultures to neurons, have been previously studied and implicated in theories of metaphorical language. However, metaphor scholars mostly privilege one of these factors, or forces, in their empirical studies and typically highlight their favorite level of analysis in their own theories of metaphor. Not only has this led to endless 'either/or' debates (e.g., metaphors are easy or difficult to interpret, embodied conceptual metaphors always or never shape verbal metaphor use), but also the focus on single causes for metaphor ignores the true complexities of how metaphors come into being and are understood via dynamical, self-organized processes. A key characteristic of the dynamical view is its proper acknowledgment of how multiple forces shape any act of human metaphorical action. Metaphorical behaviors are always emergent properties of a dynamical, self-organizing system such that no single force controls the process of metaphor production and understanding. There are ways of potentially falsifying the dynamical view of metaphor, such as showing that this approach is incapable of explaining how different cognitive and linguistic factors independently operate to shape immediate verbal metaphor use. But metaphor scholars, and psycholinguistic researchers more generally, never attempt to examine the empirical predictions of dynamical systems theory in studies on linguistic processing. Nonetheless, the mathematical tools associated with dynamical systems provide a tool-kit for showing in precise detail how multiple forces shape people's behaviors in psychological experiments (Gibbs & Van Orden, 2010). My advocacy of the dynamical view is intended as a prompt to metaphor researchers, and others, to begin thinking of metaphor performance in dynamical terms and to create experimental tests which compare this theory against more traditional, modular models of metaphor use and understanding.

Readers of this chapter may be dismayed by my message that many forces interact to create metaphorical thoughts, language, and actions. After all, how can any single scholar study all the multiple forces that give rise to metaphor in mind and language? Can't each of us focus on the level of description that most interests us or is directly relevant to our disciplinary backgrounds as linguists, psychologists, anthropologists, philosophers, neuroscientists, and so on? My answer to these questions is that scholars can still embrace disciplinary approaches to particular topics in the study of metaphor. Adopting a dynamical view of metaphor only demands recognition of how metaphor is an adaptive human behavior that is consistent with much else we know about the science of living systems. Embracing this perspective offers us a very different perspective on many of the debates that unnecessarily plague the field of metaphor scholarship and opens up scholars to exploring the real-life complexities of metaphorical thought, language, and action as a fully human, completely contextualized, enterprise. In more specific theoretical terms, scholars can no longer maintain that synchronic and diachronic aspects of metaphor use are completely separate, that there is a rigid distinction between automatic and consciously controlled facets of metaphor production and understanding, or that embodied and discourse perspectives on metaphor are opposing, to name just a few of the cherished divides that are now seen in the field. A dynamical view forces everyone to consider, and at least acknowledge, the complex interacting forces that situate how metaphors are created and used.

Further reading

Dale, R. (2015). An integrative research strategy for exploring synergies in natural language performance. *Ecological Psychology, 27*, 190–201.
Fusaroli, R., Perlman, M., Mislove, A., Paxton, A., Matlock, T., & Dale, R. (2015). Timescales of massive human entrainment. *PLOS ONE, 10*, e0122742.
Gibbs, R. W., Jr., & Van Orden, G. (2012). Pragmatic choice in conversation. *Topics in Cognitive Science, 4*, 7–20.

References

Bak, P. (1997). *How nature works: The science of self-organized criticality*. Oxford, UK: Oxford University Press.
Barr, D., & Keysar, B. (2005). Making sense of how we make sense: The paradox of egocentrism in language use. In H. Colston and A. Katz (Eds.), *Figurative language processing: Social and cultural influences* (pp. 21–41). Mahwah, NJ: Erlbaum.
Clark, H. (1996). *Using language*. New York: Cambridge University Press.
Du Bois, J., & Englebretson, R. (2004). *Santa Barbara corpus of spoken American English, Part 3*. Philadelphia, PA: Linguistic Data Consortium.
Gibbs, R. W., Jr. (1992). What do idioms really mean? *Journal of Memory and Language, 31*, 485–506.
—— (1994). *The poetics of mind: Figurative thought, language, and understanding*. New York: Cambridge University Press.
—— (2006). *Embodiment and cognitive science*. New York: Cambridge University Press.
—— (2012). Metaphors, snowflakes, and termite nests: How nature creates such beautiful things. In F. MacArthur, J.-L. Oncins-Martinez, A. Piquer-Piriz, and M. Sancez-Garcia (Eds.), *Metaphor in use: Culture, context, and communication* (pp. 347–372). Amsterdam, The Netherlands: Benjamins.
—— (2013). Walking the walk while thinking about the talk: Embodied interpretation of metaphorical narratives. *Journal of Psycholinguistic Research, 42*, 363–378.
Gibbs, R. W., Jr., & Cameron, L. (2007). Social-cognitive dynamics of metaphor performance. *Cognitive Systems Research, 9*, 64–75.
Gibbs, R. W., Jr., & Colston, H. (2012). *Interpreting figurative meaning*. New York: Cambridge University Press.
Gibbs, R. W., Jr., Gould, J., & Andric, M. (2006). Imagining metaphorical actions: Embodied simulations make the impossible plausible. *Imagination, Cognition, and Personality, 25*, 221–238.
Gibbs, R. W., Jr., & Santa Cruz, M. (2012). Temporal unfolding of conceptual metaphoric experience. *Metaphor and Symbol, 27*, 299–311.
Gibbs, R. W., Jr., & Van Orden, G. (2010). Adaptive cognition without massive modularity. *Language & Cognition, 2*, 147–169.
Giora, R. (2003). *On our mind: Salience, context and figurative language*. New York: Oxford University Press.
Grice, P. (1975). Logic and conversation. In P. Cole and J. Morgan (Eds.), *Syntax and semantics: Vol. 3. Speech acts* (pp. 41–58). New York: Academic Press.
Haser, V. (2005). *Metaphor, metonymy, and experientialist philosophy: Challenging cognitive semantics*. Berlin, Germany: Mouton de Gruyter.
Koller, V. (2004). *Metaphor and gender in business media discourse: A critical cognitive study*. Basingstoke, UK: Palgrave Macmillan.

Kövecses, Z. (2015). *Where metaphor comes from: Reconsidering context in metaphor*. New York: Oxford University Press.

Lakoff, G., & Johnson, M. (1980). *Metaphors we live by*. Chicago, IL: University of Chicago Press.

—— (1999). *Philosophy in the flesh*. New York: Basic Books.

Larsen-Freeman, D., & Cameron, L. (2008). *Complex systems in applied linguistics*. Oxford, UK: Oxford University Press.

McKinstry, C., Dale, R., & Spivey, M. (2008). Action dynamics reveal parallel competition in decision making. *Psychological Science, 19*, 22–24.

Müller, C., & Cienki, A. (2009). Words, gestures, and beyond: Forms of multimodal metaphor in the use of spoken language. In C. Forceville & E. Urios-Aparisi (Eds.), *Multimodal metaphor* (pp. 297–328). Berlin, Germany: Mouton de Gruyter.

Ortony, A. (1975). Why metaphors are necessary and not just nice. *Educational Theory, 25*, 45–53.

Quinn, N. (1992). The cultural basis of metaphor. In J. Fernandez (Ed.), *Beyond metaphor: The theory of tropes in anthropology* (pp. 56–93). Stanford, CA: Stanford University Press.

Paxton, A., & Dale, R. (2013). Argument disrupts interpersonal synchrony. *Quarterly Journal of Experimental Psychology, 66*, 2092–2102.

Richardson, M., Marsh, K., Isenhower, R., Goodman, J., & Schmidt, R. (2007). Rocking together: Dynamics of intentional and unintentional interpersonal coordination. *Human Movement Science, 26*, 867–891.

Romero, E., & Soria. A. (2013). Anomaly in novel metaphor and experimental tests. *Journal of Literary Semantics, 42*, 31–58.

Semino, E. (2008). *Metaphor in discourse*. Cambridge: Cambridge University Press.

Semino, E., Deignan, A., & Littlemore, J. (2013). Metaphor, genre and recontextualisation. *Metaphor and Symbol, 28*, 41–59.

Shockley, K., Richardson, D., & Dale, R. (2009). Conversation and coordinative structures. *Topics in Cognitive Science, 1*, 305–319.

Sperber, D., & Wilson, D. (1995). *Relevance: Cognition and communication* (2nd ed.). Oxford, UK: Blackwell.

Svanlund, J. (2007). Metaphor and convention. *Cognitive Linguistics, 18*, 47–89.

Spivey, M. (2007). *The continuity of mind*. New York: Oxford University Press.

Steen, G. (2011). The contemporary theory of metaphor – now new and improved! *Review of Cognitive Linguistics, 9*, 26–64.

Stephens, G., Silbert, L., & Hasson, U. (2010). Speaker-listener neural coupling underlies successful communication. *PNAS, 107*, 144425–144430.

Vallacher, R., Read, S., & Nowak, A. (2002). The dynamical perspective in personality and social psychology. *Personality and Social Psychology Review, 6*, 264–273.

Wilson, N., & Gibbs, R. W., Jr. (2007). Real and imagined body movement primes metaphor comprehension. *Cognitive Science, 31*, 721–731.

Zinken, J., & Musolff, A. (2009). A discourse-centred perspective on metaphorical meaning and understanding. In A. Musolff & J. Zinken (Eds.), *Metaphor and discourse* (pp. 1–8). Basingstoke, UK: Palgrave MacMillan.

Part II
Methodological approaches to metaphor and language

5
Identifying metaphors in language

Gerard Steen

Introduction

In the summer of 2000, an international group of ten metaphor scholars came together in Amsterdam for a three-day expert meeting sponsored by the Netherlands Organization for Scientific Research (NWO) in order to discuss whether it was even possible to develop a reliable method for metaphor identification in language. At that time many linguists were not interested in the methods and techniques needed for metaphor identification, while others doubted whether one tool for all could even be developed. The expert meeting was triggered by heated discussions of this issue in the late 1990s (see Steen, 2002), indicating an intimidating number of issues. The participants of the Amsterdam meeting represented a wide range of disciplines, ranging from cognitive linguistics (Cienki, Grady and Kövecses) through stylistics (Crisp and Semino) and corpus linguistics (Deignan) to applied linguistics (Cameron and Low), psycholinguistics (Gibbs) and discourse analysis (Steen). Each of these disciplines lacked an instrument for the identification of metaphors in language. Without such an instrument, researchers were forced to rely on their own intuitions. Practice had shown that these intuitions varied wildly between disciplines, theoretical perspectives, goals of research, and individual experience. The question for the meeting was whether all of these differences could be reconciled on one common ground: if linguists can and must agree on what counts as a subject or object in grammar, why would they not make the same attempt for metaphor in semantics?

The need for a valid and reliable instrument for metaphor identification arose as a result of the success of the cognitive-linguistic approach to metaphor launched by Lakoff and Johnson (1980, 1999; see Chapter 1). This approach argued that metaphor is primarily a matter of thought: we tend to think of one thing in terms of something else, and this can then be expressed in various ways, one of which is language. Thus, we talk about argument as if it is a war with defenses and attacks, or about urgent research to develop treatment of cancer as if it is a war with gains and losses, and these linguistic facts are held to be a reflection of metaphorical models in our thought that structure arguments or urgent research as if they are wars. Inspired by this cognitive-linguistic approach, researchers in different disciplines examined all sorts of situations in which metaphors were presumably being used to talk about such abstract and complex categories in more concrete and simpler terms, in order to study the relation between metaphor in thought and metaphor in language. But they soon realized that they had a huge problem: they did not have a generally accepted method to determine what counts as a metaphor in the language data in the first place. How could a metaphor be identified in language if metaphor was theoretically re-defined as a cross-domain mapping in thought? The expert meeting in Amsterdam in 2000 was a reflection of this problematic situation and aimed to explore whether there was a chance that it could be overcome.

Fifteen years later, the problem of metaphor identification in language is by and large under control. Linguists now have a range of methods to choose from (e.g. Cameron, 1999 and Charteris-Black, 2004), and one in particular has shown high validity in that it identifies all potential metaphors in language as defined in maximally metaphorical approaches such as cognitive linguistics (Steen et al., 2010). What is more, this method can be applied with a high degree of inter-analyst agreement as measured by the statistical analysis of reliability. It can also be transferred to new users in relatively short periods of dedicated training. It has been applied in various research projects (e.g. Nacey, 2013), including to an extensive excerpt from the British National Corpus, yielding the world's first annotated metaphor corpus (Krennmayr and Steen, in press). The previous version of this procedure (Pragglejaz Group, 2007) has played a role in semi-automated approaches to metaphor identification, such as Wmatrix (Semino et al., 2009), and in modelling automated metaphor identification in selected areas (Dorst, Reijnierse and Venhuizen, 2013). Even though identifying metaphors in language is still not without its controversies, problems and difficulties (as may be expected for as varied a phenomenon as metaphor), for a language such as English and languages that are close to English the difficulties are now mainly practical. They can be addressed within a well-delineated conceptual and operational framework that makes explicit in systematic ways which decisions have to be taken in order to discuss whether a particular expression in language should be counted as an expression of metaphor in thought.

The difference between 2000 and 2015 is mainly due to the group of researchers who met in Amsterdam and who then turned into the Pragglejaz Group, the name deriving from the first letters of their first names (**P**eter Crisp, **R**ay Gibbs, **A**lan Cienki, and so on). It took the Pragglejaz Group seven years and a lot of grant money invested by various countries and institutions to produce the first reliable metaphor identification procedure, called MIP (Pragglejaz Group, 2007). This publication then sparked further research into metaphor identification in language, including MIPVU, the method I am using as the encompassing framework for this chapter (Steen et al., 2010). It is a more refined, extended, reliable and valid variant of MIP that was produced at VU University Amsterdam.

Although this chapter will also acknowledge and refer to related work, it will focus on the crucial methodological issues that have emerged as a result of the development of MIPVU.

Preliminary issues

Before going into the details of methodology and the ways in which MIP and MIPVU can be used, I first need to clarify what identifying 'metaphors in language' means (cf. Steen, 2007). For metaphor, this chapter employs the cognitive-linguistic definition of metaphor as a mapping across two conceptual domains (Lakoff and Johnson, 1980, 1999; see Chapter 1). Thinking and talking about cancer research in terms of war employs one conceptual domain, 'war', which functions as the source domain to think and talk about another domain, 'cancer research', which functions as the target domain.

In order to clarify the relation between metaphor and language, there are three issues that need to be made explicit (cf. Steen, 2007). The first issue has to do with the need to make a distinction between studying language as a matter of signs versus language as behaviour. Language as behaviour has to do with the psychological or social processes occurring in and between people using language in real time, for instance, in production, reception, interaction, acquisition, learning and so on. Language as a matter of signs, by contrast, has to do with the lexico-grammatical structures and functions that have been abstracted away from these processes by linguists, who focus on the description and explanation of signs without studying the real-time processes of use, as when they study texts or transcripts or write dictionaries and grammars. As has been noted by several researchers (e.g., Gibbs, 2006), metaphor in language approached from this sign-oriented perspective is not identical with metaphor in psychological or social processes of language. Since the sign-oriented approach to metaphor identification in language is the predominant approach in linguistics, this chapter focuses on this way of identifying metaphor in language.

The second issue concerns the need for a distinction between metaphor in language as a system versus metaphor in language as usage. In the usage approach, linguistic expressions are studied as single phenomena that function as metaphors in unique contexts where they have a specific, situated meaning. In the system approach, on the other hand, metaphorical expressions or constructions are studied as part of a postulated network of constructions (or grammatical rules and lexical items) with which they contrast and from which they can be selected and combined in usage. The usage perspective examines metaphor in language as an expression that is situated in one concrete utterance and discourse context, whereas the system perspective examines metaphor as a construction in the language system that has resulted from development over time or displays variation over geographical, social and institutional space. For instance, the words *fervent* and *ardent* used to be polysemous between an emotion sense ('intense') and a temperature sense ('hot'), the emotion sense presumably being a metaphorical derivation from the temperature sense. In English as a language system, therefore, *fervent* and *ardent* can be identified as diachronically metaphorical. In language usage, however, the temperature sense has fallen out of use, and when these words are used to talk about emotions, they cannot be identified as metaphorical, since there is no contrast with the more basic temperature sense anymore. In this chapter we will discuss metaphor identification in language only from a usage-oriented perspective.

The third issue concerns the need for a distinction between metaphorical language use on the one hand and language as an expression of an underlying cross-domain mapping on the other. If metaphor in language is an expression of a cross-domain mapping in thought, then it may be expressed in a number of different ways, not all of which can be called metaphorical language use in the strict sense of the term; thus, a simile (e.g., *You are like a hurricane*) also counts as metaphor in language, even though it is not metaphorical language use: *hurricane* means what it basically or literally says, 'hurricane'. An extended metaphorical comparison (e.g., Shakespeare's *Shall I compare thee to a summer's day?*) also expresses an underlying cross-domain mapping in thought and therefore counts as metaphor in language; yet the utterance by itself simply asks whether the speaker can compare his beloved to a summer's day, which in itself does not comprise metaphorical language use. Given the re-definition of metaphor as a matter of thought, any expression in language that can be related to a cross-domain mapping in thought must be included as a target for metaphor identification in language.

This chapter hence looks at the identification of metaphor in language, focusing on language as a matter of usage from a sign-oriented perspective. This raises a methodological problem for those who define metaphor as a cross-domain mapping in thought, since linguists and other researchers of language use in the other sciences only have access to language, not thought – they need to have an instrument to bridge this gap. Such a metaphor identification procedure has to be valid and reliable if linguists wish to contribute to the interdisciplinary debate about metaphor across the humanities and the social and cognitive and computer sciences, as well as make their work applicable in concrete real-world interventions.

Main methodological aspects of metaphor identification

There are four major aspects of identifying metaphors in language (Steen, 2007):

- Metaphor identification involves a move from conceptualization to operationalization in research.
- Once a method of operationalizing the identification of metaphor in language is clear, it can be applied in two rather distinct approaches, which may be labelled as deductive versus inductive.
- Irrespective of these two approaches, there are currently two versions of the operationalization process, which are more or less explicit in the details of their decision making for identifying metaphor in language.
- Whichever method for metaphor identification is used, it needs to be subjected to quality control to determine its validity and reliability.

This section addresses each of these in turn.

Identifying metaphors in language is a form of scientific process that should follow a number of conventions. The first convention is that identification proceeds by the application of clear criteria for the phenomenon that is the target of investigation, in this case metaphor in language, and that these criteria have to be derived from a theoretical definition of that phenomenon, or 'conceptualization', that can be made operational in this way. Since metaphor in language is conceptualized as an expression of metaphor in thought, we need to begin with the conceptualization of metaphor in thought. For the purposes of this chapter, metaphor in thought is defined as a mapping across two conceptual domains that are distinct from each other but can be connected by a set of correspondences that show that they are metaphorically alike. To prevent too long and abstract an exposition, let us consider one of the famous cognitive-linguistic examples, the conceptual metaphor ARGUMENT IS WAR (Lakoff and Johnson, 1980: 4):

> Your claims are *indefensible*
>
> He *attacked every weak point* in my argument.
>
> His criticisms were *right on target*.
>
> I *demolished* his argument.
>
> I've never *won* an argument with him.
>
> You disagree? Okay, *shoot!*
>
> If you use that *strategy*, he'll *wipe you out*.
>
> He *shot down* all of my arguments.

In order to agree that all of the words in italics can be identified as metaphors in language, the following theoretical assumptions are tacitly made:

1. We have a mapping in our thought that goes from one conceptual domain, WAR, to another conceptual domain, ARGUMENT; these two conceptual domains are distinct but can be compared to each other as structurally alike, the WAR domain functioning as a source to provide comparable conceptual structure to the ARGUMENT domain as a target. Relevant concepts in the WAR domain include entities such as POINTS or TARGETS or STRATEGIES, actions such as ATTACK or DEMOLISH, and qualities such as INDEFENSIBLE or WEAK; these can be used to project corresponding relevant concepts (entities, actions and qualities) in the target domain of ARGUMENT. This is how metaphor enables thought about one thing (ARGUMENTS) in terms of another (WAR).

    Note that this assumption does not necessarily commit us to the prior, long-term existence of such cross-domain mappings in our long-term memory, nor to the on-line activation of such cross-domain mappings in our short-term memory. This is an assumption that most cognitive linguists make, but it is not a prerequisite for other researchers to accept this assumption as the basis for a metaphor identification procedure that acknowledges that metaphor is a matter of thought – as in fact happened between different participants in the Pragglejaz Group. The alternative is to see metaphors in thought as analytical reconstructions on the basis of linguistic data whose psychological validity is an empirical issue.

2. There is a whole range of linguistic expressions that belong to the WAR domain that are employed by language users to talk about aspects of war but also about aspects of argument. These are the lexical items corresponding to the concepts mentioned under (1) just now: *indefensible, attacked,* and so on. The structural polysemy of these lexical items is motivated by conventionalized metaphorical relations between argument and war in thought.

3. Since the linguistic expressions presumably belonging to the source domain of 'war' analytically stand out as incongruous or different than the other linguistic expressions properly belonging to the target domain of 'argument', and since the 'war' domain units seem to speak indirectly about the target domain 'in terms of' the source domain, there are two operational criteria for the identification of metaphors in language: indirectness and incongruity. However, there may be more forms of indirectness and incongruity in language use, for instance, in paradox and oxymoron; therefore, incongruity and indirectness point to metaphor only if there is some form of similarity between the source domain they directly express and the target domain they indirectly express.

    Note that the emphasis is on '*analytically* stand out as incongruous or different': it is precisely the main tenet of the cognitive-linguistic revolution that the bulk of metaphor is conventional and the only way to talk about a particular target domain referent or topic, which suggests that metaphors are *not* incongruous or different from that perspective. The identification of metaphor in language cannot follow the everyday experience of metaphor in language, which is a very different affair altogether.

These are the three core assumptions endorsed by most linguists inspired by the cognitive-linguistic approach that enable the move from conceptualization to operationalization. It will be appreciated that they harbour a minefield of problems, which have all been hotly debated in the literature (cf. Steen, 2007):

1. How can one demarcate, define and describe one conceptual domain as distinct from another (Croft, 2002)?
2. What is the relation between concepts and words (Evans, 2009; Murphy, 2002)?
3. When is a linguistic expression incongruous, indirect and when is one conceptual domain similar or comparable to another (Cameron and Maslen, 2010; Charteris-Black, 2004)?

Any metaphor identification procedure will be influenced by the answers given to these questions. The less idiosyncratic or more general these answers are in terms of encompassing theories of language and thought (that is, independent of the specific metaphor project that the identification procedure is needed for), the more valid and reliable the identification of metaphors in language will be.

The second major methodological aspect of metaphor identification is the distinction between the deductive approach and the inductive approach to finding metaphors in language (Steen, 2007; Krennmayr, 2013). In the deductive approach, researchers assume that there is a conventionalized cross-domain mapping in thought, such as ARGUMENT IS WAR, and then examine language to find expressions that may be related to this cross-domain mapping. They can do this in two different ways. The first involves constructing an a priori list of lexical items that are seen as bona fide expressions of the concepts in the source domain (in our example, 'war' language) and then examining how these are used in language data to talk about the target domain (in our example, language about arguments) (e.g., Koller, 2004). Re-examining the examples from Lakoff and Johnson above, it is interesting in this context to consider how words like *point*, *target* or *wipe out* could end up on such a list. The crucial question arises of whether these are linguistic expressions that are typical 'war' language – after all, *point* seems a word that is more closely related to mathematics, while *target* may be primarily related to games and sports and *wipe out* is an action applied to ovens and sinks more than anything else. In other words, how does the researcher decide on a priori grounds that a particular linguistic expression is primarily the expression of one specific conceptual domain as opposed to another? They need to do so before they can apply the deductive approach.

If this becomes too problematic, researchers can take a second route for the deductive approach. They can forget about an a priori list of key words and instead decide on a case-by-case basis whether they think that a specific linguistic expression can be classified as belonging to a particular conceptual domain that they are deductively interested in (e.g., Charteris-Black, 2004). The practical decision for specific lexical items will eventually remain the same, though. Suppose the researcher following this second route encounters the expression *He attacked every weak point in my argument*. The issue will then still remain whether *point* is to be seen as a reflection of ARGUMENT IS WAR, even though it may primarily be a word from mathematics.

In the inductive approach, researchers do not make assumptions about the prior existence of a particular cross-domain mapping such as ARGUMENT IS WAR. Instead, all language use is examined and tested for whether it contains expressions that can be seen as indirect and incongruous in context while the conceptual domain they relate to is somehow similar or comparable to the domain of that context (Pragglejaz Group, 2007; Steen et al., 2010; Cameron and Maslen, 2010). To illustrate, a researcher could encounter the first utterance of the above list, *Your claims are indefensible*, and then query whether the word *indefensible* in this context is analytically indirect and incongruous language use that can be resolved by comparison. This is a question that according to cognitive linguists can be answered affirmatively for this case. The concrete domain that *indefensible* seems to belong to is the one of averting a physical attack, while the abstract domain it is here applied to is the abstract domain of verbal criticism – this makes its use indirect and incongruous, while the defense against verbal attack can be seen as similar to the defense against physical attack.

The third major methodological issue has to do with the degree of explicitness of the procedure that needs to be followed. Degree of explicitness is best explained with reference to the Metaphor Identification Procedure (MIP) published by the Pragglejaz Group (2007: 3):

1. Read the entire text-discourse to establish a general understanding of the meaning.
2. Determine the lexical units in the text-discourse.
3. (a) For each lexical unit in the text, establish its meaning in context, that is, how it applies to an entity, relation, or attribute in the situation evoked by the text (contextual meaning). Take into account what comes before and after the lexical unit.
   (b) For each lexical unit, determine if it has a more basic contemporary meaning in other contexts than the one in the given context. For our purposes, basic meanings tend to be
   –more concrete; what they evoke is easier to imagine, see, hear, feel, smell, and taste,
   –related to bodily action,
   –more precise (as opposed to vague),
   –historically older.
   Basic meanings are not necessarily the most frequent meanings of the lexical unit.
   (c) If the lexical unit has a more basic current meaning in other contexts than the one given, decide whether the contextual meaning contrasts with the basic meaning but can be understood in comparison with it.
4. If yes, mark the lexical unit as metaphorical.

Thus, for *Your claims are indefensible*, we can assume that it occurs in a discussion of some argument (step 1), each of the orthographically distinct words constituting distinct lexical units (step 2). The contextual sense of one of these words, *indefensible*, applies to argumentation (3a), while it has a more basic sense that has to do with war (3b). The contextual sense contrasts with the basic sense but can be understood in comparison with it (3c). This lexical unit is consequently metaphorical.

This procedure may be experienced as conceptually clear and compatible with the preceding considerations. However, it is operationally minimal, as it does not give explicit criteria for what counts as a lexical unit, what counts as meaning in context, and so on. These operational gaps were acknowledged by the Pragglejaz Group (2007) but deliberately left undecided to allow for maximum freedom among metaphor researchers. However, this created too much variation between applications of MIP, a problem which MIP was precisely designed to resolve. The decisions left open were hence explicitly addressed from one consistent perspective in a further large research project which led to the development of MIPVU (Steen et al., 2010). As a result of the consistent and exhaustive application by five researchers of MIP to a corpus of almost 200,000 words excerpted from a sample of the British National Corpus called the BNC Baby, the brief instructions in MIP turned into an 18-page manual in MIPVU. Each of the major operational concerns with MIP was separately addressed and further explained, the most important of which include lexical units, contextual meanings, basic meanings and the distinctness between contextual and basic meanings.

The MIP notion of lexical units was fine-tuned by adopting the following rules:

- Phrasal verbs (marked as such in many dictionaries, but often requiring additional linguistic testing) like *turn up* do not count as two units but as one.
- Idioms like *spill the beans* do count as more lexical units, in this case as three.
- Polywords like *of course* do not count as two units but as one.
- Compounds like *brain-drain* count as one, except when they are novel and not listed in the dictionary, in which case they count as two (e.g. *honey-hunting*).

The rationale for these rules lies in the idea that metaphor identification must be relatable to concept identification (as metaphors are a matter of mapping between domains of concepts) and in the additional assumption that concepts are used in utterances (like in the ARGUMENT IS WAR examples) to set up referents (which play a role in people's mental pictures of the situation evoked by the utterance). From that perspective, *turn up* indicates one action, while *of course* indicates one meta-comment, whereas *spill the beans* indicates more than one referent (an action and an affected entity). These conceptual as well as operational decisions become crucial when metaphor use is to be compared across languages, as there are differences between languages ranging from small to fundamental in the way they organize the expression of referents and concepts in words, and the same level of measurement for metaphor in language has to be pitched for any such cross-linguistic study.

The MIP notion of contextual meaning had to be managed for cases where the data posed insuperable problems. One example is when people do not finish their utterances, as in *Yeah I had somebody come round and <u>stuck their bloody</u> . . .* The underlined words are part of an aborted utterance where it is impossible to assess their contextual meaning in the same way as elsewhere. For this reason, MIPVU suggests that these data be discarded for metaphor analysis, a decision which has to be made only very seldomly (less than one per cent of all words in regular spoken language use; Steen et al., 2010). Another example is when the analyst lacks sufficient situational knowledge, as when a text says that somebody goes *up the path* and it is unclear whether the person is moving on a rising path (not metaphorical) or not (possibly metaphorical). In that case, such metaphors can be marked as borderline and when needed can be treated as a special category – this too occurs only very seldomly.

The MIP notion of basic meaning first of all ran into the problem of 'basic meaning of what, exactly'? MIP takes lexical units as its units of analysis, but it turns out that some researchers interpret lexical units as lemmas whereas others interpret them as word class. Consider the word *key*: as a lemma in the Macmillan dictionary (Rundle, 2002), it displays uses as a noun and as an adjective, the adjective manifesting only one sense: 'important' (as in *key variable*). If lexical units are viewed simply as lemmas, then *key* used as an adjective is always metaphorical, derived from the more basic *key* as a noun. However, if lexical units are operationalized as word classes, then *key* as an adjective has one conventionalized sense, 'important', which cannot be compared to another more basic sense (instrument to open a door with), since that is in another word class; in that case, *key* will hardly ever be metaphorical. Since MIPVU has explained that metaphor identification is related to broader issues of language use, including the relation between words, concepts and referents, it interprets the MIP notion of lexical units as word classes, making a distinction between the word, concept and referent of 'key' as an entity (instrument) as opposed to a quality (important).

Another important issue in fine-tuning the notion of basic meaning concerns the role of etymology as a criterion for metaphor identification in MIP. Although it may be true that most metaphorical senses in English vocabulary are more recent than their related non-metaphorical, more basic senses, this raises at least two issues. First of all, this is not true across the board: the word *power*, for example, has an older abstract sense than physical sense in the *Oxford English Dictionary*. And secondly, etymology is an aspect of vocabulary that is basically irrelevant to the contemporary language user and language usage: people do not know which word sense came first in which century. Etymology belongs to the study of language as a system and was therefore removed from MIPVU as a criterion for metaphor identification in contemporary usage.

The last operational issue to be addressed here pertains to the MIP notion of distinctness: when are two senses sufficiently distinct? This is an important issue, as metaphor in language is supposed to reflect metaphor in thought, where two distinct domains are contrasted, aligned and compared. If two senses are not sufficiently distinct, the two corresponding conceptual domains are presumably not sufficiently distinct. This problem was addressed by making use of the way dictionaries order their sense descriptions of words: if a lexical unit, and in particular a word class, has more than one numbered sense description, these senses are taken as being sufficiently distinct for contrasting and comparison. Of course, not all dictionaries allot the same amount of space or the same conventions for using that space, but this can be negotiated by making additional arrangements, for instance, for the way sense descriptions are read and the way in which additional dictionaries may be brought in when problems arise. However, the big advantage of using a dictionary as an independent and stable frame of reference for deciding about distinct senses of individual lexical units is of paramount importance.[1]

All in all then, when considering variations in the explicitness of procedures, the comparison between MIP and MIPVU may serve as an interesting case for good practice. Most of the explications added in MIPVU are theoretically and methodologically motivated and were derived from the same principles as MIP but just taken a little further—including being based in the relation between words, concepts and referents (lexical units, word class), and in usage rather than language system (etymology), and being concerned with methodological constancy and replicability (distinctness of senses and use of dictionaries). All of these are in the same spirit as MIP and can be discussed and criticized regarding their suitability in general or for specific research projects. MIPVU does not claim to have the last word or to be error free but puts its methodological cards on the table for explicit and systematic rational criticism. Metaphor identification still requires further research and development, but the fault lines of the decisions are relatively clear and can be addressed by every researcher.

Finally, this discussion must tackle the issues of quality control, which is the fourth and last major methodological aspect of metaphor identification. When six Pragglejaz Group members looked at the following text excerpt, the following total scores for metaphor identification per lexical unit were obtained (NB: numbers within round brackets indicate how many analysts identified that word as metaphorical):

> In(5) October 1991 Secretary James Baker was able to take(6) advantage of the momentum(6) created(5) by Arab support(6) for the use of force to liberate Kuwait from(1) the clutches(6) of Saddam Hussein to cajole a reluctant Likud Israeli prime minister and skeptical Arab leaders to participate in(5) an US-USSR-sponsored Middle East Peace conference.

Most lexical units were unanimously judged to be non-metaphorical—these do not have a zero score attached to them in order not to clutter the example. Some lexical units received unanimous agreement between the six members that they were metaphorical: *take, momentum, support,* and *clutches.* However, some words got one score for metaphoricity (*from*) while other words got five (*in, created,* and *in*). This suggests that there was not complete agreement between all six judges over this short excerpt, and raises the question of the reliability of the procedure and the quality of its application by trained and expert judges (which is also partly a matter of performance).

Reliability is a crucial property of any instrument for content analysis (Krippendorf, 2010), including metaphor identification. It involves various aspects (analysis of agreement on particular cases versus analysis of agreement between analysts; analysis before discussion and agreement after discussion; complete perfection versus high reliability) and can be assessed in various ways. It typically requires quantitative statistics, which enforces more precision in data analysis and facilitates testing against chance agreement. When MIP was published, reliability by statistical measurement was modest. MIPVU increased reliability to the level of good (Steen et al., 2010; for more detail on the statistical approach to reliability, see Landis and Koch, 1977).

Validity is the second dimension of quality control. This has to do with the question of whether the metaphor identification procedure covers all cases generally counted as manifesting metaphor in language, and no more. Consider the following well-known poem by Ezra Pound:

> In a station of the metro
> The apparition of these faces in the crowd;
> Petals on a wet, black bough

It is clear that the first line presents the context for a possible target domain, people in a metro station, while the third line presents a source domain with which the target domain is compared. However, from the perspective of MIP, none of the lexical units in the third line is used indirectly or displays incongruity—they simply talk about some other domain than the station of the metro directly, the referential domain of petals on a bough which is presented in its own right. If all lexical units in the third line are not related to metaphor because they do not display a contrast between a contextual and a basic sense, an important manifestation of metaphor would be missed. For this reason, MIPVU did not only explicate some of the operational criteria that were left undecided in MIP, but it also added more categories of metaphor that could be identified in the same procedure. Because of this, MIPVU is not just more reliable but also more valid than MIP.

I have discussed four major methodological issues with metaphor identification: the move from conceptualization to operationalization, the distinct approaches within metaphor identification labeled deductive versus inductive, the distinct levels of explicitness in setting up a procedure for metaphor identification exemplified by MIP versus MIPVU, and the way in which any outcome of all of these issues in the form of some procedure for metaphor identification must be evaluated for reliability and validity. These are the foundations for any discussion of metaphor identification, and it has taken fifteen years of research to get them out into the open. Against this background we can now briefly highlight some of the critical issues in the field.

Critical issues, debates, controversies

There are a number of critical issues in the field of metaphor identification, of which I will briefly discuss four. First of all, there is the question of how the identification of metaphor relates to metonymy. This question was placed on the agenda in cognitive linguistics by a number of researchers who see both metaphor and metonymy as forms of mapping between conceptual domains and have constructed scales with distinct categories ranging from metaphor to metonymy in various ways (see Steen, 2007, for discussion). Does metaphor identification involve one scale with metaphor and metonymy at two extreme ends so that researchers have to choose between metaphor and metonymy or combinations, or does metaphor identification involve one variable that is independent from metonymy and its identification, but interacting with it? This question has been answered in different ways by different researchers (for a representative overview, see Barcelona, 2000). In my view, the same data can be both metaphorical and metonymic, either metaphorical or metonymic, or neither metaphorical nor metonymic, which suggests that metaphor identification and metonymy identification should each be carried out independently and then crossed with each other.

A second issue is whether we can identify all metaphor in language in one way even though there are several subdivisions of metaphor. The above discussion of the Ezra Pound poem already suggested that some classes of metaphor require slightly different identification procedures than others, since MIP was unable to cater for this type of metaphor. As a result, not only was MIP expanded, but also its theory was conceptualized slightly differently, locating the notion of incongruity and indirectness not in word use but at the level of concepts and referents: even though 'Petals on a wet, black bough' was not indirect and incongruous in the same way as *indefensible* in 'Your claims are indefensible', 'Petals on a wet, black bough' is indirect and incongruous when we look at this poem at the level of conceptual domains and referents in the situation model. This led to an expansion of MIP in MIPVU which catered for this type of indirectness and incongruity while redefining their basis in conceptual structure, not in the linguistic forms of metaphor in language (Steen, 2007). Similar challenges may be put to any metaphor identification procedure by other classes of metaphor. The crucial issue will always be to keep one all-encompassing theoretical model as a basis for identifying all linguistic manifestations of metaphor in thought, so that the link between conceptualization and operationalization stays firm and explicit. That such metaphors in language, once identified, may be further classified as, for instance, novel or conventional, or apt and less apt, or deliberate or non-deliberate, is a separate issue that needs to be addressed in subsequent steps.

A third issue concerns how we divide 'language' into appropriate units of analysis so that we can say that we are measuring metaphor at one and the same 'level' of language. Here Cameron and Maslen (2010) have taken issue with MIP's proposal to take lexical units as the unit of analysis: 'If the discourse dynamics framework is adopted, then a metaphor may extend beyond a single word to surrounding language, and the researcher has to decide on the beginning and ending of the stretch of language that comprises the vehicle term' (108). As a result, they propose to identify metaphor vehicles which may comprise any number of words. The unit of analysis therefore shifts from single lexical units to variable sets of lexical units which are demarcated on the basis of their metaphorical coherence. However, this approach seems to put metaphorical coherence within the vehicle up front and then asks for the decision that the words in the set are to be identified as metaphorical. In MIP and MIPVU, by contrast, metaphor identification is applied to one consistent level of linguistic expression, in this case lexical units (or simply, 'words'), which then offers a dataset that may facilitate subsequent grouping into variable sets of lexical units that may function as metaphor vehicles. This type of grouping is a procedure, however, for which we need a means of identifying the single and coherent underlying conceptual domain of the vehicle, which is a problematic and different issue.

The fourth issue has to do with the tools for metaphor identification – what help is there for applying our criteria for metaphor in language? Handling word senses is greatly facilitated by the use of dictionaries, but such dictionaries have their practical limitations (Deignan, 2005) and are only helpful if they are based on contemporary corpus work which lists senses in terms of real use and frequencies (cf. Deignan 2005; Dorst and Reijnierse, 2015; Pasma, 2011). Most languages other than English lack such dictionaries, and so they have to solve the problem of sense demarcation in a different way. Corpus work would be a good alternative, were it not for the fact that most languages other than English do not have comparable corpora to the BNC, for instance, either. Moreover, additional decisions have to be made about the number of citations needed before a word can be sensibly analyzed, and additional decisions have to be made about the number of citations there must be for a particular sense before it can count as a separate and conventionalized word sense. There is much progress to be made here.

Example(s) of current research

The most ambitious attempt at metaphor identification with maximum validity and statistical reports on (high) reliability can be found in the research done on the VU Amsterdam Metaphor Corpus (Krennmayr and Steen, in press). Four publicly available PhD theses applied MIPVU to sets of texts excerpted from the BNC Baby, averaging 45,000 words per register. The studies examined metaphor in conversation (Kaal, 2012), in fiction (Dorst, 2011), in news (Krennmayr, 2011) and in academic texts (Herrmann, 2013). A comparable PhD study on Dutch language texts, comprising conversations and news, can be found in Pasma (2011). The main finding of this work is that the incidence of metaphor largely co-varies with the first dimension of Biber's (1988) multi-dimensional/multi-feature framework for register analysis: the more informational a register is, the more metaphorical it is, and vice versa, the more involved a register is, the less metaphorical it is. In particular, academic texts exhibit the highest percentage of metaphor-related words (18.5 percent), followed by news (16.4 percent) and fiction (11.9 percent), while conversation has the lowest percentage (7.7 percent). This raises the question of whether metaphor's main function is to express information, as would be compatible with the major cognitive-linguistic tenet that we need metaphors to achieve conceptualization across domains. At the same time, the association between metaphor and information production is only partial, as there are also associations between metaphor and word class and metaphor and type of figure of speech. As is discussed in great detail in the five PhD theses, there is a four-way interaction between metaphor, register, word class and figure of speech, which pre-empts any simple descriptions and explanations of the way metaphor works in language use.

Most other metaphor studies depend on the application of MIP or comparable identification procedures, such as Charteris-Black (2004), but do not focus on the methodological issues of metaphor identification at great length nor report analyses of quality control that enable assessment of the success of the procedure. One notable exception is Susan Nacey (2013), who devotes three chapters to a discussion of methodological issues in MIP and MIPVU and their application to written English-language data produced by advanced Norwegian learners of English. Another is Littlemore et al.'s (2013) adjusted application of MIPVU to the written English produced by Greek- and German-speaking learners of English, with sensitive discussion of the reasons for adjustment. In general, however, the identification of metaphor in language still has some way to go before it can be regarded as fully conventionalized according to one agreed-upon set of principles and techniques and decisions.

Future directions

The main challenge for future research will be to extrapolate the principles behind MIP and MIPVU to languages other than English and closely related languages like Dutch. This first of all raises the question of whether researchers of other languages can agree with the overall methodological assumptions that were outlined above. Second, equivalents of lexical units, basic and contextual senses and so on have to be established across languages, just like operational criteria for determining their identity in language research. This, again, is intimately connected with the overall dearth of corpora and contemporary user dictionaries based on corpora, which presents a massive practical problem for linguistic metaphor research. It is up to the metaphor research community to address these problems in such a way that comparison of findings across languages can be achieved, which is a tremendous but exciting challenge.

One way of addressing this challenge is by making use of current attempts at automating metaphor identification in language. While the VU Amsterdam Metaphor Corpus has not been used as training data for a machine learning algorithm, there have been attempts by colleagues in computational linguistics to use it for devising tools for automatic metaphor identification (e.g., Berber Sardinha, 2009; Dunn, 2013; Florou, 2013; Niculae and Yaneva, 2013). If these attempts become successful, they may perhaps also be applied to big datasets of texts in other languages, as in Russian (Badryzlova et al., 2013).

These are just two of the most important options for metaphor identification research in the near future. Their materialization depends on a wide range of factors that have to do with fundamental theoretical assumptions and principles, generally accepted norms and values of methodological quality across the sciences, and practical problems in terms of resources and funding in the world of present-day academic research. The interaction between these issues may now be understood much better than some fifteen years ago.

Note

1 Of course, the contextual meanings of metaphorical expressions may not necessarily be found in dictionaries, especially when the particular metaphorical use is not conventional.

Further reading

Cameron, L., and Maslen, R. (Eds.) (2010) *Metaphor Analysis: Research Practice in Applied Linguistics, Social Sciences and the Humanities*, Sheffield, UK: Equinox.

Pragglejaz Group (2007) 'MIP: A method for identifying metaphorically used words in discourse', *Metaphor & Symbol* 22: 1–39.

Steen, G. J. (2007) *Finding Metaphor in Grammar and Usage*, Amsterdam, The Netherlands: John Benjamins.

Steen, G. J., Dorst, A. G., Herrmann, J. B., Kaal, A. A., Krennmayr, T., and Pasma, T. (2010) *A Method for Linguistic Metaphor Identification: From MIP to MIPVU*, Amsterdam, The Netherlands: John Benjamins.

References

Badryzlova, Y., Isaeva, Y., Shekhtman, N., and Kerimov, R. (2013) 'Annotating a Russian corpus of conceptual metaphor: A bottom-up approach', *Proceedings of the Workshop on Metaphor in NLP*, pp. 77–86.

Barcelona, A. (Ed.) (2000) *Metaphor and Metonymy at the Crossroads*, Berlin, Germany: Mouton de Gruyter.

Berber Sardinha, T. (2009) 'A tool for finding metaphors in corpora using lexical patterns,' paper presented at the Corpus Linguistics Conference 2009, Liverpool, UK.

Biber, D. (1988) *Variation across Speech and Writing*, Cambridge, UK: Cambridge University Press.

Cameron, L. (1999) 'Identifying and describing metaphor in spoken discourse data,' in L. Cameron and G. Low (Eds.), *Researching and Applying Metaphor*, Cambridge, UK: Cambridge University Press.

Cameron, L., and Maslen, R. (2010) 'Identifying metaphors in discourse data,' in L. Cameron and R. Maslen (Eds.), *Metaphor Analysis: Research Practice in Applied Linguistics, Social Sciences and the Humanities*, Sheffield, UK: Equinox.

Charteris-Black, J. (2004) *Corpus Approaches to Critical Metaphor Analysis*, Basingstoke/New York: Palgrave Macmillan.

Croft, W. (2002) 'The role of domains in the interpretation of metaphors and metonymies,' *Cognitive Linguistics* 4: 335–370.

Deignan, A. (2005) *Metaphor and Corpus Linguistics*, Amsterdam, The Netherlands: John Benjamins.

Dorst, A. G. (2011) *Metaphor in Fiction: Linguistic Forms, Conceptual Structures, Cognitive Representations*, Oisterwijk, The Netherlands: BOXpress.

Dorst, A. G., and Reijnierse, W. G. (2015) 'A dictionary gives definitions, not decisions: On using a dictionary to identify the basic senses of words,' *Metaphor and the Social World* 5: 137–144.

Dorst, A. G., Reijnierse, W. G., and Venhuizen, G. (2013) 'One small step for MIP towards automated metaphor identification? Formulating general rules to determine basic meanings in large-scale approaches to metaphor,' *Metaphor and the Social World* 3: 77–99.

Dunn, J. (2013) 'What metaphor identification systems can tell us about metaphor-in-language,' *Proceedings of the Workshop on Metaphor in NLP*, pp. 1–10.

Evans, V. (2009) *How Words Mean: Lexical Concepts, Cognitive Models and Meaning Construction*, Oxford, UK: OUP.

Florou, E. (2013) 'Detecting metaphor by contextual analogy,' *Proceedings of the ACL Student Research Workshop*, pp. 23–30.

Gibbs, R. W., Jr. (2006) *Embodiment and Cognitive Science*, Cambridge, UK: Cambridge University Press.

Herrmann, J. B. (2013) *Metaphor in Academic Discourse: Linguistic Forms, Conceptual Structures, Communicative Functions and Cognitive Representations*, LOT Dissertation Series 333, Utrecht, The Netherlands: LOT.

Kaal, A. A. (2012) *Metaphor in Conversation*, Oisterwijk, The Netherlands: Uitgeverij BOXpress.

Koller, V. (2004) *Metaphor and Gender in Business Media Discourse: A Critical Cognitive Study*, Basingstoke/New York: Palgrave Macmillan.

Krennmayr, T. (2011) *Metaphor in Newspapers*, LOT Dissertation Series 276, Utrecht, The Netherlands: LOT.

—— (2013) 'Top-down versus bottom-up approaches to the identification of metaphor in discourse,' *Metaphorik.de* 24: 7–36.

Krennmayr, T., and Steen, G. J. (In press) 'The VU Amsterdam Metaphor Corpus,' in N. Ide and J. Pustejovsky (Eds.), *Handbook of Linguistic Annotation*, Berlin, Germany: Springer.

Krippendorf, K. (2010) *Content Analysis: An Introduction to its Methodology*, 3rd ed., London: Sage.

Lakoff, G., and Johnson, M. (1980) *Metaphors We Live By*, Chicago, IL: University of Chicago Press.

—— (1999) *Philosophy in the Flesh: The Embodied Mind and Its Challenge to Western Thought*, Chicago, IL: University of Chicago Press.

Landis, J. R., and Koch, G. G. (1977) 'The measurement of observer agreement for categorical data,' *Biometrics* 33(1): 159–174.

Littlemore, J., Krennmayr, T., Turner, S., and Turner, J. (2013) 'An investigation into metaphor use at different levels of second language writing,' *Applied Linguistics* 35: 117–144.

Murphy, G. (2002) *The Big Book of Concepts*, Cambridge, MA: MIT Press.

Nacey, S. (2013) *Metaphors in Learner English*, Amsterdam, The Netherlands: John Benjamins.

Niculae, V., and Yaneva, V. (2013) 'Conceptual considerations of comparisons and similes,' *Proceedings of the ACL Student Research Workshop*, pp. 89–95.

Pasma, T. (2011) *Metaphor and Register Variation: The Personalization of Dutch News Discourse*, Oisterwijk, The Netherlands: BOXpress.

Pragglejaz Group (2007) 'MIP: A method for identifying metaphorically used words in discourse,' *Metaphor & Symbol* 22: 1–39.

Rundle, M. (2002) *Macmilllan English Dictionaary for Advanced Learners*, Oxford, UK: Macmillan.

Semino, E., Hardie, A., Koller, V., and Rayson, P. (2009) 'A computer-assisted approach to the analysis of metaphor variation across genres,' paper presented at the Corpus Linguistics Conference 2009, University of Birmingham, UK.

Steen, G. J. (2002) *Metaphor Identification*, special issue of *Language and Literature* 11(10).

—— (2007) *Finding Metaphor in Grammar and Usage*, Amsterdam, The Netherlands: John Benjamins.

Steen, G. J., Dorst, A. G., Herrmann, J. B., Kaal, A. A., Krennmayr, T., and Pasma, T. (2010) *A Method for Linguistic Metaphor Identification: From MIP to MIPVU*, Amsterdam, The Netherlands: John Benjamins.

6
Finding systematic metaphors

Robert Maslen

Introduction and definitions

Our experience of the world, like the world itself, is complex and somewhat chaotic. Yet we strive instinctively to put things in some kind of order, to explain our experience and understand it. Since the way we go about this is often far from objective (see Kahneman, 2011, for an account of heuristics and biases in human cognition), and our discourse influenced by all kinds of social factors (see, for example, Fine, Campion-Vincent and Heath, 2005), it follows that multiple, subjective understandings of a given aspect of experience will always be part and parcel of being human. It also follows that the task of finding out 'what people think' is not straightforward. Metaphors are one possible avenue for exploring people's 'ideas, attitudes and beliefs' (Cameron, 2010), and feelings, even when they are not directly expressed; Systematic Metaphor is an applied linguistic approach to analysing metaphors in discourse. It was developed by Cameron and colleagues (Cameron, 1999a, 1999b, 2003, 2007; Stelma and Cameron, 2007; Cameron, et al., 2009; Cameron and Maslen, 2010; but cf. Schmitt, 2005) as one part of a metaphor-led discourse analysis within a broader Discourse Dynamics approach (Cameron, 2010).

Systematic Metaphor research takes as its starting point one of metaphor's more intriguing characteristics: the fact that in everyday use, however random and disjointed they may seem, our metaphors often fall into patterns. When people engage in a discourse event – when they talk or write, have a conversation or deliver a speech, contribute to a debate or craft an editorial, and so on – certain kinds of metaphoric terms can be used to refer to certain kinds of things in ways that become systematic. Identifying systematic relationships between the semantics of linguistic metaphors and the 'topics' they refer to has the potential to tell us something about the way a speaker or writer conceptualises the world, or about how they want us to conceptualise it.

This might suggest that a systematic metaphor analysis turns out some kind of artefact, a fixed chunk of language representing a fixed chunk of thought. This is not the case and it is important to keep in mind from the outset the fact that discourse, an iterative system of mental, physical and physiological processes, is anything but static; on the contrary, it is noisy, dynamic, constantly flowing and changing, subject to an immense number of social, cognitive and bodily influences that bear on it moment to moment in ways that are impossible to fully account for (Larsen-Freeman and Cameron, 2008). What Systematic Metaphor analysis does is offer an insight into the sea-state of this complexity at a particular point. It allows us to say something about the participants in a particular discourse – *those* people, in *that* place, at *that* time – and draw inferences about their thoughts and feelings, their conceptualisations and communicative intentions, from the language they used *then*. It also allows us to observe developments within a particular text, to show how robust connections between vehicles (words and phrases used metaphorically) and topics (the 'real' things or concepts which are being talked about through metaphor) are arrived at as speakers interact or a piece of written argument unfolds, and how those connections vary, how they expand, overlap or sharpen in contrast with one another. 'Thought' in this sense does not exist in isolation, but rather in live interaction with discourse, what Cameron (2003) has termed 'talking-and-thinking'.

At this point it might be useful to see an example of what 'systematic' means in practice. The language of politics is, of course, rich ground for linguists and psychologists, as well as political scientists and communication scholars, and keynote speeches in particular tend to be riddled with metaphor. Here is British Prime Minister David Cameron beginning his speech to the UK Conservative Party's conference in 2014 (the referendum in question concerned Scottish independence, and the Scots had voted 'No' about a week earlier):

> I am so proud to stand here today as Prime Minister of four nations in one United Kingdom. I was always clear about why we called that referendum. Duck the fight – and our union could have been taken apart bit by bit. Take it on – and we had the chance to settle the question. This Party has always confronted the big issues for the sake of our country.

The Prime Minister's first metaphors introduce a pattern that resonates through the speech. *Duck the fight*; *Take it on*; *confronted* – these vehicle terms use the semantics of physical violence to represent the notion of competing ideas, and their proponents, as participants in a physical fight. Each instance, though the metaphors are related, carries its own specific nuance. One who *duck[s] the fight* is at best timid, at worst a coward. Mr Cameron's government, in contrast, *take it on*, showing character and pluck. And it is not just any issue his government *confronted*. This one was *big*, like bullies are.

Context amplifies the metaphorical rhetoric. The government's bravery, Mr Cameron tells us, is *for the sake of our country*. He then speaks about the anniversary of D-Day that summer, and the end of British operations in Afghanistan, and mentions soldiers he has met during the year. Thus the government's figuratively constructed bravery is conflated with the courage of people whose fights were for real.

Over the course of the speech, we hear a number of metaphors like the following:

[on practitioners of domestic slavery]: *we're coming after you*

[on hospitals]: *we protected the NHS budget* (to *save lives*)

[on hate preachers]: *we kicked out people who don't belong here*

[on the Home Secretary]: [she is] *crime-busting*

[on EU negotiations]: *we're going to go in as a country, get our power's back, fight for our national interest*

[on the 2015 UK election]: *this is a straight fight*

In nuanced and varying ways, a systematic relationship develops between vehicle terms referring to *VIOLENCE* and the topic of the government and what it does. This contributes to the following systematic metaphors:

> PERPETRATORS OF SOCIAL ILLS ARE VIOLENT OPPONENTS
> POLITICAL OBSTACLES ARE VIOLENT OPPONENTS
> GOVERNMENT (POLICY) IS A PHYSICAL PRESENCE PREPARED TO USE VIOLENCE TO REPRESENT CITIZENS
> GOVERNMENT IS A BRAVE FRIEND WHEN YOU NEED ONE.

There are several stages of analysis between identifying individual metaphoric terms in a text and being able to postulate systematic metaphors. But this simplified example highlights a key principle: systematicity emerges through repeated, coherent connections between topics and vehicles in the text itself. Analysis starts with the discourse and works upwards, and for its conclusions to be meaningful, generalisations which emerge have to be traceable back to the text.

Not all data are as tidy as a political speech. Speech writers, like novelists and poets, spend long hours crafting their figurative worlds; patterns are, to an extent, deliberate and there to be perceived, which makes them somewhat more amenable to scholarship. But in fact, much of the work on systematic metaphor looks at spontaneous spoken discourse, using transcripts of group discussions or interviews. 'Live' data can reveal most fully the dynamic processes that underlie the formation of systematic connections, but bring with them certain obstacles and analytical dangers.

Systematicity is a central issue in cognitive science. Our sensitivity to patterns starts early. It contributes to language acquisition, for example (Tomasello, 2003), but extends far beyond language. It helps us to recognise group membership and otherness, and changes to normal environments that might signal danger. And much of this attendance to systematicity takes place sub-consciously – we do it all the time without realising.

So by analogy with general cognition, there are good grounds for attaching significance to systematic patterns in metaphor use. Patterns may require some analytical excavation, but this in no way undermines claims of their potential to carry meaning. Indeed, as a – to some extent – sub-conscious phenomenon, such elusiveness is to be expected.

Establishing systematic metaphors is not so much an end in itself as a jumping-off point for further analysis or a parallel strand in a broader study, such as a metaphor-led analysis of discourse (Cameron et al., 2009; Maule et al., 2007). It is a widely applicable tool, but pressing social concerns, which so often boil down to human relationships and mutual (mis-)understanding, have been a particular focus to date. There are good reasons for this. Human decision-making is riddled with demonstrable mis-conceptions, cognitive biases (Kahneman, 2011) which have their social corollary in prejudice. Language interacts in the most intimate causal way with our decisions and behaviour. Systematic metaphor analysis is one way of trying to get at the thoughts, feelings, and beliefs that lead us to make the decisions we do.

In sum, systematic metaphor can be thought of both as a phenomenon of human communication and a tool for research. So long as its findings are grounded in robust – and robustly handled – data, they may contribute not just to the work of linguists, social scientists and psychologists, but also to health science, legislation and political communications, marketing and corporate communications, indeed to the work of anyone who needs to get beneath the surface of discourse.

Overview of relevant research to date

The term 'systematic metaphor' as it is used here originated in Cameron's work as a name for the outcome of a set of techniques for 'operationalising' metaphor to understand people's 'ideas, attitudes and values' from discourse data (Cameron, 1999b, 2010, p. 10). Schmitt uses the same term for his techniques of metaphor analysis, and although he draws on a somewhat different theoretical background and has, to an extent, different aims from the work set out in this chapter, Schmitt (2005) chimes with Cameron and colleagues in certain ways, notably on the subject of empirical rigour.

Like so much contemporary metaphor research, Cameron and colleagues' approach grew partly out of a response to Conceptual Metaphor Theory (CMT; see Chapter 1), and particularly to the fact that some a priori conceptual metaphors proved elusive in actual discourse (Cameron, 2003). What spontaneous spoken data appeared to show instead (Cameron, 2003, 2007) were systematicities arising out of numerous local discourse processes. A growing body of research was elucidating the importance of factors such as culture (Gibbs, 1999; Quinn, 1991; Slobin, 1996), embodied processes (Barsalou, 2008; Gibbs, 2006) and affect (Damasio, 2003) in metaphor use, suggesting that discourse should be approached in a more holistic way. This in turn informed an account of metaphor use as one part of a dynamic linguistic system (Cameron, 2008, 2010; Larsen-Freeman and Cameron, 2008). These developments were concurrent with a rigorous approach to identifying metaphor in discourse, culminating in the Pragglejaz (2007) methodology (see Chapter 5).

Analysis of systematic metaphor is an applied linguistic technique. It tends to be part of research that asks questions about social issues, such as education, terrorism, and post-conflict reconciliation, and thus has implications beyond the academic community. For this reason, in a broader account of the literature, it is more realistic to talk about the influence of the approach, since studies draw on the methodology without explicitly calling themselves systematic metaphor studies. The most extensive piece of research to date, in terms of the volume of data and number of metaphors involved, was a multi-method analysis of perceptions of the risk of terrorism (Maule et al., 2007; Cameron et al., 2009). Systematic metaphor analysis has also informed work on urban violence (Cameron, Pelosi and Moraes Felta, 2014; Pelosi et al., 2014), media discourse (Chwesiuk, 2011; Pelosi et al., 2014) and welfare and employment (Woodhams, 2012), as well as studies of discourse relating to psychotherapy (Tay, 2010; see also Chapter 25) and physical health issues (Plug, Sharrack and Reuber, 2011). In Maule et al. (2007) it was used along with other techniques, such as causal attribution analysis (Stratton et al., 1988), as one strand among several under the *Social Amplification of Risk* Framework (Pidgeon, Kasperson and Slovic, 2003). Using metaphor alongside other strands of enquiry puts it in a realistic perspective, since, though it offers remarkable insights, metaphor – systematic or otherwise – is never the whole story.

Critical issues

Systematic Metaphor faces the same fundamental challenge as any qualitative research: its claims involve interpretation and cannot be tested statistically (e.g. Kirk and Miller, 1986). In many regards the response, too, is that of the broader qualitative research community: if you want to find out about feelings, attitudes, and so on, there is no fully objective way to go about it. Of course, one's approach must still be methodologically rigorous. In the case of Systematic Metaphor, this means ensuring that data are appropriate to the aims of research; keeping records of decisions made during coding and analysis; ensuring that decisions are reliable and replicable (or, to avoid a term that suggests statistical testing, that they are 'trustworthy' [Schmitt, 2005]), so that two or more people working independently on the same data produce comparable results; and tying analytical conclusions to source texts (Cameron and Maslen, 2010).

When it comes to demonstrating the validity of systematic metaphors that emerge from analysis, one must look beyond the bounds of any single piece of work. A growing number of psycholinguistic studies support the thesis that metaphor has a profound, symbiotic connection to cognitive and behavioural processes (see Chapter 4 and Barsalou, 2008, for examples). In the light of this evidence, a qualitative study of systematic metaphor use examines metaphoric potential – the potential of metaphors in a specific context to be significant in cognitive and behavioural terms (Pragglejaz Group, 2007; Cameron and Maslen, 2010).

Though research findings are partly expressed in the form of somewhat static-looking statements of metaphor, it is important to remember that systematic metaphors are not abstractions in the same sense as conceptual metaphors. A systematic metaphor is not a permanent fixture in the mind. On the contrary, systematic metaphors emerge from discourse, in a specific context, and have no meaning without reference to that context. They are local phenomena, subject to potential change as the discourse unfolds, and if a vehicle–topic connection becomes systematic, it is only, as Larsen-Freeman and Cameron (2008) might have it, as a local, temporary stability in the discourse. Systematic Metaphor analysis gives an account of how such stability develops. And the account is important, since it captures something of the dynamic processes involved.

Main research methods

This section will focus on an analysis which formed part of the research project *The Perception and Communication of Terrorist Risk* (PCTR) (Cameron et al., 2009). At the time of writing it is the most extensive piece of research of its kind, analysing some 12,000 identified metaphors in 190,000 words of transcribed talk. Working at this scale, PCTR researchers were able to develop a robust methodology and to provide answers to many of the difficulties likely to crop up in an analysis of systematic metaphors. However, the methods described here are not intended to be prescriptive, but rather a guide to refer to in context.

The project's aim was to investigate people's perceptions of the risk of terrorism following the 7/7 bombings in London, in 2005, and from this to develop recommendations for public communications about ongoing risk and specific risk events. The data came from focus group discussions with members of the public and research interviews with experts in various fields (chiefly politics, the media, and the UK Security Service [MI5]). Recordings were transcribed and analysed according to two approaches: Systematic Metaphor and Causal Attribution (a technique which explores people's explanations of causality [Stratton et al., 1988]). The analyses were combined to inform field experiments which tested responses to risk communications containing varying metaphorical and attributional content. Finally, recommendations about how best to communicate terrorist risk were presented to end users from various fields.

Data collection

Analysing metaphors poses specific challenges for the design of focus group and interview schedules. On top of the usual issues (anonymity, social profiling, etc.) is the added problem of priming effects. People are apt to pick metaphors up – indeed, this kind of research presumes they may do just that – but the metaphors must originate with the group or interviewee, not the moderator. Given the ubiquity of metaphor, this is virtually impossible to control, and so potential examples of priming need to be acknowledged when transcripts are analysed.

Transcription

One point to consider when transcribing spoken data for metaphor analysis is whether to use *intonation units* (Chafe, 1994; Du Bois et al., 1993). Transcribing into intonation units requires extra time and training (Stelma and Cameron, 2007), but there are good grounds for doing it. When we talk, we tend to deliver chunks of speech under distinct intonation contours, each corresponding, more or less, to a breath, and to limit the amount of new information per unit. Giving each unit its own line in a transcript is a way of representing the passage of time in a discourse event, as well as showing detail, such as pauses and repairs, in as faithful a context as possible. This may be especially important when research is focused on dynamic processes (e.g. Cameron, 2010).

Metaphor vehicle coding

Metaphor identification is covered in Chapter 5 of this volume and so will not be described in detail here. (A full account can be found in Cameron and Maslen, 2010, chapter 6.) With one significant variation, coding followed the widely used and robust methodology established by the Pragglejaz Group (2007), later refined, as MIPVU, in Steen, Dorst, Herrmann, Krennmayr and Pasma (2010).

While the Pragglejaz (2007) methodology hones a text down to 'metaphorically used words', PCTR's researchers, following Cameron (2003), identified metaphor vehicle terms, allowing the possibility that metaphoric potential is carried by longer stretches of language – chiefly, phrases. This is appropriate if one conceives of discourse in dynamic system terms (Cameron, 2010; Larsen-Freeman and Cameron, 2008), since in that framework, where multiple associations can be active at once, processing would not take place exclusively at word level.

To give an example, when a PCTR participant talked about *opposing sides* in a conflict, the phrase was treated as a single vehicle for coding purposes, rather than as two distinct metaphorically used words. Qualities of individual words are not lost in this approach, but instead are explored when data are analysed and synthesised.

Once metaphors have been identified, vehicle terms are grouped together according to their semantic characteristics. This brings the 'metaphorical world' more sharply into focus, but it is important that vehicle group labels are not too far removed from the text. Generalising is the point, at this stage, but it should proceed parsimoniously as a set of recorded decisions.

Table 6.1 shows a sample of vehicle groups and their constituents from the PCTR research. Group terms are in the left-hand column, vehicle terms contributing to the group on the right.

As well as showing how vehicle terms come together semantically, this table highlights how type frequencies can vary. *SYSTEM* contains only one term (the only token that occurred in that group) while *MOVEMENT* contains numerous terms (and several tokens of most types). Highly frequent metaphors, such as instances of *go*, tend to turn up in conventional phrases that we hardly notice are metaphors at all. Nonetheless, they have to be included, not just for reasons of rigour, but because one does not know at first which conceptualisations might prove important.

Table 6.1 Sample vehicle groups in PCTR research

THING	thing, things, anything, everything, something, nothing, nowt (Yorkshire dialect form of 'nothing'), stuff
MOVEMENT	comes into, from, the end, comes, from behind, go, go away, go by, go for, go off, go up, goes off, going off, gone off, gone on, gone too far, lost the way, running, to a halt, to a standstill, went off, went on, went up, carry on, keep going, make a move, down the line, progressed, sliding, starts from, towards, went through
CONCEALMENT	sneaky, cover-up
CONTAINER	comes into, in, out, out of
WAY	Way
PHYSICAL ACTION	like bullying, formed, hold onto, turned, work, flattened, hit, kicking back, hammered, knocking about, breaking, wrecks, a smacked hand, hit back, slapped down, stamping on
CONTROL	Control
LOCATION	opposing sides, in the first place, on, situation, somewhere, there, where, nowhere near, positions
SEEING	invisible, look, look at, see, seeing, staring, point of view, graphic, views, brilliant, show
MILITARY	not like war, enemy, target, war

Source: Cameron and Maslen (2010).

Selecting vehicle groups is an iterative process. The group you begin with is not necessarily the one you end up with. To guarantee trustworthiness as a balance to imagination, coding should ideally be collaborative, with a portion of one person's work being checked by another, and reflective, in that one should be open to applying changes back through the data if it appears an earlier decision was not the best one. Keeping notes during coding is invaluable when it comes to checking how you got to where you are, especially when a lot of data are involved. Some of the metaphors in Table 6.1 were re-coded during the course of the study. The group *THING*, for example, was broadened to *CONCRETISE* to encompass a range of vehicles representing concepts in physical terms. *Control* did not in the end justify a group of its own and was moved to a related *PHYSICAL ACTION* group. This kind of 'principled flexibility' (Cameron, 2007) is a necessary part of the process, and in fact desirable, since it prevents bad decisions getting embedded in the analysis.

Topics

Deciding what a metaphor vehicle is being used to talk about can present a problem. Topics are often treated as 'given' information, and thus do not need to be expressed and repeated. In addition, the dynamic nature of spontaneous speech, in particular, means that topics can shift and evolve very quickly, making them harder to pin down, other than by offering an account for each instance. The decision about how precise to be is likely to be driven by resources – how much time and money and how many people you have.

After close reading of the transcripts, PCTR researchers were able to identify a number of 'Key Discourse Topics', one or other of which was active for every metaphor in the dataset. These included:

1. acts and perpetrators of terrorism;
2. communications – by the authorities and the media;
3. responses to terrorism – by the authorities and by, or especially affecting, Muslims;
4. society and social groups.

Table 6.2 Metaphors of government responses to terrorism as violent physical action

Topic	Metaphor	Line	Speaker	Intonation unit
3A	a smacked hand	3850	Eddie	is <u>a smacked hand</u>.
3A	banged up	3873	Phil	. . . to get <u>banged up</u>.
3A	hit back	136	Eddie	. . so there's no <u>way</u> you can <u>hit back</u>.
3A	kick out	2618	Finn	<u>kick</u> 'em all <u>out</u>.
3A	kick out	2625	Finn	why <u>kick</u> 'em all <u>out</u>,
3A	kick out	2636	Pat	<u>kick</u> 'em all <u>out</u>.
3A	kicking out	2605	Eddie	or <u>kicking</u> people <u>out</u>.
3A	kicking	2610	Finn	or <u>kicking</u> people,
3A	slapping down	5396	Eddie	they need <u>slapping down</u>.
3A	stamping on	1514	Josh	. . and . . they're <u>stamping on</u> it,

Source: Adapted from Cameron and Maslen (2010).

Rationalising topics in this way makes data much more amenable to coding, but it is very important not to lose sight of the more complex reality. This is accomplished partly as a habit of mind, but more reliably by always having the original text to hand, so when a vehicle and its topic are being considered, it is always in the context of the words people actually used.

With topics coded, systematic connections can be explored. What makes a metaphor systematic is the stable, repeated use of metaphors with particular semantic characteristics to talk about a particular topic. Table 6.2 shows metaphors from one of PCTR's focus groups on the topic of government responses to terrorism (see 3 above; 'A' refers to 'Authorities').

These participants consistently characterise the topic in terms of *VIOLENT ACTION*, which allows us to suggest the systematic metaphor: *GOVERNMENT RESPONSES TO TERRORISM ARE VIOLENT PHYSICAL ACTION*. This conception of what a government does (or ought to do) chimes with the Prime Minister's from the first example, which suggests, on the one hand, that political speech writers know their audience, and on the other that the audience are influenced by the systematic metaphors they routinely hear.

Talking about terrorism, and responses to it, in terms of violence is of course not a great leap in semantic terms. Other systematic metaphors in the PCTR data made connections between more distant domains. In one focus group, participants repeatedly used *GAME* metaphors, such as <u>*kicking off*</u>, <u>*level playing field*</u>, <u>*pawns in a game*</u>, <u>*our team*</u>, and <u>*your team*</u>, which contributed to a pair of related systematic metaphors: *VIOLENT CONFLICT IS A GAME WITH RULES* and *TERRORISTS BREAK THE RULES*. Another set of examples came from metaphors of *SOCIAL LANDSCAPE*, including *GROUPS WHO THINK DIFFERENTLY ARE PHYSICALLY SEPARATED* and *POLITICAL / PHILOSOPHICAL / RELIGIOUS BELIEFS ARE PHYSICALLY LOCATED*.

The systematic metaphors emerge from a number of specific, related metaphors, each contributing to a broader, but coherent conception of a topic. The contributing metaphors have specific semantic qualities – *smacked*, *banged*, *hit*, *kick*, *slapping* and *stamping*, for example, are closely related, but not the same. The characteristics of systematic metaphors will vary in other ways, too. They are not usually produced by every speaker, and different ones will emerge from different combinations of participants; they emerge at different points in a discourse – sometimes being widely distributed, sometimes appearing in clusters during a brief flurry of talk. These details are necessary for interpreting findings, both for researchers and their audiences, and so it is important to log speaker names, group details, line numbers, together with the metaphor and its context, in whichever software package is being used.

Systematic metaphors can also serve as a basis of comparison between texts, and as a starting point for fresh analysis or data collection. Having found that one group of people conceptualise a topic a certain way, you can ask whether similar conceptualisations show up in the metaphors of other groups. By comparing across groups in the PCTR data, we found a systematic metaphor which, though it drew on similar metaphor vehicles to those found across the dataset, was unique to Muslim groups: *RESPONSES TO TERRORISM ARE VIOLENT ACTIONS AGAINST MUSLIMS* (e.g. [the official response] *is thrown at us*; [our] *human rights have been squashed*). Another interesting comparison came from a suite of systematic metaphors which talked about *RESPONSES TO TERRORISM AS THEATRE*. While expert participants tended to view their actions as being on a stage addressing an audience in serious terms, members of the public spoke of the authorities' actions with metaphors such as *pantomime, farce* and *catch-phrase*. As well as having implications for official communications, this kind of variation shows how careful one has to be in drawing generalisations at the level of a whole speech community (Cienki, 2005).

Directions for further analysis include looking at the *stories* and *narratives* systematic metaphors form part of, or the *metaphor scenarios* they might contribute to (Cameron, Maslen and Low, 2010). Narrative is a key means by which we make sense of the world, while scenarios offer an insight into the way conceptualisations can be shared very broadly, even across national boundaries (see Chapters 21 and 23).

When reporting findings, it is good practice to give some quantitative detail to show where systematic metaphors have come from (see Todd and Low, 2010, for a fuller discussion). At the very least readers should be told the overall size of a dataset – word counts for transcripts, number of participants in focus groups and interviews – along with the number of metaphor vehicles identified. This can serve as a baseline for more involved quantitative measures, such as analyses of metaphor densities and clusters, as well as a point of comparison between studies.

There are numerous software platforms available to support qualitative research and this is not the place to review them. But certainly packages such as ATLAS and NVivo offer possibilities for drawing categories out of data and manipulating them. Software often presents the researcher with abstractions without the original data (although there is usually a link). This is both good and bad. It facilitates the more imaginative, associative processes necessary for a deep interpretation of data, but it also increases the danger of making unjustified claims.

Example of current research

Background

Speaking on his radio show about the recently published Apostolic Exhortation *Evangelii Gaudium*, American pundit Rush Limbaugh said the following: 'This is just pure Marxism coming out of the mouth of the Pope' (Burke, 2013). He was not alone in interpreting the document as an attack on capitalism. The Vatican (see e.g. Grant, 2014) responded that this was quite wrong, that the document was a call for a renewed focus on the plight of the poor, not an attempt to undermine the economic system. Against this background, this extract from a work-in-progress (Maslen, in preparation) asks the question: how do metaphors in *Evangelii Gaudium* represent current socio-economic circumstances? The methodology is a systematic analysis of the metaphors, following the procedure set out above.

Table 6.3 Data from analysis of *Evangelii Gaudium*

Text	Page	Section	Lines in section	Mets in section	Mets per line	Metaphor	Vehicle group	Topic
#	67	83	18	24	1.33	degenerating	NATURE	'Tomb psychology'
#	3	1	9	15	1.67	accept his offer	GIVE–TAKE	Gospels
#	45	53	28	22	0.79	feed upon (the powerful on the powerless)	PREY–HUNT	Current socio-economic model
#	62	75	23	20	0.87	ills	BODY–HEALTH	Urban culture
#	50	59	29	26	0.9	explode	VIOLENCE	Current socio-economic model / consequences

Source: Maslen (in preparation).

Data

An Apostolic Exhortation is an odd sort of document. For most of its addressees, it is a translation (from Latin or, more recently, Italian). It is written down, but takes the form of an extended address, making it a hybrid text, the more so since it is elaborated in homilies and public statements by the Pope (sometimes quite informal ones) and is read from, quoted and interpreted at Catholic gatherings. This means that for its intended audience, the document is something more than a piece of writing; it is not spontaneous speech, but it 'speaks' with a familiar voice, adapting a considerable body of shared language to contemporary concerns. Many of the metaphors in a religious message are likely to be highly conventionalised, indeed historically so, drawing on sacred texts, and this is the case here. It is the systematic use of innovative metaphors – or innovative extensions of existing ones – which is of key interest.

Evangelii Gaudium is divided into two main parts. The first addresses the laity, the second the clergy. This analysis only looks at the first, some ninety pages and approximately 25,000 words. There are 108 subsections, each addressing a separate theme, such as social exclusion and materialism.

Method

Metaphor vehicles were identified according to the method set out above. Vehicles were then grouped according to semantics, and topics were identified. Portions of identification and coding were checked by a trained assistant, and a record of coding decisions was kept. The data were kept in an Excel spreadsheet, with each metaphor coded for vehicle group, topic, page in text, section in text, number of lines in section and number of metaphors in section. The latter two items gave a rough measure of metaphor density – metaphors per line – for each section of the text. Table 6.3 shows an extract from the coded data.

The Exhortation is rich in metaphor. 1,814 metaphor vehicles were identified – about 70 per thousand words of text. Semantic coding of vehicles yielded 86 categories, ranging from a few items to high-frequency conventionalised groups with over a hundred individual metaphors (e.g. *JOURNEY, SEEING*).

Topics were identified broadly according to the themes in each section. Eighty-nine were used in the analysis and they ranged in frequency from a single item to larger categories (such as 'the current socio-economic model') with close to a hundred associated metaphors.

Several systematic relationships were excluded from the analysis because they did not inform the research theme, i.e. current socio-economic circumstances. These included *THE CHURCH AS A WOMAN*, and *FAITH AS A JOURNEY*, rich scenarios made up of several related systematic metaphors, but not relevant to the study. Relevant metaphors were identified in several ways: by sorting the data according to topic; sorting by vehicle; taking metaphor density – or clustering – as a guide to places where intensive metaphor 'work' was being done; and looking at those vehicle terms which seemed most incongruous. When systematic vehicle–topic connections had been established, they were tracked through the text to observe the way they developed and interacted with other metaphors and other aspects of the data.

Some findings

The critique of contemporary socio-economic relations is fierce. It is accomplished partly by use of non-metaphorical rhetoric (e.g. *How can it be that it is not news when an elderly homeless person dies of exposure [. . .]?* [*Evangelii Gaudium*, §53]), but chiefly the Pope's arguments employ metaphor.

PREY–HUNT metaphors personify the financial system in terms of a predator. They occur in an intense cluster (ibid., §53–70) during which the text deals with the financial system and its moral and social consequences. In this system, *the powerful feed upon the powerless*; [*the powerless*] *fall prey* to the system; rejection of ethics *lurks*; the system's influence is *baneful* and *unbridled*. The systematic metaphor that emerges – THE SYSTEM IS A STEALTHY PREDATOR WITHOUT MORALS (where system stands for financial and socio-economic structures) – clearly draws on a rich background lexis relating to the devil, and in §59 the system is directly called *evil*. But it also chimes with – and interacts in the text with – systematic vehicle-topic connections that look more like the sort of things humans do. For example, the system also *threatens*, *attacks*, and *distorts family bonds*, which inter alia leads to: THE SYSTEM IS PHYSICALLY VIOLENT. The *BODY* and physical *HEALTH* are a frequent source of vehicle terms, and the victims of *VIOLENCE* – broadly the poor – are *debilitated*, *bruised*, *hurting*, and require *healing* and *remedies*. This physical, visceral imagery, intrinsically tied to empathic processes (Cameron, Maslen and Todd, 2013; Chapter 29) contributes to the systematic metaphor NOT BENEFITING FROM THE SYSTEM IS PHYSICAL HARM, among others. There is also a powerful confluence of *LANDSCAPE* and *CONTAINMENT* metaphors in which those not benefiting from the system are *excluded*, or *outcasts*, *marginalised* on the *fringes of humanity*, leading to the systematic metaphor NOT BENEFITING FROM THE SYSTEM IS PHYSICAL SEPARATION and SUCCESS IN THE SYSTEM IS A CONTAINED EXCLUSIVE SPACE.

This research does not address the question of whether or not the Pope is a Marxist. But it does offer insights into current Vatican thinking on the state of social relations in the world today. This thinking is in some regards radical, since it conceptualises the beneficiaries of the status quo – powerful individuals, large financial concerns – in pronounced, critical terms. To answer the question posed above, the metaphors employed systematically in *Evangelii Gaudium* represent current socio-economic circumstances as parlous, bestial, and in need of immediate, fundamental change. The next stage is to look for wider evidence of these conceptualisations in the homilies of the current papacy, in other sources relating to the Catholic Church, and elsewhere.

Future directions

There is enormous scope for systematic metaphor analyses in languages other than English (but see Pelosi, de Moraes Feltes and Cameron, 2014; also, Schmitt, 2010) and for cross-linguistic analyses of conceptualisations in comparable discourses.

Systematic metaphor analysis, in combination with analysis of other aspects of language, is potentially a powerful tool to aid public/political and corporate communications. Lakoff (2005) and Luntz (2007) show two very different existing approaches to metaphor as a communications tool, but the efficacy of more bottom-up techniques in these fields is largely unexplored. The nexus of language and human decision-making is fertile territory for systematic metaphor. Systematic metaphorical conceptualisations in discourse offer potential insight into sub-conscious/heuristic decision-making processes. This could be pursued in social science and commercial contexts.

Whatever the future of systematic metaphor analysis, it will have at its heart the original motivating concern of the field – to get a truer idea of how we understand and relate to the world and one another.

Acknowledgements

The research project *The Perception and Communication of the Risk of Terrorism* was funded by the UK's Economic and Social Research Council (ESRC). RES-228-25-0053.

Extracts from: Francis. *Evangelii Gaudium* [Apostolic Exhortation]. (December 2013). London: CTS by kind permission of Libreria Editrice Vaticana, Vatican City.

Further reading

Cameron, L. and Maslen, R. (eds) 2010. *Metaphor Analysis.* London: Equinox. Especially Chapters 5, 6 and 7.
Cameron, L., Maslen, R., Todd, Z., Maule, J., Stratton, P. and Stanley, N. 2009. The discourse dynamics approach to metaphor and metaphor-led discourse analysis. *Metaphor and Symbol*, 24(2), 63–89.
Cameron, L., Maslen, R. and Todd, Z. 2013. The dialogic construction of self and other in response to terrorism. *Peace and Conflict*, 19(1), 3–22.
Larsen-Freeman, D. and Cameron, L. 2008. *Complex Systems and Applied Linguistics.* London: Oxford University Press. Especially Chapter 6 (Complex systems in discourse).

References

Barsalou, L. 2008. Grounded cognition. *Annual Review of Psychology*, 59, 617–645.
Burke, D. 2013. Rush Limbaugh: Pope is preaching 'pure Marxism'. *CNN*, 2 December 2013. http://religion.blogs.cnn.com/2013/12/02/rush-limbaugh-vs-the-pope/. [Accessed 1 September 2014]
Cameron, L. 1999a. Identifying and describing metaphor in spoken discourse data. In Cameron, L. and Low, G. (eds) *Researching and Applying Metaphor*, pp. 105–132. Cambridge, UK: Cambridge University Press.
—— 1999b. Operationalising metaphor for applied linguistic research. In Cameron, L. and Low, G. (eds) *Researching and Applying Metaphor*, pp. 3–28. Cambridge, UK: Cambridge University Press.
—— 2003. *Metaphor in Educational Discourse.* London: Continuum.
—— 2007. Patterns of metaphor use in reconciliation talk. *Discourse and Society*, 18(2), 197–222.
—— 2008. Metaphor shifting in the dynamics of talk. In Zanotto, M., Cameron, L. and Cavalcanti, M. (eds) *Confronting Metaphor in Use: An Applied Linguistic Approach*, pp. 45–62. Cambridge, UK: Cambridge University Press.

—— 2010. The discourse dynamics framework for metaphor. In Cameron, L. and Maslen, R. (eds) *Metaphor Analysis*. London: Equinox.

Cameron, L. and Maslen, R. (eds) 2010. *Metaphor Analysis*. London: Equinox.

Cameron, L., Maslen, R. and Low, G. 2010. Finding systematicity in metaphor use. In Cameron, L. and Maslen, R. (eds), *Metaphor Analysis*. London: Equinox.

Cameron, L., Maslen, R. and Todd, Z. 2013. The dialogic construction of self and other in response to terrorism. *Peace and Conflict*, 19(1), 3–22.

Cameron, L., Maslen, R., Todd, Z., Maule, J., Stratton, P. and Stanley, N. 2009. The discourse dynamics approach to metaphor and metaphor-led discourse analysis. *Metaphor and Symbol*, 24(2), 63–89.

Cameron, L., Pelosi, A. and Moraes Felta, H. 2014. Metaphorizing violence in the UK and Brazil: A contrastive discourse dynamics study. *Metaphor and Symbol*, 29(1), 23–43.

Chafe, W. 1994. *Discourse, Consciousness and Time*. Chicago, IL: University of Chicago Press.

Chwesiuk, J. 2011. A discourse dynamics approach to metaphor in talk: A case study of a BBC radio talk. *Anglika*, 20, 53–66.

Cienki, A. 2005. Metaphor in the 'strict Father' and 'Nurturant Parent' cognitive models: Theoretical issues raised in an empirical study. *Cognitive Linguistics*, 16, 279–312.

Damasio, A. 2003. *Looking for Spinoza: Joy, Sorrow and the Feeling Brain*. New York: Harcourt.

Du Bois, J., Schuetze-Coburn, S., Cumming, S. and Paolino, D. 1993. Outline of discourse transcription. In Edwards, J. and Lampert, M. (eds) *Talking Data: Transcription and Coding in Discourse Research*. Hillsdale, NJ: Lawrence Erlbaum.

Fine, G., Campion-Vincent, V. and Heath, C. 2005. *Rumour Mills: The Social Impact of Rumor and Legend*. New Brunswick, NJ: Transaction.

Gibbs, R. W., Jr. 1999. Taking metaphor out of our heads and putting it into the cultural world. In Gibbs, R. W., Jr. and Steen, G. (eds) *Metaphor in Cognitive Linguistics*, pp. 145–166. Amsterdam, The Netherlands: John Benjamins.

—— 2006. *Embodiment and Cognitive Science*. New York: Cambridge University Press.

Grant, M. 2014. I'm not a communist, just following the Gospel, says Pope Francis. *Newsweek*, 29 October 2014. http://www.newsweek.com/im-not-communist-just-following-gospel-says-pope-francis-280848. [Accessed 1 November 2014]

Kahneman, D. 2011. *Thinking, Fast and Slow*. London: Penguin.

Kirk, J. and Miller, M. 1986. *Reliability and Validity in Qualitative Research*. London: Sage.

Lakoff, G. 2004. *Don't Think of an Elephant: Know Your Values and Frame the Debate*. White River Junction, VT: Chelsea Green.

Larsen-Freeman, D. and Cameron, L. 2008. *Complex Systems and Applied Linguistics*. London: Oxford University Press.

Luntz, F. 2007. *Words that Work: It's Not What You Say, It's What People Hear*. New York: Hyperion.

Maslen, R. J. C. (in preparation). "... where the powerful feed upon the powerless": Systematic metaphor use in the Apostolic Exhortation Evangelii Gaudium.

Maule, J., Cameron, L., Stanley, N. and Todd, Z. 2007. *Perception and Communication of the Risk of Terrorism*. Full Research Report, ESRC End of Award Report, RES-228-25-0053. Swindon, UK: ESRC.

Pelosi, A., de Moraes Feltes, H. and Cameron, L. 2014. Urban violence in Brazil and the role of the media. *Metaphor and the Social World*, 4(1), 27–47.

Pidgeon, N., Kasperson, R., and Slovic, P. (eds) 2003. *The Social Amplification of Risk*. Cambridge, UK: Cambridge University Press.

Plug, L., Sharrack, B. and Reuber, M. 2011. Metaphors in the description of seizure experiences: Common expressions and differential diagnosis. *Language and Cognition*, 3(2), 209–234.

Pragglejaz Group. 2007. MIP: A method for identifying metaphorically used words in discourse. *Metaphor and Symbol*, 22(1), 1–40.

Quinn, N. 1991. The cultural basis of metaphor. In Fernandez, J. (ed.) *Beyond Metaphor: The Theory of Tropes in Anthropology*, pp. 56–93. Stanford, CA: Stanford University Press.

Schmitt, R. 2005. Systematic metaphor analysis as a method of qualitative research. *The Qualitative Report*, 10(2), 358–394.

—— 2010. Metaphernanalyse. In Bock, K. and Miethe, I. (eds) *Handbuch Qualitative Methoden in der Sozialen Arbeit*, pp. 325–335. Opladen, Germany: Verlag Barbara Budrich.

Slobin, D. 1996. From 'thought and language' to 'thinking for speaking'. In Gumpertz, J. and Levinson, S. (eds) *Rethinking Linguistic Relativity*, pp. 70–96. New York: Cambridge University Press.

Steen, G., Dorst, A., Herrmann, J., Kaal, A., Krennmayr, T. and Pasma, T. 2010. *A Method for Linguistic Metaphor Identification.* Amsterdam, The Netherlands: John Benjamins.

Stelma, J. and Cameron, L. 2007. Intonation units in research on spoken interaction. *Text and Talk*, 27(3), 361–393.

Stratton, P., Munton, T., Hanks, H., Heard, C. and Davidson, C. 1988. *Leeds Attributional Coding System (LACS) Manual*. Leeds, UK: Leeds Family Therapy and Research Centre.

Tay, D. 2010. THERAPY IS A JOURNEY as a discourse metaphor. *Discourse Studies*, 13(1), 1–21.

Todd, Z. and Low, G. 2010. A selective survey of research practice in published studies using metaphor analysis. In Cameron, L. and Maslen, R. (eds) *Metaphor Analysis.* London: Equinox.

Tomasello, M. 2003. *Constructing a Language: A Usage-based Theory of Language Acquisition.* Cambridge, MA: Harvard University Press.

Woodhams, J. 2012. A journey towards employment: Metaphorical representations of social welfare in New Zealand. *Metaphor and the Social World*, 2(1), 41–60.

7
From Linguistic to Conceptual Metaphors

Alice Deignan

Introduction

From the earliest writing on Conceptual Metaphor Theory (CMT; see Chapter 1, this volume) to the present, linguistic metaphors have been the main type of evidence provided in support of the existence of conceptual metaphors. For instance, the classic work by Lakoff and Johnson (1980) begins with a discussion of the well-known ARGUMENT IS WAR mapping. Lakoff and Johnson write that 'this metaphor is reflected in our everyday language by a wide variety of expressions' (4) among which they list 'your claims are indefensible ... He attacked every weak point in my argument ... His criticisms were right on target' (ibid.). In 1993, by which time CMT had become the established paradigm in metaphor studies, Lakoff published a book chapter setting out his position on metaphor in thought and language. He cited five types of evidence for the existence of conceptual metaphors. Of the three that he describes as 'the most robust' (1993: 205), two are linguistic: 'Generalizations governing polysemy' and 'Generalizations governing novel metaphorical language' (ibid.). He goes on to cite many lists of linguistic metaphors as evidence for the conceptual metaphors believed to underlie and motivate them. To date, numerous other publications in this tradition have cited lists of linguistic metaphors as evidence for conceptual metaphors. In 2014, for instance, Rojas-Sosa proposed twelve conceptual metaphors for love based on Spanish language data. These included THE OBJECT OF DESIRE IS A FIELD, for which the evidence cited is the linguistic metaphors in the expression 'Un terreno fértil donde dejar huellas' translated by the author as '[I am looking for] a fertile terrain where I can leave footprints' (2014: 205).

In many studies within the discourse tradition, proposing conceptual metaphors is part of a larger set of claims. One tenet of CMT is that metaphors are ideological, and there is a rich strand of literature in which the analysis of linguistic metaphors to identify conceptual metaphors is taken a step further, to identify and analyse ideological positions. The conceptual metaphors constructed through the analysis of linguistic metaphor are examined for evaluative stance and entailments, and the ideology apparently standing behind the text is then described. An important early example of this is Lakoff's discussion of the metaphors and metonymies used to talk about the 1990 war in the Gulf (1991). Lakoff analysed linguistic metaphors to construct conceptual metaphors through which domains such as SPORT,

FAIRY TALES and BUSINESS were mapped onto war, and, he claimed, used to justify the 1990 war and to play down the resulting casualties and suffering.

Despite the number of studies using this methodology, relatively few writers have raised questions about the apparently straightforward – but very subjective – analytical process of moving from the linguistic to the conceptual. The purpose of this chapter is to discuss this methodological issue. I begin by considering how linguistic data are selected for analysis. I then describe Steen's (1999) five-step method, which is the most well-known procedure for working from linguistic to conceptual metaphors, and discuss some difficulties with it. I then explore ways in which detailed analysis of linguistic data using corpora can help with these difficulties.

Methodology

The data used to identify linguistic metaphors

The first step in considering methodology is a critical look at data. The linguistic examples cited in the classic CMT literature were for the most part generated intuitively, either by the researchers themselves or by their students. They are initially convincing, but as far back as 1999, Steen pointed out that they 'serve the purpose of demonstration; they have not been systematically and exhaustively collected from large stretches of discourse but they have been selected for their persuasive power' (1999: 57).

Partly in reaction to this perceived problem, a number of applied linguists have examined metaphors in naturally occurring language data. These data are of two broad types: corpus data and discourse data (Deignan, 2015a). Examinations of corpus data usually seek to uncover general patterns in the meaning, semantic domains and form of linguistic metaphors, that is, they take a language perspective to finding and testing conceptual metaphors. Corpus data are usually examined via concordances, that is, multiple very short extracts from different texts. For instance, Deignan (2005) has conducted a number of corpus studies exploring how words from everyday source domains such as PLANTS, THE BODY and TEMPERATURE are used with figurative meaning. Stefanowitsch (2006) used corpus data to investigate metaphors of emotion. He started from concordances of the target domain words 'anger', 'fear', 'joy', 'sadness' and 'disgust' and searched for metaphorical uses of any other words nearby, as opposed to Deignan's procedure of starting with source domain words and searching for any metaphorical uses.

Examinations of discourse data tend to focus on how people use metaphors to achieve their communicative goals and negotiate meaning; that is, they take a speaker perspective. Discourse data are usually analysed as single extended stretches, in contrast with the analysis of corpus data. Discourse approaches can thus allow for researchers to see how metaphorical meaning is built up over an interaction, and researchers often bring to the analysis their knowledge about context and the history of the speakers and writers. The resulting analysis of linguistic metaphors is thus more richly grounded, but researchers are less likely to attempt language-wide generalizations. Researchers working in this tradition include Cameron and her colleagues (e.g. Cameron et al., 2009; Cameron et al., 2014). One of Cameron's early studies was a detailed analysis of the metaphors used by children and teachers in a British primary school (2003). She analysed around 27,000 words of spoken data, from eight discourse events. She identified linguistic metaphors and traced their development through the discourse events. On the basis of her analysis, Cameron constructs some underlying generalizations, which she cautiously suggests could be conceptual metaphors. This process enabled her to hypothesize not only about the ideational meaning (Halliday and Matthiessen, 2004) of the metaphors used (that is, what they refer to or name) but also to demonstrate the important role of metaphor in building shared understanding and negotiating interpersonal tensions in the classroom. She shows how metaphorical expressions are frequently used in suggesting how pupils' work and behaviour could be improved. For example, a teacher gives feedback on a task saying 'I saw the people who <u>used their heads</u>' (2003: 136) and to an individual 'think before you speak, <u>give yourself a little time</u>. You should watch the others to find out all the strategies they have for <u>buying time</u>' (2003: 135).

There is some crossover between the corpus and discourse approaches, where scholars compile relatively small datasets examined using a combination of corpus and discourse methods. This hybrid approach is often used in the analysis of the metaphors of specific genres and registers, for instance in the studies described by Deignan, Littlemore and Semino (2013).

Having collected a linguistic dataset, the analyst normally begins by identifying linguistic metaphors. This process has been the topic of much debate in the metaphor literature in the last ten years (e.g. Steen, 2008; Steen et al., 2010). This is discussed elsewhere in this volume by Steen (Chapter 5), so it will not be dealt with in this chapter. The following section looks at the next step: the move from the linguistic metaphors that have been identified to constructing conceptual metaphors.

Steen's five-step method

Steen was the first writer in the cognitive and applied linguistics tradition to tackle the difficult question of demonstrating rigorously the analytical move from linguistic to conceptual metaphor. He described the challenge as 'to explicate the assumptions that lead linguists to arrive at ... conceptual mappings in departing from metaphorical expressions in discourse' (1999: 58). In 1999, he published the first version of his five-step method, with the aim, as he described it later, of forging 'a connection between the linguistic forms of metaphor in text and talk, on the one hand, and the conceptual structures of metaphor as assumed in cognitive linguistics in the form of conceptual metaphors such as ARGUMENT IS WAR on the other' (2011: 93). His five steps are:

1. metaphor focus identification;
2. metaphorical idea identification;
3. non-literal comparison identification;
4. non-literal analogy identification;
5. non-literal mapping identification.

1999: 73

The first step, identifying linguistic metaphor, involves a choice of several methods (see Chapter 5). In general terms, these methods require the identification of the contextual meaning of each word, and then establishing whether or not there is another meaning of that word that could be considered to be its literal counterpart.

For step 2, Steen uses propositional analysis, a technique used in discourse psychology, to capture the structure of concepts. Semino, Heywood and Short write of this that: 'what is involved is no longer words but the concepts ... activated by the words of the original expression' (2004: 1275). For the purposes of metaphor study, Steen supplements standard propositional analysis by indicating whether words evoke the source domain (s) or target domain (t). For instance, Steen gives the propositional analysis for the sentence 'Lakoff attacked Glucksberg' as:

P1 (ATTACKs LAKOFFt GLUCKSBERGt) (2011: 94)

P1 signals that this is Proposition 1, while *s* and *t* stand for source and target domain: 'Lakoff' and 'Glucksberg' evoke the target domain, while 'attack' evokes a source domain. The propositional analysis makes no claims about processing or mental mappings; it is purely an attempt to state as logically and simply as possible how concepts relate to each other in a sentence. Steen writes that this step 'lays bare how metaphors can differ from each other with respect to conceptual structure' (1999: 64).

Step 2 produces input for step 3. For metaphorical sentences, step 2 will have produced a propositional analysis with elements from incongruous domains, a problem which step 3 tackles. In step 3, the proposition is rewritten as two incomplete propositions, one for the source domain, one for the target domain. For 'Lakoff attacked Glucksberg', step 3 produces:

SIM {F, x, y
[F (LAKOFF, GLUCKSBERG)]t
[ATTACK (x, y)]s}

The notation indicates a relationship of similarity shown by SIM in line 1, between the two propositions in lines 2 and 3. *F* indicates an activity that is not explicitly denoted, and *x* and *y* indicate entities that are not explicitly denoted. These gaps are implicit in the metaphor. Line 2 expresses the entities and activities in the target domain; the unspecified target domain activity being signaled by *F*. Line 3 expresses the entities and activities in the source domain, the unspecified source domain entities being signaled by *x* and *y*.

Step 4 produces an analogy from this comparison, filling in terms that are implicit in the previous steps: *F*, *x*, and *y*. For 'Lakoff attacked Glucksberg', the analogy is filled out as follows:

SIM
[CRITICIZE (LAKOFF, GLUCKSBERG)]t
[ATTACK (ATTACKER, ATTACKED)]s} (ibid.)

In step 5, the source–target domain mapping is constructed, which, in terms of CMT, generates a conceptual metaphor. Steen summarizes the aim of step 5 in the early version of the five-step method as follows: 'to capture the full cross-domain mapping that might be related to the local analogy derived in step 4, so that "Lakoff attacked Glucksberg" could be connected in some controllable fashion to ARGUMENT IS WAR' (2011: 103). Step 5 is thus the fleshing out and extending of the metaphor; it 'takes each of the correspondences projected by the analogy of step 4 and lines them up as a list of entailments' (Steen, 2011: 96).

Table 7.1 shows Steen's full analysis of 'Lakoff attacked Glucksberg'. The descriptions of the steps in column 1 are worded slightly differently from the 1999 descriptions cited above, but the essentials are unchanged.

A. Deignan

Table 7.1 Using the five steps to analyse war metaphors

Steps	Analysis
Text	Lakoff attacked Glucksberg
1. Identification of metaphor-related words	Attacked
2. Identification of metaphor-related propositions	P1 (ATTACKs LAKOFFt GLUCKSBERGt)
3. Identification of open metaphorical comparison	SIM{F, x, y [F (LAKOFF, GLUCKSBERG)]t [ATTACK (x, y)]s}
4. Identification of analogical structure	SIM [CRITICIZE (LAKOFF, GLUCKSBERG)t [ATTACK (ATTACKER, ATTACKED)]s}
5. Identification of cross-domain mapping	TARGET < SOURCE DOMAIN CRITICIZE < ATTACK LAKOFF < ATTACKER GLUCKSBERG < ATTACKED Possible inferences ARGUMENTS < WEAPONS

Source: From Steen (2011: 94).

By 2011, Steen had modified his view of step 5, writing, 'I now feel that a more interesting use of step 5 would be to see it as representing the communicative dimension of metaphor, which would be useful as input for the ongoing construction of a context model for the discourse as a whole' (2011: 103). He reframes the output of step 5 in terms of what the speaker is doing with the analogy: 'the context model might read something like "the sender is informing the addressee that Lakoff criticized Glucksberg in order to add this event to a developing account"' (2011: 101–104). In this version, the five steps start from language in use, as before, and also finish there, widening back to context, informed by the deeper analogical analysis.

Problems with the five-step method

The five steps make the structural and logical aspects of the process of working from linguistic to conceptual metaphor very clear, but the method in itself does not resolve every difficulty. The major problem for the analyst is that the method as set out here still does not provide an answer to the problem of how we can formulate one particular conceptual metaphor rather than another, based on language data. This leap, which takes place between steps 4 and 5, is dependent on the intuitions of the researcher. The issue arises not just when following the five-step method, but in all attempts to generalize from linguistic to conceptual metaphors. Cameron notes the problem in her discussion of her classroom data. She asks, 'How far do the analyst's expectations about the data shape the interpretations of linguistic metaphor?' (2003: 252). In her data, a teacher said 'I think you all deserve a medal'. She analysed 'deserve a medal' as a linguistic realization of an EFFORTFUL JOURNEYS mapping, but she notes that 'it could also be linked to fighting in a war, competing in an art show or a dog show' (ibid.).

Steen acknowledges that the move from a specific linguistic metaphor to a particular concept, and thence to a particular mapping, is the least robust of the five steps. He writes that the 'last two steps of the procedure form the weakest parts of the chain with step 5 being the weakest of all' (1999: 73). Indeed, there seems to be a danger of circularity: in the example described above, Steen is careful not to start from the assumption that there is a mapping from ARGUMENT to WAR, but it is easy to imagine how an analyst could be influenced by his or her reading about conceptual metaphors in the literature, or their assumptions about conceptual metaphors. If this were to happen, the analysis would simply demonstrate the starting assumptions of the analyst.

A few studies have applied the five-step method in detail and discussed difficulties encountered, the problem described above being the focus of most discussion. Krennmayr used the five steps to analyse linguistic metaphors including 'winning' in the citation

> Container group Tiphook yesterday said it was still confident of *winning* its joint 643 million bid for Sea Containers . . .
>
> *2011: 219*

She notes that the difficulty of deciding what conceptual metaphor underlies the linguistic one is not specific to this example but is a general problem. She decided on the mapping SUCCEEDING IS WINNING, but notes that a more specific mapping SUCCEEDING IN A BID IS WINNING A COMPETITION is possible. Her reason for choosing the former is that her 'primary interest in this example lies in the conceptual structure of *winning*' (ibid.), that is, it is based on her analytical goals, not on a claim to have uncovered speakers' conceptual structures. Indeed, she notes of the five-step method that 'No claims are being made as to how people process semantically related expressions' (2011: 21). However, as Krennmayr and Steen repeatedly make reference to the identification of conceptual metaphors, they are of necessity making claims at some level about mental mappings, albeit not always accessed during online production and processing.

The step from linguistic to conceptual becomes even more difficult if there is only one, or a very small number of linguistic metaphors from a particular source domain. Semino, Heywood and Short (2004) explored and critiqued Steen's model when they applied it to the analysis of conversations about cancer, using a combination of the corpus and discourse approaches described above. They reported relatively little difficulty with the first three steps of the five-step method, but more complications arose with steps 4 and 5. They discuss the linguistic metaphor 'galloping away', of which there are two citations in their data, used to talk about cancer spreading quickly through the body. Intuitively, 'galloping' seems to come from the source domain of horses, and Semino, Heywood and Short's search in three contemporary corpora found that in over 80 per cent of citations, it is in fact associated with horses. These seem to be grounds for postulating a conceptual metaphor linking the source domain of HORSES with the target domain of CANCER, but there are several possibilities for the exact wording, including FAST DEVELOPMENT OF CANCER IS GALLOPING AWAY or CANCER IS A HORSE. With only two citations of a single linguistic metaphor from the source domain in their data, there is no real way of establishing which of these is closer to the internal reality of speakers.

Another issue that the analyst needs to consider is that there may be no other linguistic metaphors from the source domains of HORSES or GALLOPING that are used to talk about cancer. Not all metaphors are mappings of entire domains, with structural relationships between entities, actions and attributes. In 1987, Lakoff discussed the notion of 'one-shot' metaphors, which he initially applied mainly to 'image metaphors'. He exemplified these by literary images, including Breton's line 'My wife whose waist is an hourglass' (1987: 220). Image metaphors are 'to be distinguished from very general conceptual metaphors like DEATH IS DEPARTURE in important ways:

1. One-shot mappings, as their name implies, are not used over and over again; that is, they are not conventionalized.
2. They are not used in everyday reasoning.
3. There is no system of words and idiomatic expressions in the language whose meaning is based on them.
4. They map image structure instead of propositional structure.
5. They are not used to understand the abstract in terms of the concrete.
6. They do not have a basis in experience and commonplace knowledge that determines what gets mapped onto what.

1987: 221

While 'galloping away' is clearly not an image in quite the way that 'hourglass' is, some or all of these characteristics might apply. Items 1 and 3 can be tested using linguistic data and are therefore considered the most robust here. Within Semino, Heywood and Short's dataset, there is no evidence of conventionalization (item 1) or of other words and idiomatic expressions that are semantically related (item 3). However, their corpus is not a vast dataset, and it is possible that evidence relating to these items might be found in similar texts or a general corpus. In considering Item 1, I note that the 100-million-word British National Corpus contains 16 citations of 'galloping away', all of which are literal, and 121 citations of 'galloping', some of which are metaphorical, but none describing illness; there are a small number of citations where 'galloping' describes illness in the Oxford English Corpus, but here it refers to illnesses spreading rapidly through a population rather than in an individual's body. This suggests, but does not prove, that the metaphor is not strongly established. Regarding the third characteristic, the data studied by Semino, Heywood and Short do not contain linguistic metaphors from the same semantic field. Although dependent on introspective data, we can consider items 4 and 5. For item 4, 'galloping' possibly conveys an image. For item 5, it could be argued that the development of cancer is concrete, not abstract albeit something that is not visible in normal circumstances. There is thus a tentative case for considering 'galloping away' to be a one-shot metaphor, if not actually an image metaphor.

This, however, does not necessarily mean that there is no conceptual metaphor; Steen argues (1999: 59) that one-shot metaphors are conceptual. Further, in contrast with Lakoff (ibid.), he implies that the difference between one-shot metaphors and sets of metaphors that all appear to be mapped from the same source domain onto the same target domain is relatively unimportant. He proposes that if the researcher is concerned with this difference, it should be dealt with by a sixth step, after the five-step procedure has been followed:

> If one insists on regarding as conceptual metaphors only those metaphors which are systematic (as opposed to one-shot metaphors), which I do not, then a sixth step will have to be added to the procedure, saying that the output of the first five steps is to be compared over large numbers of metaphors in order to establish more or less systematic groups of metaphorical concepts, labeling the largest systematic groups as conceptual metaphors.
>
> *1999: 59*

There is thus some ambivalence about the conceptual status of one-shot metaphors, and it is not a question easily resolved using linguistic data. The linguistic evidence usually put forward for the conceptual nature of mappings is the range and systematicity of their linguistic realizations, which by definition are not found for one-shot metaphors. The issue, for the example of 'galloping', is whether we believe that 'the question "How is cancer conceptualized within this metaphor?" would be answered by saying that cancer is conceptualized as a horse running around in the body' (Semino, Heywood and Short, 2004: 1283). If it is accepted that a one-shot mapping from the fast movement of a horse to the fast progression of cancer may be conceptual to some degree, there seems no need to generalize away from the linguistic metaphor itself. To paraphrase 'galloping away' as CANCER IS A HORSE, for example, seems inelegant, and also would generate predictions about language that are not borne out. CANCER IS A HORSE would generate a different set of entailments from those generated if the source is considered to be GALLOPING AWAY, as I show using corpus data in the following section.

We thus have two inter-connected problems with moving from an identified linguistic metaphor to a conceptual metaphor:

1. Is this linguistic metaphor a realization of a conceptual metaphor at all? If there is only one instance of the possible conceptual metaphor in the dataset, it is possible that it is a one-shot mapping. As noted, whether or not a one-shot mapping is conceptual cannot be determined using linguistic data.
2. What domains are metaphorically mapped? At what level of specificity should this be described?

In the next section, I offer some suggestions for how corpus linguistic data can be used to tackle these two problems.

Using corpus evidence to formulate conceptual metaphors

In this section I discuss my own and others' work using various synchronic corpora to explore metaphor patterns in an attempt to tackle the above questions. The first, 'Is this linguistic metaphor a realization of a conceptual metaphor at all?', clearly cannot be answered by linguistic data alone. Language cannot provide definitive proof of conceptual structures and processes. It can however corroborate or contradict hypotheses. Where a conceptual metaphor has been proposed on the basis of a small number of linguistic metaphors found in a limited number of texts, corroboration can be sought by examining a larger corpus of similar texts. The existence of more instances of the same linguistic metaphor provides some support, but may demonstrate a one-shot mapping. The existence of other linguistic metaphors apparently realizing the same source and target domains offers support for a more widespread mapping.

Early studies that tackled this issue using large datasets include work on ARGUMENT IS WAR by Deignan (2008) and Vereza (2008). Deignan (2008) examined large random samples of concordance data from the Bank of English for 'attack', 'defend', 'strategy' and other WAR lexis cited by Lakoff and Johnson (1980), and Vereza (2008) examined the metaphoricity of collocates of 'war' (2008). The general finding from both studies was that the data are not directly contradictory of the proposed conceptual metaphors ARGUMENT IS WAR. However, they reveal a more complex picture: they suggest mappings at both more general and more constrained levels than those proposed in the classic CMT works. For example, WAR lexis such as 'attack', 'defend' and 'strategy' is used to talk about a very wide range of topics besides argument, suggesting that some—but not all—WAR metaphors are often used about a much wider range of topics than just argument; other semantic areas they describe include planning, strategy and all kinds of competition and sport (Deignan, 2008). Ritchie (2003) made a similar observation about the difficulty of formulating the WAR conceptual metaphor.

The quite general reference of these metaphors contrasts with another lexical item from the source domain of WAR, the verb 'fire', as used with 'gun' and similar nouns. This verb is rarely used with a metaphorical meaning, and when it is, it is almost always in the string 'fire/fires/fired/firing a warning shot'. In the metaphorical use, the 'shot' is almost always singular, and is always premodified by 'warning'. The meaning of the metaphor is something close to 'take an aggressive action with the intention of starting an argument'. For this linguistic metaphor then, the mapping is formally and semantically more specific and constrained than the conceptual metaphor ARGUMENT IS WAR would predict. Similarly, the metaphorical meaning of 'shoot down' is mostly confined to arguments, but only within the collocation 'shoot down in flames'. When not followed by 'in flames', 'shoot down' is usually literal (Deignan, 2008). This restriction is similar to that noted above for 'fire a warning shot', where the plural form, 'warning shots', or 'fire' with a different object or used intransitively, is usually associated with a literal meaning (ibid.). In the studies generating these observations, neither Deignan nor Vereza attempt to reformulate a conceptual metaphor from the source domain of WAR/WEAPONS/VIOLENCE using their linguistic data, and their findings suggest that there may be several related mappings at work, at different levels of generality.

With regard to Semino, Heywood and Short's (2004) data from discussions of cancer, and the possible existence of a GALLOPING or HORSE mapping, I noted above that 'galloping' itself as a linguistic metaphor does not seem well established with this meaning in the two large general corpora that I searched (the British National Corpus and the Oxford English Corpus). A search of a larger corpus of medical and doctor–patient discourse, or a general corpus, could show whether there are other linguistic metaphors that seem to realize a possible conceptual metaphor. The more linguistic metaphors that are found from apparently the same source domain, the more evidence the analyst has corroborating (but not, as noted, proving) the conceptual metaphor that he/she proposes. For instance, if alongside 'galloping', it is found that 'rider', 'race' and 'horse' are also used with apparently related metaphorical meanings, we would have stronger evidence for the conceptual metaphor CANCER IS A HORSE. However, my searches of the British National Corpus and Oxford English Corpus suggest that these and related source domain words are not used metaphorically with this meaning.

A dictionary that was written using corpus data can be a short cut to such corpus searches, but it can only give positive evidence: that is, if a dictionary attests the existence of other metaphors apparently realizing a conceptual metaphor, this can be seen as demonstrating that the linguistic metaphor in question is not one-shot. If the dictionary does not attest other linguistic metaphors though, this cannot be taken as evidence that they do not exist. They may not be frequent enough to warrant their own sense in a dictionary entry.

The second question raised at the end of the previous section was:

'What domains are metaphorically mapped? At what level of specificity should this be described?'

This concerns the exact formulation, or wording, of a proposed conceptual metaphor. This is important, because even very closely related words can have very different associations for language users. As I noted above, when analysts propose a conceptual metaphor, they often go on to discuss its entailments. A small change in the wording of a mapping can result in major changes to its entailments. I illustrate this by examining citations of 'horse' and 'galloping', as examples of the possible mappings FAST DEVELOPMENT OF CANCER IS A GALLOPING HORSE or CANCER IS A HORSE (Semino, Heywood and Short, 2004).

I searched for 'horse', and 'galloping' in the 2.4-billion-word Oxford English Corpus, using the software Sketchengine (Kilgarriff et al., 2014). I focused on specific word forms

Table 7.2 Most significant collocates of 'horse' and 'galloping'

	Horse	Galloping
1	Racing/race	Hooves/hoofs (sic)
2	Riding/ride/rode	Cantering
3	Cart	Horses/horse
4	Rider	Horsemen
5	Trainer	Horseback
6	Carriage	Bareback
7	Saddle	Trotting
8	Pommel	Gait
9	Bolted	Furlongs
10	Dark	Bipedal

rather than all inflections because it has been shown that different inflections of a word can have different patterns of meaning and form (Deignan, 2005). There were 101,714 citations of 'horse' and 2,367 citations of 'galloping' at the time of my searches. I then examined words that occurred frequently alongside the words under study, i.e., its collocates. Collocates can be significant clues to meaning and context (Sinclair, 1991), and they can be identified automatically using corpus software. There are various ways of calculating the significance of collocates; here 'logdice', as recommended by Sketchengine (Kilgarriff et al., 2014), is used. The ten most significant collocates of 'horse' and 'galloping', ignoring proper names, are shown in Table 7.2:

Table 7.2 suggests that 'horse' collocates significantly with words associated with humans riding them, for racing, or leisure, and with objects associated with the domestication of the horse, such as 'saddle', 'pommel' and 'carriage'. 'Cart', 'bolted' and 'dark' owe their frequency largely to the idioms 'put the cart before the horse', 'close the barn/stable door after the horse has bolted' and 'dark horse'.

The collocates of 'galloping' are rather different. It tends to collocate with words associated with the movement of horses: 'cantering', 'trotting' and 'gait', and the technical 'bipedal' (of which there are only four citations). It also collocates with words about riding, but evoking a less domesticated picture than the collocates for 'horse' do: the 'horsemen' that collocate with 'galloping' are either the 'four horsemen of the Apocalypse' or are in citations such as:

... framing the silhouettes of three Mongolian *horsemen galloping* across the steppes.

Citations in which 'bareback' and 'horseback' collocate with 'galloping' also suggest exotic and dangerous scenes; they include:

... a warrior, *galloping bareback* with flying hair

... setting fire to a petrol tanker and *galloping* around it on *horseback*, bottles in hand.

In 25 of the 38 citations in which 'galloping' collocates with 'hooves' or 'hoofs', it is in reference to their sound, for example: 'The next thing I knew, I was woken up by the sounds of galloping hooves and ripping canvas'. As was the case for the some of the other collocates, the source texts tend to be narrative and fictional. These Oxford English Corpus collocations suggest that 'horse' and 'galloping', although apparently from the same source domain, are part of different schemata at the level of detail: the former evokes riders and racing in a controlled way, while some citations of 'galloping' evoke danger and lack of control, and others are from technical discussions of horses moving. (Because 'galloping' is a relatively infrequent word, the words towards the bottom of the list represent fewer than 10 citations and not too much weight should be placed on these as collocates.) The metaphorical entailments of the two scenarios are very different: a metaphorical entailment of CANCER IS A HORSE might therefore involve riders controlling it, while scenarios from DEVELOPMENT OF CANCER IS GALLOPING AWAY might involve danger and lack of control.

Dancygier and Sweetser (2014: 199–200) take a related approach, to the analysis of literary metaphor. They consider Emily Dickinson's nineteenth-century poem 'Over the fence', which 'appears to be about a small girl wishing she dared to be disobedient and climb over a fence to steal some strawberries' (199). They suggest the poem may be a metaphor for more adult activities that were forbidden or censored in unmarried females, such as being sexually active and having a career. The writers do not use corpus data, but in common with my arguments above, they speculate about associations between concepts, in attempting to reconstruct the metaphorical mappings behind the language. Dickinson writes, 'Over the fence. I could climb if I tried, I know'; Dancygier and Sweetser write that the mention of 'climbing' suggests a career. They do not offer corpus evidence for this, and I am unable to find any collocational evidence that climbing is especially associated with progress in a career, or was in nineteenth-century English, but this seems intuitively plausible. The other possible interpretation, that the poem refers to forbidden sexual activity, is evoked, they say, by the reference to strawberries, which may suggest the notion of forbidden fruit.

In this section, I have argued that corpus data should be consulted when attempting to hypothesize about the existence of a conceptual metaphor from linguistic expressions. Corpus citations can provide insights into the conventionalization, frequency and range of metaphorical uses from a source domain. Although not sufficient as proof of a conceptual mapping, it can help with its formulation, and can demonstrate what the entailments of various alternative formulations may be. This leads to the issue of the level of specificity required in formulating a conceptual mapping, which I now discuss.

Conceptual mappings at other levels

The early works in CMT identified intuitively satisfying mappings such as ARGUMENT IS WAR, LIFE IS A JOURNEY and THEORIES ARE BUILDINGS, but, as described above, closer linguistic analysis of expressions from domains such as WAR suggests that the boundaries around the mappings are, at very least, hazy, and variable for different linguistic expressions. Scholars from different traditions have suggested mappings that are both more general and more specific than traditional conceptual metaphors.

Grady (1997) argues that cognitive mappings work at a deeper and more general level than the kind of conceptual metaphors described by Lakoff and Johnson (1980). He works within the cognitive tradition, and used Lakoff and Johnson's original linguistic data, supplemented with other intuitively derived expressions. One of the examples he works with is the conceptual metaphor THEORIES ARE BUILDINGS put forward by Lakoff and Johnson. Grady explored the linguistic examples given by Lakoff and Johnson, such as 'She's on very solid ground with her latest theoretical work'. He also discusses linguistic metaphors that might have been predicted by the conceptual metaphor but which do not occur, such as 'This theory has French windows', and other linguistic metaphors that are used to talk about theories but are apparently from different source domains, such as 'They tore the theory to shreds'. Grady argues that the data are better explained by the existence of 'something like a compound metaphor – a metaphor composed of separate and independently motivated metaphorical correspondences' (1997: 273). In this view, THEORIES ARE BUILDINGS is not the primary mapping, but a compound of the correspondences ORGANIZATION IS PHYSICAL STRUCTURE and PERSISTING IS REMAINING ERECT. He notes that the source and target of these primary, or basic metaphors (both terms are used) would not be considered to be 'domains'. Grady's hypothesis is regarded as both credible and important within cognitive linguistics, but for an applied linguist, the problems of arriving at primary metaphors from linguistic data are the same as, but greater, than for conceptual metaphors.

In contrast, Musolff (e.g. 2006) has proposed a more detailed unit of analysis. He analysed corpora consisting of the texts of public debates in English and German on the topic of the European Union. He found that a large number of linguistic metaphors can be related to the source domain of LOVE-MARRIAGE FAMILY, explained at the most basic level by Lakoff's A NATION STATE IS A PERSON (24). He examined the large number of linguistic metaphors that seem to be realizations of these source domains in a good deal of detail, considering who had produced them, and what detailed meanings and evaluative stance they seemed to convey. Within this general mapping, Musolff finds mini-narrative structures, which he terms 'scenarios', in which

> the characterization of the participants in terms of their roles, intentions, and states of minds, as well as the assessment of their actions in terms of chances of success, are in fact highly specified.
>
> 27

Different scenarios can be developed to reflect speakers' stance towards the topic. Britain's traditional euro-scepticism is reflected in texts from British publications, which tended to develop separation and divorce narratives.

Conceptual metaphors are at a mid-level of specificity between primary metaphors and scenarios. In terms of linguistic evidence, the case is no more compelling for conceptual metaphors than for the other two, but they remain apparently the most intuitively attractive, and easily the most frequently used concept in the metaphor literature.

Another possibility for the analyst is to recognize that many linguistic metaphors seem to fall into semantic groupings but without making a strong commitment to the existence of long-standing conceptual mapping. Cameron and Maslen (2010) have done this with the notion of systematic metaphors (see Chapter 6). Cameron, Pelosi and Pedroso de Moraes Feltes (2014) describe a methodology for identifying systematic metaphors, and identify some smaller, scenario-like units. They argue that very abstract generalizations should be avoided; we should abstract only as far as strictly necessary from the actual words used in the talk. 'The operating principle at this step is to stay as close to the language used by participants as possible, generalizing a label from the talk only as far as is needed to include related vehicles' (2014: 29). They specifically distance themselves from claims about a conceptual level: 'The labels given to groupings are not intended to reflect assumptions about levels of cognitive processing or the nature of mappings' (2014: 30). However, what they find about general metaphors 'supports the idea that large-scale, generalized metaphors can emerge from human embodied experience and social interaction, and overlap with 'conceptual metaphors' (2014: 40). While Cameron, Pelosi and Pedroso de Moraes Feltes are not explicitly aligned with Conceptual Metaphor Theory, their methodology constitutes good practice for researchers who are attempting to identify conceptual metaphors.

Current research and future directions

Current research focuses on a number of areas. Researchers continue to debate which tools and methods should be used in metaphor identification, and how they should be used to develop generalizations about linguistic and conceptual metaphor. For example, MacArthur (2015) writes of inconsistencies and problems with the use of dictionaries in metaphor identification. Dorst and Reijniersi (2015) and Deignan (2015b) responded, and the debate raised once more the status of data, and the danger of allowing the analysts' preconceptions about conceptual metaphors to cloud the data analysis.

Research into metaphor is increasingly recognizing that every language community is composed of different speakers, with different experiences and interests, and that we cannot assume a shared, static set of conceptual structures. Recent research has considered different genres and registers, and has suggested that linguistic metaphors vary a good deal across these even where the subject matter of texts is closely related. This would suggest that different groups of people call on different conceptual metaphors for the same topics, and that we seem to access different conceptual metaphors when speaking or writing at different levels of formality or for different audiences. For example, Deignan, Littlemore and Semino (2013) present a series of studies of the metaphors of different but related genres and registers. They show how different groups of language users have different metaphorical resources to think and talk about the same topics, and how they can misunderstand each other's uses of metaphorical language. Methodologically, such work requires carefully compiled datasets, and, increasingly, researchers are talking to members of the language community that they are studying rather than relying on their own interpretation of texts.

Extending the exploration of figurative language in other directions, Dancygier and Sweetser (2014) discuss the crossover between creative and conventional uses, and the nature of multimodal figurative expression. They also consider how longstanding metaphorical mappings, while persisting in language over decades or centuries, may mean very different things to language users in different times and places: 'the metaphor GOD IS A FATHER is surely not the same blend for modern English speakers as it was for ancient Near Eastern cultures where a father could sell his children' (2014: 216). In their discussion of metaphor in literature they suggest a fascinating reversal of the interpretation process usually suggested. As noted above, they discuss Dickinson's 'Over the fence'. They note that a mention in the poem of God's disapproval ('God would certainly scold') would suggest to the reader that the target domain is LIFE. The reader's knowledge of the existing mappings LIFE IS A JOURNEY, PURPOSES ARE DESTINATIONS and DIFFICULTIES ARE OBSTACLES will then suggest metaphorical interpretations for some of the language. This is a reversal of the process usually described; here it is suggested that the reader's interpretation will proceed from guessing about the target domain through knowledge of existing conceptual metaphors, to an interpretation of the language: from conceptual to linguistic rather than the other way round.

Conclusion

The notion of conceptual metaphors is problematic for many researchers, and has become more so in recent years. However, even for the most sceptical, there remains a valuable insight, that generalizations can be detected from linguistic metaphors and that these generalizations seem able to generate novel metaphors, and probably frame world-views. These points are important for all metaphor researchers regardless of their level of adherence to CMT. While the imaginative leap of CMT rightly generated much excitement, for a time methodological rigour lagged behind creativity. The work of Steen and his colleagues, among others, has shown that methods need to strive to be rigorous and replicable in this area as in other scientific work, while the contributions of corpus and text analysts have suggested some ways forward.

Further reading

Musolff, A. (2006) 'Metaphor scenarios in public discourse', *Metaphor and Symbol*, 21: 23–38.
Semino, E., Heywood, J. and Short, M. (2004) 'Methodological problems in the analysis of metaphors in a corpus of conversations about cancer', *Journal of Pragmatics*, 36: 1271–1294.
Steen, G. (2011) 'From three dimensions to five steps: The value of deliberate metaphor', *Metaphorik. de*, 21.

References

Cameron, L. (2003) *Metaphor in Educational Discourse*, London: Continuum.
Cameron, L. and Maslen, R. (eds) (2010) *Metaphor Analysis*, London: Equinox.
Cameron, L., Maslen, R., Todd, Z., Maule, J., Stratton, P. and Stanley, N. (2009) 'The discourse dynamics approach to metaphor and metaphor-led discourse analysis', *Metaphor and Symbol*, 24(2): 63–89.
Cameron, L., Pelosi, A. and Pedroso de Moraes Feltes, H. (2014) 'Metaphorising violence in the UK and Brazil: A contrastive discourse dynamics study', *Metaphor and Symbol*, 29: 23–54.
Dancygier, B. and Sweetser, E. (2014) *Figurative Language*, New York: Cambridge University Press.
Deignan, A. (2005) *Metaphor and Corpus Linguistics*, Amsterdam, The Netherlands: John Benjamins.
—— (2008) 'Corpus linguistic data and Conceptual Metaphor Theory', in M. S. Zanotto, L. Cameron and M. C. Calvacanti (eds) *Confronting Metaphor in Use: An Applied Linguistic Perspective*, Amsterdam, The Netherlands: John Benjamins.
—— (2015a) 'Figurative language and lexicography', in P. Hanks and G.-M. de Schryver (eds) *International Handbook of Lexicography*, Berlin, Germany: Springer.
—— (2015b) 'MIP, the corpus and dictionaries: What makes for the best metaphor analysis?', *Metaphor and the Social World*, 5: 145–154.
Deignan, A., Littlemore, J. and Semino, E. (2013) *Figurative Language, Genre and Register*, Cambridge, UK: Cambridge University Press.
Dorst, A. and Reijniersi, G. (2015) 'A dictionary gives definitions, not decisions: Response 1 to "On using a dictionary to identify the basic senses of words"', *Metaphor and the Social World*, 5: 137–144.
Grady, J. (1997) 'THEORIES ARE BUILDINGS revisited', *Cognitive Linguistics*, 8(4): 267–290.
Halliday, M. A. K. and Matthiessen, C. (2004) *An Introduction to Functional Grammar*, London: Edward Arnold.
Kilgarriff, A., Baisa, V., Bůsta, J., Jacubíček, M., Kovář, V., Michelfeit, J., Rychlý, P. and Suchomel, V. (2014) 'The Sketchengine, ten years on', *Lexicography*, 1: 7–36.
Krennmayr, T. (2011) *Metaphor in Newspapers*, Utrecht, The Netherlands: LOT.
Lakoff, G. (1987) 'Image metaphors', *Metaphor and Symbolic Activity*, 3: 219–222.
—— (1991) 'Metaphor and war: The metaphor system used to justify war in the Gulf', Paper presented at the University of California, January 1991. Online. Available at http://www2.iath.virginia.edu/sixties/HTML_docs/Texts/Scholarly/Lakoff_Gulf_Metaphor_1.html (accessed 1 December 2015).
—— (1993) 'The contemporary theory of metaphor', in A. Ortony (ed.) *Metaphor and Thought*, Cambridge, UK: Cambridge University Press.
Lakoff, G. and Johnson, M. (1980) *Metaphors We Live By*, Chicago, IL: University of Chicago Press.
MacArthur, F. (2015) 'On using a dictionary to identify the basic senses of words', *Metaphor and the Social World*, 5: 124–136.

Musolff, A. (2006) 'Metaphor scenarios in public discourse', *Metaphor and Symbol*, 21: 23–38.

Ritchie, D. (2003) 'ARGUMENT IS WAR – or is it a game of chess? Multiple meanings in the analysis of implicit metaphors', *Metaphor and Symbol*, 18: 125–146.

Rojas-Sosa, D. (2014) 'Traditional and not so traditional metaphors of love in Spanish: A way to spread and create ideologies about romance and gender on the Internet', *Metaphor and the Social World*, 4: 199–224.

Semino, E., Heywood, J. and Short, M. (2004) 'Methodological problems in the analysis of metaphors in a corpus of conversations about cancer', *Journal of Pragmatics*, 36: 1271–1294.

Sinclair, J. (1991) *Corpus, Concordance, Collocation*, Oxford, UK: Oxford University Press.

Steen, G. (1999) 'From linguistic to conceptual metaphor in five steps', in R. W. Gibbs, Jr. and G. Steen (eds) *Metaphor in Cognitive Linguistics*, Amsterdam, The Netherlands: John Benjamins.

—— (2008) *Finding Metaphor in Grammar and Usage*, Amsterdam, The Netherlands: John Benjamins.

—— (2011) 'From three dimensions to five steps: The value of deliberate metaphor', *Metaphorik.de*, 21.

Steen, G., Dorst, A., Herrmann, J. B., Kaal, A., Krennmayr, T. and Pasma, T. (2010) *A Method for Linguistic Metaphor Identification*, Amsterdam, The Netherlands: John Benjamins.

Stefanowitsch, A. (2006) 'Words and their metaphors: A corpus-based approach', in A. Stefanowitsch and S. Th. Gries (eds) *Corpus-based Approaches to Metaphor and Metonymy*, Berlin, Germany: Mouton de Gruyter.

Vereza, S. (2008) 'Exploring metaphors in corpora: A study of "war" in corpus-generated data', in M. S. Zanotto, L. Cameron and M. C. Calvacanti (eds) *Confronting Metaphor in Use: An Applied Linguistic Perspective*, Amsterdam, The Netherlands: John Benjamins.

8
Corpus-linguistic approaches to metaphor analysis

Heli Tissari

Introduction

Corpora should be used to study metaphors for the same reasons that they should be used for any linguistic research. They help us to search through a lot of data with great speed, they make research replicable, and they give us access to statistics on linguistic phenomena. This chapter will discuss and demonstrate how best to make use of corpora in metaphor research.

What is a corpus and why should we use one to study metaphors?

A corpus is a collection of texts, and an electronic corpus is a computer-readable corpus,[1] which, when fed into appropriate software, makes searching and comparing different texts easy and fast. You can search corpora in many different ways. You can search them for words, morphemes, colligations, collocations and syntactic structures. Moreover, many corpora come with so-called annotation, i.e. they contain information about the syntactic or semantic features of their contents. *Colligation* refers to a grammatical combination of two or more words. For example, the verb *agree* tends to go together with the preposition *to*. *Collocation* refers to the habitual co-occurrence of words. For example, the adjective *auspicious* tends to go together with such nouns as *occasion* and *event* (Crystal 2008: 86). Corpus-based research becomes particularly replicable if you use a publicly available corpus, such as the 100-million-word *British National Corpus* BNC or the 450-million-word *Corpus of Contemporary American English* COCA (Davies 1990–2012). A corpus interface often gives us direct access to statistics. For example, the BNCWeb (CQP edition) (Hoffmann 1996–2013) tells us which words we should expect to go together and which actually do.

When using a corpus, it is important to know what kind of texts it consists of. If you search a corpus for something, you need to know which variety, genre and topic the samples represent, and then you can count likelihoods for the occurrences of certain phenomena in certain types of text. For example, the *Brown Corpus* was created in the 1960s by collecting samples of many different genres in order to represent then current American English, and the *Corpus of Early English Correspondence Sampler* (1418–1680) represents letters. Moreover, we can distinguish between small and big corpora. The one-million-word

Brown Corpus is small while, for example, the BNC is big, not to mention the 650-million-word *Bank of English* (see *The Collins Corpus* 2007–2013). The bigger a corpus is, the more likely one is going to find rare words in it.

Corpus studies on metaphor can be divided into three types (Semino 2008: 199). In the first type, researchers use general-purpose corpora such as the *Brown Corpus* to search for patterns of conceptual metaphors which could be relevant for the development of Conceptual Metaphor Theory (CMT; see Chapter 1). In the second type, researchers choose corpora representing text types, genres or particular periods, in order to investigate similarities and differences between these. In the third type, researchers compare metaphors occurring in corpora representing different languages (examples of all these types of studies will be given below). Bigger corpora would seem to lend themselves better to metaphor research than small ones, because they contain more data even on rare expressions. However, sometimes the amount of data in a big corpus is too much. Koller (2006: 242) notes that large amounts of corpus can be an obstacle for meticulous metaphor analysis. However, large and small corpora can also be combined in research (e.g. Cameron and Deignan 2003).

In the following sections, I will provide a sample method for how corpora can be used in metaphor research and outline previous studies where this has been done. I will then move on to demonstrate what can be gained from a corpus approach to metaphor analysis with a case study of recent research. The final section will briefly outline the development of corpus linguistic research on metaphor in the past and how I expect it to develop in the future.

How to use corpora to study metaphor: in a nutshell

To use corpora to study metaphor, you need to consider the following questions (not necessarily in this order):

1. What is your topic (e.g. metaphors realized by verbs, metaphors of emotion)?
2. Which corpus or corpora will you use as data? Why?
3. How does your research relate to previous studies?
4. How do you define metaphor?
5. How are you going to identify the metaphors in the data? (What are you going to search for in the corpus and how are you going to process the search results?)

Overview of previous research

A preliminary note and a definition of metaphor

My overview of previous research mostly relates to CMT as developed by Lakoff and Johnson (e.g. 1980, 1999). Many pioneering studies on conceptual metaphors from the 1980s and 1990s did not use corpora as data (e.g. Kövecses 1986, 1990; Lakoff 1987: 380–415). We need not dismiss those studies even if we embrace corpora. On the contrary, we can use corpora to check theories and hypotheses which have been created without them (e.g. Deignan 2005; Stefanowitsch 2006b).

According to CMT, a metaphor consists of a source domain and a target domain. The target domain is the concept which we understand in terms of the other concept, the source domain (Lakoff 1987: 384). For example, the conceptual metaphor LOVE IS A PHYSICAL FORCE consists of the source domain PHYSICAL FORCE and the target domain LOVE. It may be realized in the form of example (1) (Lakoff and Johnson 1980: 49):

(1) I could feel the <u>electricity</u> between us.

We could find this metaphor in a corpus by searching for the source domain word *electricity*, but not necessarily by searching for the target domain word *love*. To be precise, CMT suggests that metaphors exist primarily in the mind, although they are expressed in language.

Examples of previous research

Deignan (e.g. 1999, 2005, 2008) showed an early interest in combining metaphor research with corpus linguistics. She was both supportive and critical of CMT. One of her major aims was to show that authentic corpus data behaves differently from data gathered by introspection. She was interested, for example, in how frequently different parts of speech occur with a metaphorical sense. She suggested that, for example, animal metaphors such as *Richard is a gorilla* where the metaphorical word, *gorilla*, is a noun, are rare. On the other hand, many animal metaphors occur in the form of verbs (e.g. *to horse*) or adjectives (e.g. *sheepish*) (Deignan 2005: 152–5). She also studied colligation and collocation, including the words occurring together with the noun *price*, and noticed that some colligates, such as the preposition *of* in *price of*, primarily represented literal meanings, while some collocates, such as *heavy* in *a heavy price to pay*, primarily represented metaphorical meanings (Deignan 2005: 203–9).

Recent innovative corpus-linguistic work on metaphors includes Philip's (2011) research on idioms and collocations. She studied such expressions as *caught red-handed*, *once in a blue moon*, *red tape* and *the grass is always greener*, discovering, for example, that although *red-handed* in *caught red-handed* would seem to refer to violence, people typically caught red-handed in a crime have been 'dealing or using drugs, smuggling arms, stealing, [or] committing fraud' (Philip 2011: 91). As regards the expression *the grass is always greener*, Philip (2011: 146–8) searched for variant forms noting, for example, that people never said *the grass is still green*, *the grass is usually green* or *the grass tends to be green*, and that they replaced the adjective *green* only once with another adjective denoting colour, i.e. *black*.

You can also use corpora to compare different languages with each other. Ureña Gómez-Moreno and Faber (2011) studied metaphorical terminology in a corpus of marine biology journals written in English and Spanish. They searched for species names based on resemblance metaphors, such as *harvest fish* and *hammerhead shark*. They found three kinds of metaphorical terms: exact pairs, in which the English and Spanish terms were based on the same metaphors, separate pairs, in which the English and Spanish terms were based on different metaphors, and unbalanced pairs, in which only one language used a metaphor.

The corpus-linguistic method has also been used to complement manual analyses. Hardie et al. (2007) and Koller et al. (2008: 153–6) studied the metaphorical source domains in Ken Kesey's novel *One Flew over the Cuckoo's Nest*. They established that Semino and Swindlehurst's (1996) manual analysis of the machinery metaphors in the novel was correct and that the metaphors PEOPLE ARE MACHINES and INSTITUTIONS ARE MACHINES often occurred in the first half of the text. Hardie et al. (2007) also compared Koller's (2004b) manual analysis of 40 different articles on 20 different businesswomen with a computerized analysis and found that the latter method yielded 'two to three times more results'.

Sometimes we find a series of articles on a topic, such as emotion. The seminal study was by Lakoff and Kövecses on the American English concept of ANGER (Lakoff 1987: 380–415). Kövecses continued working on emotions, publishing, among other things, a book called

Emotion Concepts (1990), where he defined a prototype of emotion on the basis of metaphors of emotion. Corpus-based studies have also investigated metaphors for target domains that received a lot of attention in the CMT literature, such as emotions (e.g. Lakoff 1987; Kövecses 2000). For example, Stefanowitsch (2006b) searched for some emotion words in the BNC and identified some metaphors that had not been noted in the literature. Tissari (2003) first continued Kövecses's (1988) work on love and then turned to other emotions, such as pride (Tissari 2006b). Her work on pride in Late Middle (1418–1500) and Early Modern English (1500–1710) was followed by Fabiszak and Hebda's (2010) work on pride in Old (–1150) and Middle English (1150–1420).

How to find metaphors in corpora

The definition of conceptual metaphor suggests two ways to find metaphors in corpora. You can search for linguistic items which relate to the source domain or search for linguistic items which relate to the target domain (Stefanowitsch 2006a: 2–4). Charteris-Black (2004) searched for source domain lexis when he studied e.g. the metaphors of New Labour, metaphor in British party political manifestos and metaphor in sports reporting. He first read a sample of a certain text type in order to identify expressions suggesting metaphor sources, and then searched for similar expressions in a larger corpus. For example, he read a 'sample of 100 sports reports from popular and broadsheet newspapers' to compile a lexicon listing conflict terms which could be used to metaphorically suggest that SPORT IS WAR (Charteris-Black 2004: 117). The list included such words as *war, attack, fight, kill, campaign, army, battle, victory, victim* and *struggle*. He then searched for these words in *The Times* and *The Sun* newspapers to see how often sports was characterized as war (Charteris-Black 2004: 116–17). Koller (2004a) and Hintikka (2013) used variants of this approach in order to study metaphor and gender in business media discourse and BODY metaphors for society and the mind in four corpora representing Early Modern and Present-Day English. The reverse method of searching for target domain lexis and identifying metaphors occurring with it has been pioneered by Stefanowitsch (2006b) and Tissari (2003). It will be described below.

To find metaphors in a corpus, you can also search for so-called tuning devices of metaphors, i.e. words which can be used to introduce metaphors. Cameron and Deignan (2003: 152) used a small corpus consisting of talk recorded in a primary school to identify such devices and came up with the set: *actually, almost, imagine, just, kind of, a little, really, sort of*. These words were found to serve two functions in teachers' speech: they directed the pupils to a particular interpretation, and they adjusted the strength of the metaphor, as in the following example which related to dancing practice:

(2) ... can you go back *just* a "whisper."

Cameron and Deignan 2003: 153

Cameron and Deignan (2003: 154–9) then searched for the same tuning devices in a large corpus, finding more uses to which the tuning devices were put: they were again used to direct the interpretation of metaphors and to adjust the strength of the metaphor, but they were also used to signal something unexpected like "*midwife*" in example (3) (Cameron and Deignan 2003: 156):

(3) Fryer he was the he was er *in a way* our "midwife" because he was Secretary of the Agricultural Research Council.

Berber Sardinha (2012) compared the success rates of different types of searches for metaphors in corpus data. First, he tested the method of reading samples of text and then searching for the same metaphors in the entire corpus. His findings suggested that you should read at least 30 per cent of a corpus, which, in his test, produced 55.2 per cent of the metaphors in the entire data (Berber Sardinha 2012: 28–31). Second, he tested searches with single words and different combinations of words such as two-word bundles and five words to the left of a chosen node word. He found that searches for two-word bundles, three-word bundles and four-word bundles attested the most precision in identifying metaphors, 100 per cent, while single word searches attested the least precision, 73.2 per cent (Berber Sardinha 2012: 31–4). Third, he experimented with metaphor clustering, testing different windows within which to find more metaphors around a metaphor. He naturally found more metaphors when he enlarged the window size from 5 to 20 words. However, even a 20-word window size, which almost meant reading through the corpus, did not yield all the metaphors there. Consequently, he recommended a 5- or 10-word window size, which would be likely to retrieve 20 per cent to 40 per cent of the metaphors (Berber Sardinha 2012: 34–6). In contrast, Berber Sardinha (2012: 36–8) found that a keyword analysis using a standard corpus comparison tool is not an efficient way to find metaphors.

Until now, we have dealt with searches which can be conducted by using basic corpus tools. The next section will introduce more computational approaches, which combine several tools and/or require programming skills.

How to find metaphors in the data: going more computational

Early attempts to program metaphor detection and identification included Martin (1990) and Fass (1991). Both involved a previously programmed knowledge representation system and had some measure of success. More recently, Mason (2004) proposed a different approach based on a simple idea: to compare different text types representing potential source and target domain concepts such as LABORATORY and FINANCE in terms of their frequent lexis, and then see where there was overflow of lexis from one domain to another. He used the Internet as a source of data. Mason (2004: 29) detected an asymmetric structure of transfer between the domains LABORATORY and FINANCE: verbs which often occurred with liquids in the LABORATORY domain, for example, *pour, flow* and *evaporate*, also occurred with money in the FINANCE domain, but the reverse did not happen: verbs which often occurred with money, for example, *spend, invest* and *deposit*, did not occur with liquids. This is how Mason (2004: 35) detected the metaphor MONEY IS A LIQUID. His finding corroborated the unidirectionality of metaphor as postulated in CMT: the relationship between the source and target domains cannot be reversed (e.g. Sweetser 1990: 30). Mason's approach (2004) did not require any previously programmed knowledge representation system, but he did use the WordNet lexical database for English as a knowledge base (Fellbaum 2006).

In an alternative approach, Berber Sardinha (2012: 44–7) tested the idea that metaphors could be found by locating two semantically unrelated words near each other. He used software called WordNet::Similarity to identify word pairs which were semantically distant from each other (cf. Pedersen 2014). The words in his data had so many different senses in the WordNet lexical database that the number of word pairs studied multiplied from 12,055 to 343,347. The top 1,000 word pairs produced only seven unique metaphors, although the precision was 100 per cent. He eventually suggested that a 15 per cent sample of the output would be ideal, revealing about 85 per cent of the metaphors in the data (Berber Sardinha 2012: 44–7).

Reining and Lönneker-Rodman (2007) introduced corpus-driven metaphor harvesting. They combined a search for a target domain word, *Europe*, with searches for source domain lexis in a corpus of articles on the European Constitution in the French newspapers *Le Monde* and *Figaro*. They conducted a statistical analysis to see which hundred collocates typically occurred with the word *Europe* in each newspaper. They then evaluated the top collocates to see which lemmas could be used metaphorically and came up with such words as *construire* 'construct' and *traverser* 'traverse'. They then returned to the corpus to check if these lemmas were used metaphorically. As a result, they were able to postulate four tentative source domains, among them BUILDING and MOTION. Next, they went back to their lists of a hundred collocates and collected further collocates suggesting these source domains, such as *maison* 'house' and *progresser* 'progress'. They also compared their list of source domain lemmas against EuroWordNet which suggested connections and relationships between these and further lemmas.[2] On the basis of these comparisons, they compiled lists of about 20 key lemmas conveying the source domains BUILDING and MOTION. Lastly, they searched for these lemmas in the corpus and found many new occurrences of metaphors.

Finally, Semino et al. (2005) exploited the semantic annotation tool in the online software Wmatrix software to compare the metaphors in a scientific journal, *Nature Immunology*, with a popular scientific journal, *New Scientist* (cf. Rayson 2015). Their software automatically categorized their data into semantic domains, and they then used it to see which semantic domains were over-represented in each journal. The idea was that some of these semantic domains could represent metaphorical source domains. They found out, for example, that the popular science articles were richer in some metaphoric source domains, such as WAR (e.g. 'how the immune system's <u>front-line</u> <u>troops</u> recognise the <u>enemy</u>').

An example of current research: a case study on hope

Let us now turn to a case study of recent research. Building on an earlier diachronic study of metaphors of love in English (Tissari 2003) I set out to investigate metaphors of hope in four corpora – two representing Early Modern English and two representing Present-Day English: the 450,000-word *Corpus of Early English Correspondence Sampler* (CEECS, 1418–1680); the 551,000-word Early Modern English period of the *Helsinki Corpus of English Texts* (HCE, 1500–1710); the one-million-word corpora the *Freiburg-LOB Corpus of British English* (FLOB, 1991); and the *Freiburg-Brown Corpus of American English* (FROWN, 1991).

In an earlier unpublished study on Old English, Fabiszak and Hebda (2009) suggested that hope was a 'peripheral emotion': it shared some metaphors with other emotions, but not the EMOTION IS FORCE metaphor, because 'hope is not conceptualised as a dynamic force influencing human lives at the present moment, but rather as a foundation for structuring these lives in the future'. I thus set out to see whether the same would apply to hope later in the history of English. My method was based on searching for particular target domain words in corpora. I chose to investigate the verb and noun *hope* and their derivatives to see what kind of metaphors of hope occurred with them.

To search for a word in historical English data is not as simple as to search for a word in Present-Day English data, because not only different forms but also many spelling variants occur. I therefore created an alphabetical word list of each historical corpus, read through the words beginning with *ho-* and collected the *hope* words. To be sure I covered all the spelling variants, I checked the *Oxford English Dictionary* (2015) for them. All the variant forms given for the noun and verb *hope* in it began with *ho*.

Eventually, the noun and verb *hope* and their derivatives were found to occur 603 times in CEECS, with many variants: *hoape, hooge, hop, hope, hoped, hopefull, hopefullness, hopeing, hopeles, hopes, hopet, hopeth, hopid, hoping, hopinge, hoppe, hoppes, hopping, hops, hopyd, hopyng* and *hopyt*. In all, the *hope* words occurred 1.34 times per 1,000 words in CEECS, which was far more often than in the other corpora. The number of occurrences of the *hope* words in the Early Modern English period of HCE was 222 and comprised the spelling variants: *hope, hoped, hopefull, hopeing, hopeles, hopes, hopeth, hoping, hopinge, hopynge* and *hoope*. This was 0.40 occurrences per 1,000 words. The total of *hope* words in FLOB was 341, which was 0.34 times per 1,000 words. Lastly, the total of *hope* words in FROWN was 320, yielding a frequency of 0.32 occurrences per 1,000 words.

Before any research on metaphor was conducted, there was an important finding: The *hope* words were more frequent in CEECS and HCE than in FLOB and FROWN, although the difference between HCE and the Present-Day English corpora was not as notable as that between CEECS and the rest of the corpora. A look at the data suggested that people often reported their own hopes in CEECS and HCE: 73 per cent of all the occurrences of the form *hope* in CEECS and 60 per cent of those in HCE occurred in the phrase *I hope*, while the corresponding figures for FLOB and FROWN did not rise over 30 per cent. It thus seemed that letters especially invited reports of personal hope, but also that the early corpus data as a whole behaved differently from the Present-Day English data. The same had already been observed in my research on *fear, love* and *shame* – these words were more frequent in CEECS and HCE than in FLOB and FROWN (Koivisto-Alanko and Tissari 2006: 196; Tissari 2006a: 144). Why this should be so remains something of a mystery: there might be one overarching reason, but the reasons could also vary from emotion to emotion.

I conducted the actual analysis by reading all the sentences in which the *hope* words occurred in order to see if hope was conceptualized metaphorically. Stefanowitsch (2006b) called this method metaphorical pattern analysis (MPA). He defines a metaphorical pattern as 'a multi-word expression from a given source domain (SD) into which one or more specific lexical item [sic] from a given target domain (TD) have been inserted' (Stefanowitsch 2006b: 66). For example, I identified a metaphorical pattern in the following sentence (the pattern is underlined, and the *hope* word in italics):

(4) Many others, though, have lost the houses that were home, that were <u>built with</u> *hope*, sweat, and large, scary mortgages.

FROWN: The Miami Herald 19

This pattern was considered metaphorical because houses are not literally built with hope, but, rather, with machines and tools. In line with an earlier study (Koivisto-Alanko and Tissari 2006: 197–8), I labelled the relevant source domain INSTRUMENT and the underlying conceptual metaphor HOPE IS AN INSTRUMENT.

The naming of the metaphors was nevertheless a challenging task. A choice to call a particular source domain INSTRUMENT, for example, ruled out other options. Example (4) could also have been analysed as HOPE IS A TOOL or HOPE IS A MACHINE. Even HOPE IS BUILDING MATERIAL and HOPE IS MONEY appear viable. I googled *build a house with* and found websites dedicated to building houses with hemp, pallets, straw etc., while a search for *built with* in the BNC produced examples where, for example, schools were '*built with* public rather than private money' (*Converting Old Buildings* 1985–1993: 772). For the sake of comparison, example (5) is an Early Modern instance of the metaphor HOPE IS AN INSTRUMENT:

(5) Sir, I was muche <u>comforted and refreshed with</u> *hope* that, by your good meanes and your sonne's, my brother should have had present delyverye from his long and tedious imprisonment . . .

CEECS: 1627 Talbot Bowes 315

It should be mentioned that the metaphorical patterns I identified were not always multi-word expressions. Even Stefanowitsch (2006b: 74) accepted *burning anger* and *fierce anger* as metaphorical, although they attested only one source domain word. A relevant example from the present data was:

(6) A solid performance, particularly up front, will <u>give</u> Wales *hope* and open the way for a better World Cup challenge next month.

FLOB: Evening Standard 23

This metaphor, signalled by the verb *give*, was labelled HOPE IS A VALUABLE COMMODITY. It was modelled after the metaphor LOVE IS A VALUABLE COMMODITY (cf. Kövecses 1986: 95; Tissari 2003: 159, 380).

Eight main categories of metaphors were distinguished in the data: HOPE IS A VALUABLE COMMODITY, HOPE IS A CONTAINER, HOPE IS A FLUID IN A CONTAINER (IN THE BODY), HOPE IS AN INSTRUMENT, HOPE IS A MEASURABLE QUANTITY, HOPE IS AN INANIMATE ENTITY (OTHER than e.g. COMMODITY, CONTAINER), HOPE IS AN ANIMATE ENTITY and HOPE IS UP. I have already given examples of two metaphors. Below, I will give examples of the rest.

The metaphor HOPE IS A CONTAINER suggested that someone can be inside hope:

(7) But we lyue <u>in</u> *hope* that we shall shortly receiue you againe, I pray God hartely we may, if it be his holy wyll.

HCE: Private letter by Margaret Roper 511

The metaphor HOPE IS A FLUID IN A CONTAINER (THE BODY) occurred only once in the early data, but several times in the Present-Day English data:

(8) For poor people, seeking medical care from the marketplace <u>drains</u> them <u>of</u> *hope* and resources (Trevino and Moss 1983).

FROWN: See, 'African-American Society and Education' 22

The metaphor HOPE IS A MEASURABLE QUANTITY was frequent in the early data, but rare in the Present-Day English data:

(9) As for ther beegninninge, it is but vntoward, wth <u>lyttle</u> *hope* of good suckses.

CEECS: 1625 Thomas Meautys 1 117

(10) Still, reading autobiography, while it does not <u>increase</u> one's *hope* for the race, does lend vast amusement in watching it all pass in review from the rail.

FROWN: Epstein, 'First Person Singular' 15

I had not used the source domain label MEASURABLE QUANTITY in my previous research, but I had paid attention to emotions being quantified (Tissari 2003: 336–8; Tissari 2006a: 147, 149; Tissari 2006b: 24, 26, 33, 41). In a way, this metaphor went together with HOPE IS A VALUABLE COMMODITY, because the more hope there was, the better. It was nevertheless important to distinguish between these two metaphors, because greater amount does not

Table 8.1 Metaphors of hope in the corpora per 10,000 words

Corpus	COMM	CONT	FLUID	INSTR	QUANT	INAN	ANIM	UP	Total
HCE	0.22	0.27	0.00	0.05	0.40	0.15	0.07	0.02	1.18
CEECS	0.73	0.87	0.02	0.20	0.93	0.13	0.11	0.07	3.07
Total HCE + CEECS	0.45	0.54	0.01	0.12	0.64	0.14	0.09	0.04	2.03
FLOB	0.21	0.13	0.04	0.04	0.02	0.15	0.04	0.05	0.67
FROWN	0.21	0.16	0.02	0.04	0.04	0.04	0.06	0.03	0.60
Total FLOB + FROWN	0.21	0.15	0.03	0.04	0.03	0.10	0.05	0.04	0.64

Abbreviations of source domains: COMM = VALUABLE COMMODITY, CONT = CONTAINER, FLUID = FLUID IN A CONTAINER, INSTR = INSTRUMENT, QUANT = MEASURABLE QUANTITY, INAN = INANIMATE ENTITY (OTHER), ANIM = ANIMATE ENTITY and UP = UP.

always equal greater value. Consider shame, for example: More shame tends not to be better than less shame.

The metaphor category HOPE IS AN INANIMATE ENTITY (other than e.g. COMMODITY, CONTAINER) comprised sub-metaphors such as HOPE IS A ROCK and HOPE IS A FRAGILE OBJECT:

(11) ... God doeth nothing else but lead vs along by the hand, til he haue setled vs vpon <u>the rocke</u> of an assured *hope*, that no one iote or title of his word shall passe till all be fulfilled?
HCE: Hooker, Two sermons upon part of S. Judes Epistle 8

(12) But councillors in Warwick <u>have dashed</u> the club's *hopes*.
FLOB: Coventry Evening Telegraph 7

The metaphor label HOPE IS AN ANIMATE BEING did not specify whether this entity was a human, an animal or a plant. I had made such distinctions in previous research but found them problematic (e.g. Tissari 2003: 372–3). In example (13), hope was clearly an animal, but in example (18), it could be any animate being:

(13) *Hope* is a <u>curtall-dog</u> in some affaircs: Sir Iohn affects thy wife.
HCE: Shakespeare: The Merry Wives of Windsor 44

(14) Faith and charity were in eclipse and even *hope* <u>died</u> at last.
FLOB: Candour 8

The metaphor HOPE IS UP is related to the metaphors HAPPY IS UP and GOOD IS UP which, according to Lakoff and Johnson (1980: 14–21) are based on physiological well-being being signalled by an upward posture:

(15) True, Linda had had a few boyfriends and had <u>high</u> *hopes* of at least two of them resulting in the kind of close, loving, long-term relationship she really wanted, but somehow it didn't happen.
FLOB: Dryden, How to Untangle Your Emotional Knots 23

Table 8.1 shows the occurrences of each metaphor category per corpus. These are reported as instances per 10,000 words in each corpus, because the Late Middle and Early Modern English corpora are not directly comparable with the Present-Day English corpora, being only about half the size of FLOB and FROWN.

I used raw figures of metaphors per corpus to statistically compare the findings for the two periods with each other. A chi square test suggested that there was a statistically highly significant difference between them ($x^2 = 47.65857$, df = 7, p = 4.15E-08). In other words, the meaning of the *hope* words, "measured" in terms of metaphors, had changed between the two periods studied.

Table 8.1 can be used to zoom in on the differences between the two periods. It seems that these differences were greater with respect to some metaphor categories than others. There were more than twice as many VALUABLE COMMODITY metaphors, three times as many INSTRUMENT metaphors, more than three and a half times as many CONTAINER metaphors and 21 times as many MEASURABLE QUANTITY metaphors in the early data than in the Present-Day English data. The only metaphor that was more frequent in the Present-Day English data than in the early data was HOPE IS A FLUID IN A CONTAINER, which was three times more frequent in the former than in the latter.

Table 8.1 also suggests that the difference between HCE and the Present-Day English corpora was small as regards the metaphors HOPE IS A VALUABLE COMMODITY and HOPE IS AN INSTRUMENT, but bigger as regards the metaphor HOPE IS A CONTAINER, and substantial as regards the metaphor HOPE IS A MEASURABLE QUANTITY. This indicated that the meaning of the *hope* words may have changed less than a comparison between CEECS and the Present-Day English data would suggest.

Taking the data as a whole, to what extent is HOPE metaphorically conceptualized like other emotions? Lakoff, Espenson and Schwartz's Master Metaphor List (1991: 140–7) contains nine general metaphors for emotion, such as EMOTIONS ARE FORCES (*She was carried away by the song*) and INTENSE EMOTIONS ARE HEAT (*The crowd was all fired up*). Of these, only three occur in my data as a whole: EMOTIONS ARE ENTITIES WITHIN A PERSON (HOPE IS A FLUID IN A CONTAINER), EMOTIONS ARE LOCATIONS (HOPE IS A CONTAINER) and EMOTIONAL SELF IS A BRITTLE OBJECT (≈HOPE IS A FRAGILE OBJECT), the HOPE IS A CONTAINER metaphor being a subcategory of the more general STATES ARE CONTAINERS metaphor (Lakoff and Johnson 1980: 30). The Master Metaphor List also listed three metaphors of hope: HOPE IS A BENEFICIAL POSSESSION (*I have hope that he will return*), HOPE IS A CHILD (*I'm nursing a hope for a better life*) and HOPE IS LIGHT (*He has bright hopes*; Lakoff, Espenson and Schwartz 1991: 151–2). Of these, only the metaphor HOPE IS A BENEFICIAL POSSESSION (HOPE IS A VALUABLE COMMODITY) occurred in the present data.

The present data corroborated Fabiszak and Hebda's suggestion (2009) that hope was a peripheral emotion which did not attest all the metaphors of emotions, and particularly not the EMOTIONS ARE FORCES metaphor. This applied to all the data. However, as usual in research, this study also suggested new research questions, especially the following: (1) It would have been possible to compare the metaphors found in the present data with other listings of metaphors of emotions, for example Kövecses's description of emotion (1990: 144–81). That being the case, how do we know which list is closest to describing emotions as against other concepts? (2) If HOPE is not conceptualized like an emotion, is it conceptualized like something else, for example, like a virtue?[3] Question two also has a follow-up question which has not been researched within cognitive linguistics: How is virtue conceptualized?

A further question is whether we would have found all the metaphors characterizing emotions in the vicinity of *hope* words if we had had large enough data. As Stefanowitsch (2006b: 91) suggested: '[G]iven a large enough corpus, all metaphors will be instantiated for all emotions'. I used the examples in the Master Metaphor List to Google words and phrases (underlined) occurring with the noun *hope*, and found all the missing metaphors for emotions online:[4] EMOTIONS ARE ENTITIES WITHIN A PERSON (*God wants you to be filled with* hope[5]), EMOTIONS ARE FORCES (*Carried Forward By Hope*, a book title[6]), INTENSE EMOTIONS ARE HEAT (*Burning Hope Ministries*[7]), EMOTION IS MOTION (*Moved by Hope*: Burlington Hope Run/Walk set for May 17[8]), EFFECT ON EMOTIONAL SELF IS CONTACT WITH PHYSICAL SELF (*Touched By Hope*, free medical clinic[9]),

STRONG EMOTIONS ARE MADNESS (*Dreams Gone Mad With Hope*, book title[10]) and STRONG EMOTION IS BLINDING (*Blinded by Hope, Dazzled by Detail*, title of a CNN news story[11]). This confirmed Stefanowitch's suggestion (2006b: 91). However, it seemed that several of these metaphors were what you might call creative metaphors. The metaphors which were gleaned from the corpora were thus likely to represent the more frequent varieties of metaphors of hope.

Reflections on the past, present and future of corpus linguistic research on metaphors

When I was a PhD student at the turn of the millennium, one of my colleagues said that I could not use electronic corpora to study metaphors. Today, however, it is no longer a novel idea to use an electronic corpus to study metaphors. To mention a milestone in the field, Stefanowitsch and Gries (2006) were able to bring together a number of researchers combining research on metaphor with corpus linguistics. Their volume combined softer, more qualitative approaches to the topic such as Semino's work on metaphors for speech activity (2006) with more quantitative and computational work such as Martin's on context effects on metaphor comprehension (2006). More importantly, Stefanowitsch and Gries (2006) were able to show that corpus linguistics had become part and parcel of metaphor research and that there were many potential ways of approaching metaphors in corpora, ranging from considering metaphors as fuzzy categories (Hanks 2006) to including the study of metaphor in discourse analysis (Koller 2006; Partington 2006).

Moreover, Stefanowitsch (2006a, b) was able to suggest that there was still much to do in the field. For example, he proposed that the method of searching for metaphors occurring together with target domain lexis should be systematically applied to a large number of concepts (Stefanowitsch 2006b: 102–3). He also envisioned that corpus-based research on metaphor should involve more elaborate statistical methods (Stefanowitsch 2006a: 12). These goals still seem worth aspiring to. The first one relates to my case study on hope: we still do not have exhaustible corpus evidence of which metaphors distinguish emotions from other concepts, for example. The second one relates to what has been called the "quantitative turn" in cognitive linguistics (Janda 2013), which is increasingly affecting metaphor research.

What I have to say about the future of corpus linguistic research on metaphor concerns small corpora and big corpora or, even more generally, small data and big data. We have just seen how even small corpora can be used to study conceptual metaphors and how metaphor can be an indicator of semantic change. We indeed seem to be at an interesting juncture where things are happening both on a small scale and a large scale. Small data can be analysed by hand when there is a need to conduct analyses which computers cannot perform yet. In particular, new approaches to metaphors can be tested on small data. Examples of important "experiments" on small data include the Hamburg Metaphor Database whose compilers collected and analysed metaphors from a French corpus to create a metaphor resource which could be used, for instance, to predict metaphors in other data (Lönneker-Rodman 2008); and the even more recent VU Amsterdam Metaphor Corpus which is the 'largest available corpus hand-annotated for *all* metaphorical language use, regardless of lexical field or semantic domain', 'based on a systematic and explicit metaphor identification protocol' and which 'covers about 190,000 lexical units from a subset of four broad registers from the BNC-Baby' (Welcome to the VU Amsterdam Metaphor Corpus *Online*! 2015; see also Steen et al. 2010).

Even small data do not exclude statistical analysis, but it is big data which especially require quantitative methods. As bigger and bigger data become available, research on metaphor is likely to develop towards more and more linguistic computing. And vice versa, advances in linguistic computing facilitate the conducting of research on metaphor on a large scale (e.g. see the 'Mapping Metaphor' project described in Chapter 16). It is to be expected that data mining techniques will be used more and more to find metaphor in big data and that the automatic detection of metaphor will be significantly improved even in the near future. To conclude, if you want to be innovative in corpus-based metaphor research, I suggest that you study a concept that has not been studied yet, do something that has not been manually done yet, or venture to develop the large-scale statistical analysis of metaphors.

Notes

1 From now on, I will use the term *corpus* to refer to an electronic corpus.
2 See EuroWordNet (2001) for further information on EuroWordNet.
3 I thank prof. Dirk Geeraerts for this suggestion.
4 On 23 June 2015.
5 http://www.joycemeyer.org/ProductDetail.aspx?id=006932.
6 http://www.amazon.com/Carried-Forward-Bregdan-Chronicles-Historical-ebook/dp/B00K6IBRYE.
7 http://www.burning-hope-ministries.org/Burning_Hope_Ministries/Welcome.html.
8 http://journaltimes.com/lifestyles/health-med-fit/moved-by-hope-burlington-hope-run-walk-set-for-may/article_e28b108c-cfea-11e3-b2b2-0019bb2963f4.html.
9 http://www.wakeforestnc.gov/3rd-annual-free-medical-clinic-touched-by-hope-2013-11-02.aspx.
10 http://www.goodreads.com/book/show/21433371-dreams-gone-mad-with-hope.
11 http://edition.cnn.com/HEALTH/bioethics/9903/research.dangers/template.html.

Further reading

Deignan, A. (2005) *Metaphor and Corpus Linguistics*, Amsterdam, The Netherlands: John Benjamins.
Loenneker-Rodman, B. and Narayanan, S. (2012) 'Computational approaches to figurative language', in M. Spivey, K. McRae and M. Joanisse (eds) *The Cambridge Handbook of Psycholinguistics*, New York: Cambridge University Press, pp. 485–504.
Stefanowitsch, A. and Gries, S. Th. (eds) (2006) *Corpus-based Approaches to Metaphor and Metonymy*, Berlin, Germany: Mouton de Gruyter.

References

Berber Sardinha, T. (2012) 'An assessment of metaphor retrieval methods', in F. MacArthur, J. L. Oncins-Martínez, M. Sánchez-García and A. M. Piquer-Píriz (eds) *Metaphor in Use: Context, Culture, and Communication*, Amsterdam, The Netherlands: John Benjamins, pp. 21–50.
British National Corpus (BNC), *The*. Online. Available at: http://corpus.byu.edu/bnc/.
Cameron, L. and Deignan, A. (2003) 'Combining large and small corpora to investigate tuning devices around metaphor in spoken discourse', *Metaphor and Symbol*, 18(3): 149–60.
Charteris-Black, J. (2004) *Corpus Approaches to Critical Metaphor Analysis*, Basingstoke, UK: Palgrave Macmillan.
Collins Corpus, The. (2007–2013) Online. Available at: http://www.collins.co.uk/page/The+Collins+Corpus.
Crystal, D. (2008) *A Dictionary of Linguistics and Phonetics*, 6th edn, Oxford, UK: Blackwell.
Davies, M. (1990–2012) *The Corpus of Contemporary American English* (COCA). Online. Available at: http://corpus.byu.edu/coca/.
Deignan, A. (1999) 'Corpus-based research into metaphor', in L. Cameron and G. Low (eds) *Researching and Applying Metaphor*, Cambridge, UK: Cambridge University Press, pp. 177–99.
—— (2005) *Metaphor and Corpus Linguistics*, Amsterdam, The Netherlands: John Benjamins.

—— (2008) 'Corpus linguistics and metaphor', in R. W. Gibbs, Jr. (ed.) *The Cambridge Handbook of Metaphor and Thought*, New York: Cambridge University Press, pp. 280–94.
EuroWordNet: Building a multilingual database with wordnets for several European languages. (2001) Online. Available at: http://www.illc.uva.nl/EuroWordNet/.
Fabiszak, M. and Hebda, A. (2009) 'Hope in Old English', an unpublished manuscript.
—— (2010) 'Cognitive historical approaches to emotions: Pride', in M. E. Winters, H. Tissari and K. Allan (eds) *Historical Cognitive Linguistics*, Berlin, Germany: De Gruyter Mouton, pp. 261–97.
Fass, D. (1991) 'met*: A method for discriminating metonymy and metaphor by computer', *Computational Linguistics*, 17(1): 49–90.
Fellbaum. C. (2006) 'WordNet(s)', in K. Brown, A. Anderson, L. Bauer, M. Berns, J. Miller and G. Hirst (eds) *Encyclopedia of Language and Linguistics*, 2nd edn, Oxford, UK: Elsevier, pp. 665–70.
Hanks, P. (2006) 'Metaphoricity is gradable', in A. Stefanowitsch and S. Th. Gries (eds) *Corpus-based Approaches to Metaphor and Metonymy*, pp. 17–35.
Hardie, A., Koller, V., Rayson, P. and Semino, E. (2007) 'Exploiting a semantic annotation tool for metaphor analysis'. Online. Available at: http://eprints.lancs.ac.uk/13010/1/49_Paper.pdf.
Hintikka, M. (2013) *The Well-Being of the Body as Metaphor for Society and Mind: A Corpus-based Comparison of Early Modern and Present-Day English*, Helsinki, Finland: Société Néophilologique.
Hoffmann, S. (1996–2013) *The BNCWeb (CQP edition)*. Online. Available at: http://bncweb.lancs.ac.uk/bncwebSignup/user/login.php.
Janda, L. A. (2013) 'Quantitative methods in *Cognitive Linguistics*: An introduction', in L. A. Janda (ed.) *Cognitive Linguistics: The Quantitative Turn: The Essential Reader*, Berlin, Germany: De Gruyter Mouton, pp. 1–32.
Koivisto-Alanko, P. and Tissari, H. (2006) 'Sense and sensibility: Rational thought versus emotion in metaphorical language', in A. Stefanowitsch and S. Th. Gries (eds) *Corpus-based Approaches to Metaphor and Metonymy*, pp. 191–213.
Koller, V. (2004a) *Metaphor and Gender in Business Media Discourse: A Critical Cognitive Study*. Basingstoke, UK: Palgrave Macmillan.
—— (2004b) 'Businesswomen and war metaphors: "Possessive, jealous and pugnacious"?', *Journal of Sociolinguistics*, 8(1): 3–22.
—— (2006) 'Of critical importance: Using electronic text corpora to study metaphor in business media discourse', in A. Stefanowitsch and S. Th. Gries (eds) *Corpus-based Approaches to Metaphor and Metonymy*, pp. 237–66.
Koller, V., Hardie, A., Rayson, P. and Semino, E. (2008) 'Using a semantic annotation tool for the analysis of metaphor in discourse', *Metaphorik.de*, 15: 141–60. Online. Available at: http://www.metaphorik.de/sites/www.metaphorik.de/files/journal-pdf/15_2008_koller.pdf.
Kövecses, Z. (1986) *Metaphors of Anger, Pride and Love: A Lexical Approach to the Structure of Concepts*, Amsterdam, The Netherlands: John Benjamins.
—— (1988) *The Language of Love: The Semantics of Passion in Conversational English*, Lewisburg, PA: Bucknell University Press.
—— (1990) *Emotion Concepts*, New York: Springer.
—— (2000) *Metaphor and Emotion: Language, Culture, and Body in Human Feeling*, Cambridge, UK: Cambridge University Press.
Lakoff, G. (1987) *Women, Fire, and Dangerous Things: What Categories Reveal about the Mind*, Chicago, IL: University of Chicago Press.
Lakoff, G., Espenson, J. and Schwartz, A. (1991) *Master Metaphor List*, second draft copy, Berkeley, CA: University of California at Berkeley. Online. Available at: http://araw.mede.uic.edu/~alansz/metaphor/METAPHORLIST.pdf.
Lakoff, G. and Johnson, M. (1980) *Metaphors We Live By*, Chicago, IL: University of Chicago Press.
—— (1999) *Philosophy in the Flesh: The Embodied Mind and Its Challenge to Western Thought*, New York: Basic Books.
Lönneker-Rodman, B. (2008) 'The Hamburg metaphor database project: Issues in resource creation', *Language Resources & Evaluation*, 42: 293–318.

Martin, J. H. (1990) *A Computational Model of Metaphor Interpretation*, San Diego, CA: Academic Press.

Mason, Z. J. (2004) 'CorMet: A computational, corpus-based conventional metaphor extraction system', *Computational Linguistics*, 30(1): 23–44.

Oxford English Dictionary, The. (2015) Online. Available at: http://www.oed.com/.

Partington, A. (2006) 'Metaphors, motifs and similes across discourse types: Corpus-Assisted Discourse Studies (CADS) at work', in A. Stefanowitsch and S. Th. Gries (eds) *Corpus-based Approaches to Metaphor and Metonymy*, pp. 267–304.

Pedersen, T. (2014) Wordnet::Similarity. Online. Available at: http://wn-similarity.sourceforge.net/.

Philip, G. (2011) *Colouring Meaning: Collocation and Connotation in Figurative Language*, Amsterdam, The Netherlands: John Benjamins.

Rayson, P. (2015) Wmatrix corpus analysis and comparison tool. Online. Available at: http://ucrel.lancs.ac.uk/wmatrix/.

Reining, A. and Lönneker-Rodman, B. (2007) 'Corpus-driven metaphor harvesting', in *Proceedings of the HLT/NAACL-07 Workshop on Computational Approaches to Figurative Language*, Rochester, NY, April 26, 2007, pp. 5–12. Online. Available at: http://dl.acm.org/citation.cfm?id=1611530.

Semino, E. (2006) 'A corpus-based study of metaphors for speech activity in British English', in A. Stefanowitsch and S. Th. Gries (eds) *Corpus-based Approaches to Metaphor and Metonymy*, pp. 36–62.

—— (2008) *Metaphor in Discourse*, New York: Cambridge University Press.

Semino, E., Hardie, A., Koller, V. and Rayson, P. (2005) 'A computer-assisted approach to the analysis of metaphor variation across genres', in J. Barnden, M. Lee, J. Littlemore, R. Moon, G. Philip and A. Wallington (eds) *Corpus-based Approaches to Figurative Language*, Birmingham, UK: University of Birmingham School of Computer Science, pp. 145–53. Online. Available at: http://eprints.lancs.ac.uk/33493/1/SeminoEtAl.pdf.

Semino, E. and Swindlehurst, K. (1996) 'Metaphor and mind style in Ken Kesey's *One Flew over the Cuckoo's Nest*', *Style*, 30(1): 143–66.

Steen, G., Dorst, A. G., Hermann, J. B., Kaal, A. A., Krennmayr, T. and Pasma, T. (2010) *A Method for Linguistic Metaphor Identification: From MIP to MIPVU*, Amsterdam, The Netherlands: John Benjamins.

Stefanowitsch, A. (2006a) 'Corpus-based approaches to metaphor and metonymy', in A. Stefanowitsch and S. Th. Gries (eds) *Corpus-based Approaches to Metaphor and Metonymy*, pp. 1–16.

—— (2006b) 'Words and their metaphors: A corpus-based approach', in A. Stefanowitsch and S. Th. Gries (eds) *Corpus-based Approaches to Metaphor and Metonymy*, pp. 63–105.

Stefanowitsch, A. and Gries, S. Th. (eds) (2006) *Corpus-based Approaches to Metaphor and Metonymy*, Berlin, Germany: Mouton de Gruyter.

Sweetser, E. (1990) *From Etymology to Pragmatics: Metaphorical and Cultural Aspects of Semantic Structure*, Cambridge, UK: Cambridge University Press.

Tissari, H. (2003) *LOVEscapes: Changes in Prototypical Senses and Cognitive Metaphors Since 1500*, Helsinki, Finland: Société Néophilologique.

—— (2006a) 'Conceptualizing shame: Investigating uses of the English word *shame*, 1418–1991', in R. W. McConchie, O. Timofeeva, H. Tissari and T. Säily (eds) *Selected Proceedings of the 2005 Symposium on New Approaches in English Historical Lexis (HEL-LEX)*, Somerville, MA: Cascadilla Proceedings Project, pp. 143–54. Online. Available at: http://www.lingref.com/cpp/hel-lex/2005/index.html.

—— (2006b) 'Justified pride? Metaphors of the word *pride* in English language corpora, 1418–1991', *Nordic Journal of English Studies*, 5(1): 15–49. Online. Available at: https://gupea.ub.gu.se/handle/2077/204/simple-search?query=tissari.

Ureña Gómez-Moreno, J. and Faber, P. (2011) 'Strategies for the semi-automatic retrieval of metaphorical terms', *Metaphor and Symbol*, 26(1): 23–52.

Welcome to the VU Amsterdam Metaphor Corpus *Online*! (2015) Online. Available at: http://www.vismet.org/metcor/documentation/home.html.

9
Analysing metaphor in gesture
A set of metaphor identification guidelines for gesture (MIG-G)

Alan Cienki

Introduction

While many metaphor scholars nowadays might find it natural, and even expected, that there would be a chapter in a volume such as this concerning the analysis of metaphor in gesture, this view is relatively recent in the field of metaphor studies. Though the idea that gestures could constitute a form of metaphoric expression was suggested at least as early as Wundt (1922), it was McNeill's (1992) book *Hand and Mind* which brought the different functions of gestures, including metaphoric representation, to a broad audience. (See Cienki and Müller 2008b for more historical background on the field of study.) However, in order to sensibly look for metaphor in gesture, the first issue to consider is how one is understanding the term 'metaphor'.

The study of metaphor as 'seeing as'

Let us begin with an example from Cienki (2010: 203–204), where someone speaking about making a decision between what is morally right to do and what is wrong says, 'you have to draw your line, and figure out on which side of it you fall'. We might understand a metaphor in this context in how the phrase 'draw your line' can refer to the demarcation of two physically separated spaces, which in the context of a binary opposition (between right and wrong) can be seen as a metaphorical separation of the moral categories in terms of a spatial division. However, if we think about the relevant words that were uttered in English ('draw your line'), they are just symbols for the ideas expressed (de Saussure 1959 [1916]); the sounds of the words have an arbitrary relation to the concepts 'draw', 'your', and 'line'. Contrast this with the phenomenon of onomatopoeia, as in the English words 'buzz' to describe the sound of a bee flying or 'meow' for the sound that a cat makes. The sound of the word maps onto the sound of the referent; the constant sound of the bee is represented through the 'continuant' consonant 'zz', and the change in the sound uttered by a cat is expressed with the two vowel sounds in 'meow'. Onomatopoeia relies on iconicity: a

A. Cienki

Figure 9.1 Gesture produced when saying 'draw your line'.

Source: Cienki (2010: 204).

relation between the form of an expression and the referent of the expression. However, the sounds of the words 'draw your line' do not iconically represent the spatial action of drawing something. Speech is sonic in nature and drawing is visual. The spoken words 'draw your line' are arbitrary symbols for the concepts they represent.

When gestures represent concepts, however, they often do so iconically. The iconic images they form can then serve as the bases of metaphors. Figure 9.1 shows the gesture produced by the speaker in the example above.

While saying 'you have to draw your line', he held the extended index finger of his right hand outward and moved it from shoulder-height straight downward to waist level. The form of the movement with that articulator, the tip of his index finger, affords visualization of a trace from the movement (what Leyton [1992: 145] calls recovering shape from motion) in the form of a vertical line. In the context of the previous and co-occurring talk, the creation of two physically separated spaces with the fingertip can be understood as a metaphor, as physically separating two spaces that symbolically stand for what is right and what is wrong. In this case, making a moral decision can be understood as dividing by means of a line. With this example, we already see a hint of how researching metaphor in gesture differs from researching metaphor in spoken words.

For some theoretical background we can turn to Burke's (1945: 503) description of metaphor as 'a way of seeing one thing in terms of something different'. When researching visible forms of expression, like gesture, his wording has special significance: when viewing speakers' gestures, we may see some characterization of the ideas they are expressing via the forms and movements of the hands. The hand shapes, orientations, and movements relate in various ways to the speakers' ideas (McNeill 1992, 2005). As the explication above also makes clear, we can understand Burke's words not just in terms of the physical seeing of imagery on which a metaphor is based, but also through the metaphor involved in Burke's own use of the word 'seeing', namely, 'seeing' as a metaphor for understanding.

In this way, the present chapter follows some aspects of the approach of Lakoff (1993) and Lakoff and Johnson (1980, 1999) by making a distinction between conceptual metaphors and metaphoric expressions: the former as conceptual mappings of elements of one (Source) domain onto another (Target) domain (see Chapter 1), and the latter as expressions in words, gestures, or other media that can be construed as metaphorical. Caveats here about both of these levels are that I am not assuming that conceptual mappings need to be made consciously, nor am I assuming that every use of an expression that can be analysed by a researcher as metaphorical necessarily entails a conceptual mapping on the part of the producer or the perceiver of the expression. I follow the interpretation implicit in Lakoff and Johnson's approach, which is made explicit in Müller (2008a), that metaphor involves not just Source and Target domains, but also an agent (usually a person) who makes the mapping. This approach grounds the notion of metaphor by specifying it relative to an interpreter. The interpreter can take various forms. It can be the producer of an expression, the one who perceives and comprehends it as metaphoric, someone who reasons in terms of a metaphor in a given moment (even without speaking), a computer that analyses an expression as metaphoric, or a researcher applying a procedure in terms of which an expression can be categorized as metaphoric, such as the Metaphor Identification Procedure or MIP of the Pragglejaz Group (2007).

Finally, metaphor – both on the conceptual level and on the level of expression – is approached here as a quality that can vary in terms of its degree of entrenchment within a given culture (in terms of fixedness versus novelty), its degree of saliency or prominence in its use in a given context, and its degree of 'richness' (that is, how much it is fleshed out, as opposed to how schematic it is). These points will be elaborated upon in the remainder of the chapter. What the researcher should bear in mind, however, is that what is at issue is the quality of 'metaphoricity', rather than a simple binary categorization of 'being' a metaphor or not. This is in line with viewing metaphor more as a process than as a product (Corradi Fiumara 1995; Gibbs 1994). We are therefore dealing with a dynamic view of metaphor (Kyratzis 1997; Müller 2008a; Stibbe 1996).

The study of gesture

With the term 'gesture', many people immediately think of the manual signs people make that have fixed meanings, such as holding up a closed fist with just the thumb extended upward to indicate one's positive evaluation of something. These kinds of gestures are described as 'emblems' (Efron 1972 [1941]), as they have fairly fixed forms and meanings within a given culture and are produced to intentionally communicate specific ideas. The fact that the form-meaning relation is fixed in such a conventional way allows for the production of dictionaries to illustrate them. See, for example, Saitz and Cervanka (1972) for U.S. American and Colombian, Wylie (1977) for French, and Monahan (1983) for

Russian. However, such gestures actually constitute only a small portion of the behaviours that speakers engage in most of the time, and as such, they will not be the focus of this chapter.

Much of the gesturing that speakers do spontaneously is behaviour that they are not even aware of; when seeing a video of themselves talking, people are often surprised to see that they were gesturing. By contrast, neurotypical adults are normally aware of the fact that they are talking, even if they are not normally aware of the details of their speech production.

Speech and gesture also have different semiotic statuses from each other. In the context of face-to-face conversation between people who can hear and see each other, gesture is a semiotic system that is normally more dependent on speech than speech is on gesture; speech generally provides more information than gesture (Kibrik 2010; Kibrik and Èl'bert 2008). We can see this difference if we watch a video recording of a conversation with the sound off versus if we hear it without looking at the video. A basic point is that whereas most morphemes, words, and some fixed phrases and constructions in a given language have shared, conventional meanings, with gesture, this is only clearly the case with the small category of gestural emblems. The rest of our gestural behaviour appears to range in degrees of conventionality of communicativeness. Some recurrent gestures within a culture constitute families of gesture types (Kendon 2004; Müller 2004), whereby each gesture family is used with a limited range of meanings or functions. Examples include a brushing away gesture to indicate dismissal of an idea, or a gesture with a loose hand rotating forward cyclically at the wrist to indicate some kind of continuing process (at least for speakers of many European languages) (Bressem and Müller 2014; Ladewig 2014). However, more idiosyncratic gestures (such as depiction of a strangely shaped object) are unique to particular contexts and therefore do not express entrenched meanings with conventionalized forms. As Kendon (1980) discusses, gesture types fall along a range of different degrees of conventionality with which they are used communicatively, leading McNeill (1992) to dub this scale 'Kendon's Continuum'. This range of conventionality in gestural form-meaning pairings raises questions about how one can make a judgement about whether a gesture is being used metaphorically or not, or to what degree, which we will explore below.

Analysing metaphor in gesture

Metaphor as used in gesture versus metaphor as used in words

At one end of the continuum, gestures that are more idiosyncratic are ones more uniquely determined by the communicative context, e.g. tracing a form in the air with one's fingertip to show the outline of a strangely shaped object's surface. Recurrent gestures hold an intermediate position on the scale of conventionality of their mappings between gestural forms and their meanings. At the other end of the continuum, the use of emblems involves behaviour that is determined more by convention, and these gestures are used across different contexts with less variability.

We might draw a comparison with verbal equivalents: the idiosyncratic kinds of gestural behaviours are more like onomatopoeic sounds in spoken language discussed above (e.g. imitating the sound of a car that won't start easily); such vocal sounds are more closely tied to the sound-form of the referent, and in that sense, they show great variance in how they are produced, depending on the referent. Nevertheless, speakers are normally not totally unconstrained in how they produce such sounds. Sound-production patterns from the language of the culture speakers are working within provide an implicit framework which one can test the boundaries of; sounds can be more 'tame' or 'wild' within a given language-culture (Rhodes 1994). In contrast, the category of emblem gestures, discussed above, is more like that of conventional lexical forms in a given language in terms of the relation between form and meaning. Recurrent gestures, an in-between category, and one that often expresses pragmatic functions (Kendon 2004), can be compared to some degree with several lexico-grammatical categories in speech (including evaluatives and stance-taking devices), but in general the functions such gestures express are often more diffuse. The fact that various types of recurrent gestures appear to constitute a large proportion of what we are doing when we are gesturing in everyday conversation (Ladewig 2014) has interesting implications for metaphor studies.

Analysing metaphors in a written text involves looking at the use of fairly conventionalized signs (words). This allows one to use procedures which assume that there are fixed forms of expression, such as lexical items (the MIP of Pragglejaz Group 2007; the MIPVU of Steen et al. 2010; see Chapter 5), or words and multi-word units (Cameron and Maslen 2010). Analysis of metaphor in spoken language can be performed similarly in many respects to the analysis of metaphor in written texts. However, there are a number of issues that complicate the picture, such as the underspecification of referents and the speakers' use of elements in their shared context for purposes of communication that may not be referenced verbally (Cameron 2003, 2008; Kaal 2012). This raises questions for the analysis of metaphor in talk beyond those encountered in analysing written texts, especially texts written for more traditional means of distribution (news print, novels, etc.). The forms of 'language' represented by sound imitations (shrieks, grunts, or saying 'whoosh') simply occur less frequently in most contexts of talk than do the more conventional lexical symbols. Analysis of metaphor in the use of these forms on the periphery of language is a more esoteric endeavour. Yet if we turn to analysing metaphor in gesture, it is much more akin to analysing metaphor in the highly iconic onomatopoetic forms than it is to analysing metaphor used in words on a page. Most of the time, speakers' gestures do not constitute the kinds of manual form-meaning pairings that are used in the sign languages of the Deaf (see Chapter 18 for details on metaphor in sign language).

This is what makes researching metaphor in gesture interesting and challenging, but it also means the process cannot be guided as easily by a clear, linear formulaic set of instructions. For example, the MIP procedure (Pragglejaz Group 2007) relies upon the ability to establish a word's conventional basic meaning. This is not possible for most gestures; they are not signs of a sign language. The notable exception is the category of emblems, but that is the exception that proves the rule.

The method below is therefore presented as a set of guidelines – points to consider in analysing metaphor in gesture, rather than as a procedure or recipe that one could follow in a linear fashion with gestures as input and metaphors versus non-metaphors as output. One could say that the research in the relatively young field of gesture studies has not developed to such a state to allow for that yet. But in fact, if such a procedure could even be developed, it would not do justice to the reality of the phenomenon of speakers' gestures.

Gestures are inherently multifunctional (Kok et al. 2016) and can be highly dependent on the co-gesture speech for their interpretation.

Preliminary considerations: the scope of the claims in research on metaphor in gesture

In observing gestural behaviours in context, the researcher can make claims about what the spatio-motoric forms of the gestures might represent – but it is important to bear in mind that this is an interpretive act on the part of the researcher. This brings to light the point that we can think of the gestural behaviour from the (at least) three perspectives of different types of 'interpreters' (to use the term introduced earlier):

- that of the producer of the behaviour (the first-person role);
- that of the observer in context (if there was one); observers can also be distinguished in terms of different roles, such as that of intended addressee (the second-person role), eavesdropper, passer-by, etc. (Clark 1996); or
- that of one viewing the video-recorded behaviour in a different place and at a later time than that in which it was produced (third-person role). This role can also be subdivided into gesture researcher, film viewer, viewer of a video posted on the internet, viewer of the video at an art installation, etc. One of several important factors here is the manner in which the video is viewed: how many times, with what technology, with what level of attention, for what purpose, etc.

It is important and useful for the researcher to make clear to him/herself (if not also to mention this in one's published analyses) which of these roles one is playing with respect to the behaviours one is making claims about. This can help make the scope of one's claims clearer and can thereby avoid misinterpretations of one's analyses.

In addition, the analysis involves trying to see when gesture is being used in a way that can be construed as representing a mapping of a concept from one domain to that of another domain. This is one point of using the guidelines below. Again, it is useful to make clear in one's work what claim the researcher is making about the interpretations being presented; we can observe and analyse behaviours, and make claims from our perspective as researchers, but we also need to spell out how we reached those conclusions through use of explicit methods. Ultimately, this can help the gesture researcher avoid the appearance of claiming to be a mind-reader.

Details of the proposed guidelines

There is currently no explicit, replicable procedure for identifying and analysing metaphor in gesture. Methods that are stated in published research for how gestures were categorized as metaphoric vary greatly, if they are mentioned at all. Indeed, many scholars, particularly in psychological research, following McNeill's (1992) analysis, count only gestures expressing the 'CONDUIT' metaphor as being metaphoric. The CONDUIT metaphor was first analysed by Reddy (1979/1993) and later picked up by Lakoff and Johnson (1980).

The metaphor is actually a set of metaphors (a metaphorical model; see also the Epilogue) that has to do with how we (in English and many other languages) talk about language itself – as if words or texts were containers that held meaning, and as if communication involved transferring these meaning-containers from one person to another, through a conduit. As Reddy notes, this tacit model is both powerful and pernicious in that it makes the process of communication appear deceptively simple. Gestures claimed to express this model are usually ones in which the palm of the open hand is held up, or the palms face each other as if holding something, when the speaker is discussing a genre or text type ('it was a Sylvester and Tweety cartoon' [McNeill 1992: 14]) or when the speaker is representing a unit of language as if it contained an idea; in these contexts, the hand shape and hand orientation could represent the holding of an object. However, as much other research has shown, the CONDUIT metaphor is not the only one we see in gesture; there are many ways in which gesture is used to represent ideas that can be construed as metaphoric (see, for example, Calbris 1990; Cienki 1998, 2013a; Cienki and Müller 2008a, 2008b).

Building on Cienki (2010), the following is a proposed set of heuristics that can help pave the way towards metaphor identification guidelines for gesture (MIG-G). The hope is that, at the very least, it can help guide researchers in considering factors in their coding that they might not have otherwise considered. It draws upon elements of the Method of Gesture Analysis developed in the project 'Towards a grammar of gesture' (http://www.togog.org), outlined in Bressem, Ladewig and Müller (2013). One could implement the guidelines using annotation software such as ELAN (http://tla.mpi.nl/tools/tla-tools/elan/; Wittenburg et al. 2006), which has become a standard means of coding video data for gesture research.

In applying the guidelines, one should be aware that there can be great differences between how people gesture in different cultures, in different contexts, in different genres of communication, and that there are considerable differences between individual styles of behaviour. It is helpful to view an extended portion of the video you will be analysing before you begin, in order to become accustomed to the speakers' style(s). In addition, the first two steps below are best done with the sound turned off, to help the analyst focus on the visible forms of the gestures without distraction or influence from the accompanying speech. An overview of the proposed set of guidelines is presented first, followed by an explication of it.

The guidelines are structured as follows:

1. identify the gesture strokes;
2. describe the four form features of each stroke;
3. identify if the gesture serves any referential function. If so,
4. identify the mode(s) of representation;
5. identify the physical referent(s) depicted in the gesture(s) (the potential Source domain);
6. identify the contextual topic being referenced (the potential Target domain);
7. is the topic being identified via a resemblance in experience to the referent depicted via the gesture? If so, the gesture can be identified as metaphorically used via the mapping that the topic [This Target Domain] is being likened to the referent depicted [This Source Domain].

A. Cienki

Explication of the steps.

1. *Identify the gesture strokes*

   The first step identifies units of analysis in gesture. This step can be done well when viewing the video without sound and in slow motion. Following Kendon (1980, 2004) and McNeill (1992), a simple prototypical manual gesture consists of initial movement of the hand from a rest position (preparation), a more dynamic phase of movement and tension in the hand (stroke), after which the hand may maintain the position reached at the end of the stroke (post-stroke hold). Then the hand either returns to a rest position (retraction) or proceeds to make a new gesture stroke. The stroke phase will provide the focus for analysis, as it is where the greatest amount of effort is exerted and it is the most significant phase of the gesture in terms of its function in relation to the discourse. Figure 9.2 shows the three main phases of a gesture unit: preparation, stroke and retraction. In this case the (left-handed) speaker is talking about writing, and produces a complex stroke, with a quick back-and-forth motion.

2. *Describe the four form features of each stroke*

   Many scholars in gesture studies have adopted the system developed in sign language research (from Stokoe 1960) of describing the manual forms involved according to a set of parameters (see Chapter 18). The details of form feature analysis can be found in Bressem (2013), but in brief, the features are:

   - hand shape (e.g. flat hand, single finger extended, etc.);
   - orientation (palm orientation [towards the speaker's own body, upward, etc.] and orientation of the phalanges of the hand [lateral, vertical, diagonal]);
   - movement (path, quality and direction); and
   - location in gesture space (centrally in front of the torso, peripheral beyond the shoulders, etc.).

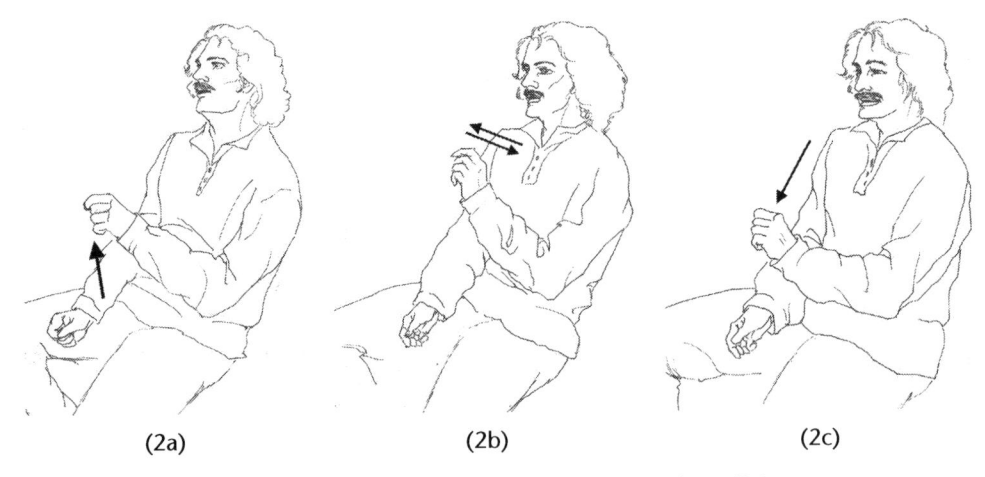

(2a) (2b) (2c)

Figure 9.2 Preparation phase (2a), stroke phase (2b), retraction phase (2c).

Source: From Cienki and Mittelberg (2013: 233).

While details will differ depending on how fine-grained the chosen system of description is for one's research project, for Figure 9.2b, we can say roughly that the handshape of the left hand is a relaxed fist, the palm faces the central space in front of the speaker and the phalanges of the hand are oriented upward, the movement of the stroke is back and forth laterally, and the location of the stroke is in the upper central space. For Figure 9.1, the handshape is such that the index finger is extended while the other fingers are curled, the palm is oriented diagonally between facing the centre gesture space and facing down while the phalanges of the hand point away from the body, the movement is straight down, and the location moves from upper to lower central gesture space. Making the form features of gestures explicit in this way, establishes an observable, verifiable starting point for the interpretations involved in the following steps.

3. *Identify if the gesture serves any referential function*
    For this and the following steps, one needs to hear the speech accompanying the gestures in order to carry out the interpretation. Most gestures can be seen as serving more than one function at once. They may relate to the topic of what the speaker-gesturer is saying, they may relate to the discourse itself and/or they may be orienting in some way towards the addressee (Kendon 2004). But one can at least begin with what the researcher sees from the context as the primary function of the given gesture. Below we will consider three functions of gesture which may be interpreted as involving some kind of reference: (a) primarily referential gestures, (b) gestures that highlight the structure of one's discourse, and (c) gestures that serve a pragmatic function.
    a) The gesture may represent some feature(s) of a referent in the verbal utterance that occurs with the gesture or in some temporal proximity to it. The qualification 'in some temporal proximity to it' concerns the fact that gestures often slightly precede the verbalization of concepts that they relate to. The referent may be a physical entity, relation, or action, in which case the gesture normally involves some kind of iconic representation of some feature(s) of the referent. For example, you might show the path that a ball took when rolling down a ramp by extending your index finger and moving it from upper left in a straight diagonal line down to your lower right side (see further details in step 4). On the other hand, the referent may be an abstract concept, which could be stative, relational, or processual in nature (like those represented by the words *devaluation*, *devaluating*, and *devalue*, respectively). In this case, the gesture may iconically represent some feature(s) of a physical referent in order to indicate the abstract referent, e.g. using one's extended finger to trace a line in the air that goes downward from left to right to indicate the devaluation undergone by a country's currency. As is made clear at later steps in these guidelines, this representation of the abstract (loss of value) in the physical forms of gestures (movement downward from left to right, as if a line on a graph) is a very common way in which metaphor appears in gesture. Note that the iconicity (here, the relation between the physical form of the referent and the spatial form of the gesture) with which gestures can represent something is a matter of degree. In minimal cases, the iconicity may be very schematic, such as with a raised extended finger itself standing for an idea when one is enumerating ideas on individual fingers.

Reference can also be accomplished by pointing, that is, deictically rather than through iconic representation. While it will be mentioned here only briefly, the complexity of the phenomenon should not be underestimated (see, e.g. Cienki 2013b, Clark 2003, Kita 2003 for details). Pointing for physical reference can be accomplished with a motion in the direction of the intended referent (or to put it more precisely: in the direction of where one conceptualizes the physical referent to be, as in pointing at a building that one cannot see at the moment) or in the direction one associates with the referent by metonymy (pointing at an empty chair when referring to someone who had just been sitting there). Pointing for abstract reference involves pointing at a space (or pointing at a finger on one's other hand, when counting off ideas) to refer to an abstract idea (McNeill, Cassell and Levy 1993). Abstract reference can include pointing to a space to refer to a physical referent when the space is not construed by the speaker as metonymically grounded by the referent, e.g. pointing to a space on the left to refer to one character and a space on the right to refer to another character in a story that one is telling.

b) Gesture can also refer to the structure of one's own discourse while one is talking. It can serve a parsing function (Kendon 1995, 2004), indicating one idea unit versus another by pointing to one space or another, via the speaker as if touching a space on one side next to him first and then the other side, or by holding out one's open hand palm up when presenting an idea (Müller 2004). Anticipating the other steps in these guidelines below, all of these types of parsing could be interpreted as involving reference to an idea as if it were a space: a kind of ontological metaphor (Lakoff and Johnson 1980: ch. 6). This kind of metaphoricity is thus more schematic than the more fully fleshed out iconic representations in category (a) above.

'Beat' gestures (usually involving a small rhythmic movement back and forth) can also structure discourse, usually through use coinciding with syllables that are stressed prosodically. They could be interpreted as also involving some reification of the discourse, and in that way, involving a schematic metaphoricity on the discourse level. But there is some indication that the structure of beats may even relate to metaphoric concepts potentially associated with the referents in the accompanying speech. Casasanto (2008) reported beats with the stress in the upward direction occurring at statistically significantly higher levels when people were talking about topics such as the weather becoming hotter and beats in the downward direction when talking about wanting to buy a cheaper car, even though the speakers were not using related verbal metaphoric expressions (such as *higher temperatures* or *a lower price*). In that regard, such beats can be viewed as involving backgrounded metaphoric reference to hotter temperatures as 'higher' and cheaper prices as 'lower'.

c) Some gestures primarily serve a pragmatic function, performing a speech act in relation to the accompanying talk, e.g. correlating with rejection of an idea by rapidly flapping the open hand downward from the wrist; showing that the speaker will continue one's idea soon by rotating a hand outward at the wrist; or indicating that feedback from the addressee is desired by holding out an open hand, palm up, oriented toward the addressee (Kendon 2004; Ladewig 2014). However, certain aspects of the gesture's use can be construed as entailing reference to the discourse or the ideas being expressed. For example, the 'throwing away' gesture of rejecting an idea involves a hand shape and motion that would be used with throwing down something small, and the cyclic rotating gesture can be seen as relating the ongoing talk to the mechanical process of a wheel or gear rotating. In this way, these gestures may involve a kind of backgrounded metaphoricity (Teßendorf 2014).

What we already see with these categories (which are not exhaustive of the possibilities) is a gradedness of possible metaphoricity. These factors can make a simple yes or no decision about metaphor in gesture problematic in that the quality (clarity of the identity of the source domains) of gestures then coded as metaphoric can differ so greatly. Note, though, that one could argue that there are some similar problematic aspects in making a binary yes/no decision about the metaphoric use of words as well (Müller and Tag 2010).

4. *Identify the mode(s) of representation*

    This step concerns moving from the manual forms in step 2, taking those gestures that serve referential functions determined in step 3 (other than the pointing gestures; for them, move directly to step 5), and articulating how they iconically refer to some referent and/or action or quality. The issue has been discussed in various ways in the literature, e.g. LeBaron and Streeck's (2000) analysis of motivations for gesture formation and Streeck's (2008) discussion of means of depicting by gestures. The following is based on Müller's (1998a, 1998b, 2014) characterization of the four means by which the hands are capable of depiction (in German: *Darstellungsweisen*). The names for them have varied over the years; here they will be called: enacting, embodying, holding/touching, and tracing.

    Enacting: The hand or hands move such that they represent engagement in a functional act, often one involving manipulating something, e.g. moving as if twisting open a bottle cap or as if writing with a pen (as seen in Figure 9.2), even though the speaker is not holding a bottle or a pen.

    Embodying: The hand stands for the entity it represents. Examples include when one moves one's extended pointer and forefinger in alternation across a surface, pretending they are the legs of a person walking, or if one holds one's two hands flat with palms pressed together to represent two pieces of bread that make a sandwich.

    Holding/touching: The palm-side of the hand or hands is as if adjacent to and conforms to an imagined entity. It might be as if holding something in mid-air (the curved hands facing each other as if holding a ball) and/or moving as if following the contour of the object's surface.

    Tracing: The hand or hands move as if to draw a form, usually with the tip(s) of the extended finger(s) being the 'active zone', moving so as to leave an imagined trace of the form being depicted. This is illustrated in the gesture in Figure 9.1, tracing a vertical line.

The modes need not be mutually exclusive categories. The hands positioned as if holding a ball could also be construed as if embodying the outer surface of the ball; dynamic holding/touching involves tracing in a three-dimensional way (see discussion in Cienki 2013b).

Metonymy plays a constitutive role in how the representing is done in all of these modes. In enacting, part of the whole action scene is represented (e.g. any objects one is representing themselves as manipulating are absent; the speaker in Figure 9.2 holds his hand as if writing, but is not actually holding a pen). In embodying, the hand cannot take on the complete form of another entity (the exception being if it is embodying another hand). In tracing and holding/touching, only a salient part of any form is shown. See Cienki (2013b) and Mittelberg and Waugh (2009) for details on the constitutive role played by metonymy in gestural reference.

5. *Identify the physical referent(s) referred to with the gesture(s)*

For representational gestures, state the entity being represented with the mode(s) determined in step 4. As stated above, this step clearly requires the accompanying speech in order to perform the necessary interpretation. For the gesture shown in Figure 9.1, the speaker said 'draw your line', indicating that it is the imagined trace left by the moving fingertip that is relevant. For the gesture made in Figure 9.2, the speaker said 'you have to write fast' when talking about writing an essay during an exam at the university, which supports the interpretation that the hand shape and movement have to do with writing by hand.

For pointing gestures, use the determination from step 3a as to whether physical or abstract pointing was involved and state the target of the point: a physical entity or a space.

If metaphoricity is established for the gesture in step 7 below, the referent identified in step 5 will be the potential Source Domain.

6. *Identify the contextual topic being referenced*

The contextual referent is often the idea being referred to in speech in temporal proximity to the gesture. However, for categories 3b and 3c above, it is the talk itself; the fact of a discourse unit being uttered may be the contextual topic of the gesture.

For representational gestures, state what the contextual referent is from the speech. For the gesture in Figure 9.1 this is the abstract idea of making of a decision between right and wrong, and for the one in Figure 9.2 it is the physical process of writing (by hand).

For pointing gestures, if the referent in step 6 is not physical, state what the contextual referent is (the relevant idea that is being referred to) in the speech.

If metaphoricity is established for the gesture in step 7, the contextual topic being referenced in step 6 will be the potential Target Domain.

7. *Is the topic being identified in step 6 related via a resemblance in experience to the referent* indicated with the gesture (step 5)? ('Resemblance in experience' should be understood here as: similarity that one could conceive of, such as an abstract process being like something moving through space, or a concept itself being like an object one could hold in one's hand.) If the answer to this question is yes, the gesture can be identified as metaphorically used. The mapping is: that [This Target Domain] is being likened to the referent depicted with [This Source Domain]. Most often with metaphorically used gestures, the Target is an abstract referent being depicted in spatial form (the Source) via the gesture. The gesture in Figure 9.1 becomes categorized as metaphorically used in terms of the mapping Making a Moral Decision is (like) Drawing a Line. The gesture in Figure 9.2, however, does not qualify as metaphorically used. It is representing writing by showing a characterization of the physical process of writing.

Critical issues

Gesture can be studied for many purposes, such as to find out more about discourse participants' roles in interaction (as explored in multimodal approaches to conversation analysis) or for typological analysis of how speakers of different languages conceptualize spatial motion events (as pursued in psycholinguistics and cognitive anthropology). But the study of a behaviour that has a different sign status than that of spoken or written words also raises some fundamental issues for metaphor theory. As noted above, researching metaphor in gesture makes questions about the possible *gradedness* of metaphor as a category even more salient. This issue comes to the fore from several perspectives.

One is the fact that, at least from the researcher's perspective, some gestures can be related more clearly to the topics being mentioned in the accompanying talk than others; that is, some gestures are more clearly playing a referential role. Whereas it is easier for two domains of experience to be invoked with referential gestures (one domain from the context and some aspect of another one depicted with the gesture), we have seen that even gestures that relate mainly to the discourse structure itself can be construed as involving metaphoricity in less obvious ways. Other gestures, though, may not relate to metaphor at all, such as those referring to physical objects or acts that are not being referred to metaphorically in the accompanying speech (gesturing as if writing with a pen when talking about physically writing with a pen is not metaphorical according to our guidelines).

Another way in which metaphor can be seen in a graded fashion in gestures is in the degree of specificity with which a Source Domain is depicted or not. Contrast (a) a detailed gestural form that clearly illustrates a point being made at the same time in speech (such as Müller's (2008b) example of someone illustrating her tumultuous first love relationship by tracing a wavy line up and down in the air that increasingly trends downward) with (b) a simple form of a hand turned outward (palm up) and back (palm down) when mentioning a problem that one is trying to solve. In the former case, the form of the Source Domain concept is depicted more specifically, and so it is clearer what it might be; in the latter case, the form of the gesture is not as clearly articulated, and consequently, any Source Domain concept being depicted is more vague (the problem being mentioned might be construed simply as a THING). In line with this, the former representation has more salient properties; as Müller (2008b) argues, the fact that the gesture is produced using a large amount of space, with great dynamism, and attracts the eye gaze of the producer as well as of the addressee is evidence of it being in the focus of attention of the speaker/gesturer and the listener/viewer. By contrast, the simple turning of one's hand outward and back, especially if it is done in the space near one's waist, is not salient visually. In addition, the former type of gesture is more effortful to produce, and may entail a more tense hand shape; the latter type is more relaxed and involves less effort. Expending greater versus lesser effort with a gesture is a way in which the Source Domain may be experienced with more or less awareness.

These different ways of analysing gesture – in terms of the level of detail in representation, the salience of its production, and the effort with which it was produced – all involve distinctions that are graded in nature, and can be interpreted as involving metaphor in a way that is more clear or less clear, to the producer and/or to the viewer, including to the researcher. This means there are different degrees of difficulty (or ease with which individual gestures may be interpreted as involving metaphor or not).

Implications for the study of metaphor in thought and future directions

Let us now return to the discussion at the beginning of the chapter about metaphor in gesture versus metaphor in spoken or written words. One hypothesis in cognitive psychological research is that gesture both reflects speakers' mental simulations of actions (Hostetter and Alibali 2008) and, in turn, influences listeners'/viewers' mental simulations (Cook and Tanenhaus 2009; see Marghetis and Bergen 2014 for an overview). This makes a strong case for the potential of gesture to communicate not just iconic representations of the physical world, but also iconic representations of things, relations, and actions that the speaker/gesturer is mapping onto concepts of abstract entities, relations, and processes – what we can call metaphoric conceptualizations. It is worth bearing in mind, however, that both the speaker/gesturer and the hearer/viewer may have various degrees (from extremely high to zero) of being consciously aware of engaging in such metaphoric conceptualization. Speakers are often not even aware of the gestures that they are producing (McNeill 1992), and as Beattie and Shovelton (1999) demonstrate, listeners/viewers can acquire spatial information from speakers' gestures without conscious awareness of it. This raises interesting questions for future research about what kinds of metaphors we live by in gestures and about the influences metaphorically used gestures may have on those who produce them and those who perceive them, both unwittingly in everyday talk and through intentional use in genres of persuasive discourse.

Acknowledgements

This research was supported by Russian Science Foundation grant #14-48-00067. Thanks to Yoriko Dixon for the illustrations for Figure 9.2.

Further reading

Cameron, L. and Maslen, R. (eds) (2010) *Metaphor Analysis: Research Practice in Applied Linguistics, Social Sciences and the Humanities*. London: Equinox.
Cienki, A. (2013) 'Conceptual metaphor theory in light of research on gesture with speech', *Cognitive Semiotics*, 5(1–2): 349–366.
Cienki, A. and Müller, C. (eds) (2008) *Metaphor and Gesture*. Amsterdam, The Netherlands: Benjamins.
Müller, C. et al. (eds) (2013 and 2014) *Body – Language – Communication*. Berlin, Germany: Mouton de Gruyter.

References

Beattie, G. and Shovelton, H. (1999) 'Mapping the range of information contained in the iconic hand gestures that accompany spontaneous speech', *Journal of Language and Social Psychology*, 18: 438–462.
Bressem, J. (2013) 'A linguistic perspective on the notation of form features in gestures', in C. Müller, A. Cieni, E. Fricke, S. Ladewig, D. McNeill and S. Teßendorf (eds) *Body – Language – Communication, Volume 1*. Berlin, Germany: De Gruyter Mouton, pp. 1079–1098.
Bressem, J., Ladewig, S. H. and Müller, C. (2013) 'Linguistic annotation system for gestures (LASG)', in C. Müller, A. Cienki, E. Fricke, S. Ladewig, D. McNeill and S. Teßendorf (eds) *Body – Language – Communication, Volume 1*. Berlin, Germany: De Gruyter Mouton, pp. 1098–1124.
Bressem, J. and Müller, C. (2014) 'A repertoire of German recurrent gestures with pragmatic functions', in C. Müller, A. Cienki, E. Fricke, S. Ladewig, D. McNeill and J. Bressem (eds) *Body – Language – Communication, Volume 2*. Berlin, Germany: De Gruyter Mouton, pp. 1575–1591.

Burke, K. (1945) *A Grammar of Motives*. New York: Prentice Hall.
Calbris, G. (1990) *The Semiotics of French Gestures*. Bloomington, IN: Indiana University Press.
Cameron, L. (2003) *Metaphor in Educational Discourse*. London: Continuum.
—— (2008) 'Metaphor and talk', in R. W. Gibbs, Jr. (ed.) *The Cambridge Handbook of Metaphor and Thought*. Cambridge, UK: Cambridge University Press, pp. 197–211.
Cameron, L. and Maslen, R. (2010) 'Identifying metaphors in discourse data', in L. Cameron and R. Maslen (eds) *Metaphor Analysis: Research Practice in Applied Linguistics, Social Sciences and the Humanities*. London: Equinox, pp. 97–115.
Casasanto, D. (2008) 'Conceptual affiliates of metaphorical gestures'. Paper presented at the international conference *Language, Communication and Cognition*. Brighton, UK, August 2008.
Cienki, A. (1998) 'Metaphoric gestures and some of their relations to verbal metaphoric expressions', in J.-P. Koenig (ed.) *Discourse and Cognition: Bridging the Gap*. Stanford, CA: Center for the Study of Language and Information, pp. 189–204.
—— (2010) 'Multimodal metaphor analysis', in L. Cameron and R. Maslen (eds) *Metaphor Analysis: Research Practice in Applied Linguistics, Social Sciences and the Humanities*. London: Equinox, pp. 195–214.
—— (2013a) 'Conceptual metaphor theory in light of research on gesture with speech', *Cognitive Semiotics*, 5(1–2): 349–366.
—— (2013b) 'Gesture, space, grammar, and cognition', in P. Auer, M. Hilpert, A. Stukenbrock and B. Szmrecsanyi (eds) *Space in Language and Linguistics: Geographical, Interactional, and Cognitive Perspectives*. Berlin, Germany: Walter de Gruyter, pp. 667–686.
Cienki, A. and Mittelberg, I. (2013) 'Creativity in the forms and functions of spontaneous gesture with speech', in T. Veale, K. Feyaerts and C. Forceville (eds) *The Agile Mind: A Multi-disciplinary Study of a Multi-faceted Phenomenon*. Berlin, Germany: De Gruyter Mouton, pp. 231–252.
Cienki, A. and Müller, C. (eds) (2008a) *Metaphor and Gesture*. Amsterdam, The Netherlands: Benjamins.
—— (2008b) 'Metaphor, gesture, and thought', in R. W. Gibbs, Jr. (ed.) *The Cambridge Handbook of Metaphor and Thought*. Cambridge, UK: Cambridge University Press, pp. 483–501.
Clark, H. H. (1996) *Using Language*. Cambridge, UK: Cambridge University Press.
—— (2003) 'Pointing and placing', in S. Kita (ed.) *Pointing: Where Language, Culture, and Cognition Meet*. Mahwah, NJ: Lawrence Erlbaum, pp. 243–268.
Cook, S. W. and Tanenhaus, M. K. (2009) 'Embodied communication: Speakers' gestures affect listeners' actions', *Cognition*, 113: 98–104.
Corradi Fiumara, G. (1995) *The Metaphoric Process: Connections between Language and Life*. London: Routledge.
de Saussure, F. (1959 [1916]) *Course in General Linguistics*. New York: Philosophical Library.
Efron, D. (1972) *Gesture, Race, and Culture*. The Hague, The Netherlands: Mouton. First published as *Gesture and Environment*. New York: King's Crown Press [1941].
Gibbs, R. W., Jr. (1994) *The Poetics of Mind: Figurative Thought, Language, and Understanding*. Cambridge, UK: Cambridge University Press.
Hostetter, A. B. and Alibali, M. W. (2008) 'Visible embodiment: gestures as simulated action', *Psychonomic Bulletin and Review*, 15(3): 495–514.
Kaal, A. A. (2012) *Metaphor in Conversation*. Oisterwijk, The Netherlands: BOXpress.
Kendon, A. (1980) 'Gesticulation and speech: Two aspects of the process of utterance', in M. R. Key (ed.) *The Relation between Verbal and Nonverbal Communication*. The Hague, The Netherlands: Mouton, pp. 207–227.
—— (1995) 'Gestures as illocutionary and discourse structure markers in Southern Italian conversation', *Journal of Pragmatics*, 23(3): 247–279.
—— (2004) *Gesture: Visible Action as Utterance*. Cambridge, UK: Cambridge University Press.
Kibrik, A. A. (2010) 'Mul'timodal'naya lingvistika [Multimodal linguistics]', in Yu. I. Aleksandrov and V. D. Solovyev (eds) *Kognitivnye Issledovaniya. Sbornik nauchynx trudov. Vyp. 4*. Moscow, Russia: Psychology Institute of the Russian Academy of Sciences, pp. 134–152.

Kibrik, A. A. and Èl'bert, E. M. (2008) 'Understanding spoken discourse: The contribution of three information channels', in *Third International Conference on Cognitive Science*. Moscow, Russia: Russian Academy of Sciences, pp. 82–84.

Kita, S. (ed.) (2003) *Pointing: Where Language, Culture, and Cognition Meet*. Mahwah, NJ: Lawrence Erlbaum.

Kok, K., Bergmann, K., Cienki, A. and Kopp, S. (2016) 'Mapping out the multifunctionality of speakers' gestures', *Gesture*, 15(1): 37–59.

Kyratzis, A. (1997) *Metaphorically Speaking: Sex, Politics, and the Greeks*. Ph.D. Lancaster University, UK.

Ladewig, S. H. (2014) 'The cyclic gesture', in C. Müller, A. Cienki, E. Fricke, S. Ladewig, D. McNeill and J. Bressem (eds) *Body – Language – Communication, Volume 2*. Berlin, Germany: De Gruyter Mouton, pp. 1605–1617.

Lakoff, G. (1993) 'The contemporary theory of metaphor', in A. Ortony (ed.) *Metaphor and Thought*, 2nd edn. Cambridge, UK: Cambridge University Press, pp. 202–251.

Lakoff, G. and Johnson, M. (1980) *Metaphors We Live By*. Chicago, IL: University of Chicago Press.

—— (1999) *Philosophy in the Flesh*. New York: Basic Books.

LeBaron, C. and Streeck, J. (2000) 'Gestures, knowledge, and the world', in D. McNeill (ed.) *Language and Gesture*. Cambridge, UK: Cambridge University Press, pp. 118–138.

Leyton, M. (1992) *Symmetry, Causality, Mind*. Cambridge, MA: MIT Press.

Marghetis, T. and Bergen, B. (2014) 'Embodied meaning, inside and out: The coupling of gesture and mental simulation', in C. Müller, A. Cienki, E. Fricke, S. Ladewig, D. McNeill and J. Bressem (eds) *Body – Language – Communication, Volume 2*. Berlin, Germany: De Gruyter Mouton, pp. 2000–2007.

McNeill, D. (1992) *Hand and Mind: What Gestures Reveal about Thought*. Chicago, IL: University of Chicago Press.

—— (2005) *Gesture and Thought*. Chicago, IL: University of Chicago Press.

McNeill, D., Cassell, J. and Levy, E. (1993) 'Abstract deixis', *Semiotica*, 95: 5–19.

Mittelberg, I. and Waugh, L. R. (2009) 'Metonymy first, metaphor second: A cognitive-semiotic approach to multimodal figures of thought in co-speech gesture', in C. Forceville and E. Urios-Aparisi (eds) *Multimodal Metaphor*. Berlin, Germany: Mouton de Gruyter, pp. 329–356.

Monahan, B. (1983) *A Dictionary of Russian Gestures*. Tenafly, NJ: Hermitage.

Müller, C. (1998a) 'Iconicity and gesture', in S. Santi, I. Guaïtella, C. Cavé and G. Konopczynski (eds) *Oralité et Gestualité: Communication multimodale, interaction*. Paris, France: L'Harmattan, pp. 321–328.

—— (1998b) *Redebegleitende Gesten. Kulturgeschichte – Theorie – Sprachvergleich*. Berlin, Germany: Berlin Verlag A. Spitz.

—— (2004) 'Forms and uses of the Palm Up Open Hand: A case of a gesture family?', in C. Müller and R. Posner (eds) *The Semantics and Pragmatics of Everyday Gestures: The Berlin Conference*. Berlin, Germany: Weidler Buchverlag, pp. 233–256.

—— (2008a) *Metaphors Dead and Alive, Sleeping and Waking: A Dynamic View*. Chicago, IL: University of Chicago Press.

—— (2008b) 'What gestures reveal about the nature of metaphor', in A. Cienki and C. Müller (eds) *Metaphor and Gesture*. Amsterdam, The Netherlands: Benjamins, pp. 219–245.

—— (2014) 'Gestural modes of representation as techniques of depiction', in C. Müller, A. Cienki, E. Fricke, S. Ladewig, D. McNeill and J. Bressem (eds) *Body – Language – Communication, Volume 2*. Berlin, Germany: De Gruyter Mouton, pp. 1687–1701.

Müller, C. and Tag, S. (2010) 'The dynamics of metaphor: Foregrounding and activating metaphoricity in conversational interaction', *Cognitive Semiotics*, 6: 85–120.

Pragglejaz Group. (2007) 'MIP: A method for identifying metaphorically used words in discourse', *Metaphor and Symbol*, 22: 1–39.

Reddy, M. (1993 [1979]) 'The conduit metaphor: A case of frame conflict in our language about language', in A. Ortony (ed.) *Metaphor and Thought*, 2nd edn. Cambridge, UK: Cambridge University Press, pp. 164–201.

Rhodes, R. (1994) 'Aural images', in L. Hinton, J. Nichols and J. J. Ohala (eds) *Sound Symbolism*. Cambridge, UK: Cambridge University Press, pp. 276–292.

Saitz, R. L. and Cervanka, E. J. (1972) *Handbook of Gestures: Colombia and the United States*. The Hague, The Netherlands: Mouton.

Steen, G. J., Dorst, A. G., Herrmann, J. B., Kaal, A. A., Krennmayr, T. and Pasma, T. (2010) *A Method for Linguistic Metaphor Identification: From MIP to MIPVU*. Amsterdam, The Netherlands: Benjamins.

Stibbe, A. (1996) *Metaphor and Alternative Conceptions of Illness*. Ph.D. Lancaster University, UK.

Stokoe, W. C. (1960) 'Sign language structure: An outline of the visual communication systems of the American deaf', Buffalo, NY: Dept. of Anthropology and Linguistics, University of Buffalo.

Streeck, J. (2008) 'Depicting by gestures', *Gesture*, 8(3): 285–301.

Teßendorf, S. (2014) 'Pragmatic and metaphoric – combining functional with cognitive approaches in the analysis of the "brushing aside gesture"', in C. Müller, A. Cienki, E. Fricke, S. Ladewig, D. McNeill and J. Bressem (eds) *Body – Language – Communication, Volume 2*. Berlin, Germany: De Gruyter Mouton, pp. 1540–1557.

Wittenburg, P., Brugman, H., Russel, A., Klassmann, A. and Sloetjes, H. (2006) 'ELAN: A professional framework for multimodality research', in *Proceedings of LREC 2006, Fifth International Conference on Language Resources and Evaluation*. http://www.lrec-conf.org/proceedings/lrec2006/.

Wundt, W. (1922) *Völkerpsychologie: Eine Untersuchung der Entwicklungsgesetze von Sprache, Mythus und Sitte, Vol. 2: Die Sprache*. Leipzig, Germany: Alfred Kröner Verlag.

Wylie, L. (1977) *Beaux Gestes: A Guide to French Body Talk*. Cambridge, MA: Undergraduate Press.

10
Analysing metaphors in multimodal texts

Elisabeth El Refaie

Introduction and definitions

Metaphor has been the object of human reflection and study for many centuries, yet it is only in the last 20 years or so that scholars have begun to pay detailed attention to nonverbal manifestations of the phenomenon. One of the drivers of this new focus of inquiry has been the striking proliferation of visual metaphors in advertising, which has elicited a number of studies by rhetoricians and marketing experts (McQuarrie and Mick 1999; Phillips 2003; Phillips and McQuarrie 2004). These researchers regard visual metaphors as effective tools of persuasion, which, by deviating from expected conventions, induce people to engage both cognitively and emotionally with the intended messages. Other scholars have been inspired by the key claim of Conceptual Metaphor Theory (CMT) that metaphor is a fundamental property of human thought that allows us to understand something abstract (the 'target') in terms of something more concrete and familiar (the 'source') (Lakoff and Johnson 1980; see Chapter 1). If metaphor is, indeed, a conceptual phenomenon, these scholars realised, it must be expressible in many different modes, not just language.

Human beings use all kinds of bodily actions, such as speaking, gesturing, mime, and dancing, and both natural and human-made materials, including images, music, and clothes, in order to communicate with one another. When any such resource is developed and organised by a particular culture into a coherent meaning-making system, it may be called a 'mode' (Kress 2009: 58–9). It is not possible to draw up a comprehensive list of all the different modes available to us, because their number and delineation will shift and change over time and across different cultures and communities. However, we can distinguish, at the very least, between the following modes: speech, writing, still images, moving images, sound, music, and gesture. Accordingly, a multimodal text is one that combines two or more different modes, such as writing and still images in the case of a poster, or moving images, sound, music, and speech in a film, for example.

In such texts, metaphorical meaning may be evoked by any individual mode on its own or through a combination of modes. Forceville (2009: 24) draws a useful distinction between 'monomodal' metaphors, where both the source and the target are represented in the same mode (e.g. through sound only), and 'multimodal' metaphors, where the target and source 'are each represented exclusively or predominantly in different modes' (e.g. in a picture and written language, respectively).

Most existing studies of nonverbal metaphor focus on advertising (Alousque 2014; Forceville 1996, 2002, 2007; Jeong 2008), but there is also a growing body of work on multimodal metaphor in political cartoons (El Refaie 2003, 2009), film (Rohdin 2009; Urios-Aparisi 2010; Winter 2014), animation (Popa 2013; Forceville 2013), comics (El Refaie 2014), corporate branding (Ng and Koller 2013), visual art (Parsons 2010), experimental literature (Gibbons 2013), and co-speech gesture (Mittelberg and Waugh 2009). The ubiquity of nonverbal metaphors across so many different genres suggests that they are capable of fulfilling important conceptual and communicative functions.

Details of methodology

The first challenge facing anyone who wishes to analyse metaphors in multimodal texts is how to identify and categorise them. As will be shown below, this can be done on the basis of the formal qualities of a particular representation, or by trying to identify the thought patterns it appears to invite. Another important area of research concerns the way in which multimodal metaphors are interpreted by audiences. To date, this has been investigated through the use of experiments, surveys, interviews, and focus groups; these methodologies will also be reviewed below.

Categorising nonverbal and multimodal metaphor

According to social semiotic theory (Kress and van Leeuwen 2001, 2006; van Leeuwen 2005), any fully developed mode must be able to fulfil the same three 'metafunctions' as language does: to represent states and events, convey a sense of the relationships between sign producers and their audiences, and create a recognisable kind of text out of individual parts. However, each mode has developed distinct ways of expressing these meanings, based on differences in the potentials and limitations of their material properties and the way they have been used over many generations in specific cultures and contexts. Language is particularly well suited to the representation of actions and causality, for instance, while the spatial organisation of still images may 'lend itself with greater facility to the representation of elements and their relation to each other' (Kress 2000: 147). Written language, in particular, is also traditionally accorded greater respect than images, which still tend to be associated with popular culture and childish entertainment. Accordingly, nonverbal metaphors never express exactly the same meanings as their linguistic counterparts, even if the underlying thought patterns are similar. Moreover, when several semiotic modes are brought together in a metaphor, the possible meanings are 'multiplied' rather than simply added together (Lemke 1998: 92).

Of all the different types of metaphor in multimodal texts, visual forms have received by far the most scholarly attention, with the main focus often being on pinpointing the specific formal qualities that allow us to recognise such metaphors. One of the first writers to consider this issue was art historian E. H. Gombrich (1971: 134), who noticed that many portrait caricatures contain a form of visual fusion, where the face of a particular politician is visually amalgamated with the body of an animal, for example. Similarly, Carroll defines visual metaphors as instances where 'physically noncompossible elements' (1994: 214) from two separate areas of reality 'are fused or superimposed or otherwise attached as parts of a recognizably integrated or unified entity' (1996: 812). He gives the example of a scene in Fritz

Lang's classic film *Metropolis*, in which the image of a gigantic machine is blended with that of a man-eating monster:

> The machine, or at least parts of it, have been transformed into parts of a monster, Moloch. Nevertheless, the machine is still recognizable as a machine. The monster elements and the machine elements are co-present – or homospatial – in the same figure.
> *Carroll 1996: 810*

This, Carroll argues, invites the viewer to regard factory machines as man-eating monsters and, more broadly, to consider the inhuman working conditions of factory workers.

Blending Theory (Fauconnier and Turner 2002; see Chapter 2) provides a useful framework for analysing such examples of visual fusion. According to this theory, we are able to generate and understand metaphorical creations like these by integrating in our minds two or more conceptual 'input spaces', which share a 'generic space' of common characteristics but are also unique in certain respects, into a new, ad hoc 'blended space'. Monsters and factory machines are both large, powerful and potentially dangerous entities that must consume energy in order to function, for instance, but only monsters are living creatures with thoughts, feelings, motivations and the ability to act without human intervention or control, while only machines are used in factories to increase production. The Moloch in *Metropolis* represents a creative blend of some of these shared and distinctive characteristics.

While fusion is certainly one of the forms a visual metaphor may take, most scholars agree that it is not the only, nor, indeed, necessarily the most common one. Charles Forceville (1996, 2002, 2007, 2009) has spent the past two decades developing and refining an influential taxonomy of what he calls 'pictorial' metaphor. He distinguishes between the following five categories:

- *Hybrid metaphor*: In hybrid metaphors, both the source and target are at least partially pictured and joined together into one figure that is perceived as a single, unified object. Gombrich's (1971) and Carroll's (1994, 1996) examples of fusion or homospatiality would fall into this category, as would the instances of visual metaphor in advertising that Gkiouzepas and Hogg (2011) refer to as 'synthesis'.
- *Pictorial simile*: Pictorial similes are characterised by both the source and target being visually depicted in their entirety as two separate figures, but in a way that emphasises their similarity. In such metaphors, which are sometimes discussed under the alternative labels of 'juxtaposition' (Gkiouzepas and Hogg 2011), or 'symmetric image [object] alignment' (Schilperoord et al. 2009; Teng and Sun 2002), the resemblance can either be inherent in the two objects or created through the manner in which they are presented. Schilperoord et al. (2009: 158) draw a helpful distinction between 'object-constitutive attributes', of the entities involved, such as size, shape, colour, and texture, and their 'object-depictment attributes', which concern their manner of representation, including the background, distance from the viewer, lighting, and alignment. For example, a black sports car may be shown next to a panther, with both depicted in the same size and from an angle that accentuates pre-existing similarities of colour and shape.
- *Contextual metaphor*: In contextual metaphors, only the source or the target is depicted, in a context where normally something else would be expected; the replacement of the anticipated element encourages viewers to interpret one thing in terms of another. An advertisement for exclusive male footwear, for instance, shows a male torso adorned with a shoe in place of a tie, inviting the viewer 'to perceive the phenomenon SHOE not in its usual, "literal" sense, but in terms of the very different phenomenon TIE' (Forceville 1996: 109).

- *Integrated metaphor*: In this type of metaphor, which is also sometimes referred to as a 'perceptual echo' (El Refaie 2013: 240), '[a] phenomenon that is experienced as a unified object or gestalt is represented in its entirety in such a manner that it resembles another object or gestalt even without contextual cues' (Forceville 2007: 18). For example, in an ad for all-weather tyres, a wild seascape is depicted in such a way that it can also be seen as a landscape with a road winding its way up the side of a mountain.
- *Verbo-pictorial metaphors*: Either the source or the target is not pictured but is implied instead by the verbal message. An example would be a photograph of a naked woman's body with insects crawling all over it. What might be seen as a literal depiction is transformed into a metaphor through the addition of a verbal caption that compares the woman's predicament to the discomfort suffered by people with skin disease.

Only metaphors in this final category are multimodal, since they alone draw on both the visual and the verbal mode. In the example given, the source (INSECTS CRAWLING OVER THE SKIN) is conveyed both visually and verbally, while the target (SKIN DISEASE) is not represented directly in the image and thus depends heavily upon the verbal cue. As Table 10.1 shows, there are, in fact, seven different ways in which the two modes can work together to cue metaphorical meaning in verbo-pictorial metaphors (see also Alousque 2014: 161).

Even within each of the options listed in Table 10.1, the exact relationship between the two modes may vary considerably from one concrete instance of metaphor to another. Roland Barthes (1977) coined the influential terms 'anchorage' to describe the way that language is often needed in order to fix the meaning of images, and 'relay' to refer to a situation, for example in many films and comics, where 'text (most often a snatch of dialogue) and image stand in a complementary relationship' (41). The notion of anchorage is applicable to verbo-pictorial metaphors in which the words perform the role of securing a metaphorical reading of an image that could, potentially, be interpreted in several different ways, including as a literal representation. In other cases, the two modes have a more equal, complementary function, with both supplying essential information about either the source or the target domain of the metaphor. It is also possible for one of the modes to perform a 'modifying' role, by specifying or accentuating a particular aspect of the metaphor. In the example discussed above, the metaphorical identity relationship between insects crawling over one's body and skin disease would be clear from reading the verbal caption alone, but the visual image has an important augmenting effect, in that it draws in additional connotation by showing a large number of particularly repulsive, oversized bugs. Finally, one of the two modes may also be at least partially 'redundant' in that it just repeats aspects of meaning conveyed perfectly adequately by the other mode (El Refaie 2013: 241; see also Popa 2013).

Table 10.1 Possible distribution of roles in verbo-pictorial metaphors

Option	Source		Target	
	Visual cue	Verbal cue	Visual cue	Verbal cue
1	x	x	x	x
2	x	x	x	
3	x	x		x
4	x		x	x
5		x	x	x
6	x			x
7		x	x	

Another unique verbo-visual relationship can be identified in cases of what Rohdin (2009: 408) terms 'verbal images', whose metaphoricity relies on the evocation of a well-known metaphorical expression, idiom, cliché, or proverb, which they visualise literally. For example, a cartoon showing a man holding a large key and looking puzzled may, in certain contexts, evoke the metaphorical notion of something being the 'key question' (El Refaie 2003: 89). In such cases the verbal mode is not literally present in the text, but it nevertheless plays an essential part in inviting viewers to interpret an image figuratively rather than literally, by evoking the relevant expression in the viewer's mind.

Moving beyond (verbo-)pictorial metaphors to a consideration of metaphors in a wider range of multimodal texts, Forceville (2009: 31–2) suggests that there are three main formal signals that encourage people to interpret representations metaphorically:

- *Simultaneous cueing* is the equivalent of 'fusion', when applied to temporally based texts such as film or dance. It refers to cases where the target and source are represented saliently at the same time, as for instance when a video of a woman entering her house and closing the front door is accompanied by the sound of a heavy iron door clanking shut, thereby suggesting that she feels imprisoned in her own home.
- *Filling a schematic slot unexpectedly* describes instances where something is placed in a context that deviates from common expectations. For instance, if a man is shown taking his dog for a walk in a pram, this might encourage the metaphorical interpretation DOG IS BABY.
- *Perceptual resemblance* refers to monomodal texts where the source and target are presented in a way that emphasises their similar appearance, sound, smell, etc., depending on the mode of representation. For example, listeners to a radio play might be invited to draw analogies between a group of women and a flock of birds when hearing the similar sounds produced by both.

However, such formal cues are only part of the story. First, not every representation that contains one or more of the characteristics discussed above is necessarily intended to be understood metaphorically in context. For instance, if the right-hand side of a presidential candidate's face is merged with the left-hand side of his or her main opponent, the resulting hybrid face is more likely to be construed as representing the contrasting options available to voters than as a genuine metaphorical blend of the two politicians' characteristics. Similarly, in some contexts the alignment of objects in a way that emphasises their visual resemblance may be interpreted not as a metaphor, but rather as a literal categorisation, visual paradox, or oxymoron, for example (Teng and Sun 2002; Schilperood et al. 2009).

Second, the formal cues that indicate the presence of a metaphor may be more or less explicit. According to Forceville (1996: 143), visual hybrids leave the viewer no choice but to understand one thing in terms of another, whereas pictorial similes merely 'invite' a metaphorical interpretation, particularly if there is also a perfectly plausible literal explanation for the juxtaposition of the two entities. Following a similar line of argumentation, Gkiouzepas and Hogg (2011: 105–6) categorise visual metaphors on the basis of 'the extent to which the relation between the two objects complies or fits with real-life visual experience': in the case of 'realistic symbiosis', there is a real-life scenario that is able to account for the combination of the two objects; in contrast, 'replacement' refers to cases where one object intrudes on a scene where it is not expected; and 'artificial symbiosis' is based on entirely unrealistic combinations of objects. Aspects of style and composition may also play a role in determining whether or not a metaphor cue is picked up by viewers. If images are designed in a way that downplays their literal, denotative meanings and foregrounds their more abstract connotations, by manipulating the colours or background detail, for instance, this may subvert people's expectations of what is 'natural' and thereby encourage a metaphorical interpretation (Ng and Koller 2013).

Third, even the most explicit cue will only have the desired effect if the receiver is aware that a metaphorical reading is intended. This recognition of intentionality is related to genre and the expectations it produces, as well as depending upon the individual receiver's knowledge, interests and familiarity with conventions. In political cartoons, metaphor is so common that most people are likely to be more alert to cues to nonliteral meaning than if the same forms are encountered in an illustrated children's book, for example.

Fourth, and perhaps most importantly, the ability of multimodal representations to evoke a metaphorical interpretation is not necessarily dependent upon the presence of specific formal cues at all. If we take seriously CMT's claim that metaphor is a cognitive phenomenon rather than simply a matter of poetic or rhetorical style, we must accept that any sign, in whatever mode, can be regarded as a metaphor, 'provided that its use is intended to occasion a metaphoric thought' (Kennedy et al. 1993: 244). Accordingly, the task of the metaphor analyst is to try and identify all those representations which, regardless of their formal properties, appear to invite people to consider one thing in terms of another.

Most of the instances of multimodal metaphor discussed so far compare two concrete entities based on perceptual similarity. Such 'resemblance' metaphors are often highly unconventional and creative, since the human imagination 'is boundless in its capacity to impose resemblance on disparate objects' (Grady 1999: 96). However, according to CMT, the vast majority of metaphors we use in our daily life are 'correlation' metaphors (ibid.), which involve drawing on concrete, clearly structured experiences of our bodily actions and perceptions as a way to understand abstract, non-physical domains such as mental states, emotions, and social relations. For instance, we project our experience of being able to see something clearly onto our sense of understanding it well, thus forming the metaphorical concept UNDERSTANDING IS SEEING. Many of these correlation metaphors are thought to be deeply embedded in our basic reasoning and conventionalised in everyday language, often generating clusters of related linguistic expressions (e.g. 'I see what you mean'; 'His arguments are so obscure').

Such correlation metaphors have also been noted in multimodal texts. Parsons (2010), for instance, identifies verticality as an expressive feature of many visual art works, suggesting that its association with possessing 'grandeur of character' (233) originates in our sensorimotor experience of standing upright when we are feeling confident. Many of the meaning potentials of perspective and composition described by social semioticians Kress and van Leeuwen (2005) also appear to be derived from our embodied experiences. For example, the fact that we feel more involved with the people depicted in an image if they are shown making eye contact and from a fully frontal angle 'is based on real life situations where we face the person we want to interact with and gaze at him/her, and turn our face (gaze) away if we don't want to interact' (Feng and O'Halloran 2013: 330).

Visual correlation metaphors abound in the cinema, too. Ortiz (2011) demonstrates how film-makers commonly exploit the conceptual metaphor IMPORTANCE IS SIZE/VOLUME by changing the perceived size of characters relative to each other and their surroundings in order to convey subtle messages about their significance. In horror movies the correlation metaphors EVIL IS DOWN and EVIL IS DARK are ubiquitous (Winter 2014), while films about human relationships often use spatial closeness or distance between characters to indicate how they feel about each other (Coëgnarts and Kravanja 2012). As will be shown in the Current Research section, correlation metaphors can also be identified in autobiographical comics.

Studying audience responses

It is important for metaphor analysts to remember that not everything they identify as a multimodal metaphor will necessarily be interpreted as such by other readers or viewers. Moreover, even if everybody agrees that a particular representation *is* a metaphor, it is still likely that the meanings it generates will vary considerably from one individual to another. Although the same is true to some extent of all forms of communication, nonverbal and multimodal metaphors are thought to be especially polysemous. In relation to advertising, for instance, Phillips (2003) makes the point that 'it is the consumer and not the advertiser who ultimately controls the meaning of the visual metaphor' (302).

There is a range of methodologies available in order to study the question of how people understand nonverbal metaphor, including written surveys, focus groups, interviews, and experiments. A questionnaire study by Forceville (1996: 165–99) invited two groups of academics to describe their own thoughts and feelings about the pictorial metaphors used in three Dutch billboard advertisements, before identifying the messages the advertisers were apparently trying to convey. Although there was considerable agreement among participants regarding the main messages in each case, some of the more associative meanings generated by the billboards varied greatly from one participant to another.

Research using focus groups composed of young people in the UK and Cyprus yielded similar results (Proctor et al. 2005). A magazine advert featuring a cheetah at the wheel of a car was interpreted by all the participants as suggesting that the car is fast and a pleasure to drive, for example. However, at the level of more connotative and narrative meanings, clear differences emerged, depending on the individual participant's gender, cultural values, interests and experiences.

Another empirical study used semi-structured one-to-one interviews with 25 young people between the ages of sixteen and nineteen to explore their readings of British newspaper cartoons about the 2004 US presidential elections (El Refaie 2009). The cartoonists were also interviewed to establish their intentions. Basic correlations between the size of cartoon characters and their power/status, and between their implied movement through space and the passing of time, for instance, were understood easily and at an intuitive level by all the young people. However, there was much more variation with regard to the interpretation of more elaborate metaphors, such as one that used the image of a giant cowboy boot crushing the inhabitants of other countries to castigate George W. Bush's foreign policy. Such metaphors could only be read in the way intended by the cartoonist if participants had a certain level of general knowledge and a familiarity with the conventions of the political cartoon genre.

There have also been several experimental studies that have compared the responses of audiences to different types of visual metaphor. Jeong (2008) used three distinct versions of the same magazine advertisement and found that ads containing visual metaphors are likely to be more persuasive and lead to greater cognitive elaboration than adverts with purely literal images. Gkiouzepas and Hogg (2011), who tested the effects of manipulating the mode of representation and the 'life-likeness' of several magazine advertisements on Greek students, discovered that visual fusion metaphors were more successful than juxtaposition metaphors in eliciting positive attitudes towards both the advert itself and the promoted brand. A similar experiment was conducted by van Mulken et al. (2010) in order to study the effects of complexity, deviation from expectations, and comprehension on the extent to which participants appreciated a visual metaphor in an advert. One of their most interesting findings was that, contrary to established beliefs in rhetorical theory, understanding a relatively complex visual metaphor did not necessarily lead to greater liking of the ad. Audiences of advertisements appear to be unwilling, the authors conclude, to 'waste time and energy going beyond a certain level of interpretative complexity' (3427).

The results of these studies demonstrate that analysts of multimodal metaphor must guard against taking their own interpretations for granted. They also underline the importance of trying to replicate the ordinary reading situation as closely as possible when studying audience responses, as the context of reception may have a big influence on people's willingness to engage with particular texts and to generate detailed interpretations.

Critical issues, debates and controversies

As mentioned in the overview above, research into metaphor in multimodal texts has tended to focus on striking and unconventional instances of resemblance metaphors in artistic or persuasive genres such as advertising, film and cartoons. Although there is now a growing body of work on other types of multimodal metaphor as well, there is still a danger that some scholars may be tempted to draw conclusions about apparent essential differences between verbal and nonverbal metaphor based on the evidence from a limited set of examples of just one type of metaphor in a specific genre.

A case in point is the debate surrounding the notion of 'reversibility.' Based on examples of fusion-type metaphors drawn from film and surrealist art, Carroll (1994, 1996) proposed that visual metaphors invite a bidirectional exploration of the similarities between the two objects more frequently than linguistic metaphors do. However, Forceville (2002) refutes this suggestion, arguing instead that 'prototypical metaphors of all kinds and occurring in all media have clearly distinguishable target and source domains, which in a given context cannot be reversed' (7). In advertising, for instance, it is almost always the product or service being advertised that is the target of a metaphor, while the source is typically drawn from an area of life that is likely to evoke positive associations in the viewer. Correlation metaphors are also non-reversible, since the target is an abstract concept that cannot be represented at all without recourse to some form of metaphor, metonymy or symbol (El Refaie 2009). In horror movies, the evil nature of a particular character can only be shown indirectly through their appearance and actions, for instance, as well as through the way they are presented through camera angle, size and lighting (Winter 2014).

A similar issue concerns the question of whether multimodal metaphors are inherently more creative than verbal metaphors. Lakoff and Turner (1989) believe that even the most celebrated examples of verbal metaphor in literature are usually based on the same conventional metaphorical patterns that underlie our ordinary, everyday thinking, although poets are often able to find ways of extending, elaborating, or combining such metaphors in novel ways. By contrast, pictorial and multimodal metaphors are typically of the OBJECT IS OBJECT variety, 'many of which function in contexts creating highly specific, *ad hoc* metaphorical resemblances' (Forceville 2009: 28). The purpose of such creative resemblance metaphors is often not to make an abstract concept easier to grasp, but rather to *defamiliarise* the target for persuasive or poetic purposes (Feng and O'Halloran 2013: 323).

But even in such cases where the metaphors are based on conventional correlations between an embodied and a more abstract experience, multimodality appears to offer unique opportunities for creativity at the level of representation, due to the distinctive properties of the different modes and the possibility of combining them in unexpected ways (El Refaie 2013). An example of this will be given in the following section, where I show how the creators of autobiographical comics are able to transform dominant cultural metaphors about mental illness into something new and unexpected by exploiting the formal properties of the medium.

Example of current research

Depression is a good example of an experience that cannot be communicated easily without recourse to more concrete source domains. The most common metaphors that people use when talking about the disease are to do with darkness, descent, being trapped, and bearing a heavy burden (Charteris-Black 2012; Schoeneman et al. 2004).

Recently, several artists have turned to the comics medium as a way of representing their experiences of mental illness. In a previous study (El Refaie 2014) of *Depresso* by Brick (2010) and *Psychiatric Tales* by Darryl Cunningham (2010), I discovered that they draw on many of the dominant verbal metaphors listed above. However, by expressing their thoughts and feelings through vivid imagery, these artists are often able to transform conventional correlation metaphors into something much more original.

A similar pattern of metaphor use can be found in Ellen Forney's (2012) graphic memoir *Marbles*, in which the author describes her experience of bipolar disorder. She uses a range of multimodal metaphors to represent her mental illness, but the most frequent ones are based on correlations between the spatial orientation of up and down, and positive or negative emotions (HAPPINESS IS UP/SADNESS IS DOWN) (Gibbs 1994: 414). In one instance, this conceptual metaphor is translated by Forney into the concrete image of a woman riding on an old-fashioned carousel, with horses mounted on poles (see Figure 10.1).

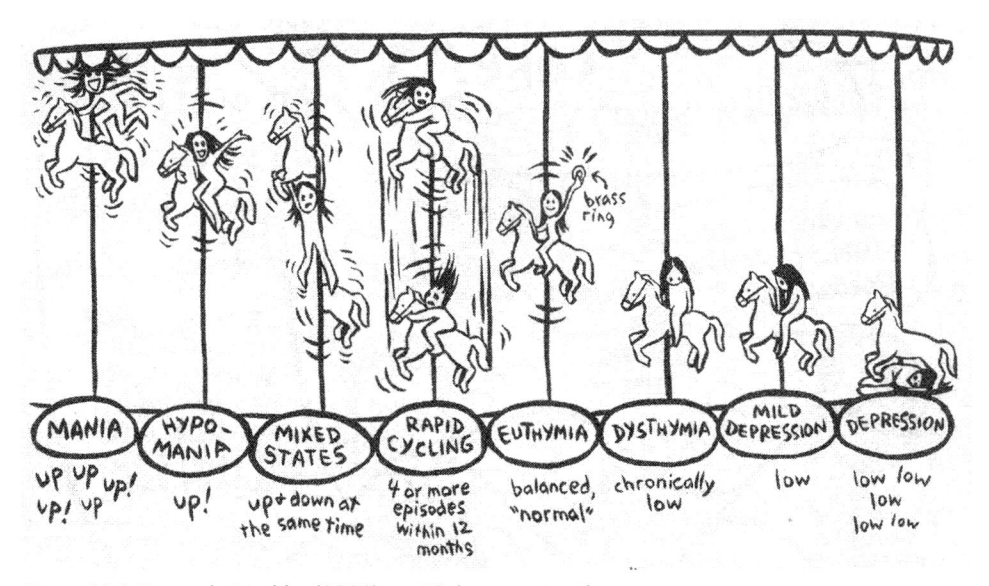

Figure 10.1 Forney's *Marbles* (2012), p. 59 (page extract).

This is a good example of a verbo-pictorial metaphor of the type I have labelled Option 3 (see Table 10.1), where the target is just given verbally, whereas the source domain is represented both verbally and visually, with the image performing a modifying role. The verbal mode explicitly identifies mental illness as the target, by providing the medical labels for various disorders (e.g. 'hypomania', 'dysthymia', 'depression'), and links this with the general source domain of spatial movement on a horizontal axis. Mania, for instance, is described through the repetition of the word 'up' and depression is labelled 'low'. The picture of a carousel elaborates the spatial source domain by emphasising the cyclical nature of many mood disorders and adding further narrative detail. The upwards and downwards motion of the horses is complemented by the actions and posture of the rider, who, in the case of mania, is standing on the horse's back and touching the ceiling, while the depressed rider has slid down onto the floor and is curled up under her wooden steed. The condition of 'mixed states' is represented through the image of a bisected horse, whose upper half is moving in one direction, while the lower half is sinking to the floor, with the rider desperately trying to hold the two parts together. By adding these visual details, the author has thus extended and complicated a simple spatial metaphor to express subtler truths about the experience of mental illness.[1]

The representation of mania through the image of the author herself riding a wooden horse on top of a high pole is repeated on two consecutive pages towards the end of the book (Forney 2012: 231–2), although here the horse is no longer attached to the carousel. On the first page, the artist has drawn herself in a racy outfit perched on top of the horse with her arms spread wide in an attitude of ecstasy and a joyful expression on her face. However, on the next page the horse is bucking violently and she is holding on for dear life, her clothes ripped and her face frozen in terror. This provides a compelling visual metaphor for the way in which a person with bipolar disorder may quickly slide from manic euphoria into hyper-anxiety and then depression, or may even experience these conflicting feelings simultaneously.

Further elaborations of the correlation metaphor HAPPINESS IS UP/SADNESS IS DOWN include the recurring image of a balloon floating up above the clouds to represent the manic person's sense of elation (Forney 2012: 13, 23, 173), and a line graph that compares the range of positive and negative feelings experienced by a 'normal' person with the extreme 'peaks' and 'troughs' that are characteristic of people suffering from bipolar disorder (153).

The artist also uses elements of visual style and composition in order to evoke metaphorical meanings. When she draws herself during one of her manic episodes, she typically employs loose brush strokes, densely packing the pages of her book with lots of detailed figurative drawings, 'pictorial runes' (Forceville et al. 2014), such as whirls, stars, and spikes, and hand-written words. As can be seen in Figure 10.2, these elements are sometimes arranged in a spiral pattern around her head.

According to Kress and van Leeuwen (2006: 196), in circular visual compositions the element in the centre is typically 'presented as the nucleus of the information to which all other elements are in some sense subservient'. In this case, the author's face, which is depicted at a slight angle and wearing a euphoric expression, forms the most salient central element, which suggests that her overexcited state of mind determines her thoughts, perceptions, feelings, and speech patterns. Specific elements of visual style and layout, such as the haphazard arrangement of an overabundance of pictorial runes and words in irregular handwriting around a central element, thus help to convey Forney's subjective experience of the manic phases in her life.

Figure 10.2 Forney's *Marbles* (2012), p. 49 (page extract).

In contrast, Forney's states of depression are typically drawn very simply, with lots of empty space on the page between self-portraits that are arranged in a regular pattern and often show little variation from one drawing to the next. In Figure 10.3, for example, the near-identical image of her small figure in bed is repeated six times in the two top rows, with her head and shoulders appearing and then disappearing again under the duvet as she struggles to muster all her willpower in order to get up and leave the room, before returning to her prostrate position on the sofa in the final row.

Forney has drawn herself from a great distance, so that her facial expressions are invisible to us. As we know from everyday interactions, the distance we keep from one another is determined by our social relations and feelings for one another. Only our most trusted, cherished friends and relations are allowed within touching distance, whereas strangers are expected to stand back. In visual images, this experience of literal physical closeness or distance is projected onto how we feel about the depicted people (Kress and van Leeuwen 2006: 124–9). Accordingly, Forney's portraits of herself as a tiny figure provide a powerful sense of the numbness and detachment, both from her own thoughts and emotions and from the rest of the world, which she experiences during her periods of depression and which are apparently very common symptoms of the disease (Demjén 2014: 45–6).

It is important to note, however, that such stylistic features are only able to cue a metaphorical reading if they deviate sufficiently from the expected norms associated with the comics medium in general and with the graphic memoir genre, as well as with the more specific baseline style of a particular work of art. If Forney always drew herself as a tiny, faceless figure in the distance, the self-portraits in Figure 10.3 would not be able to function as effectively as visual metaphors for her depression, for example.

Figure 10.3 Forney's *Marbles* (2012), p. 77 (full page).

Future directions

Since the study of multimodal metaphor is a relatively young field of inquiry, there are still many gaps in our collective knowledge and understanding of this phenomenon. One of the most important goals over the next few years will be to gather as much evidence as possible about the forms and functions of metaphor across a broad range of multimodal media and genres. An example of a small step in this direction is the VisMet project (http://vismet.org/VisMet/), hosted by the Faculty of Arts at the VU University Amsterdam. The aim is to build an online corpus of annotated visual metaphors from a variety of different styles and genres that can be used freely by students and researchers from different academic disciplines.

Another important avenue of future study is the way in which multimodal metaphors may combine with other rhetorical forms. The relationship between metaphor and symbol, for instance, has so far been almost totally ignored by the scholarly community. Forceville (2013) suggests two possible reasons for this. First, CMT has always focused on the embodied basis of metaphor and been less interested in its socio-cultural dimension, which means that the deeply cultural phenomenon of symbolism has tended to fall outside the perceived remit of scholars in this tradition. Secondly, the study of symbols has traditionally been seen as a suitable topic mainly for art history, 'a discipline that has hitherto not engaged much with CMT, or vice versa' (Forceville 2013: 251). Although the interplay between metaphor and metonymy has received some scholarly attention in recent years, for instance in relation to television commercials (Yu 2009), feature films (Urios-Aparisi 2010), and co-speech gesture (Mittelberg and Waugh 2009), this is such an important issue that it deserves much more detailed scrutiny in other media and genres as well.

It is also vital that future researchers of multimodal metaphor find ways to combine insights from theoretical and empirical studies in order to increase our still limited understanding of how people actually recognise and interpret such metaphors. Much of the empirical work in this area has been conducted by experts in the fields of marketing and communication studies (see overview section above), whose grasp of metaphor theory tends to be fairly rudimentary, while many metaphor scholars are deeply rooted in the arts and humanities tradition and are often ill-equipped to conduct vigorous experiments or quantitative surveys, for example. The study by van Mulken et al. (2010) mentioned above is a good example of the benefits that can be obtained from the judicious collaboration between scholars with a metaphor theoretical background and those with experience of designing and running experiments.

Note

1 I am very grateful to Ellen Forney for expounding her thoughts and intentions behind some of the metaphors used in *Marbles* in a personal communication (24 May 2015).

Further reading

Forceville, C. (1996) *Pictorial Metaphor in Advertising*, London and New York: Routledge.
Forceville, C. and Urios-Aparisi, E. (eds) (2009) *Multimodal Metaphor*, Berlin and New York: Mouton de Gruyter.
Hidalgo-Downing, L. and Kraljevic-Mujic, B. (eds) (2013) *Metaphorical Creativity across Modes*, special issue of *Metaphor and the Social World*, 3(2).
Pinar Sanz, M. J. (2013) *Multimodality and Cognitive Linguistics*, special issue of *Review of Cognitive Linguistics*, 11(2).

References

Alousque, I. N. (2014) 'Verbo-pictorial metaphor in French advertising', *Journal of French Language Studies*, 24(2), 155–180.
Barthes, R. (1977) *Image, Music, Text*, London: Fontana.
Brick (2010) *Depresso. Or: How I Learned to Stop Worrying and Embrace Being Bonkers!*, London: Knockabout.
Charteris-Black, J. (2012) 'Shattering the bell jar: Metaphor, gender, and depression', *Metaphor and Symbol*, 27(3), 199–216.
Carroll, N. (1994) 'Visual metaphor', in J. Hintikka (ed.) *Aspects of Metaphor*, Dordrecht, The Netherlands: Kluwer, pp. 189–218.

—— (1996) 'A note on film metaphor', *Journal of Pragmatics*, 26(6), 809–822.
Coëgnarts, M. and Kravanja, P. (2012) 'From thought to modality: A theoretical framework for analysing structural-conceptual metaphors and image metaphors in film', *Image & Narrative*, 13(1), 96–113.
Cunningham, D. (2010) *Psychiatric Tales*, London: Blank Slate.
Demjén, Z. (2014) 'Drowning in negativism, self-hate, doubt, madness: Linguistic insights into Sylvia Plath's experience of depression', *Communication and Medicine*, 11(1), 41–54.
El Refaie, E. (2003) 'Understanding visual metaphor: The example of newspaper cartoons', *Visual Communication*, 2(1), 75–96.
—— (2009) 'Metaphor in political cartoons: Exploring audience responses', in C. Forceville, and E. Urios-Aparisi (eds) *Multimodal Metaphor*, Berlin and New York: Mouton de Gruyter, pp. 173–196.
—— (2013) 'Cross-modal resonances in creative multimodal metaphors: Breaking out of conceptual prisons', *Review of Cognitive Linguistics*, 11(2), 236–249.
—— (2014) 'Looking on the dark and bright side: Creative metaphors of depression in two graphic memoirs', *a/b: Auto/Biography Studies*, 29(1), 149–174.
Fauconnier, G. and Turner, M. (2002) *The Way We Think: Conceptual Blending and the Mind's Hidden Complexities*, New York: Basic Books.
Feng, D. and O'Halloran, K. L. (2013) 'The visual representation of metaphor: A social semiotic approach', *Review of Cognitive Linguistics*, 11(2), 320–335.
Forceville, C. (1996) *Pictorial Metaphor in Advertising*, London and New York: Routledge.
—— (2002) 'The identification of target and source in pictorial metaphors', *Journal of Pragmatics*, 34(1), 1–14.
—— (2007) 'Multimodal metaphor in ten Dutch TV commercials', *The Public Journal of Semiotics*, 1(1), available at: http://pjos.org/index.php/pjos/article/view/8812/7894 (accessed 30 August 2016).
—— (2009) 'Non-verbal and multimodal metaphor in a cognitivist framework: Agendas for research', in C. Forceville and E. Urios-Aparisi (eds) *Multimodal Metaphor*, Berlin and New York: Mouton de Gruyter, pp. 19–42.
—— (2013) 'Metaphor and symbol: SEARCHING FOR ONE'S IDENTITY IS LOOKING FOR A HOME in animation film', *Review of Cognitive Linguistics*, 11(2), 250–268.
Forceville, C., El Refaie, E. and Meesters, G. (2014) 'Stylistics and comics', in M. Burke (ed.) *The Routledge Handbook of Stylistics*, London: Routledge, pp. 485–499.
Forney, E. (2012) *Marbles: Mania, Depression, Michelangelo and Me*, New York: Gotham/Penguin.
Gibbons, A. (2013) 'Multimodal metaphors in contemporary experimental literature', in L. Hidalgo-Downing and B. Kraljevic-Mujic (eds) *Metaphorical Creativity across Modes*, special issue of *Metaphor and the Social World*, 3(2), 180–198.
Gibbs, R.W., Jr. (1994) *The Poetics of Mind: Figurative Thought, Language, and Understanding*, Cambridge, UK: Cambridge University Press.
Gkiouzepas, L. and Hogg, M. K. (2011) 'Articulating a new framework for visual metaphors in advertising', *Journal of Advertising*, 40(1), 103–120.
Gombrich, E. H. (1971) 'The cartoonist's armoury', in E. H. Gombrich (ed.) *Meditations on a Hobby Horse and Other Essays on the Theory of Art*, 2nd edn, London: Phaidon, pp. 127–142.
Grady, J. (1999) 'A typology of motivation for conceptual metaphor: Correlation vs. resemblance', in R. W. Gibbs, Jr. and G. Steen (eds) *Metaphor in Cognitive Linguistics*, Amsterdam, The Netherlands: John Benjamins, pp. 79–100.
Jeong, S.-H. (2008) 'Visual metaphor in advertising: Is the persuasive effect attributable to visual argumentation or metaphorical rhetoric?', *Journal of Marketing Communications*, 14(1), 59–73.
Kennedy, J. M., Green, C. D. and Vervaeke, J. (1993) 'Metaphoric thought and devices in pictures', *Metaphor and Symbolic Activity*, 8(3), 243–255.
Kress, G. (2000) 'Text as the punctuation of semiosis: Pulling at some of the threads', in U. H. Meinhof and J. Smith (eds) *Intertextuality and the Media: From Genre to Everyday Life*, Manchester, UK: Manchester University Press, pp. 132–154.

—— (2009) 'What is mode?', in C. Jewitt (ed.) *The Routledge Handbook of Multimodal Analysis*, London and New York: Routledge, pp. 54–67.

Kress, G. and van Leeuwen. T. (2001) *Multimodal Discourse: The Modes and Media of Contemporary Communication*, London: Arnold.

—— (2006) *Reading Images: The Grammar of Visual Design*, 2nd edn, London: Routledge.

Lakoff, G. and Johnson, M. (1980) *Metaphors We Live By*, Chicago, IL, and London: University of Chicago Press.

Lakoff, G. and Turner, M. (1989) *More Than Cool Reason: A Field Guide to Poetic Metaphor*, Chicago, IL: University of Chicago Press.

Lemke, J. L. (1998) 'Multiplying meaning: Visual and verbal semiotics in scientific text', in J. R. Martin and R. Veel (eds) *Reading Science: Critical and Functional Perspectives*, London: Routledge, pp. 87–113.

McQuarrie, E. F. and Mick, D. G. (1999) 'Visual rhetoric in advertising: Text interpretive, experimental, and reader-response analyses', *Journal of Consumer Research*, 26(1), 37–54.

Mittelberg, I. and Waugh, L. R. (2009) 'Metonymy first, metaphor second: A cognitive-semiotic approach to multimodal figures of thought in co-speech gesture', in C. Forceville and E. Urios-Aparisi (eds) *Multimodal Metaphor*, Berlin and New York: Mouton de Gruyter, pp. 329–356.

Ng, C. J. W. and Koller, V. (2013) 'Deliberate conventional metaphor in images: The case of corporate branding discourse', *Metaphor and Symbol*, 28(3), 131–147.

Ortiz, M. J. (2011) 'Primary metaphors and monomodal visual metaphors', *Journal of Pragmatics*, 43(6), 1568–1580.

Parsons, M. (2010) 'Interpreting art through metaphors', *International Journal of Art & Design Education*, 29(3), 228–235.

Phillips, B. (2003) 'Understanding visual metaphor in advertising', in L. M. Scott and R. Batra (eds) *Persuasive Imagery: A Consumer Response Perspective*, London: Lawrence Erlbaum, pp. 297–310.

Phillips, B. J. and McQuarrie, E. F. (2004) 'Beyond visual metaphor: A new typology of visual rhetoric in advertising', *Marketing Theory*, 4(1–2), 113–136.

Popa, D. E. (2013) 'Multimodal metaphor in political entertainment', *Review of Cognitive Linguistics*, 11(2), 236–249.

Proctor, T., Proctor, S. and Papasolomou, I. (2005) 'Visualizing the metaphor', *Journal of Marketing Communications*, 11(1), 55–72.

Rohdin, M. (2009) 'Multimodal metaphor in classical film theory from the 1920 to the 1950s', in C. Forceville and E. Urios-Aparisi (eds) *Multimodal Metaphor*, Berlin and New York: Mouton de Gruyter, pp. 403–428.

Schilperoord, J., Maes, A. and Ferdinandusse, H. (2009) 'Perceptual and conceptual visual rhetoric: The case of symmetric object alignment', *Metaphor and Symbol*, 24(3), 155–173.

Schoeneman, T. J., Schoeneman, K. A. and Stallings, S. (2004) '"The black struggle": Metaphors of depression in Styron's *Darkness Visible*', *Journal of Social and Clinical Psychology*, 23(3), 325–346.

Teng, N. Y. and Sun, S. (2002) 'Grouping, simile, and oxymoron in pictures: A design-based cognitive approach', *Metaphor and Symbol*, 17(4), 295–316.

Urios-Aparisi, E. (2010) 'The body of love in Almodóvar's cinema: Metaphor and metonymy of the body and body parts', *Metaphor and Symbol*, 25(3), 181–203.

van Leeuwen, T. (2005) *Introducing Social Semiotics*, London and New York: Routledge.

van Mulken, M., le Pair, R. and Forceville, C. (2010) 'The impact of perceived complexity, deviation and comprehension on the appreciation of visual metaphor in advertising across three European countries', *Journal of Pragmatics*, 42(12), 3418–3430.

Winter, B. (2014) 'Horror movies and the cognitive ecology of primary metaphors', *Metaphor and Symbol*, 26(4), 272–298.

Yu, N. (2009) 'Nonverbal and multimodal manifestations of metaphors and metonymies: A case study', in C. Forceville and E. Urios-Aparisi (eds) *Multimodal Metaphor*, Berlin and New York: Mouton de Gruyter, pp. 119–143.

Part III
Formal variation of metaphor in language

11
Metaphor and parts-of-speech

Tina Krennmayr

Introduction

Metaphor is part and parcel of everyday language use and can be found across all major parts-of-speech (word classes). For example, shares can <u>rise</u>; one can feel <u>down</u> or find a <u>way</u> to make things possible. Even prepositions can be metaphorical, though they are unlikely to be recognised as such (e.g. to be <u>on</u> time). Goatly (1997) was one of the first scholars to devote attention to the relationship between metaphor and parts-of-speech. He suggests that part-of-speech has an influence on the interpretation of metaphor, claiming that metaphorical nouns are particularly noticeable. Whether this is indeed the case, however, can only be verified by experimental research on metaphor and parts-of-speech, which is scarce. What research does exist (e.g. Steen, 2004), points to word class as an influencing parameter on metaphor recognition. Yet part-of-speech is a variable seldom considered in experimental studies on metaphor recognition, comprehension and interpretation, and is often neglected in the design of stimulus texts.

Research approaching metaphor from a corpus-linguistic perspective has also revealed interesting connections between metaphor and parts-of-speech. Corpus-linguistic approaches can reveal larger patterns that may go unnoticed when examining hand-picked examples. Deignan (2005) has made inroads into a largely neglected area of research, revealing important connections between metaphor and word class such as changes in metaphoricity when a lexical item shifts part-of-speech (e.g. 'a cute <u>ferret</u>' versus 'to <u>ferret</u> out the truth').

Both experimental and corpus work on metaphor and parts-of-speech may have implications for theory development, design of experimental materials and interpretation of metaphor use in discourse. The notion of parts-of-speech also plays an important role in the early stages of metaphor analysis, namely when collecting metaphorical lexis in natural language data. First, different parts-of-speech pose unique challenges for metaphor identification (for details, see the section on 'Methodological challenges and debates'). Second, a researcher will need to decide whether to consider word formation processes when determining if meanings are related via metaphor (e.g. is the verb *to dog* metaphorically related to the noun *dog*?) (Steen *et al.*, 2010a).

More generally, metaphor in discourse cannot be treated as a phenomenon isolated from word class. Steen et al. (2010a) have demonstrated that metaphor shows interesting interactions with word class and different kinds of discourse. Since each register exhibits its own unique distribution of word classes, the frequency and distribution of metaphor in discourse is heavily influenced by the kind of discourse analysed.

Given these important findings and crucial methodological considerations, there is surprisingly little corpus-based or experimental research on the relation between metaphor and word class. Notable exceptions are: Goatly (1997, 2011) on the interpretation of metaphors, and metaphor and word formation processes; Deignan (2005, 2007) on literal versus metaphorical uses of lexis; Cameron (2003) on metaphor and word class in spoken educational discourse; Steen (2004) on the recognition of metaphors in song lyrics; Steen et al. (2010a) on the relation between metaphor, word class and register; Krennmayr (2011, 2014) on word class and metaphor in news texts; Dorst (2011) on fiction; Pasma (2011) on Dutch news and conversations; Kaal (2012) on conversations; and Herrmann (2013) on academic writing.

This chapter will first give an overview of research on metaphor and word class, including experimental and corpus-linguistic approaches. This will be followed by a discussion of methodological challenges that will be encountered by any researcher identifying metaphor in natural discourse or selecting lexical items for experimental stimulus materials. The chapter will conclude with an example from recent research that takes word class into account, in the entire research process from beginning to end. The goal of this chapter is to show that the relation between part-of-speech and metaphor deserves greater attention when researching metaphor in language use.

Overview of research on metaphor and parts-of-speech

As mentioned above, there is surprisingly little research on the relationship between metaphor and parts-of-speech, even though part-of-speech has been shown to play an important role in metaphor recognition, identification, interpretation, and distribution in discourse, and has valuable practical relevance, such as in foreign language teaching.

Goatly (1997, 2011) focuses on word formation processes and on how the consequences of choosing a particular word class influences metaphor interpretation. He argues that adverbial and prepositional metaphors are less forceful and less likely to be recognised as metaphors than verbal and adjectival ones. Nominal metaphors are described as the most powerful category, as they prompt richer interpretations than other word classes. They are more recognisable as metaphors, since the clash between metaphorical and non-metaphorical meanings is particularly strong and the referents are easily imaginable, giving them greater metaphorical force. Goatly argues that this is even true for nouns describing processes, such as *tennis* or *gurgling*, because they are commonly used to refer to a schema or script, which can also prompt rich interpretations.

Metaphorically used verbs can also evoke imagery through a process Goatly (2011) calls 'vehicle construction', that is, a connection to their conventional 'colligate', i.e. a lexical unit with which it is syntactically connected. For example, in 'the gills <u>kneading</u> quietly' (85), metaphoricity is evoked through the evocation of the conventional colligate of *kneading*, i.e. *hands*. The structure of gills and their movements are compared to the structure and the movement of hands. This works similarly for adjectives such as in '<u>naked</u> shingles of the world' (81), for which the conventional colligate is *body* (human-related) and not an inanimate object (*shingles*). Adverbs and prepositions belong to what Goatly calls 'inactive' metaphors, which have noun or verb colligates that are too general to yield any imagery.

Goatly gives a rich collection of examples to illustrate his argument, and his claims on metaphor interpretation are often intuitively plausible. However, they cannot be verified by his hand-picked assortment of examples. Is it indeed the case, as Goatly claims, that nouns are most powerful and most easily recognised as metaphors and give rise to rich interpretations? In order to answer questions like these, experimental approaches are required.

Parts-of-speech and metaphor recognition and processing

In order to determine how metaphors used in different parts-of-speech influence the way we perceive their metaphoricity, recognise them in texts, or process them, it is necessary to go beyond examining linguistic examples. Jamrozik et al.'s (2013) experimental results, for example, call for a more nuanced interpretation of Goatly's (1997, 2011) prediction that more concrete and imaginable words such as nouns have greater metaphoricity. For instance, they discovered that there is a difference between, on the one hand, nouns and verbs that take more than one argument, so-called relational nouns (e.g. *friend*) or relational verbs (e.g. *know)*, and, on the other hand, so-called entity words (e.g. *zebra, thing*). Test subjects rated relational words as more metaphorical than entity words. While Jamrozik et al.'s (2013) research underlines that word class and relationality matter, their test sets consisted of only one sentence with an underlined and bolded word; participants were asked to judge the word's metaphoricity. What happens when people confront words in a more elaborate context, as in their everyday lives? Is metaphor more easily recognised in some parts-of-speech than in others in natural language discourse? In other words, does part-of-speech affect how people pick out metaphors from a text if asked to look for them? Attempting to answer these questions, Steen (2004) conducted a study in which he asked test subjects to underline metaphors in song lyrics by Bob Dylan. His results suggest that nouns and noun phrases are more easily recognised as metaphorically used than verbs and verb phrases. This was counter to the expectations. All verbal metaphors were explicit (i.e. the utterance contained both the literal and the non-metaphorical word) and most of the nominal metaphors were implicit (and thus needed to be reconstructed through inferencing). The result may be influenced by the fact that most nominal metaphors in the data occurred after the verb, and metaphors were more likely to be recognised in post-verbal position than when they occurred pre-verbally or in verbal position (Steen, 2004). Moreover, noun metaphors have a higher imagery value and may therefore be more richly interpretable and thus recognised more frequently as metaphorically used, as Goatly (1997, 2011) claims. Based on Jamrozik et al.'s research (2013), it may be worthwhile to explore whether the results of their rating study also hold for metaphor recognition in experimental setups such as Steen's (2004).

Steen's (2004) results clearly suggest that word class influences metaphor recognition, though further research is needed. For example, his work did not consider the factors of novelty and conventionality of the metaphors in the stimulus text, while Krennmayr et al. (2014), for example, have shown that recall of metaphorically used words in a text is influenced by their degree of conventionality. Novel metaphors are more often recalled than conventional ones. In Steen's text, novel metaphors may thus be more likely to be recognised than conventional ones. Further research needs to uncover if/how word class interacts with the degree of conventionality in metaphor recognition.

Cameron's (2003) research takes a different focus: she is interested in what happens when people reason about topics that have been described in metaphorical terms. Using goal-directed interactive think-aloud tasks in which children were asked, for example, to help the researcher decide if a book on the ozone layer was suitable for a younger child, she investigates the processes involved when students make sense of the metaphors they come across. For example, do metaphors lead to new understandings and do they help to recall new information? She found that nominal and verb metaphors were comprehended and interpreted differently. Nominal metaphors tended to be explicitly referenced and positively evaluated: they were restated, contextualised and reformulated, and could even become the focus of discussion. They turned out to be good examples of deliberate use, i.e. they were used 'for a particular purpose on a particular occasion' (Cameron, 2003). An example of deliberate metaphor use in Cameron's data came from a teacher, who made an explicit comparison between distinct domains when describing lava as being like 'sticky treacle' or like 'runny butter' (103).

Verb metaphors showed a different pattern. If a verb metaphor was commented on, the comment was usually about the larger phrase or sentence; it did not concern the metaphor directly but was rather about the topic. Verb metaphors were repeated and re-lexicalised (mostly as phrasal verbs) but were not taken up for discussion, which remained focused on the topic rather than the metaphor. Cameron suggests that verb metaphors are less stable, more flexible and more likely to be extended than those involving nouns, which may be why their effects differ from noun metaphors. In particular, their combination with prepositions dramatically increases the range of meanings that can be expressed.

All these findings suggest that word class is a factor that cannot be ignored when examining perceived metaphoricity, and when looking at how metaphors are recognised in discourse and how people interpret, understand and process information drawing on metaphorical language use. In order to get a better understanding of qualitative and quantitative differences between metaphors in different parts-of-speech as they occur in everyday language use, it is necessary to go beyond experimental approaches. Through corpus-linguistic studies, it is possible to detect larger patterns of metaphorical and literal uses of different parts-of-speech.

Parts-of-speech and corpus research

Examining metaphors in large corpora can reveal patterns that may not be apparent from a handful of examples. For example, through her corpus research, Deignan (2005) realised that literal and metaphorical meanings of a word often belong to different word classes. She also noticed that the relative frequencies of metaphorically used words of different word classes seem to vary across source domains (see Chapter 1). In her data the source domain of ANIMALS tended to be realised by nouns, the source domain of MOVEMENT featured a prominent use of verbs, and the source domain of CLEANLINESS AND DIRT contained a high incidence of adjectives.

By examining concordance data, Deignan found that words derived from nouns were often used metaphorically. For example, an examination of concordances of *fox*, *foxes*, *foxing*, and *foxed* revealed that of the over 400 uses of the noun, only three were metaphorical, while all of the uses of verbs derived from the noun *fox* were metaphorical. The adjective *foxy* was also exclusively metaphorically used. Note that there is no unanimous agreement between researchers on whether or not there is a metaphorical relationship between the noun and the adjective or verb. For details, refer to the section on 'methodological challenges and debates' below. According to Deignan, grammatical conversion in metaphorical mappings may be expected in cases where entities that are easy to imagine are used metaphorically to talk about abstract qualities, such as, for example, behaviour.

Thus changes in word class and metaphoricity appear to correlate. Subtler differences can be detected when the use of metaphors within a certain word class is examined.

For example, in Deignan's data the verbs *rock*, *shake* and *stir* tended to occur in the passive when used metaphorically to express emotions, while for their literal uses both passive and active forms were employed. As was the case with verbs, detailed analysis of adjectival metaphors of cleanliness and dirt (e.g. *clean, dirty, spotless, filthy*) also revealed different patterns for literal versus metaphorical usage. Metaphorical uses tended to occur as relatively fixed expressions, while in their literal sense these adjectives were often part of clear-cut pairs of antonyms (e.g. you can talk dirty but not talk clean, while dishes can be *clean* or *dirty*). Overall, corpus evidence suggests that metaphorical uses are more restricted in terms of their grammatical choices than their literal counterparts.

These findings have clear applications in foreign language learning and instruction. Words can often extend their meaning via a change in word class, but the principles whereby this change takes place may differ across languages, leading to problems for learners. For example, MacArthur and Littlemore (2008) report that Spanish learners of English could not figure out the meanings of metaphorically used *mushroom* or *weather* when used as verbs. Interestingly, even though A = B metaphors (e.g. 'My lawyer is a shark') are rare in natural language data (Deignan, 2005), this pattern seemed particularly salient to Spanish learners. As a consequence, non-native speakers tended to use nominal rather than verbal metaphors in their first language for guessing the meaning of unknown verbs (e.g. 'I think it probably means something like "be a bad person" because in German we say someone is a snake when we mean he's bad').

Word class also seems to play a role in the production of metaphors. Native and non-native speakers have been shown to exhibit diverging distributions of metaphors across word class in their production of written texts. For example, while Norwegian non-native writers of English use fewer adjectives and nouns than native speakers do in their writing, the ones they do produce are more often used metaphorically than those employed by native speakers (Nacey, 2013).

While there are differences in patterns for literal versus metaphorical uses within word classes, as Deignan has shown, there can also be differences in their patterns of use across different registers. For example, examining a corpus of news texts and conversations from the VU Amsterdam Metaphor Corpus (Steen *et al.*, 2010b), Krennmayr (2011) showed that the verb *come* is typically used metaphorically in news, but almost exclusively literally in everyday conversation. In conversation data, the literal use of *come* is dominated by people seeing each other or making other people go somewhere (e.g. 'But at least when this bloke *comes* tonight you've got something for him'). The few metaphorical uses can be attributed to personification, connecting the human-related *come* to a non-human entity such as in 'the rain came tumbling down splish, splash'. Most metaphorical uses in news are of this type, giving the impression of objective information by concealing human responsibility for decisions and actions (e.g. 'tax rebellions come in crests').

Since metaphorical expressions as used in real discourse are always embedded in a specific communicative context, their functions may vary depending on, for example, the goal of the speakers or writers, the audience, and/or the production circumstances of the discourse. This also becomes clear in Cameron's (2003) research on metaphors in a corpus of spoken classroom discourse. She found that the bulk of all metaphorically used words in her data of classroom talk were prepositions and verbs, followed by nominal metaphors and a small proportion of adjectives and adverbs, which accounted for less than 5 per cent of all metaphorically used words. Verbs, by contrast, made up almost half of the metaphors in her dataset. Such unequal distribution may point to different functions of metaphorically used words across different parts-of-speech. While these figures are representative of classroom talk, the results cannot be extrapolated to other kinds of discourse.

The difference in situational characteristics between different kinds of discourse is reflected in diverging distributions of word classes (Biber, 1988). In other words, word class interacts with register. For instance, conversations are characterised by a high incidence of verbs, whereas nouns dominate in informational registers such as news or academic texts. Consequently, Cameron may have found a high incidence of verb metaphors because her data contained a high proportion of verbs in the first place. This illustrates the importance of taking into account metaphor, word class, and register when interpreting results. A concrete example of current research that takes word class into account right from the start – from collecting data to data analysis – will be presented below. Taking part-of-speech into account poses some methodological challenges, however, mainly concerning decisions a researcher faces when identifying metaphor in data.

Methodological challenges and debates

Parts-of-speech and metaphor identification: the unit of analysis

Every researcher working on metaphor in discourse encounters the issue of part-of-speech in the very first stages of data collection. For example, is the verb to *squirrel* in 'to squirrel away a fortune' metaphorically connected to the noun *squirrel*, which refers to an animal? A clear decision on whether or not to consider metaphorical connections across word classes is crucial, because it will impact the number and kinds of metaphors that will be found in the data, as well as the steps and procedures that will have to be followed when determining the metaphoricity of lexical units. A researcher must therefore decide early on whether to cross word class boundaries when determining the metaphoricity of lexical units. This section will focus on two main approaches. It will highlight the similarities and differences between them and will illustrate the debates surrounding the choice of approach. Ultimately, the approach best followed will depend on the kind of research questions and data the researcher wants to analyse.

Two established methods for metaphor identification, MIP (Pragglejaz Group, 2007) and MIPVU (Steen *et al.*, 2010a), a more elaborate and refined protocol than MIP, can be used to analyse texts for metaphor on a word-by-word basis. For each lexical unit, the analyst must determine its contextual meaning, check if it has a more basic meaning, and decide if the two meanings contrast and whether the contextual meaning can be understood in comparison with the more basic meaning. For example, the contextual meaning of the adjective *high* in 'high standard' is 'very good, or excellent'. The lexical unit also has a more concrete, basic meaning, namely 'large in size from the top to the ground'. The two meanings contrast, but the contextual meaning can be understood in comparison with the more basic meaning. Therefore, in this context, *high* is metaphorically used.

One main distinction between the two procedures is that MIP crosses word class boundaries, while MIPVU does not. In other words, MIPVU takes the grammatical word class as a unit of analysis, while MIP takes the broader lemma (headword in the dictionary). This has repercussions for the selection of relevant contextual and basic senses that need to be compared and contrasted with each other.

To illustrate the process and potential differences in outcome based on the chosen approach, consider the verb *to dog* as in 'Photographers *dogged* the princess all her adult life' (Macmillan English Dictionary for Advanced Learners). Both the MIP and the MIPVU approach will first establish the contextual meaning of the verb, namely, 'to follow someone closely in a way that annoys them'. The verb has no more basic sense, but the noun does: 'an animal kept as a pet, for guarding buildings, or for hunting'. Approaches such as MIP, which take the broader lemma as a unit, compare and contrast the contextual meaning (a typically human action) with the noun's basic referent (the animal). This approach leads one to conclude that the verb *to dog* is metaphorically used in the present context. When noun and verb are considered to be distinct lexical units, as in MIPVU, the meaning of the noun cannot act as a basic sense to which the verb's sense can be compared. In order for the verb to be metaphorically used, there would need to be another, more basic, sense for the verb (not the noun) that could be contrasted with the contextual sense of 'following someone'. Since the verb *to dog* does not have such a more basic sense, MIPVU concludes that it is not metaphorically used in the example above.

While the MIPVU approach does not deny that there is a metaphorical connection between different word classes, the approach emphasises a discourse perspective; it regards this connection as irrelevant for the use in discourse where a word applies to a specific referent. The focus is thus on a word's use in discourse and not on word formation processes. It also has a practical advantage. The researcher only needs to check the meanings of one word class instead of two or more. For example, the noun *break* has 9 sense descriptions in Macmillan; the verb has 13. A researcher crossing word class boundaries has to systematically check all word classes of the lemma and thus a much larger number of meanings. This needs to be done for each and every lexical unit and not just for cases where this may seem convenient (such as the example of *to dog* above). Clearly, such an approach is more time-consuming.

Deignan (2005) presents arguments against considering the noun and the verb separately, giving an example of animal metaphors which are metaphorical as a verb but literal as a noun. She points out that staying within the same word class leads an analyst to label non-metaphorical many uses that most language users would consider to be metaphorical. This applies to many mappings from animals onto humans, e.g. *weasel, horse, ferret,* or *hound*. Deignan (2005) further notes that meaning differences are reflected in form differences. This suggests that metaphorical senses often differ formally from their literal counterparts. For example, the noun *rock* used in its singular form, tends to carry a positive connotation ('the rock on which our society is built'), while in its plural form it has a negative one ('the marriage has been on the rocks for a while').

The examples above illustrate that varying choices for a protocol's basic lexical unit can lead to different outcomes for metaphoricity. Whether the lemma or the grammatical word class is best taken as the unit of analysis will be determined by the research questions and data analysed. For example, in their work on the development of metaphor across different levels of proficiency among learners of English, Littlemore *et al.* (2013) follow the MIPVU procedure but deviate from its instructions by allowing crossing of word classes when identifying metaphor in the corpus. This is because metaphorical senses often differ formally from their literal counterparts and because there is evidence that metaphoricity underlying language is more salient to learners than to native speakers. Learners may therefore benefit from any meaningful metaphorical connections between word senses, whether they belong to the same word class or not. Crossing word class for the identification of metaphor, therefore, better fits with the learner data Littlemore *et al.* analyse. While there may be several ways of operationalising units of analysis, what is most important is to be explicit about what kind of measure is selected and to be consistent and systematic in applying whatever approach was chosen.

Parts-of-speech and metaphor identification: open- and closed-class lexical units

Metaphor is a gradable phenomenon, so the metaphorical status of a lexical unit is not always straightforward to pinpoint. Metaphorical nouns are often relatively easy to identify because they refer to entities, but adjectives, which typically denote properties, may be more difficult (Semino *et al.*, 2002). Other researchers list delexicalised verbs such as *give*, *get*, *have*, *make* or *put* as being particularly difficult for metaphor identification because they are relatively empty semantically (e.g. Cameron, 2003; Deignan, 2005).

Nevertheless, Steen *et al.* (2010a) show that it is possible to locate contextual meanings of delexicalised verbs in the dictionary and to determine their basic senses, which can then be contrasted with more abstract senses. In metaphor identification, they are therefore treated like any other verbs. Consider the following examples taken from a subcorpus of the British National Corpus, the BNC-Baby: in 'We will tackle putting our economy in order [. . .]', *putting* is used in its abstract sense of 'to cause someone or something to be in a particular situation or state'. But *put* does have a more concrete, basic meaning: 'to move something to a particular position, especially using your hands'. In the present context it is thus metaphorically used. The same even goes for *have*, such as in 'I didn't know if I would ever have a chance again'. Though semantically empty, it is possible to identify a meaning that fulfils the criteria of 'more basic', i.e. a meaning that is more concrete and body-related. This is the third sense in the Macmillan dictionary: 'used for showing possession' with two subentries 'to own something' and 'to be holding something or to be carrying something with you'. While *having* a concrete thing like having a pen or a computer is literal, *having* something abstract such as 'a chance' is metaphorical.

Closed class items, such as prepositions, are regarded as particularly semantically empty. And indeed, for prepositions like *of* and *for*, it is difficult to determine a basic meaning, and even more difficult to decide how the multiple senses are related. Consider *of*, for example. We may argue that the sixth sense in Macmillan fulfils the criteria for a more basic sense ('used for saying what something is part of', e.g. 'She sat at the edge of the chair'). However, determining how the other twenty senses are related to that basic meaning is a daunting task for which it is difficult to achieve reliability between different coders.

Many other prepositions, such as *over* or *on*, have clear spatial meanings alongside their numerous abstract uses. A more basic meaning of *on* is 'touching a surface or an object'. References to time, such as 'He is coming home on Wednesday' (Macmillan), are therefore metaphorical. There are some cases that may seem less straightforward, such as determining the metaphorical status of *on* in 'a school on the outskirts of Glasgow' (Macmillan). However, it can be argued that as long as a concrete object (school) and a concrete location (outskirts) are involved, the preposition is not metaphorically used.

Parts-of-speech and metaphor identification: personification

When the use of particularly verbs, adjectives and adverbs normally requires a human entity but a non-human entity replaces the human one, this results in personification. An example is the verb *decide* in 'A party can't even decide its name [. . .]' (BNC-Baby). Taking the noun *party* as a starting point, we can interpret this example as people in the party not being able to decide its name. In this case *party* is interpreted metonymically and *decide* is not used figuratively, since 'deciding' is a human activity referring to the behaviour of people in the party. Starting out from the verb, however, *decide*, should be marked as metaphorically used.

This is because its basic sense is human-related ('to make a choice what you are going to do') and thus requires the presence of a human agent. In this case, there is no human agent but an abstract group – the party. The possibility of metaphorical usage of this type of personification thus depends on analyst perspective (see also Low (1999) and Dorst (2011)). Researchers identifying metaphors need to show awareness of this type of figurative language use, make clear decisions on how to mark it, and follow their decisions consistently.

Current research on metaphor, part-of-speech and register variation

There has long been a lack of corpora annotated exhaustively for metaphor. Responding to this, Steen and colleagues built the VU Amsterdam Metaphor Corpus (Steen *et al.*, 2010b), which consists of texts from four different registers: news, academic texts, fiction, and conversation taken from the BNC-Baby corpus, totalling almost 200,000 lexical units. Each lexical unit has a part-of-speech tag and has been manually coded for metaphor use, taking the grammatical word class as a unit of analysis. Steen *et al.*'s (2010a) goal was to compare metaphor use across different registers. Unlike previous studies, their analysis simultaneously took the variables metaphor, register, and word class into account, allowing them to identify a three-way interaction among these variables. This suggests that one cannot conclude that English tends to place metaphoricity in the verb, as may seem evident from Cameron's (2003) research, without controlling for varying word class distribution among registers. Each register is composed of groups of metaphors per word class that exhibit divergent distributions across different registers. Linguistic metaphor thus cannot be looked at simply as a matter of metaphor in word classes, since such a perspective ignores the functional variation of metaphor across word classes in different registers. In other words, associations between metaphor and register cannot be interpreted directly but need to be interpreted by looking at the distribution of metaphor across word classes per register.

Each register has its own typical distribution of word classes (Biber, 1988; Biber *et al.*, 1999). Highly informational texts such as news reports or academic writing are characterised by a high proportion of nouns, prepositions and adjectives and a low number of verbs and adverbs. This picture is reversed in highly involved discourse such as conversations, with a low proportion of nouns, prepositions and adjectives and a high proportion of verbs and adverbs. Thus word classes are not equally distributed across registers, and merely reporting on frequencies of metaphors in a certain type of discourse cannot give the full picture (see Table 11.1).

In academic discourse, for example, the metaphorical use of prepositions, nouns and verbs dominates in absolute numbers (raw count). A large number of, for example, metaphorical verbs may reflect the fact that verbs are especially likely to be metaphorical in academic discourse. Or it could be because both metaphorical and non-metaphorical verbs in general appear frequently. To distinguish these effects, it is useful to consider metaphor in relative terms, that is to consider the proportion of metaphors within a specific word class (e.g. verbs in academic discourse), rather than the entire register (academic discourse). In relative terms, metaphorical prepositions and verbs are most often metaphorically used in the academic register, followed by adjectives (Herrmann, 2013). News texts display a similar pattern to academic texts. The most frequently used metaphorical words in absolute terms are verbs, prepositions and nouns. In relative terms, metaphorical prepositions are followed by verbs, while adjectives come in third position (Krennmayr, 2011, 2014). In fiction, metaphorical verbs, prepositions and nouns are most dominant, in absolute numbers. In relative terms, metaphorical verbs drop to third place, preceded by adjectives and

Table 11.1 Absolute numbers and percentages of metaphorically used words in four different registers in the VU Amsterdam Metaphor Corpus

	Academic	News	Fiction	Conversation
Metaphorical adjectives	818	791	575	233
% in register	17.6	21.0	19.4	13.3
Metaphorical adverbs	252	241	264	321
% in register	10.1	11.0	9.3	7.5
Metaphorical conjunctions	41	22	25	35
% in register	1.4	0.9	1.0	1.5
Metaphorical determiners	544	339	378	654
% in register	8.1	5.9	7.6	15.6
Metaphorical nouns	2,345	1,701	1,016	461
% in register	17.6	13.2	10.5	8.3
Metaphorical prepositions	2,750	1,958	1,411	838
% in register	42.5	841.7	33.4	33.8
Metaphorical verbs	2,255	2,172	1,555	1,110
% in register	27.7	27.6	15.9	9.1
Metaphorical remainder	117	118	69	35
% in register	2.6	2.5	0.9	0.2
Metaphorical total	9,122	7,342	5,293	3,687
	18.5	16.4	11.9	7.7

prepositions (Dorst, 2011). The conversation register, as the only spoken register in the VU Amsterdam Metaphor Corpus, deviates strongly from the three written registers. In terms of overall frequencies, verbs, prepositions, and determiners belong to the most metaphorical word classes. In relative terms, metaphorical prepositions again come out at the top, followed by determiners and adjectives. Metaphorical verbs, nouns and adverbs are lowest on the list (Kaal, 2012).

How the type of discourse along with its unique distribution of word classes shapes the use of metaphor can also be seen in Berber Sardinha's (2008) investigation of metaphor in both a general corpus and a specialised corpus of Portuguese. He calculated the probability of a metaphorically used lexical unit belonging to a particular part-of-speech. Words in the general corpus were most likely to be metaphorical when they were adjectives, followed by verbs, adverbs, nouns, and prepositions. Metaphorically used words in the specialised corpus were most likely to be nouns, followed by adverbs, adjectives, and verbs, with prepositions being the least probable.

If a word class is typical of and has an important function in a specific type of discourse, it is consequently more frequent and more prominent in comparison to other word classes. This will naturally raise the absolute number of metaphorically used words in that word class. What is more revealing, then, is to examine if and how certain parts-of-speech are metaphorical in ways that go against the distributional grain. For example, nouns are a prominent feature of news texts. Are metaphorically used nouns also more frequent in news texts? Verbs are not particularly frequent in news texts, but perhaps they are when they are metaphorically used? Below are examples of two studies focusing on the (non-)metaphorical use of two selected word classes in newspapers, and on how their use differs from their use in academic writing (nouns) and conversations (verbs). For a detailed discussion and analysis of word classes refer to Krennmayr (2011) for news, Dorst (2011) for fiction, Kaal (2012) for conversation, and Herrmann (2013) for academic texts. For metaphor and word class in Dutch news texts and conversations, see Pasma (2011).

Nouns

As informational registers, both academic texts and news texts are characterised by a dominant use of nouns, which allows for dense information packaging. Within news texts, there is a contrast between metaphorical nouns and non-metaphorical ones. Metaphorical nouns are used less frequently and non-metaphorical ones more frequently than expected. Journalists typically make use of non-metaphorical nouns designating concrete people and places. Many abstract nouns refer to institutions (e.g. *government*) or points in time (e.g. *day*, *week*) and societal issues (e.g. *problem*). They do not have a more basic meaning and are never metaphorically used in this particular dataset (Krennmayr, 2011).

Compared to other registers, academic writing exhibits an underuse in literal nouns and overuse in metaphorical ones. Metaphor is needed for information packaging of complex content, textual cohesion and organisation of arguments. Nouns also seem to play a particular role in direct comparisons as part of deliberate metaphor use (e.g. 'almost as if it were a piece of engineering') (Herrmann, 2013).

Even metaphorically used items frequent in both registers, such as *way* or *point*, are employed in different ways. For example, the metaphorical use of *way* in news often describes the one and only approach to address a societal problem (e.g. 'the only way to develop a prototype' or 'the only way to remove the Government'). In academic writing, *way* tends to be metaphorically used in order to highlight different angles of discussion ('to frame the law in such a way' or 'there is no precise way of describing those non-intentional killings'). Overall, news texts are characterised by a higher type-token ratio (*way* and *ways* are tokens of the same type) of metaphorical nouns than academic texts. A high type-token ratio indicates large variability; a low type-token ratio signals low variability. The results thus suggest that journalists draw on a variety of metaphorical lexical items to transfer a message to the audience, while writers of academic texts tend to reuse metaphorical nouns that are perceived as conventional by the expert audience. Thus academic writers seem to value consistency, whereas journalists tend to aim for stylistic variation.

Verbs

Newspaper texts and spontaneous conversations exhibit contrasting patterns for both metaphorically and non-metaphorically used verbs. While a high frequency of verbs is characteristic of spontaneous conversation, metaphorical verbs are atypical. Highly informational texts such as newspaper articles, on the other hand, are characterised by a low incidence of verbs; metaphorical verbs, however, are highly prominent.

Close inspection of the metaphorical verbs in news texts shows that personification is a major contributor to their high number. Half of the metaphorical uses of *say*, for example, can be attributed to personification. While journalists report on what people *say*, the individuals are frequently hidden behind parties, companies or agencies (e.g. 'the Roman Catholic Church says this is a deterrent to unity'). At the same time, this has a simplifying function when the identity of individual actors is not directly relevant for comprehension. In face-to-face conversation, by contrast, only one fifth of the metaphorical uses of *say* can be attributed to personification. This is because conversations revolve around individual people talking about what they or other people say.

The top metaphorical verbs in both news texts and conversations are mostly delexicalised (e.g. *have*, *get*, *give*) and are mainly attributable to the semantic domains of movement and perception. Overall, news makes use of a greater variety of verbs than conversations and even more distinct lemmas are involved when verbs are metaphorical (Krennmayr, 2011, 2014).

These examples give a glimpse of how metaphor, while present across all major word classes and part of all types of natural discourse, reveals its unique distribution in different registers across different word classes. As a result, a researcher interpreting the use of metaphors in a text needs to show awareness of both the register he or she is analysing and the word classes that are typical of that register.

Conclusion and future directions

Recent corpus-linguistic approaches have shown interesting and strong connections between metaphor and word class in terms of their forms, their grammatical patterns, their distribution, or their relation to different registers. Apart from some attempts to learn more about which word classes are recognised more frequently as metaphors, psycholinguistic research and cognitive metaphor theory have so far neglected the richness of results obtained in corpus-linguistic studies. This is particularly apparent in the stimulus materials created in many experimental setups. Such materials often involve noun metaphors in A = B structures (e.g. 'My life is a jail'), which are not very frequent in natural discourse. Experimental studies on metaphor processing in discourse especially stand to benefit from the findings of corpus linguistics for both the generation of experimental material and the interpretation of the data. Future experimental research on metaphor recognition, understanding, processing or appreciation also needs to aim at uncovering if/how the degree of conventionality of metaphorically used words interacts with word class.

While research, particularly by Cameron (2003), Deignan (2005), Dorst (2011), Krennmayr (2011), Kaal (2012), Pasma (2011), and Herrmann (2013), has revealed rich and interesting connections between metaphor and part-of-speech in natural discourse, much more work is needed. In particular, there is urgent need for further in-depth corpus studies that explore the distribution and function of different word classes across different kinds of registers and the differences in grammatical form between literal and metaphorical uses.

Findings on metaphor and part-of-speech also have practical relevance, in particular for foreign language learning and instruction. This is because principles of meaning extension, for example through a word's change of grammatical class, are not always the same across different languages. Teachers and learners would benefit from cross-linguistic research on meaning extensions as well as phraseological patterns.

Further reading

Cameron, L. (2003) *Metaphor in Educational Discourse*, London/New York: Continuum. (Chapter 4)
Deignan, A. (2005) *Metaphor and Corpus Linguistics*, Amsterdam/Philadelphia: John Benjamins. (Chapter 7)
Goatly, A. (2011) *The Language of Metaphors*, 2nd edn. London/New York: Routledge. (Chapter 3)
Krennmayr, T. (2014) 'What corpus linguistics can tell us about metaphor use in newspaper texts', *Journalism Studies*. DOI: 10.1080/1461670X.2014.937155.
Steen, G. J., Dorst, A. G., Herrmann, J. B, Krennmayr, T. and Pasma, T. (2010) *A Method for Linguistic Metaphor Identification: From MIP to MIPVU*, Amsterdam, The Netherlands: John Benjamins.

References

Berber Sardinha, T. (2008) 'Metaphor probabilities in corpora', in M. S. Zanotto, L. Cameron and M. C. Cavalcanti (eds) *Confronting Metaphor in Use: An Applied Linguistic Approach*, Amsterdam/Atlanta: John Benjamins, pp. 127–148.

Biber, D. (1988) *Variation across Speech and Writing*, Cambridge, UK: Cambridge University Press.

Biber, D., Johansson, S., Leech, G., Conrad, S. and Finegan, E. (1999) *The Longman Grammar of Spoken and Written English*, London: Longman.

Cameron, L. (2003) *Metaphor in Educational Discourse*, London/New York: Continuum.

Deignan, A. (2005) *Metaphor and Corpus Linguistics*, Amsterdam/Philadelphia: John Benjamins.

—— (2007) 'The grammar of linguistic metaphors', in A. Stefanowitsch and S. Th. Gries (eds) *Corpus-based Approaches to Metaphor and Metonymy*, Berlin, Germany: Mouton de Gruyter, pp. 106–122.

Dorst, A. G. (2011) *Metaphor in Fiction: Linguistic Forms, Conceptual Structures, Cognitive Representations*, Oisterwijk, The Netherlands: BOXpress.

Goatly, A. (1997) *The Language of Metaphors*, London/New York: Routledge.

—— (2011) *The Language of Metaphors*, 2nd edn, New York: Routledge.

Herrmann, J. B. (2013) *Metaphor in Academic Discourse: Linguistic Forms, Conceptual Structures, Communicative Functions and Cognitive Representations*, Utrecht, The Netherlands: LOT dissertation series.

Jamrozik, A., Sagi, E., Goldwater, M. and Gentner, D. (2013) 'Relational words have high metaphoric potential', in E. Shutova, B. Beigman, J. Klebanov, J. Tetreault and Z. Kozareva (eds) *Proceedings of the 2013 Meeting of the North American Association for Computational Linguistics: Human Language Technologies, First Workshop on Metaphor in NLP*, Atlanta, GA: Association for Computational Linguistics.

Kaal, A. A. (2012) *Metaphor in Conversation*, Oisterwijk, The Netherlands: BOXpress.

Krennmayr, T. (2011) *Metaphor in Newspapers*, Utrecht, The Netherlands: LOT.

—— (2014) 'What corpus linguistics can tell us about metaphor use in newspaper texts', *Journalism Studies*, 16(4), 1–17.

Krennmayr, T., Bowdle, B. F., Mulder, G. and Steen, G. J. (2014) 'Building metaphorical schemas when reading text', *Metaphor and the Social World*, 4, 65–89.

Littlemore, J., Krennmayr, T., Turner, S. and Turner, J. (2013) 'An investigation into metaphor use at different levels of second language writing', *Applied Linguistics*, 1–29.

Low, G. D. (1999) '"This paper thinks . . .": Investigating the acceptability of the metaphor AN ESSAY IS A PERSON', in L. Cameron and G. Low (eds) *Researching and Applying Metaphor*, Cambridge, UK: Cambridge University Press, pp. 221–248.

MacArthur, F. and Littlemore, J. (2008) 'Figurative language learning with the use of corpora', in F. Boers and S. Lindstromberg (eds) *Cognitive Linguistic Approaches to Teaching Vocabulary and Phraseology*, Berlin, Germany: Mouton de Gruyter, pp. 159–188.

Nacey, S. (2013) *Metaphor in Learner English*, Amsterdam, The Netherlands: John Benjamins.

Pasma, T. (2011) *Metaphor and Register Variation. The Personalization of Dutch News Discourse*, Oisterwijk, The Netherlands: BOXpress.

Pragglejaz Group (2007) 'MIP: A method for identifying metaphorically used words in discourse', *Metaphor and Symbol*, 22, 1–39.

Semino, E., Heywood, J. and Short, M. H. (2002) 'Linguistic metaphor identification in two extracts from novels', *Language and Literature*, 11, 35–54.

Steen, G. J. (2004) 'Can discourse properties of metaphor affect metaphor recognition?', *Journal of Pragmatics*, 36, 1295–1313.

Steen, G. J., Dorst, A. G., Herrmann, J. B., Kaal, A. A. and Krennmayr, T. (2010a) *A Method for Linguistic Metaphor Identification: From MIP to MIPVU*, Amsterdam, The Netherlands: John Benjamins.

—— (2010b) VU Amsterdam Metaphor Corpus. http://ota.ahds.ac.uk/headers/2541.xml.

12
Textual patterning of metaphor

Aletta G. Dorst

Introduction

Prototypical studies in the Conceptual Metaphor Theory (CMT) tradition are often mainly interested in relating any identified linguistic metaphors to a relatively fixed set of conceptual metaphors (see Chapter 1). That is, in most of these studies, the textual patterning and systematicity of linguistic metaphors serves only as evidence for the existence of conventional patterns of thought, rather than being the object of study themselves. As pointed out by Semino (2008), among others, this has led to a systematic neglect of the specific forms, functions and effects of linguistic manifestations of metaphor.

Yet metaphors in language vary depending on whether and how they pattern, and these patterns can reveal the connections between local, individual uses of metaphor and the contextualized discourse event. Studying metaphor patterns allows us to determine how language users introduce, develop, negotiate, challenge, reject and adapt metaphors within the context of the discourse event in order to achieve their rhetorical goals and meet the needs of their addressees. For example, a writer or speaker may continue to use the same metaphor to talk about the same topic, or may use a related or different one. Or they may use the same metaphor to talk about a different topic. In spoken interaction particularly, studying metaphor patterns reveals whether and how speakers use each other's metaphors, and how metaphors are introduced, developed and dropped dynamically (e.g. Cameron 2003, 2007; see Chapters 4 and 29).

Analysing the patterns of metaphor in a single text (whether written or spoken) or a group of texts can help us deduce why the writer or speaker uses them, i.e. what their rhetorical goal is and what effect those patterns may have on the reader or listener. For instance, a pattern may be aimed at grabbing the readers' attention and entertaining them through the creation of humour (see Semino 2008 on punning in newspaper headlines), or at creating coherence between different parts of the discourse in order to help readers understand a complex issue (see Semino 2008 on political discourse). Patterns can also be used to signal similarities or differences between topics in order to add symbolic meaning to a text, for instance, in literature (see Goatly 1997, 2011), or to persuade readers to adopt a particular point of view or ideology (see Krennmayr 2011 on news texts). Unlike conceptual metaphors, such patterns of metaphor in language generally are flexible, varied, dynamic and specific to the discourse context in which they are used, rather than serving general language functions. At the same time, they can also be relatively stable and fixed across one or several discourse events; this temporary stability is captured by labels such as 'systematic metaphors' (e.g. Cameron 2007; see Chapter 6) or 'discourse metaphors' (e.g. Zinken et al. 2008).

This chapter will first present an overview of some of the main types of metaphor patterns that occur in authentic discourse, as well as their functions and effects. Then a number of methodological issues will be addressed. The Current Research section will first discuss a recent experimental study that investigated how metaphor patterns are received by readers of news texts. The reception of metaphor patterns remains an exciting, under-researched area of interest, as most studies on patterns of metaphor focus primarily on determining their purpose and the rhetorical aims of the producer. The section will then offer a discussion of current research on how the use of signalling devices interacts with register, and how signalled metaphor in fiction often occurs in specific types of patterns that have a function in the narrative or are characteristic of the author's style.

Overview of metaphor patterns in discourse

Establishing patterns of metaphor in language helps the researcher determine the function of linguistic metaphors and can serve as the basis for assumptions about the possible reasons the writer/speaker may have had in using them (e.g. to create cohesion, grab attention), as well as about any possible effects they may have on readers/listeners (e.g. the reader is entertained or persuaded). To understand the functions and effects of metaphor in discourse, researchers need to take into consideration the many different textual realizations of linguistic metaphors, and the many different types of patterns they can form. The unit of analysis is usually a single text or interaction, though these patterns can also be studied across larger datasets depending on the aims of the project. Most publications on metaphor patterns focus on the function of a specific type of patterning in a specific type of discourse; for instance, Cameron and Stelma (2004) show how metaphor clusters in conciliation talk occur when speakers present their opinions and perspectives to 'the Other', or when they appropriate metaphors originally used by 'the Other'; Corts and Pollio (1999) show how clusters in college lectures orient the listeners to the structure and flow of the lecture and are used to present and emphasize novel perspectives on important topics. More-encompassing studies of metaphor patterns are offered by Goatly (1997, 2011), who offers an extensive overview of different types of metaphor 'interplay' in literary texts, and Semino's (2008) comprehensive study on metaphor in literary texts, news texts, political discourse, scientific texts, medical texts and advertising. The following sections provide an overview of some of the main types of metaphor patterns.

Repetition

In the case of repetition, the text or stretch of discourse contains several instances of the same metaphorical expression (which need not be a single word) in reference to the same topic, such as the word 'progress' in the following excerpt from a news article:

> [...] And as for trade, even the prime minister conceded that he had failed to make progress. [...] Mr Blair conceded modestly: "What this is is the possibility of re-establishing a consensus." But together with Africa, he insisted: "Politics is about getting things done step by step, this is progress, and we should be proud of it." The bottom line is this. On Africa, the G8 made progress that, if implemented, will be substantive and meaningful, particularly on the issues of aid and debt relief. On trade, the buck was passed onto the trade talks in Hong Kong later this year. The least progress was made on combating climate change, but then there wasn't a big concert in London for that, was there?
>
> *http://news.bbc.co.uk/2/hi/uk_news/politics/4665923.stm;*
> *quoted in Semino 2008: 23*

Semino (2008) shows how this type of repetition is 'closely related to the topic and argument of the text, and contribute[s] to its internal coherence' (23); this type should be distinguished from repetitions that are 'indicative of the metaphorical productivity of particular concepts, such as size, which can be applied metaphorically to a variety of other, more abstract, concepts' (23). The repeated metaphorical use of adjectives such as 'big', 'small', 'long' and 'short' is often of the second type, with different instances involving different metaphorical contextual meanings and relating to different underlying conceptual metaphors such as IMPORTANT IS BIG, QUANTITY IS SIZE, TIME IS SPACE, etc.

Semino also points out that while the noun 'progress' is repeated four times in the article, only the first and second occurrence can be attributed to Blair; the third and fourth occurrence should be considered to express the journalist's own opinion. This raises an interesting issue with regard to the function of repetition, as repetitions may in fact be used to either agree or disagree with someone else's metaphor (see Cameron 2007). For the example above, the instances of 'progress' all express the same contextual meaning of realizing positive change, and there is no indication that the author disagrees with Blair that the current developments should be seen as progress, but this is certainly not always the case.

In relation to repetition in literary texts, Goatly (1997, 2011) points out a number of interesting issues. First is the phenomenon which he refers to as 'the law of diminishing signaling/Specification' (2011: 274): when a specific metaphor is used for the first time, it is often signalled and expressed as a simile, rather than as a metaphorical expression. Then, each time the metaphor is repeated, the topic and the grounds for the comparison will become less specific, as in the following examples from William Golding's *Darkness Visible*:

> p. 18 It seemed that a word was an object ... round and smooth, a golf-ball of a thing that he could just about manage to get through his mouth.
>
> p. 23 The golf-balls emerged from his mouth.
>
> *Goatly 2011: 272*

Second, Goatly points out that it is unusual for 'active' metaphors (e.g. 'golf-balls' for words) to be simply repeated. If they are, then the vehicle or source-domain term is usually repeated immediately and often involves some form of extension, as in the following examples from D.H. Lawrence's *The Rainbow*:

> p. 346 She had the ash of disillusion gritting under her teeth.
>
> p. 347 Always she was spitting out of her mouth the ash and grit of disillusion, of falsity.
>
> *Goatly 2011: 272*

Both the 'law of diminishing signalling' and repetition involving extension can easily be linked to the reputation literary metaphor has of being novel, creative and aesthetic (see Dorst 2011; Semino and Steen 2008; see also Chapter 14). One reason for expressing metaphorical comparisons as similes when they are first introduced may be their novelty and creativity – the reader needs to be told quite explicitly what is being compared to what and why or the metaphor might fail.

Recurrence

Semino (2008: 23) defines recurrence as involving 'the use of different expressions relating to the same broad source domain in different parts of the text'. In the news article cited above, she identifies a number of metaphorical expressions that all relate to the source domain of WAR, namely 'battle of metaphors', 'army of charity workers' and 'combating climate change'. Semino points out that while the source-domain terms all draw on the WAR domain, the topic is different each time. Such recurrences 'reflect a general conventional tendency to construct difficult enterprises in terms of struggle and military action' (Semino 2008: 23). In other words, recurrence may result from the fact that some source domains tend to be used to describe a wide range of topics. In Goatly's (1997, 2011) framework, repetition of the same metaphorical expressions to talk about different topics is called multivalency. Goatly points out that multivalency in literature is often used to indicate a character's lack of lexical resources to describe complex experiences and to create metaphorical parallels between topics, or suggest thematic equivalences (2011: 275).

Darian (2000) emphasizes the noticeable recurrence of a number of metaphors related to the themes of war, hunting and relationships in his introductory science texts on biology. He argues that war is 'the central metaphor in discussions of the immune system' (171), with nearly 40 words and phrases from the WAR domain occurring throughout the corpus. The expressions cover different aspects of the domain, such as 'weapons and targets, attacking and defending, invading and destroying' (172). He also notes that these expressions often occur in collocations that are part of the language of warfare, such as 'take up stations' and 'mount an attack', but sometimes result in awkward collocations, such as 'mount a response' and 'a captive photosynthetic partner' (172). In relation to the function of these recurring metaphors and their influence on the reader's understanding of the workings of the immune system, Darian warns that this textual pattern creates 'an intense *reciprocity* between the two elements, each influencing the other. A danger of such an approach is that one comes to perceive the process through the metaphor' (173).

Clustering

Many researchers identifying metaphors in authentic texts have noticed that some stretches seem to contain hardly any metaphors, and then suddenly there's a burst or cluster of metaphors (Cameron 2003; Cameron and Stelma 2004; Corts and Pollio 1999; Koller 2003). Metaphor clusters often stand out and draw attention to themselves because they are used in strategic positions which can be related to specific rhetorical aims. For business texts, Koller (2003) found that clusters occurring at the beginning of texts have a framing function and offer a particular way of viewing the issues to be addressed. Clusters at the end of texts, on the other hand, often help authors to 're-instantiate and reinforce their particular metaphoric constructions and thus "drive the point home" to their readers' (120). Corts and Pollio (1999) found that, in their corpus of university lectures, metaphor clusters were often used in relation to the contents of the lecture and 'served as a reference point for the remainder of the lecture' (96); if such clusters involved novel metaphors, the cluster provided both 'a definition and a heuristic' and 'the core metaphor provided a new understanding for the topic in question' (97). The following cluster was used to introduce the novel metaphor ALCOHOLISM IS A GAME (94):

> He was saying that many of the ills that afflict us can be understood as games.
> ... not games like silly ones, but games in which there are players that follow rules.
> If you can change the players or change the rules, we have a different game, a better game.

Similar to the novel metaphors in Goatly's (1997, 2011) literary texts, this novel metaphor is introduced in the form of a simile first ('understood as games') and is then both repeated and extended, though in this case the extension is meant to increase comprehensibility rather than add creative variation. As mentioned above, Cameron and Stelma (2004) found that clusters in conciliation talk often occurred when a speaker presented his or her own point of view, or when speakers appropriated the Other's metaphors or explored alternative scenarios.

Extension

Semino defines extension as when 'several metaphorical expressions belonging to the same semantic field or evoking the same source domain are used in close proximity to one another in relation to the same topic, or to elements of the same target domain' (25). She provides the following example from a newspaper article:

> The Tories start their conference ... desperately sick – and tired. Leading lights in the party are crippled by life-threatening anaemia, loss of appetite and delusions of grandeur. Troops have been laid low by the UKIP superbug, which devastated the Hartlepool byelection and threatens to spread its spores nationwide.
>
> *Quoted in Semino 2008: 25*

In this example, several metaphorical expressions that evoke the source domain of ILLNESS are used to describe the state of the Tory members at the start of their conference. As pointed out by Semino, some of these metaphorical expressions are clearly related to illness and viruses (such as 'anaemia' and 'superbug') while others are less clearly part of the source domain (such as 'delusions of grandeur'). In addition, some of these words refer to a particular illness (e.g. 'anaemia') while others refer to symptoms (e.g. 'loss of appetite') or causes (e.g. 'spores'). And in terms of conventionality, some of these words are conventional metaphorical expressions (e.g. 'crippled') while others are novel (e.g. 'superbug'). In this example, the fact that 'sick' sets up an interpretation in terms of the ILLNESS domain will facilitate the interpretation of any subsequent expressions that are only loosely related to illness in terms of this domain, while they would easily fit into other source domains in other contexts. That is, once readers have activated a certain domain, they may try to fit other potentially related metaphorical expressions into the same domain. This issue is more explicitly addressed in the experimental study by Krennmayr et al. (2014) discussed in the section below on the recognition and processing of metaphor patterns.

Combination and mixing

When metaphorical expressions that evoke different source domains occur in close proximity to each other, they can interact in various ways, and the mappings they evoke may be either compatible or incompatible. When metaphor clusters evoke different source domains that can be merged meaningfully, this is called combination. When the domains clash, on the other hand, and the expressions cannot be combined meaningfully, this is called mixing. Mixed metaphors are traditionally seen as a characteristic of poor or sloppy writing. However, some experiments (e.g. Quinn 1991; Shen and Balaban 1999) have shown that such mixing often does not harm the coherence of the text and goes unnoticed, especially when the metaphors involved are not signalled (see also Gibbs 2016). Moreover, it may at times be very difficult to determine whether two domains are in fact compatible or not, and this may differ per text and context.

Kimmel's (2010) study of clustering in newspaper texts convincingly challenges the view that mixed metaphors result in awkward or confusing expressions. His results showed that 76 per cent of all the identified clusters were in fact ontologically mixed but posed no problems in terms of comprehension. In the following example from Kimmel's data, the source domains of GAMBLING, WARFARE, LIFE AND DEATH, FORCE-RELATIONS, VISUAL PERCEPTION, and JOURNEYS are mixed 'in a quite skilful way that supports a complex argument connected to EU politics' (2010: 98):

> He [British Prime Minister Tony Blair] has had to play his difficult hand with due diplomacy, and not risk finding himself too far in the vanguard. So he was reluctant to say out loud that the British referendum on the constitution was suspended, let alone dead. Instead, he worked the Danes – the next in the firing line – to agree that further plebiscites would be masochism, thus countering the French view that the referenda should continue. In the words of the former Foreign Office minister Denis MacShane: 'Even lemmings have got a right to stop at the edge of a cliff'.
>
> *Quoted in Kimmel 2010: 97–98*

Kimmel argues that mixing normally poses no problems to discourse coherence or reader comprehension because the metaphors 'are typically embedded in separate clauses situated at different temporal, causal, speaker, or belief-related conceptual planes' (97). As a result, the different source domains are not experienced as 'clashing' and the mixing actually supports the complex argument being built up in the text.

Literal–metaphorical interplay

In some texts, both the metaphorical and non-metaphorical meaning of certain words may be evoked simultaneously. Koller (2004) calls this phenomenon 'topic-triggered metaphor', as the topic of the text 'triggers' the use of a particular metaphor. Topic-triggered metaphor often occurs in newspaper headlines in the form of puns that have a clear function in grabbing the attention of the reader and creating humour, as in the following example from Krennmayr's newspaper corpus: 'Crossed lines over the toytown tram: City transport could soon be back on the right track' (2011: 160). However, creating humour is not the only function such topic-triggered metaphors may have. Krennmayr also discusses a text on the development of a Palestinian state in which the author uses metaphorical expressions from the semantic field of physical conflict and violence to describe the Palestinians, alongside semantically related expressions that are used literally to describe the actions of the Israelis. As pointed out by Krennmayr, this interplay between literal and metaphorical violence is not meant to create humorous effects. Instead, it reveals the author's subjective position on the matter and indicates that the rhetorical purpose of these expressions is to persuade the readers to sympathize with the Palestinians, a function clearly related to the creation of ideology (Charteris-Black 2004: 7–8).

In relation to literary texts, Goatly describes the closely related phenomenon of 'literalization of vehicles' (2011: 290–298), in which a lexical item is first used literally in the text and then in a metaphorical expression (or vice versa). Goatly argues that readers will only notice such literalizations if the literal and metaphorical instance are relatively close together and if the literal referent, or the source domain it belongs to, is central to the plot or setting of the narrative (292). In some cases, an image may be presented that is too powerful not to notice. The possible effects of such literalizations of vehicles are the revitalization of normally inactive metaphors, a blurring of the distinction between literal and metaphorical, and symbolism, in which case the literal becomes symbolic or leads to an allegorical interpretation of the text.

Signalling

Metaphorical expressions in texts can also be accompanied by what is commonly referred to as 'signals' (Goatly 1997, 2011) or 'tuning devices' (Cameron and Deignan 2003). Such signals may be used to draw the attention of the reader or listener to the fact that a metaphor is being used, and as such, emphasize the metaphorical status of the expressions, as in 'as it were'. Other signals seem to 'hedge or tone down the force of the metaphor' (Semino 2008: 28), such as 'kind of' or 'sort of'. As pointed out by Semino, these signals may play an important role in guiding the reader or listener in their interpretation of the subsequent metaphorical expressions. Goatly (1997, 2011) offers an extensive overview of different signalling devices found in his literature corpus, including 'like', 'literally', 'as it were', 'sort of', 'imagine', 'compare', and so on. He argues that different signalling devices have different purposes and effects and their own patterns of use (1997: 168–197). This issue will be considered in more detail in the Current Research section below.

Intertextual relations

The final pattern is that of intertextual relations, where metaphorical expressions are re-used across different texts or discourse events. For instance, a particularly interesting metaphor may be repeated or further developed in a different text in order to express agreement with the metaphor or to contradict or nuance it (see also Musolff 2004). One example in Semino (2008) is the use of the metaphorical expression 'reverse gear', which was used by British Prime Minister Tony Blair during a conference speech:

> Get rid of the false choices: principles or no principles. Replace it with the true choice. Forward or backward. I can only go one way. I've not got a reverse gear.
> *Quoted in Semino 2008: 81*

This metaphor was later exploited by a BBC anchorman in order to criticize Blair, saying 'but when you're on the edge of a cliff it is good to have a reverse gear'. While Blair's use of 'reverse gear' relied on a general JOURNEY scenario in which forward movement is considered to be good and backward movement is considered to be bad, the BBC anchorman's use of the same metaphor evokes a different JOURNEY scenario, focusing on a specific situation in which any forward movement would be catastrophic and the reverse gear is the only way to prevent a dangerous situation. Some metaphors may even become so closely associated with a particular issue that they become part of the dominant way to talk about the issue, a so-called 'discourse metaphor' (Zinken et al. 2008). Semino shows how this has happened in the case of the 'Road Map' metaphor in the Israeli–Palestinian conflict, which was first used in an official document but then became 'a central component of the discourse surrounding problems in the Middle East' (Semino 2008: 29).

Methodological challenges

Researchers working with naturally occurring data may run into various challenges when trying to identify metaphor patterns in language. A first issue relating to the nature of repetition in authentic discourse is that repetitions are rarely verbatim but often involve a shift in word class or inflection (e.g. Cameron 2007; Goatly 1997, 2011) – for example, a shift from singular to plural or a shift from present to past tense. Researchers working with large datasets from which instances of a particular metaphor are retrieved automatically through the use of software need to think carefully about any possible variations when looking for repetitions in their corpus, and they need to decide which forms still count as repetitions. Moreover, researchers need to decide what kind of repetition they are interested in. Most will be interested in repetitions with a clear rhetorical function in the specific text and context, which means that they may wish to disregard the repetition of conventional metaphorical expressions that cannot be avoided when a certain topic is discussed, as in the case of the repetition of metaphorical technical terms such as 'field' or 'flow' in a text on electricity. Researchers may decide to leave out highly frequent metaphors that are inherent in the discourse on a specific topic, or which serve general language functions, in order to focus more specifically on metaphors that are more clearly related to optional choices made by the speaker, though the issue of how to determine which metaphors are deliberate and which are not remains controversial (see issue 1:1 of *Metaphor and the Social World* for a discussion between Deignan, Gibbs, Müller and Steen on the notion of 'deliberateness').

Another challenge to overcome is that many of the patterns discussed above overlap and interact (see Semino 2008), and it may at times be very difficult to decide whether the pattern observed is in fact a case of recurrence, extension or clustering. Recurrence is distinguished from extension partly in terms of distance between related metaphorical expressions: the further the expressions are apart, the more likely they are to be treated as recurrence. As for clustering, Cameron and Stelma (2004) point out that it is difficult to determine exactly how many metaphorical expressions need to occur and how close to each other the expressions need to be for a number of metaphorical expressions to be called a cluster. This is because little is known about the 'normal' density of metaphor in authentic texts, although some studies have started to calculate such percentages. For instance, Cameron found a density of 90.3 linguistic metaphors per 1,000 words of transcribed talk for reconciliation conversations, 27 per 1,000 words for classroom talk, and 55 per 1,000 words for talk between doctor and patient (Cameron 2007: 203). Steen et al. (2010), using a different methodology, found that, on average, one in every seven and a half words was related to metaphor in their 200,000-word corpus, though the percentages differed considerably per register: 18.5 per cent in academic texts, 16.4 per cent in news texts, 11.7 per cent in fiction, and 7.7 per cent in conversation. Such calculations can provide a useful baseline for researchers to estimate whether a particular stretch of texts contains more metaphorical expressions than would 'normally' occur.

A final important issue for researchers trying to label the patterns they find in naturally occurring discourse is whether or not the individual words all belong to the same semantic field. Cameron and Low (2004) have argued that metaphors have the ability to 'attract' one another. For example, in Semino's example of extension discussed above, the fact that 'sick' sets up an interpretation in terms of the ILLNESS domain will facilitate the interpretation of any subsequent expressions that are only loosely related to illness in terms of this domain, while they would easily fit into other source domains in other contexts. Semino emphasizes that such examples show that conceptual domains should not be considered to be entirely fixed. Whether or not individual words are considered to belong to a particular domain depends to a certain degree on the text and context in which these words are used.

Current research on metaphor patterns

Recognition and processing of metaphor patterns

Various studies have provided useful descriptions of the different kinds of textual patterns that linguistic metaphors may form in texts. These patterns tend to be related to different rhetorical purposes, such as creating symbolism in literature (Goatly 1997, 2011), creating coherence in news texts (Semino 2008), summarizing explanations in classroom interaction (Cameron 2003), presenting and emphasizing novel perspectives in college lectures (Corts and Pollio 1999), and signalling agreement and disagreement between speakers (Cameron and Stelma 2004). One question that remains, however, is the extent to which readers and listeners become aware of such metaphor patterns. Do they recognize them when they occur, and also, does the presence of carefully constructed metaphor patterns influence their processing, reasoning and understanding?

Many psychologists (e.g. Bowdle and Gentner 2005; Gibbs 1994; Glucksberg and Haught 2006) have pointed out that the fact that metaphor is pervasive in everyday language does not automatically mean that metaphorical expressions are processed metaphorically, that is, via comparison. And while many critical discourse studies have convincingly demonstrated the persuasive and ideological potential of metaphor (e.g. Charteris-Black 2004; Musolff 2006; Santa Ana 1999), the influence of metaphor patterns on the reception of authentic texts is rarely tested. It is easy to see why text producers, especially those of persuasive texts such as advertisements and speeches, would assume that their carefully crafted metaphor patterns will entice readers and listeners to think of particular topics in particular ways, but experimental evidence is needed to reveal if and to what degree readers and listeners are in fact influenced. The experimental study described below addresses these issues from a linguistic, text-based perspective.

Recall of extended metaphors in news texts

Krennmayr et al.'s study (2014) addresses the question 'Under which conditions do readers think metaphorically about a topic when they read a text containing an extended metaphor?' More specifically, they investigated under which conditions extension, signalling and conventionality influenced readers of short news passages on economic development to think of economic competition in terms of auto racing. Rather than focusing on reading times – whether a compatible or incompatible metaphor facilitated or slowed down the reader – the study used a memory or recall task. It was expected that participants who had read a passage with an extended racing metaphor would recall more racing expressions than participants who had read a passage without an extended metaphor; in addition, it was expected that signalling would also have an effect, in that participants who had read the passage in which the extended metaphor was signalled by a simile would recall more expressions than participants who had read a passage without signalling. If textual patterns do indeed influence readers in such a way that they understand the topic, economic development, in terms of the metaphor, auto racing, then readers should also be tempted to incorrectly identify racing expressions that were not actually in the passage as having occurred in the text, so-called 'intrusions'.

The results showed first of all that participants who had read the control passage without the extended metaphor produced virtually no race metaphors in their recalls. For the passages containing the extended metaphor, a clear main effect of conventionality was found, as participants recalled more items when they had read a passage with a novel racing metaphor than a passage with a conventional racing metaphor. The results of the study also showed that participants produced more intrusions when they had read the passage with signalling than when they had read the text without signalling. Interestingly, participants produced more intrusions during delayed recall than during immediate recall. In addition, signalling also had a reverse effect on metaphor conventionality: the presence of a signalled simile actually led to an increase in the number of intrusions that were produced when a passage with novel metaphors had been read. Overall, the results of the recall study indicate that extended metaphor patterns in text do affect readers' text representation but that this effect is strongest when the metaphorical expressions are novel and explicitly signalled.

The relatively large number of intrusions in the novel + signalled condition that were produced during delayed recall suggests that when participants were presented with novel metaphorical expressions and an explicit signal of the mapping, they were more likely to draw on the racing metaphor while they had already forgotten the actual wordings used in the text. This finding is in line with both the Career of Metaphor (Bowdle and Genter 2005; Gentner and Bowdle 2001) and the Paradox of Metaphor (Steen 2008). As pointed out by Steen (2008), metaphorical expressions are more likely to be processed as metaphors, i.e. via comparison, when the reader is invited to perform a cross-domain mapping, and extended metaphors are likely to be experienced as such invitations. Krennmayr et al.'s (2014) results show that this claim needs to be formulated more carefully, as extended metaphors must also be divided into conventional extended mappings and novel extended mappings, and extension alone may not be enough for a metaphor to be experienced as deliberate. They argue that if writers intend to make their readers think of a particular topic in terms of a particular metaphor:

> it may not be enough to indicate a mapping by playing on words through extended conventional mappings – the data indicate that integration of metaphor in the reader's model of the text is most effectively achieved with signalled *novel* metaphors.
>
> *Krennmayr et al. 2014: 82*

The results demonstrate that formal characteristics of metaphor interact with conceptual characteristics, and more research is still needed to determine under which conditions textual patterns influence readers and listeners in complex and contextualized discourse events.

Metaphor patterns and register variation: signalled metaphor in fiction

As illustrated above, most studies on metaphor patterns focus on patterns found in individual texts or specific genres. Although these studies convincingly describe and illustrate different functions and effects for the identified patterns, there are few studies which investigate metaphor usage across different texts, registers and genres (but see Deignan et al. 2013; Semino 2008). One project that includes a cross-register comparison is Steen et al. (2010), which compared and contrasted the frequency, forms and functions of linguistic metaphor in academic discourse (Herrmann 2013), conversations (Kaal 2012), fiction (Dorst 2011) and news texts (Krennmayr 2011).

This cross-register comparison showed, first of all, that fiction was not the register with the highest number of words that were related to metaphor (i.e. metaphorical expressions, similes, or signalling words): with a percentage of 11.8 per cent metaphor-related words, fiction contained fewer metaphors than academic discourse (18.5 per cent) and news (16.4 per cent), though more than conversation (7.7 per cent). The results showed that there was a significant interaction between register and word class (see Chapter 11), and that one type of metaphor, namely signalled metaphor (or 'direct' metaphor in MIPVU [Steen et al. 2010]), interacted significantly with register. Although the overall occurrence of signalled metaphor in all four registers was extremely low (less than 1 per cent), almost 50 per cent of all the signalled metaphors identified in the 200,000-word corpus occurred in the fiction sample, followed by 30 per cent in news, and a virtual absence in conversations and academic discourse. In addition, the signalled metaphors in news occurred in 'soft' news (i.e. arts and leisure) rather than 'hard' news (Krennmayr 2011), and the signalled metaphors in academic discourse occurred mostly in arts and humanities (Herrmann 2013). As argued by Dorst (2015), this suggests that signalled metaphor may be more associated with literary and creative writing styles, and may therefore be avoided in more formal writing.

The cross-register comparison revealed that signalling, as a pattern, is a register characteristic and is most typical of the language of fiction. A further comparison of the signalled metaphors (i.e. similes) across the 12 excerpts included in the fiction sample revealed interesting findings in terms of register patterns that appeared to be typical of the fiction texts. The signalled metaphors in fiction often combined with other patterns such as repetition and extension to form complex patterns that were typical of individual texts and can therefore be seen as a style characteristic rather than a register characteristic. For example, the signal 'like' was found to be the preferred signal across all excerpts, accounting for 35 out of 64 instances of metaphor signalling, followed by 'as' with 11 occurrences. Other signals appeared to be more typical of individual texts, suggesting that these are more closely related to the personal style of the author. For instance, one excerpt did not contain any signalled metaphors with 'like' or 'as' but did contain three potentially metaphorical comparisons with 'as if':

1) 'I am the centre of my existence,' Clare sang, <u>as if chanting a psalm</u> [. . .].
2) Clare felt <u>as if she had won a sweepstake</u>.
3) [. . .], Miranda felt <u>as if she were breathing the air of the gods</u>.

Similarly, three of the four occurrences of the signal 'with the X of a Y' in the sample were all found in the same excerpt:

4) They briefly appeared on deck for lunch; a meal which Rickie hardly touched, while Robin-Anne, despite her apparent frailty, attacked the sandwiches and salad <u>with the savagery of a starving bear</u>.
5) At supper, as at lunch, Robin-Anne ate <u>with the appetite of a horse</u>, though her brother hardly touched his chicken and pasta salad.
6) 'He's precisely what anyone would expect of a drop-out Phys Ed basketball-playing retard,' Ellen said scornfully, 'by which I mean that he's a jock <u>with the brains of a dung beetle</u>. He reminds me of your Neanderthal friend, the Maggot, except Rickie is a great deal more handsome.'

Examples (4)–(6) immediately reveal that these three signalled metaphors form not only a pattern in terms of the specific signal that is used – the repetition of 'with the X of a Y' – but also a pattern in terms of the recurrence of the semantic fields involved (a human is compared to an animal), and in terms of the function these signalled metaphors have in the narrative. While the use of 'like' emphasizes a similarity between two entities, the use of 'with the X of a Y' allows the author to emphasize a similar characteristic between two *dissimilar* entities, which makes this similarity all the more surprising and unexpected: Robin-Anne eats like a bear and like a horse but she is not otherwise like a bear or like a horse and, in fact, looks nothing like these animals, given that she is described as being 'frail'. Similarly, Rickie is stupid like a dung beetle but 'a great deal more handsome' and therefore not likely to be considered creepy or disgusting.

Such combinations of signalling, repetition, recurrence and extension occurred several times in the fiction sample and appeared to be closely related to the author developing characters or scenery throughout the text. Another example is the use of 'like' in a text in which the main characters are trying to catch and kill a 'monster', which is described in terms of several animal metaphors that involve signalling, repetition and recurrence:

7) Was it even now shadowing them, moving soundlessly from cover to cover, <u>like a tiger in the steel jungle</u>?
8) 'I feel <u>like a Maharajah waiting for the tiger to pounce on the tied-up goat</u>,' Forster grinned.
9) <u>Like a chameleon</u>, it moved out of the aisle between machines, then stopped, and became utterly motionless.
10) When she checked through the spyhole it was standing in exactly the same spot, unmoving, <u>like a lizard</u>.
11) But it struck <u>with the speed of an attacking snake</u>.

While it is hard to imagine a monster that looks like a tiger and like a chameleon and like a lizard and like a snake all at the same time, each of these animal metaphors provides another piece to the overall description of what the monster looks like and behaves like. The consistency in form and function of these signalled animal metaphors carefully prepares the reader for the great shock the characters will feel later on when they find out that the monster is 'unmistakably human'. Throughout the text, the readers have been 'trained' to see the monster explicitly in terms of different animals, but now they suddenly have to adjust the mental image they have constructed to conform to the revelation that the monster is in fact a human being.

Most of these examples also illustrate an interaction between narrative and extension (see also Chapter 23) for the signalled metaphors in fiction: signalled metaphors in the narrative prose were often extended into rather elaborate and complex comparisons involving whole scenarios (see Musolff 2006; Semino 2008) rather than single entities, as in example (12). In contrast, the signalled metaphors in the fictional dialogues were normally not extended but short and simple comparisons involving single entities, as in example (13):

12) Only once had he returned after they all left and that had been bad enough, <u>like a dream – no, like stepping into the set and scenario of some frightening film, a Hitchcock movie perhaps</u>.
13) 'You look, how you say?, <u>as a raccoon</u>.'

The cross-register comparison revealed that short and simple signalled metaphors were typical not just of fictional dialogue but also of real face-to-face conversations, and that long and complex signalled metaphors were typical not just of fictional narrative but also of narrative news texts, which suggests that the extension of signalled metaphor patterns interacts with (sub-)register.

Most signalled metaphors in fiction occurred across the text excerpts at a relatively large distance from each other, and only one instance was found in which they clustered, with four similes in eight consecutive sentences. It is likely that clustering of signalled metaphors is less likely to occur because signalled metaphors stand out and tend to draw attention to themselves, so using too many in close proximity would probably create a sense of 'overkill'. Nevertheless, signalled metaphors do often combine with unsignalled metaphorical expressions, as in (14) and (15). These clusters of signalled and unsignalled metaphor often have a clear function in creating vivid imagery, and adding emotion to the text.

> 14) Now the nearest tree is an enormous trunk, <u>struck</u> by lightning and sawed-off. But one side branch shoots up very high and lets fall an <u>avalanche</u> of dark green pine needles. This <u>sombre giant – like a defeated proud man</u> – contrasts, when considered in the nature of a living creature, with the <u>pale smile</u> of a last rose on the fading bush in front of him.
>
> 15) At the top they came out into <u>uncompromising</u>, bright grey light, the bleak, hedgeless lane, the flat meadows where here and there stunted trees <u>squatted like old men in cloaks</u>.

Overall then, signalled metaphor can be seen as forming a register pattern in the sense that it is more typical of fiction than of news, academic discourse or spoken conversations, and more typical of narrative prose than dialogues in fiction. In addition, signalling combines with repetition, recurrence, clustering and extension to form more specific metaphor patterns within individual fiction texts that can be related to specific functions, effects and styles. The signalled metaphors in fiction have a strong visualization function in the sense that they create vivid, rich imagery that helps the reader imagine what the characters and their surroundings look like. In this sense, the function of signalled metaphor in combination with repetition and recurrence is strongly related to characterization and scene setting. The clear interaction with extension suggests that authors also try to be as creative and original as possible, which can be related to the aesthetic and entertaining function of fiction: the signals themselves are repeated, but the signalled metaphor that follows is varied through recurrence, embellished through extension, and combined with clusters of metaphorical expressions. The resulting rhetorical weight and noticeability of such signalled metaphors may be the main reason why they are more suitable to texts that involve openly creative, aesthesic or persuasive uses of metaphor. This in turn could contribute to the belief that such metaphors are appropriate only in literature or soft news, and not in any form of serious, objective writing.

Conclusion and future directions

The above discussion of the different patterns of metaphor illustrates what a rich and varied field of investigation this is, and how important these patterns are to understanding the functions and effects of metaphor in varied and complex discourse events. Both the experimental study on extended metaphor in news texts and the current research on signalled metaphor in fiction suggest that metaphor patterns should also be analysed more explicitly from the perspective of conventionality and creativity. In addition, more systematic comparisons are needed of how the different metaphor patterns work in similar or different ways across texts, registers and genres, and perhaps even across languages and cultures.

Further reading

Cameron, L. (2007) 'Patterns of metaphor use in reconciliation talk', *Discourse and Society*, 18(2): 197–222.
Cameron, L. and Stelma, J. (2004) 'Metaphor clusters in discourse', *Journal of Applied Linguistics*, 1(2): 107–136.
Goatly, A. (2011) *The Language of Metaphors*, 2nd edn, London and New York: Routledge. (Chapter 9)
Kimmel, M. (2010) 'Why we mix metaphors (and mix them well): Discourse coherence, conceptual metaphor, and beyond', *Journal of Pragmatics*, 42: 97–115.
Koller, V. (2003) 'Metaphor clusters, metaphor chains: Analysing the multifunctionality of metaphor in text', *Metaphorik.de*, 5: 115–134.
Semino, E. (2008) *Metaphor in Discourse*, Cambridge, UK: Cambridge University Press. (Chapters 2–5)

References

Bowdle, B. F. and Gentner, D. (2005) 'The career of metaphor', *Psychological Review*, 112(1): 193–216.
Cameron, L. (2003) *Metaphor in Educational Discourse*, London and New York: Continuum.
—— (2007) 'Patterns of metaphor use in reconciliation talk', *Discourse and Society*, 18(2): 197–222.
Cameron, L. and Deignan, A. (2003) 'Combining large and small corpora to investigate tuning devices around metaphor in spoken discourse', *Metaphor and Symbol*, 18: 149–160.
Cameron, L. and Low, G. (2004) 'Figurative variation in episodes of educational talk and text', *European Journal of English Studies*, 8(3): 355–373.
Cameron, L. and Stelma, J. (2004) 'Metaphor clusters in discourse', *Journal of Applied Linguistics*, 1(2): 107–136.
Charteris-Black, J. (2004) *Corpus Approaches to Critical Metaphor Analysis*, London: Palgrave Macmillan.
Corts, D. P. and Pollio, H. R. (1999) 'Spontaneous production of figurative language and gesture in college lectures', *Metaphor and Symbol*, 14(2): 81–100.
Darian, S. (2000) 'The role of figurative language in introductory science texts', *International Journal of Applied Linguistics*, 10(2): 163–186.
Deignan, A., Littlemore, J. and Semino, E. (2013) *Figurative Language, Genre and Register*, Cambridge, UK: Cambridge University Press.
Dorst, A. G. (2011) *Metaphor in Fiction: Linguistic Forms, Conceptual Structures, Cognitive Representations*, PhD thesis, Oisterwijk, The Netherlands: BOXpress.
—— (2015) 'More or different metaphors in fiction? A quantitative cross-register comparison', *Language and Literature*, 24(1): 3–22.
Gentner, D. and Bowdle, B. F. (2001) 'Convention, form, and figurative language processing', *Metaphor and Symbol*, 16: 223–247.
Gibbs, R. W., Jr. (1994) *The Poetics of Mind: Figurative Thought, Language and Understanding*, Cambridge, UK: Cambridge University Press.
—— (ed.) (2016) *Mixing Metaphor*, Amsterdam, The Netherlands: John Benjamins.
Glucksberg, S. and Haught, C. (2006) 'On the relation between metaphor and simile: When comparison fails', *Mind and Language*, 21(3): 360–378.
Goatly, A. (1997) *The Language of Metaphors*, London and New York: Routledge.
—— (2011) *The Language of Metaphors*, 2nd edn, New York: Routledge.

Herrmann, J. B. (2013) *Metaphor in Academic Discourse: Linguistic Forms, Conceptual Structures, Communicative Functions and Cognitive Representations*, PhD thesis, Utrecht, The Netherlands: LOT dissertation series.

Kaal, A. A. (2012) *Metaphor in Conversation*, PhD thesis, Oisterwijk, The Netherlands: BOXpress.

Kimmel, M. (2010) 'Why we mix metaphors (and mix them well): Discourse coherence, conceptual metaphor, and beyond', *Journal of Pragmatics*, 42: 97–115.

Koller, V. (2003) 'Metaphor clusters, metaphor chains: Analysing the multifunctionality of metaphor in text', *Metaphorik.de*, 5: 115–134.

—— (2004) Businesswomen and war metaphors: 'Possessive, jealous and pugnacious?', *Journal of Sociolinguistics*, 8(1): 3–22.

Krennmayr, T. (2011) *Metaphor in Newspapers*, PhD thesis, Utrecht, The Netherlands: LOT.

Krennmayr, T., Bowdle, B. F., Mulder, G. and Steen, G. J. (2014) 'Building metaphorical schemas when reading text', *Metaphor and the Social World*, 4: 65–89.

Musolff, A. (2004) *Metaphor and Political Discourse: Analogical Reasoning in Debates about Europe*, Basingstoke, UK: Palgrave Macmillan.

—— (2006) 'Metaphor scenarios in public discourse', *Metaphor and Symbol*, 21(1): 23–38.

Quinn, N. (1991) 'The cultural basis of metaphor', in J. Fernandez (ed.) *Beyond Metaphor: The Theory of Tropes in Anthropology*, Stanford, CA: Stanford UP.

Santa Ana, O. (1999) '"Like an animal I was treated": Anti-immigrant metaphor in US public discourse', *Discourse and Society*, 10(2): 191–224.

Semino, E. (2008) *Metaphor in Discourse*, Cambridge and New York: Cambridge University Press.

Semino, E. and Steen, G. J. (2008) 'Metaphor in literature', in R. W. Gibbs, Jr. (ed.) *The Cambridge Handbook of Metaphor and Thought*, pp. 232–246, Cambridge, UK: Cambridge University Press.

Shen, Y. and Balaban, N. (1999) 'Metaphorical (in)coherence in discourse', *Discourse Processes*, 28: 139–153.

Steen, G. J. (2008) 'The paradox of metaphor: Why we need a three-dimensional model of metaphor', *Metaphor and Symbol*, 23(4): 213–241.

Steen, G. J., Dorst, A. G., Herrmann, J. B., Kaal, A. A. and Krennmayr, T. (2010) *A Method for Linguistic Metaphor Identification: From MIP to MIPVU*, Amsterdam, The Netherlands: John Benjamins.

Zinken, J., Hellsten, I. and Nerlich, B. (2008) 'Discourse metaphors', in R. Dirven, R. Frank, T. Ziemke and J. Zlatev (eds) *Body, Language, and Mind. Vol. 2: Sociocultural Situatedness*, pp. 363–385, Berlin, Germany: Mouton.

13

Genre and metaphor
Use and variation across usage events

Rosario Caballero

Introduction

In this chapter, I explore how and why people use metaphor differently in different communicative contexts. The main objective is to discuss the advantages of incorporating the notion of genre into metaphor research and the possible issues and lines of research current in the field. Genres are systematic ways of doing things with language, and both their purposes and participants influence the use of metaphor. The sensitivity of metaphor to context or situation will be illustrated by describing how architects use metaphor in one of their typical genres.

In the next two sections, I define metaphor, discourse and genre. I then provide an overview of research on metaphor from a discourse and genre perspective, divided into generalist approaches and specific studies. The main section, drawing on my own research, features a specific study, describing how metaphor is used in the genre of architectural reviews. The chapter ends by providing an agenda for future genre-based research on metaphor.

Metaphor and metaphor variation

Metaphor is symptomatic of people's systematic ways of interacting with the world. A standard definition of metaphor is that it involves transferring or *mapping* knowledge from a familiar domain of experience known as the *source* onto a less-known domain called the *target* (Lakoff and Johnson 1980; see also Chapter 1). This re-use of knowledge helps us understand our experience in and with the world, and share such experiences with others. The sharing dimension is important since it is through use that metaphors become entrenched in culture(s). Put differently, our ability to think in metaphors is intrinsic to being human and, therefore, is universal; however, metaphor cannot be dissociated from the complex and socially acquired beliefs, knowledge and world view(s) intrinsic to our belonging to and interacting within one or several communities. All of this results in variation.

Metaphors vary according to (a) our belonging to different cultural backgrounds (both representative of a single culture or of the various cultures it subsumes), and/or (b) the pragmatic constraints imposed by the contexts where we use metaphor – which roughly correspond to what Kövecses (2005) refers to as *cross-cultural variation* and *within-culture variation* respectively. Cross-cultural variation may be illustrated by the ways in which Spanish and English construe the notion of spinsterhood as suggested by the idioms *quedarse para vestir santos* (literally, 'to remain/be left to dress saints') and *to be left on the shelf*. The Spanish expression draws on the old-fashioned practice of some single women of helping priests to take care of the ornaments and religious images in churches. In contrast, the English idiom *to be left on the shelf* brings to mind unwanted goods that nobody has bought in a shop, and hence remain on the shop's shelf. These examples illustrate two diverse culturally specific metaphors underlying common expressions in two languages and cultures.

In turn, within-culture variation results from pragmatic factors, and concerns cases where conventional, highly pervasive metaphors are adapted to suit particular communicative situations. For instance, the notion of JOURNEY motivates descriptions of our personal and professional lives as purposeful experiences, which involve following a given *direction*, choosing among various *paths* of action or *reaching* a set of *goals*. However, JOURNEY metaphors in more specific contexts do not always focus on the purposeful quality of a course of action. For instance, when researching the role of metaphor in wine discourse (Caballero 2007) and architectural discourse (Caballero 2006, 2009, 2013, 2014), I found examples such as the following:

(1) [F]lavours carry the palate to a finish that is tart and tight. Seems to pick up speed along the way, and finishes better than it starts.
(2) "From one building to another, you're experiencing movement as part of a journey," claims the architect, who always deploys orientation devices – views, openings, corridors – to make the path of the constantly changing officescape self-guiding and cogent.

In example 1, the sensory profile of a wine is described as a journey taking place in the critic's nose and mouth; that is, the metaphor is concerned with sensory perception rather than with purposeful activities. In turn, the movement-related expressions in example 2 suggest the architects' views of three-dimensionality as necessarily involving motion – both literal and metaphorical. Both examples illustrate different versions of JOURNEY metaphors used for describing two different targets and, therefore, meaning different things and meeting different purposes.

In this chapter I describe ways to approach the kind of within-culture variation illustrated in examples 1 and 2, which, in my view, covers people's use of metaphor according to *both* their belonging to a particular discourse community (professional or otherwise) and the pragmatic constraints imposed by the genres where metaphor occurs. Indeed, while knowledge of the communities involved is a necessary first step towards understanding the mechanics of metaphor, it is not enough. It does not explain why some metaphors are favoured at the expense of others, or how people tune metaphor in agreement with the specific characteristics of the discourse interaction – usage event – in which they participate. Here I argue that genre provides an operative framework to explore which notions (targets) are being construed and discussed by means of metaphor within a particular discourse community, the reasons motivating this metaphorical rendering, and how such metaphors appear in texts. A genre approach to metaphor illustrates what is variously referred to as *discourse-based, situated* or *socio-cognitive* metaphor research (see the papers in Low et al. 2010), and is particularly useful to explore metaphor in professional discourses and genres.

Discourse and genre

The term 'discourse' is employed in different disciplines where it covers different things. Two of the disciplines where the concept occupies a central role are linguistics and social theory. In linguistics, discourse is broadly defined as the use of language in social contexts (see, for instance, the definition in Crystal 1985). In social theory, it refers to the ways in which knowledge and social practice are structured and manifest themselves through the different symbolic forms (e.g. language) available (Foucault 1969). My take on discourse follows a combination of both views, and is the way a group of people with similar interests and/or occupation (i.e. a 'discourse community') represents the areas of knowledge they are interested in ('topics') and shares them in various interactions and resulting texts (written and oral). For instance, architectural discourse deals with the various ways in which space can be organized for social uses. The technical, methodological, aesthetic, etc. dimensions of space are, in turn, communicated by means of the typified communicative routines and texts – 'genres' – whereby architects interact among themselves and/or with people outside the community like, for instance, their customers. These include technical genres such as competition briefs, theoretical genres such as design manuals, and critical genres such as architectural reviews. In other words, the genres used by architects are highly typified usage events or routines defined by formal (textual) features, functions or communicative purposes, and the relationship between those interacting in and through them. Architectural discourse arises from the 'sum' of those genres.

The notion of genre is critical in research on professional communication, where it is seen as mediating the process of building the 'professional view' characterizing professional communities (Goodwin 1994). Accordingly, it is also a critical enculturation and insertion tool for their new members. One of the most fruitful insights of scholars dealing with specific discourses has been the provision of an analytical procedure for describing how topic, goal and audience factors motivate the prototypical structure or textual patterning of the genres characterizing professional communication (Swales 1990). This is described as consisting of recognizable functional units or textual stretches (called 'moves' and 'steps') representing the diverse ways chosen by authors for accomplishing rhetorical goals in agreement with the author–reader relationship mediated by the genre. For instance, a genre scholar dealing with metaphor in architectural communication would pay attention to the fact that the JOURNEY metaphor in example 2 opens the review's descriptive part, which is organized as a virtual tour inside the building. Likewise, a genre scholar would note that the sensory journey of the wine in example 1 is an iconic representation of what happens in real tasting events, and communicates the evolution of the wine's flavour from the opening of the bottle to the final impressions left in the taster's mouth. Exploring the role of metaphor in this text, then, would involve relating its occurrences at different textual stages to the stages in the tasting event.

The question to answer, then, is what are the benefits of a genre approach to metaphor? On the one hand, both metaphor and genre are important cognitive socio-cultural tools contributing to the content and formal schemas involved in communication (i.e. what we talk about and how we do it). Accordingly, combining them should help us understand the way different peoples and cultures interact with, and in, the world through metaphor. On the other hand, genre may be used as a blueprint for researching metaphor in an organized fashion: because the structure of genres reflects the purpose(s) of the people participating in them and their relationship (who writes for whom), locating metaphorical expressions in the rhetorical structure of genres may help explain people's choice and use of metaphors in them (Halliday 1984).

An overview of discourse-based approaches to metaphor

Discourse-based approaches to metaphor, that, implicitly or explicitly, consider genre, fall into what may be called either generalist or specific studies, depending on their different research concerns and the level of generality of the language context under analysis.

Generalist approaches to metaphor considering genre

A common concern within generalist approaches is to limit the role of intuition in metaphor research, and the first step in this direction is the provision of methods for identifying metaphorical uses in texts (e.g. Pragglejaz Group 2007; Cameron and Maslen 2010; Steen et al. 2010; see also Chapter 5). Here we also find proposals discussing the benefits of using software-assisted methods for exploring the diversity or variation of metaphor across different types of text (Stefanowitsch and Gries 2006; Koller et al. 2008; Kimmel 2012).

Of course, exploring metaphor in real communication involves dealing with genre, irrespective of whether this notion provides an explicit research rationale. This is the case in Goatly's (2011) study of the form and function of metaphors in six different genres (conversation, news reports, popular science articles, adverts, novels and poems). Drawing insights from cognitive and functional approaches to language, Goatly explores whether certain discourses and genres favour some metaphors over others, the reasons underlying any preferences, and the genre-specific effects of a metaphor's occurrence (e.g. ideological, stylistic, etc.). Goatly applies Halliday's (1984) distinction between the ideational, interpersonal and textual metafunctions of language, i.e. how people represent their experience in the world, communicate it to others, and organize those ideas in texts. On this basis, he provides a classification of metaphors, describes the metaphorical motivation of some word-formation processes, and discusses the role of metaphor in the texts under study. Among the functions of metaphors in texts, Goatly discusses their role in filling lexical gaps or in explaining specialized concepts and/or theories for a non-specialized audience in, for instance, popular science articles (ideational metafunction); in expressing emotional attitude, typically in literary genres (interpersonal metafunction); or in providing lexical cohesion – structure – to all sorts of texts (textual metafunction).

More recent studies include Charteris-Black (2004), Semino (2008) and Deignan et al. (2013). These describe how metaphors are used across a range of discourses, genres and texts while, at the same time, setting methodological outlines for the principled study of metaphor variation. Charteris-Black (2004) combines critical discourse analytical procedures and concerns with those of corpus and metaphor research in order to discuss the persuasive and ideological role of metaphors found in some of the typical genres in the media, politics and religion. As is the case with most discourse-based metaphor research, Semino (2008) draws upon various research traditions (e.g. Cognitive Metaphor Theory, Stylistics, Critical Discourse Analysis and Corpus Linguistics) in order to approach metaphor variation in texts from discourse contexts as different as literature, politics, science and education, and advertising. For instance, she describes how a metaphor drawing upon the notion of WASTE DISPOSAL is used by scientists communicating with their peers to discuss the cell processes causing ageing and, therefore, fulfils a theory-constitutive role. This changes when the same metaphor is re-used in popular science articles aimed at non-specialist audiences. Here, the metaphor is tweaked to perform a more explanatory, pedagogic function which, in some cases, also meets persuasive goals – for instance, validating and/or promoting certain courses of action by convincing readers of the benefits of scientific research.

Although genre plays a categorizing role, none of the aforementioned studies explicitly draws on insights from genre research in order to discuss choice of texts or their findings. In contrast, Deignan et al. (2013) bring genre research and methodology into their exploration of metaphor variation across oral and written texts. Their book offers a good panoramic view of research dealing with several aspects of metaphor use and variation in diverse discourses and text-types, which is then used to introduce their model of analysis. This model rests upon a combination of genre and register. Genre provides the broad context for studying how specific groups of language users (discourse communities) use metaphors in oral and written texts to fulfil the specific goals of some of their specific interactions. In order to provide a fine-grained analysis of metaphor at the lexico-grammatical level, however, Deignan et al. draw upon Systemic Functional Linguistics (e.g. Halliday 1984) and use the notion of 'register' – i.e. what results from combining the categories of 'field' (the subject matter or 'what' of texts), 'tenor' (the participants or 'who'), and 'mode' (the communication mode and channel or 'how'). In Deignan et al.'s view, combining genre and register is most advantageous since:

> a single model, of either genre or register, cannot handle analyses from the broad context of culture through to linguistic detail. Register and genre are both necessary as perspectives onto text, and they influence each other in a recursive process.
> *Deignan et al. 2013: 49*

Their model is illustrated through several case studies focusing on the metaphorical language found in oral and written genres from academic, political, scientific, journalistic and literary discourse, as well as less-regulated speech events from oral interaction.

Metaphor research in specialized discourses and genres

Other studies are narrower in scope, and explore the metaphors used in specific – usually professional – genres and discourses. These have been approached in two ways. On the one hand, metaphor has caught the attention of scholars belonging to the very communities under study – for instance, the metaphors of Biology (Liakopoulos 2002), Physics (Mirowski 1989) or Economics (McCloskey 1994). Their research draws from classical discussions of the role of metaphor in science (Gentner 1980; Boyd 1993), where it functions as a problem-solving strategy and, therefore, is critical to both thought and discourse. Drawing upon Boyd (1993), metaphors are shown to (a) provide new insights into scientific phenomena and, by so doing, help develop and articulate scientific theories (*theory-constitutive* metaphors), (b) inform specialized terminology (*catachretic* metaphors), and (c) contribute to explaining and disseminating scientific theories both within and outside the scientific realm (*exegetical* or *pedagogical* metaphors).

Specialized communication has also been explored by linguists and discourse analysts. Because no discourse can be analysed in its entirety, their work focuses on the metaphors found in some of the genres used by the communities under study. Among the many functions fulfilled by metaphor in these genres, most research has focused on the figurative motivation of professional jargon (often considering further applications to the Language for Specific Purposes [LSP] classroom; see Chapter 19), or on metaphor's persuasive and/or ideological potential (e.g. Musolff 2004; Lu and Ahrens 2008; see Chapters 21 and 22). Koller's (2003, 2004) research on metaphor in business communication offers a more comprehensive view of metaphor use. As well as focusing on the ideational and interpersonal dimensions of metaphor, she describes the way metaphors cluster at certain points in the structure of texts. For instance, Koller shows that SPORTS metaphors tend to cluster in the middle of the texts she analyses, where they perform an interpersonal, argumentative role, whereas WAR metaphors provide a frame for the texts by opening and closing them, and fulfil an ideational and persuasive (interpersonal) function respectively. In other words, while metaphors may meet many needs, their tendency to cluster at certain points helps scholars better determine and explain their roles in texts.

The notion of genre is explicitly used in research into the exegetical function of metaphor, that is, the role of metaphor in disseminating knowledge across communicative contexts or situations involving different purposes and participants. This 'relocation' of knowledge from one place to another is known as 'recontextualization' (Linell and Sarangi 1998), and typically happens when ideas from specialized scientific contexts are communicated to non-expert audiences in non-specialist texts (e.g. those published in popular science journals and magazines, the science sections in newspapers, etc.). For instance, Knudsen (2003) compares the metaphorical use of the notion of translation for discussing DNA in scientific articles from *Science* and popular-scientific articles from *Scientific American* (e.g. the description of amino acids as if they were letters, words or sentences). She explains how the TRANSLATION metaphor is originally used in specialized scientific texts and, then, is recycled in popular texts where it plays a pedagogical function, and is more abundantly used and visible than in the 'expert' version' (i.e. it is often typographically marked and/or explicated). Similar views and results can be found in Wee's (2005) exploration of Physics and Management genres, Skorczynska and Deignan's (2006) study of metaphor in Economics genres, Semino's (2011) study of pain metaphors and Caballero's (2013) discussion of architectural metaphors.

In the following section, I describe some of my own research on the metaphors used in a genre from architectural discourse.

An example of current research: metaphor in architectural communication

Architecture is a complex affair that cannot do without metaphor. Our experience of buildings is embodied. We experience buildings by looking at them and, above all, by moving into them and then inside, which allows for a rich input of sensory data about their properties (i.e. what their spaces look, smell and feel like). Likewise, when architects design a building, they consider these features and assemble spatial elements in a way that affords their prospective users those embodied experiences. Architects' and users' experiences are reflected in architectural texts and, of course, in the metaphors used in them. Thus, architects' metaphors carry diverse types of information (abstract, visual or a combination of both) about buildings and may focus on the buildings themselves or on the processes architects undergo to achieve particular spatial solutions. For instance, the metaphor ARCHITECTURE IS LANGUAGE portrays buildings as intelligible and readable *texts* that result from combining *lexical* devices in accordance with *grammatical* rules; ARCHITECTURAL PRACTICE IS CLOTH-MAKING presents architects as manipulating space as if it were cloth and motivates technical terms such as *cladding, jacketing, sheathing, sheeting* and *curtain wall*; and ARCHITECTURAL PRACTICE IS MUSICAL PRACTICE describes architects' work as *orchestrating* or *choreographing* spaces, and refers to the sequential arrangement of structural and ornamental elements in buildings as *rhythm*. The following examples further illustrate these three metaphors:

(3) In what would seem to be a tradition already crowded by modernist masters, the very literate Myers has succeeded through a process of commentary, reference, and cross-fertilization in writing a sequel chapter in steel house design.
(4) A building protects itself from water by wearing three garments. A vapor barrier lining creates a raincoat around all extremities and appendages of the space, a rubberlike membrane provides a boot around the foot of the structure, and a variety of materials are stitched together to make an umbrella of protection around the top.
(5) Each level of columns follows its own regular rhythm; together, the layers read as simultaneous melodies or separate instruments playing their own part of a symphony. This facade is Goethe's credo of frozen music.

In turn, product-focused metaphors usually draw upon organic, inorganic and motion sources, which help architects to refer to, describe and assess buildings according to their functional or 'behavioural' properties (e.g. *breathing* or *fatigue*), their external appearance (e.g. reference to building parts as *lozenges*, *wedges* or *boxes* or to whole buildings as *the Gherkin* or *the Cheesegrater* – two iconic buildings in London's financial centre) or a combination of both (e.g. *skeleton*, *rib*, *skin* or *apron*). Finally, MOTION metaphors are used in two ways: on the one hand, they carry visual information and describe particular layouts as reminiscent of the motion expressed by motion verbs (e.g. buildings described as *hunkering down, easing into* or *heaving up* in their sites); on the other hand, we find the more holistic metaphor MOVING WITHIN A BUILDING IS MAKING A JOURNEY where people's experiences inside buildings are described as different types of travel – referred to as *routes* (usually co-occurring with *circulation*), *itineraries*, *paths* or *promenades*. Some such metaphors are illustrated in the following assessment of a school in Berlin:

(6) Arriving in front of the school in the suburban Berlin neighborhood, you do not see what is going on inside; the building does not reveal itself immediately. The design, based on the sunflower, unfolds its petals to form "a village for children." [. . .] I was very lucky. Zvi Hecker took the time to show me around. It was a joyful experience being led into one of Hecker's colored pencil drawings where a curving "snake" intercepts with the sunflower theme. The petals form the classrooms; the curving snake connects and conceals them at the same time [. . .] you move through a landscape of walls and roofs, alleys and corners. It is always about light and how the light penetrates the building; direct light, reflected light, diffused light. The sunflower is a metaphor, not in some abstract geometry, but because of the way the building absorbs the light and projects it inside. There are no parallel walls, the sunflower is actually catching the sun [. . .] it turns with the sun. The spaces between the walls form the "canyons," the stairways are the "mountains," the windows frame views or open up to balconies and roof terraces. One never comes directly to an empty space, but arrives slowly. [. . .] At the end of our visit, a bell rang and the corridors were suddenly filled with children laughing and running. We followed them through the slightly sloping snake-like corridors out into the "village" square.

This review starts by presenting the Heinz-Galinski school as a SUNFLOWER, which is the metaphor originally used by the architect in its design and further (verbal) explanations. This metaphor informs the reference to classrooms as *petals* and is implicit in remarks on the role of light and directionality in the school's internal organization – both notions befitting the SUNFLOWER metaphor. This is complemented by: a TOWN metaphor also attributed to Hecker

Table 13.1 Rhetorical structure of architectural reviews

TITLE + LEAD
INTRODUCTION
Move 1: Creating Context

- Step 1: Building a situation (e.g. generalizations; background information; preliminary description)
- Step 2: Evaluating the situation (problem spotting; claiming importance)

Move 2: Introducing the building

- Step 1: Positioning the building in the previous context
- Step 2: Highlighting a specific trait of the building

Move 3: First evaluation of the building
DESCRIPTION
Move 1: Providing technical/budget/construction details of the building

- Step 1: Siting details
- Step 2: Information on budget and/or construction phases

Move 2: Outlining the building's general organization and/or appearance (overall plan)
Move 3: Describing the parts/components of the building
Move 4: Highlighting parts of the building
CLOSING EVALUATION
TECHNICAL CARD
VISUAL DATA + CAPTIONS

Source: Caballero (2006).

and portraying the building as *a village for children*; and a LANDSCAPE metaphor informing the description of the building's internal spaces as *canyons* and *mountains*. These three metaphors appear alongside the reviewer's more ad-hoc image-schematic reference to corridors as *curving snakes* due to their physical resemblance to this animal.

Architectural genres are also suitably multimodal in that they combine images and verbal language in order to communicate the functional, interactive and sensory properties of buildings before, during and after their construction. One of the genres that best illustrates the complexities of both architectural practice and communication is the architectural review (henceforth AR). ARs are written by and for architects, and are published in specialized magazines concerned with architectural design. The genre describes and evaluates buildings regarded as noteworthy, and both purposes are reflected in its textual organization. As shown in Table 13.1, this typically relies upon three distinct parts (Introduction, Description and Closing Evaluation) which are further organized in various moves and steps in agreement with the way reviewers choose to accomplish those goals.

A conspicuous trait of the genre is its twofold concern with showing and telling: ARs always incorporate graphic representations of the buildings at hand alongside the verbal commentary, which allows their expert readers to go back and forth between the images and the text and, most importantly, judge the buildings for themselves. The multimodal and professional qualities of ARs influence the way(s) in which assessment is couched in the texts and, of course, the reviewers' choice and use of metaphorical language. Thus, although reviewers must take into account intellectual and technical aspects when assessing spatial arrangements, these appear to be best illustrated in what the building under focus looks like – a visual bias acknowledged by architects themselves.

Both architects' visual thinking and the genre's idiosyncrasies appear to motivate the reviewers' choice and use of metaphors to present their views in the texts. For instance, as discussed elsewhere, my exploration of a 95-text corpus of ARs showed that visually informed or 'image' metaphors and conceptual metaphors were evenly distributed (46 per cent and 54 per cent respectively) even if this may not be the case with more theoretical genres such as architectural treatises and/or manifestos. Thus, image metaphors not only inform a large part of architectural jargon (e.g. *cross tee*, *I-beam*, *I-joist*, *barrel vault*, *curtain wall*, etc.), but are often used to handle different dimensions and perspectives when representing and describing space in texts, as shown in the following example:

(7) As a free-standing element, [the building] needed to be curved for stability, and the curve chosen prompted the development of a tadpole-like plan with entrance and social centre in the head. [...] The thick, solid brick wall is visibly the spine of the whole, emerging naked externally in the tail. It contrasts everywhere with the flimsiness of the timber parts that butt up against it [...] The combination of radial and linear principles in the plan allows transition between centrality in the head and a route distributing to either side in the tail. [...] The wall runs north–south. [...] The spatial organization presented to a small child could scarcely be simpler: from a distance the building is a kind of mound or crouching creature with very low eaves to bring the scale down.

This building is first introduced in two-dimensional, flat terms (*tadpole-like*) in agreement with the shape suggested by its ground plan. Likewise, its two furthermost extremes are later referred to as the *head* and *tail* respectively. The shift towards three-dimensionality occurs by qualifying the central wall in the complex as a *spine emerging naked*, and by comparing it to a *mound or crouching creature*. These metaphor clusters are usually found in the Description section of ARs and in the captions of the visuals accompanying the main text.

Nevertheless, since architects cannot do without metaphor, metaphorical language used for descriptive purposes occurs everywhere in ARs and remains fairly inconspicuous. A different matter are the metaphor clusters found in textual stretches functionally related to evaluation, namely: titles and leads; problem spotting and first evaluations in the Introduction; the move in Description concerned with highlighting specific aspects of a building; and the Closing Evaluation. In other words, metaphor is a critical evaluation tool, and this role is often textually marked in the genre. For instance, many ARs open with a metaphor, and the frame thus set is further elaborated throughout the ensuing text. This is shown in example 8, where I have indicated the different sections of the text:

(8) TITLE
Church and State
INTRODUCTION, move 1, step 2 (Evaluating the situation)
How does one build in a space like the Plaza Cardenal Belluga? asked Rafael Moneo when he began designing an annex to the city hall of Murcia [...] What Moneo faced was in many ways a thoroughly European problem of adding new uses and structures to ancient environments – but with a few twists. In the case of the Plaza Cardenal Belluga, the buildings surrounding the plaza were as strong in character as the irregular space they described [...] And the site of the new city hall annex would put it squarely opposite and on axis with the cathedral, creating an urbanistic tension that Americans might find troubling: a direct confrontation of church and state. In a country where the Catholic Church wielded so much power for so many centuries, the relationship is even more loaded.

INTRODUCTION, move 3 (First Evaluation)
Moneo claims to have created a building "content in its role as spectator, without seeking the status of protagonist held by the cathedral and the palace." The building may have been cast as a supporting player in the urban drama of its surroundings, but it has strong character and authority.

DESCRIPTION, move 4 (Highlighting parts of the building)
Within a single flat plane, Moneo's civic annex becomes as affected and self-conscious as the baroque cathedral – but never relinquishes its sense of order and rationality.

CLOSING EVALUATION
Although Moneo wanted his addition to defer to its historic setting, it's not as reverent as he claims. The building makes a clever game of playing order against disorder to assert its own identity among its ornamented neighbors.

This extract also shows the reviewers' use of metaphor to negotiate their views (and assert their authority) in the genre. The review opens with the name of the institutions standing metonymically for the religious and civic buildings that 'cohabitate' in the same urban space – the latter being the object of assessment in the review. The evaluation focuses on the aesthetic clash caused by a modern building in a baroque environment, a confrontation theatrically described as an *urban drama* after the architect's own metaphor. This theatrical metaphor creates a frame for the ensuing commentary, providing the means whereby the reviewer will contrast his or her own opinion with the views held by the architect. The metaphor is consistently used in such critical loci as the first evaluation in the text's Introduction, the highlighting move in the Description part, and the Closing Evaluation. Interestingly, the reviewer's views appear hidden behind the personified view of the building suggested by the statement: *the building makes a clever game of playing order against disorder to assert its own identity among its ornamented neighbors.*

The use of metaphor for evaluative purposes is heavily determined by both the visual weight of the genre and the expertise of its readers: since architects may read and interpret visual data without the reviewers' mediation, their commentary needs to be mitigated rather than categorically presented if it wants to avoid being dismissed as inappropriate when compared to the information provided graphically. Among the resources used in this endeavour, we find personification (as in example 8), the manipulation of citation (usually, the reviewer's borrowing of the architect's metaphors to reinforce his/her views) and the use of orthographic devices (inverted commas) and lexical devices such as *metaphorically, literally, visually, architecturally, almost,* and *a kind of* to underlie the metaphorical quality of the critics' commentary:

(9) Glazed walls and doors dividing the living areas from the sun balconies would be backed below waist height by a vertical layer of sand-coloured terracotta 'baguettes' (bars measuring about 1200 × 40 × 40 mm) set apart in a 50 per cent transparent pattern.

(10) Metaphorically, the mass is supposed to have been eroded by time and weather, so revealing its strata, and allowing openings to be, created for access and light.

Interestingly, most language thus marked – and, as a result, hedged or downscaled – has to do with the visual properties of buildings, which suggests that, of all the traits susceptible to being commented upon in ARs, it is the aesthetics of a given design that appears to be particularly face-threatening for the participants in the genre – all equally literate in visual terms. In other words, since the genre's audience can read the images in the texts and, therefore, agree or disagree with the corresponding verbal explanation, one way to avoid confrontation is to keep the commentary as non-categorical as possible. In contrast, metaphors concerned with abstract properties (e.g. the theatrical metaphor in example 8) are less hedged: given the impossibility of comparing the assessment thus articulated with the visuals in the texts, the audience's disagreement remains a personal matter.

What does a genre approach to architectural metaphors tell us? In the first place, while architects use various types of metaphor to discuss space, ARs typically yield a large number of metaphors concerned with what buildings look like and, in this regard, illustrate – indeed, respond to – the aesthetic concerns of the genre. Choice and clustering of metaphors in the textual reconstruction of built spaces can also be explained by taking into account the purposes of the genre. On the one hand, image metaphors help architects 're-view' the buildings under focus from different perspectives – a descriptive role seldom noticed by people outside the community and often taken for granted by professionals, yet a necessary prerequisite for evaluation. On the other hand, metaphor is an important evaluation strategy and, therefore, tends to cluster at those moves and steps explicitly concerned with evaluation. Finally, the symmetry between the participants in ARs in terms of status and knowledge is reflected in the way metaphors of various sorts are used in the genre.

Conclusions and future directions

Despite its importance, the notion of genre is still under-exploited in research on metaphor in professional contexts – whether this involves metaphor's role in intra- or inter-disciplinary communication. My contention here, and elsewhere, is that in order to understand the mechanics of metaphor, we need to take into account the topic(s) it helps articulate, the people using it to communicate, and the goals fulfilled by the interaction where it plays a role. Since all three are defining traits of genre, an approach relating to all three is seen as worth trying in metaphor research.

How may knowledge of genre help metaphor scholars? In the first place, genre may help researchers to build hypotheses about the types of metaphorical expressions likely to appear in the context under focus, or about the motivations underlying their presence as specified by the genre's rhetorical goals. Second, analysts may check those hypotheses, and explain that presence and role in a more situated, informed way. They can therefore discuss the relevance of metaphorical language by relating it to the intentions underlying the author's use of metaphor and the audience's expectations when dealing with the texts (both constrained at a very basic, general level by the genre's communicative purpose). Finally, relating the textual staging of metaphor to the goals and participants of the genre in question may contribute to improved identification and lead to a more systematic understanding of the communicative function of metaphorical language. This is important because, although research on metaphor in professional genres has grown in the past two decades, the textual dimension of metaphor is still often overlooked. Given that the main assumption in genre research into professional communication is that textual structure is constrained by and reflects the genre's topic, goals and author–reader relationship, it seems odd that the interest in how metaphor fulfils these aspects in specific genres has not also provoked some reflection upon how it actually appears within their rhetorical structure.

Acknowledgement

Research funded by the Spanish Ministerio de Economía y Competitividad MINECO (reference: FFI2013-45553-C3-2-P).

Further reading

Caballero, R. (2006) *Re-viewing Space: Figurative Language in Architects' Assessment of Built Space*, Berlin, Germany: Mouton de Gruyter.
Caballero, R. and Suárez Toste E. (2010) 'A genre approach to imagery in winespeak', in G. Low, Z. Todd, A. Deignan and L. Cameron (eds), *Researching and Applying Metaphor in the Real World*, Amsterdam, The Netherlands: John Benjamins, pp. 265–287.
Koller, V. (2004) *Metaphor and Gender in Business Media Discourse: A Critical Cognitive Study*, Basingstoke, UK: Palgrave Macmillan.
Deignan, A., Littlemore, J. and Semino, E. (2013) *Figurative Language, Genre and Register*, Cambridge, UK: Cambridge University Press.

References

Boyd, R. (1993) 'Metaphor and theory change: What is "metaphor" a metaphor for?', in A. Ortony (ed.) *Metaphor and Thought* (2nd edn), Cambridge, UK: Cambridge University Press, pp. 356–408.
Caballero, R. (2006) *Re-viewing Space: Figurative Language in Architects' Assessment of Built Space*, Berlin, Germany: Mouton de Gruyter.
—— (2007) 'Manner-of-motion verbs in wine description', *Journal of Pragmatics*, 39, 2095–2114.
—— (2009) 'The role of metaphor in architectural appreciation: A look at reviews from the 19th and 20th centuries', in S. Radighieri and P. Tucker (eds), *Point of View: Description and Evaluation across Discourses*, Rome, Italy: Officina.
—— (2013) 'The role of metaphor in architects' negotiation and (re)construction of knowledge across genres', *Metaphor and Symbol*, 28(1), 3–21.
—— (2014) 'Language, space and body: Sensing and construing built space through metaphor', in J. Bamford, F. Poppi and D. Mazzi (eds), *Space, Place and the Discursive Construction of Identity*, Berna, Switzerland: Peter Lang, pp. 107–134.
Cameron, L. and Maslen, R. (2010) 'Identifying metaphor in discourse data', in L. Cameron and R. Maslen (eds), *Metaphor Analysis: Research Practice in Applied Linguistics, Social Science and the Humanities*, London: Equinox, pp. 97–115.
Charteris-Black, J. (2004) *Corpus Approaches to Critical Metaphor Analysis*, Basingstoke, UK: Palgrave Macmillan.
Crystal, D. (1985) *A Dictionary of Linguistics and Phonetics* (2nd edn), New York: Basil Blackwell.
Deignan, A., Littlemore, J. and Semino, E. (2013) *Figurative Language, Genre and Register*, Cambridge, UK: Cambridge University Press.
Foucault, M. (1969) *L'Archéologie du savoir*, Paris: Éditions Gallimard.
Gentner, D. (1980) *The Role of Analogical Models in Learning Scientific Topics*, Cambridge, MA: Bolt Beranek and Newman Report.
Goatly, A. (2011) *The Language of Metaphors* (2nd edn), London: Routledge.
Goodwin, C. (1994) 'Professional vision', *American Anthropologist*, 96, 606–633.
Halliday, M. A. K. (1984) *Language as Social Semiotic: The Social Interpretation of Language and Meaning*, London: Edward Arnold.
Kimmel, M. (2012) 'Optimizing the analysis of metaphor in discourse: How to make the most of qualitative software and find a good research design', *Review of Cognitive Linguistics*, 10(1), 1–48.
Knudsen, S. (2003) 'Scientific metaphors going public', *Journal of Pragmatics*, 35, 1247–1263.

Koller, V. (2003) 'Metaphor clusters, metaphor chains', *Metaphorik.de*, 5, 115–134. http://www.metaphorik.de/sites/www.metaphorik.de/files/journal-pdf/05_2003_koller.pdf.

—— (2004) *Metaphor and Gender in Business Media Discourse: A Critical Cognitive Study*, Basingstoke: Palgrave Macmillan.

Koller, V., Hardie, A., Rayson, P. and Semino, E. (2008) 'A computer-assisted approach to the analysis of metaphor variation across genres', *Metaphorik.de*, 15, 141–160.

Kövecses, Z. (2005) *Metaphor in Culture: Universality and Variation*, Cambridge, UK: Cambridge University Press.

Lakoff, G. and Johnson, M. (1980) *Metaphors We Live By*, Chicago and London: University of Chicago Press.

Liakopoulos, M. (2002) 'Pandora's box or panacea? Using metaphors to create the public representations of biotechnology', *Public Understanding of Science*, 11(5), 5–32.

Linell, P. and Sarangi, S. (eds) (1998) *Discourse across Professional Boundaries*, special issue of *Text*, 18(2).

Low, G., Todd, Z., Deignan, A. and Cameron, L. (eds) (2010) *Researching and Applying Metaphor in the Real World*, Amsterdam, The Netherlands: John Benjamins.

Lu, L. and Ahrens, K. (2008) 'Ideological influence on building metaphors in Taiwanese presidential speeches', *Discourse and Society*, 19(3), 383–406.

McCloskey, D. N. (1994) *Knowledge and Persuasion in Economics*, Cambridge, UK: Cambridge University Press.

Mirowski, P. (1989) *More Heat Than Light: Economics as Social Physics, Physics as Nature's Economics*, Cambridge, UK: Cambridge University Press.

Musolff, A. (2004) *Metaphor and Political Discourse: Analogical Reasoning in Debates about Europe*, Basingstoke, UK: Palgrave Macmillan.

Pragglejaz Group. (2007) 'MIP: A method for identifying metaphorically used words in discourse', *Metaphor and Symbol*, 22(1), 1–39.

Semino, E. (2008) *Metaphor in Discourse*, Cambridge, UK: Cambridge University Press.

—— (2011) 'The adaptation of metaphors across genres', *Review of Cognitive Linguistics*, 9(1), 130–152.

Skorczynska, H. and Deignan, A. (2006) 'Readership and purpose in the choice of economics metaphor', *Metaphor and Symbol*, 21(2), 87–104.

Steen, G., Dorst, A., Herrmann, J., Kaal, A. Krennmayr, T. and Pasma, T. (2010) *A Method for Linguistic Metaphor Identification: From MIP to MIPVU*, Amsterdam, The Netherlands: John Benjamins.

Stefanowitsch, A. and Gries, S. T. (eds) (2006) *Corpus-based Approaches to Metaphor and Metonymy*, Berlin, Germany: Mouton de Gruyter.

Swales, J. (1990) *Genre Analysis: English in Research and Academic Settings*, Cambridge, UK: Cambridge University Press.

Wee, L. (2005) 'Class-inclusion and correspondence models as discourse types: A framework for approaching metaphorical discourse', *Language in Society*, 34, 219–238.

14
Creative metaphor in literature

Marco Caracciolo

Introduction

As she drives along a provincial road in Scotland, Isserley – the protagonist of Michel Faber's novel *Under the Skin* (2000) – spots two young men walking in the heavy rain:

> They had turned at her approach and shouted something too heavily accented for her to understand. Their rain-soaked heads looked like a couple of peeled potatoes, each with a little splat of brown sauce on top; their hands seemed gloved in bright green foil: the wrappers of crisps packets. In her rear-view mirror, Isserley had watched their waddling bodies recede to coloured blobs finally swallowed up in the grey soup of the rain.
>
> *2000: 24–5*

This description of rain-soaked pedestrians is rich in figurative language: the second sentence is structured around two similes ('looked like a couple of peeled potatoes', 'their hands seemed gloved in bright green foil'), building up to the metaphors of the last sentence ('swallowed up', 'the grey soup of the rain'). As the reader can hardly fail to notice, these expressions have something in common: they all point to the semantic domain of food; they present the human body as something that can be eaten, wrapped in foil and 'washed down' with soup-rain. Further, these comparisons originate in Isserley's own changing perceptions while driving past the pedestrians – hence the dynamic quality of the description: we imagine Isserley focusing first on the men's potato heads; then turning her attention to their gloves' foil-like shine; and finally seeing them being 'swallowed up' by the rain as they gradually disappear in the rear-view mirror. When reading this passage, especially in the context of Faber's novel, readers are thus encouraged to connect the metaphorical language – and its underlying comparison between human bodies and food – with Isserley's consciousness. This metaphorical mapping is, of course, no coincidence in a novel whose plot revolves around an alien race coming to Earth to 'farm' human beings and ship their meat to a distant planet. Isserley herself, as the reader soon discovers, is an alien involved in this business, since her job is to pick up male hitch-hikers, sedate them and take them to a secret underground facility to be fattened and slaughtered.

Creative metaphor in literature

Faber's passage neatly illustrates many of the issues surrounding the literary use of metaphorical language. First, its similes and metaphors are an example of stylistic foregrounding, or the creative deviation from ordinary language that has often been seen as the hallmark of literary texts (see Miall and Kuiken 1994). Jan Mukařovský, one of the exponents of the Prague Linguistic Circle in the late 1920s and 1930s, is generally associated with the term 'foregrounding', but similar theories about the deviation of literary language (including metaphor) can be found in Russian Formalism and even in the ancient rhetorical tradition. Yet not all metaphorical expressions occurring in a literary context are equally creative, and therefore likely to be seen as foregrounded: compare, for instance, the conventional 'swallowed up' (which could easily appear in everyday speech) with the relative novelty of 'the grey soup of the rain'. Second, through its focus on the protagonist's subjective experience, Faber's description exemplifies how metaphors may become bound up with the perspectival nature of literary discourse: they participate in readers' engagement with perspectives on the world (in this case, the protagonist's) that differ from those of the text's flesh-and-blood author. Finally, Faber's passage shows how figurative language can coalesce around particular semantic domains, contributing to broader interpretations and evaluations as readers connect a set of metaphorical expressions with other aspects of literary discourse. All of these issues will be explored in the following pages, which aim to introduce work on literary metaphor at the crossroads of linguistics, stylistics, literary studies and narrative theory. In the first section I will provide a historical overview of theories of literary metaphor, from Aristotle to modern-day cognitive models. For obvious reasons, this won't be a comprehensive account but rather a series of strategic 'samples' in a particularly long, and complex, history. The questions raised in this introduction will be further discussed in the section on 'Critical issues and debates'. I will then come back to Faber's novel, offering a 'hands-on' analysis which builds on the core ideas advanced in this chapter.

Before moving on, let me spell out the working definition of literature I will adopt. Obviously, this question has been the object of much controversy, but for our purposes I will define literature as a practice involving written – and typically, but not necessarily, fictional – texts that are thought to have special value in a given community. In today's world, literary texts are seen as possessing *artistic* value: they are expected to reward a specific kind of attention focusing on style, themes, depth of characterization and so on (see Lamarque 2008: 61).

Historical overview

Before metaphor became an autonomous object of enquiry in twentieth-century linguistics and cognitive science, it is difficult to disentangle accounts of metaphor in literature from accounts of metaphor as such. This duality is already evident in the father of Western literary theory, Aristotle, who treated metaphor in both the *Poetics* and the *Rhetoric*. As Paul Ricoeur puts it, for Aristotle metaphor 'belongs to both domains' (1977: 12), straddling the divide between the art of persuasive argumentation (rhetoric) and the study of artistic creativity (poetics). Metaphor is thus presented as an intrinsically 'interdisciplinary' phenomenon, reflecting both its flexibility as a cognitive and linguistic tool and the difficulty of grasping it from within a single conceptual framework. According to Aristotle, 'A metaphor is the application of a word that belongs to another thing: either from genus to species, species to genus, species to species, or by analogy' (1995: 105). In Aristotle's language, a 'species' is a subset of a 'genus': his first example is the sentence 'my ship stands here', where – Aristotle argues – the verb 'stands' is metaphorical because being moored is a way of standing, so the metaphor replaces the specific (being moored) with the general (standing). Aristotle's definition of metaphor, as modern commentators have noted (Levin 1982), is quite unsystematic, since it appeals to two different criteria: (1) a relationship between conceptual categories (i.e. 'species' and 'genera') reminiscent of what we would now call 'metonymy'; (2) an analogical relationship. This definitional ambiguity anticipates some of the more recent debates (see Glucksberg 2008) on whether metaphor understanding relies on a process of categorization (the extension of pre-existing conceptual categories) or cross-domain mapping (Aristotle's analogy).

In the twentieth century, I. A. Richards – the English literary scholar who founded New Criticism – also combined rhetoric and poetics in the influential account of metaphor he offered in *The Philosophy of Rhetoric* (1936). Richards is known for introducing the distinction between 'tenor', 'vehicle' and 'ground', a terminology that has been widely adopted in literary criticism. In short, 'tenor' is the target of the comparison, 'vehicle' is what the tenor is being compared to, while 'ground' is what tenor and vehicle have in common. For instance, in the phrase 'the grey soup of the rain' (from Faber's novel) the rain is the tenor, the soup is the vehicle, and the ground – we imagine – is the greyness and thickness of the downpour as seen from Isserley's car. But Richards' account of metaphor goes well beyond this familiar distinction, zooming in on the psychological and interpretive processes underlying literary metaphor; Richards insisted that – at one level – all thought is metaphorical, and that metaphorical meaning is always a function of context (see West 2007: 11–12). In this sense, Richards' theory of metaphor is a 'protocognitivist' one, anticipating many of the concerns of today's cognitive approaches.

Another important milestone is Paul Ricoeur's *The Rule of Metaphor* (1977). Ricoeur also takes his cue from Aristotle and the rhetorical tradition, and in fact his study has been seen as the 'hallmark of traditional metaphor research' (Biebuyck and Martens 2011: 58) before the advent of Lakoff and Johnson's conceptual metaphor theory (see Chapter 1). Drawing on a wide variety of sources, from Saussurean linguistics to the philosophy of language and literary theory, Ricoeur anchors his conception of metaphor to a hermeneutic account of literary mimesis – a view that he would articulate more fully in the three volumes of *Time and Narrative*. For Ricoeur, 'metaphor is the rhetorical process by which discourse unleashes the power that certain fictions have to redescribe reality' (1977: 5). Not only do fictional representations reflect existing conceptions of the world and human action, but by giving rise to an imaginary domain – a fictional world – they can disclose novel perspectives and therefore enrich our understanding of reality. This 'redescription' or 'reconfiguration' of the real world is what metaphor can achieve on a smaller scale by presenting the target (Richards' tenor) from new and unexpected angles (the vehicle). In the next section I will have more to say about this analogy between literary representation and the workings of metaphor.

A different tradition, that of Anglo-American stylistics (see, e.g. Leech 1985), also calls attention to the link between metaphor and literary language. Mick Short's (1996: 9–13) account of metaphor, for instance, ties in with the notion of stylistic foregrounding – i.e. the use of 'marked', unconventional language in literary texts. Metaphor is the foregrounding device *par excellence*, since it is defined in terms of a semantic deviation from the linguistic norms that underlie 'literal' language use. One of the assumptions behind stylistics is that the linguistic description of literary texts should precede and 'ground' interpretation *qua* the construction of complex meanings (Short 1996: 2–3). Hence, stylistics posits that metaphorical language interacts with interpretive judgements in both poetry and prose fiction.

The last act in this (inevitably condensed) overview of approaches to literary metaphor coincides with the surge of interest in metaphor in the 1970s and 1980s (Lakoff and

Johnson 1980; Ortony 1979). This movement, originating in psychology and philosophy, saw metaphor as a conceptual tool which *precedes* concrete metaphorical expressions in language. Even as it uncoupled metaphor from both rhetoric and poetics, this cognitive turn was not without repercussions for the study of metaphor in literary contexts. We can distinguish here between two relatively independent lines of inquiry. On the one hand, in *Understanding Metaphor in Literature* (1994) Gerard Steen explores various aspects of literary metaphor – and particularly the distinction between metaphor in literature and metaphor in other discourse domains – from an empirical standpoint. Steen's study is premised on a sharp distinction between traditional literary-critical approaches to metaphor and his own empirical account, which investigates the reading strategies of non-professional readers (Steen 1994: 30; cf. also Steen and Gibbs 2004: 339).

A second strand of literary scholarship inspired by cognitive metaphor theory takes a more traditional, stylistic approach, looking at the conceptual metaphors underlying individual literary texts (Popova 2003) or, possibly, entire corpora (Kimmel 2008). The emphasis here does not fall on reader-response, but on how literary texts reflect cognitive-level constraints on the production and understanding of metaphor. This project can be more easily reconciled with the close reading of individual texts than with Steen's empirical studies. Yet neither approach has managed to win over literary scholars working outside of the cognitivist paradigm. The title of the volume recently edited by Monika Fludernik, *Beyond Cognitive Metaphor Theory* (2011), is symptomatic of the discontent with cognitive metaphor theory existing within some areas of literary studies. Just as it straddled the divide between rhetoric and poetics in Aristotle's work, the theory of literary metaphor has become a battlefield for different conceptions of literature and methodologies of literary enquiry.

Critical issues and debates

I have made several references to literary metaphor in the previous section, but what exactly is a literary metaphor? Answers to this question fall between three possibilities. First, one could argue that literary metaphors are particularly novel and creative, and can therefore be distinguished from non-literary metaphors on these grounds. This view, of course, goes hand in hand with the Formalist idea of literary language as involving a deviation from everyday language (foregrounding). Second, we could think that a literary metaphor is just a metaphor occurring in a literary context – for instance, a poem or short story – without there being anything specific or distinctive about it. Third, it is conceivable that literary reading as a specific practice calls for a certain attitude in readers: a literary metaphor is a metaphor approached in certain ways, which differ from how we make sense of metaphors in other contexts. All of these claims have merit. Indeed, different approaches place different emphases on continuities and discontinuities between metaphor in literature and metaphor in everyday language (see Semino and Steen 2008).

Let's start from the claim that there is something unique about literary metaphors. A version of this view has been defended by Lakoff and Turner in *More than Cool Reason* (1989). According to Lakoff and Turner, poetic language builds on conceptual metaphors that are commonly found in everyday language, but offers creative variations on such metaphors. In particular, Lakoff and Turner (1989: 67–72) argue that literary language can extend ordinary metaphors, develop them in unconventional ways, question them by calling attention to their inadequacy, or combine metaphors belonging to different conceptual domains. These four strategies, which Lakoff and Turner label 'extending', 'elaborating', 'questioning' and 'composing', account for the specificity of literary metaphors. The metaphors appearing in literary contexts are, therefore, thought to be particularly creative both conceptually (in terms of how they relate to established conceptual metaphors) and linguistically.

It is not difficult to come up with counter-examples to this claim (see also Chapters 15 and 23). As I noted above, while Faber's 'grey soup of the rain' meets these criteria, his 'swallowed up' (in the sense of 'vanished') does not, and could easily appear in a non-literary text or even in speech. Two conclusions can be drawn from this observation. One is straightforward: the metaphors appearing in literary contexts may be more creative than (most of) the metaphors we use in everyday language, but this is a probabilistic tendency rather than a hard-and-fast rule. 'Literary metaphors' should then be taken as shorthand for 'metaphors appearing in a literary context', even if such metaphors *can*, in some scenarios, differ from everyday metaphors. The second conclusion has to do with literary genre. Literature is an umbrella term for a large variety of texts falling in categories such as 'drama', 'the novel', 'the short story', 'lyric poetry', etc. Each of these categories follows different conventions and exhibits different stylistic patterns. Andrew Goatly (2011: 333–40) has studied the frequency of what he calls 'active' (i.e. unconventional) metaphors across literary genres. Perhaps unsurprisingly, active metaphors are especially dense in lyric poetry, amounting to 56 per cent of the metaphors used. The novel comes in second (28 per cent) and is comparable to magazine advertising (22 per cent). In popular science, news reports and conversation, active metaphors are respectively at 18 per cent, 10 per cent and 4 per cent of the total. While Lakoff and Turner's creative variations frequently appear in poetic language, novels like Faber's *Under the Skin* prefer conventional metaphors (e.g. 'swallowed up') over novel ones, and are in this sense closer to other discourse types. Yet we shouldn't forget that even conventional metaphors can have distinctive effects when they are used deliberately (Ng and Koller 2013) – for example, Faber's 'swallowed up' helps evoke associations between human beings and food.

Readers of Faber's novel may notice this conceptual connection because the *context* in which we encounter literary metaphors favours a specific kind of attention. Indeed, as an artistic practice, literature is likely to call for reading strategies distinct from those we adopt in engaging with other discourse types. Steen's (1994) study confirms this hypothesis. Comparing readers' responses to metaphor in both literary and journalistic texts, Steen found differences in five areas. Readers of literature are more likely to: focus on metaphors, identify them explicitly, evaluate them according to aesthetic criteria, interpret them by referring to authorial intentions, and 'refunctionalize' them later on in the act of reading (Steen 1994: 142). These findings suggest that metaphors embedded in a text that readers consider – or have been asked to consider – literary are interpreted in partially different ways from metaphors appearing in other contexts. This interest in the context of metaphor and in its effects underlies Steen's (2008) more recent 'three-dimensional' model of metaphor. Steen aims to account for metaphor not just as a cognitive and linguistic tool, but also as a communicative phenomenon. In particular, he insists on the 'deliberateness' of creative metaphors, arguing that this deliberateness depends on the author's communicative intention:

> I propose that a metaphor is used deliberately when it is expressly meant to change the addressee's perspective on the referent or topic that is the target of the metaphor, by making the addressee look at it from a different conceptual domain or space, which functions as a conceptual source.
>
> *2008: 222*

Through its 'perspective-changing' function, metaphor may thus invite readers to see a particular object or topic in a new light. In this respect, metaphor is closely aligned with the potential effects of literature as such. At different levels, both metaphor and literature can bring about a form of conceptual change by inviting readers to look at aspects of reality from novel and unexpected perspectives. Guy Cook (1994) has called this effect of literature 'schema refreshment', which ties in with Ricoeur's conception of literary mimesis as a 'reconfiguration' of the world: literary representation allows authors and readers to experiment with beliefs, values and worldviews from a 'safe' distance, potentially gaining insight into aspects of their own everyday reality. This structural resemblance between metaphorical and literary perspective-changing is one of the reasons for the deep connection between literature and creative metaphor, and explains why metaphor can become a privileged object of readers' attention in literary contexts.

We'll see this kind of literary perspective-changing at work in my reading of Faber's novel in the next section. Before turning to the case study, however, it is worth commenting on an important divide in the contemporary study of metaphor. The approach to literary metaphor advocated by linguistically oriented scholars (Steen 1994; Goatly 2011) is empirical and nomothetic – i.e. it aims at drawing generalizing conclusions based on statistically significant corpora or populations of readers. By contrast, literary scholars (Biebuyck and Martens 2011; Pettersson 2011) tend to place the emphasis on idiographic, bottom-up research that starts from the close reading of individual texts. Scholarly interpretations of this kind are *not* likely to be shared by most readers, and therefore cannot be generalized in the same way as the findings of an empirical study (Steen and Gibbs 2004). This tension between the interpretive and the empirically oriented approach represents a potential stumbling block for interdisciplinary collaboration. One way to sidestep it is to look at the processes – both textual and psychological – that guide the interpretive strategies of readers (including literary critics). This is what I will attempt in the next section.

An example of current research: embodiment and metaphorical 'paranarratives'

Metaphor is typically associated with – and analysed in connection to – poetic language. Indeed, as pointed out in the previous section, creative metaphors do appear to be more frequent in lyric poetry than in other literary genres. But metaphor, and especially 'extended metaphors' or the concatenation of semantically related metaphorical expressions, can play an equally important role in narrative texts. Biebuyck and Martens describe this network of connected metaphors under the heading of 'paranarrative' (2011: 65–6), contending that the metaphorical paranarrative stands in a complex relation to other aspects of literary narrative, enriching and complicating its meanings. Using Faber's *Under the Skin* as a case study, this section explores how metaphorical language can modulate readers' engagement with characters and shape their overall interpretation of a given narrative.

I argued in the introduction that narrative representation can convey mental states (e.g. perceptions, emotions, beliefs and desires) of beings distinct from the narrative's flesh-and-blood author. These (fictional) beings are what we call characters (see Jannidis 2013), and the technique through which third-person narrative renders a character's mental life as if 'from the inside' is called 'internal focalization' (see Jahn 2005). Consider, for instance, the following passage from *Under the Skin*:

> Normally, [Isserley] would sleep only a few hours during the night, and then discover herself lying wide-eyed in the claustrophobic dark, her contorted back muscles keeping her hostage in her bed with the threat of needle-sharp pains.
>
> *Faber 2000: 49*

By focusing on Isserley's proprioceptive experience, these lines give readers access to the character's mental processes in ways that – we imagine – would be barred from an external observer. Like most of Faber's novel, the passage can thus be said to be internally focalized through Isserley's eyes. While internal focalization is a *narrative* strategy, patterns at the stylistic level can also serve to flesh out a character's mental perspective. Literary stylistician Roger Fowler (1977: 76) used the term 'mind style' to refer to a coordinated set of stylistic cues reflecting a character's worldview. In *Under the Skin* we find contrasts in mind style whenever Isserley picks up a hitch-hiker: the focalization temporarily switches from Isserley to the passenger's mind, resulting in a sense of more or less marked deviation from the articulate language we have come to associate with Isserley. For instance, one of the hitch-hikers thinks:

> This girl who'd picked him up, now. She'd probably be all right. As a girlfriend, like. She'd let him sleep when he was dying for it, he could tell. She wouldn't poke him just when he was drifting off and say, 'You're not falling asleep are you?' Kind eyes, she had. Bloody big knockers, too.
>
> *Faber 2000: 80–1*

The combination of lexical choices, elementary syntax and colloquialisms paints a fairly detailed picture of the character's background, level of education and attitude towards women.

Research in literary stylistics has shown that recurring metaphorical patterns may, in themselves, contribute to a character's distinctive mind style. Building on Elizabeth Black's (1993) work, Semino and Swindlehurst argue that 'consistent metaphorical patterns can be employed to project a characteristic and partly deviant mind style' (1996: 164). They exemplify this idea through Ken Kesey's novel *One Flew Over the Cuckoo's Nest*, where the narrator often uses metaphorical expressions comparing animate beings to pieces of machinery. According to Semino and Swindlehurst, this metaphorical pattern dovetails with the mechanistic worldview of the mentally deviant narrator. Something similar happens in *Under the Skin*. In my analysis of a passage from Faber's novel in the introduction, I have already called attention to the incongruous comparison between human beings and processed food (peeled potatoes). This association turns out to be part of a larger network of metaphorical mappings involving the external appearance of human beings and inanimate objects. For instance, looking at the bodies of four dead prisoners, Isserley observes that '[pale] and glistening with frost, the foursome looked like massive effigies made of candlefat, unevenly melted from their hairy wicks' (1996: 114). Candlefat is an industrial product, and can be made from animal fats, thus serving as reminder of how human bodies are turned into food by the aliens. Even when humans *are* compared to animate beings, Isserley's choice falls on invertebrate animals that are biologically far removed from us. When watching a TV show, Isserley notes that one of the actors 'resembled a giant insect and waved pincers like a crab, but advanced clumsily on two legs' (1996: 146). Isserley's objectifying gaze expresses her indifference towards the suffering of her victims, the hitch-hikers who are fattened and slaughtered by the aliens. These estranging metaphors for human embodiment can imaginatively distance readers from Isserley, prompting their ethical condemnation of the character. Put otherwise: not only does metaphorical language point to Isserley's ethical and emotional attitude towards humans, but it may also shape readers' attitude towards her.

However, other textual strategies counterbalance this effect, potentially *reducing* the distance between readers and the protagonist. Before being forcefully sent to Earth by a powerful corporation, Isserley had to undergo extensive surgery in order to resemble human beings; these bodily alterations give her chronic pain. Through the internal focalization, the novel lingers in often excruciating detail on Isserley's bodily discomfort. Metaphorical language plays a key role in these descriptions, reflecting a well-known link between metaphor and the representation of pain (see Kövecses 2008; Semino 2010). Consider again the passage quoted above: 'Normally, [Isserley] would sleep only a few hours during the night, and then discover herself lying wide-eyed in the claustrophobic dark, her contorted back muscles keeping her hostage in her bed with the threat of needle-sharp pains' (2000: 49). Isserley's pain is rendered through the conventional image of the needle's sharpness, which synaesthetically maps tactile experience onto pain. But the metaphors of the 'claustrophobic' dark and (especially) of Isserley being kept 'hostage' are far more significant: they present Isserley's body as a prison, as if she herself were a victim of dark forces, not unlike the human hitch-hikers. The same metaphorical motif is developed in a later scene. Isserley is lying in bed when she thinks:

> [She] would have to get up and do her exercises, regardless of what time it was, or she would end up unable to get up at all, trapped in a cage of her own bone and muscle.
> *Faber 2000: 143*

Isserley's body becomes a trap: despite her apparent lack of empathy towards her human victims, Isserley lives under similarly captive conditions, except that her prison is internalized through metaphorical language. More specifically, Isserley's pain can be read as a bodily manifestation of her emotional distress, as she herself recognizes: 'Lately, she suspected her feelings were getting swallowed up, undigested, inside purely physical symptoms' (Faber 2000: 39).

In *Under the Skin*, metaphors for embodiment become a site of negotiation of interpretive meanings: while the human body is de-anthropomorphized through comparisons with non-human objects, the metaphors surrounding Isserley's surgically modified – and superficially human-like – body open a window onto her alienation. It is because of this existential wound that Isserley becomes a more relatable character than we could expect, given her 'job' and lack of concern for human suffering. The ethical distance between the audience and the protagonist is thus partly counterbalanced by strategies that – like the 'body as prison' metaphor – may foster in readers the sympathy Isserley is unable to feel for our conspecifics. In being confronted with Isserley's bodily and perceptual experience, readers are thus given the chance to bridge the interspecies gap that Isserley herself cannot bridge: they can imaginatively take on the experiential perspective of an alien creature. This perspective-taking is a form of empathy, and – as psychologists and literary scholars have convincingly shown – it plays a central role in engaging with the protagonists of narrative (Hakemulder 2000; Keen 2007). But relating to characters, and especially complex characters such as Isserley, is a multidimensional or 'aspectual' (Gaut 1999) process: readers may feel close to some aspects of a character's mental life – for example, Isserley's bodily pain and emotional traumas – while condemning her lack of compassion for her victims. Though more empirical research is needed to confirm this hypothesis, we may suggest that metaphorical 'paranarratives' are among the textual strategies that shape readers' attitude towards a fictional character. They may express a character's worldview by creating an idiosyncratic 'mind style' (in this case, through cues conveying Isserley's perception of the human body as non-human), but they may also evoke a sense of closeness and intimacy between readers and characters.

In a recent article (Caracciolo 2013), I tried to account for this power of metaphorical language in terms of an underlying connection between metaphor and experience. Basic bodily and perceptual sensations as well as emotional feelings can be difficult to describe.

Philosophers make a similar point when they argue that the qualitative properties of experience – known as 'qualia' (see Tye 2009) – tend to be ineffable. As already noted by David Lodge (2002: 13), creative metaphors often serve to fill this gap: they enable us to talk about experiences that seem to resist capture in standard, 'literal' language. This account of Isserley's disgust for one of the hitch-hikers, for instance, is highly metaphorical: 'The sheer brute alienness of him hit her like a blow; and, with a heady rush like the nausea after a sudden loss of blood, she hated him' (Faber 2000: 206). Isserley's emotional response is rendered in terms of physical sensations such as a blow or the nausea caused by bleeding. Faber's language creatively leverages these images of violence and internal motion in order to convey the character's unique emotional feeling. Why is metaphorical language of this kind so effective at creating the illusion that we can share Isserley's experience in a relatively 'raw', unmediated form? The answer, I suggest, can be found in the structure of conscious experience itself. Consciousness is a stream – to use a famous Jamesian image – where sensations of different kinds are dynamically blended together (Pred 2005). In experience, the difference between – say – emotional feelings and tactile sensations is by no means as clear-cut as concepts and language make it seem. This is where metaphorical language comes in: by integrating linguistically distinct semantic domains, metaphors are particularly effective at rendering the integratedness of experience itself. As psychologist Cristina Cacciari puts it, 'metaphorical language is pervaded by cross-modality references that mirror, at a linguistic level, our neural architecture' (2008: 468). Hence, metaphors blending different aspects of characters' inner experiences can create an illusion of privileged access to their mental life, especially when the metaphorical language does not seem to originate from an explicit comparison drawn by the character, but from the external narrator's attempt at conveying 'what it is like' to be that character (see Caracciolo 2013: 63–6). This is what happens in *Under the Skin* through Faber's detailed – and highly metaphorical – descriptions of Isserley's bodily sensations and feelings. Faber's novel complicates our engagement with the protagonist, asking us to 'try on' her perspective at the bodily level – possibly through a mechanism of 'embodied simulation' (see Gibbs 2005; Semino 2010) – even as we realize the ethical undesirability of her actions.

This dynamic of readers' responses to Isserley seems to refunctionalize the novel's title: going 'under the skin' becomes another embodied metaphor for a form of empathetic engagement with the character, where readers are given the chance to imagine the bodily experience of an alien creature. But as we do so, we can never leave behind the ethical condemnation that usually goes with the idiom (in itself a conventionalized metaphor) 'getting under someone's skin'. The upshot of this process may well be that readers discover how, as one of the novel's characters explicitly states, we're 'all the same under the skin' (Faber 2000: 164), with Isserley's emotional struggles and even, perhaps, indifference towards others' pain mirroring our own. *Under the Skin* stages a tension not only between different characters and worldviews, but between strands of metaphors centring on the body and its multiple meanings. All in all, the novel exemplifies how metaphorical paranarratives may interact with characterization and other aspects of narrative, working as a catalyst for readers' meaning-making. In this way, Faber's novel explores the limits of empathy as well as the potential role of metaphorical language in enabling it (see Cameron 2011).

Directions for future research

As this handbook as a whole demonstrates, metaphor is a highly interdisciplinary topic, attracting interest in fields as diverse as linguistics, psychology, philosophy and literary studies. Metaphor thus offers a unique test bed for the rising field of the 'cognitive humanities' (see Hogan 2003; Stafford 2011), highlighting both the immense potential and the difficulties involved in interdisciplinary research. I have shown in this chapter that the investigation of creative metaphor in literature often reflects the diverging interests of literary studies and psychological or linguistic research on metaphor. While the heuristic value of the close reading of individual literary texts is undeniable, empirically oriented research can help 'ground' and systematize the intuitions of literary scholars. What is needed, then, is research capable of bridging the gap between these approaches through what Liesbeth Korthals Altes (2014) would call a 'metahermeneutic' method – one that looks at the structures underlying the diversity of readers' interpretations, investigating how specific stylistic and narrative strategies may shape readers' meaning-making. The analysis of *Under the Skin* I have sketched out in the previous section works along these lines, though of course it would have to be extended, and its hypotheses would have to be examined empirically, to be fully convincing. Studies of this kind would help develop an account of literary metaphor where the textual expertise of literary scholars and empirical methods are cross-fertilized rather than segregated, thus addressing the unease with cognitive metaphor theory expressed by many of the contributors to Fludernik (2011).

Most work on literary metaphor has so far concentrated on poetry (Lakoff and Turner 1989; Steen 2014). More research is needed on the connection between metaphorical paranarratives and other dimensions of literary narrative (e.g. characterization and plot dynamics). Kimmel's (2008) cognitive-stylistic approach, which distinguishes between *classes* of metaphor through ad-hoc qualitative coding, could be extended to account for other dimensions of narrative and their interrelation with figurative language. Moreover, metaphors and similes have typically been conflated in accounts of literary metaphor, but the explicitness of similes (*qua* marked comparisons) is likely to have distinctive effects, which call for both textual and empirical research (see Michael, Harding and Tobin 2005; Glucksberg and Haught 2006). Readers' interpretive strategies should also be taken into account, along with the broader communicative context in which literary texts are embedded (Yacobi 2011): for instance, how does metaphorical language contribute to thematic or satirical readings? At another level, it would be interesting to look into the connection between metaphorical language and the *experience* of literature. Talk about literary texts is rich in more or less conventional metaphors such as 'immersion' (Ryan 2001) or being 'lost in a book' (Nell 1988). To what extent do these metaphors structure readers' interpretation of literary works? Are they helpful or unhelpful in theorizing readers' engagement with literature? From a historical perspective, the impact of literary metaphor on everyday metaphor (i.e. how literary imagery enters language use) deserves further consideration. These questions open up new perspectives on metaphor in literature, offering fertile ground for interdisciplinary research at the intersection of literary scholarship and metaphor studies. As I have tried to show in this chapter, such research should be able to integrate multiple dimensions of metaphor – and different methodological tools – in theoretically sophisticated ways, exploring continuities *and* discontinuities between metaphor in literature and the uses of metaphor in other discursive contexts.

Further reading

Lakoff, G. and Turner, M. (1989) *More than Cool Reason: A Field Guide to Poetic Metaphor*, Chicago, IL: University of Chicago Press. (The first book-length attempt at applying conceptual metaphor theory to the study of metaphor in poetry.)

Steen, G. (1994) *Understanding Metaphor in Literature: An Empirical Approach*, London: Longman. (Steen's study offers an empirical account of metaphor understanding, comparing the effects of metaphor in literary and non-literary contexts.)

Semino, E. and Steen, G. (2008) 'Metaphor in Literature', in R.W. Gibbs, Jr. (ed.) *The Cambridge Handbook of Metaphor and Thought*, New York: Cambridge University Press. (A comprehensive account of metaphor in literature, encompassing both traditional, stylistic approaches and empirical trends.)

Fludernik, M. (ed.) (2011) *Beyond Cognitive Metaphor Theory: Perspectives on Literary Metaphor*, New York: Routledge. (An important edited collection, aiming to assess the impact of cognitive theories of metaphor on literary studies.)

References

Aristotle (1995) *Poetics*, in S. Halliwell (ed.) *Aristotle, Poetics; Longinus, On the Sublime; Demetrius, On Style*, Cambridge, MA: Harvard University Press.

Biebuyck, B. and Martens, G. (2011) 'Literary Metaphor between Cognition and Narration: The Sandman Revisited', in M. Fludernik (ed.) *Beyond Cognitive Metaphor Theory: Perspectives on Literary Metaphor*, New York: Routledge.

Black, E. (1993) 'Metaphor, Simile and Cognition in Golding's *The Inheritors*', *Language and Literature* 2(1): 37–48.

Cacciari, C. (2008) 'Crossing the Senses in Metaphorical Language', in R.W. Gibbs, Jr. (ed.) *The Cambridge Handbook of Metaphor and Thought*, New York: Cambridge University Press.

Cameron, L. (2011) *Metaphor and Reconciliation: The Discourse Dynamics of Empathy in Post-Conflict Conversations*, New York: Routledge.

Caracciolo, M. (2013) 'Phenomenological Metaphors in Readers' Engagement with Characters: The Case of Ian McEwan's *Saturday*', *Language and Literature* 22(1): 60–76.

Cook, G. (1994) *The Discourse of Literature: The Interplay of Form and Mind*, Oxford, UK: Oxford University Press.

Faber, M. (2000) *Under the Skin*, Edinburgh: Canongate.

Fludernik, M. (ed.) (2011) *Beyond Cognitive Metaphor Theory: Perspectives on Literary Metaphor*, New York: Routledge.

Fowler, R. (1977) *Linguistics and the Novel*, London: Methuen.

Gaut, B. (1999) 'Identification and Emotion in Narrative Film', in C. Plantinga and G.M. Smith (eds) *Passionate Views: Film, Cognition, and Emotion*, Baltimore, MD: Johns Hopkins University Press.

Gibbs, R.W., Jr. (2005) 'Embodiment in Metaphorical Imagination', in D. Pecher and R.A. Zwaan (eds) *Grounding Cognition: The Role of Perception and Action in Memory, Language, and Thinking*, Cambridge, UK: Cambridge University Press.

Glucksberg, S. (2008) 'How Metaphors Create Categories – Quickly', in R.W. Gibbs, Jr. (ed.) *The Cambridge Handbook of Metaphor and Thought*, New York: Cambridge University Press.

Glucksberg, S. and Haught, C. (2006) 'On the Relation between Metaphor and Simile: When Comparison Fails', *Mind & Language* 21(3): 360–78.

Goatly, A. (2011) *The Language of Metaphors*, New York: Routledge.

Hakemulder, F. (2000) *The Moral Laboratory: Experiments Examining the Effects of Reading Literature on Social Perception and Moral Self-Concept*, Philadelphia, PA: John Benjamins.

Hogan, P.C. (2003) *Cognitive Science, Literature, and the Arts: A Guide for Humanists*, New York: Routledge.

Jahn, M. (2005) 'Focalization', in D. Herman, M. Jahn and M.-L. Ryan (eds) *Routledge Encyclopedia of Narrative Theory*, New York: Routledge.

Jannidis, F. (2013) 'Character', in P. Hühn (ed.) *The Living Handbook of Narratology*, Hamburg, Germany: Hamburg University Press. Online. Available at: http://www.lhn.uni-hamburg.de/article/character (accessed 21 November 2014).

Keen, S. (2007) *Empathy and the Novel*, Oxford, UK: Oxford University Press.

Kimmel, M. (2008) 'Metaphors and Software-Assisted Cognitive Stylistics', in S. Zyngier, M. Bortolussi, A. Chesnokova and J. Auracher (eds) *Directions in Empirical Literary Studies*, Philadelphia, PA: John Benjamins.

Korthals Altes, L. (2014) *Ethos and Narrative Interpretation: The Negotiation of Values in Narrative Fiction*, Lincoln, NE: University of Nebraska Press.

Kövecses, Z. (2008) 'The Conceptual Structure of Happiness and Pain', in C. Lascaratou, A. Despotopoulou and E. Ifantidou (eds) *Reconstructing Pain and Joy: Linguistic, Literary and Cultural Perspectives*, Cambridge, UK: Cambridge Scholars Publishing.

Lakoff, G. and Johnson, M. (1980) *Metaphors We Live By*, Chicago, IL: University of Chicago Press.

Lakoff, G. and Turner, M. (1989) *More than Cool Reason: A Field Guide to Poetic Metaphor*, Chicago, IL: University of Chicago Press.

Lamarque, P. (2008) *The Philosophy of Literature*, Malden, MA: Wiley-Blackwell.

Leech, G.N. (1985) 'Stylistics', in T.A. van Dijk (ed.) *Discourse and Literature: New Approaches to the Analysis of Literary Genre*, Philadelphia, PA: John Benjamins.

Levin, S.R. (1982) 'Aristotle's Theory of Metaphor', *Philosophy & Rhetoric* 15(1): 24–46.

Lodge, D. (2002) 'Consciousness and the Novel', in *Consciousness and the Novel: Connected Essays*, Cambridge, MA: Harvard University Press.

Miall, D.S. and Kuiken, D. (1994) 'Foregrounding, Defamiliarization, and Affect: Response to Literary Stories', *Poetics* 22(5): 389–407.

Michael, I., Harding, J.R. and Tobin, V. (2005) 'On Simile', in S. Kemmer and M. Achard (eds) *Language, Culture, and Mind*, Stanford, CA: CSLI Publications.

Nell, V. (1988) *Lost in a Book: The Psychology of Reading for Pleasure*, New Haven, CT: Yale University Press.

Ng, C.J.W. and Koller, V. (2013) 'Deliberate Conventional Metaphor in Images: The Case of Corporate Branding Discourse', *Metaphor and Symbol* 28(3): 131–47.

Ortony, A. (ed.) (1979) *Metaphor and Thought*, Cambridge, UK: Cambridge University Press.

Pettersson, B. (2011) 'Literary Criticism Writes Back to Metaphor Theory', in M. Fludernik (ed.) *Beyond Cognitive Metaphor Theory: Perspectives on Literary Metaphor*, New York: Routledge.

Popova, Y. (2003) '"The Fool Sees with His Nose": Metaphoric Mappings in the Sense of Smell in Patrick Süskind's *Perfume*', *Language and Literature* 12(2): 135–51.

Pred, R. (2005) *Onflow: Dynamics of Consciousness and Experience*, Cambridge, MA: MIT Press.

Richards, I.A. (1936) *The Philosophy of Rhetoric*, Oxford, UK: Oxford University Press.

Ricoeur, P. (1977) *The Rule of Metaphor: Multi-disciplinary Studies of the Creation of Meaning in Language*, Toronto, Ontario: University of Toronto Press.

Ryan, M.-L. (2001) *Narrative as Virtual Reality: Immersion and Interactivity in Literature and Electronic Media*, Baltimore, MD: Johns Hopkins University Press.

Semino, E. (2010) 'Descriptions of Pain, Metaphor, and Embodied Simulation', *Metaphor and Symbol* 25(4): 205–26.

Semino, E. and Steen, G. (2008) 'Metaphor in Literature', in R.W. Gibbs, Jr. (ed.) *The Cambridge Handbook of Metaphor and Thought*, New York: Cambridge University Press.

Semino, E. and Swindlehurst, K. (1996) 'Metaphor and Mind Style in Ken Kesey's *One Flew over the Cuckoo's Nest*', *Style* 30(1): 143–66.

Short, M. (1996) *Exploring the Language of Poems, Plays and Prose*, London: Longman.

Stafford, B.M. (ed.) (2011) *A Field Guide to a New Meta-Field: Bridging the Humanities-Neurosciences Divide*, Chicago, IL: University of Chicago Press.

Steen, G. (1994) *Understanding Metaphor in Literature: An Empirical Approach*, London: Longman.

—— (2008) 'The Paradox of Metaphor: Why We Need a Three-Dimensional Model of Metaphor', *Metaphor and Symbol* 23(4): 213–41.

—— (2014) 'Metaphor and Style', in P. Stockwell and S. Whiteley (eds) *The Cambridge Handbook of Stylistics*, Cambridge, UK: Cambridge University Press.

Steen, G. and Gibbs, R.W., Jr. (2004) 'Questions about Metaphor in Literature', *European Journal of English Studies* 8(3): 337–54.

Tye, M. (2009) 'Qualia', in E.N. Zalta (ed.) *The Stanford Encyclopedia of Philosophy*. Online. Available at: http://plato.stanford.edu/archives/sum2009/entries/qualia/ (accessed 21 November 2014).

West, D. (2007) 'I. A. Richards' Theory of Metaphor: Between Protocognitivism and Poststructuralism', in L. Jeffries, D. McIntyre and D. Bousfield (eds) *Stylistics and Social Cognition*, Amsterdam, The Netherlands: Rodopi.

Yacobi, T. (2011) 'Metaphor in Context: The Communicative Structure of Figurative Language', in M. Fludernik (ed.) *Beyond Cognitive Metaphor Theory: Perspectives on Literary Metaphor*, New York: Routledge.

15
Conventional and novel metaphors in language

Gill Philip

Introduction

Metaphor drives innovation in language. New meanings are not necessarily metaphorical, but metaphor provides the grounds for new referents to be identified using old words. Speakers 'stretch' the meanings of the words they know when they need to communicate something that they have no existing word for. If that stretched meaning fills a vocabulary gap in the language, making it possible for speakers to talk about an object or concept that had no previously established wording, it gets absorbed into the language system where it becomes available for further exploitation, and the process starts all over again.

An example of this can be shown with the term 'hotbed', using diachronic data from the *Corpus of Historical American English* (Davies 2010). In its literal use, a hotbed is an area of warmed manure in which plants are cultivated, the heat ensuring that plants grow more quickly than they would at normal temperatures (i.e. their growth is 'forced'). This meaning is present from the start date of the corpus (1810) until the mid-1920s. Contemporaneously (from the 1820s onwards) we can find evidence of 'hotbed' referring metaphorically to schools which 'force' their pupils' precocious intellectual growth, and another metaphorical use in the field of medicine. This refers to environments in which germs and infections can flourish, typically warm, damp, overcrowded conditions, which recall the fertilizer and plants of the literal sense, although the causative 'forcing' seems to be lost. Over the course of the twentieth century, the literal meaning drops out of use (except in specialized horticultural texts), the medical sense consolidates into the fixed phrase 'hotbed of infection', and the education sense stretches to incorporate ideological education (from about 1970 onwards it has a distinct subsense relating to political or religious extremism). In the early years of the twenty-first century, 'hotbed' appears again with reference to plants, but has the 'infection' meaning within the metaphor CRIME IS A DISEASE: all the plants are involved in narcotics. And so it goes on.

Central to the contemporary view of metaphor proposed in Conceptual Metaphor Theory is that our thought processes are structured metaphorically and that the linguistic realization of non-literal metaphor (and many literary ones too) stems from such metaphorical cognition (see Chapters 1 and 14). In this chapter I present a different viewpoint, arguing that language does not merely provide evidence of the underlying metaphorical thought processes but is, in itself, a net contributor to our metaphorical modes of thinking, and acts as a bridge between the individual's cognition and that individual's need to communicate meaningfully with others.

Contrastive linguistics studies indicate that many of the concepts we use to shape our world are shared across languages and cultures, but shared concepts are no guarantee of mutual comprehension, as can easily be demonstrated in cross-linguistic studies and language acquisition research. For example, in Italian BEGINNING IS BIRTH, regardless of what is beginning. Therefore, in Italian, I would normally express the beginnings of such diverse entities as a cultural association, a misunderstanding, or an idea, as 'nascita' ('birth'). In English the BEGINNING IS BIRTH metaphor exists but is much more restricted in scope (Philip 2010), and would not be appropriate if used for the same contexts as the Italian: associations are formed or started, misunderstandings arise, ideas are conceived (but do not progress through gestation to birth).

Habitual language use as represented by conventional lexicalizations of concepts undeniably plays a part in selecting which aspects of a broad concept are relevant for the speakers of any given language: some features are core, some are peripheral, some are absent. Speakers tend to know when they are overstepping the boundaries of conventional language use and will typically remain within the confines of the linguistic and conceptual norms that have built up in their minds. Ideas are not 'born' in English: they are conceived. They may then have an embryonic form or a period of gestation before they finally emerge, fully formed, into the world – and yet English eschews the lexicalization of that final phase as 'birth'. It is not that the BIRTH metaphor is inappropriate in itself, it just does not fit with the way that ideas are conceptualized in English. There are in fact several metaphors available, including seeds which develop into plants, and they share a common conceit: they start small and develop in a dark place, hidden from view (e.g. underground or in the womb). For 'ideas', reaching maturity is not marked as a transitional event, as 'birth' would imply, but simply as part of a continual progression: this may be why ideas are not 'born' in English.

The conventions of our language and how it allows us to express concepts are a constraining factor in linguistic creativity. It is important to appreciate this before venturing into the study of novel metaphors, because although metaphor allows us to stretch the meanings of words so that they can also refer to new things, it is subject to the same rules and norms as any other aspect of the language. Most cognitive linguists prefer to operate at the abstract level of the conceptual metaphor, accounting for variation and novelty at the conceptual level (see especially Kövecses 2010 in this regard). I argue here that the lexical level cannot be overlooked, and that contextually determined *lexical* creativity must also be taken into consideration in any account of metaphor production and comprehension. The balance is a delicate one. In the course of this chapter, we focus on metaphor as expressed through linguistic forms, and how conventionality and novelty can be identified using linguistic parameters. We first look at some of the theoretical debates surrounding cognitive versus linguistic accounts of metaphor. We then discuss what is meant by 'conventional' or 'novel' in the context of metaphor, how we can measure degrees of novelty, and how novel linguistic forms and novel concepts interact. To finish up, two short case studies are provided to illustrate recent research into novel metaphor.

The data divide: conflicting and converging viewpoints

In the discussion of conventional and novel metaphor in this chapter, novelty is measured with reference to the conventional. How conventionality is determined, however, depends very much on the theoretical stance of the researcher. Some researchers appeal to a conventional form that all speakers of the language are expected to know; others make constant reference to corpus data and lexicographical (dictionary) evidence. Experts in the field have already decided which path to tread; it is determined by their background and method of investigation. Newcomers are often unaware of the 'data divide' which separates theoretical and descriptive linguistics, and as a result often fail to appreciate the deep divisions in theory and analysis that arise from the use of different sources of metaphorical examples. This section addresses some of the larger questions which affect the analysis of novel and conventional metaphors, namely: where do linguistic examples come from? What do we compare them to? How do we compare them, and why?

Intuitive and empirical metaphor studies

A first glance, the lists of linguistic examples provided as evidence of conceptual metaphors that abound within the conceptual metaphor literature seem convincing. Consider the following examples of the LOVE IS A JOURNEY metaphor (Lakoff and Johnson 1980: 44–45).

Look how far we've come.

We're at a crossroads.

We'll just have to go our separate ways.

We can't turn back now.

I don't think this relationship is going anywhere.

Examples such as these serve their illustrative purpose and are usually taken at face value – as instances of real language use. But on closer inspection, a number of problems emerge. One is that the examples are not gathered and transcribed from actual conversations or texts. They are, instead, idealized versions of real language, drawn from memory. The second issue is that they are decontextualized snippets of language, severed from their linguistic and extra-linguistic context. Mention is made of their context but it is not visible in the citations. With no concrete evidence to go on, we must assume that the context, like the examples themselves, is idealized. A third issue is that the examples are gathered serendipitously, not methodically: we cannot know how frequent they are, either in the language as a whole, or with respect to other uses of the JOURNEY metaphor (see also Chapters 7 and 8).

'Look how far we've come' (ibid.) is, of course, familiar and clearly refers to the JOURNEY source domain. But decontextualized, it is impossible to prove whether its target domain is indeed LOVE (from the expressions listed, it appears to be more specifically RELATIONSHIPS), and if so, how often it is used metaphorically with that target domain. That it *can* be used to talk about love is deemed sufficient. But if we turn to data, we can see why the idealized, decontextualized phrase might be problematic. A search of the *Corpus of Contemporary American English* (Davies 2008) for 'how far we've come' provides 89 examples of the phrase. Only one refers to an actual journey; of the remaining metaphorical instances, three refer to relationships, only one of these to a romantic relationship. The vast majority of the examples instead refer to social progress, predominantly improved rights for women and black Americans. Now, while we cannot say that 'look how far we've come' *cannot* be used when talking about LOVE, the data tell us that the expression prefers another target domain – (SOCIAL) PROGRESS, and a different sort of relationship (COMMUNITIES). This is observable in the data but less visible to our introspection.

There are two main counter-arguments to corpus-based claims such as this one. The first is that the actual occurrence of the form in the language is not important: metaphor is a feature of thought which can be examined *through* language but is not *derived from* language. The other argues that absence in a corpus is not evidence of absence in the language. Both arguments are valid to a certain extent, yet both miss the point somewhat. Linguistic data are extensively drawn upon to illustrate conceptual metaphors; indeed, cognitive linguistics relies heavily on examples found in 'everyday language' (Lakoff and Johnson 1980: 3). It should follow, then, that this 'everyday language' is conventional, typical, and normal, used in equally conventional, typical, normal contexts of use. The implications made in published studies are that this is the case, but it is easy to demonstrate the contrary. A corpus is only a sample of language, not the entirety of the language, so it cannot reveal whether a metaphor *can* exist, but it does tell us how frequent the metaphor is in the language, the approximate proportion of literal vs. metaphorical uses, and what target domain(s) it typically refers to. While it may not be necessary to consult a corpus all the time, it is somewhat churlish to sweep aside the details of language use that a corpus makes accessible, rather than using that information to further refine and define conceptual metaphor theory.

Metaphors, meanings and lexical patterns

The connections between linguistic and conceptual metaphor are discussed at length in Deignan (2005); here I will limit myself to explaining why authentic, attested text data are important in determining whether a metaphor is conventional or novel. As we have just seen, corpus data provide information about frequency of occurrence, typical phraseology and the range of contexts of use – information that is missing with decontextualized, idealized examples.

Corpus research over the past quarter century has demonstrated beyond doubt how close the connection is between context, lexical patterning (phraseology) and meaning. Each meaning of a word tends to avoid the phraseology associated with other meanings of that word so as to avoid ambiguity and misunderstanding (Hoey 2005). Returning to 'look how far we've come', we can note that although it typically refers to social or community relationships, this does not mean that it cannot be used to refer to a romantic relationship, only that it is *primed* (ibid.)[1] to occur in society- or community-related contexts. If it is found elsewhere this expectation will linger, triggering an ambiguous or fuzzy interpretation (*neighbourly* LOVE as a JOURNEY?).

Novel metaphors cannot be profiled because they have no recurrent lexical patternings, so they are usually compared and contrasted with similar forms – either established (conventional) metaphors drawing on the same source domain or lexical set, or, in the case of metaphorical idioms, the 'canonical form' (used in dictionaries). But meaning exists both in instantiation and in memory. Metaphors exploit this interplay, drawing on, enhancing and building up mental images through words in context. So while data are clearly necessary for the identification of both conventional forms and novel ones, there are some aspects of metaphor interpretation and production that are invisible, existing in the mind of individual speakers, which data can do little to prove or disprove.

Overview of the field

A conventional metaphor may be a conventional wording or a conventional concept. In both cases it is characterized by established (or *institutionalized*) ways of saying things. Institutionalization means that the language community as a whole has accepted the word,

> 1. **Bananas** are long curved fruit with yellow skins.
> 2. If someone is behaving in a silly or crazy way, or if they become extremely angry, you can say that they are **going bananas**. (INFORMAL)

Figure 15.1 Definition of 'banana' (Sinclair 2001). Cobuild.

expression or conceptual frame and has incorporated it into the standard repertoire of the language. The most straightforward way of attesting the conventionality of a linguistic metaphor is to look for it in a dictionary. For conceptual metaphors, there is no equivalent repository.[2] This section therefore starts by explaining how 'conventionality' is established, then looks at how novelty emerges from the conventional.

What is a conventional metaphor?

Conventional language use can be established in two ways. The first has just been mentioned and is based on frequency of occurrence and word patternings (phraseology), and is favoured by lexicographers and descriptive linguistics. The second, psycholinguistic, approach focuses on salience, a concept which encompasses familiarity, frequency, aptness in context and prominence in the mind (Giora 2003). The factors contributing to salience overlap substantially with those found in the lexicographical approach. What differentiates them is the focus on the language system as a whole (lexicographic) or on the individual's knowledge and use of language (psycholinguistic).

To see how salience and phraseology interact, we can consider the figurative meaning of 'banana' listed in a dictionary definition (Figure 15.1). Some language users may not know the expression 'go bananas' (familiar/unfamiliar parameter); some speakers encounter it more frequently than others (frequent/infrequent parameter). For the individual speaker, these factors contribute to the expression's overall salience: if you were to list all the expressions you know that include the word 'banana', you will include 'go bananas' only if you already know it, and how far down your list it appears gives an indication of its familiarity for you. It is included in the dictionary definition because it occurred frequently enough in the lexicographers' reference data for it to be 'profiled'.[3] In other words, it recurs in similar contexts, expressing a similar meaning, making it possible to formulate a definition which includes context of use (describing a person's behaviour) and register (informal).

On the other hand, there are other figurative meanings for 'banana' which are established and which appear in corpus data, e.g. 'banana' (or 'banana-brain') meaning 'idiot', which is current in British English and attested (nine occurrences) in the *British National Corpus*. It is salient for me, but does not feature in the entry in Figure 15.1, presumably because it was not present with sufficient frequency in the data consulted by the lexicographers.

Established meanings occur – and are identified – thanks to their occurrence in particular contexts and phraseological configurations. 'Banana' will be interpreted literally if it co-occurs with 'apple' or 'orange', but not if it co-occurs with 'brain'. This is partly due to juxtaposition – the proximity of other fruits in the immediate context makes us interpret 'banana' as a fruit – but it is also a product of phraseology. Corpus-based phraseological research has highlighted that conventional meanings occur in stable and distinctive phraseological patternings which differentiate literal and figurative meanings (Deignan 2005; see also Chapters 7 and 8). In fact, it is quite possible to *predict* one or the other, before the appearance of the metaphorical word, on the basis of the preceding text. Thus, 'Roy's customers think the council has gone . . . ' (*British National Corpus*) already provides us with a predictive context where 'bananas' will be interpreted as meaning 'crazy', just as 'otherwise I would have looked a right . . . ' (*British National Corpus*) predicts the meaning 'idiot', which in this example is lexicalized as 'banana'. The more common the metaphor in the language, the greater the regularity in its patterning (Deignan 2005). For instance, 'heart' is a body part, but when metaphorical it can be a location or an emotion – as encoded and identified in the syntax ('be <u>at</u> the heart of something', 'take something <u>to</u> heart'; '<u>in</u> my heart of hearts', etc.).

Conventional linguistic metaphors have predictable contextual and phraseological constraints which signal not only semantic meaning, but pragmatic intentions too.[4] Moon (1998) is one of the first corpus studies to investigate the interplay between word choice and communicative intention. While dealing with figurative expressions in general, not metaphor alone, her data indicate that as well as expressing a semantic meaning, figurative expressions usually carry out one or more text functions – informational, evaluative, situational, modalizing, text-organizational are the five main functions she cites (ibid. 219). In her data, 51 per cent of the figurative expressions were primarily evaluative (conveying speaker attitude) or modalizing (expressing truth values, etc.), and that score rises when those expressions which are also (but not mainly) evaluative or modalizing are added into the calculation (ibid.). Moon's research offers important evidence showing that metaphorical meaning is not simply figurative in semantic terms, but loaded pragmatically, evaluatively and/or epistemically.

What is a novel metaphor?

Kövecses (2005: 52) makes the point that 'accumulating evidence suggests that "creative" people make heavy use of conventional, everyday metaphors and that their creativity and originality actually derive from them'. At the level of language, novelty (the product of a creative mind) occurs when words are used metaphorically in ways which differ from their conventional applications, sometimes as substitutions for part of the wording of an existing linguistic metaphor. At the level of thought, novelty introduces new elements into the existing conceptual frame which force the concept to be re-elaborated. We can see this at work in a recent news item in which an executive from one broadcasting company describes his rival as a 'massive <u>gorilla</u> on the block'.[5] We glean from the subsequent context that the relevant features to bear in mind are power and aggression (the speaker specifies: 'they are trying to smash and crush us'). But since broadcasters are not normally spoken of in terms of animal attributes, it is difficult to assess precisely how to interpret '<u>gorilla</u>'. The potential entailments of this metaphor are manifold and richly complex – King Kong springs to mind – but since the expression is not institutionalized, we each have to interpret it in our own way.

Novelty is not a clear-cut category, but one which operates along a conventionality cline with the utterly predictable at one end, and the previously inconceivable at the other. Novel metaphors are infrequent and unfamiliar in the language at large. Given these criteria, we should be able to say that they are not salient either. But the brain is pre-programmed to notice the unusual, so novel metaphors – once encountered – stick in our mind. We are apt to forget the circumstances in which we come across everyday conventional language, but we remember instances of unusual language, even years after our (one) encounter with them and long after their textual or communicative purpose has been served.

A metaphor is novel when it is 'similar-but-different'. It has to be close enough to existing ways of speaking or thinking about a topic in order to achieve successful communication, but it has to be different enough for the speaker to have to put in some cognitive effort to fully comprehend it. By 'similar', I mean that the principal meaning-making parameters can still be identified, even if they do not appear exactly as we might have expected. In the case of word-play in idioms, catch-phrases and the like, the wording needs to be partially preserved so that we can retrace the 'original' form. If we are looking at new wordings for existing concepts, the underlying conceptual metaphor has to be recognizable even if some elements of the metaphor frame or image schema are introduced, modified or eliminated. As for the intended meaning, both semantic and pragmatic aspects have to be contextually relevant, pertinent to the interlocutors and/or to the situation in which it is used (Kövecses 2010). The conventional counterpart must be profiled, only after which is it possible to pinpoint how and where the novel instance deviates from it (Philip 2011; Hanks 2013). The extent to which it deviates is also significant: a certain degree of variety is normal even in conventional expressions, but novel elements are more radically divergent. Detailed lexicographical discussions of variation types can be found in Hanks (2013: 174–210), Moon (1998: 120–177) and Philip (2011: 143–165), while for discussions focusing on the conceptual level the reader is pointed to Fauconnier and Turner (2002), Lakoff and Turner (1989) and Kövecses (2010). The following discussion of variants of 'see red' illustrates some of the mechanisms that come into play.

It is fairly common in English to change the colour word in the expression 'to see red' ('to be very angry'), but there are some constraints, the most important of which being that the red spectrum is obligatory. 'Pink', 'deep red' and 'dark red' are all allowed, although they change the meaning slightly (lighter colours mitigate the intensity of the expression, while darker and more intense colours are emphatic) (Philip 2011: 152–160), but 'purple' or 'black' stand out because they do not belong to the red spectrum (ibid.). Going into further detail, 'scarlet' and 'salmon pink' are also marked because they change the basic colour term into a specific one, but they are less marked than 'purple' (red plus blue) or 'black' (the extreme depth of any colour), which in turn are less marked and less novel than 'blue', found in 'Jeans ads dropped after protestors see blue' (ibid. 187). This is a significant change and consequently requires a lot of cognitive effort on the part of the reader. It is not even apparent on the surface that it is a variant of 'see red', but when compared to the profile of conventional 'see red', everything is in its place except for the colour word. There is a strong supporting context for comprehension – 'Jeans' are both blue in colour *and* the cause of the anger – so 'blue' is coerced to mean what 'red' normally means in this phrase (ibid.).

Gradations of novelty

As we have just seen, the meaning of familiar metaphors can often be predicted from the preceding context. The meaning of unfamiliar metaphors can also be predicted by the preceding context, but psycholinguistic research has shown that when the expected word fails to appear and an unexpectedly different one takes its place, comprehension is delayed ever so slightly (a matter of milliseconds) as we rapidly try to connect the meaning we expected and the word that actually appears, running through our mental repository of meanings of the unexpected word, starting with the most salient, until we find something that fits in the context (Giora 2003) and then continue with our task of comprehension. The production of novel metaphors in spontaneous speech follows the same principles as those found for lexical access in general. If a word is used in a new way (i.e. its phraseology and meaning are different from normal), there is typically a hesitation before it is uttered (Hartsuiker and Notebaert 2010). This perceptible silence represents thinking time while the speaker searches for the most apt word to use, and is a counterpart of the pause that appears in comprehension.[6] If no pause is detectable in the speech, then likely the speaker has already used (or mentally rehearsed) the metaphor, i.e. it is already familiar to him/her. Written language allows us no such insight into the production of novel metaphors. We cannot know if a poetic metaphor came in a flash of inspiration or after hours of tortured reworking. But the delay that occurs between the production of a written text and its reception allows the writer time to refine and perfect a metaphor before it is encountered by a reader, so novel written metaphors can be far richer and more complex than spoken ones. They are also more likely to be classed as 'good' metaphors, a vague concept which encompasses aptness, intertextuality and satisfaction, which has been called 'optimal innovation' (Giora 2003).

Repetition and reuse of a metaphor lessen its impact, and facilitate and speed up its comprehension. As a result, some metaphors are more metaphorical than others. The criterion of resonance, first introduced in Black (1993) and revisited in Hanks (2006), comes into play here. Sometimes the components of the metaphor – its topic (thing referred to) and vehicle (word used to refer to it) (Richards 1936) – share many features, and/or have 'obvious' connections; other times it is difficult to link the two together. In the first case, the metaphor is understood quickly and with relatively little effort. As a consequence, it is not perceived as rich (or resonant), e.g. when we speak of discourse as a 'flow of words'. However, when the parallels are not so obvious and we are forced to engage more actively in the search for the metaphor's meaning, it seems more metaphorical (ibid. 22–23), e.g. calling a business competitor a 'massive gorilla'. A very resonant metaphor draws on multiple correspondences from a plurality of frames of reference, is semantically and cognitively complex, and takes time to process. The kind of novel metaphors that we find in high-quality literature belong to this type (Lakoff and Turner 1989; see also discussion in Kövecses 2005: 50–58).

The more conventional a metaphor is, the less metaphorical (resonant) its meaning. But this should not be taken to mean that all novel metaphors are perceived to be highly metaphorical and resonant: they are not. Novelty, like metaphoricity itself, is gradable. It runs the gamut from nonce-forms (i.e. those which have never previously been documented in the language), to metaphors which exist in the language and are familiar to the speaker but not to the interlocutor (e.g. 'go bananas' above). In practical terms, we can only say that a metaphor is novel in relation to our personal experience of the language. Absolute novelty is a moot point, virtually impossible to prove, although reference to corpus data lends a degree of objectivity to the matter because it allows us to recognize variations of familiar patterns as opposed to forms with no apparent precedent.[7]

Novel linguistic metaphors and novel conceptual metaphors

The vast majority of novel metaphors are identified by virtue of being similar-but-different with respect to existing forms, both linguistic and conceptual. The need for novelty arises when the existing expressive repertoire fails us, and this can happen equally well in spontaneous speech as in pondered literary creation, by expert users of language and by novices, including children and non-native speakers.

A novel linguistic metaphor which can be matched to an existing conceptual metaphor can be viewed as an exploitation (Hanks 2013) of a metaphor norm, and is typically interpreted as 'normal form + new information'. It may also be viewed as a purely conceptual process (e.g. Lakoff and Turner 1989; Fauconnier and Turner 2002), though how wise it is to remove the linguistic aspect from metaphor linguistically expressed is questionable.

Given that this aspect is covered elsewhere in this volume (see Chapter 14), I will focus here on the combination of the linguistic and the conceptual in a recent news event. An off-the-cuff comment made by the British Prime Minister, David Cameron, caused a stir in the media: 'you have got a <u>swarm</u> of people coming across the Mediterranean, seeking a better life'. Both journalists and contributors to online forums were quick to pick up on the unusual metaphor. The day after, in a live BBC interview, the Prime Minister denied having intended to demean migrants, stressing that he wanted to convey the idea of a 'very large number of people'.

Here we are confronted with an interesting situation. The person who produced the metaphor insists that it refers to quantity and nothing else. There is no denying that quantity is one feature associated with 'swarm', but it is not the most salient element of the image schema. There was a flurry of interest in this metaphor and its potential meanings. Nobody failed to identify its relation to insects (cf. 'a <u>swarm</u> of flies/bees/locusts'). Following on from this, it was also presumed that the expression is negative, because 'swarm' defines not only large groups of insects, but particularly those which bite, sting or otherwise cause harm to humans. Some also insisted that it was insulting, saying that a conflation of 'immigrant' with 'insect' was implied, thus dehumanizing the people and casting them as 'undesirables'. Indeed, one journalist went so far as to suggest that 'David Cameron used "swarm" instead of "plague" in case it implied that God had sent the migrants' (*The Guardian*, 2015) thus pairing 'swarm' with 'locusts' and recasting the metaphor within a biblical context (where the plague of locusts, sent by the Almighty, caused devastation).

This situation provides us with documentation of what happens with novel metaphors. There is evidence in these various interpretations that words remind people of how they are used in other contexts; that those remembered contexts remind people of alternative words which might have been used; and that both of these processes activate memories and projections of potential contexts and frames of reference for interpretation. What 'swarm' was initially intended to mean becomes irrelevant, because this unusual choice of words led to conjecturing as to what the Prime Minister really *felt* about immigration. Going by the forum posts, some people approved of the metaphor, finding it an apt description of the situation as viewed through their personal lens. These people may well reuse it, thus bringing it into their active lexical repertoire and conventionalizing it to some extent. The more liberal-minded, however, were the ones who recalled that the more conventional metaphor is 'wave', declaring 'swarm' inappropriate, unacceptable, demeaning, even dehumanizing. They are unlikely to reuse the metaphor and will resist attempts to 'normalize' it.

Current research on conventional and novel metaphors in language: some examples

From conventional metaphor to optimal innovation and beyond

At the heart of novelty in language is a desire to communicate something in a manner that is both familiar and new. The familiar aspect – be it reference to a well-known phrase, and/or to a recognizable situation or concept – is necessary to ensure that the speaker's intended meaning gets through. Sometimes the novel aspect fails to achieve its desired communicative effect, so the familiar element ensures that at least a watered-down version of the intended meaning comes across. The novel aspect personalizes that more familiar meaning, pulling in aspects of context which are relevant to the message we wish to convey, or that we think we are understanding (Kövecses 2005 calls this 'pressure of coherence'). The specific nature of these contextual elements changes every time we use a phrase, and the effects they have on meaning are equally varied and unique. The best results are had when a metaphor induces multiple meanings to be activated simultaneously. This enriches the quality of communication, its aesthetic appreciation, and the metaphor's resonance, and is what Giora (2003) calls 'optimal innovation'. Others cause meaning malfunction, whether because the purpose of the novelty cannot be grasped or, indeed, because it is too obvious and therefore aesthetically unpleasing. There are clearly a myriad shades in between. Most studies of linguistic and metaphorical creativity focuses on optimal innovation.[8] Here I try to redress the balance by also examining some unsuccessful novelty.

We have already established that conventional metaphors sit at one end of a cline, ad-hoc coinings of novel metaphors at the other. It should come as no surprise, then, that the space in between these extremes is populated with all sorts of variant forms which deviate to a greater or lesser extent from the norm. To illustrate this, we can consider a proverb, 'the grass is always greener', because in fixed phrases such as this it is relatively easy to pinpoint where novelty is being introduced and to comment on the effect it has on meaning (cf. Philip 2011: 188–195).

'The grass is always greener' is a metaphorical proverb which makes reference to a real-world scenario which can be easily imagined: the grass growing on a neighbour's land is (perceived to be) more luxuriant than the grass on one's own land. The upshot of such a situation is to make the speaker feel dissatisfaction, and it is this meaning which underpins the choice to use the proverb and which needs to remain even when the word choice is altered. In the data examined,[9] the word 'greener' was the most likely component of the phrase to be changed, usually by substitution with another colour word, normally one associated with grass. 'The grass is always goldener' connotes positively (despite the strange form of the colour word); here the positive values associated with gold transfer well: golden grass or cereal is ripe for harvest; gold also indicates wealth; both are potential causes for dissatisfaction if they are missing in our lives. In other words, it *resonates* with the conventional form and with other levels of meaning which are brought into play when it appears in place of 'greener'. 'Yellow' or 'brown' as colours for grass, however, do not have this enriching, emphatic effect: quite the contrary. When these words appear, they mark a shift: a neighbour's dry or sickly grass is no cause for dissatisfaction but rather, perhaps, for smugness or self-satisfaction. Thus a simple word-substitution can change the polarity of the proverb, reverse the direction of its sentiment and alter its pragmatic implications. The novelty is therefore successful on a superficial level, i.e. as word-play, but the ambiguities it introduces compromise its communicative effectiveness.

Another colour change involved the substitution of 'green' with 'blue', which is not a normal grass colour. In every instance, in the surrounding cotext of this variant form, a reference can be found to bluegrass music, from the Appalachian region which takes its name from a native grass, the Kentucky bluegrass. This renews the connection with the lexeme 'grass', but not in a way that allows the novel element – 'blue' – to be fully absorbed back into the underlying concept. The sense of dissatisfaction is no longer supported, because there is no precedent in real life: if my neighbour's grass is blue, how should I feel? This makes it possible to cast 'the grass is always bluer' in a positive light, and also helps to explain why this novel form can be used to talk about a place (where bluegrass is played) rather than an emotion. The change of colour to 'blue' causes the metaphorical aspect of the proverb to collapse and its meaning to fragment. It is not meaningless, because meaning can be inferred from the words and the context, but having altered the context of reference, the words, and the underlying pragmatic meaning normally associated with the original proverb, the meaning this variant expresses has lost much of its connection with 'the grass is always greener' and is therefore difficult to interpret.

Computing creative metaphors and similes: current research in AI

Successful communication using metaphor is thought to be bound up with human expressivity, so it may come as a surprise to discover that computers can coin metaphors too. Metaphor, particularly novel metaphor, is something that humans generate when their expressive needs are not served by their existing language resources. We delight in the many-layered meanings of optimally innovative metaphors, but they are the exception to the rule. Many of the metaphors that humans create are very mundane, and amount to a mere stretching of an existing meaning to cover a new area of reference. Others are apt without being particularly memorable. Most novel metaphors draw on what is already known, exploiting the linguistic and conceptual knowledge that speakers of a language share, and add to it. Computers exploit this fact of language use to generate metaphors and similes, and do so quite successfully.

Computational models of language have advanced to such an extent that it is now possible to generate novel figurative language using algorithms. One of the masterminds in this field is Tony Veale, whose team of researchers has created a suite of programs which generate novel, creative language on demand.[10] The work behind these web applications is rooted in AI research and demonstrates that it is possible to create novel, apt metaphors without the help of a brain, a personality, life experience or human cognition. It is based on language data alone, but not in the form of a corpus. Its data are, in many ways, much more like the data that humans refer to, infinitely larger in size and many, many times more varied: the World Wide Web.

As critics of corpora are quick to point out, even a large corpus can represent only a tiny sample of the language that any person encounters in a year, let alone a lifetime. But if the web is used as a corpus, the amount of data available increases exponentially. The 100m-token *British National Corpus* occupies about 4 gigabytes on a PC. The web, in contrast, is colossal, with many exabytes (billions of terabytes) of data potentially available for the English language alone. Humans cannot process such quantities of data, but computers can. Veale's (2013) research demonstrates that, when they do, they can exploit that linguistic information to generate creative language that seems as if it has been produced by humans.

Metaphor exploits commonplace, stereotypical features of words and their semantic associations (Black 1962: 44), and this principle underlies Veale's work, which is based on the concept of the 'linguistic readymade' (Veale 2013). Stereotypical knowledge about words and the world can be extrapolated from language data by computers, but as well as profiling words, the quantity of data available on the web makes it possible to profile conceptual spaces, and it is this aspect that allows the computer to be creative rather than merely regurgitating expressions that it has already encountered.

At the time of writing, Veale's team have made available six fully functioning applications. Not only are they interesting in how they function (described in Veale 2013), but also in terms of the range of figurative language that they generate. The output is admittedly variable in appeal and communicative success – it is not always 'optimally innovative' – but although it cannot imitate the refined and sophisticated language which we associate with the very best of creative writers, its language fragments do mimic human output fairly convincingly (see Figure 15.2).

> Logic competes with the arts that express dreams. Chaos diminishes the beauty that inspires dreams. Take your pick. #Logic=#Chaos?
>
> Pleasure, relaxing holiday that you are, please refresh me with your welcome delight. #Pleasure=#Holiday
>
> When it comes to the treatises they publish, some academics are little more than imitative parodists. #Academic=#Parodist #Treatise=#Parody

Figure 15.2 Output from @MetaphorMagnet.

Source: https://twitter.com/MetaphorMagnet (retrieved 5 November 2014).

These web applications reveal that metaphor can bypass cognition and emerge from language alone. 'Can', not 'does': they also show that successful figurative language requires human judgement in addition to language skills. Previous language use, as represented here by corpora or web data, and for humans in their memories, allows us to interpret metaphorical language, to predict which kinds of appropriate linguistic expressions are likely to be interpreted metaphorically, and to generate such expressions. But the fine-tuning required goes beyond the current capabilities of computers, because their world knowledge is not individual but collective. They have no personality to express nor experiences to allude to, and as a result they are unable to tailor their output to a particular audience, in short, to guarantee appropriateness in context.

Future directions

The contribution of data-based studies to the field of metaphor research in recent years has been felt in several areas, two related aspects of which are particularly relevant to this chapter. The first is that 'conventional' and 'novel' are not clear-cut classes, but simply extremes on a cline whose middle ground is usually ignored by language users and scholars alike; the second is that investigating the interplay between conventional metaphors (cognitive and linguistic) and novel variants in attested language use reveals that most novelty is highly principled and actually quite limited in scope because it has to conform to pre-existing and intertwined semantic, cognitive and pragmatic schemata.

The variety of lexicalizations found in corpus data, in web data, or in the memory of a language user, is too great for humans to process consciously, and this fact leads us to assume that 'there can be no rules for "creatively" violating rules' (Black 1993: 24). Yet close analysis of data reveals that parameters are indeed present, and that humans follow them intuitively when creating and when decoding novel forms. Novelty is highly context-centric: contextual features and constraints provide grounds for users to adapt existing metaphors and coin novel forms which fit better. This is something that happens all the time, but only rarely do we notice it because an adaptation has to differ significantly from more commonly encountered forms to merit our attention. We need to turn our attention to the swathe of moderately novel metaphors if we are ever to truly understand what makes some forms stand out and others pale into insignificance. Similarly, since not all novel metaphors are also communicatively successful, a far greater number of moderately novel forms, including those generated by Veale's AI systems, need to be analysed. To date, quite a lot of attention has been paid to successful novel forms – 'optimal innovations' – and we now have a good understanding of how these work. Yet at present we are unable to explain why some novel metaphors are successful and others are not. Unlocking this conundrum will lead to a leap forward in understanding creativity in language communication.

Notes

1 In Hoey's (2005) theory of lexical priming, 'priming' refers to our repeated exposure to particular linguistic forms. This influences how we understand their meaning and how, in turn, we reformulate those meanings through the same (or very similar) wordings.
2 Several conceptual metaphor lists are available (e.g. Lakoff et al. 1991, Goatly 2002–2005); some also feature example sentences but these are rarely drawn from attested data (Goatly's *Metalude* is an exception in this regard).
3 For a comprehensive discussion of lexical profiling, see Hanks (2013: Chapters 4 and 5).
4 Conceptual metaphors are much more ephemeral. In the absence of well-delimited contexts of use and communicative purpose, they can be said to be semantically rich, but pragmatically poor.
5 'ITV executives criticise "arrogant" BBC as *News at Ten* row escalates' (*The Guardian*, 2015)
6 The same is true of carefully chosen words in general, as anyone listening to spontaneous speech (live or broadcast) can notice if they pay close attention.
7 See especially Hanks (2013) on the relationship between 'norms' and their variants ('exploitations') in corpus data; see also Veale (2013) and below for a discussion of how the World Wide Web, if used as a source of linguistic data, can contribute to the computational modelling of lexical creativity within syntactic patterns.
8 See, for example, Hanks (2013), Giora (2003), Müller (2008), Philip (2011), Veale (2013), to mention only a few of the book-length works on the topic.
9 The initial analysis was carried out using *WordBanks Online*, a 56-million-token sample of the *Bank of English* (no longer available); the World Wide Web was used as a 'corpus' for supplementary data featuring variant forms (see Philip 2011: 146–148).
10 http://afflatus.ucd.ie/.

Further reading

Giora, R. (2003) *On Our Mind: Salience, Context, and Figurative Language*. Oxford, UK: Oxford University Press.
Hanks, P. (2013) *Lexical Analysis: Norms and Exploitations*. Cambridge, MA: MIT press.
Philip, G. (2011) *Colouring Meaning: Collocation and Connotation in Figurative Language*. Amsterdam, The Netherlands: John Benjamins.
Veale, T. (2013) *Exploding the Creativity Myth: The Computational Foundations of Linguistic Creativity*. London: Bloomsbury.

References

Black, M. (1962) *Models and Metaphors*. Ithaca, NY: Cornell University Press.
—— (1993) 'More about metaphor'. In A. Ortony (ed.) *Metaphor and Thought*, 2nd edn, pp. 19–41. Cambridge, UK: Cambridge University Press.
British National Corpus, version 2 (BNC World). (2001) Oxford, UK: Oxford University Computing Services.
Davies, M. (2008–) *The Corpus of Contemporary American English*. Online. Available at: http://corpus.byu.edu/coca/ (accessed 4 August 2015).
—— (2010–) *The Corpus of Historical American English*. Online. Available at: http://corpus.byu.edu/coha/ (accessed 4 August 2015).
Deignan, A. (2005) *Metaphor and Corpus Linguistics*. Amsterdam, The Netherlands: John Benjamins.
Fauconnier, G. and M. Turner (2002) *The Way We Think*. New York: Basic.
Giora, R. (2003) *On Our Mind: Salience, Context, and Figurative Language*. Oxford, UK: Oxford University Press.
Goatly, A. (2002–2005) *Metalude*. Online. Available at: http://www.ln.edu.hk/lle/cwd/project01/web/home.html (accessed 4 August 2015).

Hanks, P. (2006) 'Metaphoricity is gradable'. In A. Stefanowitsch and S.Th. Gries (eds) *Corpus-based Approaches to Metaphor and Metonymy*, pp. 17–35. Berlin, Germany: Mouton de Gruyter.

—— (2013) *Lexical Analysis: Norms and Exploitations*. Cambridge, MA: MIT Press.

Hartsuiker, R.J. and L. Notebaert (2010) 'Lexical access problems lead to disfluencies in speech'. *Experimental Psychology* 57: 169–177.

Hoey, M. (2005) *Lexical Priming*. London: Routledge.

Kövecses, Z. (2010) 'A new look at metaphorical creativity in cognitive linguistics'. *Cognitive Linguistics* 21(4): 663–697.

—— (2005) *Metaphor: A Practical Introduction*. Oxford, UK: Oxford University Press.

Lakoff, G. and M. Johnson (1980) *Metaphors We Live By*. Chicago, IL: University of Chicago Press.

Lakoff, G. and M. Turner (1989) *More Than Cool Reason: A Field Guide to Poetic Metaphor*. Chicago, IL: University of Chicago Press.

Lakoff, G., J. Espenson, and A. Schwartz (1991) *Master Metaphor List*, 2nd edn. Online. Available at: http://araw.mede.uic.edu/~alansz/metaphor/METAPHORLIST.pdf (accessed 4 August 2015).

Moon, R. (1998) *Fixed Expressions and Idioms in English*. Oxford, UK: Clarendon.

Müller, C. (2008) *Metaphors Dead and Alive, Sleeping and Waking*. Chicago, IL: University of Chicago Press.

Philip, G. (2011) *Colouring Meaning: Collocation and Connotation in Figurative Language*. Amsterdam, The Netherlands: John Benjamins.

—— (2010) '"Drugs, traffic, and many other dirty interests": metaphor and the language learner'. In G. Low, A. Todd, A. Deignan and L. Cameron (eds) *Researching and Applying Metaphor in the Real World*, pp. 63–79. Amsterdam, The Netherlands: John Benjamins.

Richards, I.A. (1936) *The Philosophy of Rhetoric*. Oxford, UK: Oxford University Press.

Sinclair, J. (ed.) (2001) *Collins COBUILD on CD-ROM v1.0*. Glasgow, UK: HarperCollins.

Veale, T. (2013) *Exploding the Creativity Myth: The Computational Foundations of Linguistic Creativity*. London: Bloomsbury.

16
Metaphor and diachronic variation

Wendy Anderson

Introduction and definitions

The title 'Metaphor and diachronic variation' brings together a number of related linguistic issues. On the one hand, metaphor is a major mechanism of semantic change and there is a substantial literature tracing its contribution to language. On the other hand, the metaphorical expressions used to convey concepts within particular semantic domains themselves change over time, reflecting changes in society. So too do the conceptual metaphors which may underlie these metaphorical expressions (see Chapter 1). Taking these aspects together, a consideration of the diachronic dimension of metaphor in language offers a fuller understanding of the nature and importance of metaphor and of language itself.

Several quite different, although closely interrelated, senses of 'metaphor' are at play here, and it is useful to begin with some explanation and examples to differentiate them. First, metaphor (or 'metaphorisation' – see e.g. Traugott 2006) is one of the most commonly recognised mechanisms behind semantic change, which in turn results in metaphorical polysemy in language. To take a straightforward example, the adjective *sunny* with the meaning 'bright, cheerful, joyous' (*Oxford English Dictionary* [OED], *sunny*, adjective, sense 5a)[1] represents one of several senses of this polysemous word, a metaphorical sense. The core, literal sense of *sunny*, 'characterized by or full of sunshine' (ibid., sense 1), is older, being attested from 1300 according to the OED, while the metaphorical extension is more recent: the OED gives the earliest metaphorical attestation as 1616, in Shakespeare's *Comedy of Errors*: 'A sunnie looke of his'.

The extension from the literal to the metaphorical sense of *sunny* is not, however, a narrow phenomenon limited to this word. Rather, it is an example of a broader driving force, or of 'characteristic patterns of thought' (Durkin 2009: 240), and this brings us to a second understanding, in which metaphor can be used as shorthand for *conceptual metaphor* (see Chapter 1). The figurative sense of *sunny* instantiates the HAPPINESS IS LIGHT conceptual metaphor, which also underlies many other words and expressions in English, including: *beam* ('Of a person: to smile radiantly, broadly, or good-naturedly', OED, *beam*, verb, sense 3), *sparkling* ('Of pleasure: characterized by a high degree of delight or enjoyment', OED, *sparkling*, adjective 1, sense 6), *light up* (see the OED citations for *light*, verb 2, sense 3c), and arguably even *cloudless*, the figurative sense of which is recorded in the OED in the 1867 example 'Whose life has been cloudless as one long summer's day'.[2] Such conceptual metaphors, following the terminology set out by Lakoff and Johnson (1980, 2003), are the conventional metaphorical patterns of thought shared by speakers of a language, which are instantiated by metaphorical words and expressions and often lie at the heart of examples of semantic change.

Both of these understandings of metaphor relate to the mass noun, *metaphor*. A further frequent use is as a count noun, *metaphor(s)*, referring to metaphorical words and expressions, whether novel or conventionalised, which are surface linguistic features, the result of the underlying mechanism of semantic change. Dancygier and Sweetser express some disapproval for this usage, commenting that 'the linguistic form itself is not a metaphoric structure; it is its usage in context which prompts a metaphoric construal rather than a literal one' (2014: 49). Nevertheless, this usage is common and is often the intended one outside of linguistics, typified by classic literary examples like Shakespeare's 'Juliet is the sun' (from *Romeo and Juliet*, act 2, scene 1). It is striking, however, that even such examples as these are often underpinned by the same conceptual metaphors that have such a strong influence on our everyday vocabulary. The conceptual metaphor in this example is BEAUTY IS LIGHT, which is just as pervasive as HAPPINESS IS LIGHT: consider such examples as *lustre*, in the sense of 'radiant beauty or splendour' (OED, *lustre*, noun 1, 4a) or *radiant* when applied figuratively to beauty (OED, *radiant*, adjective and noun, 2b).

In what follows, I first offer an overview – necessarily selective – of relevant theoretical work to date on diachronic variation in relation to metaphor. I then discuss in more detail some of the critical issues and debates in this area, including the question of dead metaphor, the nature of semantic domains and the directionality of metaphor. I go on to present some examples from a current data-driven research project which focuses on the nature and extent of metaphor across the history of English. In the final section, I suggest some future directions for the study of metaphor.

Overview of the literature on metaphor and language change

This chapter as a whole, including, broadly speaking, the specific research project discussed below, sits within Conceptual Metaphor Theory, initiated in the late 1970s and 1980s by George Lakoff and Mark Johnson, and developed and refined by many others (see Chapter 1).[3] This section focuses on work on the role of metaphor in semantic change and change in metaphor itself.

Metaphor as a mechanism of semantic change

It has long been recognised that metaphor is a very productive mechanism of semantic change, that is, the change in meaning of words over time. In this respect it is typically listed alongside specialisation, generalisation and metonymy. Some scholars also highlight further processes of semantic change: Durkin, for example, identifies broadening, narrowing, pejoration and amelioration alongside metaphor and metonymy as processes which are commonly identified in the scholarly literature, although he notes that these 'are not hard and fast categories' (2009: 235).[4]

The result of the mechanism of metaphor over time is a state of synchronic polysemy, or the fact that many words exist at the same time with distinct but related senses. This can be more precisely called 'metaphoric polysemy' as polysemy also results from other processes of change. As Geeraerts explains, 'the synchronic links that exist between the various senses of an item coincide with diachronic mechanisms of semantic extension such as metaphor and metonymy' (1997: 6). Dirven (1985: 101–4) too illustrates the centrality of metaphor to the development of the lexicon of a language, revealing for instance that metaphor accounts for around half of the meaning extensions of *cup* (e.g. 'bra cup', where there is metaphorical transfer of the shape), and that metonymy (including synecdoche) accounts for another third or so (e.g. 'cupful', where the whole is used for a contained part). Overall, 'metaphorisation processes can logically be seen as an integral part of the rules of the lexicon' (ibid.: 115).

Many scholars have suggested that semantic change, unlike phonetic change, generally does not follow easily identifiable patterns (e.g. Trim 2007; Kay and Allan 2015). For a long time, therefore, attempts to find regular patterns of semantic change were largely abandoned, though with some notable exceptions (e.g. Stern [1931] 1968, cited in Trim 2007). However, more recent work has turned attention back to the possibility of regularity, especially in relation to metaphor. Sweetser, in her ground-breaking work (1990), tackled the issue of systematicity in metaphorical connections, in English as well as other Indo-European languages. In particular, she surveyed the metaphorical connections between the domains of physical perception and mental processing (as instantiated in metaphors like KNOWING IS SEEING and UNDERSTANDING IS GRASPING). Indeed, this is part of a wider phenomenon: just as lexical polysemy can be accounted for by cross-domain structuring, so too can grammatical phenomena like the diachronic extension from root modality to epistemic modality, as exemplified in the distinct senses of *will* in the following examples:

John will come.

'The present state of affairs will proceed to the future event of John's arrival.'

(hearing phone ring) That will be John.

'My present theory that that is John will proceed to future verification/confirmation.'

Examples from Sweetser 1990: 62

A significant point in Sweetser's work is that the regularities observed in synchronic polysemy can also be used to account for diachronic change. Metaphor, therefore, is an extremely significant factor in both synchronic and diachronic models of language, and one with vast explanatory power.

Traugott and Dasher too offer persuasive evidence of regularity in semantic change, though they play down the role of metaphor, stressing that the most salient mechanisms of change are dependent on one's perspective: with regard to metaphor, this 'may be a function of focusing on comparison of synchronic stages, and therefore on sources and targets (beginnings and endings) rather than on fine-grained intermediate stages of development' (2002: 282). Finally, Haser's work on metaphor and semantic change (2003) aims to fill out some of the detail of such broad-brush studies, with reference to a larger range of languages, and drawing on lexicographical and etymological works, supplemented by interviews with native speakers.

Change in metaphor and metaphorical expressions

As noted above, for example from Sweetser's work (1990), there is evidence that conceptual metaphors motivate language change. Once a metaphorical pathway has been well established, as Kay (2000: 277) explains, 'then a new metaphor [i.e. metaphorical expression] following the same path will also be understood'. For example, the long-established metaphorical pathway between concepts of weather and concepts of commotion and confusion (as instantiated by *storm, hurricane, tempest* and *whirlwind*) has allowed for easy integration of new words used with the same metaphorical meaning. An example is *tsunami*, which is first attested in English in 1897 with the sense of waves caused by an earthquake, and as recently as 1972 with the metaphorical sense of an overwhelming and uncontrollable quantity of something (OED, *tsunami*, noun).

Considerable work in this area, emphasising the interconnected nature of metaphor over time, has been carried out by Trim (2007, 2011). In line with Kay, he finds that 'Despite the complexities and fluctuations in evolutionary paths, it appears that the same networking processes have been at work since time immemorial' (Trim 2007: xiii; see also 148), and it is not only over time that the same processes occur, but also across languages. Trim gives the example of the BUSINESS CORPORATION IS FAMILY metaphor in French and English, in which concepts including baptism and marriage/divorce have been drawn on historically in the metaphorical connection in both languages. Trim argues, however, that such metaphors have maintained a stronger hold in French than in English, perhaps because of the additional reinforcement provided by the stronger influence of Catholicism in France (ibid.: 86–90). The conceptualisation of the splitting of an institution into two as a divorce, for example, is common in French but 'has not occurred in English', and Trim gives in support of this the French example *il est en train de se produire entre le service postal et le public un divorce grave*, with a suggested translation 'a serious split [i.e. not *divorce*] is taking place between the postal service and the public' (ibid.: 88).

A reliance on large quantities of data, whether from corpora or lexicographical resources, has characterised recent work on change in conceptual metaphor.[5] This is true of Allan's work (2008), which exploits the recently completed *Historical Thesaurus of English* (see also the 'Current research' section below). The *Historical Thesaurus*, which is based on the complete second edition of the *Oxford English Dictionary* (OED2), supplemented by *A Thesaurus of Old English* (TOE, Roberts and Kay 1995) for the earlier period c700–1150AD, sets out a detailed, hierarchical semantic framework capturing the complete recorded vocabulary of English.[6] Allan provides a diachronic analysis of metaphors in English relating to the target concept of INTELLIGENCE and the source domains of DENSITY, THE SENSES and ANIMALS. All three are long-standing source domains for conceptual metaphors, and all three show clearly the productivity of new metaphorical expressions exploiting the same underlying conceptual connection. For example, Allan identifies the words from the domain of DENSITY used to express the concept of STUPIDITY: the words and expressions *thickwit, thickie, as thick as (two) plank(s)* and *thicko* all take on the meaning 'stupid' in the twentieth century, exploiting a conceptual link which can be traced back to the sixteenth century when forms such as *gross, grosshead, thick(-)skin* and *thick* began to be used with this sense (2008: 119).

A recent corrective to work on the driving force of conceptual metaphor is provided by Evans (e.g. 2013), who claims that conceptual metaphor is only one part of figurative meaning construction: alongside it he argues that we also have to take account of 'discourse metaphor', a different class of metaphor which inheres in the language system rather than the conceptual system. For Evans, 'the linguistic facts are better accounted for by assuming that language change is effected at the linguistic level' (ibid.: 88). While conceptual metaphor has been a seductive focus of investigation over the last few decades, and is likely to remain so, we may nevertheless therefore see something of a reconsideration of the lexical and discourse aspects of metaphor over the coming years.

Change can also be viewed on the level of individual linguistic expressions. Bowdle and Gentner present a detailed account of this phenomenon in their 'career of metaphor' hypothesis (e.g. 2005), which seeks to account for the 'lifespan' of metaphorical expressions: they are novel at one stage, become conventional at a later stage, and eventually die. At different stages in their 'career', metaphors require different types of conceptual processing by language users: comparison when they are novel and categorisation when they have become conventionalised. Bowdle and Gentner give the example of a novel metaphorical expression, *Science is a glacier*, in which the term *glacier* has a literal sense ('body of ice') but no conventionalised metaphorical sense: language users interpret the expression through a process of comparison 'in which the target concept is structurally aligned with the literal base concept' (2005: 199). When a metaphor has become conventionalised, on the other hand, it has a recognised separate sense. To illustrate this, they use the example of *blueprint*: this is like other conventional metaphors which, they suggest, language users may interpret 'as categorizations, by seeing the target concept as a member of the superordinate metaphoric category named by the base term [here, *blueprint*]' (ibid.: 199).

Critical issues and debates

There are a number of issues that have prompted discussion among scholars in the area of diachronic metaphor. As is common in linguistics more broadly, much of the difficulty stems from the impossibility of identifying clear-cut categories into which linguistic phenomena can be placed. Language is not appropriately described or accounted for by a traditional category model; rather, a model which allows for fuzziness and prototypicality is required.[7]

The boundaries of metaphor

A significant issue is how to delimit the boundaries of metaphor (see Grady 2007: 206). Synchronically, this manifests itself in the nature of the relationship between metaphor and other phenomena such as metonymy. The latter is traditionally seen as transfer within, rather than across, conceptual or semantic domains: however, in practice this distinction is less clear and recent research has found much metaphor to be based on metonymy (see the discussion in Geeraerts 2010: 212–22, and also Goossens 1990; Barcelona 2000, 2003). Diachronically, we encounter the very significant difficulty of the boundaries between metaphorical and literal expression, mentioned above in relation to Bowdle and Gentner's 'career of metaphor' hypothesis (2005). While research so far has shown quite conclusively that conceptual metaphors can be long-standing, continuing to drive metaphorical thought and language production beyond the lifetime of individual metaphorical expressions, speakers consider metaphorical expressions to be more or less 'alive' at different times, and perhaps more problematically, speakers vary in their judgements of what is metaphorical. Trim expresses this as follows:

> [. . .] there are very many conventionalised metaphors in our language that started off with a metaphoric origin but would not normally be considered today as metaphors. To make matters more complicated, apparently conventional metaphors may vary considerably in their degree of *metaphoricity*, that is, there is often a gradation of how metaphoric each metaphor might look in a given conceptual cluster.
>
> *Trim 2007: 9*

An early attempt to delimit 'dead metaphor' is made by Lakoff, who argues that what had previously been called dead metaphors 'have turned out to be a host of quite disparate phenomena, including those metaphors that are most alive' (1987: 143). The latter category includes items like *grasp* which – while not being novel – represent systematic, conventional metaphors (in this case UNDERSTANDING IS GRASPING) which are still productive in language and thought. Allan (2013) provides an up-to-date survey of definitional work on 'dead metaphor' and offers lexicographical case studies of four words (*pedigree, comprehend, ardent* and *muddle*) with metaphorical senses which may be considered to have 'died'. She maintains that metaphor death 'cannot be considered separately from the individual histories of lexemes and the languages in which they are found' (2013: 308).

The nature of semantic domains

In much of the early work on metaphor which followed Lakoff and Johnson's *Metaphors We Live By* (1980, 2003), the notion of a conceptual domain, on which the theory depended heavily, was under-specified. The nature of domains raises questions for both the synchronic and diachronic study of metaphor. Synchronically, the boundaries of domains are significant for the distinction between metaphor and metonymy. As we have seen, metaphor is traditionally defined as cross-domain semantic extension, and metonymy as within-domain semantic extension. However, Geeraerts (2010: 215–16) draws attention to both cross-domain semantic extensions that are not metaphorical and within-domain semantic extensions that are not metonymic. He remarks that 'the notion of domain is not well defined, neither theoretically nor methodologically: there is no stable and well-established heuristic in cognitive semantics to distinguish one domain from the other or to determine a generally acceptable ontology of domains' (2010: 215).

Similarly, domains are problematic from a diachronic perspective because, regardless of where the boundaries between them may lie synchronically, domains shift over time. This is highlighted by the difficulties faced by the editors of the *Historical Thesaurus of English*: Kay and Wotherspoon (2005) discuss the quite different shapes of the category of couches and seats in their Old English data specifically (drawn from *A Thesaurus of Old English* [Roberts and Kay 1995]) compared with the entire *Historical Thesaurus* (see also Kay 2016, on the necessarily static nature of the HT categories). Clearly, then, an intuitive sense of what constitutes a domain is not sufficient. Later work has refined the notion, as explained by Taylor:

> One of the firmest results to have come out of the Cognitive Linguistics enterprise over the past couple of decades has been the realization that word meanings need to be understood against broader knowledge configurations, variously studied as 'frames', 'scenes', 'domains', and 'idealized cognitive models'.
>
> *Taylor 2003: 31*

To this list we might add 'domain matrix' (e.g. Croft 1993). While the realisation that word meaning requires a background against which to understand it may be firm, nevertheless work remains to be done on the delimitation of such configurations, especially in relation to their dynamic qualities over time.

Directionality of metaphor

A further issue which has seen increasing discussion over recent years is that of the directionality of metaphor. This can be understood in two senses. On the one hand, it relates to whether metaphorical mappings are unidirectional (e.g. the conceptual metaphor BEAUTY IS

LIGHT is well attested, but LIGHT IS BEAUTY is not) or bidirectional (few examples are discussed in the literature; although PEOPLE ARE COMPUTERS / COMPUTERS ARE PEOPLE has been suggested as an example, the frames are different in each case; see Dancygier and Sweetser 2014: 30–1). On the other hand, it also relates to the direction of metaphorical transfer, which is commonly accepted to be from a concrete source domain to a more abstract target domain, and there is little doubt that this is the general tendency (see for example Lakoff and Johnson 1980, 2003; Kövecses 2010: 7).

Nevertheless, a considerable amount of work has challenged this assumption. Drawing on evidence from the *Historical Thesaurus* and the OED, Allan (2008) flags a possible counter-example with the word *dull*, in which the arguably more abstract sense related to slowness of understanding appears from the date evidence to be the source of the more concrete sense 'blunt' (Allan 2008: 186; see also Allan 2012). Similarly, Lehrer suggests that some derivational affixes (*pre-* and *post-*) may present a challenge to the concrete–abstract direction of change (2003: 230).

Some researchers have pointed out that the distinction between concrete and abstract is itself problematic, and that at the very least a more nuanced model of directionality is needed. Szwedek, for example, proposes the physicality of objects (or density of touch) in place of 'the vague and undefined general distinction between the abstract and concrete domains' (2011: 360). Dancygier and Sweetser (2014: 25–31) summarise the issue especially as it relates to Primary Metaphors, that is, the physical correlations we become aware of early in our lives, such as that between affection and warmth in the experience of being cuddled as infants (see also Grady 1997, 2007). These domains, which cannot easily be distinguished on a scale of concreteness, are initially conflated by the individual and only at a later stage of development are understood to be independent (see also Allan 2008: 187). Dancygier and Sweetser suggest that we interpret this as 'understanding a more subjective and less mutually accessible domain in terms of a more intersubjectively accessible domain', which they paraphrase helpfully as 'I can see what you see (and that you see it), but not what you know (or that you know it)' (2014: 27).

A current research project

This section explores the changing metaphorical patterns in a selected semantic area, drawing on the data from a current research project, 'Mapping Metaphor with the *Historical Thesaurus*'. This is predominantly an onomasiological approach to diachronic metaphor, that is, one that takes conceptual domains to be more or less constant, and considers forms with metaphorical senses which are gained or lost in these domains. Such an approach is typically opposed to a semasiological approach, or one that takes a single word form and investigates the meaning changes associated with that form.[8]

Mapping Metaphor

The aim of the 'Mapping Metaphor with the *Historical Thesaurus*' project has been to establish an overview of metaphorical connections made by speakers and writers of English over the entire history of the language.[9] The starting point for the project is the fact that metaphorical connections between semantic areas can be identified from their shared lexis. For example, the metaphorical connection which links the semantic area of textiles with those of intellect and imagination in English can be glimpsed in words and expressions such as *spin (a yarn)* (meaning both 'to draw out the fibres of a material like wool to form thread'

Table 16.1 Senses of *inflame* in the *Historical Thesaurus of English* with corresponding Mapping Metaphor category headings

Sense of inflame	OED dates of attestation	Mapping Metaphor semantic category
inflame (with) passion	c1340–	2D02 Strong emotion and lack of emotion
inflame with passionate desire	a1340–	2E03 Willingness and desire
set on fire	1382–	1J03 Weight, heat and cold
illuminate with/as with fire	c1477–	1J27 Illumination
make red	c1477–	1J35 Individual colours
inflame (cause to be ill)	1530–	1C02 Ill-health
make (a person) warm/hot	1530–	1J03 Weight, heat and cold
become inflamed with passion	1559–	2D02 Strong emotion and lack of emotion
make hot (of a stimulant)	1560–	1J03 Weight, heat and cold
excite	1560–	2D03 Excitement
become inflamed	1607–	1C02 Ill-health
make (more) violent	1607–	1O20 Vigorous action and degrees of violence
make more severe	1607–	1O20 Vigorous action and degrees of violence
become very hot	1638	1J03 Weight, heat and cold
increase (prices)	1672–1773	3L02 Money
catch fire/begin to burn	1783–	1J03 Weight, heat and cold

and 'to tell a story'), *woolly* (meaning both 'made of wool' and 'confused or muddled'), and *fustian* (meaning both 'a coarse cloth' and 'unintelligible language'). Lexicographical evidence shows that these polysemous items have their source in the domain of textiles and have later figurative senses relating to mental processes.

Using the electronic database of the *Historical Thesaurus*, the project team automatically compared all of the word forms in every one of around four hundred semantic categories based primarily on the HT categorisation system and together covering the entire thesaurus, with those in every other such category, thus generating sets of shared word forms for every category pair. A large proportion of these shared word forms do not owe their presence to metaphor. The word form *bat*, for example, appears among animals and sporting equipment but there is no metaphorical, or even semantic, connection between them: the two senses of *bat* are homonymous. Similarly, highly polysemous words like *sound* or *set* appear in lots of semantic categories but the connection between any pair of categories containing these items is only rarely metaphorical. Therefore, a labour-intensive process of manual analysis was undertaken to pick out the metaphorical connections from the sets of shared word forms.

This process is a step in the direction that Sweetser pointed to in saying that 'Studies of systematic metaphorical connections between domains are thus needed, in addition to local studies of relevant semantic contrasts, to help us understand what is a likely relationship between two senses' (1990: 19). In then returning to the OED date information which the *Historical Thesaurus* contains, it was possible for the project researchers to identify the most likely direction of metaphorical transfer from the 'historical order in which senses are added to polysemous words' (ibid.: 9), and to select lexical items to illustrate each metaphorical connection. This was not always straightforward, and some of the challenges of the task can be exemplified by a glance at the senses of the word *inflame* in the OED, a word which can be traced etymologically to Latin and occurs in English as both a transitive and intransitive verb. The senses in Table 16.1 above are ordered chronologically from oldest to newest.

Perhaps surprisingly, the earliest use in this list is of a metaphorical sense, 'inflame with passion'. However, this should be treated with caution. The OED contains evidence of the corresponding nominal form with a literal sense also from 1340 (*flame*, noun and adjective, sense 1b), and we might argue that metaphorical extensions do not respect part-of-speech distinctions.[10] Further metaphorical senses appear in the sixteenth and seventeenth centuries: indeed, further literal senses also appear. A fuller analysis would also need to take account of related items in the lexical field (*flame, fire, inflammation,* etc.). Nevertheless, this example shows the complex interplay of literal and metaphorical senses over time and illustrates the sort of data that the project was handling, albeit in much greater quantities.

The results of the Mapping Metaphor lexical analysis can be seen in the project's online 'Metaphor Map' resource, an interactive visualisation which gives a picture of the overall patterning of metaphorical connections over the history of English. Ongoing analysis suggests that, once complete, the Map will show quite clearly the general concrete–abstract tendency to which metaphor researchers have consistently pointed. Given that the project has identified well over 10,000 category pairs with metaphorical links, it would clearly be impossible to give a full overview in the space available here. Instead, a single semantic category is selected to illustrate the types of metaphorical patterning that emerge. This is the category of 'Illumination'.[11]

A source category: 'Illumination'

For a semantic category which is predominantly the target of a metaphorical connection, such as the highly abstract categories of 'Success' or 'Fear', for example, the benefit of the Mapping Metaphor project methodology is the possibility of viewing and analysing an organised set of lexemes shared between this category and every other category in turn. This allows metaphorical tendencies to emerge much more clearly and reliably than simply scanning with the eye through the relevant category in the *Historical Thesaurus*, keeping thousands of possible metaphors in mind at once. However, where the Mapping Metaphor methodology really comes into its own is in the investigation of areas of semantic space which are predominantly *source* domains for metaphor. Identifying entirely manually those categories which are predominantly used as the source of metaphors would involve scanning through the entire *Historical Thesaurus* – nearly 800,000 word forms, arranged in close to a quarter of a million semantic categories, across the different levels of the nested hierarchy.

'Illumination' is one such category, and one of several Mapping Metaphor categories in the wider domain of 'Light', sitting alongside 'Reflection', 'Natural light' and 'Artificial light'. While these categories are closely related – indeed slightly overlapping in places – the decision was made to treat them separately as it was anticipated that the general concept of light was likely to be metaphorically interesting and therefore to repay a more fine-grained analysis. This proved to be true: despite the small size of this category, measured in terms of the number of lexemes it contains, metaphorical connections were found with around fifty other categories, with some connections naturally better substantiated than others.

In all but one case, 'Illumination' was found to be the source of the metaphor. The single instance where it is the target is in the connection found with the categories of 'Flowing and floating' and 'Movement in a specific direction', and visible in the lexeme *stream* ('be suffused with radiant light', OED *stream*, verb, sense 6b). With 'Illumination' as the source, the metaphorical category connections can be easily grouped to show a number of families of metaphors relating in particular to: life and movement; the mind and thought; emotion; aesthetics; and authority. For reasons of space, only the first two of these are shown here.

Table 16.2 Connections between 'Illumination' and categories in the area of life and movement

Category label	Example lexemes with dates of metaphorical senses from HT/OED
1B01 Life	*spark* ('vital or animating principle in man', 1382–)
1O20 Vigorous action and degrees of violence	*inflame* ('make more severe/violent', 1607–); *spark* ('a trace of spirit, courage, etc.', 1942–)
1N04 Rate of movement and swift movement	*flash* ('a fit of activity', 1706)
1N06 Movement in a specific direction	*spark* ('to issue in the manner of sparks', 1513–); *irradiate* ('to send forth as in rays', a1617–); *radiate* ('to spread or disseminate as from a centre', 1821–)

The lexical connections between 'Illumination' and several other categories can be seen to offer evidence for a metaphorical connection concerning concepts of life and movement (see Table 16.2).

As the fuller Metaphor Map makes clear, this is only part of a broader picture. The general metaphorical connection between categories related to light on the one hand and those representing aspects of life and movement on the other is also supported by lexemes from closely related categories such as 'Artificial light' (e.g. *candle*, 'the "light" of life', 1535–1768) and 'Natural light' (e.g. *lightning*, adjective, 'Moving or flashing by with the rapidity of lightning', 1640–). This is a long-standing connection: the specific connection from 'Illumination' can be traced at least as far back as the late fourteenth century and it is probably still productive (cf. *spark* with the sense of 'a trace of spirit, courage, etc.', attested for the first time from as late as the mid-twentieth century). Not surprisingly, given that many of the lexemes above relate specifically to illumination from firelight, there is also evidence of this connection from the Mapping Metaphor category of 'Weight, heat and cold', where the concept of 'fire' is located.

By far the strongest links with 'Illumination' are those which centre on concepts of the mind and thought, as represented in several categories, including those shown in Table 16.3.

As with the connections to life and movement above, there is additional support for this metaphorical connection from semantically adjoining categories, such as 'Artificial light' and the general category of 'Light' itself. There is wide support for the metaphorical connection which can be traced right back to the Old English period: see the example lexemes in 'Knowledge and experience' and 'Education' above, and also *leoht* (with various senses including 'famous/eminent' and 'inspiration/revelation'), which is more naturally a connection between the general category of 'Light' and those of 'Esteem', 'Faith' and 'Information and advertising'. The connection is still productive: in addition to the metaphorical senses of words attested first in the nineteenth and early twentieth centuries above, other words from the same general semantic area occur with even later first dates of attestation (e.g. *light* with the minor sense of 'word to be guessed in an acrostic poem', from 1954–).

Looking at the source domain of 'Illumination' specifically allows us to focus in on this narrow area. The examples in Table 16.3, and the wider data from which they are drawn, show a network of polysemous words. Some, like *enlighten* and *illuminate*, have many related senses stretching across the semantic space of the *Historical Thesaurus*, while others, like *irradiate* and *flare*, play a rather smaller part, but still contribute to the extremely strong and systematic metaphorical connection between types of light and knowledge.

Table 16.3 Connections between 'Illumination' and categories in the area of the mind and thought

Category label	Example lexemes with dates of metaphorical senses from HT/OED
2A10 Cleverness	*illuminate* (noun, 'intellectual person', 1600– arch.)
2A18 Intelligibility	numerous, including *enlumine* ('explain', 1393); *illuminate* ('explain', 1586–); *irradiate* ('explain', 1627–); *luminousness* ('lucidity of explanation', 1873)
2A20 Knowledge and experience	numerous, including, from Old English data, *onlihtan* ('enlighten', OE) and *illustrate* ('enlighten', 1526–1872); *illuminate* ('enlighten, intellectually', c1566–); *enlightened* ('having great knowledge', 1663–)
2A22 Truth and falsity	*flash* ('not genuine', 1812–, colloquial)
2B07 Esteem	numerous, including *enlumine* ('make famous', c1386–1579); *emblaze* ('make famous', 1596–1630)
3G01 Education	numerous, including, from Old English data, *onlihtan* ('enlighten', OE) and *enlumine* ('throw light upon a subject', c1400–1581); *enlightening* ('imparting of knowledge', 1561–); *illuminated* ('enlightened intellectually', 1661–)
3H01 Faith	numerous, including *illumine* ('inspire', c1340–1554 + a1900); *illustration* ('inspiration', c1375–1653); *illuminate* ('inspire', 1538–); *enlighten* ('inspire', 1577–)
3I01 Communication and disclosure	*shine* ('to stand out clearly', c1340–); *flare* ('to spread out to view', 1862)
3I05 Information and advertising	numerous, including *illighten* ('to enlighten', 1555–1693); *irradiate* ('to throw light upon something intellectually obscure', 1627–a1710); *enlighten* ('to impart wisdom to', 1667–); *illume* ('enlighten', a1764–, chiefly poet.)

Current research: conclusion

In aiming for a global overview of metaphor in English across more than a millennium, the project has inevitably sacrificed some detail. Strategic decisions were made to focus on metaphor of a certain level of systematicity, typically setting aside potential metaphorical connections which were based on only a one-off or highly specialised citation. Human error and judgement are also relevant factors: it is inevitable that, over the course of several thousand hours of analysis of millions of pieces of data, coders will have overlooked some metaphors and classed as metaphorical some connections that others would see as literal or metonymic. These matters aside, the Metaphor Map offers a bird's-eye view of metaphor which has not previously been possible, giving firm evidence that, as Trim (2007: 211) says: 'Metaphors may continue indefinitely, appear more salient at one period of time than another, become conventionalised or completely die out'. The detail and the theoretical implications of data-driven research remain to be filled out: this is likely to form just one strand in the research into diachronic metaphor over the coming years.

Conclusion and future directions

Metaphor researchers find themselves in a very exciting place right now. As this volume makes evident, a very significant amount of scholarship on metaphor has been amassed over the past decades. Metaphor has been probed from various angles and quite thoroughly dissected. However, significant questions still remain, many of these related to diachronic aspects of metaphor. Further work is needed on the issues mentioned above.

First, the concept of 'dead metaphor' has not died, despite efforts by Lakoff and others to lay it to rest: this suggests that to language users it represents an intuitively real phenomenon – or acts as an umbrella term for more than one intuitively real phenomenon – and this therefore requires further investigation. Greater quantities of lexicographic and textual evidence, as well as insights from psycholinguistics and neurolinguistics, are likely to shape the future of this endeavour. Second, despite significant advances, we are still at an early stage of understanding the nature of semantic domains, and especially the dynamic quality of domains over time. While evidence from texts may be part of the picture here, more revelatory work is likely to be located within the cognitive sciences. Third, recent work has questioned the ubiquity of the concrete–abstract directionality of metaphor: further research, especially that driven by large quantities of authentic data, is needed to add the appropriate nuance to the model.

While the discussion in this chapter has focused on English, all of these questions would benefit immensely from fuller data-driven work on other languages. Complementary data for other languages, typologically both related and unrelated, would facilitate analysis of possible universal tendencies in the role of metaphor in language change and the nature and extent of conceptual metaphor in language.

Notes

1. In the OED, the different senses of a word are numbered, broadly in order of historical attestation. Sub-senses are indicated by lower-case letters. Separate entries are given for different parts of speech under the same lemma (e.g. *light* as a noun or an adjective), and usually for homonymous forms (e.g. *light*, adjective 1, for 'of little weight' and *light*, adjective 2, for 'bright').
2. See also Sullivan (2013, chapter 3) for an analysis of *sunny* and semantically related words from the perspective of Frame Semantics.
3. For a detailed overview of metaphor theory in recent years, see Ruiz de Mendoza Ibáñez and Pérez Hernández (2011), who explain the ways in which the theory has evolved since Lakoff and Johnson (1980), integrating (among other aspects) Grady's theory of primary metaphor (1997, 2007) and Fauconnier and Turner's conceptual blending (e.g. 2002). See also the Afterword in the second edition of *Metaphors We Live By* (Lakoff and Johnson 2003).
4. See also Samuels (1972) for foundational work on semantic change, and Traugott and Dasher (2002: 51–104) for a detailed literature review of semantic change.
5. See also the work on metaphor and semantics by Lehrer (1985).
6. *The Historical Thesaurus of English* is freely available online at http://historicalthesaurus.arts.gla.ac.uk (accessed 16 June 2015), and in print form as the *Historical Thesaurus of the Oxford English Dictionary* (Kay et al. 2009).
7. For a prototype model of semantic change, see Geeraerts (1997).
8. On the distinction between onomasiology and semasiology, see the explanations in Traugott (2006: 124) and Geeraerts (1997: 17).
9. 'Mapping Metaphor with the *Historical Thesaurus*', of which the current author was the Principal Investigator, was funded by the UK Arts and Humanities Research Council between 2012 and 2015. More information and project outputs can be found at www.glasgow.ac.uk/metaphor (accessed 16 June 2015).
10. This is, however, controversial. See Deignan (2005: 35) who argues that for some researchers the lack of a literal verb use of *dogged* excludes it from being a metaphor, despite the semantic connection with the noun *dog*. For both practical and theoretical reasons, the Mapping

Metaphor project adopted a definition of metaphor which ignored such grammatical distinctions in identifying metaphor.
11 Semantic categories defined for the Mapping Metaphor project are in inverted commas here, except in Tables.

Further reading

Allan, K. (2008) *Metaphor and Metonymy: A Diachronic Approach*, Oxford, UK: Blackwell.
Geeraerts, D. (2010) *Theories of Lexical Semantics*, Oxford, UK: Oxford University Press.
Sweetser, E. (1990) *From Etymology to Pragmatics: Metaphorical and Cultural Aspects of Semantic Structure*, Cambridge, UK: Cambridge University Press.
Traugott, E. C. and Dasher, R. B. (2002) *Regularity in Semantic Change* Cambridge, UK: Cambridge University Press.
Trim, R. (2011) *Metaphor and the Historical Evolution of Conceptual Mapping*, Basingstoke, UK: Palgrave Macmillan.

References

Allan, K. (2008) *Metaphor and Metonymy: A Diachronic Approach*, Oxford, UK: Blackwell.
—— (2012) 'Using *OED* data as evidence for researching semantic change', in K. Allan and J.A. Robinson (eds) *Current Methods in Historical Semantics*, Berlin, Germany: Mouton de Gruyter, pp. 17–39.
—— (2013) 'An inquest into metaphorical death: Exploring the loss of literal senses of conceptual metaphors', in R. Fusaroli and S. Morgagni (eds) *Conceptual Metaphor Theory: Thirty Years After*, special issue of the *Journal of Cognitive Semiotics*, 5(1–2): 291–311.
Barcelona, A. (2000) *Metaphor and Metonymy at the Crossroads: A Cognitive Perspective*, Berlin, Germany: Mouton de Gruyter.
—— (2003) 'Metonymy in cognitive linguistics: An analysis and a few modest proposals', in H. Cuyckens, T. Berg, R. Dirven and K.-U. Panther (eds) *Motivation in Language: Studies in Honor of Günther Radden*, Amsterdam, The Netherlands, and Philadelphia, PA: John Benjamins, pp. 223–55.
Bowdle, B.F. and Gentner, D. (2005) 'The career of metaphor', *Psychological Review*, 112(1): 193–216.
Croft, W. (1993) 'The role of domains in the interpretation of metaphors and metonymies', *Cognitive Linguistics*, 4: 335–70.
Dancygier, B. and Sweetser, E. (2014) *Figurative Language*, New York: Cambridge University Press.
Deignan, A. (2005) *Metaphor and Corpus Linguistics*, Amsterdam, The Netherlands, and Philadelphia, PA: John Benjamins.
Dirven, R. (1985) 'Metaphor as a basic means for extending the lexicon', in W. Paprotté and R. Dirven (eds) *The Ubiquity of Metaphor*, Amsterdam, The Netherlands, and Philadelphia, PA: John Benjamins, pp. 85–119.
Durkin, P. (2009) *The Oxford Guide to Etymology*, Oxford, UK: Oxford University Press.
Evans, V. (2013) 'Metaphor, lexical concepts, and figurative meaning construction', in R. Fusaroli and S. Morgagni (eds) *Conceptual Metaphor Theory: Thirty Years After*, special issue of the *Journal of Cognitive Semiotics*, 5(1–2): 73–105.
Fauconnier, G. and Turner, M. (2002) *The Way We Think: Conceptual Blending and the Mind's Hidden Complexities*, New York: Basic Books.
Geeraerts, D. (1997) *Diachronic Prototype Semantics: A Contribution to Historical Lexicology*, Oxford, UK: Clarendon Press.
—— (2010) *Theories of Lexical Semantics*, Oxford, UK: Oxford University Press.

Goossens, L. (1990) 'Metaphtonymy: The interaction of metaphor and metonymy in expressions for linguistic action', *Cognitive Linguistics*, 1(3): 323–342.

Grady, J. (1997) 'Foundations of meaning: Primary metaphors and primary scenes', unpublished thesis, University of California: Berkeley, CA.

—— (2007) 'Metaphor', in D. Geeraerts and H. Cuyckens (eds) *The Oxford Handbook of Cognitive Linguistics*, Oxford, UK: Oxford University Press, pp. 188–213.

Haser, V. (2003) 'Metaphor in semantic change', in A. Barcelona (ed) *Metaphor and Metonymy at the Crossroads: A Cognitive Perspective*, Berlin, Germany, and New York: Mouton de Gruyter, pp. 171–94.

Kay, C. (2000) 'Metaphors we lived by: Pathways between Old and Modern English', in J. Nelson and J. Roberts (eds) *Essays on Anglo-Saxon and Related Themes in Memory of Lynne Grundy*, London: King's College London Medieval Studies, pp. 273–85.

—— (2016) 'Food as a fruitful source of metaphor', in W. Anderson, E. Bramwell and C. Hough (eds) *Mapping English Metaphor Through Time*, Oxford, UK: Oxford University Press, pp. 66–78.

Kay, C. and Allan, K. (2015) *English Historical Semantics*, Edinburgh, UK: Edinburgh University Press.

Kay, C., Roberts, J., Samuels, M. and Wotherspoon, I. (eds) (2009) *Historical Thesaurus of the Oxford English Dictionary*, Oxford, UK: Oxford University Press.

Kay, C. and Wotherspoon, I. (2005) 'Semantic Relationships in the *Historical Thesaurus of English*', *Lexicographica*, 21: 47–57.

Kövecses, Z. (2010) *Metaphor: A Practical Introduction*, 2nd edn, Oxford, UK: Oxford University Press.

Lakoff, G. (1987) 'The death of dead metaphor', *Metaphor and Symbolic Activity*, 2(2): 143–7.

Lakoff, G. and Johnson, M. (1980) *Metaphors We Live By*, Chicago, IL: University of Chicago Press.

—— (2003) *Metaphors We Live By*, 2nd edn, Chicago, IL: University of Chicago Press.

Lehrer, A. (1985) 'The influence of semantic fields on semantic change', in J. Fisiak (ed) *Historical Semantics: Historical Word-Formation*, Berlin, Germany: Mouton de Gruyter, pp. 283–96.

—— (2003) 'Polysemy in derivational affixes', in B. Nerlich, Z. Todd, V. Herman and D. D. Clarke (eds) *Polysemy: Flexible Patterns of Meaning in Mind and Language*, Berlin, Germany, and New York: Mouton de Gruyter, pp. 217–32.

Oxford English Dictionary online (OED), http://www.oed.com (accessed 1 June 2015).

Roberts, J. and Kay, C., with Grundy, L. (1995) *A Thesaurus of Old English* (= King's College London Medieval Studies XI.), Amsterdam, The Netherlands, and Philadelphia, PA: Rodopi.

Ruiz de Mendoza Ibáñez, F. J. and Pérez Hernández, L. (2011) 'The Contemporary Theory of Metaphor: Myths, developments and challenges', *Metaphor and Symbol*, 26(3): 161–85.

Samuels, M. L. (1972) *Linguistic Evolution: With Special Reference to English*, Cambridge, UK: Cambridge University Press.

Sullivan, K. (2013) *Frames and Constructions in Metaphoric Language*, Amsterdam, The Netherlands, and Philadelphia, PA: John Benjamins.

Sweetser, E. (1990) *From Etymology to Pragmatics: Metaphorical and Cultural Aspects of Semantic Structure*, Cambridge, UK: Cambridge University Press.

Szwedek, A. (2011) 'The ultimate source domain', *Review of Cognitive Linguistics*, 9(2): 341–66.

Taylor, J. R. (2003) 'Cognitive models of polysemy', in B. Nerlich, Z. Todd, V. Herman and D. D. Clarke (eds) *Polysemy: Flexible Patterns of Meaning in Mind and Language*, Berlin, Germany, and New York: Mouton de Gruyter, pp. 31–47.

Traugott, E. C. (2006) 'Semantic change: Bleaching, strengthening, narrowing, extension', in K. Brown (ed) *Encyclopedia of Language and Linguistics*, Vol. 11, 2nd edn, Amsterdam, The Netherlands, and Boston, MA: Elsevier, pp. 124–31.

Traugott, E. C. and Dasher, R. B. (2002) *Regularity in Semantic Change*, Cambridge Studies in Linguistics 96, Cambridge, UK: Cambridge University Press.

Trim, R. (2007) *Metaphor Networks: The Comparative Evolution of Figurative Language*, Basingstoke, UK: Palgrave Macmillan.

—— (2011) *Metaphor and the Historical Evolution of Conceptual Mapping*, Basingstoke, UK: Palgrave Macmillan.

17
Metaphor in Translation

Christina Schäffner

Introduction

Translation plays a significant role in our global world, assuring communication across linguistic and cultural boundaries. In these processes, information initially produced in one language (the source language) is transferred into a new language (the target language) for a new audience in a different culture. Although translation is much more complex, it is this element of transfer from a source to a target which is also often central to characterising metaphor (see Chapter 1). The two concepts, metaphor and translation, are etymological cognates. 'Metaphor' originates from Greek, with 'meta-' indicating a change (e.g. of place) and 'pherein' a process of carrying. 'Translate' originates from the Latin 'transferre', with 'trans-' meaning across, and 'ferre' meaning to bear, or to carry (see also e.g. Guldin 2010: 161–191; Shuttleworth 2014b: 53–65).

In addition to the idea of transfer, the notion of similarity has been used for the characterisation of both concepts. In the traditional understanding of metaphor, similarities and/or analogies are supposed to hold between the image and the object.[1] For translation, the key word for the relationship between source text and target text is 'equivalence', although variously described as, e.g. equivalence of meaning, of communicative function, of effect, if not even totally rejected as the defining criterion (e.g. Halverson 1997).

It is now generally recognised in Translation Studies that translation is not a simple replacement of linguistic signs of the source language by equivalent signs of the target language, but a far more complex process. In addition to the change in language, the audience and the purpose for which the text is to be produced are to be taken into consideration, alongside the socio-cultural, ideological, and institutional factors that play a significant role in the production, dissemination, and reception of translations. These developments within Translation Studies are reflected in its different definitions, from the more traditional view of translation as meaning transfer to more recent views of translation as a purposeful activity (Vermeer 1996), as norm-governed behaviour (Toury 1995), as a socio-cultural practice (Venuti 1995), or as socially regulated behaviour (Wolf 2002).

Whatever the definition of translation, metaphor is a phenomenon which has regularly attracted the interest of Translation Studies scholars. A search in the online Benjamins

Translation Studies Bibliography (https://benjamins.com/online/tsb/) showed many more results for 'metaphor and translation' than for 'metaphor and interpreting', signalling that more attention has been given to the phenomenon of metaphor in the context of translation (even if this Bibliography is not exhaustive). This chapter will therefore focus only on translation. After a brief illustration of metaphors which have been used to conceptualise translation, the chapter will give an overview of relevant research conducted to date, comment on critical issues, illustrate some current research, and suggest future directions.

Relevant research to date: questions and methods

Metaphors of translation

The discourse about translation is itself characterised by metaphorical reflection. Translation has been conceptualised as transfer, as a mirror imitation, as deception (cf. the well-known adage of the translator as a traitor: *traduttore traditore*), as refraction, as action, and so on (for more details see the chapters in St André 2010). Metaphors which are linked to the aspect of faithfulness indicate the dominant status awarded to the source text, from which translations are derived as secondary objects. This is also the case in the metaphorical reflections of a gender-biased nature, in particular the tradition of the *belles infidèles* which compares translations to women and argues that beautiful women are not faithful (on criticism of such views see e.g. Chamberlain 2000: 314–329; Godayol i Nogué 2013).

Transfer metaphors conceptualise movement to a different place and thus give attention both to the source text and to the target culture. A famous metaphor in the tradition of German Translation Studies is Jakob Grimm's comparison of translating to ferrying across the sea, exploiting the polysemy of the German word 'übersetzen' (Störig 1963: 111). The translator is perceived as a navigator who transports the word-freight safely from one shore to the other.

Translation has also often been conceived of as a bridge which connects cultures, or as bridge-building for communication. The bridge links two different cultures and linguistic communities, thus enabling the free exchange of texts and ideas. Constructing the bridge is a complicated and time-consuming endeavour, but once it has been erected, no user needs to think about its construction and the material used. As Hönig (1997) argues, a translator as a bridge-builder needs to have a sound knowledge of the material, i.e. language, and also needs to feel responsible for constructing a bridge which is appropriate for its intended purpose.

The traditional assumption of the translator as a non-involved conduit has been challenged by more recent reflections of their active role as mediators, 'go-betweens', or 'gatekeepers' (e.g. Heimburger 2012: 21–34). Research informed by postcolonial theories and Cultural Studies in particular has shown that translation is never neutral or innocent, that translators can also deliberately misinform or pursue specific agendas (e.g. feminism). Translators are situated within socio-cultural contexts, which has implications for their work. This social situatedness of the production and reception of translation makes spatial metaphors such as 'the third space' or 'in-betweenness', used in postcolonial theories, problematic (see Tymoczko 2003: 181–201; Medendorp 2013).

The metaphors used to conceptualise translation illustrated above are not universal, and not even shared among European languages and cultures. Guldin (2010: 180), for example, comments that the Hungarian word 'forditás' reflects the notion of a turning, rotating movement. Tymoczko (2010: 109–143) provides examples of words for 'translation' and their metaphorical potential from non-European languages. For example, the Arabic word 'tarjama' has 'biography' as an early meaning, and the most common Chinese term 'fanyi' literally means 'turning over'. Tymoczko (2010) argues that the Western metaphorical view of translation as carrying across is entangled with the history of Christianity and Western colonisation. Such culturally different traditions in the conceptualisation of translation thus highlight the constructed nature of prevailing concepts and provide rich material for exploring the history of Translation Studies.

In addition to framing the discourse on translation, metaphors themselves have often been the object of scholarly research within Translation Studies. The next section will present some of the main issues that have been addressed. It will illustrate that both the theoretical approach to translation and the respective definition of metaphor used by scholars have influenced their research questions, methods of analysis, and interpretation of results.

Overview of how metaphor has been addressed in Translation Studies

In the literature on metaphor and translation, two major threads can be identified: (1) the translatability of metaphor, and (2) methods of metaphor translation. The discussion on whether and how metaphor can be translated was predominantly informed by the more traditional definition of metaphor as a figure of speech. Conceptual theories of metaphor (mainly the theoretical framework first proposed by Lakoff and Johnson 1980; see Chapter 1), which describe metaphors as basic resources for thought processes in human society and not just as decorative elements in a text, entered Translation Studies only in the 1990s.

Translatability of metaphor

The translatability of metaphor concerns questions such as: Can metaphor be translated? Can it be transferred into another language without any loss? Metaphor as a translation problem was articulated particularly in equivalence-based approaches to translation and linked to both the traditional view of metaphor as a purely linguistic phenomenon and a narrow definition of translation as meaning transfer. The underlying assumption was that a metaphor, once identified, should ideally be transferred intact from source language (SL) to target language (TL). Such an intact transfer was perceived as problematic because of the inherent differences between languages and cultures.

A key paper in respect of translatability is Dagut (1976). For Dagut, metaphor is an individual flash of imaginative insight whose main function is to provide a shocking effect for its readers. Since metaphors are viewed as the products of the creative violation of the semantic rules of a linguistic system, they are highly culture-specific. Dagut argues that the shocking effect is to be retained in a translation, and if linguistic and cultural factors hinder this, the metaphor cannot be translated. Reflecting on translatability in such terms of yes or no, however, has not been the main focus in Translation Studies. Since linguistic and cultural differences always play a role in translation, and an 'intact' transfer is thus impossible anyway, other scholars have devoted their attention to the exploration of such cultural differences and suggested translation procedures.

Translation procedures for metaphor

There is a significant body of literature that presents categories of translation procedures, alternatively labelled as translation methods, or strategies, derived either on the basis of comparisons of isolated linguistic units of languages (and thus more of a speculative nature) or on the basis of authentic translations. Some of these typologies are of a didactic nature (how metaphor could, or even should, be translated) meant to help translators and students of translation. Most of these typologies are based on the identification of metaphor in the source text as a problem for which a solution has to be found. The most frequently suggested procedures can be summarised as follows:

(i) metaphor into same metaphor – direct translation;
(ii) metaphor into different metaphor – substitution of the image in the SL text by a TL metaphor with the same or similar sense;
(iii) metaphor into sense – paraphrase, shift to a non-figurative equivalent.

Newmark (1981) defines five types of metaphors (dead, cliché, stock, recent, original) and reflects on the most appropriate translation method for each type. In his discussion of stock metaphors, he develops seven translation procedures which have frequently been taken up in the literature to date (e.g. Oliynyk 2014). Newmark arranges these procedures in order of preference of use, with the examples given (reproduced below) not extracted from authentic translations (Newmark 1981: 87–91):

1. reproducing the same image in the TL, e.g. 'golden hair – goldenes Haar';
2. replace the image in the SL with a standard TL image which does not clash with the TL culture, e.g. 'other fish to fry – d'autres chats à fouetter [literal translation: other cats to whip]';
3. translation of metaphor by simile, retaining the image, e.g. 'Ces zones cryptuaire où s'élabore la beauté – the crypt-like areas where beauty is manufactured';
4. translation of metaphor (or simile) by simile plus sense (or occasionally a metaphor plus sense), e.g. 'tout un vocabulaire moliéresque – a whole repertoire of medical quackery such as Molière might have used';
5. conversion of metaphor to sense, e.g. 'sein Brot verdienen [literal translation: to earn one's bread] – to earn one's living';
6. deletion, if the metaphor is redundant;
7. same metaphor combined with sense, in order to strengthen the image.

Newmark also argues that the function of a metaphor in a text (i.e. its cognitive and/or emotive function) should be the basis for the translator's decision. For example, the fourth procedure could be used as a compromise solution in order to avoid comprehension problems, although it results in the loss of the intended effect. The fifth procedure is recommended when the TL image is not appropriate to the register, although the emotive effect may get lost. A deletion, however, should only be used, according to Newmark, if the text is not authoritative or expressive.

Toury (1995: 81ff) points out that translation procedures like those suggested by Newmark typically start from a metaphor (i.e. a metaphorical expression) as identified in the source text (ST) which is treated as a unit of translation. Toury contrasts this retrospective view with his own prospective view. Starting from the target text (TT), he identifies two additional cases: the use of a metaphor in the TT for a non-metaphorical expression in the ST (metaphor for non-metaphor), and the addition of a metaphor in the TT without any linguistic motivation in the ST (metaphor for zero).

Toury's comments reflect the perspective of Descriptive Translation Studies, with its interest in the actual form of translations. The question thus becomes 'How is metaphor translated?', with actual procedures identified on the basis of a descriptive comparative analysis of source texts and their authentic translations. Strategies identified in that way, however, also apply to metaphorical expressions and thus to the micro-level. Some research has been conducted to explore the function of metaphors within and throughout a specific text. For example, based on the interaction theory of metaphor (Black 1962: 218–235; see also Goatly 1997: 117ff) and on scenes-and-frames semantics, Kurth (1995) illustrates how several metaphors interact in the construction of a macro-scene. He shows which TL frames had been chosen for an SL scene in German translations of Charles Dickens' early work and comments on the consequences for the effect of the text. He derives nine basic types of translational behaviour for metaphors: deletion, compression, levelling of the image, weakening of the image, image shift, image preservation, enhancement of the image, new metaphorisation, and elaboration of the metaphor (Kurth 1995: 187).

In the last two decades, the conceptual theory of metaphor (see Chapter 1) has become more widely used in Translation Studies research, and the methodology is predominantly a descriptive comparative analysis of source texts and their authentic translations. Among the first studies is the work by Stienstra (1993) who analysed several Bible translations into English and Dutch, with a particular focus on the conceptual metaphor YHWH IS THE HUSBAND OF HIS PEOPLE.[2] She illustrates that this central metaphor of the Old Testament was preserved in the translations at the macro-level, even if specific textual manifestations were changed or not accounted for in each individual occurrence. She differentiates between universal, culture-overlapping, and culture-specific metaphors and argues that it is not the conceptual metaphor that is culture-dependent, but its linguistic realisation.

Some studies that take a conceptual metaphor perspective have also presented lists of translation procedures, which are significantly different from those previously produced on the basis of more traditional metaphor theories. For example, based on the analysis of English translations of Arabic political speeches, Al-Harrasi (2001) suggested a very extensive list which includes procedures such as Instantiating the Same Conceptual Metaphor (with sub-procedures such as Concretising an Image Schematic Metaphor, or Same Mapping but a Different Perspective), Using a Different Conceptual Metaphor, and Deletion of the Expression of the Metaphor (Al-Harrasi 2001: 277–88). The cognitive approach to metaphor has thus already contributed new insights to translation, and investigating authentic translations can also contribute to a better understanding of metaphor as a phenomenon. In the next section, some critical issues and debates will be addressed.

Critical issues and debates

Definition of metaphor and evaluation of metaphor translation

Although the conceptual theory of metaphor has become more widely used in Translation Studies, this is not the case for every analysis. There are still publications in which a more traditional definition of metaphor is used, or which aim to combine linguistic and conceptual metaphors. The main reason for this is that translators encounter the linguistic realisations of conceptual mappings in the texts they are dealing with, and not the mappings as such.

There are only relatively few publications of general reflections on metaphor theories, definitions, and classifications that discuss their consequences for translation (e.g. Prandi 2010), in contrast to the large body of research investigating how metaphors – i.e. metaphorical expressions – have been translated. These studies are often combined with an evaluative element, that is, scholars comment on the accuracy, appropriateness, or effectiveness of the translational choices. This is sometimes done in a didactic or prescriptive way, aiming at suggestions for translating metaphors. Examples of such studies are El-Zeiny (2011) and Zahid (2009), who both investigated metaphors in the Qur'an. El-Zeiny (2011) compared six different approaches to the translation of Qur'anic metaphors to arrive at principled criteria to recommend for their translation, and Zahid (2009) uses data from translations of the Qur'an into English to build up a comprehensive model for metaphor translation. Similarly, Tan's description of strategies for metaphor translation in different translations of Chinese novels into English has the aim of finding out 'how best metaphors are handled in translation' (Tan 2004: 219).

Culture-specific or universal metaphors and consequences for translation

Cultural factors have been addressed quite frequently in Translation Studies, with cultural differences being identified as obstacles to the semantic transfer of metaphors. Already back in 1976, Dagut had argued that 'what determines the translatability of an SL metaphor is not its "boldness" or "originality", but rather the extent to which the cultural experience and semantic associations on which it draws are shared by speakers of the particular TL' (Dagut 1976: 28). It is therefore no surprise that culture as a major problem has remained at the centre of attention. Moreover, it has predominantly been addressed in research involving non-European languages, such as Arabic (with a specific focus on the Qur'an) or Chinese. For example, Fagong (2009) identified image losses in Chinese–English metaphor translation and recommends a literal translation of the vehicle in combination with an indication of its cultural implications. Al-Kharabsheh (2011) investigates the conceptualisation and translation of euphemistic metaphorical expressions for death in obituaries in Jordanian newspapers, identifying conflicting cultural models of agency in Arabic and English as the main hurdles to translation. Although these studies make reference to conceptual metaphor theory, they evaluate the results of their analysis in terms of loss, i.e. loss in meaning, and/or in cultural implications, and/or in effect, thus reflecting a traditional view of translation as meaning transfer.

In investigating cultural differences, Translation Studies scholars also build on Metaphor Studies research into the ways conceptual metaphors are expressed linguistically in different languages. For example, based on a comparison of the linguistic expressions of particular conceptual metaphors in English and Hungarian, Kövecses (2005) identified four possible patterns:

(i) metaphors of similar mapping conditions and similar lexical implementations;
(ii) metaphors of similar mapping conditions but different lexical implementations;
(iii) metaphors of different mapping conditions but similar lexical implementations;
(iv) metaphors of different mapping conditions and different lexical implementations.

These patterns were tested by Al-Hasnawi (2007) with authentic examples from English and Arabic and their translations, and he found examples for each one of them. However, even metaphorical linguistic expressions which have been identified as being similar across two languages cannot be treated as ready-made translation equivalents, since a variety of factors impact translation production. Further evidence that translators do not necessarily opt for similar metaphorical expressions, even if they exist, has been provided by research which makes use of corpus analysis software and is thus based on extensive data. Researchers often extend the metaphor identification procedure proposed by the Pragglejaz Group (2007; see Chapter 5) by a stage in which source text and target text segments are aligned in order to see how the metaphorical expression has been translated. They then proceed to establish whether the translation is metaphorical, and, if so, they infer the underlying conceptual metaphor. An example of such an approach is the study by Rodríguez Márquez (2010), who used an extensive bidirectional corpus of US-English and Mexican-Spanish annual business reports to investigate how the linguistic metaphors identified in the source texts were translated in the target texts. She refers to the patterns identified by Deignan et al. (1997), which are similar to the ones by Kövecses above. Rodríguez Márquez did find evidence for a pattern of 'same conceptual metaphors and same/similar linguistic metaphors' in her corpus, but no examples of the other three patterns. Instead, she discovered two new patterns: (i) the translation of the source linguistic metaphor is not metaphorical and, thus, no conceptual metaphor is instantiated in the target text, and (ii) the source linguistic metaphor is not translated at all in the target text. She argues that 'none of the cases where the translation is not considered to be metaphorical indicates that culture is the reason for the lack of metaphoricity of the translation and, in turn, the absence of a conceptual metaphor' (Rodríguez Márquez 2010: 131). Rather, she explains such differences in source text and target text with additional changes translators made to the syntactic structure of a sentence, or their choice of established terminology in the specialised domain of business.

Descriptive analysis of translations and wider implications

Despite the limitations of a text-based analysis, a description of translation procedures used by translators provides interesting results for both Translation Studies and metaphor research. Differences in the metaphorical expressions in source texts and target texts can reflect cultural differences, but they can also be the result of genre conventions (as found by Rodríguez Márquez 2010), time constraints, institutional arrangements, or other factors.

Lindquist's study (2014: 167–180) is interesting in this respect. She analysed a corpus of cookery books and their translations from English into Swedish, focusing on grammatical metaphors. Grammatical metaphor is used in Halliday's (1994) sense as a departure from the unmarked, congruent structures and wordings. Lindquist discovered examples of both congruent translation (e.g. 'my interest in cooking' – 'mitt interest för matlagning') and non-congruent translation (e.g. 'the various book signings I have done' – 'när jag var ute och signerade böcker' [literal translation: when I was out signing books]). She explains the lower frequency of grammatical metaphors in the Swedish target texts with reference to the language planning initiatives of the Swedish government. These initiatives resulted in guidelines which, among others, state preferences for finite clauses (Lindquist 2014: 178). Grammatical metaphors, however, are less frequently analysed from a translation perspective compared to lexical metaphors.

The identification of translation procedures can thus lead a researcher to formulate new research questions, or to use additional research methods, or to resort to different theoretical frameworks for exploration and/or explanation. Such a process of question generation is illustrated in Carter (2014) with her analysis of the English translation of the novel *Utu* by the French crime fiction writer Caryl Férey. In a first step, she conducted a quantitative analysis of the linguistic metaphors, discovering that the translation contains 31 per cent fewer metaphors than the source text, and that, for example, a large number of the stock metaphors had been converted to sense in the target text (e.g. 'Il suivait les cours du bout des neurones' [literal translation: He followed the class by the tips of his neurons] rendered as 'He paid little attention in class'). Comparing this translation to two other translated novels by Férey, she noticed the same reduction in metaphors in the English target texts. She then moves on to reflect on the potential reasons for such quantitative differences, mainly by putting forward hypotheses. One hypothesis is linked to genre conventions and target culture norms, suggesting that translators of crime fiction into English might reduce metaphors in order to meet the perceived expectations of their readers. With reference to research in cognitive literary studies and cognitive narratology, she moves on to ask whether reading popular genres which employ familiar repertoires requires less cognitive effort. The final considerations concern the low status of crime fiction as a genre and the working conditions of translators. Although her hypotheses are not tested further, her main argument is that translators should be encouraged to retain metaphors in crime fiction because metaphors influence readers' emotional engagement with the texts.

Examples of current research: multilingual translation

Current research into metaphor in translation is of a diverse nature, but most prominently it is based on empirical analyses of authentic texts. Most of the work does make reference to cognitive metaphor theories, most frequently to Lakoff and Johnson (1980). In this section, only one area of current research will be illustrated since it has added new methods and new perspectives to investigating metaphor in translation: the analysis of multilingual translations. Analysing how one source text has been translated into several languages can bring insights in respect of culture specificity and contexts of translation production.

Shuttleworth (2011, 2014a), for example, uses a multilingual corpus to study the translation of metaphor in popular-scientific texts. His data come from the official published translations into French, Italian, German, Russian, and Polish of articles in the magazine *Scientific American*. He explores how metaphorical expressions have been dealt with both at the micro-level (translation procedures for individual metaphorical expressions) and at the macro-level (clusters of mappings). Shuttleworth notices both similarities and differences in how translators dealt with individual metaphorical expressions across the five target languages analysed. Retention of the metaphorical expression was identified as the default procedure across all languages, whereas modification was used only rarely. In respect of differences, he notices, for example, that the translations into Polish display the greatest number of modifications, and that the translations into German show the largest number of omissions and removals of metaphorical expressions, but also the largest number of newly added metaphorical expressions. Comparing the metaphorical expressions to the mappings they represent, he concludes that what is 'lost' in translation are individual metaphorical expressions rather than entire mappings. The main advantage of such multilingual studies is the richness of data they produce, which can allow researchers to draw conclusions based on results that go beyond a single translation context, and also identify tendencies that appear to be common to translators' behaviour regardless of the target language and the subject domain.

Translators' behaviour, however, is also determined by the context in which they operate, as illustrated by Tcaciuc (2012, 2014: 99–112) with financial documents translated within the European Central Bank (ECB). She noticed, for example, more similarity in the French and Spanish translations of the English source texts compared to the translations into Romanian, as illustrated below with a phrase from a text in the *Monthly Bulletin* of June 2008:

English: The ongoing "health check" of the EU common agricultural policy
French: «bilan de santé» en cours de la politique agricole commune de l'UE
Spanish: el «chequeo» al que está siendo sometida la política agrícola común de la UE
Romanian: evaluarea politicii agricole comune a UE.

This excerpt reflects the conceptual metaphors POLICY IS A PERSON or HEALTHY IS GOOD. Although the four versions are nearly identical to each other, the Romanian translation is the only one which uses an explicitation and thus demetaphorises the expression ('evaluarea' corresponds to 'evaluation'). Tcaciuc noticed that translators into Romanian generally tend to demetaphorise the English economic metaphors or add explanations, especially in cases of novelty (e.g. 'helicopter money' rendered as 'bani-cadou' [literal translation: money gift]). Tcaciuc comments that the institutional translation process at the ECB requires translators to work with translation memory tools, to use databases, glossaries, and previous documents in order to ensure consistency across the texts. Since Romania joined the European Union at a later stage, the Romanian translators do not yet have the same large body of reference material at their disposal. Moreover, due to the 'newness' of Romanian as a working language in the European Union, the revision of the translations is often done by the translators of the Romanian national bank, who tend to avoid metaphorical expressions, considering figurative language to be inappropriate for such official documents.

In my own research on political texts, I also identified differences in the various language versions of the same document (Schäffner 2004). For example, the English, French, and German versions of the Manifesto of the European People's Party (EPP) for the 1999 Elections to the European Parliament employ expressions that are realisations of a movement metaphor (POLITICS IS MOVEMENT TOWARDS A DESTINATION: 'taken a step forward' corresponds to 'Schritt nach vorn getan', 'faire un pas'). However, in the subsequent sentence, the beginning of a new project is conceptualised as the start of a construction process in the English text ('foundation stone'), whereas the French text continues the movement metaphor ('une étape sur la voie' [literal translation: a stage on the path]), and the German text uses a more general expression ('Beginn' [literal translation: beginning]). Otherwise the three language versions are identical.

English: We have already taken a great step forward towards European integration by introducing the Single Currency. But the euro is ... the foundation stone of what we intend to be a new era,

French: Nous venons de faire un grand pas vers l'intégration européenne avec l'instauration de la monnaie unique. Mais l'euro ... est une étape sur la voie d'une union politique, ...

German: Mit der Einführung des EURO haben wir einen großen Schritt nach vorn getan. Der EURO ... Die EVP sieht darin den Beginn eines neuen Projektes, ...

This analysis, however, was based purely on the texts. In recent studies, I have tried to go beyond the text by investigating the contexts and conditions in which the translations were produced. For example, translations of speeches by the German Chancellor and the Federal President are produced by the translation service of the German Foreign Office. Comparing the English and French versions of a speech by the German Federal President Joachim

Gauck, delivered on 22 February 2013, and of an interview that the Federal Chancellor Angela Merkel gave to several European newspapers on 25 January 2012, I noticed more liberty in English in using metaphors (e.g. 'enter unchartered territory' for the more neutral formulation 'Neues' [literal translation: something new]), more verbal style (e.g. 'move forward' for the noun 'Weg' [literal translation: path]), and often more literal renderings into French compared to the English translations, as illustrated in the extracts below. In the second example, the French translation is identical to the original German [but above all we must agree on one common path in Europe].

> German: Wir halten inne, um uns gedanklich und emotional zu rüsten für den nächsten Schritt, der <u>Neues</u> von uns verlangt (http://www.bundespraesident.de/SharedDocs/Reden/DE/Joachim-Gauck/Reden/2013/02/130222-Europa.html).
>
> English: we are pausing to reflect so that we can equip ourselves both intellectually and emotionally for the next step, which will require us to <u>enter unchartered territory</u> (http://www.bundespraesident.de/SharedDocs/Downloads/DE/Reden/2013/02/130222-Europe-englisch.pdf?__blob=publicationFile).
>
> French: Nous marquons une pause pour nous préparer mentalement et émotionnellement à la prochaine étape qui nous conduira sur de <u>nouvelles voies</u> (http://www.bundespraesident.de/SharedDocs/Downloads/DE/Reden/2013/02/130222-Europa-Rede-Franzoesisch.pdf?__blob=publicationFile).
>
> German: aber vor allem müssen wir uns in Europa auf einen gemeinsamen <u>Weg</u> verständigen (http://www.bundesregierung.de/ContentArchiv/DE/Archiv17/Interview/2012/01/2012-01-26-merkel-sueddeutsche-zeitung.html).
>
> English: but the main thing we need to be doing in the EU is finding consensus on how we are going to <u>move forward</u> together (http://www.london.diplo.de/Vertretung/london/en/03/__Political__News/01/Merkel__Interview.html).
>
> French: mais nous devons avant tout nous accorder en Europe sur une <u>voie</u> commune (http://www.cidal.diplo.de/Vertretung/cidal/fr/__pr/actualites/nq/Dossier__Eurokrise/2012-01-27-merkel-interview-pm.html).

By doing fieldwork in the offices of the translation service and interviewing translators and other staff members, more information could be gathered about translation practices and institutional procedures. Translators reported that their overall translation method is a reader-oriented approach and their guiding principle is comprehensibility. They also make systematic use of previously translated texts and are supported by a terminology section. A very thorough system of checking and revision is in operation to ensure quality. However, if one text is to be translated into several languages (as was the case with the Merkel interview which was translated into English, French, Spanish, Italian, and Polish), there is normally no time to have regular joint meetings of all translators involved or for close cooperation since the sheer volume of work does not allow for this. This also means that translators would not normally consult each other in how to deal with metaphors. Combining text analysis with ethnographic fieldwork in the actual institutional contexts can thus result in a better understanding of the complexity of translation, also in respect of dealing with metaphorical expressions and conceptual metaphors (see also Schäffner, Tcaciuc and Tesseur 2014).

Future directions

Future research can be most productive if it involves empirical research and combines methods, genres, languages, and contexts. In this final section, this will be briefly illustrated for (i) translation process studies, (ii) multilingual data, and (iii) professional practices, although these three aspects can be combined.

Translation process studies

On the basis of comparing authentic source and target texts, we can see how metaphorical expressions were handled, but we cannot retrace the actual pathways of the translator's decision-making procedures. Investigations into translation processes conducted so far have tried to fill this gap in our knowledge. Methods used in order to get insights into actual cognitive processes include think-aloud protocol studies, keystroke logging, and eye-tracking, sometimes in combination. However, only very few of such process studies were exclusively devoted to investigating metaphor in translation, and there is thus scope for future research.

Think-aloud studies are experimental procedures in which translators are asked to think aloud as they are performing their translation task. These oral comments are audio-recorded (sometimes combined with video recordings) and transcribed by the researcher, resulting in a think-aloud protocol (TAP). TAP-based research has been employed, for example, to test the Cognitive Translation Hypothesis, which states that 'metaphorical expressions take more time and are more difficult to translate if they exploit a different cognitive domain than the target language equivalent expression' (Tirkkonen-Condit 2001: 11). Martikainen (1999) and Tirkkonen-Condit (2001, 2002) measured the time and the length of TAP segments, counted the lines of target text produced, and asked the translators to comment on their own satisfaction with their translations. They found that metaphorical expressions with different domains took longer to translate and resulted in more verbalisation and more potential translation solutions. They interpreted their findings as evidence of concept mediation and thus confirmation of the Cognitive Translation Hypothesis.

Keystroke logging records (or logs) every key which is struck by a translator when translating a text using a computer, thus providing detailed information about duration, timing, and position of pauses and corrections. Using the keystroke logging software TRANSLOG, Jakobsen et al. (2007: 217–249) measured processing time and noticed that idiomatic expressions (which are often metaphorical) slow down the translation process, which also lends support to the Cognitive Translation Hypothesis.

Eye-tracking is the most recent addition to translation process research. Translators work in front of a computer screen, with an eye-tracker device recording the translator's eye movements, fixation durations, number of fixations, and pupil dilation. This research is based on the assumption that there is a correlation between the time readers fixate on a word and the amount of processing that takes place. Of particular interest for metaphor in translation are the experiments conducted by Sjørup (2008: 53–77, 2011: 197–214) who discovered that there was indeed a longer fixation time for metaphors compared to non-metaphorical language. Her studies also led her to conclude that the choice of paraphrase as a translation strategy is linked to a higher cognitive load compared to the use of a direct metaphorical equivalent or the use of another metaphorical phrase as alternative strategies, since paraphrase involves two shifts: a shift from one domain to another, and a shift from metaphorical expressions to literal ones.

Process research has revealed that the translation of metaphors does indeed seem to be linked to greater cognitive load, evident in longer pauses, total length of task completion, and more uncertainty (verbalised in TAPs and/or noticeable in TRANSLOG reports). However, a number of questions remain. For example, although Sjørup (2008) identified longer fixation times for metaphorical expressions, she still concedes that it is impossible to determine how this greater cognitive processing load is distributed between metaphor interpretation and the choice of a translation strategy and a target text formulation.

In respect of the question of whether translators actually access the conceptual level, the data gathered from process studies are not conclusive either. TAPs do reflect that thought processes are happening at conceptual levels, but they also indicate that these processes are often triggered by linguistic expressions. TAPs and keystroke logging reports also show that translators initially attempt to provide a target language equivalent for a linguistic metaphor. This seems to lend support to literal translation as the default strategy. However, both TAPs and retrospective interviews provide evidence that translators' decisions are also informed by considering the purpose of the translation, intra-textual coherence and stylistic considerations, etc., thus confirming that the factors that influence the decisions for dealing with metaphors are manifold.

In Schäffner and Shuttleworth (2013), we argued that data gathered through various process methods could be scrutinised more systematically to get deeper insights into translation procedures, and we made some suggestions for experimental studies. Our main argument was that a combination of methods and datasets, i.e. triangulation, would lend more weight to hypotheses and explanations.

Multilingual data

Metaphor researchers have often been interested in detecting cross-cultural similarity and variation in metaphor, reflected, for example, in different linguistic expressions for the same conceptual metaphor (Kövecses 2005). A comparative analysis of authentic texts in several languages is a good method to achieve such an aim. However, an analysis of translations will not necessarily lead to the same results as the analysis of authentic texts in several languages. Metaphor in translation is a matter of discourse and social context, which means that translation strategies are not only determined by the availability of a corresponding conceptual metaphor and/or a metaphorical expression in the target language. Purely product-oriented analyses of multilingual translations would thus also need to consider the text production conditions. Moreover, even for translated magazine articles (such as the different language versions of popular scientific magazines such as *Scientific American* or *National Geographic*), the final structure of the texts is the result of translation followed by additional processes (especially editing) in their respective socio-cultural and institutional contexts.

Process studies could identify differences in the way translators take decisions. In Schäffner and Shuttleworth (2013), we suggested that experiments could be set up to produce multilingual texts in identical conditions. For example, a number of translators could be asked to translate the same source text into several target languages, with all translators working at the same time in the same setting, and researchers ideally combining methods (e.g. keystroke logging and/or eye tracking and/or TAPs and/or retrospective interviews). Analysing the data gained in this way should not only give us more insights into cross-cultural variation in metaphors and metaphorical expressions, but also reveal whether translators operate at the lexical or the cognitive level, whether they are conscious of their decisions, how the cognitive load is distributed between comprehension and formulation, and which subjective variables (e.g. background, training and habitus) impact their decisions.

Researching professional practices

Future research could also focus on investigating the professional practices in various environments. Research could be conducted, for example, to see whether institutional procedures and requirements lead to specific ways of dealing with metaphors in translation. There could be studies into the potential effects of working with translation memory systems and machine translation, or analyses of specific documents such as institutional style guides to see whether they explicitly refer to metaphors. In my own work on political and journalistic texts, I discovered, for example, that translations done by the translation department of the German government showed more consistency as compared to more variability in translations done by media institutions (Schäffner 2014: 69–84). For example, the German *Spiegel International* opted for 'bailout fund', 'rescue fund', or 'backstop fund' for the metaphorical expression 'Rettungsschirm' (literal translation: rescue umbrella), whereas translations produced by the government's translation department use 'rescue package' consistently. These differences in the texts reflect differences in institutional practices. As said above, the translation department of the German government operates a very thorough checking system. Translation processes for mass media, however, are governed by the values of journalism, that favours, above all, speed, newsworthiness, and understandability for a broad international audience. For this reason, journalists as translators survey the press in their respective target cultures to follow their usage in the translations they produce.

Similar research into professional contexts could investigate whether proof-reading and revision processes affect metaphors – whether, for example, proof-readers and/or revisers change, add, or omit metaphorical expressions in the translations. Finally, longitudinal studies could be conducted to see whether translators change the way/s they deal with metaphor in translation in the course of their professional career and if so, why. Such studies could combine product and process studies, and would also benefit from ethnographic fieldwork.

Notes

1 In the literature on metaphor research, various terms have been used, such as 'image' or 'vehicle' for the source referent, 'object' or 'topic' for the target referent, and 'sense', 'grounds', or 'tenor' for the relationship between the two (see e.g. Goatly 1997 for such terminology in metaphor definitions). Translation Studies scholars too have used these various labels in line with the respective metaphor theory they subscribe to.
2 YHWH is God's name in original Hebrew.

Further reading

Miller, D. R. and Monti, E. (eds) (2014) *Tradurre figure / Translating figurative language*, Bologna, Italy: Bononia University Press.
Schäffner, C. (2004) 'Metaphor and translation: Some implications of a cognitive approach', *Journal of Pragmatics*, 36: 1253–1269.
Shuttleworth, M. (2011) 'Translational behaviour at the frontiers of scientific knowledge: A multilingual investigation into popular science metaphor in translation', *The Translator*, 17: 301–323.

Sjørup, A. C. (2011) 'Cognitive effort in metaphor translation: An eye-tracking study', in S. O'Brien (ed.) *Cognitive Explorations of Translation*, London: Continuum, pp. 197–214.

St André, J. (ed.) (2010) *Thinking through Translation with Metaphor*, Manchester, UK: St Jerome.

References

Al-Harrasi, A. (2001) 'Metaphor in (Arabic-into-English) translation with specific reference to metaphorical concepts and expressions in political discourse', unpublished PhD thesis, Aston University.

Al-Hasnawi, A. R. (2007) 'A cognitive approach to translating metaphor', *Translation Journal*, 11 http://www.bokorlang.com/journal/41metaphor.htm (accessed 22 July 2015).

Al-Kharabsheh, A. (2011) 'Arabic death discourse in translation: Euphemism and metaphorical conceptualization in Jordanian obituaries', *Across Languages and Cultures*, 12: 19–48.

Black, M. (1962) 'Metaphor', in M. Margolis (ed.) *Philosophy Looks at the Arts*, New York: Temple University Press.

Carter, E. (2014) 'Why not translate metaphor in French crime fiction? The case of Caryl Férey's *Utu*', *The Journal of Specialised Translation*, 22: 44–56. Online. Available at: http://www.jostrans.org/issue22/art_carter.pdf (accessed 15 May 2015).

Chamberlain, L. (2000) 'Gender and the metaphorics of translation', in L. Venuti (ed.) *The Translation Studies Reader*, London and New York: Routledge.

Dagut, M. (1976) 'Can "metaphor" be translated?', *Babel*, 22: 21–33.

Deignan, A., Gabryś, D. and Solska, A. (1997) 'Teaching English metaphors using crosslinguistic awareness-raising activities', *ELT Journal*, 51: 352–360.

El-Zeiny, I. (2011) 'Criteria for the translation and assessment of Qur'anic metaphor: A contrastive analytic approach', *Babel*, 57: 247–268.

Fagong, L. (2009) 'Making up for image losses in Chinese-English translation of metaphors', *Chinese Translators Journal*, 6: 52–56.

Goatly, A. (1997) *The Language of Metaphors*, London and New York: Routledge.

Godayol i Nogué, P. (2013) 'Metaphors, women and translation: From les belles infidèles to la frontera', *Gender and Language*, 7: 97–116.

Guldin, R. (2010) 'Metaphor as a metaphor for translation', in J. St André (ed.) *Thinking through Translation with Metaphor*, Manchester, UK: St Jerome.

Halliday, M. (1994) *An Introduction to Functional Grammar*, 2nd edn, London: Arnold.

Halverson, S. (1997) 'The concept of equivalence in translation studies: Much ado about something', *Target*, 9: 207–233.

Heimburger, F. (2012) 'Of go-betweens and gatekeepers: Considering disciplinary biases in interpreting history through exemplary metaphors. Military interpreters in the allied coalition during the First World War', in B. Fischer and M. Nisbeth Jensen (eds) *Translation and the Reconfiguration of Power Relations: Revisiting Role and Context of Translation and Interpreting*, Graz, Austria: LIT Verlag.

Hönig, H. G. (1997) 'Positions, power and practice: Functionalist approaches and translation quality assessment', *Current Issues in Language and Society*, 4: 6–34.

Jakobsen, A. L., Jensen, K. T. H. and Mees, I. M. (2007) 'Comparing modalities: Idioms as a case in point', in F. Pöchhacker, A. L. Jakobsen and I. M. Mees (eds) *Interpreting Studies and Beyond: A Tribute to Miriam Shlesinger*, Copenhagen, Denmark: Samfundslitteratur Press.

Kövecses, Z. (2005) *Metaphor in Culture: Universality and Variation*, Cambridge, UK: Cambridge University Press.

Kurth, E.-N. (1995) *Metaphernübersetzung. Dargestellt an grotesken Metaphern im Frühwerk Charles Dickens in der Wiedergabe deutscher Übersetzungen*, Frankfurt am Main, Germany: Peter Lang.

Lakoff, G. and Johnson, M. (1980) *Metaphors We Live By*, Chicago, IL, and London: University of Chicago Press.

Lindquist, Y. (2014) 'Grammatical metaphors in translation: Cookery books as a case in point', in D. R. Miller and E. Monti (eds) *Tradurre Figure / Translating Figurative Language*, Bologna, Italy: Bononia University Press.

Martikainen, K. (1999) 'What happens to metaphorical expressions relating to "comprehension" in the processes and products of translation? A think-aloud protocol study', Pro Gradu Thesis, University of Savonlinna.

Medendorp, L. (2013) 'The power of the periphery: Reassessing spatial metaphors in the ideological positioning of the translator', *TranscUlturAl*, 5: 22–42.

Newmark, P. (1981) *Approaches to Translation*, Oxford, UK: Pergamon.

Oliynyk, T. (2014) 'Metaphor translation methods', *International Journal of Applied Science and Technology*, 4: 123–126.

Pragglejaz Group. (2007) 'MIP: A method for identifying metaphorically used words in discourse', *Metaphor and Symbol*, 22: 1–39.

Prandi, M. (2010) 'Typology of metaphors: Implications for translation', *Mutatis Mutandis*, 3: 304–332.

Rodríguez Márquez, M. (2010) 'Patterns of translation of metaphor in annual reports in American English and Mexican Spanish', unpublished doctoral thesis, University of Surrey.

Schäffner, C. (2004) 'Metaphor and translation: Some implications of a cognitive approach', *Journal of Pragmatics*, 36: 1253–1269.

—— (2014) 'Umbrellas and firewalls: Metaphors in debating the financial crisis from the perspective of translation studies', in D. R. Miller and E. Monti (eds) *Tradurre Figure / Translating Figurative Language*, Bologna, Italy: Bononia University Press.

Schäffner, C. and Shuttleworth, M. (2013) 'Metaphor in translation: Possibilities for process research', *Target*, 25: 93–106.

Schäffner, C., Tcaciuc, L. S. and Tesseur, W. (2014) 'Translation practices in political institutions: A comparison of national, supranational, and non-governmental organisations', *Perspectives: Studies in Translatology*, 22: 493–510.

Shuttleworth, M. (2011) 'Translational behaviour at the frontiers of scientific knowledge: A multilingual investigation into popular science metaphor in translation', *The Translator*, 17: 301–323.

—— (2014a) 'Scientific rich images in translation: A multilingual study', *JoSTrans*, 2: 35–51. Online. Available at: http://www.jostrans.org/issue21/art_shuttleworth.pdf (accessed 15 May 2015).

—— (2014b) 'Translation studies and metaphor studies: Possible paths of interaction between two well-established disciplines', in D. R. Miller and E. Monti (eds) *Tradurre Figure / Translating Figurative Language*, Bologna, Italy: Bononia University Press.

Sjørup, A. C. (2008) 'Metaphor comprehension in translation: Methodological issues in a pilot study', in S. Göpferich, A. L. Jakobsen and I. M. Mees (eds) *Looking at Eyes: Eye-Tracking Studies of Reading and Translation Processing* [Copenhagen Studies in Language 36], Copenhagen, Denmark: Samfundslitteratur.

—— (2011) 'Cognitive effort in metaphor translation: An eye-tracking study', in S. O'Brien (ed.) *Cognitive Explorations of Translation*, London: Continuum.

St André, J. (ed.) (2010) *Thinking through Translation with Metaphor*, Manchester, UK: St Jerome.

Stienstra, N. (1993) *YHWH is the Husband of His People: Analysis of a Biblical Metaphor with Special Reference to Translation*, Kampen, The Netherlands: Kok Pharos.

Störig, H. J. (ed.) (1963) *Das Problem des Übersetzens*, Darmstadt, Germany: Deutsche Buchgemeinschaft.

Tan, Z. (2004) 'Chinese and English metaphors in comparison: As seen from the translator's perspective', in S. Arduini and R. Hodgson (eds) *Similarity and Difference in Translation*, Rimini, Italy: Guaraldi, pp. 219–243.

Tcaciuc, L. S. M. (2012) 'Translation practices at the European Central Bank with reference to metaphors', unpublished PhD thesis, Aston University.

—— (2014) 'The conceptual metaphors "money is a liquid" and "economy is a living organism" in Romanian translations of European Central Bank documents', in D. R. Miller and E. Monti (eds) *Tradurre Figure / Translating Figurative Language*, Bologna, Italy: Bononia University Press.

Tirkkonen-Condit, S. (2001) 'Metaphors in translation processes and products', *Quaderns. Revista de traducció*, 6: 11–15.

—— (2002) 'Metaphoric expressions in translation processes', *Across Languages and Cultures*, 3: 101–116.

Toury, G. (1995) *Descriptive Translation Studies and Beyond*, Amsterdam, The Netherlands, and Philadelphia, PA: John Benjamins.

Tymoczko, M. (2003) 'Ideology and the position of the translator: In what sense is a translator "in between"?', in M. Calzada-Pérez (ed.) *Apropos of Ideology: Translation Studies on Ideology – Ideologies in Translation Studies*, Manchester, UK: St Jerome.

—— (2010) 'Western Metaphorical Discourses Implicit in Translation Studies', in J. St André (ed.) *Thinking through Translation with Metaphor*, Manchester, UK: St Jerome.

Venuti, L. (1995) *The Translator's Invisibility*, London: Routledge.

Vermeer, H. J. (1996) *A Skopos Theory of Translation (Some Arguments For and Against)*, Heidelberg, Germany: TEXTconTEXT.

Wolf, M. (2002) 'Translation activity between culture, society and the individual: Towards a sociology of translation', *CTIS Occasional Papers*, 2: 33–43.

Zahid, A. (2009) 'A model for metaphor translation: Evidence from the holy Quran'. Online. Available at: http://zahid66.arabblogs.com/archive/2009/2/808744.html (accessed 15 May 2015).

18
Metaphor in sign language

Michiko Kaneko and Rachel Sutton-Spence

Introduction

This chapter discusses metaphor in sign language, which has gained increasing interest among cognitive linguists due to its unique way of representing human thought processes through visual language.

Sign languages are natural human languages developed and used by deaf communities around the world. They use the hands, face and body as articulators to convey linguistic meaning through a visual, spatial, and kinetic modality, as opposed to spoken languages, which rely primarily on sound patterns created by the speech articulators. Such fundamental differences in the mode of representation have made sign languages particularly relevant for linguists who are interested in mode-specific and/or mode-independent features of metaphors. While we will mostly focus on metaphor in everyday signing in relation to conceptual metaphor theory (see Chapter 1), the specific question of literary metaphors in sign language is also a fascinating topic that has been addressed in recent years (see Christie and Wilkins 1997; Taub 2001a; Wilcox 2000; Sutton-Spence and Kaneko 2016).

Research to date has shown that the essence of conceptual metaphor theory – the claim that humans understand and express one thing in terms of another – holds true for sign languages. Many conceptual metaphors identified in spoken languages have been observed in sign languages as well. Orientational metaphors (e.g. GOOD IS UP, BAD IS DOWN) and ontological and conduit metaphors (MIND IS A CONTAINER, IDEAS ARE OBJECTS, COMMUNICATION IS SENDING) are well-established in the different sign languages researched to date (Wilbur 1987; Wilcox 2000; Taub 2001b; Roush 2011). It is clear from the presence of these metaphors that deaf people conceptualise the world in a similar way to hearing people because, CMT argues, all humans interact with the physical environment in essentially the same way.[1]

What makes sign language metaphor intriguing, then, is not so much the underlying conceptual metaphors but *how* they are instantiated in the visual modality. Although the major claim of conceptual metaphor theory is that metaphor is not simply a matter of language (as accepted since the age of Greek philosophers) but is deeply rooted in our cognition, applying theories about metaphor as a linguistic phenomenon to signed languages can help us understand their structure better, and applying what we see of how signed languages realise metaphor can contribute to an overall understanding of metaphor.

Two unique features of sign language metaphor are particularly relevant in our discussion here. First of all, *iconicity*, a non-arbitrary correspondence between a linguistic form and its referent, plays a crucial role in sign language metaphor. Although iconicity and metaphor are separate phenomena, the prevailing iconic forms in sign language structure blur the distinction. In almost all examples of metaphors identified in sign language so far, the direct metaphorical representations are made by visually motivated modifications to signs. How metaphors emerge out of iconic forms is crucial in our discussion of sign language metaphors.

The second characteristic of metaphors in sign language is that they mostly occur at *lexical and sub-lexical levels*. English combines existing words to create metaphorical meaning as in 'Life's but a walking shadow' (from Shakespeare's *Macbeth*). On the other hand, sign language metaphors are observed within one sign or even at the smaller level of phonological parameters. Partly, this is because one sign can encapsulate the information that English expresses in a phrase or sentence, as the iconic nature of the handshape, location or movement of the sign can add meaning simultaneously (Johnston and Schembri 2010). These components of the sign play a crucial role in the construction of metaphorical meaning in sign language.

In this chapter, we will first explain the relevant basic formational features of sign language for readers unfamiliar with the structure of sign languages. We then provide an overview of studies in signed metaphors to date, and discuss critical debates in the research of sign language metaphor. This is followed by examples of some current research in this area. The final section provides some conclusions and reflections on future directions.

Formational features of sign languages

Glossing

Signed glosses are conventionally written with small capitals – e.g. BOOK, HOUSE, DOG, EAT, THINK.[2] Sign languages have rich and complex phonological and morphological systems in which a great deal of information is packaged simultaneously rather than sequentially. Thus, in many cases, one sign corresponds to several English words. A hyphen connects these English words in the gloss – e.g. WALK-SLOWLY (which does not consist of two separate signs WALK and SLOWLY but is expressed by inflecting the verb sign WALK with a repeated slow and circular movement) and I-ASK-YOU (the subject and object of the verb are incorporated in the movement from the signer to the recipient).

Parameters

Sign languages are governed by the same fundamental organising principles as spoken languages despite the difference in the way they are organised and their visual motivation. Signs are decomposable into *parameters* underpinning a phonological system (Stokoe 1960). Five parameters are now understood to be important: handshape; location of articulation of the hands; path movement of the hands; palm orientation and non-manual features. For example, a British Sign Language (BSL) sign WHAT (Figure 18.1) consists of the following parameters:

- Handshape[3]: '1' (an extended index finger of the dominant hand with all the other fingers closed)
- Location of the hand: in neutral space
- Movement: small, repeated side to side

Figure 18.1 The BSL sign WHAT.

- Palm orientation: palm facing forward
- Non-manual feature: mouthing derived from the English word 'what' or pursed-lips mouth gesture.

These parameters are *phonemic* in that changing one of them will result in a different sign (minimal pairs). For example, if we produce the above sign with an open '5' handshape instead of the single-finger '1' handshape, it will be a sign NOT-AT-ALL.

Established and productive lexicons

The native lexicon of a sign language can be divided into two types of signs: established and productive signs. Whereas most of the world's dominant spoken languages, including English, rely heavily upon the established lexicon, sign languages use productive signs extensively for visual description of a referent.

Established signs form the language's vocabulary. Their form and meaning are well-established and agreed upon in the community, and thus are not easily changed. Established signs refer to general ideas of a concept, rather than a specific example of that concept. For example, the sign DOG does not specify the size and appearance of a particular dog, but rather refers to what we understand as 'dogs' in general. These signs are frequently iconic but based on prototypical metonyms that have become conventionalised and the iconicity has degenerated over time so that its meaning is not immediately transparent (Figure 18.2a shows a widely used BSL sign for 'dog', based on the dog's paws). The signers' intention when using established signs is non-illustrative (Cuxac and Sallandre 2007), such that they do not deliberately set out to create a visual image, even if the sign might be perceived as being one.

Productive signs are new signs created ad hoc to describe the appearance, movements and locations of a particular referent or scene. Unlike established signs, they do not identify the

Figure 18.2 (a) an established sign for DOG in BSL; (b) productive sign showing the dog enthusiastically wagging its tail at a human beside it; (c) productive sign showing the dog running.

general concept and it is the signer's intention to provide an illustrative representation and image by describing specific features of an individual referent. In case of a dog, signers can present details about a *particular* dog (their own dog, a dog they saw on the way to work one morning, and so on) by describing the outline of its body, its size, the length of its legs and tail, the shape of its ears, how they walk and run, and so on. While speakers of English would have to use a string of established words to describe its appearance, signers have a more direct means of producing clear visual descriptions of the referents (Figures 18.2b and 18.2c show productive signs describing a dog's behaviour).[4]

Classifiers

Productive signs make use of signed elements that are frequently termed *classifiers* in sign linguistics research. Classifiers use parameters to provide an accurate visual description of the appearance, movement and location of the referent. The handshape used in a classifier construction 'classifies' referents according to their physical appearance (for example, an open flat handshape represents flat objects, whereas a closed fist represents spherical objects), although the precise nature of signed classifiers and their linguistic status has been the object of active discussion among sign linguists (see Schembri 2003 for a summary). For the purpose of our discussion of signed metaphor, we will provide a simplified account of three types of classifiers:

Handling classifiers show how we handle objects. The handshape and movement of the signer's hand represent the hand of a person manipulating or touching an object. Examples are HOLD-A-NEEDLE, CARRY-A-BIG-BOX, and CUDDLE-A-CAT. The handshape will reflect the size and shape of the referent. Signers are likely to use an 'F' handshape, with the finger and thumb in a precision grip, in HOLD-A-NEEDLE or HAND-OVER-A-FLOWER (because they involve handling something fine) and use a slightly bent '5' handshape in CARRY-A-BIG-BOX and HAND-OVER-A-SOCCER-BALL (because they involve handling something large). This type of classifier is relevant in the discussion of ontological metaphors as signers literally 'handle' many abstract concepts (including thoughts and emotions) as if they were objects that can be manipulated.

Entity classifiers show an object's movement or location by using the entire hand as the surrogate of the object. For example, a flat handshape facing down can represent a car, and the signer can move it around in the signing space to show its location and path of movement.

It is essential to note that classifiers are highly *context-dependent*. A flat handshape can represent any flat object – a car, a wall, a flag or a sheet of paper – depending on the context. Similarly, an extended index finger can represent *any* long thin object (a person, a pencil, an antenna), and a closed fist can represent any spherical object (a planet, a rock, a head).

Many signed metaphors are represented through entity classifiers. For example, the American Sign Language (ASL) sign THINK-PENETRATE ('to get one's point across'), used as an example of metaphor by Wilcox (2000) and Taub (2001b), is extended from the iconic representation of a long thin object such as a drill bit (representing the idea or thought) piercing through a flat wall (representing an obstacle in communication). Both the long thin object (the index finger of the dominant hand) and the flat wall (the non-dominant hand) are examples of entity classifiers.

Size and Shape Specifiers (SASS) use the hand to trace the outline of the referent. They can trace the surface of the referent (such as rolling mountains), emphasise the depth and width of the referent (a thin tree trunk will be traced differently from a thick tree trunk), or trace the external shape of the object such as the frame of a mirror.

The SASS classifier can be used metaphorically as well. When describing someone who knows a lot, the signer may specify the invisible outline of that person's knowledge in the same manner as describing a thick tree trunk (KNOWLEDGE IS SUBSTANCE).

Semiotic basis for signs

The selection of elements that create the form of a sign is either *arbitrary* or *motivated* – and in the case of the latter, it can be motivated through iconicity, metonymy or metaphor, or selected by conventional association.

All sign languages studied so far use *arbitrary* signs where there is no immediately obvious link between the linguistic form and the referent. The above-mentioned BSL sign WHAT is an example of arbitrary sign – the '1' handshape moving repeatedly from side to side has no obvious motivating link with the meaning of 'what'.

However, sign languages also exhibit a large number of *iconic* signs. Taub (2001b) defines iconicity as follows:

> In iconic items, some aspect of the item's physical form (shape, sound, temporal structure, etc.) resembles a concrete sensory image. That is, a linguistic item that involves only iconicity can represent only a concrete, physical referent.
>
> *Taub 2001b: 20*

For example, the English onomatopoeic word 'hiss' resembles the actual sound snakes make (sound–sound correspondence), while the BSL sign SNAKE represents the fangs striking forward (visual–visual correspondence). However, although there are many possible iconic choices for a referent, the form which is actually used is determined by the community – and thus different sign languages have different forms. For example, the sign for SNAKE in Japanese Sign Language does not depict the fangs but focuses more on the movement of the snake. As Taub (2012: 388) has phrased it, '[i]conicity motivates but does not determine the form of iconic signs'.

Some early researchers of sign languages tried to downplay the pervasive presence of iconicity in sign languages, emphasising instead the more arbitrary elements, perhaps for fear that acknowledging iconicity would reinforce misconceptions that sign languages cannot express abstract thoughts. However, over the last few decades, iconicity has become the centre of the discussion of sign linguistics as its indispensable role in the structure of sign language is recognised (Taub 2012).

Almost every iconic established sign is *metonymic* in some way, as a part of the referent stands for the whole. In many sign languages, for example, the sign CAT represents the whiskers of the cat, and the sign CAR represents the act of holding the steering wheel.

While iconicity is based on *physical* resemblance between the form and the referent, *metaphor* is based on the *conceptual* resemblance between two ideas, involving two distinct semantic domains (Lakoff and Turner 1989; Hiraga 2005). Usually one of the domains, the source domain, is more concrete and is used to facilitate our understanding of the target domain, which is more abstract and difficult to grasp. In the metaphor LIFE IS A JOURNEY, the source domain is a physical journey, which is used to facilitate our understanding of the abstract notion of how we live our 'life' (the target domain).

There are many signs whose forms are metaphorically motivated. For example, in BSL the sign REMEMBER takes the form of holding an object in the mind, whereas FORGET imitates the act of letting go of an object from the head. They both utilise the metaphor of THE MIND IS A CONTAINER and IDEAS ARE OBJECTS.

Conventional association means that there is no natural (physical) link between the form and the meaning. Instead, the speakers (signers) of the community agree to make a systematic association between certain forms and what they refer to. For example, the ASL sign SHEEP is represented by the act of cutting off the sheep's fleece with shears while the BSL sign SHEEP is represented by the curling shape of a ram's horns. Both signs are based on prototypical metonyms, but whereas the BSL SHEEP depicts the physical feature of the referent itself, the ASL SHEEP is based on the action *associated* with sheep shearing (and thus may not be immediately transparent in communities where the sheep industry is not common).

Overview of research on signed metaphor to date

Early research on sign language metaphors (1980–1990s)

The initial work on sign language metaphor developed as part of the earlier exploration of sign language lexicons in the 1980s–1990s, and analysis was threefold: researchers focused on the role of metaphor in the organisation of 'sign families', as a semiotic basis for lexical signs, and in meaning extension.

First of all, researchers suggested that signs can be grouped together ('sign families') based on certain meanings associated with the handshapes, movements, directions or locations, and some of these associations can be regarded as metaphoric. For example, in many sign languages, the location on the temple is used in a group of signs whose meaning is related to mental activities (such as THINK, KNOW, REMEMBER, UNDERSTAND), while a group of signs made on the chest often refer to emotion (FEEL, LIKE, LOVE, HATE, ENJOY). Frishberg and Gough (1973) noted that the closed-fist handshape (with an extended thumb) is often used in signs with negative meaning in ASL. Although they did not explore this metaphorical link in detail, it is related to a later claim that the closed handshape, as opposed to open handshape, may denote negative meaning (Sutton-Spence 2005). This approach to regard metaphors as organisers of sign families is still popular in recent works on metaphor in sign language lexicons (see Cabeza-Pereiro 2014).

Other studies of signed metaphor in this period focused on its role as a semiotic basis for the sign lexicon (see Boyes Braem 1981 for ASL, Brennan 1990 for BSL, and Bouvet 1997 for French Sign Language). During this period, ideas of metaphor and iconicity were often conflated. Boyes Braem (1981), for example, provides an extensive analysis of handshape features which instantiate what she calls 'visual metaphor'. However, 'visual metaphor' here refers not only to metaphorical association of certain handshapes, but also to other types of semiotic basis (such as iconicity, metonymy, conventional association). In other words, any motivation between an underlying concept and the selected surface form is termed as 'metaphorical'. Similarly, Brennan (1990) provided an extensive analysis of BSL morphology, in which she used the term 'metaphorical' for iconic motivation behind the formation of a sign. For example, she described the BSL sign GRASS as a 'metaphor' in that one set of upright long thin objects (blades of grass) is represented by another set of upright thin objects (fingers). In current research, this is seen as a purely iconic form.

This conflation of the two terms is because both iconicity and metaphor represent one object in terms of another, their only difference being 'the concrete or abstract nature of the represented object' (Cabeza-Pereiro 2014: 305). There are very few examples of iconic words in spoken languages, and thus mainstream linguistic theories in the 1980s were not equipped to make finer distinctions between different types of symbolic associations between form and meaning.

Finally, several researchers have used the notion of 'metaphorical extension' (based on more concrete/iconic signs) from the beginning of metaphor studies in sign languages. Gee and Kegl (1982) compare abstract verbs of emotion, perception and cognition with concrete verbs of location and direction, and claim that the former are formed by metaphorically extending the latter. For example, the abstract verb IMPRESS in ASL has more or less the identical form of the sign LETTER which represents the act of putting a stamp on the envelope. The concrete notion of 'fixing something on a flat surface' is literally used in the case of LETTER and is metaphorically extended in the case of IMPRESS (in which the flat surface represents a human mind).

Woll (1985) also briefly discussed metaphorical extensions in BSL. She distinguished metaphorical extensions based on existing iconic signs (such as ENOUGH and FED-UP, both of which are based on the sign FULL which literally refers to 'my stomach is full'), and those based on iconic forms which do not derive from existing signs (such as the sign CONCENTRATE, which is based on the image of blocking unnecessary visual input from the side to the eyes, although there is no existing sign NO-VISION-FROM-SIDE in BSL). This allows us to explore metaphoric extension regardless of whether or not the original iconic forms exist as established signs. This becomes relevant in our later discussion of the interplay of iconicity and metaphor, as they suggest a strong motivation, or a necessity, for signed metaphors to develop out of iconic forms.

Wilbur (1987) and Wilcox (2000)

These earlier studies on metaphor confirmed the ubiquity of metaphorical operation in sign languages, but they were not based on any particular theoretical framework. The study by Wilbur (1987) was the first major systematic analysis of metaphor based on a cognitive linguistic framework, followed by Wilcox's (2000) in-depth analysis of signed metaphors. Both researchers explored three types of metaphors identified by Lakoff and Johnson (1980): orientational, ontological and structural metaphors. Although they looked at American Sign Language, their essential arguments can be applied to other sign languages.

Orientational metaphors use directions as the source of metaphors. Both Wilbur and Wilcox found many examples of these in ASL – noting that 'ASL uses space in a variety of ways to carry information, both literal and metaphorical' (Wilbur 1987: 173).

Up-down direction is the most common source of this type of metaphor, as in HAPPY IS UP, SAD IS DOWN (expressed in English with 'She perked up', 'I'm very depressed'), EMOTIONAL IS UP, CALM IS DOWN ('I felt fired up', 'Please calm down'). Wilbur presented a variety of examples, many of which are formational opposites, such as HAPPY, RICH and SUCCESS with an upward movement, and SAD, POOR and FAIL with a downward movement (HAPPY/POSITIVE IS UP, SAD/NEGATIVE IS DOWN). Wilbur also found that not only the direction of the movement but also the palm orientation can be associated with this up-down metaphor, as in the pair GOOD (with the palm facing up) and BAD (with the palm facing down).

Front-back direction is often associated with the notion of time. For speakers of many languages, the orientational metaphor of FUTURE IS AHEAD, PAST IS BEHIND is well-established ('Let's put this *behind us* and *move forward*'). Wilbur and Wilcox identified that the association of front-back direction with temporal information is prominent in ASL. Signs that denote future tend to move forward (e.g. FUTURE, TOMORROW, NEXT-WEEK, NEXT-YEAR) and signs that denote past move backward (e.g. PAST, HISTORY, YESTERDAY, LAST-WEEK, LAST-YEAR).

Ontological metaphors treat abstract ideas, events and states as tangible objects which we can manipulate (e.g. 'I didn't *grasp* what he said'). Wilbur illustrates this using an ASL sign CLEVER, which is made with a 'C' handshape at the forehead. This handshape represents a sort of a container, so this sign literally means 'holding something (=information, knowledge) in the mind' (MIND IS A CONTAINER, IDEAS ARE OBJECTS). Collapsing of this container handshape, on the other hand, indicates 'a momentary lapse in thought or an incomplete understanding of a topic' (ibid.: 177).

Wilcox analysed IDEAS ARE OBJECTS in great depth, showing a complex semantic network of metaphorical mappings within this metaphor. Through the use of entity classifiers (see above), ideas can be represented as objects which are subject to physical force such as gravity (thus can 'fall out' of one's head). They can also be grasped, manipulated or carefully selected as if they were tangible objects, using handling classifiers (such as INFORM, which resembles the act of passing a flat object from the signer's mind to the recipient's mind).

Structural metaphors use one conceptual domain systematically in order to explore another. They are called 'structural' because the mapping between these two domains is not a single, one-to-one correspondence (as in the case of preceding types) but multiple elements and their structure are systematically mapped. In the case of a common structural metaphor LOVE IS A JOURNEY, lovers are mapped onto travellers, the development of a relationship is seen as a journey, problems in a relationship are explained in terms of obstacles and so on.

According to Wilbur, identifying structural metaphors in ASL was 'the hardest search' (ibid.: 179). Common structural metaphors in English identified by Lakoff and Johnson (1980) (such as LIFE IS A JOURNEY, IDEAS ARE FOOD) can be *translated* into ASL and understood by deaf signers, but they do not seem to occur spontaneously in ASL. Wilbur did not discuss why this is the case, but it may highlight an interesting difference between metaphors in spoken and signed languages, which we will return to later.

Wilcox was more successful in identifying structural metaphors in ASL. Although she also did not find examples of common English metaphors (such as LIFE IS A JOURNEY), she identified a metaphor THOUGHT IS A JOURNEY in ASL.[5] Logic and the process of thinking are perceived as following a unidirectional path along time. ASL has signs such as OFF-THE-SUBJECT in which 'the index finger makes a dramatic 90-degree shift from a front-moving path' (101) to show one's thought is (literally) 'off the track'. Other examples she gives are BACK-UP (go back to the previous point and explain again) and LEAP-AHEAD (jump to the conclusion), which make use of the backward/forward movement in front of the body.

Taub (2001b)

Taub (2001b) identified a range of conceptual metaphors in American Sign Language, but her approach is driven by the need to explain the close relationship between metaphor and iconicity. Inspired by cognitive linguistic theories, Taub states that iconicity 'is not an objective relationship between image and referent; rather, it is a relationship between our mental models of image and referent' (19). She proposes the *analogue building model* for iconicity and the *double-mapping model* for metaphor in sign language. Most importantly, she points out that both iconic and metaphorical mappings need to preserve their structure.

Her analogue building model (for iconic signs) consists of the following three stages:

1. *image selection* of a mental image that is associated with the original concept;
2. *schematisation* of essential features;
3. *encoding* of the schema using the appropriate parts of the sign language.

Taub explains her model using the example of an ASL sign TREE (the same sign is used in many sign languages and BSL has borrowed it from ASL – see Figure 18.3). The first stage, image selection, selects a prototypical sensory image of a tree (for TREE, a visual image of a tree that consists of the trunk, spreading branches, and the ground in which it is rooted). In the second stage of schematisation, the essential features of the visual image are extracted to form a simplified framework that can be represented in a sign language. In her example of TREE, only three fundamental features are selected: a long vertical shape representing the trunk, spreading branches, and a flat surface. Finally, at the encoding stage, appropriate parts of sign languages are chosen to represent the schematised elements: the upright forearm for the trunk, open palm and fingers for spreading branches, and the horizontal forearm of the signer's non-dominant hand for the flat surface. The possible building blocks for encoding are language-specific, and thus different sign languages may choose to select/schematise/encode the image of tree differently. For example, Chinese Sign Language chooses to schematise the outline of the trunk and not the branches or the ground.

Figure 18.3 The sign TREE.

Taub further claims that metaphorical signs also go through these three stages like iconic signs, but there is an additional stage at the beginning in which an abstract target concept is mapped onto a concrete source concept (i.e. it is a conceptual mapping). Once this mapping is done, the source concept undergoes the above-mentioned analogue building process for iconic items. In other words, metaphors in sign languages undergo *a double mapping process*: metaphorical (conceptual) mapping and iconic mapping.

Taub uses the example of an ASL sign THINK-PENETRATE ('to get one's point across'), which involves the idea of an object transferred, as part of a common metaphor COMMUNICATION IS SENDING. In the process of forming this sign, the abstract concept of successful communication (an utterance understood by the addressee) is first mapped onto a concrete concept of successful sending of an object (the object manages to get through a physical barrier). Then this concrete concept is given an appropriate image, schematised, and encoded into ASL. The last encoding stage involves encoding of the object as the index finger, the barrier as the palm of the non-dominant hand (which looks like a wall), and the penetrating movement as the index finger gets through between the fingers of the non-dominant hand.

In summary, Taub explains that both iconicity and metaphor require a mapping between our mental image and the linguistic form. Metaphor requires an extra mapping from abstract concept to concrete concept, before going through the iconic mapping and being assigned a linguistic form. This is in sharp contrast to spoken languages, in which, according to Conceptual Metaphor Theory, metaphorical mapping takes place primarily at the conceptual level, not at the linguistic level, as metaphorical expressions are built on a single mapping between abstract and concrete concepts.

Critical issues, debates, and controversies

Iconicity and metaphor

As Taub's research clearly suggests, iconicity plays a significant role in metaphorical constructions in sign languages. In spoken languages, the impact of iconicity on metaphorical expressions has not been discussed widely, due to the fact that the number of iconic expressions at the vocabulary level in most spoken languages is seen to be limited. However, sign languages display a rich and complex relationship between iconicity and metaphor, and how metaphorical mapping can be *constrained* or *motivated* by iconic forms is one of the biggest debates in the research of sign language metaphor.

Meir (2010), in her attempt to explain why some conceptual metaphors common in spoken languages cannot be expressed in sign languages, proposes a *double-mapping constraint* in metaphorical extension in sign languages, based on Taub's double-mapping mechanism.

> The Double-Mapping Constraint: A metaphorical mapping of an iconic form should preserve the structural correspondences of the iconic mapping. Double-mapping should be structure-preserving.
>
> *Meir 2010: 18*

When signs are formed based on iconic mapping, any further mapping (metaphorical mapping) needs to preserve the structure that corresponds to the iconic mapping. When this is not possible, the metaphorical extension of iconic form will be blocked. This explains why some conceptual metaphors common in spoken languages cannot be meaningfully expressed iconically in sign languages while others can.

Metaphor in sign language

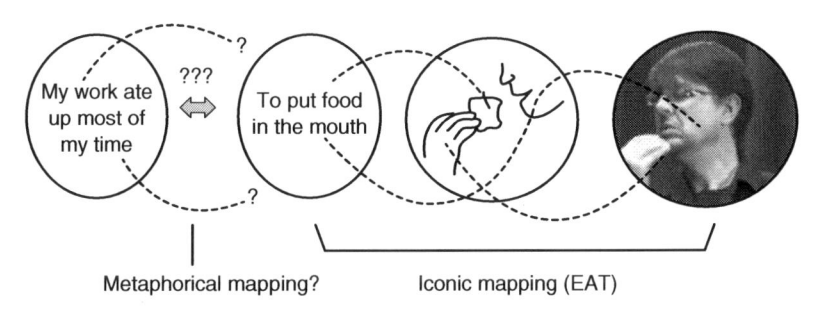

Figure 18.4 Metaphorical and iconic mappings for the sign EAT.

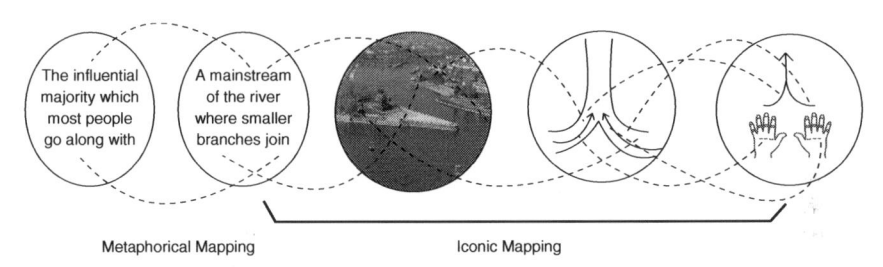

Figure 18.5 Metaphorical and iconic mappings for the sign MAINSTREAM.

For example, the sign EAT in many sign languages cannot express an abstract notion of consumption as in the English sentence 'My work ate up most of my time'. This is because the sign EAT has a set of structural correspondences (the hand represents the holding of a piece of food; its movement represents the act of putting the food into the mouth; the mouth represents the mouth of the person who is eating) which cannot be preserved in the abstract notion of consumption.[6] Consumption is entailed as the result of EAT, but it has no structural elements that correspond to the details in the original iconic mapping (Figure 18.4).

There are examples in which iconic mapping allows further metaphorical extension. The sign MAINSTREAM (commonly used in many deaf communities to specifically refer to 'mainstream' schools in which deaf children are educated together with hearing children) represents small branches of the river joining together to become the mainstream. The target meaning ('an influential majority with which most people go along') has corresponding elements with the original iconic form (hands = small branches of the river = different groups of people, hands joining together = branches joining to become a main river = people joining the most influential group), allowing the form of this sign to be metaphorically extended (Figure 18.5).

Iconicity may restrict certain metaphorical extensions which are possible in spoken languages. However, it also allows many unexpected liaisons of two concepts based on visual iconicity, especially in creative sign language (poetry, jokes, and storytelling). Kaneko and Sutton-Spence (2012) explore a wide range of creative signing to identify various examples in which iconic forms motivate or facilitate metaphorical interpretation. For example, in a Christmas story told in BSL by Richard Carter, Father Christmas' reindeer can 'talk' (sign) using his antlers as his 'hands' because the antlers *look like* hands, which motivates the personification of the reindeer into a signing person (Figure 18.6, modelled here by Tim Northam). Such examples are possible and lead to a poetic effect because they are motivated by iconicity, and they only make sense in sign languages.

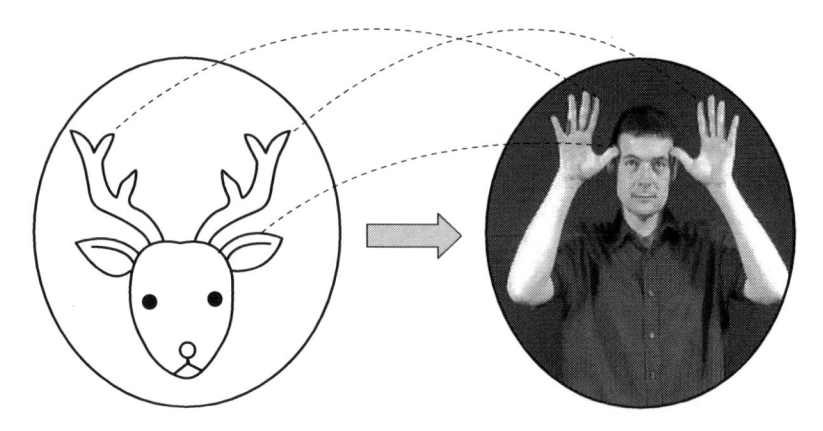

Figure 18.6 The sign REINDEER.

The way sign language metaphors can be constrained or motivated by iconicity may explain part of the reason why sign languages have a different set of conceptual metaphors to those found in spoken languages. Many of these structural metaphors in English, such as TIME IS MONEY and IDEAS ARE FOOD, are based on the non-visual notion of the source domain. The TIME IS MONEY metaphor is based on the notion that money can be spent, saved or wasted, which is extended to describe our experience with time. The metaphor is not based on the physical aspect of money – what it looks like or how it is physically manipulated. Similarly, the IDEAS ARE FOOD metaphor is not based on the act of putting the food into the mouth, but is extended on the less-concrete notion of consumption and nutrition. In other words, aspects of the source domain highlighted in these metaphors do not have elements that can be mapped onto the iconic elements in the source sign (MONEY and FOOD).

Metaphor at sub-lexical and discourse level

One of the current debates in the study of sign language metaphor is the linguistic level at which metaphorical analysis should take place. The majority of the studies so far (Wilbur 1987; Wilcox 2000; Taub 2001b; Meir 2010) have exclusively dealt with metaphor at a *lexical* level. Most examples are single signs in the established lexicon, which have a clear form and boundary, and have one core meaning regardless of the context in which they are used.

Creative signing within narratives and conversations, however, is frequently characterised by a mixture of these established signs and sections of *productive* signs, which cannot be separated into distinct signs, and whose metaphorical interpretation is context-dependent. For example, a signer may produce a morphologically complex sign, in which both index fingers are placed side by side, and then move forward together (away from the body) in a swaying movement. This poses several challenges to a lexical approach to metaphor. First of all, instead of building up metaphorical meaning based on distinct lexical items, this sign expresses multiple layers of information simultaneously. Second, the meaning of this sign depends on the context and the intent of the signer. It can be a purely iconic form denoting two people walking side by side along a winding road. Or it can be a metaphor referring to a pair of lovers or friends, who, despite difficulties, continue to stay together. The way the two index fingers are held close to each other represents the fact that they stick together (PHYSICAL PROXIMITY IS EMOTIONAL PROXIMITY). The movement forward is understood as their continuing relationship (LIFE IS A

JOURNEY). The difficulties they experience in their relationship may be represented by the non-smooth path (also based on LIFE IS A JOURNEY). The same expression can be a completely different metaphor in a completely different context – for example, it may be a personified representation of democracy and justice slowly and sadly walking away from a country where nobody recognises them anymore. In order to understand such potential metaphorical interpretations, analysis needs to be made at the sub-lexical level, taking into consideration metaphor at the discourse level.

Metaphor at the sub-lexical level refers to a symbolic meaning associated with each sub-lexical (phonological) parameter even before they are combined into a sign. For example, metaphorical interpretation may occur with 'emotional effects commonly associated with particular handshapes' (Sutton-Spence 2005: 26). Physical configuration of handshapes, such as open/closed, sharp/non-sharp, substantial /non-substantial, may possess a symbolic value per se. For example, open plain handshapes tend to create a more positive impression in the mind of the viewer than closed handshapes (GOOD IS OPEN, BAD IS CLOSED). Straight fingers in open handshapes are also contrasted with 'bent' fingers, which appear to be more 'tense' and negative (Kaneko 2011). Movement and location are tied with spatial metaphors: i.e. upward movement and upper location may be construed as positive (GOOD IS UP), and physical proximity (locations on or close to the body and the movement toward the body) may symbolise emotional proximity.

Kaneko and Sutton-Spence (2012) claim that such symbolic power of parameters is often dormant and is activated only when they are put into a particular context. They also point out that the same symbolic aspect of a parameter can be interpreted very differently depending on the context. While open handshapes are usually more positive than closed handshapes, Kaneko and Sutton-Spence (2012) noted one story in which closed fists are used to refer to positive concepts. Fists, which iconically represent a firm grip (as in GRAB), are used as a symbol of determination, solidarity and power in this particular story, whereas an open handshape represents helplessness and weakness.

This suggests the importance of analysing metaphor both at micro (sub-lexical) level and macro (discourse) level. Parameters are potential building blocks for metaphorical interpretation, while a discourse often imposes an overall metaphorical meaning.

Examples of current research

Recent studies on signed metaphor shift their unit of analysis from the lexical to the narrative level. One such study, the *Metaphor in Creative Sign Language* project (University of Bristol, 2009–2012), focuses on metaphor in less spontaneous, but more artistic narratives. This project is characterised by the following three features (Kaneko and Sutton-Spence 2012):

1. Instead of focusing on individual signs in the established lexicon, it accommodates the manifestation of metaphor in productive signs at various levels – especially highlighting the importance of sub-lexical metaphors.
2. Instead of treating metaphors as isolated and de-contextualised phenomena, it foregrounds the context as the essential force in creating metaphorical meaning. It is claimed that metaphorical interpretation is not inherent in signs, but is generated by each context and the intent of the signer.
3. Instead of highlighting what is essentially a translation issue between spoken languages and sign languages, which is especially the case for Meir (2010), it attempts to approach creative metaphors in sign language per se.

| SNAKE | HOLD-APPLE | WORM-CRAWLING |

Figure 18.7 The signs with bent fingers in Wim Emmerik's *Garden of Eden*.

For example, Kaneko and Sutton-Spence (2012) demonstrated that the manipulation of handshape is a powerful tool in creating metaphoric value in creative discourse. As we mentioned earlier, some handshapes have inherent semantic values, such as open handshapes can be more positive than closed handshapes; or bent fingers (claws at joints) may arouse more negative feelings than straight fingers. However, such inherent metaphorical values are 'dormant' in everyday signing. When placed into a poetic context (with the illustrative intention of the signer), they are *reactivated* and *become* metaphorical.

A brief example will highlight our point. A poem in Sign Language of the Netherlands, titled *Garden of Eden*,[7] explores the theme of lost paradise. It does not explicitly state any particular view or emotion, but through the frequent use of signs with claws at joints (such as SNAKE, APPLE, and WORM-CRAWLING), it successfully produces a negative impression in the poem (Figure 18.7). Such subtle nuance cannot be captured if we only look at individual signs. We need to see smaller building blocks that constitute metaphorical meaning. Moreover, such metaphorical meaning is not inherent in the form of the signs. Signs such as APPLE are perfectly ordinary signs used widely in everyday conversations without negative connotation. Their form *becomes* metaphorical when they are situated in a particular context. Such creation of metaphorical interpretation through the visual form of parameters is unique in sign language, and is often hard to translate into a spoken language.

Conclusion and future directions

This chapter has explored how metaphors manifest themselves in the visual modality of sign languages. A number of seminal works have confirmed the presence of common conceptual metaphors identified in spoken languages in the lexicon of sign languages. Orientational (spatial) metaphors occur extensively, as sign languages incorporate directions as part of their formational features. Ontological metaphors are also common in sign languages because they can manipulate abstract concepts through handling and entity classifiers.

We have identified two critical issues in the research on sign language metaphor: how iconicity interferes with metaphorical operation, and how sub-lexical metaphors interact with the larger discourse force in creating metaphorical understanding.

Research on sign language metaphor has a short history, and there are many potential areas for future research. First, although a variety of sign languages have been used in exploring underlying conceptual metaphors, few studies have provided direct comparisons of metaphoric manifestation between two or more sign languages (but see Cabeza-Pereiro 2014). It will be interesting to see whether there are language-specific features of metaphor in different sign languages, be it at conceptual level or at purely linguistic level.

Second, research on sign language metaphor should work closely with how it can be seen as analogous to metaphor in gestures (Cienki and Müller 2008). Both sign language and gestures exhibit the direct way of representing how we conceptualise the world through the visual modality. Together they can provide holistic and multimodal insight into how metaphor contributes to the creation of meaning in human communication.

Finally, with an increasing interest in cognitive linguistics toward metonymy, it will become essential to explore the relationship between metaphor and metonymy in sign languages. Metonymy is the basis for a large number of established signs and grammatical structures of sign languages. Together with metaphor, it contributes to an understanding of how our cognitive structures and conceptualisations derive from our everyday experience of the world.

Acknowledgements

We thank Paul Scott, Richard Carter and Tim Northam for their kind permission to use their images. Those by Paul Scott and Richard Carter were produced as part of the *Metaphor in Creative Sign Language* research project, funded by the Arts and Humanities Research Council at the University of Bristol (AH/G011672/1) between 2009 and 2012. Images of Wim Emmerik are from the Language Archive of European Community Heritage Online, openly available for educational use. Image of the confluence of the Rhine and the Mosel at Koblenz by Holger Weinandt: Creative commons licence CC BY-SA 3.0, from https://commons.wikimedia.org/wiki/File:Koblenz_im_Buga-Jahr_2011_-_Deutsches_Eck_01.jpg. Martin Haswell provided invaluable technical assistance.

Notes

1 The only difference is the presence or absence of the sense of hearing, but we know of no study to show how this impacts on the way deaf people conceptualise the world through metaphor.
2 To distinguish these from conceptual domains and conceptual metaphors (which are also written in small capitals in some chapters in this book), we will use normal capitals for the latter in this chapter.
3 The list of handshapes used in this chapter and their symbols can be found in the appendix.
4 A BSL poem 'Our Dumb Friends' by Dorothy Miles describes dogs of various size and shapes using a range of productive signs. This poem is accessible at https://youtu.be/23Pf1rjxqZE.
5 According to Wilcox (2000), while this THOUGHT IS A JOURNEY metaphor is common in ASL, a similar metaphor SPEECH EXCHANGE IS A SHARED JOURNEY does not seem to occur. Common expressions in English, such as 'I'm lost', 'Are you following me?' and 'I'm with you' are understood only in their literal sense.
6 This is perhaps a translation issue between the word 'eat' and the sign EAT. Strictly speaking, there is no sign that corresponds to the English word 'eat'. There is a sign meaning 'a human puts food in the mouth' which is conventionally glossed as EAT (a different sign would be used to illustrate how dogs, horses or birds take in food, as their manners of eating will be very different from how humans eat). There is another sign which means 'make something smaller by removing it bit by bit' which could anthropomorphise the time (and allow it to be reduced in size), but it is not the sign EAT.
7 Crasborn, O., E. van der Kooij, A., Nonhebel and W. Emmerik (2004) *ECHO Data Set for Sign Language of the Netherlands (NGT)*. Department of Linguistics, Radboud University Nijmegen. http://www.let.ru.nl/sign-lang/echo.

Further reading

O'Brien, J. (1999) 'Metaphoricity in the signs of American Sign Language', *Metaphor and Symbol*, 14(3): 159–177.

Sutton-Spence, R. (2005) *Analysing Sign Language Poetry*, Basingstoke, UK: Palgrave Macmillan.

—— (2010) 'Spatial metaphor and expressions of identity in sign language poetry', *Metaphorik.de*, 19: 1–40.

Wilcox, S. and Morford, J. (2007) 'Empirical methods in signed language research', in M. Gonzalez-Marquez, I. Mittelberg, S. Coulson and M. J. Spivey (eds) *Methods in Cognitive Linguistics*, Amsterdam, The Netherlands: John Benjamins.

References

Bouvet, D. (1997) *Le corps et la métaphore dans les langues gestuelles: à la recherche des modes de production des signes*, Paris: L'Harmattan.

Boyes Braem, P. (1981) *Features of the Handshape in American Sign Language*, unpublished doctoral dissertation, University of California.

Brennan, M. (1990) *Word Formation in British Sign Language*, Stockholm, Sweden: University of Stockholm.

Cabeza-Pereiro, C. (2014) 'Metaphor and lexicon in sign languages: Analysis of the hand opening articulation in LSE and BSL', *Sign Language Studies*, 14(3): 1–25.

Cienki, A. and Müller, C. (2008) *Metaphor and Gesture*, Amsterdam, The Netherlands: John Benjamins.

Christie, K. and Wilkins, D. (1997) 'A feast for the eyes: ASL Literacy and ASL Literature', *Journal of Deaf Studies and Deaf Education*, 2: 57–59.

Cuxac, C. and Sallandre, M. A. (2007) 'Iconicity and arbitrariness in French sign language: Highly iconic structures, degenerated iconicity and diagrammatic iconicity', in E. Pizzuto, P. Pietrandrea and R. Simone (eds) *Verbal and Signed Languages: Comparing Structures, Constructs and Methodologies*, Berlin, Germany: Mouton de Gruyter.

Frishberg, N. and Gough, B. (1973) *Morphology in American Sign Language*, La Jolla, CA: Salk Institute for Biological Studies.

Gee, J. and Kegl, J. (1982) 'Semantic perspicuity and the locative hypothesis: Implications for acquisition', *Journal of Education*, 3: 185–209.

Hiraga, M. (2005) *Metaphor and Iconicity: A Cognitive Approach to Analysing Texts*, Basingstoke, UK: Palgrave Macmillan.

Johnston, T. and Schembri, A. (2010) 'Variation, lexicalization and grammaticalization in signed languages', *Langage et société*, 1(131): 19–35.

Kaneko, M. (2011) 'Alliteration in sign language poetry', in J. Roper (ed.) *Alliteration in Culture*, Basingstoke, UK: Palgrave Macmillan.

Kaneko, M. and Sutton-Spence R. (2012) 'Iconicity and metaphor in sign language poetry', *Metaphor and Symbol*, 27: 107–130.

Lakoff, G. and Johnson, M. (1980) *Metaphors We Live By*, Chicago, IL: University of Chicago Press.

Lakoff, G. and Turner M. (1989) *More Than Cool Reason: A Field Guide to Poetic Metaphor*, Chicago, IL: University of Chicago Press.

Meir, I. (2010) 'Iconicity and metaphor: Constraints on metaphorical extension of iconic forms', *Language*, 86(4): 865–896.

Roush, D. (2011) 'Language between bodies: A cognitive approach to understanding linguistic politeness in American Sign Language', *Sign Language Studies*, 11(3): 329–374.

Schembri, A. (2003) 'Rethinking "classifiers" in signed languages', in K. Emmorey (ed.) *Perspectives on Classifier Constructions in Sign Languages*, Mahwah, NJ: Lawrence Erlbaum Associates.

Stokoe, W. C. (1960) 'Sign language structure: An outline of the visual communication systems of the American Deaf', *Studies in Linguistics: Occasional papers (No. 8)*, Buffalo, NY: University of Buffalo.

Sutton-Spence, R. (2005) *Analysing Sign Language Poetry*, Basingstoke, UK: Palgrave Macmillan.

Sutton-Spence, R. and Kaneko, M. (2016) *Introducing Sign Language Literature: Folklore and Creativity,* Basingstoke, UK: Palgrave Press.

Taub, S. (2001a) 'Complex superposition of metaphors in an ASL poem', in V. Dively, M. Metzger, S. Taub and A. M. Baer (eds) *Signed Languages: Discoveries from International Research,* Washington DC: Gallaudet University Press.

—— (2001b) *Language From the Body: Iconicity and Metaphor in American Sign Language,* Cambridge: Cambridge University Press.

—— (2012) 'Iconicity and metaphors', in R. Pfau, M. Steinbach and B. Woll (eds) *Sign Language: An International Handbook (Handbooks of Linguistics and Communication Science 37),* Berlin, Germany: Mouton de Gruyter.

Wilbur, R. (1987) *American Sign Language: Linguistic and Applied Dimensions,* Boston, MA: College-Hill Press.

Wilcox, P. P. (2000) *Metaphor in American Sign Language,* Washington, DC: Gallaudet University Press.

Woll, B. (1985) 'Visual imagery and metaphor in British Sign Language', in W. Paprotté and R. Dirven (eds) *The Ubiquity of Metaphor: Metaphor in Language and Thought,* Amsterdam, The Netherlands: John Benjamins.

APPENDIX

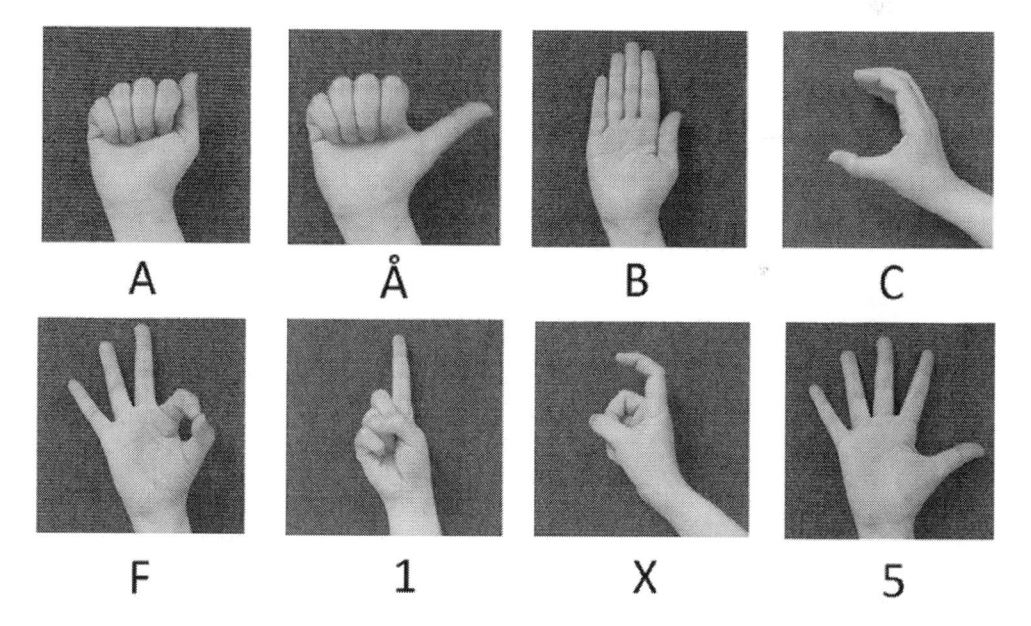

Figure 18.8 Handshapes used in this chapter.

Part IV
Functional variation of metaphor in language

19
Metaphor use in educational contexts
Functions and variations

Jeannette Littlemore

Introduction and definitions

This chapter aims to provide an overview of the research that has been conducted into the role(s) played by metaphor in a range of educational contexts, and to explain its variation across different genres and registers within education. I look at both spoken and written metaphor in educational contexts involving both children and adults, using either their first or second language. The term 'educational context' is taken to mean any communicative situation in which the intention is to extend the knowledge base of the recipient or to promote different or deeper ways of thinking about a given subject. Both formal and informal contexts are considered.

Metaphor serves a number of functions in educational contexts, one of which is to develop and frame new theories and ideas. An example of metaphor performing this function is the BRAIN AS COMPUTER metaphor, which led to a number of theories about the way in which the brain works. When metaphor is used in this way, it is normally described as 'theory constitutive' (Boyd, 2002; Knudsen, 2003). Metaphor is also used to fill terminological gaps (Black, 1962; Ortony, 1975), which means that in some cases, the terminology that is highly specific to a particular discipline will be metaphorical. Another function of metaphor in education is to express complex ideas in ways that people understand (Sticht, 2002). When it is used in this way, it is usually described as serving a 'pedagogical' function (Boyd, 2002) or an 'illustrative' function (Semino, 2008). As we will see in the chapter, metaphor serves other functions in educational contexts besides these, and as such can be a useful resource both for the educator and the student. However, as we will see below, its use is not uniform across all genres and registers, a fact which must be borne in mind when, for example, preparing students for entry into educational settings that use a language other than their own.

The organisation of the chapter is as follows: in the next section, developments in the study of metaphor in educational settings are tracked in terms of content and research methods. This is followed by the introduction of critical issues and debates along with examples provided from my own research in this area. A number of recommendations for future research are made in the final section.

Overview of relevant research to date

Evidence for the key role played by metaphor in educational contexts can be found in both written and spoken language, as well as in other forms of expression, such as images and gesture. It can be found in child and adult education, in first and additional language contexts, and in both formal and informal settings. A wide variety of research methods have been employed to investigate the use of metaphor in educational contexts. These range from discourse analysis, through corpus-based studies to more experimental studies designed to explore the extent to which metaphor presents a problem or studies involving different groups of students being shown doctored texts and asked to draw conclusions from them. This section provides an overview of the most important research findings in these areas, beginning with the use of metaphor in children's education in a first language setting.

The use of metaphor in children's education

By far the most influential and in-depth study of the use of metaphor in education in general, and in children's education in particular, is Cameron's (2003) monograph on the use of metaphor by both teachers and pupils aged 9 to 11 in a series of lessons delivered in a state primary school in the UK. I will begin by providing a detailed account of this study, as it laid the groundwork for more recent research in the area and introduced and addressed many of the issues arising in this field of research. The study consisted of a two-part investigation into the use of metaphor by teachers and pupils in a series of classes, including two mathematics classes, a geology class, a dancing class, and a grammar class, all of which were delivered at a British primary school. The first part of the study involved classroom observation. Audio recordings were made of the classes and Cameron analysed the metaphor use in these recordings. The second part of the study focused on the ways in which the pupils comprehended and interpreted the metaphors that had been employed by their teachers. In order to do this, Cameron employed a novel data-gathering technique, which she referred to as the Goal-directed, Interactive Think-Aloud (GITA) technique, which allowed her to examine the processes used by the students to interpret and learn from the metaphors. In this technique, students were encouraged to evaluate, in pairs, the suitability of a particular metaphorical text for children slightly younger than themselves. The approach was designed to draw their attention to the metaphorical language used in the text, whilst enabling them to distance themselves from any difficulties that they might themselves encounter.

Findings from the first part of the study allowed Cameron to outline the nature of metaphor in this context, the opportunities that it offers for learning, and the factors that help or prevent students from taking advantage of these opportunities. In the various lessons examined, Cameron found that the teachers made substantial use of metaphor in agenda management, summarising sequences, and when providing evaluative feedback. It was also used in explanation sequences, and in sub-technical language. Metaphors were often used affectively to mitigate potentially threatening situations, such as the giving of negative feedback, or the presentation of potentially difficult material. For example, one teacher described the characteristics of lava as being like 'sticky treacle' or 'runny butter'. The teachers also used metaphor to introduce new or difficult concepts, using language that the students would understand. These metaphors were designed to help pupils cross the gulf between their current levels of understanding and the levels of understanding desired by the teacher. In summarising sequences, evaluative metaphors were sometimes used, which according to

Cameron may have played a role in the development of shared values and attitudes between teachers and pupils. For example, in one such summarising sequence, the teacher tells the pupils: 'don't go by what you see [.] because what you see might not actually tell you the true story' (ibid., 134). Overall, Cameron points out that when it is used in educational contexts involving children, metaphor often serves an alignment function, whether to promote shared values, to simplify, or to mitigate potentially face-threatening situations. Where the students used metaphor, they tended to repeat, extend, or re-literalise conventional metaphors that had been used by the teacher, and to comment, occasionally in a somewhat subversive manner, on what the teacher had said. For example, in the following extract, the pupil plays with the metaphor that the teacher has used by re-using the vehicle term in a literal way:

> T   (to the class) where does the time go?
> (to Louise) finished?
> L: (to T) I'm having trouble with this
> T: You stuck? (.) right (.) . . .
> . . . yes Paul?
> P: I know where the time goes
> Into the past
> T: into the past (.) you're right ????
> Quickly into the past
>
> *Cameron, 2003: 141*

In the second part of the study, which explored the children's understanding of the metaphors used by their teachers, Cameron found that the pupils often discussed the vehicles of nominal metaphors at length, engaging in vehicle development and contextualisation, but when they were faced with verbal metaphors, they usually resorted to repetition and relexicalisation. For example, in a discussion about the workings of the human heart, the teacher's use of the 'body's transport system' was discussed at length by the pupils, whereas metaphorical terms such as 'relax' or 'squeeze' were simply repeated (ibid., 211). In terms of understanding, the pupils' previous knowledge of, and involvement with, the vehicles appeared to be a key factor in their ability to understand how the vehicles related to the context. Cameron found that the pupils were particularly likely to experience difficulties with verbal metaphors when they were combined with anaphoric reference. They often mistook the subject of the sentence for something else, a phenomenon that Cameron describes as 'topic reference shift'. For example, one of the pupils misinterpreted the metaphor 'it (= *heat*) doesn't escape into space' as 'none of *the atmosphere* can escape into space'. Cameron concludes that in these cases, the pupils' knowledge of the metaphor vehicle was unable to compensate for gaps in their topic knowledge. The misinterpretations in Cameron's data tended to result from a combination of inaccurate topic knowledge, earlier misleading collocations in the text, and complex referencing between the sentences. Cameron warns that misinterpreted metaphors such as these may have detrimental effects on learning.

Cameron's work has been highly influential in the field of metaphor studies, but its influence lies mainly in the area of methodology. To the best of my knowledge, there have been no other detailed studies of metaphor use in either primary or secondary education, although there have been a number of studies of teachers' own use of metaphor to conceptualise the learning and teaching environment. These are discussed in more detail below.

The use of metaphor in adult education

In comparison with children's education, there have been far more studies of metaphor use in adult education, where it has been investigated in depth from a number of angles. Extensive use of metaphor has been found in, for example, economics textbooks (Boers and Demecheleer, 1997; Henderson, 1982, 2000; McCloskey, 1986; Mason, 1990), in management science textbooks (Morgan, 1983, 2003; see also Chapter 27) and in science textbooks more generally (Brown, 2003; Mayer, 2002; Ritchie et al., 2006). Metaphor has also been investigated in university lectures. Johns (1996) looked at Science and Engineering lectures and found a substantial amount of colloquial language, much of which involved metaphor. Examples included 'a dog's breakfast', 'a paper exercise', and 'pull figures out of the air' (ibid., 3). His main finding was that metaphor was used primarily to serve evaluative functions, to emphasise not just whether the lecturer liked or disliked a particular scientific approach, but also to show whether or not he or she thought it to be central or peripheral, easy or difficult, reliable or unreliable, theoretical or practical. More recently, Carew and Mitchell (2006) found that engineering lecturers used metaphor consistently to elucidate and evaluate ideas relating to sustainability. Corts and Meyer (2002) and Corts and Pollio (1999) found that lecturers use metaphor to express conceptually or emotionally difficult concepts and that when they do so, their metaphors appear to cluster together. Low, Littlemore, and Koester (2008) followed up this work with a detailed study of metaphor use in three lectures in the British Academic Spoken English (BASE) corpus. They found that metaphoric density ranged from 10 per cent to 13 per cent, and that metaphors served a variety of functions, the most important of which were evaluation and discourse organisation. Like Corts and Meyer, they found a number of clusters, some of which were coherent, and they found that the more salient metaphors tended to be recurrent.

The use of metaphor in educational discourse is not restricted to spoken and written language. In their study of linguistics lectures, Mittelberg and Waugh (2009) found considerable evidence for the role of gestural metaphor in the teaching of grammatical concepts. For example, when talking about 'sentences', lecturers would hold their hands fairly far apart, with the palms facing each other. In contrast, the word 'morphemes' was accompanied by a gesture indicating 'small items' either in an open hand or a closed fist. Finally, embedded clauses were represented by the right hand wriggling downwards. All of these gestures reflect a metaphorical construal of grammatical features as bounded objects and involve a mapping whereby conceptual structure is mapped onto physical structure.

As with children's education, the reasons why metaphor is used in adult educational discourse vary. One reason for its use is that it serves to foster understanding. Mayer and colleagues (Mayer et al., 1995) found that in science education, the use of metaphor led to a better understanding of abstract concepts, and Williams (2005), who investigated the benefits of using metaphors in teaching psychology to nursing students, found that the use of metaphors by the lecturer enhanced students' ability to understand the subject matter as well as their ability to memorise key concepts. Other researchers have commented on the motivational impact of metaphor. Although they did not actually put this to the test, Petrie and Oshlag (2002) suggest that metaphor can provide a useful way of re-engaging students who have become disaffected, as it can allow them to connect what they are learning with their own experiences.

Although it serves as a useful device in elucidating concepts and performing a wide variety of functions, the use of metaphor can at times constitute a source of confusion in adult educational contexts, although, as one might expect, the nature of the confusion is somewhat different from that found by Cameron (2003) in her study of metaphor in children's education. Serious problems were identified by Brooks and Etkina (2007) in their study of the role played by metaphor in the context of physics students and physicists talking and writing about the subject of quantum mechanics. They found that the language employed by the physicists encoded a number of different conceptual metaphors, and argued that this reflects a covert understanding by the physicists that each metaphor only has *partial* explanatory power. For example, physicists sometimes talked about quantum mechanics in terms of 'waves' (emphasising the fact that it is a 'process'), whereas at other times, they talked in terms of 'particles' (emphasising the fact that 'matter' is involved). They reported that the students found the alternation between these different metaphors confusing. Their analysis of student writing and discussions showed that they often used them inappropriately, and that they tended to think in more literal terms than their lecturers.

The use of metaphor in academic discourse has also been found to be problematic for students who are working in their second language. For instance, research has shown that the use of metaphor by university lecturers can present considerable problems to international students attending their lectures. The first study to show this was Littlemore's (2001) examination of Bangladeshi Civil Servants taking short courses in Leadership and International Development at a British university. She found that over 70 per cent of the vocabulary items with which the students experienced difficulties involved metaphor and that, most crucially, when the students misunderstood the metaphor, they might still grasp the content of the lecture, but they misinterpreted the lecturer's stance. In a more in-depth follow-up study, Littlemore et al. (2011) investigated metaphor comprehension in international students from eight different countries, who attended four one-hour lectures from different disciplines and were tested on their understanding of the language used in these lectures. They found that metaphor accounted for 41 per cent of the items that students found problematic on a self-report task. When asked to explain metaphors in the lectures, students were only able to explain 50.6 per cent of them, and most interestingly, students were only aware of the problem in 4.2 per cent of the cases. These findings suggest that metaphor in academic lectures is often misunderstood and that, by and large, students do not even know that they have misunderstood the meaning. This is important given the aforementioned findings concerning the range of important functions that are performed by metaphor. In addition to their various findings regarding the amount and the nature of metaphor in university lectures, Low et al. (2008), in their aforementioned study, also found that in the lectures they investigated, the metaphors were never explained. These findings suggest that metaphor should be a focus in the teaching of English for Academic and/or Specific Purposes (see also Chapter 28).

Studies involving an explicit focus on metaphor in educational settings in order to improve learning

The fact that metaphor serves such important functions in educational discourse, and that it has been found to present problems to students (both native and non-native speakers), has led some researchers to investigate whether an explicit focus on metaphor in educational contexts has a positive impact on learning. The findings from such studies have tended to be encouraging. For instance, when Kamler and Thomson (2006) investigated the use of metaphor by doctoral students to conceptualise the learning process, they found that if students were encouraged to develop their own positive metaphors for learning, they were able to change their perceptions about difficulties that lay ahead, making them more positive about their ability to overcome these difficulties. More generally, in the context of academic skills training, Power, Carmichael and Goldsmith (2007) found that by encouraging students to identify the metaphors that underpin their particular disciplinary approaches and discourse, they could help them to find a useful framework for developing critical awareness and critique.

In the area of second language education, Littlemore (2004) also found that a focus on metaphor in an English for Academic Purposes (EAP) context helped develop students' critical thinking skills. The participants in her study were 30 students studying for an MBA in Public Service Administration in an International Development department at a British university. They were divided into an experimental group and a control group. Both groups participated in a general "critical thinking" session. The experimental group was also given a "metaphoric awareness-raising" session, whereas the control group was given no such session. The aim of the study was to investigate whether or not the metaphoric awareness-raising session had any lasting effect on the critical thinking abilities of the students in the experimental group. During the metaphoric awareness-raising session, the experimental group participants were introduced to conceptual metaphors and the ways in which they can shape thinking. After a significant time lag of five months, both groups were given a critical thinking test which involved analysing several texts relating to their discipline, all of which employed conceptual metaphor to persuade the reader of certain ideas. The students who had received the metaphorical awareness training were significantly more likely than those in the control group to make explicit references to metaphor in their critical analyses. While none of the students in the control group made any reference to the underlying metaphor, of the 15 students who had attended the metaphoric awareness-raising session, 7 made explicit references to the underlying metaphor and used these references to support their critical evaluations. They were able to point out how the authors used metaphor to make sweeping generalisations, and to avoid discussing specific factors. They were also able to point out that metaphors can be understood on different levels, leading to different interpretations of the text, and they were able to point out limitations of the metaphors involved.

There have been some studies of the use of metaphor in teacher training programmes. These have tended to focus on the use of metaphor by the trainees to conceptualise the teaching and learning process, and findings suggest that trainees have found this beneficial (see, for example, Stofflet, 1996). Wan (2014) explored the use of metaphor to promote critical thinking skills among language teachers on an MA Education programme at a British university. Her study explored Chinese students' conceptualisations of academic writing by means of a series of metaphor elicitation tasks. It also considered the benefits of metaphor awareness-raising training and of group discussions of metaphors. She found that this training had a beneficial effect on the students, and noted how new metaphors emerged from the group discussion. Over time, the participants in the study changed their conceptualisations of the essay-writing process and developed their levels of metaphoric awareness over the course of the year. They benefitted from the group discussions of metaphor, as they were able to use the metaphors produced by their peers, such as the 'writing as a tour' metaphor, to identify problems with their own essay writing, and refine their own metaphors. Finally, the students adapted the metaphors employed by their tutors and made them their own, and they questioned and improved their writing behaviour as a result of being exposed to other students' metaphors. Group discussions were perceived as being more valuable than the individual metaphor generation activities, which reflects the socio-cognitive nature of metaphor. This study is important as it underscores the essentially social nature of metaphor as a tool for thinking.

Critical issues and debates

There are currently two 'hot topics' in the field of metaphor and educational discourse. The first concerns the extent to which the use of metaphor can actually shape and influence thinking, and the second concerns variation in metaphor use across different genres and registers.

The question of whether metaphor use can shape or influence people's responses to the ideas presented in discourse is an interesting one. A number of studies have shown that, by adjusting the use of metaphor in texts, it is possible to radically alter the ways in which those texts are understood, and to shape the recommendations that readers make on the basis of their reading of those texts (see, for example, Boers, 2000; Kamler and Thompson, 2006). One of the most well-known studies of this type is Boers (1997). He was interested in finding out whether undergraduate students of economics would respond in different ways to text about economic competition if the ideas in the text were framed using different metaphors. The participants (100 students of economics) were asked to read a short written text about a European company that was being confronted with a cheaper Taiwanese competitor. They were then requested to write down their problem-solving suggestions for the European firm. They were told the assignment was meant to serve both as a writing task and as input for a class debate on the topic. Fifty participants received a version of the text in which the situation was described in terms of HEALTH, FITNESS, and RACING metaphors, whereas the other 50 participants received a version in which the situation was described in terms of FIGHTING and WARFARE metaphors. Participants who had been exposed to the HEALTH, FITNESS, and RACING metaphors were significantly more likely than the others to suggest reducing the size of the European company ('downsizing' the organisation) by laying off personnel ('slimming down' the organisation) or by closing down less profitable departments (using language which related to 'surgery' and 'amputations'). In accordance with the RACING metaphor, they were significantly more likely than the others to recommend more innovation and research and development (in order 'to stay ahead of' the Taiwanese competitor). In contrast, participants who had been exposed to the FIGHTING and WARFARE metaphors were significantly more likely to recommend price cuts and start a 'price war' in order to force the Taiwanese out of the European market. Boers shows convincingly how these findings fit with the 'logic' of the metaphors. It is also interesting to note that Thibodeau and Boroditsky (2011) have shown how such metaphoric framing can influence policy decisions, a finding that has clear implications for education, both in the field of Political Science and beyond.

Work in this field has been advanced in recent years by Krennmayr et al. (2014), who are interested in the interaction between the persuasive power of metaphor and its level of conventionality as well as the ways in which it is signalled. In order to test this, they used a text in which economics was described in terms of racing. They doctored the text so as to have four versions: one in which the metaphors were highly conventional and un-signalled; one in which the metaphors were highly conventional but signalled; one in which the metaphors were novel and signalled; and one in which the metaphors were novel but un-signalled. 'Signalled' metaphors were basically similes, and were indicated by the use of words such as 'like'. The hypothesis was that the racing metaphors would be more likely to shape respondents' thinking, and would thus have a positive impact on the participants' recall of the passage if they were novel and signalled. They found a significant effect for novelty but the results for signalling were less conclusive. They thus concluded that novel metaphors have the ability to shape a reader's mental representation of the content of a text, but this is less likely to happen if the metaphors are conventional.

The second area of debate in educational metaphor studies relates to the extent to which metaphor use varies across genres. This controversial topic was launched with Henderson's (2000) observation that non-expert publications such as *The Economist* have sometimes been used to teach the 'language of economics' for future students of Economics. One can see why teachers might use such texts as at first sight they appear more accessible and perhaps more 'fun' than the target texts. However, Henderson points out that there are serious problems with this approach as the metaphor use is completely different in these very different genres. *The Economist* is seen by economists as a current-affairs weekly, and thus not truly representative of the language that is used by economists in an academic context. Not only do the metaphors themselves differ between the two genres, but there is a level of sensationalism in the metaphors used in *The Economist* which is not often found in standard economics textbooks. For example, Henderson cites an article entitled 'Trapped Bubble', which appeared in *The Economist* in 1999 (*The Economist*, September 1999: 17). In this article, which assesses the state of the US economy, the author writes: 'sorry to be party-poopers, but America's still looks horribly bubble-like' (Henderson, 2000: 169). Henderson notes that sentences such as these would be very unlikely to appear in Economics textbooks, and argues that rather than giving their students texts such as these to read, EAP teachers should concentrate on helping them to understand and appreciate the textual constraints upon meanings that occur in more formal, academic Economics writing.

More recent research has explored the different ways in which both the form and functions of figurative language do indeed vary according to genre and register (see, for example, Skorczynska and Deignan, 2006; MacArthur and Littlemore, 2011). Deignan et al. (2013) showed how metaphor use is shaped at the level of genre by the role of the discourse community, communicative purpose and staging. They then focused on register, showing how there is considerable variation according to the field, which in educational contexts, can be broadly interpreted to mean the discipline. They also identified differences according to the relationship between the speakers and according to whether the communication was primarily spoken or written, and whether the metaphor was spoken or written, constitutive or ancillary, verbal or visual.

Most importantly, Deignan et al. (2013) showed how the different components of genre and register work together to shape overall metaphor use. They compared academic papers on the topic of climate change with articles on the same topic appearing in *The New Scientist*. They found very different uses of figurative language in the two genres, which, they argued, reflected the two different discourse communities, their aims, shared knowledge, assumptions and values (ibid.,123). The research articles used metaphor in precise, apparently community-sanctioned ways, with a highly restricted set of collocations. There were no explanations, and there were no extensions of source domain language. The metaphors in *The New Scientist* article displayed much more syntactic and lexical flexibility, and their meanings were much closer to the general, non-specialist senses of the words. A number of metaphors only appeared in *The New Scientist* and these tended to serve evaluative or persuasive functions.

Examples of current research: the use of metaphor in education

The largest current research project focusing on the use of metaphor in educational contexts is entitled 'Metaphor use in one-to-one academic consultations in English: Implications for

Spanish student mobility in Europe' (FFI2011-22809). This project, which is being led by Dr Fiona MacArthur at the University of Extremadura, Spain, involves a team of international researchers from the UK, Sweden, Ireland, and Holland. Researchers in the project are conducting a comparative study of the ways in which metaphors are used in academic consultations with international students at European universities. They are also investigating the interactions between verbal and gestural metaphor in these settings. The focus is on Spanish Erasmus students, and the overall aim is to identify the extent to which metaphor impedes or facilitates understanding in the cross-linguistic educational settings in which these students find themselves. In order to do this, the researchers have gathered and analysed data from interactions in four countries. They have identified the metaphors used in the academic exchanges using the Pragglejaz Group (2007) metaphor identification procedure, identified uses of metaphor that are more or less likely to lead to misunderstandings, and explored whether and how misunderstandings are resolved. The procedure was adapted slightly to account for SIGHT metaphors where both the metaphorical meaning and the non-metaphorical meaning were at work at the same time.

Interim findings from the project suggest that SIGHT metaphors are significantly more common in academic conversations than they are in spoken language more generally (MacArthur, Krennmayr and Littlemore, 2015). When the data are explored qualitatively, more details emerge. Both lecturers and students appear to be using SIGHT metaphors (such as 'focus', 'look', 'see', and so on). As expected, the lecturers use a wider range of linguistic expressions within this field than the students, which may be partly a reflection of the fact that the dyads are dominated by lecturer talk (lecturers talk for approximately 70 per cent of the time).

The researchers are interested to see whether the results from these dyads follow findings that have already been made for metaphor in native speaker exchanges. One observation that has been made for such exchanges is Cameron et al.'s (2009) finding that metaphors are often picked up on and elaborated throughout the conversation, which affords opportunities for the development of shared meaning. The researchers in this study are finding very little evidence of this. Metaphors used by the lecturers (L in the excerpt below) are very rarely taken up by the students (S), who tend to reply with minimal responses, such as 'uhu' and 'OK'. Here is an example of one such extract:[1]

L: yeah (.) so i mean in theory the seminars were there to: (.) test your knowledge from: the (.) or to give an opportunity for people to ask questions about the (.) the information in the ◇ lecture ◇
L: ◇ mhm ◇
L: and then maybe to extEND it a little bit so that there was something to discuss (.) so have a <u>look</u> at the readings
S: Hm
L: and see if there's a polemic of any kind that ◇ <u>comes out</u> ◇
S: ◇ uhu ◇
S: do you <u>see</u> what i mean
S: Yeah
L: and so (.) then THAT is the connection that you need to try and make in your mind (.) so where is the debate where is the discussion (.) 'cause that's the second half of your essay
S: so (.) the first half is just writing about the theory?
L: er the yeah (.) so the first half is present the theory ◇ the second half is ◇

> S: ◇ to pre- to present ◇ the main ◇ ideas ◇
> L: ◇ er ◇ these are the debates or this is a debate that COULD <u>arise</u> (.) out of this (.) theoretical <u>background</u> (.) this pers- these people have this <u>view</u> (.) these people have this <u>view</u> (.) this is what I think
> S: okay (.) ◇ so ◇
> L: ◇ do ◇ you¹ <u>see</u> what I mean (.) that's quite a <u>clear</u> (.)
> S: so I ◇ have to combine◇
> L: ◇ so if if ◇
> S: theory a:nd (.) ◇ personal criteria ◇
> L: ◇ and discussion ◇
> S: ◇ <soft> (yes i can surely) </soft> ◇
> L: ◇ exactly and ◇ the other thing is if you <u>look</u> HARD at (.) the (.) topic (.) and you think (.) there IS no debate here (.) it's just facts (.) it probably isn't going to be on the exam paper
> S: okay
>
> *MacArthur et al. 2015: 207*

As MacArthur et al. (2015) point out, in this extract, the lecturer (L) uses a range of sight terms with metaphorical senses ('have a look', 'view', 'look hard at') and uses 'see' to check that the student is understanding ('do you <u>see</u> what I mean'). She also uses words ('comes out', 'arise', 'clear') that can be described as being coherent with the metaphor of visual reasoning, as the object of mental attention becomes more visible or salient to the perceiver. Despite this extensive use of metaphor by the lecturer, the student (S) fails to contribute to the metaphorical framing of the task. She either responds minimally or simply rephrases what the lecturer has already said.

These findings suggest that when preparing students for their study abroad, it is worth focusing on the role of metaphor in spoken academic discourse, and training students to use it effectively in these settings. Lecturers at the receiving universities would also benefit from a focus on metaphor when being trained in the reception of international students, as opportunities for communication are clearly being missed.

Future directions

There are a number of areas where more research on the role played by metaphor in educational contexts could usefully be conducted. Apart from a few notable exceptions, much of the work to date has focused on the use of metaphor in English-speaking educational contexts, and it would be interesting to find out whether the findings to date are applicable to other languages. In relation to this, it would also be interesting to follow up the MacArthur et al. (in press) study by investigating the impact of metaphor used on returning Erasmus students. MacArthur herself notes the value of comparing metaphor use in returning Erasmus students with metaphor use before they go, in order to investigate the impact of the international educational setting on this important linguistic resource (MacArthur, 2014).

Another potentially useful future direction for research would be to evaluate the effectiveness of integrating the explicit study of metaphor into the teaching of disciplines where it plays a theory-constitutive role. This point is made very strongly in the case of architecture by Caballero (2014), who shows how metaphor informs all the stages of designing, constructing and evaluating a building, and is heavily involved in all communication with both colleagues and clients. Despite multiple instances of metaphorical language, and the fact that metaphorical thinking is implicitly built into programme aims, Caballero points out that students of architecture are never taught to use metaphor to conceptualise their buildings. If they were, they may be able to write more persuasive bids for buildings. She suggests incorporating an explicit focus on metaphor into architecture teaching in the form of a three-stage process, adapted from metaphor research. The process would involve metaphor identification, classification, in terms of its properties, and use, involving reflection on why architects use certain metaphors in certain contexts.

Other areas of educational discourse where research could usefully be conducted include the use of metaphor in different modes of expression. More consideration needs to be given to the way metaphor is used in spoken data, including gesture, as well as in visuals. This is particularly important given current developments in the use of MOOCs, virtual learning environments, and so on, where the boundaries between different modes of delivery and between 'experts' and 'non-experts' are becoming increasingly blurred, and where internationalisation and multilingualism are destined to become key test-beds for research into metaphor use.

Note

1 The transcription conventions used in this extract are as follows:

◇ Overlap
(.) Pause
CAPITALS: Words spoken with emphasis
Underlining: Metaphorically used words under discussion

Further reading

Caballero, R. (2014) Thinking, drawing and writing architecture through metaphor. *Iberica*, 28: 155–180.
Cameron, L. (2003) *Metaphor in Educational Discourse*. London: Continuum.
Ritchie, S. M., Bellochi, A., Poltl, H. and Wearmouth, M. (2006) Metaphors and analogies in transition. In P. J. Aubusson, A. G. Harrison and S. Ritchie (eds), *Metaphor and Analogy in Science Education*. Dordrecht, The Netherlands: Springer.

References

Black, M. (1962) *Models and Metaphors*. New York: Cornell University Press.
Boers, F. (1997) No pain, no gain in a free-market: A test for cognitive semantics? *Metaphor and Symbol*, 12: 231–241.
Boers, F. (2000) Enhancing metaphoric awareness in specialised reading. *English for Specific Purposes*, 19: 137–147.
Boers, F. and Demecheleer, M. (1997) A few metaphorical models in (western) economic discourse. In W.-A. Liebert, G. Redeker and L. Waugh (eds), *Discourse and Perspective in Cognitive Linguistics*, pp. 115–129. Amsterdam, The Netherlands: John Benjamins.
Boyd, R. (2002) Metaphor and theory change: What is 'metaphor' for? In A. Ortony (ed.), *Metaphor and Thought*, 3rd edn, pp. 481–531. Cambridge, UK: Cambridge University Press.
Brooks, D. T. and Etkina, E. (2007) Using conceptual metaphor and functional grammar to explore how language used in physics affects student learning. *Physical Review Special Topics – Physics Education Research*, 3(010105): 1–15.
Brown, T. L. (2003) *Making Truth: Metaphor in Science*. Urbana and Chicago, IL: University of Illinois Press.

Caballero, R. (2014) Thinking, drawing and writing architecture through metaphor. *Iberica*, 28: 155–180.

Cameron, L. (2003) *Metaphor in Educational Discourse*, London: Continuum.

Cameron, L., Maslen, R., Todd, Z., Maule, J., Stratton, P. and Stanley, N. (2009) The discourse dynamics approach to metaphor and metaphor-led discourse analysis. *Metaphor and Symbol*, 24(2): 63–89.

Carew, A. L. and Mitchell, C. A. (2006). Metaphors used by some engineering academics in Australia for understanding and explaining sustainability. *Environmental Education Research*, 12(2): 217–231.

Corts, D. P. and Meyer, K. (2002) Conceptual clusters in figurative language production. *Journal of Psycholinguistic Research*, 31(4): 391–408.

Corts, D. and Pollio, H. (1999) Spontaneous production of figurative language and gesture in college lectures. *Metaphor and Symbolic Activity*, 14(1): 81–100.

Deignan, A., Littlemore, J. and Semino, E. (2013) *Figurative Language, Genre and Register*. Cambridge, UK: Cambridge University Press.

Henderson, W. (1982) Metaphor in economics: Talking about text, discourse analysis. *Monographs*, 13. Birmingham: University of Birmingham Press.

—— (2000) Metaphor, economics, and ESP: Some comments. *English for Specific Purposes*, 19: 167–173.

Johns, T. (1996) The airy-fairy and the nitty-gritty: Colloquial language in lectures on science and technology. Available at: http://web.bham.ac.uk/johnstf/c_gloss.htm.

Koller, V., Hardie, A., Kamler, B. and Thomson, P. (2006) *Helping Doctoral Students Write*. Abingdon, UK: Routledge.

Knudsen, S. (2003) Scientific metaphors going public. *Journal of Pragmatics*, 35(8): 1246–1263.

Krennmayr, T., Bowdle, B. F., Mulder, G. and Steen, G. J. (2014) Economic competition is like auto racing: Building metaphorical schemas when reading text. *Metaphor and the Social World*, 4(1): 65–89.

Littlemore, J. (2001) The use of metaphor in university lectures and the problems that it causes for overseas students. *Teaching in Higher Education*, 6(3): 333–349.

—— (2004) Conceptual metaphor as a vehicle for promoting critical thinking skills amongst international students. In L. Sheldon (ed.), *Directions for the Future: Directions in English for Academic Purposes*, pp. 43–50. Oxford, UK: Peter Lang.

Littlemore, J., Chen, P., Koester, A. and Barnden, J. (2011) Difficulties in metaphor comprehension faced by international students whose first language is not English. *Applied Linguistics*, 32(4): 408–429.

Low, G., Littlemore, J. and Koester, A. (2008) The use of metaphor in three university lectures. *Applied Linguistics*, 29(3): 428–455.

MacArthur, F. (2014) *English as academic lingua franca and the Erasmus challenge: The use of metaphor in office hours' consultations.* Paper presented at the symposium Metaphor in Academic Conversation, AELCO Conference, Badajoz, Spain.

MacArthur, F., Krennmayr, T. and Littlemore, J. (2015) How basic is UNDERSTANDING IS SEEING when reasoning about knowledge? Lecturers' and students' asymmetric use of SIGHT metaphors in office hours' consultations in English as academic lingua franca. *Metaphor and Symbol*, 30: 184–217.

MacArthur, F. and Littlemore, J. (2011) On the repetition of words with the potential for metaphoric extension in conversations between native and non-native speakers of English. *Metaphor and the Social World*, 1(2): 201–238.

Mason, M. (1990) 'Dancing on air': Analysis of a passage from an economics textbook. In T. Dudley-Evans and W. Henderson (eds), *ELT Documents 134: The Language of Economics: The Analysis of Economics Discourse*. London: Modern English Publications, in association with the British Council.

Mayer, R. E. (2002) The instructive metaphor: Metaphoric aids to students' understanding of science. In A. Ortony (ed.), *Metaphor and Thought*, 3rd edn. New York: Cambridge University Press.

Mayer, R. E., Sims, V. and Tajika, H. (1995) A comparison of how textbooks teach mathematical problem solving in Japan and the United States. *American Educational Research Journal*, 32: 443–460.

McCloskey, D. (1986) *The Rhetoric of Economics*. Brighton, UK: Wheatsheaf Books.

Mittelberg, I. and Waugh, L. (2009) Metonymy first, metaphor second: A cognitive semiotic approach to multimodal figures of thought in co-speech gesture. In C. Forceville and M. Urios-Aparisi (eds), *Multimodal Metaphor*, pp. 336–350. Berlin, Germany: Mouton de Gruyter.

Morgan, G. (1983) More on metaphor: Why we cannot control tropes in administrative science. *Administrative Science Quarterly*, 28: 601–607.

—— (2003) *Images of Organization*. Thousand Oaks, CA: Sage Publications,

Ortony, A. (1975) Why metaphors are necessary and not just nice. *Educational Theory*, 25(1): 45–53.

Petrie, H. G. and Oshlag, R. S. (2002) Metaphor and learning. In A. Ortony (ed.), *Metaphor and Thought*, 3rd edn. New York: Cambridge University Press.

Power, C., Carmichael, E. and Goldsmith, R. (2007) Parrot poo on the windscreen: Metaphor in academic skills learning. *Journal of Academic Language and Learning*, 1(1): 18–32.

Pragglejaz Group. (2007) MIP: A method for identifying metaphorically used words in discourse. *Metaphor and Symbol*, 22(1): 1–39.

Ritchie, S. M., Bellochi, A., Poltl, H. and Wearmouth, M. (2006) Metaphors and analogies in transition. In P. J. Aubusson, A. G. Harrison and S. Ritchie (eds), *Metaphor and Analogy in Science Education*. Dordrecht, The Netherlands: Springer.

Semino, E. (2008) *Metaphor in Discourse*. Cambridge, UK: Cambridge University Press.

Skorczynska, H. and Deignan, A. (2006) Readership and purpose in the choice of economics metaphor. *Metaphor and Symbol*, 21(2): 87–104.

Sticht, T. (2002). Educational uses of metaphor. In A. Ortony (ed.), *Metaphor and Thought*, 3rd edn. New York: Cambridge University Press.

Stofflet, R. (1996) Metaphor development by secondary teachers enrolled in graduate teacher education. *Teaching and Teacher Education*, 12(6): 577–589.

Thibodeau, P. H. and Boroditsky, L. (2011) Metaphors we think with: The role of metaphor in reasoning. *PLoS ONE*, 6(2): e16782. doi: 10.1371/journal.pone.0016782.

Wan, W. (2014) Constructing and developing ESL students' beliefs about writing through metaphor: A longitudinal exploratory study. *Journal of Second Language Writing*, 23: 53–73.

Williams, G. (2005) *Using metaphor in teaching and learning: A literature review and synthesis*. Paper presented at the Sixth Learning and Teaching Conference, University of Nottingham.

20
Metaphor and the representation of scientific issues
Climate change in print and online media

Nelya Koteyko and Dimitrinka Atanasova

Introduction: rhetorical studies of public understandings of science

Metaphor is widely considered an essential tool for explaining and understanding. Just as we often use analogies in our daily lives when trying to explain and understand what we observe, hear and feel, scientists have been using metaphors for a long time to elaborate theories and to write for and speak to the public. The metaphors that scientists use for the purpose of theoretical elaboration are often the same as those used to explain scientific concepts to non-specialists (Massimiano 1998). From Newton's metaphor of the UNIVERSE AS A MACHINE (Glebkin 2013) and Dawkins' EVOLUTION AS THE PROGRESSION OF A SELFISH GENE (Journet 2010) to the more recent HUMAN GENOME AS THE BOOK OF LIFE (Nerlich et al. 2002), metaphors have been central to scientific thought and science communication. Indeed, as Pauwels (2013: 524) points out in a recent *Nature* paper: 'Faced with explaining the messy complexity and uncertainty of science to the public, it is understandable that scientists reach for metaphors'.

There are different models outlining how this process of science communication works, and the role of metaphorical thinking in it. According to Gross (1996), for example, we can distinguish between two primary models of the public understanding of science: the 'deficit model' and the 'contextual' model. The deficit model conceives of communication as a one-way flow from scientists to a passive public, who are assumed to be already persuaded of the value of science. Social scientists, however, challenged the key tenet of this model, namely that simply delivering more information about science would necessarily lead to the acceptance of scientific advances. This gave rise to the contextual model, which is, by contrast, symmetrical and implies an active public: 'it requires a rhetoric of reconstruction in which public understanding is the joint creation of scientific and local knowledge' (Gross 1996: 6). Here the rhetorical analysis of communication plays a major role, shifting the focus from the examination of a scientific field to the study of audiences' cultural, political and socio-economic conditions.

Scientific writing for the general public, described as 'popularisation discourse' has two main channels – institutional (for example, universities) and the print and online media (Calsamiglia 1997). Whereas the deficit model of public understanding relied on the notion of translation between registers, where a specialised register of science is merely reformulated for transmission to popular channels, more recent approaches have stressed the discursive nature of this process. According to Calsamiglia (1997) the communicative context determines the register in which scientific knowledge is discursively represented, leading to a re-contextualisation of knowledge. In the case of the mass media, journalists re-contextualise science writing in accordance with genre conventions, communicative norms and assumptions about the audience's prior knowledge (Cassany et al. 2000).

Scholars of science communication have examined different sites and modes of interaction between scientific and 'lay' knowledge, focusing on metaphor and metonymy as key framing devices (Condit et al. 2012). As other contributors to this volume point out, metaphors are not only explanatory tools but can be used as powerful rhetorical devices, foregrounding or backgrounding different aspects of policy and ethics. Although cognitive linguists showed the important role of metaphors in our thinking and acting (Lakoff and Johnson 1980), it was Donald Schön's work on 'generative metaphors' (1993: 137) that put the emphasis on how metaphors derive their 'normative force from certain purposes and values, certain normative images, which have long been powerful in our culture'. Schön's well-cited example of representing a slum as a disease or an ecosystem refers not only to the role that metaphors play in anchoring novel phenomena in familiar and shared ideas, but also the strategic nature of the narratives where such metaphors are embedded. A narrative about 'blight' and a narrative about 'natural community' call for different policy actions and, therefore, are crafted and used to serve political ends.

This growing body of research has therefore studied metaphors in science communication as part of a discourse analysis framework. In this regard, Zinken and colleagues speak about 'discourse metaphors'—metaphors that are conceptually grounded but whose meaning is also shaped by their use at a given time and in the context of a debate about a certain topic (Zinken et al. 2008). Attention to such 'discourse metaphors' also foregrounds the creative properties of metaphor and its ensuing potential to spark dialogue and collaboration rather than mere expressions of policy support or criticism (Russill 2011). In this regard, Väliverronen and Hellsten (2002) and Ungar (2007) explore the rhetorical properties of metaphor in the communication of environmental issues, placing emphasis on metaphors derived from popular culture and discussing the possibility that such metaphors can act as a bridge between expert and public understandings. Particular attention is paid to the online environment as a new and expanding arena for such discussions (Koteyko et al. 2015). The use of metaphors by different stakeholders in blogs, Twitter and other social media platforms, which enable interactivity and multiple possibilities for content creation, promotes dialogue and provides audiences with the opportunity to contest elite messages about science (Nerlich et al. 2010).

In this chapter we focus on the example of climate change, which, as a complex and multifaceted problem, is increasingly characterised by the involvement of a variety of stakeholders (scientists, politicians, industry representatives, but also journalists and members of the general public) resulting in rhetorical contestation. Numerous rhetorical battles have been fought over the science behind climate change, and more recently, over the social and ethical implications it has or may have. Russill (2011) has recently stressed the ubiquity of metaphor in such discourses and the importance of efforts to analyse analogical reasoning and appraise arguments that involve metaphors.

In what follows, we review the available scholarly literature on the use of climate change-related metaphors in print and online media outlets. Focusing on examples of 'discourse metaphors', we aim to draw attention to the importance of metaphors in these analyses of assumptions, disagreements and contrarian views in climate debates.[1]

Overview of relevant research

From the perspective of practices aimed at communicating the science and policy about such a complex and abstract issue as climate change, the role of metaphors as framing devices has come to be recognised as particularly important (Nerlich and Koteyko 2009a; Shaw and Nerlich 2015; see also Chapter 30). In 'Why it matters how we frame the environment', George Lakoff (2010: 70) wrote, 'Environmental framing is everywhere in the news'. According to Entman (1993: 53) framing means selecting certain aspects of a perceived reality and making them more salient in a communicating text 'to promote a particular problem definition, causal interpretation, moral evaluation, and/or treatment recommendation'. A frame is therefore a structure that can help us understand complex issues, especially what should be done about them and by whom (Nisbet and Mooney 2007). As Lakoff and others have demonstrated, metaphors are among the most potent framing devices (Lakoff 2004).

Frames, discourses and climate change metaphors

In this section we consider a line of research in which metaphors are viewed as important framing devices in discussions of climate change. Research by Tynkkynen (2010) is a case in point. Studying Russian print newspapers, Tynkkynen (2010) found that climate change was discussed in terms of MISSION, NATIONAL INTEREST and DUTY frames. In the MISSION frame, Donor and Leader metaphors were used to conceptualise Russia as an ecological power, which, with its vast forests soaking up emissions, is part of the solution to climate change. The NATIONAL INTEREST frame relied on Gulag and Marxism metaphors to undermine the scientific validity of the Kyoto protocol and highlight its costs for Russian political and economic interests. In the DUTY frame, the metaphor of a Soldier was used to conceptualise the Kyoto protocol and to present Russia as a traitor betraying its duty by delaying ratification.

Since the focus of this study was not on metaphors per se, linguistic examples were not consistently given. Among those that were included were examples related to the use of the Leader metaphor as in '[Russia] becomes the political leader in preventing the climate catastrophe' (Tynkkynen 2010: 187) and 'Russia is the de facto leader in preserving natural resources. Why not become the de jure leader?' (Tynkkynen 2010: 189).

Other research made observations about metaphor use as part of efforts to identify climate change discourses. Informed by Dryzek's (2005) components approach to discourse analysis, where rhetorical devices like metaphors are one component, Doulton and Brown (2009) studied the construction of climate change and international development in British print newspapers. They identified a *rationalism* discourse where the Flood metaphor was employed to discredit climate change as a concept 'flooded' with eco-hype and to argue that it is an important issue for developing countries, but not as important as others (Doulton and Brown 2009: 196). Additionally, the metaphor of War was found to be used in discourses of: *ethical mitigation* – to argue that it is fair for the West, as primarily responsible for current emissions levels, to 'lead the war on climate change'; *disaster strikes* – to describe climate change as 'a weapon of mass destruction'; and *potential catastrophe* – to argue that 'we are our own worst enemies in the war against climate change' (Doulton and Brown 2009: 196).

War metaphors

Much existing research with a specific focus on metaphors has, in fact, identified the use of War metaphors in climate change-related print and online media content. This should perhaps be unsurprising. Metaphorical wars have been waged against cancer (see Chapter 26), crime, obesity, poverty and terror, to name just a few examples. The widespread use of War metaphors can be speculatively attributed to their resonance with the principles of modern news making (Cohen 2011). Using War metaphors is believed to be an especially potent way to motivate action by highlighting the seriousness of an issue (Nerlich 2009). But, as the following discussion demonstrates, War metaphors have been used to achieve a variety of aims in print and online media content related to climate change.

One of the first studies to identify the use of War metaphors is Romaine's (1997) analysis of discussions at the 1992 Earth Summit and in coverage of the Summit in English-language print newspapers and news magazines. Romaine (1997: 178) found that one of the uses of War metaphors was to conceptualise discussions about global warming in terms of a liberal left attacking a conservative worldview: '[w]hat they [environmentalists] really want to do is attack our way of life. Their primary enemy: capitalism (. . .) Their appeals and their scare tactics are designed to transform people into foot soldiers in the army of doomsday environmentalism.' War metaphors were also found to be combined with Sports metaphors to conceptualise dealing with global warming as an activity in which there are winners and losers: the 'jousting grounds of negotiation' on which 'contenders [developed and developing countries] (. . .) pitched one camp' or 'pitched another [camp]' (Romaine 1997: 178).

Later research by Asplund (2010) and Cohen (2011) identified uses of War metaphors that are more in line with its potential to highlight the importance of an issue and motivate action to address it. Asplund (2010: 5) analysed Swedish print farm magazines and found that War metaphors were used to depict climate change as a 'threat' to farmers and to encourage them to address it: 'the sugar cane worker or the wheat grower. Who should be eliminated? Who will save us from the climate threat?'

Analysing British print broadsheet newspapers, Cohen (2011) showed that War metaphors were used to characterise the challenges of addressing climate change and to evoke British wartime steadfastness. For example: 'we are at war: at war against climate catastrophe, presenting us with a far greater threat towards our survival than 1939; and [that] the measures adopted must rise to this unprecedented challenge' (Cohen 2011: 206). Cohen (2011) argued that such use of War metaphors may create opportunities for British policy makers to propose greenhouse gas reduction strategies reminiscent of wartime austerity programmes. He also suggested that, if people perceive climate change in terms of war, bolder interventions like geoengineering, which refers to intentional modifications of the climate, might become more acceptable.

This may not always be the case, however, as suggested by research by Luokkanen and colleagues (2014) and Nerlich and Jaspal (2013). Luokkanen and colleagues (2014) analysed metaphor use in blog, news, opinion and editorial items about geoengineering published on the online platforms of the British *Guardian* newspaper and the American *New York Times*. They found that War metaphors were used both in arguments opposing and favouring geoengineering, as well as to simply talk about geoengineering as a possible solution to climate change without arguing for or against it. Opposing arguments discussed geoengineering using 'atomic warfare' and 'Cold War' imagery to paint the catastrophe that may follow (Luokkanen et al. 2014: 972). Favourable arguments included: '[a] group urges research into aggressive efforts to fight climate change' (Luokkanen et al. 2014: 977). A neutral use of War metaphors can be seen in: '[s]ome geoengineering schemes to fight climate change would probably succeed in cooling the planet (. . .) but whether we should ever deploy them is still an open question' (Luokkanen et al. 2014: 972).

Similarly, Nerlich and Jaspal (2013), who examined how carbon capture and storage was discussed in British print newspapers, observed that War metaphors were used to conceptualise carbon capture and storage as an effective way of addressing climate change. Carbon capture and storage was presented as 'an effective <u>weapon</u> in the <u>war</u> against climate change' (Nerlich and Jaspal 2013: 45). But War metaphors were also used to refer to carbon capture and storage implementation as a '<u>battle</u>', with expressions like 'serious <u>blow</u>' being employed to discuss decreasing support for carbon capture and storage projects (Nerlich and Jaspal 2013: 45).

In a recent analysis of the use of metaphors in editorials and op-eds published on the online platforms of the British *Guardian* and *Daily Mail*, Atanasova and Koteyko (2015) found that, in the *Guardian* opinion-page content, War metaphors were used to communicate the urgency of the need to act on climate change: 'climate change is undeniably a serious <u>threat</u> (. . .) the potential impacts of climate change on the Amazon forest must be a call to action to conserve the Amazon, not a reason to <u>retreat</u> in despair' (Atanasova and Koteyko 2015: 7). In addition, as Romaine (1997) found, War metaphors were used to conceptualise climate change politics as a battle: 'the <u>battle</u> for the green vote is on' (Atanasova and Koteyko 2015: 8).

When it comes to using War metaphors to communicate the urgency of climate change and the need to act on it, Atanasova and Koteyko (2015) also warn of possible unintended reactions. Empirical research on fear appeals in climate change communication shows that scaring people into action 'won't do it' (O'Neill and Nicholson-Cole 2009: 355). Fear appeals, which identify the existence of a threat, may result in efforts to control either the threat or the fear (Moser and Dilling 2004). Continued exposure to fear appeals may create the impression that the threat that climate change presents is impossible to control, leading to a focus on controlling fear from climate change via denial.

What all of the above studies demonstrate so clearly is that metaphors of War are far from being 'dead' (Gwyn 2002: 138). Quite the opposite – militaristic language has pervaded climate change discourse for some time and powerfully structured the public and political descriptions of the issue. The use of War metaphors characterises science communication more generally, and climate change is no exception.

Religion metaphors

In addition to War, another frequently identified conventional metaphor in discussions of climate change is Religion. Metaphors of Religion, in fact, have a long history of use in criticisms of environmentalism (Woods et al. 2012). Nerlich (2010) analysed blog entries to understand how climate sceptics (deniers or contrarians) used Climategate to undermine climate change science and justify political inaction. It emerged that it was metaphors of Religion that were used to achieve these goals. Climategate, referring to accusations that global warming is a scientific conspiracy, spurred reactions in which science was labelled as a 'fear-mongering climate-change <u>faith-system</u>', scientific theories as '<u>gospel</u>' or '<u>bible</u>', scientific consensus as 'singing from the same <u>hymn</u> sheet', scientists as '<u>prophets</u>' or '<u>high priests</u>' and scientific dissemination as a '<u>crusade</u>' (Nerlich 2010: 14).

Similarly, Woods and colleagues (2012), who analysed British print newspapers, found that metaphors of Religion were employed to denigrate climate change by presenting the science behind it as irrational and based on faith rather than facts. Climate change was a '<u>creed</u>' or '<u>cult</u>', environmentalism a '<u>crusade</u>', climate change claims '<u>sermons</u>', environmentalists '<u>zealots</u>' and pro-climate change behaviour '[buying/selling] <u>indulgences</u>' (Woods et al. 2012: 331).

One of the most recent studies in this domain additionally identified two novel mappings of the metaphor of Religion in *Daily Mail* opinion-page content published online. Atanasova and Koteyko (2015: 11) found that the concepts of conversion and recanting were used to conceptualise and welcome transitions from believing in climate change to being sceptical about it: 'green guru to <u>recant</u>' and 'Osborne's <u>conversion</u> is too little too late, but it is some small comfort'.

The Greenhouse metaphor

Also frequently identified is the Greenhouse metaphor – a metaphor with a long history of use in physics and atmospheric sciences (Nerlich and Hellsten 2014). It is among the climate change metaphors that evoke one of the most vivid understandings of what global warming means, by mapping what we know about how greenhouses work onto what happens in the earth's atmosphere as a result of human action. In an early analysis, Romaine (1997: 184) however, expressed reservations about its capability to provide 'a truly explanatory model' of climate change. In later studies of its use in media content, Asplund (2010) as well as Nerlich and Hellsten (2014) echoed this concern. Indeed, this metaphor may not be particularly conducive to understanding the negative impacts of climate change, as it contradicts common perceptions about greenhouses as places of safety (Carolan 2006) (see also Chapter 30).

Other climate change metaphors

Additional conventional metaphors that have been detected in various print and online media content include, in no particular order, Machine, Body/Patient/Health, Game/Race, Controllability, Tipping point and Footprint.

Two studies examining the use of metaphors in geoengineering-related media content identified different uses of the Machine metaphor. Nerlich and Jaspal (2012), who studied the English-language industry trade press, found that the Machine metaphor was used to argue in favour of geoengineering. Building on the familiar notion of our planet as a machine, geoengineering was conceptualised as a straightforward intervention into a machine mechanism: '[install] a dimmer <u>switch</u> on the sun', '[install] a global <u>thermostat</u>', geoengineering is needed if we 'can't <u>plug</u> the flow of carbon into the atmosphere' (Nerlich and Jaspal 2012: 135). In contrast, Luokkanen and colleagues (2014) found that the Machine metaphor was primarily used in arguments opposing geoengineering: '[t]urning down the dimmer <u>switch</u> may reduce incoming solar radiation but would do nothing to slow ocean acidification. The climate <u>system</u> is hugely complicated and <u>tinkering</u> with it might be akin to introducing cane toads to control sugarcane beetles' (Luokkanen et al. 2014: 972). Indeed, one common use of Machine metaphors is to create the impression that the task at hand is simple, but they can also be used to argue that such notions are simplistic (Warnick 2004).

The above two studies also identified divergent uses of Body, Patient and Health metaphors in geoengineering-related media content. Nerlich and Jaspal (2012) found that Body and Patient metaphors were used to emphasise the need for geoengineering. Articles spoke of having to 'apply "sunscreen" to the whole planet' where geoengineering is likened to sunscreen and the planet to a human body (Nerlich and Jaspal 2012: 138). Other articles spoke of 'manipulating the environment in a healing way' (Nerlich and Jaspal 2012: 139) and, thus, conceptualising the planet as a patient. Luokkanen and colleagues (2014), however, noticed that Health metaphors were primarily used to conceptualise geoengineering as an improper solution: '[geoengineering is] atmospheric liposuction: a retrospective fix for planetary overindulgence. (. . .) Is it time to admit defeat and check ourselves into the clinic?' (Luokkanen et al. 2014: 976). Here geoengineering is conceptualised as a solution that does not address the fundamental causes of climate change and is as much a solution to climate change as liposuction is to obesity.

Despite the latter example, Health metaphors are generally seen as powerful means of fostering concern and action by invoking universal experiences of health and illness (Nancy et al. 1997). Body/Patient metaphors in particular have been recommended as being especially effective in conveying the negative consequences of climate change and mobilising the general public (Somerville 2006).

In terms of Game/Race metaphors, Asplund (2010) observed that a Game metaphor was used to highlight the potential positive impacts of climate change on farmers. Having drawn the 'winning ticket', farmers are 'winners' in the 'climate game', who will see higher yields and income – 'the profits will be greater than the expenses for the farm and forest industries as the climate changes' (Asplund 2010: 4). This use implies no need for action, as positive effects will follow naturally from climate change. But the Game metaphor was also used to identify farmers as 'key players' in the 'climate game' who need to actively adapt to take advantage of a changing climate (Asplund 2010: 4). In a similar way, Nerlich and Jaspal (2013: 45–6), who studied carbon capture and storage, found that Race metaphors were used both to convey movement in the right direction – 'massive step forward', 'step in the right direction' and to convey the notion of losing the race – 'backsliding'.

A set of metaphors that have been identified with some regularity is what Luokkanen and colleagues (2014) call Controllability metaphors which include Backup plan, Plan B and Insurance. Geoengineering was depicted as a complementary measure: 'big ideas in reserve, a Plan B, in case nothing comes of appeals to personal abstinence' and '[geoengineering] will act like an insurance policy if the world one day faces a crisis of overheating' (Luokkanen et al. 2014: 972). Nerlich and Jaspal (2012: 140) also identified the use of the Plan B metaphor, as in 'unless we can succeed in greatly reducing CO_2 emissions we are headed for a very uncomfortable and challenging climate future, and geoengineering will be the only option left'.

Overall, Controllability metaphors were used to argue in favour of more geoengineering experiments, while also emphasising that it is a complementary measure and not a substitute for other actions. Insurance metaphors have, in fact, been used in similar ways in the context of biodiversity conservation to argue that preserving biodiversity is an insurance against unexpected disturbances (Hellsten 2002).

The use of another conventional metaphor – the Tipping point metaphor – in scientific discourse and mainstream American and British print news media was studied by Russill and Nyssa (2009). They showed how scientists, and particularly James E. Hansen, had initiated its use in a 2005 presentation to the American Geophysical Union (AGU) to draw attention to moments of sensitivity to rapid change: 'we are on the precipice of climate system tipping points beyond which there is no redemption' (Russill and Nyssa 2009: 336). Mainstream media then followed. Russill (2011) has subsequently called for a better understanding of the use of temporal metaphors like the Tipping point metaphor in scientific and policy discussions.

Critical issues, debates and controversies

Despite their widespread use in scientific description and popularisation, relying on metaphors to convey scientific phenomena has its cost. The images of the UNIVERSE AS A MACHINE, the HUMAN GENOME AS THE BOOK OF LIFE, or indeed CARBON CAPTURE AND STORAGE AS A WEAPON have the potential to bring distortion and confusion, not least because scientists themselves may sometimes overlook their metaphorical nature. Furthermore, metaphors are one of the most powerful tools that can influence the way we think about societal issues, and not always overtly. As Thibodeau and Boroditsky (2013) demonstrate in their study, people provide different responses to initiatives for combating crime when it is presented as either a 'beast' or a 'virus' ravaging society. In the former case they tend to call for strong law enforcement, whereas in the latter they respond to solutions such as rehabilitation and the understanding of underlying causes. Interestingly, the participants appeared to be unaware of how the metaphorical context affected their reasoning and rationalised their decisions appealing to statistics and other criteria they believed to be objective.

This potential of metaphors has important implications from the perspective of the contextual model of science communication, which requires taking into account the facilitation of public dialogue and the exchange of perspectives. As science communication takes the form of an active and ongoing conversation with a range of stakeholders holding different and potentially conflicting value commitments and positions, research has to pay attention to the strategic use of metaphors (by all the parties involved), which may be aimed at promoting specific value-laden assumptions.

The role of scientists in high-profile debates over climate change as well as stem cell research, food biotechnology and other policy controversies has already been subject to public scrutiny. Although many scientists define their role as creating knowledge that can be used by policymakers but not entering into policy debates themselves, in reality such a differentiation can be difficult to make. As Hellsten and Nerlich (2008) point out, scientists often engage in strategic communication as a means to promote their careers and succeed in obtaining government funding, using Breakthrough metaphors and other framing devices.

This is not to say, however, that all the uses of metaphor in science communication will be strategic or malevolent. As Lakoff and colleagues have shown, metaphors are pervasive in our language, both in 'lay' talk and in scientific articles. Rather, this means that science communication research will benefit from careful analysis and application of the ethical principles underlying the engagement of the public and policy makers with scientific advances (Nisbet 2009).

Examples of current research: metaphor use in climate change debates

An example of current research that has drawn attention to the creative capacity of metaphors and the 'novel collective and linguistic response' (Nerlich and Koteyko 2009a: 345) they can engender has focused on the word 'carbon' as a term around which metaphoric expressions are built. In the metaphorical compounds with 'carbon' as head, some aspects of the compound 'carbon dioxide' were used to concretise and make sense of the new realities emerging from what one may call the 'management' of CO_2, be it selling/buying (e.g. 'carbon trading') or reducing/increasing/calculating it (e.g. 'carbon (dioxide) footprint calculator'). In a series of papers Koteyko, Nerlich and colleagues focused on different aspects of this emerging 'carbon language' and demonstrated how it can be monitored via print and online media to shed light on how the wider public and different stakeholders may make sense of climate change (Koteyko 2012; Koteyko et al. 2010; Nerlich 2012; Nerlich et al. 2011; Nerlich and Koteyko 2009a, b; Nerlich and Koteyko 2010).

Koteyko, Nerlich and colleagues argue that, in the English language, 'carbon compounds' began their life as relatively standard or conventional compounds, such as 'carbon emission' or 'carbon dioxide emission'. 'Carbon emission' is an expression which simply integrates, blends and compresses knowledge of the emission of carbon dioxide into the atmosphere. Gradually, more creative, metaphorical carbon compounds based on this template started to appear. One example of a metaphorical carbon compound is a 'carbon criminal'. When we use metaphors, we map our existing knowledge or experience from a familiar, simpler domain onto problems or phenomena from a newer or more complex domain. In this case, we map our knowledge and maybe experience with criminals onto climate change mitigation, so that someone responsible for excessive carbon dioxide emissions becomes a 'carbon criminal' (Nerlich et al. 2011).

In one of these studies, Koteyko and colleagues (2010) identified the context and trends in the use (from 1990 to 2008) of three clusters of metaphorical carbon compounds within English-language blogs and news websites. These included finance carbon compounds like 'carbon currency', lifestyle carbon compounds such as 'carbon diet' and attitudinal carbon compounds, which is where the example of a 'carbon criminal' falls. The use of all three clusters of metaphorical compounds closely reflected different stages of public discussion around climate change mitigation. Finance and lifestyle compounds were in use mostly in the period between 1990 and 2005, when belief in political and economic solutions to climate change was still high. Around 2006, and especially around the 2008 financial crisis, negatively coloured attitudinal compounds like 'carbon indulgence' started to be used to question reliance on market mechanisms.

In several subsequent studies, the authors focused on specific clusters or individual metaphorical compounds from one of the three clusters. Koteyko (2012), for example, focused on the use of finance compounds to report on market-based solutions to climate change in British newspapers. Koteyko traced the chronological development of different metaphorical compounds – from 'carbon market' and 'carbon economy' around 1990 to 'carbon loansharks' around 2009.

Focusing on a specific metaphorical compound, Nerlich and colleagues (2011) analysed American newspapers to understand how 'carbon diet', an example of a lifestyle carbon compound, had been used in efforts to make climate change science more accessible to the general public. 'Carbon diet' allowed campaigners and journalists to reduce the complex issue of climate change to a human scale by integrating the familiar experience of dieting with the unfamiliar notion of mitigation strategies for carbon dioxide emissions reduction. Also homing in on a specific metaphorical compound, Nerlich (2012) analysed news from English-language media outlets to understand how 'low carbon future' and the related metaphorical compounds 'low carbon world' and 'low carbon society' had become prominent. As the author explains, before the 1990s 'low carbon' was used mostly in the steel industry to refer to steel that is more malleable and capable of being drawn out. Later on, however, 'low carbon' began to be used in a new type of discourse and semantic field – that of climate change. This happened gradually, starting from the use of such compounds as 'low carbon dioxide' followed by 'low-carbon fuel' and 'low-carbon alternatives' as 'dioxide' was beginning to be increasingly elided. By the late 1990s, after the Rio Earth Summit in 1992 and the Kyoto Protocol in 1997, 'low carbon' was firmly in place as a shorthand for 'low carbon dioxide' in such compounds as 'low-carbon technologies' and 'low-carbon diet'. These changes accelerated further in 2008 when the use of the compound 'low carbon' became even more frequent until it became possible to use it as a stand-alone phrase without any noun. For example, Ed Miliband, then UK Secretary of State for Energy and Climate Change, exhorted readers of *The Times* "to take full advantage" of business opportunities related to the "transition to low carbon [which] will lead to a restructuring of economies around the world" (Nerlich 2012: 24).

In another study, Nerlich and Koteyko (2009a) analysed English-language blog posts and news reports published between 1980 and 2008 which used the compound 'carbon indulgence'. The compound is used as a metaphor as it constructs climate change mitigation in terms of our knowledge of medieval papal indulgences as a way for the guilty to pay for absolution rather than change their behaviour. It also refers metonymically to self-indulgent or over-indulgent actions that result in an increase in carbon emissions. As such, 'carbon indulgence' was used to conceptualise (and criticise) carbon offsetting schemes, which promote reductions in emissions of carbon dioxide to compensate for or offset emissions made elsewhere. Used in this way, carbon offsetting was presented as a mechanism which simply makes it easier for those who pollute to continue to do so without feeling guilty. The 'carbon indulgence' compound was used in a similar way by the Carbon Rationing Action Group (CRAG) and in articles about CRAG published in English-language newspapers (Nerlich and Koteyko 2009b).

However, carbon offsetting has not been exclusively conceptualised via the 'carbon indulgence' compound. A study of British national newspapers and finance publications also identified the use of 'carbon gold rush' and 'carbon cowboy' metaphorical compounds to conceptualise carbon offsetting (Nerlich and Koteyko 2010). The gold rush compound was used to promote carbon offsetting: '[i]t's a carbon gold rush (. . .) It's very easy to set yourself up as a carbon offset provider (...) It's a booming industry' (Nerlich and Koteyko 2010: 45). The cowboy compound was, similarly to the 'carbon indulgence' compound, used to criticise carbon offsetting as an activity with dubious moral quality: '[o]ffsetting chief warns of carbon cowboys: Lack of standards a threat to fledgling business' (Nerlich and Koteyko 2010: 48).

These are just some of the many metaphorical carbon compounds that have emerged. They show how a whole new language is evolving around climate change, which needs to be monitored to understand how climate change is conceptualised by different stakeholders and how public attitudes may be shaped.

Future directions

By approaching metaphor from the perspective of its creative capacity and its potential to illuminate a range of standpoints and value commitments, we hope to have shown that the analysis of metaphors in print and particularly online media provides an opportunity to contribute to our understanding of the ethical and cultural dimensions of the climate change issue. However, several issues still need further study.

First, coming back to the point of strategic use, more attention must be paid to journalistic sources – that is, the actors behind the use of metaphors who are quoted and, thus, given voice in media content. We only identified one study which sought to link metaphor use in media content to sources. Nerlich and Jaspal (2013: 39) found that the carbon capture and storage media agenda was 'largely grounded in certain stakeholder agendas'. Such analyses can show which sources (e.g. politicians or scientists) are more predominantly used to lend credibility to arguments. Source identification and analysis can also be helpful for understanding whether certain actors are being strategically quoted to construct versions of events so that they would appear independent from the newspaper (Nerlich and Jaspal 2013).

Second, the majority of studies examining metaphor use in media content related to climate change focused on publications aimed at a general audience. Few studies analysed the metaphorical language that was employed to discuss climate change in specialised publications. These included Asplund's (2010) analysis of Swedish media outlets aimed at farmers, Nerlich and Koteyko's (2010) study of British national newspapers as well as finance publications including *Business Week*, *Environmental Finance* and the *Financial Times* and Nerlich and Jaspal's (2012) study of the English-language industry trade press. Further attention should be paid to metaphor use in specialised media outlets in order to understand whether and how different audiences may be exposed to different metaphors. This has, in fact, started to be done for other scientific issues (Skorczynska and Deignan 2006) and there is the additional argument that the sub-field of climate change should follow in the steps of research on metaphor use in the context of other scientific issues.

Third, comparative research is needed. By this we mean comparing metaphor use in climate change discourses across different national and cultural contexts and across different types of media – mainstream and new media, print and online media outlets. Metaphor use is, after all, constrained by our social and cultural environments. The communication of a complex natural, political and social issue such as climate change therefore calls for the examination of climate metaphors in a comparative context.

Note

1 In this chapter, single quote marks are used to quote linguistic expressions, and underlining is used for metaphorical expressions within quotes; small capitals indicate conceptual metaphors. In addition, we use initial capitals to label metaphors more generally; italics for discourses; and all-capitals for frames.

Further reading

Koteyko, N. (2012) 'Managing carbon emissions: A discursive presentation of "market-driven sustainability" in the British media', *Language and Communication*, 32: 24–35.

Nerlich, B. (2010) '"Climategate": Paradoxical metaphors and political paralysis', *Environmental Values*, 19(4): 419–42.

Nerlich, B. and Jaspal, R. (2012) 'Metaphors we die by? Geoengineering, metaphors, and the argument from catastrophe', *Metaphor and Symbol*, 27(2): 131–47.

Russill, C. (2011) 'Temporal metaphor in abrupt climate change communication: An initial effort at clarification', in W. Leal Filho (ed.) *The Economic, Social, and Political Elements of Climate Change*, New York: Springer.

References

Asplund, M. (2010) 'Metaphors in climate discourse: An analysis of Swedish farm magazines', *Journal of Science Communication*, 10(4): A01.

Atanasova, D. and Koteyko, N. (2015) 'Metaphors in *Guardian Online* and *Mail Online* opinion-page content on climate change: War, religion, and politics', *Environmental Communication*.

Calsamiglia, H. (1997) 'Divulgar: Itinerarios discursivos del saber', *Quark*, 7: 9–18.

Carolan, M.S. (2006) 'The values and vulnerabilities of metaphors within the environmental sciences', *Society and Natural Resources*, 19: 921–30.

Cassany, D., López, C. and Martí, J. (2000) 'La transformación divulgativa de redes conceptuales científicas. Hipótesis, modelo y estrategias', *Revista iberoamericana de Discurso y Sociedad*, 2(2): 73–103.

Cohen, M.J. (2011) 'Is the UK preparing for "war"? Military metaphors, personal carbon allowances, and consumption rationing in historical perspective', *Climatic Change*, 104: 199–222.

Condit, C., Lynch, J. and Winderman, E. (2012) 'Recent rhetorical studies in public understanding of science: Multiple purposes and strengths', *Public Understanding of Science*, 21: 386–400.

Doulton, H. and Brown, K. (2009) 'Ten years to prevent catastrophe? Discourses of climate change and international development in the UK press', *Global Environmental Change*, 19: 191–202.

Dryzek, J.S. (2005) *The Politics of the Earth: Environmental Discourses*, Oxford, UK: Oxford University Press.

Entman, R. (1993) 'Framing: Toward clarification of a fractured paradigm', *Journal of Communication*, 43(4): 518.

Glebkin, V. (2013) 'A socio-cultural history of the machine metaphor', *Review of Cognitive Linguistics*, 11(1): 145–62.

Gross, A.G. (1996) *The Rhetoric of Science*, Cambridge, MA: Harvard University Press.

Gwyn, R. (2002) *Communicating Health and Illness*, London: Sage.

Hellsten, I. (2002) *The Politics of Metaphor: Biotechology and Biodiversity in the Media*, Tampere, Finland: Tampere University Press.

Hellsten, I. and Nerlich, B. (2008) 'Genetics and genomics: The politics and ethics of metaphorical framing', in M. Bucchi and B. Trench (eds) *Handbook of Public Communication of Science and Technology*, London and New York: Routledge, pp. 93–109.

Journet, D. (2010) 'The resources of ambiguity: Context, narrative, and metaphor in Richard Dawkins's *The Selfish Gene*', *Journal of Business and Technical Communication*, 24(1): 29–59.

Koteyko, N. (2012) 'Managing carbon emissions: A discursive presentation of "market-driven sustainability" in the British media', *Language and Communication*, 32: 24–35.

Koteyko, N., Nerlich, B. and Hellsten, I. (2015) 'Climate change communication and the Internet: Challenges and opportunities for research', *Environmental Communication*, 9(2): 149–52.

Koteyko, N., Thelwall, M. and Nerlich, B. (2010) 'From carbon markets to carbon morality: Creative compounds as framing devices in online discourses on climate change mitigation', *Science Communication*, 32(1): 25–54.

Lakoff, G. (2004) *Don't Think of an Elephant: Know Your Values and Frame the Debate*, White River Junction, VT: Chelsea Green Publishing.

—— (2010) 'Why it matters how we frame the environment', *Environmental Communication*, 4(1): 70–81.

Lakoff, G. and Johnson, M. (1980) *Metaphors We Live By*, Chicago, IL: Chicago University Press.

Luokkanen, M., Huttunen, S. and Hildén, M. (2014) 'Geoengineering, news media and metaphors: Framing the controversial', *Public Understanding of Science*, 23(8): 966–81.

Massimiano, B. (1998) *Science and the Media*, London: Routledge.

Moser, S.C. and Dilling, L. (2004) 'Making climate hot', *Environment*, 34: 32–46.

Nancy, R., Eyles, J., Cole, D. and Iannantuono, A. (1997) 'The Ecosystem metaphor in science and policy', *The Canadian Geographer*, 41(2): 114–27.

Nerlich, B. (2009) '"The post-antibiotic apocalypse" and the "war on superbugs": Catastrophe discourse in microbiology, its rhetorical form and political function', *Public Understanding of Science*, 18(5): 574–90.

—— (2010) '"Climategate": Paradoxical metaphors and political paralysis', *Environmental Values*, 19(4): 419–42.

—— (2012) '"Low carbon" metals, markets and metaphors: The creation of economic expectations about climate change mitigation', *Climatic Change*, 110(1/2): 31–51.

Nerlich, B., Dingwall, R. and Clarke, D.D. (2002) 'The Book of Life: How the completion of the human genome project was revealed to the public', *Health*, 6(4): 445–69.

Nerlich, B., Evans, V. and Koteyko, N. (2011) 'Low carbon diet: Reducing the complexities of climate change to human scale', *Language and Cognition*, 3(1): 4582.

Nerlich, B. and Hellsten, I. (2014) 'The greenhouse metaphor and the footprint metaphor', *Technikfolgenabschätzung – Theorie und Praxis*, 23(2): 27–33.

Nerlich, B. and Jaspal, R. (2012). 'Metaphors we die by? Geoengineering, metaphors, and the argument from catastrophe', *Metaphor and Symbol*, 27(2): 131–47.

—— (2013) 'UK media representations of carbon capture and storage: Actors, frames and metaphors', *Metaphor and the Social World*, 3(1): 35–53.

Nerlich, B. and Koteyko, N. (2009a) 'Compounds, creativity and complexity in climate change communication: The case of "carbon indulgences"', *Global Environmental Change*, 19: 345–53.

—— (2009b) 'Carbon reduction activism in the UK: Lexical creativity and lexical framing in the context of climate change', *Environmental Communication*, 3(2): 206–23.

Nerlich, B. and Koteyko, N. (2010) 'Carbon gold rush and carbon cowboys: A new chapter in green mythology?' *Environmental Communication*, 4(1): 37–53.

Nerlich, B., Koteyko, N. and Brown, B. (2010) 'Theory and language of climate change communication', *Wiley Interdisciplinary Reviews*, 1: 1–14.

Nisbet, M.C. (2009) 'The ethics of framing science', in B. Nerlich, B. Larson and R. Elliott (eds) *Communicating Biological Sciences: Ethical and Metaphorical Dimensions*, London: Ashgate.

Nisbet, M.C. and Mooney, C. (2007) 'Framing science', *Science*, 316(5821): 56.

O'Neill, S. and Nicholson-Cole, S. (2009) '"Fear won't do it": Promoting positive engagement with climate change through visual and iconic representations', *Science Communication*, 30: 355–79.

Pauwels, E. (2013) 'Communication: Mind the metaphor', *Nature*, 500: 523–24.

Romaine, S. (1997) 'War and peace in the global greenhouse: Metaphors we die by', *Metaphor and Symbolic Activity*, 11: 175–94.

Russill, C. (2011) 'Temporal metaphor in abrupt climate change communication: An initial effort at clarification', in W. Leal Filho (ed.) *The Economic, Social, and Political Elements of Climate Change*, New York: Springer.

Russill, C. and Nyssa, Z. (2009) 'The tipping point trend in climate change communication', *Global Environmental Change*, 19: 336–44.

Schön, D. (1993) 'Generative metaphor: A perspective on problem-setting in social policy', in A. Ortony (ed.) *Metaphors and Thought*, 2nd edn, Cambridge, UK: Cambridge University Press.

Shaw, C. and Nerlich, B. (2015) 'Metaphor as a mechanism of global climate change governance: A study of international policies, 1992–2012', *Ecological Economics*, 109: 34–40.

Skorczynska, H. and Deignan, A. (2006) 'A comparison of metaphor vehicles and functions in scientific and popular business corpora', *Metaphor and Symbol*, 21: 87–104.

Somerville, R.C.J. (2006) 'Medical metaphors for climate issues', *Climatic Change*, 76: 1–6.

Thibodeau, P.H. and Boroditsky, L. (2013) 'Natural language metaphors covertly influence reasoning', *PLoS ONE*, 8(1): e52961.

Tynkkynen, N. (2010) 'A great ecological power in global climate policy? Framing climate change as a policy problem in Russian public discussion', *Environmental Politics*, 19(2): 179–95.

Ungar, S. (2007) 'Public scares: Changing the issue culture', in S. Moser and L. Dilling (eds) *Creating a Climate for Change: Communicating Climate Change and Facilitating Social Change*, Cambridge, UK: Cambridge University Press.

Väliverronen, E. and Hellsten, I. (2002) 'From "burning library" to "green medicine": The role of metaphors in communicating biodiversity', *Science Communication*, 24: 229–45.

Warnick, B.R. (2004) 'Technological metaphors and moral education: The hacker ethic and the computational experience', *Studies in Philosophy and Education*, 23: 265–81.

Woods, R., Fernández, A. and Coen, S. (2012) 'The use of religious metaphors by UK newspapers to describe and denigrate climate change', *Public Understanding of Science*, 21(3): 323–39.

Zinken, J., Hellsten, I. and Nerlich, B. (2008) 'Discourse metaphors', in R.M. Frank, R. Dirven, T. Ziemke, and E. Bernárdez (eds) *Body, Language and Mind*, 2nd edn, Amsterdam, The Netherlands: John Benjamins.

21
Metaphor and persuasion in politics

Andreas Musolff

Introduction: the role of metaphor in political discourse

In *The Art of Rhetoric*, Aristotle attributes to the Athenian leader Pericles (c. 495–429 BC) a powerful metaphorical denunciation of the enemy city of Aegina:

> Pericles told the Athenians to destroy Aegina, the eyesore of the Piraeus
> The Art of Rhetoric, *1411a; Aristotle 1991: 236*

The metaphorical description of the city as an *eyesore* is an efficient rhetorical move that kills several communication birds with one stone: it shifts the attention from military action with all its risks and ethical problems to the 'solution' of a quasi-aesthetic problem, it belittles and demeans the victim of the planned attack, and it presents the attacker, i.e. one's own side, as a problem-solver rather than as an aggressor. The *eyesore* metaphor thus works as an efficient means of legitimizing war not only at the representational level but also at emotional and interpersonal levels (Halliday 1978) insofar as it relieves misgivings about the rightfulness of one's own actions and at the same time serves to intimidate the victim as well as third parties.

Even when the intended effect is not as momentous as that of a war threat, the aptness of metaphor, metonymy, simile, analogy and related rhetorical figures of persuasive language use have made them the means of choice in public political discourse, even though there have been famous warnings against their use, e.g. by Thomas Hobbes and John Locke, precisely on account of their persuasive power (Hobbes 1661/1996; Locke 1690/1979). This chapter focuses on the multi-functionality of political metaphor as a central feature of its persuasive power. After a brief historical overview and an outline of cognitively orientated approaches since the advent of Conceptual metaphor theory (Chapter 1), it presents an exemplary analysis of metaphors in immigration debates, which illustrate the multi-dimensional character of metaphor in political persuasion. Lastly, current research desiderata and future directions are indicated.

Historical perspectives: political metaphor in the rhetorical tradition

The analysis of metaphor in public political discourse is as old as the emergence of rhetoric and its professional teaching in ancient Greece, at least as regards the Western tradition. Aristotle, in his remarks on metaphor in *The Art of Rhetoric*, which complement those in the *Poetics* (Mahon 1999), built on a tradition of devising and evaluating persuasive metaphors developed by the sophists and their critics such as Plato. In *The Art of Rhetoric*, metaphors are discussed explicitly in the third part, which deals mainly with 'style'. This apparent categorization of metaphor as a 'stylistic' feature has led to anachronistic misunderstandings of Aristotle's perspective equalling later concepts of metaphor as an ornamental epiphenomenon of language use that could be largely disregarded (Miller 1993; Lakoff and Johnson 1999). However, Aristotle's main concern in the analysis of 'style' is the clarity and perspicuity of texts as a central and integral part of the general rhetorical aim of establishing the speaker's credibility (*ethos*), move the hearers' emotions (*pathos*) and building a convincing argument (*logos*) (Charteris-Black 2013; Finlayson 2014). Metaphor is for Aristotle a means to achieve such clarity, not a mere decorative extra. As a result, he discusses metaphors in terms of the inferences that they facilitate in practical arguments (enthymemes), which suggest conclusions whose 'recognition occurs as soon as they are spoken (. . .) or (. . .) in which the intellect of the hearer is but a little behind' (Aristotle 1991: 235). He devotes a considerable amount of space on elucidating the relationship of metaphor and simile and highlights their importance for presenting arguments so that they are both vivid, succinct and hence, convincing (1991). Over-stretched metaphors and similes whose underlying analogies are either obscure or trite, i.e. those which strike hearers/readers as 'merely rhetorical' in the sense of mainly serving to show off an orator's brilliance, are discussed by Aristotle as infelicitous and inappropriate. In view of this focus on metaphor's role in achieving conceptual clarity, *The Art of Rhetoric* can serve as an example of cognition-oriented analysis that still calls for an adequate historiographic reconstruction (in place of the dismissive treatment of Aristotle as a stalking horse of a 'merely' stylistic perspective on metaphor, e.g. Lakoff and Johnson 1980/2003).

The aforementioned treatment may be understood as a reaction to traditions of referencing Aristotle, together with other famous classical authors of works on rhetoric, e.g. Cicero and Quintilian, as endorsing a reductionist view of metaphor as ornamental embellishment in 'School Rhetoric', which persisted from Antiquity up to the nineteenth century (Richards 1936). In opposition to this main trend, however, we find two famous (for some, infamous) philosophical 'warnings' against metaphor, especially in the political sphere, i.e. those by Thomas Hobbes and John Locke. Hobbes disassembled the near-identification of metaphor and simile in his *Leviathan* (1661/1996), and distinguished sharply between perspicuity-enhancing 'similitudes' (which he amply used in his own writings) and 'metaphors' which he considered to be a means to mislead, both in general communication and in particular in political discourses, to the point of fostering civil war (Musolff 2005). Locke, in his *Essay Concerning Human Understanding* (1690/1979) deepened this critique as part of a general criticism of the 'Abuse of Words' without, however, condemning all figurative language use per se (Mouton 2010). These traditions of taking metaphor seriously, i.e. as a part of a philosophical concern about the power of rhetoric to elucidate as well as confuse, were taken up in the twentieth century in various strands of a renewed, critical Rhetoric (e.g. Richards 1936; Perelman and Olbrechts-Tyteca 1971). As early as 1939 (but without sufficient political impact), Kenneth Burke applied metaphor criticism to Hitler's strategy of figuratively projecting a religious category, i.e. the devil, onto a 'visible, point-to-able form of people with a certain kind of "blood"' (Burke 1939/40), in order to warn of the genocidal dimension of Nazi metaphor use.

Overview of new perspectives: political metaphor and cognition

In the aftermath of twentieth-century totalitarian regimes, such as Nazism and Stalinism, which systematically used figurative language to publicly present and 'justify' their murderous policies by depicting supposed 'racial'- or 'class'-enemies as *parasites* that only deserved extermination, political metaphor criticism became a concern for the general critique of ideology and culture (e.g. Blumenberg 1960; Sontag 1979; Steiner 1987), but it largely lacked a basis in linguistics (for a notable exception see Weinrich 1963, 1967). In the language sciences, metaphor studies still only had an uneasy existence at the intersection (and often only at the margins) of semantics, pragmatics, analytical philosophy and philological studies (Ortony 1979).

This situation changed decisively with the publication of George Lakoff and Mark Johnson's book *Metaphors We Live By* in 1980, which established a new approach, Conceptual Metaphor Theory (CMT), as a key research area of Cognitive Linguistics (Croft and Cruse 2004, Chapter 1). It redefined metaphor as a mapping between 'domains' of knowledge and/or experience leading to systematic 'entailments', which 'framed' the respective target topic from a particular perspective. CMT thus emphasized the fundamental importance of metaphor for human thought and also highlighted its persuasive and political impact: 'Metaphors may (...) be a guide for future action. Such actions will, of course, fit the metaphor. This will, in turn, reinforce the power of the metaphor to make experience coherent. In this sense metaphors can be self-fulfilling prophecies' (1980/2003: 156). Since then, Lakoff has intervened several times in public political debates on wars in the Middle East, the so-called 'War on Terror' and the party-political divide in the US, which he interprets as competition/conflict between different versions of basic conceptual metaphors, in particular THE NATION (STATE) IS A PERSON and THE NATION (STATE) IS A FAMILY (e.g. Lakoff 1992, 1996, 2003). In addition, hundreds of books, book chapters and journal articles have been published in what has become almost an industry of applied critical metaphor studies, complete with its own discipline label, 'Critical Metaphor Analysis' (CMA), coined by Charteris-Black (2004), which suggests a combination of Conceptual Metaphor Theory and Critical Discourse Analysis (CDA). Over the past 25 years, these studies have been refined and extended by incorporating, *inter alia*, corpus-based and corpus-driven methods (e.g. Charteris-Black 2004, De Landtsheer 2009), Discourse and Conversation Analysis (e.g. Cameron and Deignan 2006), Appraisal and Empathy theory (e.g. Cameron 2011), 'Proximisation' (social and cognitive distance) theory (e.g. Hart 2010, Cap 2013; Chilton 2014) as well as experimental, psycho- and socio-linguistic and multimodal studies (e.g. Cienki and Müller 2008; Steen 2007); they have also led to further reflections on the 'rhetorical metaphor' concept (e.g. Charteris-Black 2013).

Those researchers who integrate metaphor in an overarching theory of analogical 'structure-mapping' reasoning (Gentner 1983; Gentner and Bowdle 2008) have emphasized that it is not single concepts or concept areas from different domains but rather their structural relationships that are 'aligned' with each other and give rise to inferences about the respective topics. This approach has proved fruitful in psycholinguistic experiments that try to elicit the impact of such inferences on the hearers or readers of metaphoric texts. In experiments with university students as participants, it was shown, for instance, that the inclusion of contrasting metaphor stimuli, i.e. instances of CRIME-AS-VIRUS and CRIME-AS-BEAST metaphors, in otherwise identical versions of a media crime report, led to systematically varying analogical inferences, which resulted in differing preferences for policy and prosecution strategies. When a crime surge was introduced as the effect of a 'virus', most participants tended to process further incoming information within that biological frame and to propose 'investigating the root causes and (. . .) enacting social reform', whereas when crime was framed as a 'beast', they preferred to align further information with this frame and to articulate a preference for 'catching and jailing criminals and enacting harsher enforcement laws' (Thibodeau and Boroditsky 2011: 2). For analyses focusing on the persuasive force of metaphor, it seems more promising to investigate such actually elicited analogical inferences and their impact rather than relying on vague assumptions about hypothetical 'entailments'. However, it is still an open question how results from such an experimental set-up, which is characterized by narrowly controlled stimulus input and reaction options, can be transferred to 'naturally' occurring discourse conditions.

The empirical application of CMT to political discourse and other 'real-world' discourse phenomena has led to a questioning of some fundamental assumptions in the cognitive approach. Early CMT had relied on relatively few data and had made strong predictions concerning the coherence, systematicity and psycho-linguistic automaticity of processing conceptual metaphor systems. More recent data-based empirical studies have, however, revealed a high degree of synchronic and diachronic, intra- and cross-cultural variation, not only at the production/usage level but also in the reception/interpretation of metaphors (Dirven, Hawkins and Sandikcioglu 2001; Dirven, Frank and Ilie 2001; Musolff 2004, 2010a,b). As a result, the classic CMT model has been modified and adapted in various ways to accommodate new methodologies, including quantitative approaches. The early practice of interpreting linguistic usage as a mere 'surface manifestation of conceptual metaphor' (Lakoff 1993: 244) has largely been superseded by approaches that recognize 'discourse metaphors' as constituting an analytical level in its own right, whose relationship to conceptual metaphors has to be explained rather than just assumed (Zinken 2007; Zinken et al. 2008). This issue has led to proposals for either multiple or hybrid cognitive-pragmatic methodologies in CMT applications, to account for the variation in metaphor production, understanding and effect on recipients' behaviour (Gibbs and Tendahl 2006; Gibbs and Lonergan 2009; Ritchie 2013).

The analysis of political metaphor as a discourse phenomenon certainly needs to account for their communicative multi-functionality (see introduction) and in particular the relationship to narrative text structures, argumentation and emotive-polemical genres. To capture these dimensions of persuasive political metaphor use, the category of 'scenario' has been proposed (Musolff 2006; Semino 2008) as the basic structural unit for conceptual mapping. Scenarios are mini-narratives that include a 'conclusion' or 'solution' that seems to be ethically correct, self-evident and practicable at the source level and is presented analogically as equally 'good' in all respects at the target level. Its inferences are suggested to the hearers or readers as convincing topic explanations, on account of their seeming evidentiality, and thus 'naturally' lead to recommendations for specific problem-solving actions. Such inferences deriving from metaphoric scenarios are in the first place context-specific, 'emergent' conclusions, which over time can become crystallized into figures of thought that are taken for granted in a discourse community.

Critical issues and controversies

By emphasizing the centrality and ubiquity of metaphor for conceptualization processes, CMT has greatly enhanced the appeal of metaphor analysis for discourse studies on socio-political issues. At the same time, its assumption of a 'secondary' status of discourse phenomena remains a fundamental problem. It makes CMT vulnerable to criticisms of circularity, as its data have often been collected to fit theoretically assumed conceptual metaphors but are then presented as 'proof' of those same metaphors without comparison with other, contradicting data. Some discourse phenomena predicted by CMT in political discourse, e.g. an alleged split of metaphoric STATE AS FAMILY models into STRICT FATHER and NURTURANT PARENT models in US politics, have proved hard to find in real-life discourse data (Cienki 2008), or their metaphorical status has been contested, e.g. that of the NATION AS PERSON concept (Twardzisz 2013). Another open issue is the 'deliberateness' (Steen 2008, 2011) of metaphor use and reception. From its inception, CMT has stressed the 'automatic' and 'unconscious' nature of processing metaphoric meaning and has sought to corroborate this with evidence from psycholinguistic experiments (Gibbs 1994, 2011; Glucksberg 2001). However, this assumption is counter-intuitive as regards political discourse. Genre analysis and CDA have established that politicians' and journalists' texts, which form the basis of many CMA studies, are among the most carefully prepared and edited types of discourse on the senders' side and that their conceptual content is publicly (or, where this is not possible due to authoritarian regimes, privately) scrutinized, debated and routinely contested. Any identification of the basic conceptual processing of metaphor with its emotional or political *acceptance* is highly dubious. Hence, the differentiation of various stages in the reception process – from the identification of metaphor occurrence through referent disambiguation, context-adequate interpretation to possible changes in opinion and follow-up behaviour – has to be developed further.

Closely related to this issue is the question of the 'manipulative' power of metaphor, which implies its 'persuasive' force. CMT-related statements on this topic range from assertions of ideologically loaded metaphors being used (by their producers) as a means to deceive their recipients and naïve users (e.g. Goatly 2007; Charteris-Black 2005), to positions claiming to draw a neat line between scientific cognitive analysis and its politically 'engaged' application (Lakoff 1996). More sceptical approaches refrain from jumping to conclusions about recipients' understanding of metaphors on the sole basis of metaphor production data and instead elicit and document their inferences (see above) and/or attempt a 'triangulation' (Wodak 2001a, b) that combines linguistic analyses of semantic choices at sentence level with pragmatic methods to reconstruct the co-text of the respective utterances and with historical investigations of their 'situatedness' in their socio-political contexts (Musolff 2004, 2010; Gavriely-Nuri 2010).

Furthermore, if a manipulative power of metaphor is considered to exist in a strong sense, we need to ask whether and how the 'critical' analysis of metaphor can help to enlighten the 'deceived' audience and to resist its persuasive appeal. Such attempts have indeed been made with regard to metaphors stigmatizing specific 'outsider' groups, such as migrants, minorities, people with illnesses such as cancer, AIDS, mental handicaps, etc. The legal, political and ethical implications of banning certain metaphors from public use, or advising against their use, or merely relying on a cathartic effect of public criticism of their use are controversial (e.g. Sontag 1979; Hawkins 2001; Neagu and Colipcă 2014), touching as they do on general debates over the social and ethical impact of CDA (Wodak and Chilton 2005; Wodak and Meyer 2009). The following section sketches a discourse-critical assessment of persuasive metaphor effects in the immigration debate in the United Kingdom.

Current research: metaphors in debates about immigration

Discourses about migration and in particular the effect of immigration on the 'we-group' of a 'home nation' have been a main area of interest in critical studies of metaphor use and social impact, as such debates are rife with stereotyping, xenophobia, racism and identity-construction (Messer et al. 2012; Wodak and Sedlak 2000). Conceptual and Critical Metaphor Theory have identified a limited number of 'scenarios' (see above) that are used in immigration debates, each with its own persuasive/reasoning potential (Hart 2010; KhosraviNik et al. 2012; Neagu and Colipcă 2014):

a) The SPACE-CONTAINER scenario: the nation(-state) is conceptualized as a *container* with distinct *boundaries*, which distinguish those *on the outside* from those *inside*: immigrants are thus *outsiders* that want to *come/move into the container*. The *container* has *doors* or other *openings* that can be *closed, open* or *half-open* and it is seen as having only a *limited capacity* to include people; if too many immigrants come in, this increases the *pressure* inside to *bursting point* and necessitates the erection of new *barriers*.
b) The MASS MOVEMENT scenario (specific to immigrants as PARTICIPANTS): the most prominent version is that of a *flood, tide* or *wave* that *pours/rushes* into the container. Its impact on the *insiders* is indicated by verbs such as *flock, pass through, overwhelm*.
c) The ACTION scenario (specific to CONTAINER-insiders as PARTICIPANTS): these fall into two distinct groups: on the one hand, those politicians, institutions and social groupings who are viewed as (and mostly condemned for) *inviting, letting, allowing, bringing* immigrants into the country, and on the other side those who try to *send them home, round them up, chuck* or *kick them out* or at least *limit, target* and *control* immigration. Ordinary *insider*-citizens are depicted as victims of an unwanted change in their living circumstances. A sub-scenario is that of VIOLENT ACTION, as indicated by vocabulary such as *backlash, invasion, rivers of blood, revolution, time bomb*, which legitimizes the *insiders*' defensive response to a perceived aggression.
d) The EFFECT scenario concentrates on the results of immigration as depicted in the previous scenarios. It has three sub-scenarios: MIX, GAIN and SCROUNGE. The first one depicts an alleged blending of cultures that makes them interchangeable and unrecognizable, but most importantly *submerges, dominates* or *subjugates* the traditional home culture. The GAIN sub-scenario portrays immigrants as *enriching* the home culture, mainly by providing an *economic benefit*. The third sub-scenario is that of the IMMIGRANT AS SCROUNGER who *sucks, drains* or *bleeds the country dry, aims for freebies* and, as a *parasite, lives off* or *sponges from* their *host* country.

Whilst this listing of metaphor scenarios gives an overview of the conceptual range of source concepts that are commonly brought to bear on a topic, it does not necessarily tell us much about how they are precisely understood and in which groups of recipients they find the strongest resonance. A recent study (Musolff 2015) differentiates the use of such metaphors across three genres of immigration debates in Britain, i.e. the press, online discussion fora and blogs.

The data for this analysis consist of three samples: a press sample, a sample of three online discussion fora that are maintained by the BBC under their popular 'Have your say' website (BBC 2010a–c) and 40 Internet weblogs (blogs) that included uses of the term 'parasite' for immigrants, with readers' comments (inasmuch as these have been kept accessible by the blog managers, i.e. without 'removed' postings). Table 21.1 gives an overview of the range and size of the whole corpus (word counts for blogs have been established through conversion into Word documents, which include extra website material to a greater or lesser extent; their word count is therefore not as exact as that for the other media).

When the corpus was queried specifically for instances of stigmatization of (im)migrants as *parasites* (as part of the SCROUNGE-EFFECT scenario), a differentiated picture of the immigration

Table 21.1 Range and size of the whole corpus

Media	Newspaper and magazine articles (2003–2013)	Have your say online fora (April–June 2010)	Blogs (accessed December 2013)
	Daily Express, Daily Mail, Financial Times, Guardian, Independent, Observer, Scotsman, Spectator, Sun, Telegraph, Times.	(1) Should politicians be talking about immigration? (2) How should immigration be tackled? (3) Are immigration rules fair?	40 websites, searched on WWW by key words: *immigration, parasites, UK*
No. of items	138 articles	2,473 postings (566, 881, and 1,026 for the respective fora; with altogether 81 postings removed by BBC online forum management)	40 websites
No. of words	100,756	333,518	89,950

debate in Britain emerged. *Parasite* metaphors do indeed occur across all the genres of press articles, blogs and online fora, but their frequency, collocation patterns and argumentative contexts are markedly different in each. The press sample, even though it includes texts from tabloids and broadsheets that take a strong anti-immigration stance, has only one single text in which *parasite* is used in an assertive sense to denote immigrants, and even this assertion is qualified by the distinction between 'beneficial' and 'non-beneficial' immigrants, accusing as it does the government of 'letting in parasites, [but] turning away entrepreneurs' (*Daily Telegraph* 2013). All other articles in the press sample quote *parasite* metaphors (or allege to quote them) as being used by xenophobes, with clearly negative evaluations. In the mainstream press, *parasite* metaphors seem too ideologically loaded to be used uncritically; instead, they are reported as being employed by the xenophobic part of the political spectrum in Britain. There appear thus to be only few press texts that could serve as models for readers to 'learn' the aggressive use of *parasite* metaphors from, even though the SCROUNGE-EFFECT scenario (of the UK being exploited by immigrants) is represented in about 20 per cent of all articles.

The percentage of texts invoking the SCROUNGE scenario is even smaller in the online-forum sample, i.e. about 10 per cent of all postings. In 90 per cent of all these postings, however, the scenario is used in an assertive-aggressive way to depict immigrants as scroungers, in some cases in elaborate, sarcastic versions. This use of the SCROUNGE scenario overlaps in many cases with the (INSIDER-)ACTION scenario, so that radical measures against supposedly *sponging* immigrants are advocated, e.g. using the army to 'round up immigrants who are not working and deport them immediately' (BBC 2010a). As regards the use of dehumanizing characterizations such as *parasites, leeches,* or *sucking blood/life out of [the host society]*, the picture becomes more complicated: in the first place they appear to be rare, amounting as they do to just 15 instances in the sample; of these, 50 per cent are directly targeted at immigrants. The remaining 50 per cent of instances, however, include critical thematizations of such uses within arguments defending the right of immigrants and also counter-usage, so to speak, which applies the *parasite/scrounger* image to 'indigenous' UK benefit receivers to whom the immigrants are compared favourably. Like the press, such online comments ascribe the discriminating use of *parasite* metaphors against immigrants to the xenophobic parts of the British public and political landscape. Unlike in the press, however, the forum commentators' critical perception of such metaphors does not seem to hinder them from using these same metaphors against other target groups.

In the blog sample (which is statistically incomparable to the other samples due to its pre-determined 100 per cent rate of *parasite* text occurrences), we encounter a different calibre of polemical use of *parasite* metaphors altogether. All blogs start with strong assertions of a *parasite*-status of immigrants, often in headlines such as 'Foreign Immigrants are Parasites', 'Britain: Muslim immigrants are the chief parasites'. These assertions are then followed up in more than 80 per cent of cases by emphatic endorsements and reinforcements in the main text body of the blog and its further comments, which detail the *parasites*' effect in graphic detail and combine this with racist (in one case, anti-Semitic) hate speech. Eight blogs also contain comments that are critical of the blog's main anti-immigration thrust but these are apologetic, arguing about details about exaggerated statistics, the economic benefit that immigrants bring to Britain and issues of Human Rights legislation. They do not, however, tackle the issue of stigmatizing and dehumanizing metaphors critically in the way that the press and online forum users do. The emphatic anti-immigration comments, on the other hand, use openly insulting statements about their target referents, not only describing them as criminals and scroungers but also denouncing them as being both metaphorically and literally *dirty* as well as elaborating on the bio-imagery by using *parasite*-related terminology (*leeches, locusts, rats, vermin, plague, germs, contamination*). They also include detailed analogies between the effect that bio-parasites have on their host organisms and the alleged destructive impact of immigrants on their host societies, thus maximizing the polemical and racially stigmatizing effect of the MUSLIM IMMIGRANT AS PARASITE scenario: 'During their centuries of conquest, marauding Arab tribes subjugated their neighbors, sucked them dry – as parasites do – and then moved on. And the process continues – right into the 21st century. Unable to produce much wealth, or for that matter, much of *anything*, on their own, Muslims flood into the West where they reproduce like lice and live, parasitically, on the wealth of others – what we know as welfare' (gerryporter.blogspot).

The results of our comparison of *parasite* metaphors in three media genres indicate that only the 'Blogosphere' exhibits a relatively consistent xenophobic and polemic bias insofar as the *parasite* metaphor is used to dehumanize immigrants and denounce them as not being part of the 'proper' national society. However, in the online fora, and to an even greater extent in the press, such usage is explicitly criticized and ascribed to a section of the political spectrum that the relevant journalists and commentators argue against, even when they employ the SCROUNGE scenario themselves. *Parasite* metaphors are never neutral, nor are they used 'naïvely' in the sense of non-reflective, 'automatic' usage. Whoever is employing this metaphor or its semantic 'relatives' (*bloodsucker, leech*, etc.) is doing so in the knowledge of its strongly polemical, insulting and defamatory bias. This finding also seems to provide evidence that both the production and the interpretation of explicitly quoted political metaphors is deliberate and reflective, i.e. is informed by socio-historically 'situated' knowledge of typical users and registers, ethical and legal implications and precedents in historical racist discourses. In Britain, legal actions have been brought against racist uses of *parasite* metaphors, and the evidence from online fora discussed above shows that it is not just journalists but also many members of the public who explicitly denounce its defamatory function. Even though British usage of *parasite* imagery may not be as strongly associated with Nazi-jargon as it is in Germany and Austria (Posch, Stopfner and Kienpointner 2013; Musolff 2012), its closeness to racist hate speech is familiar to the online commentators and most probably eschewed by the majority among them for this very reason (e.g. 'those who bang on about assylum [*sic*] seekers, yes some may be fraudulent but then the same points were made about Jews fleeing the Nazis').

The metaphor production and interpretation data presented here would have to be corroborated by larger corpora and by detailed socio-psychological studies of actual opinion-forming/changing power of such metaphors of the kind sketched above for CRIME-AS-VIRUS and CRIME-AS-BEAST metaphors, in order to provide reliable evidence. One result they seem to indicate relatively clearly, however, is that the usage-conditions, especially the media and text genres in which they occur, have a strong bearing on their pragmatic construction and elaboration in utterances and interpretations by recipients. The persuasiveness of political metaphor evidently depends on these factors and cannot be exclusively derived from the source-target mapping. The cognitive approach to political metaphor needs to be complemented by text-analytical, psycholinguistic and discourse-historical methods.

In the case of *parasite* metaphors, the discourse-historical aspect takes on a special importance, due to the 'live' historical memory of Nazi jargon as a precedent. In addition, an ever wider historical horizon has to be considered. According to the cognitive approach, the default metaphorization trajectory goes from a concrete source to an abstract target concept, which in our case means that the target notion of socio-parasites is derived from bio-parasites (Chilton 2005; Hawkins 2001). Curiously, however, the etymological and lexical history of the term 'parasite' points towards a diachronic precedence of socio- over the bio-parasites: the latter were only gradually identified and terminologized (as characterizing whole species) in the seventeenth and eighteenth centuries, whereas talk of *scrounging* socio-parasites predates them by at least one hundred years in English and by two full millennia in the languages it was borrowed from, i.e. Latin and Ancient Greek (Gullestad 2012; Serres 2007). The Renaissance 'parasite' was a sponging courtier, cleric or servant who earned his keep not by honest work but through flattery and servility, and he was the (conceptual) descendant of a stock figure of ancient comedy, i.e. the *parasitus* (Latin) or *parasitos* (Greek) as the hanger-on of rich people (Damon 1998). We thus have not one but two historical antecedents for *parasite* metaphors in today's usage: (a) the ancient figure of the lazy scrounger, a contemptible and ludicrous individual and (b) the popular science notion of a bio-parasite as a species, which not only damages its host (by depriving it of some of its resources) but can destroy it (e.g. by way of complete resource-consumption, or by injuring it or infecting it with fatal diseases). Both versions fit the SCROUNGE scenario as identified in our corpus; so at this point we have to consider the metaphor's collocations and argumentative contexts to arrive at a sufficiently fine-grained analysis. In our corpus, collocations of *parasite* metaphors with biological terminology (*leeches* etc.) and explicit analogies between bio- and socio-parasites occur almost exclusively in the blogs. It is these uses that can most plausibly be said to be dehumanizing, rather than the SCROUNGE scenario as such: it too is negatively stereotyping but focuses more on the *scroungers*' alleged laziness and resource-reduction for the host than on a necessarily destructive effect.

The implicit argumentative 'conclusions' and practical 'solutions' of these two versions differ drastically: the 'mere' SCROUNGER-PARASITE is, at worst, a nuisance that needs 'keeping in check', the SPECIES-PARASITE is a deadly threat that requires relentless extermination. The persuasiveness of *parasite* metaphor uses thus hangs not on the simple use of the metaphoric term but on the alleged plausibility of the source-scenario in which they are integrated and of its transfer on the respective socio-political topic issue. To define the immigration issue in terms of a SPECIES-PARASITE threat is an attempt to persuade the recipients to take violent action.

Future directions

The example of metaphors in immigration debates demonstrates several implications and desiderata for further research on metaphor in political discourse:

a) The need for genre- and register-differentiation: language in politics is not a homogenous object of investigation and consequently metaphor research in this field has to take socio-linguistic, situational and genre-dependent variation into account, both at the level of qualitative (semantic-pragmatic) and quantitative (distributional) analysis. In doing so, it will fit in with developments in recent cognitive metaphor studies that highlight intra- as well as cross-cultural variation as a central characteristic of metaphor usage and understanding (Carver and Pikalo 2008; Kövecses 2009; Low et al. 2010). A further, connected perspective is the application of this approach to multimodal studies, which might allow the analysis of converging data from different semiotic levels in metaphor usage and reception.

b) A framework to integrate qualitative-interpretative, psycholinguistic (experimental), corpus-based and corpus-driven analyses of metaphor production and reception, which have sometimes been conducted without connection. Such a multi-methodological perspective demands collaborative research projects that transcend one researcher's capacity and provide larger amounts of data to groups of researchers who can test and replicate analyses (Deignan 2005; Gibbs and Lonergan 2009; Steen 2007; Steen et al. 2010).

c) The historicity of political metaphor has been occasionally acknowledged (e.g. Musolff 2010b; Trim 2011) but, due to a synchronic bias of CMT and some of its CDA applications, is still often neglected, e.g. in references to metaphorical applications of the *Great Chain of Being* that omit the huge amount of insights available from conceptual history research (Lakoff and Turner 1989). As Rash (2006) has shown, the mere association of HUMAN-ANIMAL mappings in political discourse with the *Great Chain of Being* conceptual metaphor complex is not sufficient to describe or explain the cognitive import and persuasiveness of that metaphor as used in Hitler's *Mein Kampf*; rather, its relationship to that tradition (i.e. deliberate selective use) is highly significant for any in-depth analysis.

As a field of linguistic investigation, political metaphor analysis has the advantage of confronting any theoretical approach with empirical data that are relatively easy to access and at the same time discursively highly salient on account of their social impact and public contentiousness. The debate about persuasive political metaphor and the best methods of its analysis, which Aristotle *et al.* started, is certain to continue.

Further reading

Cap, P. (2013) *Proximization: The Pragmatics of Symbolic Distance Crossing*, Amsterdam, The Netherlands: John Benjamins.

Charteris-Black, J. (2013) *Analysing Political Speeches: Rhetoric, Discourse and Metaphor*, Basingstoke, UK: Palgrave Macmillan.

Musolff, A. (2010b) 'Metaphor in discourse history', in M. E. Winters, H. Tissari and K. Allan (eds) *Historical Cognitive Linguistics*, Berlin, Germany: De Gruyter Mouton.

—— (2012) 'Immigrants and parasites: The history of a bio-social metaphor', in M. Messer, R. Schroeder and R. Wodak (eds) *Migrations: Interdisciplinary Perspectives*, Vienna, Austria: Springer.

Semino, E. (2008) *Metaphor in Discourse*, Cambridge, UK: Cambridge University Press.

References

Aristotle (1991) *The Art of Rhetoric*, ed. H.C. Lawson-Tancred, London: Penguin.
BBC (2010a) Have your say: Should politicians be talking about immigration? Available at: http://www.bbc.co.uk/blogs/haveyoursay/2010/04/should_politicians_be_talking.html (accessed 15 December 2013).
—— (2010b) Have your say: How should immigration be tackled? Available at: http://www.bbc.co.uk/blogs/haveyoursay/2010/04/how_should_immigration_be_tack.html (accessed 15 December 2013)
—— (2010c) Have your say: Are immigration rules fair? Available at: http://www.bbc.co.uk/blogs/haveyoursay/2010/06/are_immigration_rules_fair.html (accessed 15 December 2013).
Blumenberg, H. (1960) *Paradigmen zu einer Metaphorologie*, Bonn, Germany: Bouvier.
Burke, K. (1939/40) 'The Rhetoric of Hitler's "Battle"', *The Southern Review* 5: 1–21. Reprinted in M. Shapiro (ed.) (1984) *Language and Politics*, Oxford, UK: Blackwell.
Cameron, L. (2011) *Metaphor and Reconciliation: The Discourse Dynamics of Empathy in Post-Conflict Conversations*, London: Routledge.
Cameron, L. and Deignan, A. (2006) 'The emergence of metaphor in discourse', *Applied Linguistics* 27(4): 671–690.
Cap, P. (2013) *Proximization: The Pragmatics of Symbolic Distance Crossing*, Amsterdam, The Netherlands: John Benjamins.
Carver, T. and Pikalo, J. (eds) (2008) *Political Language and Metaphor: Interpreting and Changing the World*, London: Routledge.
Charteris-Black, J. (2004) *Corpus Approaches to Critical Metaphor Analysis*, Basingstoke, UK: Palgrave Macmillan.
—— (2005) *Politicians and Rhetoric: The Persuasive Power of Metaphor*, Basingstoke: Palgrave Macmillan.
—— (2013) *Analysing Political Speeches: Rhetoric, Discourse and Metaphor*, Basingstoke, UK: Palgrave Macmillan.
Chilton, P. (2005) 'Manipulation, memes and metaphors: The case of *Mein Kampf*', in L. de Saussure and P. Schulz (eds) *Manipulation and Ideologies in the Twentieth Century*, Amsterdam: John Benjamins.
—— (2014) *Language, Space and Mind: The Conceptual Geometry of Linguistic Meaning*, Cambridge, UK: Cambridge University Press.
Cienki, A. (2008) 'The application of conceptual metaphor theory to political discourse: Methodological questions and some possible solutions', in T. Carver and J. Pikalo (eds) *Political Language and Metaphor: Interpreting and Changing the World*, London: Routledge.
Cienki, A. and Müller, C. (2008) *Metaphor and Gesture*, Amsterdam, The Netherlands: John Benjamins.
Croft, W. and Cruse, D. A. (2004) *Cognitive Linguistics*, Cambridge, UK: Cambridge University Press.
Damon, C. (1998) *The Mask of the Parasite: A Pathology of Roman Patronage*, Ann Arbor, MI: University of Michigan Press.
De Landtsheer, C. (2009) 'Collecting political meaning from the count of metaphor', in A. Musolff and J. Zinken (eds) *Metaphor and Discourse*, Basingstoke, UK: Palgrave Macmillan.
Deignan, A. (2005) *Metaphor and Corpus Linguistics*, Amsterdam, The Netherlands: John Benjamins.
Dirven, R., Hawkins, B. and Sandikcioglu, E. (eds) (2001) *Language and Ideology. Volume I: Theoretical Cognitive Approaches*, Amsterdam, The Netherlands: John Benjamins.
Dirven, R., Frank, R. M. and Ilie, C. (eds) (2001) *Language and Ideology. Volume II: Descriptive Cognitive Approaches*, Amsterdam, The Netherlands: John Benjamins.
Finlayson, A. (2014) 'Proving, pleasing and persuading? Rhetoric in contemporary British politics', *The Political Quarterly* 85: 428–436.
Gavriely-Nuri, G. (2010) 'If both opponents "extend hands in peace" – Why don't they meet?', *Journal of Language and Politics* 9(3): 449–468.
Gentner, D. (1983) 'Structure-mapping: A theoretical framework of analogy', *Cognitive Science* 7: 155–170.

Gentner, D. and Bowdle, B. F. (2008) 'Metaphor as structure-mapping', in R. W. Gibbs, Jr. (ed.) *The Cambridge Handbook of Metaphor and Thought*, Cambridge, UK: Cambridge University Press.

Gibbs, R. W., Jr. (1994) *The Poetics of Mind: Figurative Thought, Language, and Understanding*, Cambridge, UK: Cambridge University Press.

—— (2011) 'Are "deliberate" metaphors really deliberate? A question of human consciousness and action', *Metaphor and the Social World* 1(1): 26–52.

Gibbs, R. W., Jr. and Lonergan, J. E. (2009) 'Studying metaphor in discourse: Some lessons, challenges and new data', in A. Musolff and J. Zinken (eds) *Metaphor and Discourse*, Basingstoke, UK: Palgrave Macmillan.

Gibbs, R. W., Jr. and Tendahl, M. (2006) 'Cognitive effort and effects in metaphor comprehension: Relevance theory and psycholinguistics', *Mind & Language* 21(3): 379–403.

Glucksberg, S. (2001) *Understanding Figurative Language: From Metaphors to Idioms*, Oxford, UK: Oxford University Press.

Goatly, A. (2007) *Washing the Brain: Metaphor and Hidden Ideology*, Amsterdam, The Netherlands: John Benjamins.

Gullestad, A. (2012) 'Parasite' in *Political Concepts: A Critical Lexicon*, ed. by The New School for Social Research. Available at: http://www.politicalconcepts.org/issue1/2012-parasite/ (accessed 30 December 2013).

Halliday, M. A. K. (1978) *Language as Social Semiotic: The Social Interpretation of Language and Meaning*, London: Edward Arnold.

Hart, C. (2010) *Critical Discourse Analysis and Cognitive Science: New Perspectives on Immigration Discourse*, Basingstoke, UK: Palgrave Macmillan.

Hawkins, B. W. (2001) 'Ideology, metaphor and iconographic reference', in R. Dirven, R. M. Frank and C. Ilie (eds) *Language and Ideology. Volume II: Descriptive Cognitive Approaches*, Amsterdam, The Netherlands: John Benjamins.

Hobbes, T. (1661/1996) *Leviathan*, ed. Richard Tuck, Cambridge, UK: Cambridge University Press.

KhosraviNik, M., Krzyżanowski, M. and Wodak, R. (2012) 'Dynamics of representations in discourse: Immigrants in the British press', in M. Messer, R. Schroeder and R. Wodak (eds) *Migrations: Interdisciplinary Perspectives*, Vienna, Austria: Springer.

Kövecses, Z. (2009) 'Metaphor, culture, and discourse: The pressure of coherence', in A. Musolff and J. Zinken (eds) *Metaphor and Discourse*, Basingstoke, UK: Palgrave Macmillan.

Lakoff, G. (1992) 'Metaphor and war: The metaphor system used to justify war in the Gulf', in M. Pütz (ed.) *Thirty Years of Linguistic Evolution: Studies in the Honour of René Dirven*, Amsterdam, The Netherlands: John Benjamins.

Lakoff, G. (1993) 'The contemporary theory of metaphor', in A. Ortony (ed.) *Metaphor and Thought*, 2nd edn, Cambridge, UK: Cambridge University Press, pp. 202–251.

—— (1996) *Moral Politics: What Conservatives Know That Liberals Don't*, Chicago, IL: University of Chicago Press.

—— (2003) 'Metaphor and war, again'. Available at http://www.alternet.org/story.html?StoryID=15414 (accessed 15 December 2013).

Lakoff, G. and Johnson, M. (1980/2003) *Metaphors We Live By*, Chicago, IL: University of Chicago Press.

—— (1999) *Philosophy in the Flesh: The Embodied Mind and Its Challenge to Western Thought*, New York: Basic Books.

Lakoff, G. and Turner, M. (1989) *More Than Cool Reason: A Field Guide to Poetic Metaphor*, Chicago, IL: University of Chicago Press.

Locke, J. (1690/1979) *An Essay Concerning Human Understanding*, ed. P. H. Nidditch, Oxford, UK: Oxford University Press.

Low, G. D., Todd, Z., Deignan, A. and Cameron, L. (eds) (2010) *Researching and Applying Metaphor in the Real World*, Amsterdam, The Netherlands: Benjamins.

Mahon, J. E. (1999) 'Getting your sources right: What Aristotle didn't say', in L. Cameron and G. Low (eds) *Researching and Applying Metaphor*, Cambridge, UK: Cambridge University Press.

Messer, M., Schroeder, R. and Wodak, R. (eds) (2012) *Migrations: Interdisciplinary Perspectives*, Vienna, Austria: Springer.

Miller, G. A. (1993) 'Images and models, similes and metaphors', in A. Ortony (ed.) *Metaphor and Thought*, Cambridge, UK: Cambridge University Press.

Mouton, N. T. O. (2010) 'Metaphor, empiricism and truth: A fresh look at seventeenth-century theories of figurative language', in A. Burkhardt and B. Nerlich (eds) *Tropical Truths: The Epistemology of Metaphor and Other Tropes*, Berlin, Germany: W. de Gruyter.

Musolff, A. (2004) *Metaphor and Political Discourse: Analogical Reasoning in Debates about Europe*, Basingstoke, UK: Palgrave Macmillan.

—— (2005) '*Ignes fatui* or *apt similitude*? The apparent denunciation of metaphor by Thomas Hobbes', *Hobbes Studies* 18: 96–113.

—— (2006) 'Metaphor scenarios in public discourse', *Metaphor and Symbol* 21(1): 23–38.

—— (2010a) *Metaphor, Nation and the Holocaust: The Concept of the Body Politic*, London: Routledge.

—— (2010b) 'Metaphor in discourse history', in M. E. Winters, H. Tissari and K. Allan (eds) *Historical Cognitive Linguistics*, Berlin, Germany: De Gruyter Mouton.

—— (2012) 'Immigrants and parasites: The history of a bio-social metaphor', in M. Messer, R. Schroeder and R. Wodak (eds) *Migrations: Interdisciplinary Perspectives*, Vienna, Austria: Springer.

—— (2015) 'Dehumanizing metaphors in UK immigrant debates in press and online media', *Journal of Language Aggression and Conflict* 3(1): 41–56.

Neagu, M. and Colipcă, I. (2014) 'Metaphor and self/other representations: A study on British and Romanian headlines on migration', in A. Musolff, F. MacArthur and G. Pagani (eds) *Metaphor and Intercultural Communication*, London: Bloomsbury.

Ortony, A. (1979) *Metaphor and Thought*, Cambridge, UK: Cambridge University Press.

Perelman, C. and Olbrechts-Tyteca, L. (1971) *The New Rhetoric*, Notre Dame, IN: University of Notre Dame Press.

Posch, C., Stopfner, M. and Kienpointner, M. (2013) 'German postwar discourse of the extreme and populist right', in R. Wodak and J. E. Richardson (eds) *Analysing Fascist Discourse in Talk and Text*, London: Routledge, pp. 97–121.

Rash, F. (2006) *The Language of Violence: Adolf Hitler's* Mein Kampf, Oxford, UK: P. Lang.

Richards, I. A. (1936) *The Philosophy of Rhetoric*, Oxford, UK: Oxford University Press.

Ritchie, L. D. (2013) *Metaphor*, Cambridge, UK: Cambridge University Press.

Semino, E. (2008) *Metaphor in Discourse*, Cambridge, UK: Cambridge University Press.

Serres, M. (2007) *The Parasite (Posthumanities)*, Minneapolis, MN: University of Minnesota Press.

Sontag, S. (1979) *Illness as Metaphor*, New York: Farrar, Straus and Giroux.

Steen, G. J. (2007) *Finding Metaphor in Grammar and Usage*, Amsterdam, The Netherlands: John Benjamins.

—— (2008) 'The paradox of metaphor: Why we need a three-dimensional model of metaphor', *Metaphor and Symbol* 23(4): 213–241. doi: 10.1080/10926480802426753.

—— (2011) 'What does "really deliberate" really mean? More thoughts on metaphor and consciousness and action', *Metaphor and the Social World* 1(1): 53–56.

Steen, G. J., Dorst, A. G., Herrmann, J. B., Kaal, A., Krennmayr, T. and Pasma, T. (2010) *A Method for Linguistic Metaphor Identification: From MIP to MIPVU*, Amsterdam, The Netherlands: John Benjamins.

Steiner, G. (1987) 'The long life of metaphor: An approach to the "Shoah"', *Encounter* 68(2): 55–61.

Thibodeau, P. H. and Boroditsky, L. (2011) 'Metaphors we think with: The role of metaphor in reasoning', *PLoS ONE* 6(2): e16782, 1–11.

Trim, R. (2011) *Metaphor and the Historical Evolution in Conceptual Mapping*, Basingstoke, UK: Palgrave Macmillan.

Twardzisz, P. (2013) *The Language of Interstate Relations: In Search of Personification*, Basingstoke, UK: Palgrave Macmillan.

Weinrich, H. (1963) 'Die Semantik der kühnen Metapher', *Deutsche Vierteljahreszeitschrift* 37: 325–344.

—— (1967) 'Semantik der Metapher', *Folia Linguistica* 1: 3–17.
Wodak, R. (2001a) 'What CDA is about: A summary of its history, important concepts and its developments', in R. Wodak and M. Meyer (eds) *Methods of Critical Discourse Analysis*, London: Sage.
—— (2001b) 'The discourse-historical approach', in R. Wodak and M. Meyer (eds) *Methods of Critical Discourse Analysis*, London: Sage.
Wodak, R. and Sedlak, M. (2000) 'We demand that foreigners adapt to our life-style': Political discourse on immigration laws in Austria and the United Kingdom', in E. Appelt and M. Jarosch (eds) *Combating Racial Discrimination*, Oxford, UK: Berg.
Wodak, R. and Chilton, P. (eds) (2005) *A New Agenda in (Critical) Discourse Analysis: Theory, Methodology and Interdisciplinarity*, Amsterdam, The Netherlands: John Benjamins.
Wodak, R. and Meyer, M. (eds) (2009) *Methods of Critical Discourse Analysis: Introducing Qualitative Methods*, London: Sage.
Zinken, J. (2007) 'Discourse metaphors: The link between figurative language and habitual analogies', *Cognitive Linguistics* 18(3): 445–466.
Zinken, J., Hellsten, I. and Nerlich, B. (2008) 'Discourse metaphors', in R. M. Frank, R. Dirven, T. Ziemke and E. Bernárdez (eds) *Body, Language and Mind. Volume 2: Sociocultural Situatedness*, Berlin, Germany: Mouton de Gruyter.

22
Metaphor and persuasion in commercial advertising

Laura Hidalgo-Downing and Blanca Kraljevic-Mujic

Introduction and context: the role of metaphor and persuasion in commercial advertising

Commercial advertising is a persuasive genre which makes extensive use of metaphor as a strategy for engaging with potential consumers and attracting their attention to the product. Metaphor plays a crucial role in the persuasive function of this genre by appealing to the emotions and evaluative judgements of the potential buyer and by supporting claims about the positive properties of the product, often by means of creative strategies (Semino 2008: 168–75). This introductory section addresses, first, the nature of commercial advertising as a genre and, second, the persuasive function of metaphor in commercial advertising.

Commercial advertising as a persuasive genre

Advertising is a pervasive genre in our society. In our day-to-day life we are constantly being exposed to various forms of advertising in continuously changing and ever more inventive formats: printed forms such as newspapers; multi-semiotic modes which have arisen with each new technological invention, from billboards through TV ads to internet ads; and a variety of everyday advertisements on all types of objects which we see and handle daily, such as bottles, pens, cosmetics, food products, clothes, cars and ICTs (Gorman and McLean 2003). Commercial advertising, which is the focus of this chapter, needs to be distinguished from other types of advertising which are persuasive but do not pursue a commercial goal or involve a business transaction (see Geis 1998). That is, this chapter will not deal, for example, with advertisements for non-profit organisations, which appeal to the reader/viewer in order to support their social or political causes, or with political campaigning.

In brief, this chapter deals with forms of advertising in which a company with a brand name has as a primary objective the selling of a product or service, often also promoting their brand at the same time (see Cook 2001; Myers 1994; Vestergaard and Schroeder 1985; Geis 1982, 1998; Goddard 1998; Koller 2008). While there may be ads which promote brands exclusively, very often commercial advertising promotes both brands and products simultaneously.

In analysing advertising, persuasion as an effect on an audience needs to be distinguished from the strategies used to achieve that affect. Rhetorical and discursive strategies are the verbal and other semiotic means (visual, acoustic, kinetic) used by ad designers in order to achieve the desired effect of consumers buying the product (Charteris-Black 2011). More specifically, in commercial advertising the goal of persuasion may be pursued by means of two main types of rhetorical and discursive strategies: a direct appeal to the audience to buy the product, and the use of indirect strategies such as metaphor, humour and language play to engage the audience and achieve the desired effect (Cook 2001; Semino 2008). These strategies can be related to the three dimensions of traditional rhetoric: ethos, logos and pathos. With regard to ethos, which has to do with the presentation of the self of an individual, in commercial advertising this is closely linked to the identity of the brand, to what the brand is about; with regard to logos, the arguments which present the reasons that justify and legitimise the act of persuasion, commercial advertising typically makes use of the description and positive evaluation of the product; with regard to pathos, the strategies which appeal to emotions and attitudes, these are typically manifested by the use of humour, metaphor, word play and so on.

Logos and pathos in commercial advertising have been linked respectively to 'hard-sell' and 'soft-sell' techniques, or 'reason' and 'tickle' strategies (Cook 2001; Simpson 2001; Comradie 2013). As argued by Simpson, reason and tickle strategies may be used in combination to appeal both to rational argument and emotion in the consumer. However, present-day commercial advertising often makes use of 'tickle' or 'soft-sell' strategies, among which metaphor plays a crucial role (Cockroft et al. 2014; Semino 2008). In this respect, it is worth bearing in mind that commercial advertising has further persuasive goals in addition to convincing the consumer to buy a product. Thus, contemporary advertising uses techniques which are aimed at modifying consumers' behaviours and habits, offering identities and creating effects of pleasure, humour and enjoyment (Semino 2008; Burgers et al. 2015).

The persuasive function of metaphor in commercial advertising

The persuasive role of metaphor in commercial advertising may be related to two functions performed by metaphor in advertising discourse, according to Semino (2008: 169). First, metaphors can be used as attention-grabbing devices, especially when they are relatively novel and salient, and when they involve visual images. Second, metaphors can be used in order to present what is being advertised in terms of other entities that have the characteristics which the advertisers want to associate to the product.

The two strategies mentioned above are characteristic of the soft-sell strategy of persuasion in commercial advertising. This point is illustrated by Semino, who, in her analysis of a Lucozade ad, argues that 'the use of metaphor is central to the soft-sell technique used in the ad, which involves both some degree of indeterminacy and, potentially, humour' (Semino 2008: 174). As Semino explains, the Lucozade ad does not promote the drink by means of direct strategies, such as directive speech acts (e.g. 'buy Lucozade') or explicit evaluations of the product (e.g. 'Lucozade is a great drink'). Rather, it makes use of a hybrid image in which bubbles coming out of a Lucozade bottle form the shape of a fuel pump. This is reinforced by the verbal text which reads:

<blockquote>
REFUEL YOUR CAR
REFUEL YOURSELF
</blockquote>

In other words, drinking the product is presented metaphorically in terms of replenishing the person's energy. In terms of Conceptual Metaphor Theory, the drink LUCOZADE is the target domain, which is presented in terms of the RE-FUELLING source domain. The positive properties of re-fuelling mentioned above, such as re-energising and invigorating, are mapped onto the product. Semino further argues that the use of the 'fuelling' metaphor to present the properties of the drink may be seen as humorous, especially because the ad appears in a UK motorway service station, and, consequently, the metaphor is situationally relevant. The combination of metaphor and humour 'might make it more likely that viewers will find the ad appealing, and respond to it by buying the product' (Semino 2008: 175).

A further important point regarding the persuasive potential of advertising concerns the nature of creativity and novelty. In commercial advertising, novel metaphors that involve creative realisations of conventional conceptual metaphors seem to be more effective for persuasive purposes than novel metaphors that involve totally original source–target mappings (Burgers et al. 2015). While totally novel metaphors are typically attention-grabbing, they do not necessarily have more of an effect on the audience than conventional metaphors (Burgers et al. 2015). The distinction between novel and conventional metaphors is discussed in Chapters 14 and 15. Here, it suffices to say that conventional metaphors are those which make use of pairings between source and target domains/concepts which are well known and familiar in a society or community of speakers (Lakoff and Johnson 1980).

Conventional metaphors tend to be exploited in commercial advertising because, as a genre, commercial advertising, on the whole, appears to aim to maintain and reinforce the status quo and shared assumptions about reality, rather than to challenge or disrupt such assumptions and world views (Cook 2001; Koller 2008; Semino 2008). With regard to the Lucozade ad discussed by Semino, the re-fuelling metaphor, in relation to human experience, is conventional and its most common lexical or phraseological realisations even appear in some dictionaries (e.g. 'recharging one's batteries'). However, there is originality and creativity in the choice of image and in the combination of image and text. Moreover, the ad was designed to be placed in motorway service stations and the notion of re-fuelling is related to the full name of the product (Lucozade energy) (Semino 2008: 175). Indeed, creative realisations of conventional metaphors, as in this ad, are more frequent than totally novel metaphors as a persuasive strategy in commercial advertising. Additionally, the use of more than one mode in advertising, as pointed out above, can contribute to the creative exploitation of conventional metaphors.

Overview of relevant research

The present section provides an overview of the most influential approaches to the study of metaphor and persuasion in commercial advertising.

Metaphor and persuasion in commercial advertising: discourse-cognitive approaches

Much of the research on metaphor and persuasion in commercial advertising draws on Conceptual Metaphor Theory (Lakoff and Johnson 1980; Gibbs 2008; Kövecses 2002; see also Chapter 1) and from Discourse Analysis (Cameron and Low 1999; Semino 2008; Semino et al. 2013). The interaction between Cognitive Linguistics and Discourse Analysis leads to a view of metaphor as a tool for conceptualisation, as argued by Lakoff and Johnson (1980), and as an instrument for communication, as pointed out by discourse-pragmatic scholars (Semino

2008). Discourse-pragmatic studies have had a great influence on the study of the role of metaphor in communication and its relation to persuasion. According to Charteris-Black,

> what a pragmatic perspective on metaphor does is to take metaphor back to its origin in the branch of philosophy known as rhetoric – remembering that for Aristotle, rhetoric meant a theory of argumentation as well as a theory of composition and style.
>
> *2004: 10*

Charteris-Black adds that 'a pragmatic view [of metaphor] argues that speakers use metaphor to persuade by combining the cognitive and linguistic resources at their disposal' and that 'metaphor is effective in realising the speaker's underlying goals of persuading the hearer because of its potential for moving us' (2004: 11). More specifically, '[a] metaphor is an incongruous linguistic representation that has the underlying purpose of influencing opinions and judgements by persuasion; this purpose is often covert and reflects speaker intentions within particular contexts of use' (Charteris-Black 2004: 21). The incongruity mentioned by Charteris-Black can be explained in terms of the concept of solving a puzzle when facing a metaphor. Thus, although the Lucozade advertisement discussed in the introduction relies on a conventional conceptual metaphor, it involves the hybrid image of a re-fuelling pump made out of orange bubbles. The potential consumer therefore needs to solve the apparent incongruity between the shape and substance represented in the image, in order to achieve a coherent interpretation of the advertisement.

Metaphor is a crucial instrument for persuasion because it can involve both cognition and emotion (logos and pathos), as discussed above (Charteris-Black 2011: 103). Persuasion can be carried out in three ways in order to influence the audience: response shaping, response reinforcing and response changing. In all cases, a metaphor is potentially persuasive if it makes use of already known beliefs, shared knowledge, needs and desires in the audience. This is known as the 'anchor', or point of departure for the persuasive effect, since it originates in already accepted beliefs (Charteris-Black 2011: 103; Jowett and O'Donnell 1992). Metaphor is a particularly effective means of persuasion since it enables the persuader to make use of concepts and beliefs already familiar to the audience in order to present more complex, abstract or new conceptual domains.

In discourse generally, and advertising in particular, metaphors can interact by mixing, combination or repetition, thus creating patterns which spread throughout a particular discourse. These types of discursive phenomena related to metaphor have received various names, from 'extended metaphor' to 'megametaphor' (Werth 1999; see also Chapter 12)

Metaphor and persuasion in commercial advertising: critical discourse perspectives

Critical Discourse Analysis and its interaction with Cognitive Approaches to Discourse have had a great influence on the development of approaches to metaphor and persuasion in commercial advertising. The reason for this is the nature of commercial advertising as a genre, which promotes products in our present-day consumer society by associating them with values, beliefs and identities; by so doing, it reinforces and, occasionally, questions such values. In this sense, cognitive critical discourse studies view metaphor and persuasion in commercial advertising as social practices, that is, as acts which are reflected in texts, appropriated by or rejected by audiences and perpetuated by these audiences in various social environments. This may take the form of shaping particular views of reality and the social world, or the perpetuation of traditional power relationships and socio-cultural stereotypes, such as gender stereotypes (Koller 2008).

With regard to shaping views of reality, the power of metaphor as an instrument of persuasion in commercial advertising may be linked to the crucial role of metaphor 'in linking cognition with language use as social practice' (Koller 2009a: 120). For this purpose, personification metaphors have a great persuasive potential, since they represent abstract concepts and entities such as corporations and services in terms of people with specific characteristics (Charteris-Black 2004; Koller 2009b). The personification of brands is also a typical strategy in commercial advertising and marketing (Forceville 2006: 388; Koller 2009b: 51). Brands are abstract entities, but can be made concrete by metaphors such as BRANDS ARE LIVING ORGANISMS, and, more specifically, BRANDS ARE PEOPLE. In other words, brands can be presented and understood metaphorically as human beings who are positively evaluated (Koller 2009b: 45–6). In this study, Koller explores the role played by metaphor in companies' communications of their brand 'personalities' in a corpus of mission statements, logos and other features of commercial communications. Koller points out that 'brand characteristics can reflect readers' perceived personality' (2009b: 62). The author illustrates this point by a reader's description of a Volkswagen 'like a polite, good-looking person' which shows 'A nice, friendly attitude' (Koller 2009b: 62). It is argued that customers seem to be describing their own personalities when talking about the car. Personification can perform a persuasive function for several reasons. First, the personality traits which are attributed to the brand form part of our human experience and give a concrete and recognisable form to the abstract entity. Additionally, multimodal commercial advertisements which make use of personification can be particularly persuasive since the desirable characteristics of the brand 'personality' are often reinforced by both the verbal and visual modes (Charteris-Black 2011; Koller 2009b).

With regard to the perpetuation and reinforcement of social and cultural stereotypes, research has focused on the representation of gender in commercial advertising, in particular, on the representation of women. An example of this type of research is found in studies of car ads, in which the car is personified as a sexually desirable woman (Thornborrow 1998).

Metaphor and persuasion in commercial advertising: reception studies and cognitive factors

A fairly recent and very promising line of research on metaphor and persuasion in commercial advertising includes experimental studies on audience reception and the persuasive potential of metaphor. Such studies have analysed and discussed the perception of different types of metaphors and their persuasive effects on subjects according to different variables, such as familiarity with and interest in the topic, degrees of novelty and conventionality of the metaphor, and type of cognitive processing of the metaphor (Ottati and Renstrom 2010; Burgers et al. 2015). With regard to familiarity and interest, studies have revealed that these factors have a positive influence on the persuasive effects on the audience. For example, Ottati et al. (1999) show that subjects who are interested in sports are more receptive to Sport metaphors than subjects who are not interested in sports.

With regard to the degree of novelty and conventionality of metaphor, although novel and creative metaphors are proven to be attention-grabbing, various studies have demonstrated that if a novel metaphor is too complex, the desired persuasive effect is not achieved, since the audience is distracted by the metaphor itself and does not pay attention to the product

(Phillips and McQuarrie 2004; Forceville 2012). Burgers et al. argue that 'these studies unequivocally demonstrate that novel metaphors are most persuasive when they are moderately complex; when the metaphoric comparison is too complex, readers get frustrated and do not appreciate the metaphor' (2015: 516). Additionally, with regard to the position of the metaphor in the text, some studies have shown that metaphor has a greater persuasive potential when it 'appears at the onset of related arguments, or is semantically congruent with other metaphorical statements contained in the communication' and thus helps organise and encode the message (Ottati and Renstrom 2010).

The influence of other factors on the audience has also been discussed, such as the performance factor in audiovisual mediums such as TV. Caballero (2014) combines a qualitative analysis of how non-verbal modes enhance the verbal mode and interact in the metaphorical construction of TV advertisements with an experimental study of responses by 60 subjects regarding the perceived difficulty of and interest in the advertisements. Caballero analyses four advertisements: one in which the tennis player Nadal strikes a ball while a Kia car is shown running at top speed; a second one in which a wine product is metaphorically represented by means of a father–son metaphor (i.e. the wine producer is the father and the product is the son); a third one in which two computer companies, a Mac and a PC, are personified as two young men; and a fourth ad in which Freixenet cava is metaphorically represented multimodally by means of visual images of fizzing bubbles and the sound of a 'zapateado' or Spanish Flamenco dance. Caballero argues that it is not only the multimodal metaphors which have a creative and persuasive effect, but that there is a performative dimension which enhances the creativity and persuasiveness of the ads. Nadal is acting out a role in the ad, doing a performance in which a similarity is established between his speed and the speed of the Kia; the personification in the wine advertisement is enhanced by the fact that the man who represents the company performs the role of a father talking to a son; personification is also present in the computer ads, in which the two actors perform their roles showing the properties of each of the brands; finally, in the Freixenet ad, the sound of the zapateado together with the fizzing bubbles evokes the resonance of performativity both in the moving bubbles and in the dance associated with the rhythmic sound (Caballero 2014). The results of Caballero's experimental study show that the ads rated higher with regard to aesthetic quality are the Mac and Freixenet ads, which were additionally rated as easy to process and described by the subjects as making clever use of imagery, while the metaphor in the Kia advertisement is considered to be too obvious and easy to process. This study measures aspects of reception which can be linked to persuasiveness, such as how buying intentions may be conditioned by the perception of the degrees of creativity and complexity of metaphors in TV ads.

Although most of the research on metaphor and persuasion in commercial advertising has been carried out within the field of cognitive-discourse and critical discourse theories, as pointed out above, some research has been carried out within pragmatic approaches, and particularly Relevance Theoretical approaches (Sperber and Wilson 1995; see also Chapter 3). Recent studies make reference to the role played by relevance in the processing of advertisements, in particular with regard to difficulty in processing metaphors and its influence on the persuasive effect. As argued by Caballero, 'audiences confronted with advertisements relying on metaphor ultimately get a reward for their cognitive investment in interpreting them' (2014: 33). According to Relevance Theory, a greater cognitive effort in processing pays off if there is a cognitive reward (Sperber and Wilson 1995; Tendahl 2009; Tendahl and Gibbs 2008).

Critical issues, debates and controversies

Academic debates on metaphor and persuasion in commercial advertising

Academic debates on metaphor and persuasion in commercial advertising can be divided into three main groups related to the theoretical frameworks discussed in the preceding section. The first group is primarily concerned with the metaphors used to advertise abstract entities such as brands, and concrete objects such as cars and beauty products. Studies following this line of research examine the ideological implications deriving from choosing one specific metaphor instead of another (Koller 2009a; Trong Tuan 2010; Thornborrow 1998; Piller 1999; Velasco-Sacristan 2010). A critical issue is the extent to which the choice of a specific metaphor provides a frame or overall orientation in the discourse, and the effect on the direction of the persuasive act (cf. the section on reception studies above). Thus, in Caballero's example of the computer personifications mentioned above (2014), the PC has a 'virus', which is personified as a young man with a bad cold, while the Mac computer does not and is personified as a healthy man. In the study, results show that subjects find the advertisement easy to process and aesthetically pleasing because the virus metaphor clearly and cleverly evokes both the computer problem and the health problem.

A second critical issue in the study of metaphor and persuasion in commercial advertising is the relation between metaphor and other figurative phenomena, such as metonymy and irony, among others, and its possible effects on the persuasive process (Forceville 1996, 2012; Urios-Aparisi 2009; Phillips and McQuarrie 2004; Burgers et al. 2015; Hidalgo-Downing and Kraljevic-Mujic 2011). For example, Burgers et al. (2015) have shown that, while conventional metaphors enhance the persuasive potential in commercial advertising, the presence of irony in an ad does not.

A third area of current academic debate addresses the psychological factors which influence the effects of metaphor on persuasion. These studies, which are empirical in nature, have confirmed that metaphor triggers interest in advertisements and thereby increases potential persuasion in the direction advocated by the sender (e.g. Landau et al. 2009; Ottati and Renstrom 2010; Sopory and Dillard 2002). Further issues which are the object of debate are, for example, to what extent creative or conventional metaphors have an influence on the persuasive process, to what extent the distraction factor of metaphor may influence persuasion and what determines the threshold of difficulty in solving a metaphorical puzzle in order for the metaphor to be perceived as enjoyable and, consequently, to have a persuasive effect.

Media debates on metaphor and persuasion in commercial advertising

With regard to media debates, it is worth noting that a social awareness has developed regarding the potential influence on audiences of the metaphorical representations of reality in commercial advertising. This social awareness and concern for the ethical implications of commercial advertising, in particular with regard to the use of soft-sell strategies such as metaphor, has led to the creation of consumers' associations and ethical committees which can officially exercise control on what may be advertised or not and how. An example of such an entity is the UK Advertising Standards Authority (ASA), which examines whether certain topics, and, by extension, images, sounds, etc. are acceptable as instruments for the (metaphorical) construction of persuasive meanings in advertising. The UK Advertising Standards Authority and similar authorities can recommend the modification, withdrawal or banning of advertisements if a request is made by a consumers' association or on their own initiative when it is considered that an ad does not conform to ethical principles.

An example of an advertisement provoking controversy is the case of Antonio Federici's 'Immaculately conceived' ice-cream print ad, which was banned by the UK Advertising Standards Authority (ASA) in September 2010, after it received complaints from Christian consumers (Sweney 2010). These argued that the ad was offensive to their religion, in particular, to those who practice Catholicism. The image of the ad shows a young heavily pregnant nun in a church eating the advertised product with a spoon. This image was controversial because of the way in which it relies on the background knowledge shared by receivers who are familiar with the Catholic religion, according to which priests and nuns take vows of celibacy and sexual abstinence. The image suggests a metaphorical comparison between breaking the vow of celibacy and eating that particular ice-cream, on the basis that they are both pleasurable. The ice-cream is then attributed the property of being a sinful pleasure. It may be argued that the metaphor EATING ICE-CREAM IS A SIN is suggested and that it subtly situates the audience of the ad in the position and identity of the sinner. This interpretation would be based on the mapping THE POTENTIAL CONSUMER IS A POTENTIAL SINNER. The offensive potential of the ad lies precisely in this mapping, because it trivialises the vow of celibacy by comparing it to eating an ice-cream. The image is accompanied by the slogan 'Immaculately conceived', which provides an anchor for the visual image and directs the reader's interpretation in the desired direction. Thus, the interaction between the visual and verbal modes influences the assumptions and metaphorical constructs evoked by the visual mode alone. The words 'Immaculately conceived' make reference to the fact that the Virgin Mary is exempt from original sin, according to Catholic doctrine. In the popular, non-expert interpretation of 'immaculate conception', however, Jesus is conceived by the Virgin Mary without sexual intercourse. There is thus a contrast between the slogan and the image of the pregnant nun, which is open to various interpretations.

One possible interpretation of the ad is that the production of the ice-cream is not a sin, but eating it is a sin. Another possible interpretation is that the slogan is ironic in that the ice-cream was made precisely as a source of temptation. This reformulation is based on the ambiguous personification of the conceiver either as the consumer, who in the visual mode is personified by the pregnant nun, or as the company, which in the verbal mode is implicitly presented as an immaculate conceiver. As a consequence, the product itself, the ice-cream, is humorously presented as the result of immaculate conception. Here is the second controversial representation suggested by the ad: the product is potentially associated with Jesus Christ, the fruit of the Virgin Mary's immaculate conception, and the company is associated with the Virgin Mary as immaculate conceiver. This involve a pun that relies on the metaphoric polysemy of the verb 'conceive', which can mean both 'to become pregnant' and 'to think of or design something'. We therefore argue that the advertisement was perceived as offensive not only because it apparently invites the consumer to 'sin' in an initial interpretation, but also because there is an implied metaphorical equivalence between the conceived product, the ice-cream, and Jesus Christ. At the same time the company, as conceiver of the product, somehow acquires divine attributes, hence the controversial trivialisation and mockery of Catholic teaching about the importance of celibacy and abstinence.

According to Contrast Creative (2014), the agency that created this ad for the brand Antonio Federici, the marketing impact after the ASA banned the ad was huge, and they claimed that the brand enjoyed extensive coverage in the media. It was the most shared story of the day on the BBC's website, and it even made the headlines on the US comedy show, 'The Colbert Report'. Moreover, it was voted 'Best Ice Cream in the World' in 2010. The controversial ad was part of the company's 'Ice-cream is our religion' campaign, claiming that their decision to use religious imagery stemmed from their strong feelings towards their product and also from their wish to comment on and question shared assumptions, using satire and gentle humour (Sweney 2010). Metaphors with religion and politics as source domains are used frequently in present-day commercial advertising as a persuasive strategy which draws on familiar areas of shared knowledge in our society (Koller 2009a).

Examples of current research

Hidalgo-Downing et al. (2013) present the results of a study of the similarities and differences in the metaphors used in two samples of multimodal print ICT advertisements from 1990–2002 and 2009–2012. More specifically, the study focuses on JOURNEY and WAR/COMPETITION metaphors in these two periods of time. The results of the study show, first, that the JOURNEY metaphor is used in both periods of time to conceptualise e-business. The authors, following Linell (2009) and Semino et al. (2013), argue that a process of re-contextualisation has taken place. The metaphor BUSINESS IS A JOURNEY has been adapted to the new social situation witnessing the boom in new technologies, and now takes the form of E-BUSINESS IS A CYBERSPACE JOURNEY. The study shows that while the metaphor is pervasive in both samples, a difference may be observed with regard to the fact that reaching destinations is foregrounded in the first period, while speed, motion and discovering new territories are foregrounded in the second. This shift may be said to reflect an adaptation in the discourse strategies used for persuasive purposes in the two different periods of time, taking different audiences and different social realities into account. That is, while the initial period focuses on exploring new virtual territories, the new situation developing after the year 2000 generates a need to produce services which are faster and more efficient. Similarly, the WAR/COMPETITION metaphor is also shown to vary across the two time periods, with a preference for the WAR metaphor in the first period and a preference for the SPORTS/COMPETITION metaphor in the second. Once more, these changes can be said to reflect a variation in the persuader's intentions according to changes in the needs and desires of the audience a decade later. Thus, before 2000, ICT producers seem to focus on the need to modify potential buyers' perception of the new technologies as dangerous and risky, hence the WAR metaphor. The domain of the new technologies is represented as one in which there is a fear of the unknown and of safety threats, such as hacking. A decade later, potential ICT buyers have become familiarised with the new technologies, and the pervasive SPORTS/COMPETITION metaphors show the focus of ICT producers on potential buyers' needs for faster services and products.

One of the advertisements discussed in Hildago-Downing et al. (2013) is the Huawei ad reproduced as Figure 22.1.

The Huawei ad (see Figure 22.1) shows a scene with two boys who are engaged in the enterprise of trying to catch a bunch of coloured balloons, which are flying off into the sky. The context of commercial advertising as a genre makes this image work as a metaphor for ambition, namely, AMBITION IS REACHING OUT FOR FLYING BALLOONS, which can be seen as a variant of AMBITION IS REACHING FOR THE SKY. This metaphor is supported by the personification of the corporate brand as a friend (Koller 2009b). The personification of the advertised company is cognitively structured by a multimodal metaphor THE BRAND IS A FRIEND, where the friend is visually represented as the child who provides the 'leg-up' in the image. Following Barthes (1977: 38–41 in Koller 2009b: 45), the purpose of the ad is achieved by anchoring the persuasive message in the text. Consequently, the verbal mode serves to cue and restrict possible interpretations of the visual mode as expressed in extracts 1 and 2 below.

Figure 22.1 Huawei ad.

(1) We've found the way to reach for new heights. (Huawei)
(2) Just like friends who help each other to reach for the sky. Huawei can do the same for your business. [...] Proof that with good collaboration, the sky is the limit. (Huawei)

The consumer is positioned as able to 'reach for new heights' and 'to reach for the sky' with the help of the advertised company. This upward movement towards 'new heights' and 'the sky' tends to be associated with ambition and success, represented through the conventional orientational metaphors HIGH STATUS IS UP, POWERFUL IS UP and most generally, GOOD IS UP (Lakoff and Johnson 1980). The conventional conceptual metaphor POWERFUL IS UP is seen as resulting from embodied primary metaphors (Grady 1997), in the interaction of children with taller persons and caregivers. These spatial metaphors are formed in early childhood through the experience of children moving their body through space and interacting with objects and other people (Koller 2009a: 120). As argued in the study of ICT metaphor variation across time, the present advertisement illustrates the re-contextualisation of the JOURNEY and WAR metaphors as focusing respectively on MOTION rather than on REACHING A DESTINATION, and on AMBITION as COLLABORATION instead of WAR.

In a second study on both print and internet ads, Hidalgo-Downing and Kraljevic-Mujic (2015) discuss the similarities and differences in the use of metaphor in these two genres, focusing on the activation of background knowledge and positive evaluation of the products by means of non-verbal modes. One of the ads analysed is a 1.32-minute-long YouTube Coca-Cola ad with the title 'Fairy tale in a vending machine', produced in the Netherlands in 2006 ('Television commercial', 2006). The ad exploits the themes of fantasy and magic, while multimodal metaphors are based on the interaction of visual (an ideal fantasy world) and aural triggers (a jingle). There are no verbal forms of expression in the construction of meaning, and the music is particularly important. The ad starts with an everyday scene of a young man who wants to buy a bottle of Coca-Cola from a street vending machine. He inserts a coin in the vending machine. Inside the vending machine, the coin reaches the fantasy world where the bottle is filled with the advertised product. At that moment, the Coca-Cola jingle begins. The same jingle accompanies the coin on its journey through the fantasy world, during the magical production of Coca-Cola. In the final scene of the ad, the bottle of Coca-Cola comes out of the vending machine and brings us back to the frame of the world of the young man. The young man collects the product. There is a pause in which he looks at the bottle. When he opens it, the Coca-Cola theme music starts again.

The authors argue that the positive evaluation of the brand and the advertised product arises from the associations communicated primarily by the metonymy MUSIC STANDS FOR THE BRAND and the extended metaphor THE ADVERTISED PRODUCT IS A MAGIC DRINK. To sum up, the extended metaphor is achieved at the end of the ad by means of the visual mini-narrative and the music (the jingle). It may be argued that the potential persuasiveness of the ad rests upon the audience's expectations and the privileged access they are given to the world created in the ad.

Future directions

Further research is needed on the way socio-cultural factors may affect people's comprehension of ads and emotional responses to ads. This involves all the main theoretical areas discussed above: metaphor in commercial advertising within cognitive, discourse analytic and critical discourse perspectives, as well as reception studies. In a society which changes so fast, it is necessary to have further diachronic studies on how metaphors have changed over time in the representation of products and services in commercial advertising. Similarly, the tendency towards globalization, together with the need to appeal to specific cultural values, make it necessary to explore in greater depth the nature of the universality or variation of different types of metaphors and their persuasive potential in commercial advertising across cultures. The study of the reception and interpretation of metaphor and its influence on persuasion in commercial advertising is a particularly promising field of research. This applies to research that focuses on the factors that determine how choice of metaphor influences different consumers' interpretation and reception of ads, according to age, interests, social background, etc. and how this may influence their decisions on buying products.

A further promising line of research concerns the function and nature of multimodal metaphor as a persuasive strategy in new online settings, such as YouTube and other digital and virtual spaces. In these settings, there tends to be a deliberate blurring of the boundaries of genre types, in such a way that on some occasions it is not clear whether a YouTube recording is a commercial advertisement or it belongs to another genre. An example of this is the YouTube Oreo advertisement in which the protagonists are members of a music band ('YouTubers ads' 2014). The recording is performed in such a way that, as pointed out by consumers' associations, the persuasive commercial intention of the Oreo advertisement is disguised in the form of a promotional video of a music band.

Finally, an interesting future direction is the creation of further pedagogical books for students and scholars in order to study the current nature of commercial advertising and the metaphorical persuasive strategies which are arising in the new virtual commercial advertising genres. A particularly important aspect of this is the development of an awareness of the critical and ethical dimensions of metaphor as a persuasive strategy in commercial advertising. Specific social groups, such as children and young people, are particularly vulnerable as potential target audiences of advertisements which make use of metaphor as a soft-sell persuasive strategy. This makes it necessary to work in educational contexts on the development of an awareness of the power of metaphor in commercial advertising. Commercial advertising can be studied as a genre in secondary schools and in university courses as a way of exploring the metaphorical strategies used by this genre in the construction and reinforcement of social stereotypes and consumer habits.

Further reading

Koller, V (2004/2008) *Metaphor and Gender in Business Media Discourse: A Critical Cognitive Study*, Basingstoke, UK: Palgrave Macmillan.
Charteris-Black, J. (2006/2011) *Politicians and Rhetoric: The Persuasive Power of Metaphor*, 2nd edn, Basingstoke and New York: Palgrave MacMillan.
Forceville, C. 1996. *Pictorial Metaphor in Advertising*, London: Routledge.
Ottati, V., Rhoads, S. and Graesser, A. C. (1999) 'The effect of metaphor on processing style in a persuasion: A motivational resonance model', *Journal of Personality and Social Psychology*, 77(4): 688–697.
Semino, E. (2008) *Metaphor in Discourse*, Cambridge, UK: Cambridge University Press. (Chapter 5)

References

Burgers, C., Konijn, E., Steen, G. and Iepsma, M. (2015) 'Making ads less complex, yet more creative and persuasive: The effects of conventional metaphors and irony in print advertising', *International Journal of Advertising*, 34: 515–532.
Caballero, R. (2014) 'Exploring the combination of language, images and sound in the metaphors of TV commercials', *Atlantis*, 36(2): 31–51.
Cameron, L. and Low, G. D. (eds) (1999) *Researching and Applying Metaphor*, Cambridge, UK: Cambridge University Press.
Charteris-Black, J. (2004) *Corpus Approaches to Critical Metaphor Analysis*, Basingstoke, UK: Palgrave Macmillan.
—— (2011) *Politicians and Rhetoric: The Persuasive Power of Metaphor*, 2nd edn, Basingstoke and New York: Palgrave Macmillan.

Cockroft, R., Cockroft, S., Hamilton, C. and Hidalgo-Downing, L. (2014) *Persuading People: An Introduction to Rhetoric*, Basingstoke and New York: Palgrave Macmillan.
Comradie, M. (2013) 'Reason-tickle patterns in intertextual print advertising', *Language Matters: Studies in the Languages of Africa*, 44(2): 5–28.
Contrast Creative (2014) Contrast Creative Project Antonio Federici/Advertising. Available at http://www.contrastcreative.co.uk/item/antonio-federici (accessed 8 January 2016).
Cook, G. (2001) *The Discourse of Advertising*, 2nd edn, London: Routledge.
Forceville, C. (1996) *Pictorial Metaphor in Advertising*, London: Routledge.
—— (2006) 'Non-verbal and multimodal metaphor in a cognitivist framework: Agendas for research', in G. Kristiansen, M. Achard, R. Dirven and F. R. de Mendoza Ibàñez (eds) *Applications of Cognitive Linguistics*, 379–402, Berlin and New York: Mouton de Gruyter.
—— (2012) 'Creativity in pictorial and multimodal advertising metaphors', in R. Jones (ed.) *Discourse and Creativity*, 113–132, London: Longman.
Geis, M. L. (1982) *The Language of Television Advertising*, New York: Academic Press.
—— (1998) 'Advertising', in J. Mey (ed.) *Concise Encyclopedia of Pragmatics*, Oxford, UK: Elsevier.
Gibbs, R. W., Jr. (ed.) (2008) *Cambridge Handbook of Metaphor and Thought*, New York: Cambridge University Press.
Goddard, A. (1998) *The Language of Advertising: Written Texts*, London: Routledge.
Gorman, L. and McLean, D. (2003) *Media and Society in the Twentieth Century: A Historical Introduction*, Malden, MA: Blackwell Publishing.
Grady, J. 1997. 'Foundations of meaning: Primary metaphors and primary scenes', University of California, Berkeley: Ph.D. dissertation.
Hidalgo-Downing, L. and Kraljevic-Mujic, B. (2011) 'Multimodal metonymy and metaphor as complex discourse resources for creativity in ICT advertising discourse', *Special issue on Metaphor and Metonymy of the Review of Cognitive Linguistics*, 9(1): 153–178.
—— (2015) 'Recontextualizing social practices and globalization: Multimodal metaphor and fictional storytelling in printed and internet ads', *Revista Brasileira de Lingusitica Aplicada*, http://dx.doi.org/10.1590/1984-639820156096 (accessed 19 September 2015).
Hidalgo-Downing, L., Kraljevic-Mujic, B. and Núñez Perucha, B. (2013) 'Metaphorical creativity and recontextualisation in multimodal advertisements on e-business across time', in L. Hidalgo-Downing and Kraljevic-Mujic, B. (eds) *Metaphor in the Social World: Special Issue on Metaphorical Creativity Across Modes*, 3(2): 199–219.
Jowett, G. and O'Donnell, V. (1992) *Propaganda and Persuasion*, 2nd edn, 122–154, Newbury Park, CA: Sage Publications.
Koller, V. (2008) *Metaphor and Gender in Business Media Discourse: A Critical Cognitive Study*, Basingstoke and New York: Palgrave Macmillan. (paperback edition)
—— (2009a) 'Missions and empires: Religious and political metaphors in corporate discourse', in A. Musolff and J. Zinken (eds) *Metaphor and Discourse*, 116–134, Basingstoke, UK: Palgrave.
—— (2009b) 'Brand images: Multimodal metaphor in corporate branding messages', in C. Forceville and E. Urios-Aparisi (eds) *Multimodal Metaphor*, 45–71, Berlin, Germany: Mouton de Gruyter.
Kövecses, Z. (2002) *Metaphor: A Practical Introduction*, Oxford, UK: Oxford University Press.
Lakoff, G. and Johnson, M. (1980) *Metaphors We Live By*, Chicago, IL: Chicago University Press.
Landau, M., Sullivan, D. and Greenberg, J. (2009) 'Evidence that self-relevant motives and metaphoric framing interact to influence political and social attitudes', *Psychological Science*, 20(11): 1421–1427.
Linell P. (2009) *Rethinking Language, Mind, and World Dialogically: Interactional and Contextual Theories of Human Sense-Making*, Charlotte, NC: Information Age Publishing.
Myers, G. (1994) *Words in Ads*, Oxford, UK: Oxford University Press.
Ottati, V. and Renstrom, R. (2010) 'Metaphor and persuasive communication: A multifunctional approach', *Social and Personality Psychology Compass*, 49: 783–794.
Ottati, V., Rhoads, S. and Graesser, A. C. (1999) 'The effect of metaphor on processing style in a persuasion. A motivational resonance model', *Journal of Personality and Social Psychology*, 77(4): 688–697.

Phillips, B. and McQuarrie, E. (2004) 'Beyond visual metaphor: A new typology of visual rhetoric in advertising', *Marketing Theory*, 4(1/2): 111–134.
Piller, I. (1999) 'Extended metaphor in automobile discourse', *Poetics Today*, 20(3): 483–498.
Semino, E. (2008) *Metaphor in Discourse*, Cambridge, UK: Cambridge University Press.
Semino, E., Deignan, A. and Littlemore, J. (2013) 'Metaphor, genre and recontextualization', *Metaphor and Symbol*, 28(1): 41–59.
Simpson, P. (2001) '"Reason" and "tickle" as pragmatic constructs in the discourse of advertising', *Journal of Pragmatics*, 33: 589–607.
Sopory, P. and Dillard, J. P. (2002) 'The persuasive effects of metaphor: A meta-analysis', *Human Communication Research*, 28(3): 382–419.
Sperber, D. and Wilson, D. (1995) *Relevance: Communication and Cognition*, 2nd edn, Oxford, UK: Blackwell.
Sweney, M. (2010, September 15) 'Ice-cream advert featuring pregnant nun is banned', *The Guardian*, online. Available at http://www.theguardian.com/media/2010/sep/15/ice-cream-pregnant-nun-ad-banned (accessed 7 September 2015).
'Television commercial – Coca Cola – Fairy tale in a vending machine' (2011, August 6) Available at https://www.youtube.com/watch?v=7kqomBb640A (accessed 20 July 2015).
Tendahl, M. (2009) *A Hybrid Theory of Metaphors: Relevance Theory and Cognitive Linguistics*, Basingstoke and New York: Palgrave Macmillan.
Tendahl, M. and Gibbs, R. W., Jr. (2008) 'Complementary perspectives on metaphor: Cognitive linguistics and relevance theory', *Journal of Pragmatics*, 40: 1823–1864.
Thornborrow, J. (1998) 'Playing hard to get: Metaphor and representation in the discourse of car advertisements', *Language and Literature*, 7(3): 254–272.
Trong Tuan, L. (2010) 'Metaphors in advertising discourse', *Studies in Literature and Language*, 1(6): 75–81.
Urios-Aparisi, E. (2009) 'Interaction of multimodal metaphor and metonymy in TV commercials: Four case studies', in C. Forceville and E. Urios-Aparisi (eds) *Multimodal Metaphor*, 95–118, Berlin and New York: Mouton de Gruyter.
Velasco-Sacristan, M. (2010) 'Metonymic grounding of ideological metaphors: Evidence from advertising gender metaphors', *Journal of Pragmatics*, 42: 64–96.
Vestergaard, T. and Schroeder, K. (1985) *The Language of Advertising*, Oxford, UK: Blackwell.
Werth, P. (1999) *Text Worlds: Representing Conceptual Space in Discourse*, London: Longman.
'YouTubers ads for Oreo banned for not making clear purpose of videos' (2014, November 26) *The Guardian*, online. Available at http://www.theguardian.com/media/2014/nov/26/youtube-ad-oreo-banned-advertising-lick-race (accessed 8 January 2016).

23
Metaphor and story-telling

L. David Ritchie

Introduction

Metaphors often appear in stories, both in literary fiction and in more casual conversations. Often metaphors are used in story-telling for much the same reasons and with much the same effect as in other forms of discourse, e.g., to express complex or abstract ideas or to induce audiences to experience a particular relationship among apparently unrelated ideas. These uses of metaphors are treated in detail in other chapters in this volume. This chapter will focus on phenomena of a different sort, in which:

a) Stories are told with apparent metaphorical intent, as in 'George Bush <u>was born on third base</u> and thought <u>he had hit a triple</u>' (Jim Hightower at the 1988 Democratic National Convention); or,
b) Metaphors refer to, imply, or have the potential to activate stories, as in 'Mitt Romney is a <u>vulture</u> capitalist' (Rick Perry, during the 2004 Republican Presidential Primary debates), where '<u>vulture</u> capitalist' potentially activates a story about vultures and a story about a certain kind of capitalist.

Sometimes these types assume extensive background knowledge, as the first example quoted at the beginning of this chapter assumes knowledge about both the game of baseball and George Bush, and the second assumes knowledge about vultures and Mitt Romney's firm, Bain Capital. I will begin with definitions of some basic terms, then review some of the past research and controversies on the topic as a basis for discussing some of the current research and future directions.

Definitions

Narrative

Abbott (2008: 13) defines *narrative* as 'the representation of an event or a series of events,' that constitutes a 'fuzzy set,' without clear demarcation. Snaevarr (2010) includes visual and other non-linguistic representations as potential narratives. Labov (2013: 15) defines a 'minimal narrative' as 'a sequence of two independent clauses.' However, a 'fully developed narrative begins with an abstract, an orientation with information on persons, places, times and behavior involved; the complicating action; an evaluation section, which identifies the point of the narrative; the resolution; and a coda' Labov (2013: 5); at the very least a narrative will include a complicating action, an 'expectation failure' (Schank and Berman, 2002) or 'something unforeseen' (Bruner, 2002: 15).

Story

Although some researchers do not distinguish between *narrative* and *story*, for others the distinction is important. According to Snaevarr (2010: 168) 'Story is *what* is being recounted, independent of the medium used. Narrative is the *way* the story is told... narrative (or discourse) is the signifier, the story is the signified' (italics in original). Abbott (2008) makes a similar distinction. On the other hand, Labov (2013: 18) defines narrative as a subcategory of story: 'Since we have constrained narrative to mean a very particular kind of speech event, *story* may be allowed to float freely for any talk about a sequence of events' (italics in original). 'George Bush was born on third base' meets these minimal criteria to be considered a story. The second line of Hightower's quip completes a complicating action: 'he thought he had hit a triple,' thus the full quote combines two stories in a way that implies a (minimal) narrative. (For a more detailed discussion see Fludernik, 2003; Norrick, 2010; Schank and Berman, 2002.)

Metaphor

Semino (2008: 1) defines *metaphor* as 'the phenomenon whereby we talk and, potentially, think about something in terms of something else.' Lakoff and Johnson (1980) define metaphor as experiencing one concept as or in terms of another concept of a different sort (see Chapter 1). 'A substantial argument' and 'empty rhetoric' both invite the listener to experience facts and logic as 'substances'; 'A meaty argument' invites the listener to experience them as specifically 'nutritious.' 'Predatory lenders' invites the listener to experience certain business practices as 'killing and consuming the customer or customer's assets.' The first three examples, 'substantial,' 'empty,' and 'meaty,' are merely descriptive and do not imply stories, but the third example potentially goes beyond mere description, and characterizes a sequence of actions, a story about a certain kind of business practice, in terms of a very different sort of story about the behavior of certain animals.

Metaphors and stories

Snaevarr (2010) refers to stories that are in part or entirely metaphorical as *metaphoric stories*; I will use the more fluid term *metaphorical stories* suggested by Cameron, Maslen, and Low (2010). 'George Bush was born on third base (but) he thought he had hit a triple' is an example. In baseball, a *triple* refers to a hit that allows the batter to run all the way to third base. 'Hit a triple' metaphorically maps onto Bush's frequently repeated claim to have earned his fortune strictly by his own efforts. Being 'born on third base' maps onto a contrasting story about being born into a family with substantial wealth and connections. Jim Hightower's remark combines and contrasts these two metaphorical stories in a way that implies a larger, unstated narrative about Bush's oft-repeated claim to be an 'ordinary person' and a 'self-made man' for the sake of political advantage (Ritchie, 2014).

Snaevarr refers to metaphors that either explicitly or implicitly invoke or activate stories ('vulture capitalist,' 'sour grapes,' 'a Judas goat') as *storied metaphors* (2010: 233); I will use the simpler term *story metaphors*. 'Vulture capitalist' is a good example of a story metaphor. During the 2012 Republican U.S. Presidential primary debates, Rick Perry called Mitt Romney a 'vulture capitalist.' A major theme in Romney's campaign was his claim to managerial competence, based in part on his career as a co-owner of Bain Capital, a private equity / venture capital firm. One of the ways a company like Bain Capital earns money is by purchasing a failing company and either restoring it to profitability or closing it down and selling the assets. Either way, the transaction often leads to massive layoffs.

Vultures circle in the sky above a weak or dying animal, and reputedly sometimes hasten an animal's death by beginning to eat it before it is dead. This vehicle story about actions associated with vultures is easily mapped onto a topic story about actions associated with venture capitalists.[1] The story mapping is supported by Perry's statements in which he described two South Carolina companies purchased and closed down by Bain Capital, and summed up with the declaration that Romney and his company had 'picked their bones clean.'

Musolff (2006) introduced another category, the *metaphor scenario*, an often implicit mini-narrative that serves as a source domain for metaphors about a topic such as politics (see also Cameron, 2007; Cameron, Maslen, and Low, 2010). I will discuss some of Musolff's work in a later section.

Parables and proverbs

Turner defines *parable* as the projection of one story onto another, a 'basic cognitive principle,' through which we 'interpret every level of our experience' (1996: v). Snaevarr distinguishes between '*source-goal parables* and *blended parables*' and identifies three types, '*Ordinary* blended parables, Emblems, and *Metaphoric parables*' (2010: 246, italics in original). Turner defines *proverb* as a condensed parable; similarly, Snaevarr (2010: 241) defines proverb as 'a condensed implicit story to be interpreted through projection.' Most proverbs recount a sequence of causally related events, and thus qualify as metaphorical stories, for example, 'When the cat's away, the mice will play.' However, some examples such as 'A penny saved is a penny earned' are better interpreted as metonymic. In other cases, a mere reference to a fable or other kind of story has taken on the characteristics of a proverb, e.g., 'sour grapes' refers to or indexes a commonly known fable, a metaphorical story, but is in itself a story metaphor, not a complete story.

Allegory

Prior to the eighteenth century, *allegory* was understood very broadly, to include metaphor, symbol, and figurative language in general. During the Medieval period, allegory became intertwined with Christian traditions of religious symbolism and Biblical interpretation (Crisp, 2005a; Harris and Tolmie, 2011), and in the nineteenth century, it came to be associated specifically with literary works like *The Pilgrim's Progress*. *Allegory* is still sometimes used quite broadly, for example, as *any* extended or 'super-extended' metaphor (Crisp, 2008; Oakley and Crisp, 2011), any fiction that is subject to a continuous and consistent metaphorical interpretation (Crisp, 2001), any metaphorical passage in which overt reference to the target or topic domain is omitted (Crisp, 2005a), or any instance in which a metaphorical interpretation is applied to discourse containing no overtly metaphorical language (Gibbs, 2011).

Harris and Tolmie (2011: 112) propose a more limited and precise definition, consistent with the nineteenth-century usage:

> the specific genre that had its most sustained literary peak in the middle ages ... *Divine Comedy, Piers Plowman ... The Faerie Queene, ... Pilgrim's Progress* and *Paradise Lost*. The genre is characterized by abstract personifications, concepts that walk and talk, like Reason and Conscience (*Piers*), Gluttony and Lust (*Queene*) ... ; by topifications, conceptually laden landscapes like the Celestial City (*Pilgrim's*) the Cave of Error (*Queene*) ... within the frame of a journey or quest ...

I will use Harris and Tolmie's definition, since it facilitates comparisons between allegories in this narrower sense and other forms of metaphorical story. However, as Harris and Tolmie point out, *allegory* is a 'fuzzy category,' and many texts have some but not all of these specified features.

Extended metaphors and allegory

Crisp (2008: 291) defines *extended metaphor* as 'a linguistic metaphor extending over more than one clause whose language relates directly to both the metaphorical source and target.' Although he acknowledges that in previous writing (e.g., Crisp 2005b) he defined allegory as a 'super-extended metaphor,' Crisp (2008: 291) distinguishes between extended metaphor, which 'involves both source-related and target-related language' and allegory, which 'involves only source-related language.' As an example of extended metaphor that is not allegory, Crisp cites some lines from the second stanza of Causley's (1975: 14) *A Ballad for Katherine of Aragon*:

> O war is a casual mistress
> And the world is her double bed
> She has a few charms in her mechanised arms
> But you wake up and find yourself dead.

Here the common metaphor WAR IS SEX is extended in a series of metaphors. In the first half of the same stanza, Causley presents another extended metaphor, based on WAR IS MUSIC, beginning with the line 'war is a bitter bugle / That all must learn to blow' then extending the metaphor even further in the third stanza with 'His funeral knell was a six-inch shell.' One difference between this example and allegory is the appearance of the target-related phrase 'war is' at the beginning of both passages. Crisp argues that the language in allegory is presented as literal: In contrast to Jim Hightower's metaphorical story about George Bush's misrepresentation of his birth, in which being 'born on third base' is highly improbable (although possible), *Pilgrim's Progress* (Bunyan, 1678/1969) is presented as a literal story about a journey in which the protagonist '*Christian*' meets and overcomes various perils, and in *The Faerie Queene* (Spenser, 1590) a series of adventures in which Arthurian knights meet, battle, and defeat various opponents are presented as literal stories. However, Crisp's claim about this apparent literalness of language is undermined by various features observed in widely accepted examples of allegory. Prototypical allegories like *The Faerie Queene* and *Pilgrim's Progress* have 'concepts that walk and talk,' persons and places that both bear the names of and demonstrate the characteristics of abstract moral and spiritual qualities (e.g., the dragon '*Errour*,' '*Christian*,' '*Evangelist*,' the dungeon in the castle '*Despaire*,' the '*Slough of Dispond*'). Crisp argues that these are interpretable as merely nicknames, but, especially in Bunyan, the protagonist and other characters enact and often comment on the psychological and spiritual qualities implied by the names. Both Bunyan and Spenser include a preface regarding the allegorical nature of the writing, and in Bunyan, many of the adventures are followed by an apparently literal Christian homily that explicitly connects source with target.

At several points in *The Faerie Queene*, metaphorical stories are inserted that are separate from both the vehicle story (the source) and the overall metaphorical mapping. For example, near the end of Book I, Spenser (1590: 209) uses a nautical metaphorical story to describe the story-telling process:

> Now strike your sailes you jolly Mariners,
> For we be come unto a quiet rode,
> Where we must land some of our passengers,
> And light this wearie vessel of her lode.

In Book II, describing the villainous Archimage's continued scheming against the knight Redcrosse, Spenser (1590: 213) uses two separate metaphorical stories to explain why Redcrosse should be expected to be suspicious of Archimage:

> His credit now in doubtfull ballaunce hong;
> For hardly could be hurt, who was already stong.

And a few lines later, 'The fish that once was caught, new bait will hardly bite.' In these examples, the language is all apparently literal—there is no intrusion from the target domain—but the tone and intent are clearly distinct from the overall allegorical intent of the poem. Under an extremely general definition of allegory, these might be counted as allegory within allegory, but that would obscure a vital contrast that is preserved by classifying these examples as metaphorical stories within an overarching allegory.

Overall, Harris and Tolmie's (2011) more limited and precise definition of allegory is useful because it facilitates comparisons between allegory and other examples of metaphorical story, especially when they are included within an extended allegory, as in the examples discussed in the above paragraph. However, as Harris and Tolmie point out, the category is 'fuzzy,' with many marginal examples. For example, *Animal Farm* (Orwell, 1946/2008) is often classified as a political allegory, but it lacks many of the features cited by Harris and Tolmie. Many texts include elements that may usefully be analyzed as allegorical, even if we would not classify them as allegories. It is also useful to recognize the process of *allegoresis* (giving an allegorical interpretation to texts, whether or not they were intended allegorically) as distinct from the definition of allegory as a specific category of texts.

Overview of relevant research

Until quite recently the intersection of metaphors and story-telling has been dominated by discussion of how metaphors are used in formal literature. Within the study of literature, Fludernik (2010: 926) identifies a potential 'paradigm shift,' in which 'narratology, the empirical study of literature, stylistics, possible-worlds theory, and metaphor studies' may be brought together in a kind of grand synthesis based on cognitive theories. She identifies two points of caution. First is the tension between the drive toward generalization in the cognitive paradigm and the importance of attention to specific and unique cultural contexts. Second is the proliferation of overlapping and often contradictory theories and models within cognitive studies, with approaches ranging from neurology and computer simulation to sociological and psychological work.

Steen and Gibbs (2004) argue that literary critics tend to focus on creating novel and interesting readings of literary works rather than reliable and generalizable accounts of how readers actually understand these works and the metaphors they contain. However, as Fludernik argues, recent literary scholars have made good use of cognitive metaphor theory, Conceptual Metaphor Theory (CMT) in particular (see Chapter 1). Yanna Popova has applied CMT to explicating the use of metaphors in texts such as Patrick Susskind's novel *Perfume* (Popova, 2003) and Henry James' short story, 'The figure in the carpet' (Popova, 2002). Don Freeman has used cognitive metaphor theory to describe and explain Shakespeare's use of conventional metaphors in *King Lear* (1993), *Macbeth* (1995), and *Antony and Cleopatra* (1999). Fludernik (2010) has used cognitive metaphor theory and conceptual blending theory to show that the 'omniscient author' style of third-person narrative metaphorically represents a 'God's eye view' of the events depicted in a narrative. Semino (2002; Semino and Swindlehurst, 1996) used cognitive metaphor analysis to examine the narrator's mind style in Ken Keseys novel *One Flew over the Cuckoo's Nest*.

Fauconnier and Turner (1998, 2002) proposed a detailed model for analyzing how two separate concepts can be cognitively blended to form a discrete new concept, with particular application to conceptual metaphors. Conceptual blending theory does not actually explain how this happens but it does provide a useful tool for analysis and explanation. For example, Fludernik (2010) uses the conceptual blending model to provide a neat and succinct explanation of a visual metaphor in a political cartoon from the 2008 U.S. Presidential election. Fludernik also applies conceptual blending theory to explain how readers understand 'naturally impossible storytelling scenarios,' such as the 'omniscient narrator,' who is readily comprehended as a conceptual blend of God (omniscient) with the human author.

More on allegory

Much of the recent research on allegory has used the concept to examine specific texts or to examine processes of interpretation. As noted in the preceding, Crisp has defined allegory in terms of the use of overtly literal language to relate a metaphorical story, with no overt metaphorical mapping. Crisp (2008) applies this idea to William Blake's (1966: 218) 'A Poison Tree,' in part as a test of Conceptual Blending Theory (Fauconnier and Turner, 2002; see also Chapter 2). The poem begins with a simple literal statement, 'I was angry with my friend,' followed by a second line that ends with a simple lexical metaphor, 'I told my wrath, my wrath did end,' followed by a parallel but contrasting couplet that also ends with a simple lexical metaphor: 'I was angry with my foe: / I told it not, my wrath did grow.' Blake then develops the implications of the metaphor 'grow' into an extended metaphor, a metaphorical story, beginning with 'I water'd it in fears,' leading to line 10, 'Till it bore an apple bright.' At this point, according to Crisp, the poem is abruptly transformed into allegory in which the 'fruit' is 'poisonous,' culminating in 'In the morning glad I see / my foe outstretch'd beneath the tree.' Crisp's reading of the poem is interesting—but it is not clear to me that either Conceptual Blending Theory or the concept of allegory adds anything to it. The poem begins with two contrasting literal stories, then the second literal story is developed into a metaphorical story that develops the consequences of 'hiding' one's wrath.

In his analysis of Robert Frost's (1969) poem 'The Road Not Taken,' Gibbs (2011) argues that the poem can be read either as a story about a literal ride through the woods or as an allegory about the poet's 'journey' through life. To test the hypothesis that people easily provide allegorical meanings to apparently literal statements, Gibbs had college students read 'The Road Not Taken' three lines at a time and write down their thoughts, then read the poem through from beginning to ending and write down what they thought the poet was trying to communicate. The participants provided few personal associations from their own lives, but 72 percent of the participants provided allegorical interpretations based on the poet's life. An earlier study of Garner's (1994) satirical book *Politically Correct Bedtime Stories* yielded similar results: 65 percent of the responses mentioned a theme that fit Gibbs's definition of allegory.

Thagard (2011) takes a different approach to the comprehension of allegory in his analysis of *Animal Farm* (Orwell, 1946/2008). Thagard begins with a theory that analogical mapping is governed by three sets of constraints relating source (vehicle) to target (topic) – similarity, structure, and purpose – and adds an integrative theory in which emotions generated by analogies result from judgments about the source and target as well as physiological responses to the text. He uses a set of diagrams to show how these two approaches help to explain the success of the novel as a political allegory, then contrasts it with a less successful example.

Metaphorical stories and story metaphors

Ritchie (2008) analyzed a series of metaphorical stories and story metaphors in Tony Blair's speech to the 2005 Labour Party conference at Gateshead (see also Deignan and Semino, 2010). Blair related the history of his tenure as Prime Minister, beginning with a series of metaphorical phrases: 'steady hard slog of decision-making and delivery ... events that tested me ... the media mood turning, ... the thousand little things that irritate and grate'; 'things' is a simple objectification metaphor but each of the other underlined words and phrases are story metaphors, in that they imply a story. This passage was followed by a phrase that can be interpreted either metaphorically or literally: 'there you are, the British people, thinking: you're not listening and I think: you're not hearing me.' This theme led immediately into a metaphorical story about an episode of domestic violence: 'And before you know it you raise your voice. I raise mine. Some of you throw a bit of crockery.' In contrast to the allegories discussed by Crisp and Thagard, Blair explicitly mapped the vehicle story (a marital fight) onto the topic story (the dispute within the Labour Party): 'you, the British people, have to sit down and decide ... If you want to go off with Mr. Kennedy ... '

Metaphors transformed into stories

Speakers are often quite inventive in transforming common metaphors into stories. One example appears in an informal focus group conversation among scientists (Ritchie and Schell, 2009). In response to a comment about the need for research funding, one participant remarked, 'Ya. There really is no more ivory tower.' This remark itself implies a story in which there once was an 'ivory tower' (a descriptive metaphor for an idyllic form of academic science) and implicitly maps it onto a story in which it was once but is no longer possible to conduct basic research without worrying about funding. A minute later, another participant echoed this metaphor ('I've never really seen the ivory tower'), which was then spontaneously and collaboratively developed into a metaphorical story about a search for an 'ivory tower,' mapped onto the search for research funding:

> Participant 4: You haven't. They never did <u>let you in</u> did they.
> Participant 5: Is that what you <u>dream about, in the night</u>, Jim?
> <u>ivory tower</u> you just go to sleep, and the first thing you get is the seven million dollar grant from [*sic*] to do whatever you want from the MacArthur Foundation, and you <u>go up into the ivory tower</u>. What the, <u>open pit, unstable wall</u>
> Participant 1: Ya the <u>unstable</u>.
> Participant 4: Ya, instead of the <u>ivory tower</u>, we're in an <u>unstable foundation</u>.

Another example of a transformed idiomatic metaphor appeared in a conversation among a group of four African-American men about public safety and police–community relations (Ritchie, 2010). To reinforce a point about the need for the community, schools, and families to hold adolescents accountable for their anti-social activities, the speaker transformed the idiomatic story metaphors '<u>in the same boat</u>' and '<u>everybody goes down</u>' into a brief metaphorical story: 'it's like someone in a boat [*sic*] and saying, "Well look I'm just gonna <u>put a hole in the boat</u> so I can <u>get me some water</u>." No, <u>everybody goes down. Everybody goes down</u>.'

An example of a different sort comes from Cameron's (2007) analysis of the 'Reconciliation dialogues' between Pat Magee, a convicted IRA terrorist, and Jo Berry, whose father was killed by a bomb planted by Magee. Berry read a poem she had written, based on a conventional '<u>building bridges</u>' story metaphor. Magee transformed the '<u>bridge as connector</u>' metaphor into a very different sort of metaphorical story. He first pointed out that a bridge has '<u>two ends</u>'; later he further transformed the metaphor by combining it with two other story metaphors into a metaphorical story in which bridges '<u>create distances</u>' and '<u>become barriers,</u>' then returned to the initial '<u>building bridges as connecting people</u>' metaphor (see also Cameron, Maslen, and Low, 2010; Ritchie, 2013).

Metaphor scenarios

Fauconnier and Turner wrote about scenarios in terms of several blended stories, including the story metaphor '<u>digging your own grave</u>' (2002: 131) and a quip about President Bill Clinton that implies a metaphorical story, 'If Clinton were the Titanic, the iceberg would sink.' In another example, Turner and Fauconnier (1999: 406) explain how people who support free speech can also support outlawing burning or otherwise desecrating the national flag by blending the flag as a symbol of the nation with the image of people burning flags, and with stories of people attacking or betraying the nation: 'In the blend, an attack on the flag is an attack on the nation.'

Musolff (2006) developed the idea of metaphor scenarios more explicitly in his analysis of discourse about the European Union in German and British media. Musolff showed how a 'mini-narrative' or story scenario based on COURTSHIP, MARRIAGE, AND FAMILY provides a source domain for describing and analyzing the complex relationship in which France and Germany are characterized as a '<u>married couple</u>' and Britain as seeking to exploit 'apparent marriage problems of the Franco–German <u>couple</u> in order to establish a <u>ménage à trois</u>.' Other commentaries build on the same scenario to characterize the smaller members of the EU as '<u>children of the family</u>,' for whose welfare the Franco–German '<u>parents</u>' are responsible.

Critical issues

Many of the critical issues facing research on metaphorical stories / story metaphors are extensions of issues facing metaphor theory in general. Two sets of issues seem particularly salient.

Creativity

A widely shared assumption is that literary metaphors are much more creative than those used among ordinary people, and that once a metaphor is introduced into ordinary language it quickly becomes shop-worn and stale. However, Ritchie (2010, 2011) and his colleagues (Ritchie and Dyhouse, 2008; Ritchie and Negrea-Busuioc, 2014; Ritchie and Schell, 2009) provide many examples in which people in ordinary conversations have transformed familiar metaphors in creative and often spontaneous ways, usually by telling metaphorical stories. These results lead to the question, how is the creativity of ordinary language users related to the creativity of communication elites?

Comprehension and processing

Is Conceptual Blending Theory (Fauconnier and Turner, 2002) an independent theory of cognitive processing, or is it useful primarily as a system of notation (Crisp, 2008; Fludernik, 2010; Gibbs, 2011)?

To what extent are actual simulations activated by metaphors, and what role do simulations play in story-telling? Green (2004) has shown that 'transportation' into a 'story-world' (Gerrig, 1993), i.e. simulation of a vehicle narrative, enhances the persuasiveness of a narrative message. To what extent do people routinely experience or access stories implied by metaphors like 'vulture capitalist'? What role do these implicit stories play in metaphor comprehension generally?

Differences among individuals

Conceptual Metaphor Theory (Lakoff and Johnson, 1980) implies that metaphors are grounded in unique vehicle concepts—but there is evidence that individuals differ in the perceptual simulations and story schemas activated by metaphors (Ritchie, 2013). If individuals experience different simulations, what does that imply for the communicative functions of story metaphors, metaphorical stories, and metaphors generally?

Examples of current research

Both metaphor and narrative have been extensively studied in contexts such as business (Koller, 2004), climate change (McComas and Shanahan, 1999), health care (Mattingly, 2011; Semino, 2010), law (Bruner, 2002; Amsterdam and Bruner, 2002), science (Brown, 2003; Semino, 2008) and therapy (Bülow, 2004; Reissman, 2008). Although story metaphors are often implicit in these contexts, until very recently research on narrative and metaphor in contexts beyond formal literature has generally been conducted separately (Hanne, 2011).

One interesting exception to this separate treatment comes in a recent study by Mattingly (2011). She identifies three story metaphors widely used in medicine (each of which is associated with common descriptive or identity metaphors): healing is 'crime fighting' or 'sleuthing' ('the body is a crime scene' and 'the doctor is a detective'); healing is 'war' ('the body is a battlefield or war zone'); and healing is 'mechanical repair' ('the body is a machine' and 'the doctor is a mechanic').

In another commonplace medical descriptive metaphor, severe damage to the brain may turn a patient into a 'vegetable.' Mattingly relates the case of an infant born with severe spinal bifida who was kept alive solely by technology that sustained several of her vital biological functions. The medical staff wanted to withdraw artificial support and allow the infant to die a natural death, but the deeply religious parents wanted to keep the infant alive at all costs. In an attempt to convince the parents to allow them to disconnect the child from the complex machines that were keeping her alive, the medical staff compared her to 'an <u>old car</u> with <u>a bad engine</u>, too <u>broken down</u> to <u>repair</u>.' However, the parents developed the availability of this supportive technology into a contradictory narrative, about a miracle in which God used the scientists to create the technology that could keep their baby alive. Then a nurse warned that 'Your daughter's going to <u>be a vegetable</u>,' and the mother developed a second metaphorical counter-story: 'That's okay, we're going to be her <u>garden</u>. We will <u>water</u> her and she will <u>grow</u>.'

Metaphors based on truncated stories

Speakers frequently omit large parts of a story, relate events out of time order, or merely allude to the narrative implications of a metaphor. In many cases, a metaphor can be more thoroughly understood by activating an implied story or cannot be understood at all without the implied story (Ritchie and Negrea-Busuioc, 2014). The notion of *story metaphor* captures this phenomenon, and '<u>vulture</u> capitalist,' discussed in a previous section, is one example.

Another example comes from the 1984 U.S. presidential primaries, when Senator Gary Hart and former Vice President Walter Mondale were competing for the Democratic presidential nomination. Throughout the campaign, Hart repeatedly claimed to have a large list of specific policy proposals—without providing any details. During two televised debates Mondale referred to these claims and asked Hart '<u>Where's the beef</u>?' In the U.S., '<u>meaty</u>' and '<u>substantial</u>' are common descriptive metaphors for detailed and well-reasoned ideas, consistent with A DETAILED ARGUMENT IS MEAT. Thus, a satisfying interpretation of Mondale's metaphorical question is possible on this basis alone, without activating any stories. However, the question referred to and potentially activated a commercial for the Wendy's chain of hamburger restaurants, featuring an elderly lady who looked with an expression of dismay at a tiny beef patty underneath a very large hamburger bun, turned toward the camera, and exclaimed angrily, 'Where's the beef?' This intertextual reference invited a further metaphorical mapping in which the story of voters frustrated by the lack of '<u>meat</u>' in Hart's claims maps onto the fast food customer's dissatisfaction with the small amount of meat in her hamburger.

Metaphors that allude to, invite, or require stories

Gibbs (2011) argues that many idioms seem to activate story metaphors, for example, '<u>go out on a limb</u>,' '<u>skating on thin ice</u>,' and '<u>get away with murder</u>.' '<u>Vulture</u> capitalist,' discussed in a previous section, could be understood as a simple descriptive metaphor, but in the context of the political debate in which it was used, it was much more meaningful as a story metaphor.

In a conversation about incidents in which a police officer shot unarmed civilians, one participant referred to the explanation that 'I thought my life was in danger' as a '<u>get out of jail free card</u>,' which makes sense only if a story from the game *Monopoly* is activated.

The visual metaphor of 'Justice as a blindfolded goddess holding a scale' requires activation of a story in which she is unable to '<u>see</u>' the personal characteristics of the individuals whose actions are 'placed in the <u>scale</u> to be <u>weighed</u>' against the principles of law.

Stories and metaphorical images

Several researchers have recently investigated metaphors that are represented in or implied by visual images (see Chapter 10), for example, in advertising (Koller, 2009) and editorial cartoons (El Refaie, 2009a, 2009b; Schilperoord and Maes, 2009).

Editorial cartoons often build on conventional metaphors, and sometimes combine multiple metaphors. A 2013 cartoon by Rick McKee depicts an elephant (a symbol of the U.S. Republican party) waist-deep in a square hole, with a headstone labeled 'GOP' and an orange triangle (a symbol used to alert motorists to road construction projects) with the words 'Govt. shutdown strategy in progress.' This image blends '<u>digging your own grave</u>' with POLITICAL ACTION IS CONSTRUCTION and maps it onto the Republican strategy to extort concessions from President Obama by refusing to pass a resolution to increase the national debt limit. A 2013 cartoon by Tom Toles shows two miners, one dressed in the 'Uncle Sam' striped top hat and trousers, standing next to a mining car full of coal. Behind them is a bird in a cage, obviously dead; the wall of the mine is labeled 'climate.' The miner wearing a hard hat comments 'The canary died.' The 'Uncle Sam' miner replies 'kick it down the road.' A tiny figure in the corner, representing the cartoonist, suggests 'put it in a handbasket.' This cartoon blends '<u>the canary in the coal mine</u>' (a sensitive entity used to provide a warning of dangerous conditions), '<u>kick the can down the road</u>' (postpone action in a crisis until later), and '<u>going to hell in a handbasket</u>' (deteriorating rapidly) into a single vehicle story that maps onto the political gridlock over climate change.

However, in two studies of political cartoons, El Refaie (2009a, 2009b) has shown that viewers often have difficulty interpreting editorial cartoons. When they do offer interpretations, their interpretations often disagree with those of other viewers as well as with the intentions of the cartoonists, obtained through *post hoc* interviews. Although El Refaie used a non-representative sample of both cartoons and viewers, her findings raise disturbing methodological *and* theoretical issues about visual metaphors and, potentially, about metaphors in general.

Conclusion and future directions

Systematic attention to story metaphors, including stories activated by shorter metaphors and by visual metaphors, has only begun. There is need for experimental research to explore and verify when and to what extent hearers actually process stories implied by metaphors. Since many metaphors have the potential to activate multiple (and often contradictory) stories, further research is needed to examine the circumstances under which this might occur—and the consequences for communication outcomes when it does occur.

What metaphors index or activate stories: and when?

How important is the activation and blending of stories in comprehending ordinary lexical metaphors? How do metaphors differ with respect to their potential to activate stories associated with vehicle, topic, or both?

On the basis of research to date it appears that many verb metaphors have at least the potential to activate a story. Returning to the previously quoted passage from Tony Blair's (2005) party conference speech at Gateshead (Ritchie, 2008), 'events that <u>tested</u> me' does seem to imply a narrative—an encounter with (personified) '<u>events</u>' that opposed Blair's skillful execution of plans and had to be overcome. 'Media mood <u>turning</u>' presents the mood of the media as either a '<u>vehicle turning onto the wrong street</u>' or '<u>milk turning sour</u>,' itself a metaphor based on CHANGE OF STATE IS CHANGE OF DIRECTION. Both metaphor layers imply at least a brief narrative. On the other hand, '<u>irritate</u>' and '<u>grate</u>' both suggest a single continuing action, and map readily onto a topic verb such as *annoy*. They might but need not activate a story.

Nouns and adjectives also vary in the degree to which they seem likely to activate or invite activation of stories. In the context of a political debate Rick Perry's metaphor '<u>vulture</u> capitalist' seems almost to demand activation of stories associated with both topic and vehicle. On the other hand, a similar political insult from the era of the U.S. Civil War, when General McClellan repeatedly referred to President Lincoln as 'a <u>gorilla</u>,' there is no indication that he intended to activate any associated story, or anything beyond a simple descriptive insult. 'Cigarettes are <u>time bombs</u>' and '<u>coffin nails</u>' both demand activation of stories associated with both topic and vehicle—without the stories they make no sense. '<u>Dead-end</u> job' and '<u>dead-end</u> relationship' both seem likely to invite stories to complete their meaning, but '<u>dead</u> battery' does not.

The potential of a metaphor to activate a story might be assessed by three questions: Is a story necessary for the metaphor to make sense? Does the metaphor have richer or deeper meaning that rewards the extra processing effort if a story is activated? Are there indications in context that a speaker may have intended for a story to be activated (e.g., Governor Perry's contention that Romney's company had bought two companies and '<u>picked their bones clean</u>').

Perceptual simulation/transportation

Research on the use of narratives in persuasive messages (Gerrig, 1993; Green, 2004; Green and Brock, 2000) has shown that the persuasive effects of stories are increased when the story is constructed in such a way that viewers or listeners are 'transported into' the 'story world' and experience the story as if they were part of it. 'Transportation,' as described by Green and her colleagues, is a dynamic version of *perceptual simulation*, which appears to play an important role in metaphor comprehension (Gibbs, 2011), at least when the language is processed intensively (Barsalou, 2007). The relationship between transportation and perceptual simulation merits experimental research, as do the effects of perceptual simulation on the persuasiveness and enjoyment of metaphors and story metaphors in particular.

Issues related to analysis and interpretation

Both experimental and qualitative research is needed to explore the ways in which vehicle stories are mapped onto topic stories. This includes the mapping of time and space from vehicle to topic story as well as the mapping of persons, events, and concepts. The effect of context—both the immediate discourse context and the more extended cultural and historic context—on the use and interpretation of story metaphors also needs closer analysis. The motives for using story metaphors deserve more extensive research—and it is time that researchers gave serious consideration to the aesthetic and hedonic motives, the pleasure to be obtained from metaphorical stories.

Schank and Abelson (1995) argued that memory consists largely of stories. This is an interesting proposal that has not received the research attention it merits. The role of metaphorical stories and the effect of potential story activation on the recall of metaphors also merits research attention.

Telic vs. paratelic uses of story metaphors and metaphorical stories

Social theory, including discourse analysis, commonly assumes that discourse is fundamentally *telic*, or goal-oriented, that social relations are fundamentally hierarchical, and that discourse is always, at some level, motivated by competition for social dominance (e.g., Billig, 2005; Edwards, 1997). However, Ritchie and Dyhouse (2008) and Ritchie and Negrea-Busuioc (2014; Negrea-Busuioc and Ritchie, 2015) have argued that ordinary conversation is often both spontaneous and playful (*paratelic*). Consistent with Dunbar (1996), Ritchie and Negrea-Busuioc argue that metaphor and figurative language generally is often directed toward affiliative rather than dominance relations. The role of story metaphors and metaphorical stories for paratelic purposes deserves further investigation.

Note

1 A more accurate term for the economic activity Perry described is 'equity capitalist'—but that would not serve the creative alliteration required for Perry's quip.

Further reading

Harris, R. A. and Tolmie, S. (eds) (2011) Special Issue on Allegory, *Metaphor and Symbol*, 26.
Ritchie, L. D. (2011) '"*Justice is blind*": A model for analyzing metaphor transformations and narratives in actual discourse', *Metaphor and the Social World*, 1: 70–89.
—— (forthcoming) *Metaphorical Stories in Discourse*, Cambridge University Press.
Turner, M. (1996) *The Literary Mind*, New York: Oxford University Press.

References

Abbott, H. P. (2008) *The Cambridge Introduction to Narrative*, 2nd edn, New York: Cambridge University Press.
Amsterdam, A. G. and Bruner, J. S. (2002) *Minding the Law*, Cambridge, MA: Harvard University Press.
Barsalou, L. W. (2007) 'Grounded cognition', *Annual Review of Psychology*, 59: 617–45.
Billig, M. (2005) *Laughter and Ridicule: Towards a Social Critique of Humour*, London: Sage.
Blair, T. (2005) 'A fight we have to win', speech to Labour's Spring Conference, Gateshead, England.
Blake, W. (1966) *Complete Writings*, ed. G. Keynes, London: Oxford University Press.
Brown, T. L. (2003) *Making Truth: Metaphor in Science*, Champaign-Urbana, IL: University of Illinois Press.
Bruner, J. (2002) *Making Stories: Law, Literature, Life*, New York: Farrar, Straus and Giroux.
Bülow, P. H. (2004) 'Sharing experiences of contested illness by storytelling', *Discourse and Society*, 15: 33–53.
Bunyan, J. (1678/1969) *Pilgrim's Progress* (Harvard Classics series), New York: Collier.
Cameron, L. (2007) 'Patterns of metaphor use in reconciliation talk', *Discourse and Society*, 18: 197–222.

Cameron, L., Maslen, R. and Low, G. (2010) 'Finding systematicity in metaphor use', in L. Cameron and R. Maslen (eds.), *Metaphor Analysis: Research Practice in Applied Linguistics, Social Sciences and the Humanities*, London: Equinox.

Causley, C. (1975) *Collected Poems, 1951–1975*, Boston, MA: Godine.

Crisp, P. (2001) 'Allegory: Conceptual metaphor in history', *Language and Literature*, 10: 5–19.

—— (2005a) 'Allegory, blending and possible worlds', *Metaphor and Symbol*, 20: 115–31.

—— (2005b) 'Allegory and symbol—a fundamental opposition?', *Language and Literature*, 14: 323–38.

—— (2008) 'Between extended metaphor and allegory: Is blending enough?', *Language and Literature*, 17, 291–308.

Deignan, A. and Semino, E. (2010) 'Corpus techniques for metaphor analysis', in L. Cameron and R. Maslen (eds.), *Metaphor Analysis: Research Practice in Applied Linguistics, Social Sciences and the Humanities*, London: Equinox.

Dunbar, R. (1996) *Grooming, Gossip, and the Evolution of Language*, Cambridge, MA: Harvard University Press.

Edwards, D. (1997) *Discourse and Cognition*, Thousand Oaks, CA: Sage.

El Refaie, E. (2009a) 'Metaphor in political cartoons: Exploring audience responses', in C. J. Forceville and E. Urios-Aparisi (eds.), *Multi-Modal Metaphor*, Berlin and New York: Mouton de Gruyter.

—— (2009b) 'Multiliteracies: How readers interpret political cartoons', *Visual Communication*, 8: 181–205.

Fauconnier, G. and Turner, M. (1998) 'Conceptual integration networks', *Cognitive Science*, 22: 133–87.

—— (2002) *The Way We Think: Conceptual Blending and the Mind's Hidden Complexities*, New York: Basic Books.

Fludernik, M. (2003) 'Natural narratology and cognitive parameters', in D. Herman (ed.), *Narrative Theory and the Cognitive Sciences*, Stanford, CA: CSLI.

—— (2010) 'Narratology in the twenty-first century: The cognitive approach to narrative', *PMLA*, 125(4): 924–30.

Freeman, D. C. (1993) '"According to my bond": *King Lear* and re-cognition', *Language and Literature*, 2: 1–18.

—— (1995) '"Catch[ing] the nearest way": *Macbeth* and cognitive metaphor', *Journal of Pragmatics*, 24: 689–708.

—— (1999) '"The rack dislimns": Schema and metaphorical pattern in *Antony and Cleopatra*', *Poetics Today*, 20: 443–60.

Gerrig, R. J. (1993) *Experiencing Narrative Worlds: On the Psychological Activities of Reading*, New Haven, CT: Yale University Press.

Gibbs, R. W., Jr. (2011) 'The allegorical impulse', *Metaphor and Symbol*, 26: 121–30.

Green, M. C. (2004) 'Transportation into narrative worlds: The role of prior knowledge and perceived realism', *Discourse Processes*, 38: 247–66.

Green, M. C. and Brock, T. C. (2000) 'The role of transportation in the persuasiveness of public narratives', *Journal of Personality and Social Psychology*, 79: 701–21.

Hanne, M. (2011) 'The binocular vision project: An introduction', *Genre*, 44: 223–37.

Harris, R. A. and Tolmie, S. (2011) 'Cognitive allegory: An introduction', *Metaphor and Symbol*, 26: 109–20.

Koller, V. (2004) *Metaphor and Gender in Business Media Discourse: A Critical Cognitive Study*, Basingstoke, UK: Palgrave Macmillan.

—— (2009) 'Brand images: Multimodal metaphor in corporate branding messages', in C. J. Forceville and E. Urios-Aparisi (eds.), *Multi-Modal Metaphor*, Berlin and New York: Mouton de Gruyter.

Labov, W. (2013) *The Language of Life and Death: The Transformation of Experience in Oral Narrative*, New York: Cambridge University Press.

Lakoff, G. and Johnson, M. (1980) *Metaphors We Live By*, Chicago, IL: University of Chicago Press.

Mattingly, C. (2011) 'The machine-body as contested metaphor in clinical care', *Genre*, 44: 380.
McComas, K. and Shanahan, J. (1999) 'Telling stories about global climate change: Measuring the impact of narratives on issue cycles', *Communication Research*, 26: 30–57.
McKee, R. (2013, Sept. 18) 'Digging your own grave', *Augusta Chronicle*.
Musolff, A. (2006) 'Metaphor scenarios in public discourse', *Metaphor and Symbol*, 21: 23–38.
Negrea-Busuioc, E. and Ritchie, L. D. (2015) 'When "*seeking love is travel by bus*": Deliberate metaphors, stories and humor in a Romanian song', *Metaphor and the Social World*, 5: 62–83.
Norrick, N. R. (2010) *Conversational Narrative: Storytelling in Everyday Talk*, Amsterdam, The Netherlands: Benjamins.
Oakley, T. and Crisp, P. (2011) 'Honeymoons and pilgrimages: Conceptual integration and allegory in old and new media', *Metaphor and Symbol*, 26: 152–9.
Orwell, G. (1946/2008) *Animal farm*, London: Penguin.
Popova, Y. (2002) 'The figure in the carpet: Discovery or re-cognition', in E. Semino and J. Culpeper (eds.), *Cognitive Stylistics*, Amsterdam, The Netherlands: John Benjamins.
Popova, Y. (2003) '"The fool sees with his nose": Metaphoric mappings in the sense of smell in Patrick Süskind's *Perfume*', *Language and Literature* 12: 135–51.
Reissman, C. K. (2008) *Narrative Methods for the Human Sciences*, Los Angeles, CA: Sage.
Ritchie, L. D. (2008) 'Gateshead revisited: The integrative function of ambiguous metaphors in a tricky political situation', *Metaphor and Symbol*, 23: 24–49.
—— (2010) '"Everybody goes down": Metaphors, stories, and simulations in conversations', *Metaphor and Symbol*, 25: 123–43.
—— (2013) *Metaphor*, New York: Cambridge University Press.
—— (2014, June) '"Born on third base": Stories, simulations, and metaphor comprehension', paper presented at the International Conference on Researching and Applying Metaphor (RaAM), Cagliari, Italy.
Ritchie, L. D. and Dyhouse, V. (2008) '"Fine as frog's hair": Three models for the development of meaning in figurative language', *Metaphor and Symbol*, 23: 85–107.
Ritchie, L. D. and Negrea-Busuioc, E. (2014) '"Now everyone knows I'm a serial killer": Spontaneous intentionality in conversational metaphor and story-telling', *Metaphor and the Social World*, 4: 171–95.
Ritchie, L. D. and Schell, C. (2009) '"The ivory tower" on an "unstable foundation": Playful language, humor, and metaphor in the negotiation of scientists' identities', *Metaphor and Symbol*, 24: 90–104.
Schank, R. C. and Abelson, R. P. (1995) 'Knowledge and memory: The real story', in R. S. Wyer, Jr. (ed.), *Knowledge and Memory: The Real Story* (Advances in Social Cognition, Vol. VIII), Hillsdale, NJ: Lawrence Erlbaum.
Schank, R. C. and Berman, T. R. (2002) 'The pervasive role of stories in knowledge and action', in M. C. Green, J. J. Strange and T. C. Brock (eds.), *Narrative Impact: Social and Cognitive Foundations*, Mahwah, NJ: Lawrence Erlbaum.
Schilperoord, J. and Maes, A. (2009) 'Visual metaphoric conceptualization in editorial cartoons', in C. J. Forceville and E. Urios-Aparisi (eds.), *Multi-Modal Metaphor*, Berlin and New York: Mouton de Gruyter.
Semino, E. (2002) 'A cognitive stylistic approach to mind style in narrative fiction', in E. Semino and J. Culpepper (eds.), *Cognitive Stylistics: Language and Cognition in Text Analysis*, Amsterdam, The Netherlands: Benjamins.
—— (2008) *Metaphor in Discourse*, New York: Cambridge University Press.
—— (2010) 'Descriptions of pain, metaphor, and embodied simulations', *Metaphor and Symbol*, 25: 205–26.
Semino, E. and Swindlehurst, K. (1996) 'Metaphor and mind style in Ken Kesey's *One flew over the cuckoo's nest*', *Style*, 30: 143–66.
Snaevarr, S. (2010) *Metaphors, Narratives, Emotions: Their Interplay and Impact*, Amsterdam, The Netherlands: Rodopi.

Spenser, E. (1590) *THE FAERIE QUEENE: Disposed into twelve books, fashioning XII. Morall vertues*, London: William Ponsonbie. Page references are to the electronic version published on-line by the University of Oxford Text Archive.

Steen, G. and Gibbs, R. W., Jr. (2004) 'Questions about metaphor in literature', *European Journal of English Studies*, 8: 337–54.

Thagard, P. (2011) 'The brain is wider than the sky: Analogy, emotion, and allegory', *Metaphor and Symbol*, 26: 131–42.

Toles, T. (2013, Feb. 25) 'The canary in the coal mine', *Washington Post*.

Turner, M. (1996) *The Literary Mind*, New York: Oxford University Press.

Turner, M. and Fauconnier, G. (1999) 'A mechanism of creativity', *Poetics Today*, 20: 397–418.

24
Metaphor, impoliteness, and offence in online communication

Zsófia Demjén and Claire Hardaker

Introduction and definitions

What role might figurative language play in utterances that are designed to threaten or cause offence? In this chapter we tackle this question, against the backdrop of social practices around computer-mediated communication (CMC), by combining evidence in metaphor and impoliteness research. This combination is necessary because of the relative absence of studies investigating the role of metaphor in offence more broadly.

As the chapters in this book demonstrate, there are various definitions of metaphor that could be used, but for this chapter, metaphor involves talking and, potentially, thinking about one thing in terms of another on the basis of some perceived similarity between the two (Semino 2008). In addition, we will consider metonymy alongside metaphor. In metonymy one thing is used to refer to another, but the relationship between the two entities is much closer than in metaphor. While the latter usually involves a perceived similarity between (supposedly) unrelated entities – often described as a crossing of conceptual domains – in metonymy, the relationship between a vehicle and its target is one of association, often within a conceptual domain (Kövecses 2010; Littlemore 2015). This is a simplified view, but one that suits our purposes here. (For more detailed treatments, including problems with pinning down conceptual domain boundaries, see Deignan (2005); Goatly (1997); Littlemore (2015); Partington (2006).)

Despite the wealth of literature on the evaluative and persuasive power of figurative language (e.g. Chapters 21 and 22 in this volume), metaphors being used specifically to cause offence have not received much attention. This chapter is an attempt at remedying that by drawing on the links between impoliteness, evaluation, and metaphor.

Impoliteness, for our purposes, is defined as:

> [T]he issuing of intentionally gratuitous and conflictive face-threatening acts (FTAs) that are purposefully performed:
>
> 1. unmitigated, in contexts where mitigation (where mitigation equates with politeness) is required; and/or
> 2. with deliberate aggression, that is, with the face threat exacerbated, 'boosted', or maximised in some way to heighten the face damage inflicted.

> Furthermore, for impoliteness to be considered successful impoliteness, the intention of the speaker (or 'author') to 'offend' (threaten/damage face) must be understood by someone in a receiver role ... [T]he speaker must intend and successfully *project* offence while the hearer must also perceive intent and take offence.
>
> *Bousfield, 2010, pp. 120, 121*

For the purposes of this chapter, we consider that offence is the typical effect associated with impoliteness. Therefore, we use *impoliteness* to refer to the producer's language, and *offence* to refer to the target's reaction. Most often, in our data, the kind of impoliteness we see takes the form of insults.

Computer-mediated communication (CMC) – communication occurring via any mediating, networked technology such as laptops or mobile phones (Herring, 2003, p. 612) – forms a particularly interesting arena for the study of impolite metaphors. Recent government reports in the UK suggest that a large majority of Anglo-American homes are now online (Office of National Statistics, 2015). In other words, CMC has become a major aspect of our daily lives, and more importantly, it is an environment that facilitates antisocial behaviour. Factors such as anonymity combined with the linguistically, socially, and psychologically distancing and dehumanising effects of the medium (e.g. Lea & Spears, 1991; Reicher, Spears, & Postmes, 1995) all make it easier to produce impolite utterances. Effectively, CMC allows users to behave unpleasantly whilst feeling that they can evade the consequences. This makes it ideal for the exploration of figurative language (including metaphor and metonymy) in causing offence.

We begin below with work in pragmatics on impoliteness and offence, followed by an overview of literature related to figurative language and insults. We draw on discussions of the various functions of metaphor and metonymy to explain their role in this context. We outline the typical vehicle groups or source domains that occur in insults (ANIMAL, FOOD, OBJECT metaphors and body part metonymies) and consider the role of gender. We consider some of the debates and difficulties in looking at metaphor and offence before presenting an example of current research. Under Current Research, we focus on a case study of *asynchronous* CMC (ACMC), where the intended target is generally not expected to immediately respond. We specifically look at online aggression and trolling (behaving offensively online, typically for entertainment's sake) where users are seeking to cause offence, and we focus on cases where users employ metaphor as a tool with which to achieve this aim. We finish by suggesting directions that future research could take.

Overview of work on impoliteness, offence and metaphor

Impoliteness and offence

Impoliteness research initially began with the assumption that impoliteness was a deviation from 'normal' behaviour, particularly in the context of research on 'politeness' in communication (Austin, 1987, p. 5; Eelen, 2001, p. 104). In fact, whilst impoliteness may be considered *exceptional* or *abnormal* by lay interactants (Culpeper, 2010, pp. 3, 238), a growing body of research shows that it plays a central role in a large number of discourses – more than was previously thought – ranging from everyday chat (Beebe, 1995), to the media (Bousfield, 2008; Culpeper, 2005b; Hutchby, 1992, 1996), and the workplace (Andersson & Pearson, 1999; Holmes et al., 2008). It is only latterly, however, that researchers have started to take an interest in online aggression (Herring, 1999; Honeycutt, 2005; Willard, 2007),[1] which is the topic of the Current Research section below.

Researchers have studied impoliteness from broadly different perspectives, including the postmodern discursive approach (see Eelen, 2001), the interactional approach (see Haugh, 2010), and the social psychological approach (see Spencer-Oatey, 2007). Due to the expansion of research and theories, there has been an accompanying proliferation of terminology for various types of impolite behaviour. A selection of existing terms, often drawing on Goffman's (1967, p. 14) work in this area, is summarised extremely briefly below:

- **Ritual/mock impoliteness** as in 'sounding' or 'playing the dozens' (outlined below), is 'an offensive way of being friendly' (Leech, 1983, p. 144).
- **Non-malicious/incidental impoliteness** is a by-product of the speaker undertaking the task at hand (e.g. criticising a student's essay) despite being aware that she may offend the hearer (Culpeper, 2005b, pp. 36–7). Due to the lack of malicious intent, we might argue that this is not impoliteness at all.
- **Rudeness, faux pas, and failed politeness** capture the unintentional absence, or an inadequate degree of appropriately polite behaviour (Beebe, 1995, p. 166).
- **Genuine, malicious, strategic impoliteness, and instrumental rudeness** are terms by Culpeper et al. (2003, p. 1,546), R. T. Lakoff (1989), Bandura (1973) and others that refer to acts carried out with the intention of causing offence, *and* of conveying that intention (see introduction for a definition of intention).

It is this last version of impoliteness, and particularly its manifestation within aggressive trolling – i.e. deliberately and overtly impolite behaviour that is seeking to cause gratuitous offence, usually for amusement's sake (Hardaker, 2013, p. 77) – with which we are concerned in this chapter.

One commonality across much of the work in the field of impoliteness is that whilst some research has happened to look at examples that include metaphor or figurative language more generally (e.g. see Culpeper, 2005a), none of them has specifically considered the use of metaphor as a choice of impoliteness strategy.

Metaphor, evaluation, and offence

Approaching the topic from the field of metaphor, the research gap seems to be equivalent though opposite: plenty of studies focus on metaphor and its functions, but few on metaphor's direct involvement in offence. Instead studies seem to focus more on metaphors *about* arguments and disagreements – the prototypical example being ARGUMENT IS WAR (G. Lakoff & Johnson, 1980) – than on metaphors used *to undertake* disagreement, arguing, or indeed causing offence. A few studies (e.g. Gibbs, 1994; Kövecses, 2005) have, however, looked at metaphor in ritual/mock offence (cf. Leech, 1983), in the context of verbal jousting, sounding or 'playing the dozens'. For example, the following excerpt (Kochman, 1981, p. 55) involves a number of friends playing cards. A sly jibe between two participants (not shown in the excerpt) creates a bit of tension in the group, which Cunny, a third participant, defuses by making everyone laugh. Then Pretty Black and Nap, silent until now, join in:

Pretty Black:	'What'chu laughing 'bout Nap, with your funky mouth smelling like dog shit.'
Nap:	'Your mama motherfucker.'
Pretty Black:	'Your funky mama too.'
Nap (strongly):	'It takes twelve barrels of water to make a steam-boat run; it takes an elephant's dick to make your Grandmammy come; she been elephant fucked, camel fucked and hit side the head with your Grandpappy's nuts.'

The excerpt above (cited in Kövecses, 2005) includes some figurative language involved in the causing of offence, e.g. *like dog shit*; *motherfucker*; *nuts*.[2] Crucially, however, in bouts of playing the dozens, the objective is not to actually insult the opponent but to demonstrate superiority in verbal skill (Gibbs, 1994), however bold, and in this case sexist, the utterances might be.

The limited literature on metaphors specifically to cause offence however, does not mean that metaphors (and other tropes such as simile and metonymy) do not occur in insults and offensive comments. Insults and the offence they cause involve evaluation (see Culpeper, 2011, for more on this), in that the speaker is projecting a negative assessment of the target (e.g. Chan & Yap, 2015). This works on at least two levels: (a) that the speaker does not respect or care enough for the hearer's face to withhold the insult in the first place, and (b) in the substance of the insult itself.

Evaluation is also a crucial function of metaphor and metonymy (Littlemore, 2015). Recent work on metaphor and politics is explicitly based on this function of metaphor (Chan & Yap, 2015; Goatly, 2007; G. Lakoff, 2002; Musolff, 2004), but the most comprehensive review of metaphor and evaluation can be found in Deignan (2010). Based on previous studies, Deignan (2010) proposes four ways in which metaphors are used to evaluate: by creating evaluative entailments; by triggering evaluative 'scenarios' (as in 'mini-narratives': cf. Musolff, 2006); through strategic source domain choices that align the speaker with a particular group; and by exploiting the connotations of literal meanings. These are all implicit and indirect rather than explicit ways of communicating evaluative meaning, as one would expect with metaphor. Although more research has focused on evaluation in metaphor than metonymy (e.g. G. Lakoff & Turner, 1989; Maalej, 2007), Littlemore (2015) for example, has suggested that, from the point of view of the language user, metonymy actually provides subtler ways of communicating nuance and evaluation than metaphor.

Evaluation, as we discussed so far, can of course be positive as well as negative; both compliments and criticisms can be conveyed through metaphor or metonymy. It is, however, in negative evaluation that metaphors, and indeed metonymies (Levin & Lindquist, 2007; Littlemore, 2015; Obeng, 1997), can be particularly useful precisely because they are indirect. For example, Charteris-Black (2003) found that in Malay, the importance of protecting the hearer's face is paramount, so any criticism tends to be expressed via metaphor. (In English, he found a preference for metonymy.) Similarly, Semino et al. (2014) found that, in the sensitive context of end-of-life care, criticisms of patients are often metaphorical. In these studies as well, the use of figurative language seems to be motivated, in part at least, by the attempt to express a negative evaluation *without causing* offence. Sometimes, however, the objective is to attack an interlocutor's face explicitly and in earnest. In such cases one often finds Animal metaphors.[3]

At times, simply referring to humans as (other) animals conveys a negative evaluation through depersonalisation/dehumanisation, as it inverts the traditional Great Chain of Being hierarchy in which humans are positioned as superior to animals (G. Lakoff & Turner, 1989).[4] In addition, however, contextual factors influence just how offensive such HUMAN IS ANIMAL metaphors are perceived to be (Baider & Gesuato, 2003; Haslam et al., 2011). The discourse situation and manner in which they are uttered (the tone of expression, the target's gender and in/out-group status) and the cultural associations with the particular animals mentioned all play an important role. For example, Haslam et al. (2011) found that, generally speaking, the most offensive animal metaphors involve disliked animals such as snakes, rats, and leeches, which lead to moral disgust through associations of depravity and disagreeableness. Animal metaphors are also perceived as more dehumanising/degrading, and therefore more offensive, if they equate rather than compare the target with an animal (usually ape or dog). The degree of offence caused by such metaphors increases further if they are expressed in a hostile manner, towards more vulnerable individuals and traditionally marginalised groups, such as women and homosexuals.

In fact, metaphors used to abuse or insult often have a gendered element. Generally speaking, metaphor can be gendered in different ways: metaphors might be used differently by speakers of different genders; they might be used to masculinise or feminise an activity, behaviour, or person; or they might be used to represent women and men in discourse (Koller, 2011). Ostensibly offensive metaphors often involve the latter two types. With Animal metaphors, for instance, we find that these are largely directed at either women or men (only a few tend to be directed at both sexes), and that the vehicles themselves denote male or female animals (*stallion*, *stag* vs. *hen*, *bitch*, for example). The distribution, however, is not equal. Hines (1999), drawing on previous studies of Animal metaphors (e.g. Leach, 1964) and her own collection for the topic 'women-considered-sexually' from a range of published literature, suggests the following patterns:

- Women are described as sexual objects using a wider variety of Animal metaphors than men (see also Leach, 1964).
- Animal metaphors such as livestock (e.g. *cow*), game (e.g. *fox*), and pets (e.g. *pussy*) suggesting ownership, domestication, and taming, in some cases as a result of having been hunted, are used mostly for women.

Similar patterns are found in Italian, French (Baider & Gesuato, 2003), English, and Spanish (López Rodríguez, 2009; see also, Kövecses, 2006).

However, Animal metaphors are not the only ones that gender and/or are gendered. For example, in English women are also conventionally referred to via metaphors to do with food (*honey, sweetie, cookie*), playthings (*toy, doll*), personality (*ditz*), and metonymies related to clothing (*skirt*), as well as body parts (*blondie, piece of ass*) (Hines, 1999; Kövecses, 2006; López Rodríguez, 2009). While some of these can be used affectionately (depending on who utters them to whom and in what context as outlined above), they all have the potential be offensive, demeaning, or patronising.

From a conceptual metaphor theory (CMT) perspective, Kövecses (2006) examined 245 (American) English slang words for women and 95 for men, which he collected from various American English slang dictionaries. He found that four source domains dominate conceptualisations of both sexes: THING (*package, doll, piece of*. . .), FOOD (*sweetie*), ANIMAL (*cow, stud, pussycat, chick*), and KINSHIP (*baby, lad*), and a fifth group of terms draws on stereotypical social constructions of masculinity and femininity. Despite the somewhat limited dataset, Kövecses (2006), echoing Hines (1999), found that, while all of these source domains were used to describe both men and women, there tended to be a larger number, variety, and fuller metaphorical conceptualisations denoting women. For instance, both women and men were described metaphorically as THINGS, but only women were conceptualised specifically as COMMODITIES, GOODS, MERCHANDISE, and PLAYTHINGS. These items of course can be bought and owned (like livestock and pets), and in the metaphorical conceptualisations the owners are men. Essentially derogatory metaphors for women, Kövecses (2006) claims, seem to be driven by a combination of social views of women as inferior and as sexual objects. Baider and Gesuato (2003) come to a similar conclusion on much stronger linguistic evidence in both Italian and French.

Theoretical and methodological debates

Controversies and debates around impoliteness and offence are mostly not linguistic in nature (though there are attempts to change that, e.g. Graham, 2007; Shin, 2008), do not focus on metaphor, and generally centre on the legal, political, and moral aspects of what it is permissible to say. This is particularly relevant for the online context, due to the degree of ambiguity and anonymity it affords. Although most of these debates are beyond the scope of this chapter, it is worth considering the possible reasons for the dearth of linguistic research on impoliteness online, and, more specifically, on metaphor and impoliteness.

As outlined by Haugh (2010, p. 8), the surprisingly little linguistic research on impoliteness and CMC can partly be attributed to the:

> variability in the perceptions of norms and expectations underlying evaluations of behaviour as polite, impolite, over-polite and so on, and thus inevitably discursive dispute or argumentativity in relation to evaluations of im/politeness in interaction.

These problems of perceptual variability are not limited to impoliteness, but they are perhaps trickier in CMC than in other mediums. Even long-term members of a certain group may struggle to evaluate the im/politeness of a given online utterance in light of their own norms and expectations. Meanwhile, analysts may be approaching the data with far less contextual knowledge, and this gap is not necessarily filled by a significant body of theoretical work. Indeed, whilst there has been interest in *some* antisocial online behaviours, the focus – especially within the media – has tended to be on cyberbullying (Topçu et al., 2008), cyberstalking (e.g. Bocij, 2004), and latterly on trolling (Hardaker, 2010, 2013, 2015; Herring et al., 2002).

From a metaphor studies perspective, there is the added methodological question of capturing figurative language that is not easily accounted for at the lexical level, that consists of neologisms, or that perhaps emerges and changes its meaning in interaction. As the historical overview above shows, the few studies of metaphor and offence have mostly remained at the level of conceptual metaphors, focusing on specific source domains and providing linguistic examples in support. As our data in the next section shows, however, it is not easy to discuss examples from everyday online interactions in these simplified CMT terms whilst also accounting for the ways in which metaphors interact across turns/utterances, individuals, and within social and cultural norms. When it comes to impoliteness or offence, all of these aspects need to be taken into account, and the example of current research in the next section is an attempt at doing just that.

Example of current research: antisocial online behaviour

High-profile cases of, particularly, women being abused and threatened through social media (e.g. Caroline Criado-Perez, Mary Beard, Anita Sarkeesian, Zoe Quinn, etc.) have brought impoliteness and verbal offence online into the limelight. Issues around where to draw the line between humour and abuse, or an 'innocent' tweet and a very real death-threat and what to do about these kinds of behaviour, are being debated from legal, political, and moral perspectives. The specific case from the UK we discuss in this section will bring some of these issues to life.

In 2013, the Bank of England announced that they were replacing Elizabeth Fry's image on the £5 note with that of Winston Churchill, thereby leaving no notable historical women represented on any UK banknote. In response, in early July 2013, feminist activist and journalist Caroline Criado-Perez started an online petition demanding that the Bank of England include at least one woman on their banknotes. As a result, in late July, the Governor of the Bank of England, Mark Carney, announced that Jane Austen would appear on the £10 note from 2017. Whilst many responded to this success positively, Criado-Perez was also targeted with rape, death, and bomb threats on Twitter. The incident escalated such that by September 2014, three individuals had been convicted and given custodial sentences under §127 of the Communications Act 2003 for their parts in the abuse.

Brief overview of main research methods

The dataset used in this section is a subset of a larger corpus (the Criado-Perez Complete Corpus, CPCC), which was collected as part of the ESRC-funded Discourse of Online Misogyny (or DOOM) project. That project investigated the Criado-Perez case in particular, as well as the phenomenon of women being sent online rape, death, and bomb threats in general. Specifically, the project aimed to discover what we can learn about individuals who send extreme misogynistic abuse online, why they make these kinds of threats, how those threats are constructed (syntactically, semantically, pragmatically, and so forth), and what other kinds of antisocial online behaviour those individuals engage in.

The CPCC was collected using the Datasift service, which provided third party access to historical tweets (amongst other data). The dataset included all tweets and retweets sent to and from Caroline Criado-Perez's Twitter account (@CCriadoPerez) from midnight 25 June 2013 to midnight 25 September 2013 inclusive. The dates captured a month prior to the first abuse to provide a benchmark of 'normal' behaviour around this account, the month of the abuse itself, and a further month after that.

The CPCC dataset had already been separated into subcorpora for the DOOM project, and we therefore chose the already-existing *Criado-Perez Risky Corpus* subset (CPRC) for this analysis. This subcorpus was derived by extracting all tweets from each account within the complete corpus that ranged from offensive through to menacing. The CPRC contains 705 tweets aggregated from 147 low-risk accounts (i.e. these accounts sent offensive but non-illegal tweets such as insults and derision) and 61 high-risk accounts (i.e. these accounts sent rape, death, and bomb threats – linguistic behaviours which can be prosecuted under UK legislation). It is worth noting that the three individuals who subsequently received custodial sentences all feature in this dataset.

Given our interest in metaphors used for causing offence, we firstly worked through the 705 risky tweets and identified all those that could be classified as 'aggressive trolling' (see Hardaker, 2013, p. 77) – that is, deliberately and overtly impolite behaviour that is seeking to cause gratuitous offence. From this shorter list of 134 tweets, we then manually identified and coded metaphorically used words using the Metaphor Identification Procedure (MIP) (Pragglejaz Group, 2007; for details, see also Chapter 5), before performing some preliminary categorisation and analyses on them. In addition, as MIP is not designed to capture metonymy, we introduced a variant to the final step of the procedure for capturing metonymies. In step 3 of MIP, where the researcher needs to decide what the relationship is between the basic and contextual meanings of a lexical item, we introduced the following options:

i. The contextual meaning can be understood in comparison with the basic meaning.
ii. The contextual meaning can be understood/explained in terms of association with the basic meaning.

For relationship i (covered under MIP) we marked lexical items as metaphorical; for relationship ii, not covered in MIP, we marked vehicles as metonymic.

In our analysis, we focused on content rather than function words and only analysed those that were directly involved in causing the offence. This means we excluded (often conventional) metaphors that appeared in a potentially offending tweet, but were not directly involved in causing the offence (e.g. *Im not back peddling. I could care less, actually. I just hope that you die in your sleep*). This distinction was not always easy to make but was designed to ensure focus on the most critical metaphors in this intense context.

While the MIP procedure allowed us to identify the majority of impolite metaphors in the data, in some cases, the word-level analysis required by MIP could not fully account for what was actually happening (cf. Deignan, 2005). We discuss this further in the context of the social stereotype examples below. It should be noted that we found far more features than we can cover in this chapter, so we present only the most interesting results here.

Analysis

In this section, we explore how Twitter accounts within the CPRC use metaphor in the construction of their threats. Once all relevant examples of metaphor and metonymy were coded, we identified the following groups of expressions that were used repeatedly to convey impoliteness, including in the form of insults:

- **childhood and development**: *crybaby, illiterate cunt, grow up* (as a command);
- **prostitution, sex, and sexual organs**: most commonly *cunt*, but also *ass* used metonymically, and *whore* or *hooker* used metaphorically;
- **references to social activities, scenarios, and characters that metonymically stand for social stereotypes**: *cat lady, hulk, making sandwiches*;
- **animals**: by far the most common being *bitch*, but also *pussy, beast, cow*, and one instance of *deeply offended Tibetan yak*;
- **things and (often worthless) objects**: most commonly *shit, crap, trash*, but also *kumquat*.[5]

Body related metonymies, in particular *cunt*, are a frequent type of figurative reference to Criado-Perez (used 23 times in 134 tweets). Metonymies such as these generally communicate negative evaluations through depersonalisation, similarly to Animal metaphors. The choice of taboo expressions such as *cunt* moves them from simple negative evaluations into the realm of impoliteness. These are designed to achieve maximum impact in terms of offence with minimum effort. In some cases, intensity is further increased by pre-modification, e.g. *frigid cunt*. As is well-documented, women are more frequently reduced to their sexual organs via metonymy than men (Baider & Gesuato, 2003; Kövecses, 2006), foregrounding their role as objects of desire and backgrounding all other aspects of their being.

In addition, when pre-modified with *frigid* (a Temperature metaphor), the use of *cunt* not only reduces the woman to her sex, but suggests that even in that respect, she is inadequate:[6]

1. @ya____: @____ @CCriadoPerez #RapeCr3w4ever get fucked *frigid* <u>cunts</u>.

A similarly insulting description in terms of sexual activity happens when Criado-Perez is referred to as a *whore* or *hooker* – arguably some of the most offensive synonyms available from the general paradigm of negatively loaded terms ascribed to female sex-workers. Additionally, however, in these cases the woman also becomes a commodity (a type of objectification) to be purchased:

2. @ti____: @CCriadoPerez U fucking spanish <u>dirty</u> <u>hooker</u>.

Objectification is also one of the main effects of referring to people by way of metaphors involving inanimate objects. The examples in our data, however, take this one step further by mostly referring to Criado-Perez as a worthless and/or soiled object:

3. @ay____: @CCriadoPerez fuck off and die you <u>worthless</u> <u>piece</u> of <u>crap</u>, you're a <u>waste</u> of the air, you should of just jumped infront of horses, go die!
4. @5h____: Feminism does not equal woman superiority. Don't let the <u>trash</u> like @CCriadoPerez fool you on that. @____ @____
5. @ti____: @CCriadoPerez All feminists should fucking die. Males are superior to females. You fucking <u>brainless</u> <u>scum</u>.

These examples are not only dehumanising, but further derogate their target by equating them to rubbish, with all its connotations of dirt, smell, and pestilence.

As suggested by the literature on metaphor and offence, there are also plenty of animal references to Criado-Perez (and other participants in these exchanges). These further contribute to attempts to dehumanise her (cf. G. Lakoff & Turner's (1989) Great Chain of Being) and are often the highly conventional *bitch*, *cow*, and *pussy* (both in reference to the whole person and to the vagina). While Animal metaphors in reference to humans can sometimes function as terms of endearment, these examples are all extremely offensive. The chosen vehicles are often conventional insults in English and denote pets or farm animals with connotations of ownership, control, domestication, and subjugation (López Rodríguez, 2009). In addition, the use of *pussy* for an individual can be seen as doubly offensive: it is reductive in the same way as *cunt*, but also dehumanising because the metonymic vagina is represented metaphorically through a diminutive term for *cat* (Baider & Gesuato, 2003).

While not denoting ownership and domestication, a power imbalance similar to that involved in Animal metaphors is also conveyed by metaphorical expressions to do with childhood and development. Criado-Perez (and others in the interaction) are called *crybabies*, told to *grow up*, and described as *illiterate* or *retarded*.

Taken together, these Body metonymies, and Object and Childhood Development metaphors, attack several aspects of Criado-Perez's self: her status as a rounded person and as a human, her worth or value, and her intelligence and maturity. Via these means, attackers attempt to reduce her to excrement, a sex organ, or to a powerless, uneducated child. A number of non-metaphorical expressions also attack her appearance. While these metaphors and metonymies draw on a variety of source domains, the resulting entailments or implications are relatively consistent and coherent. This suggests the presence of a systematic view (both in a general sense and in the sense of Cameron et al. (2010)) of women as ownable objects of inferior value.

In addition to the metaphors above, we also found figurative patterns that were more difficult to capture using MIP. Some, for example, involved neologisms not recorded in dictionaries, making the identification of a basic meaning less straightforward (they may instead be discussed in terms of conceptual blending for example, as in Chapter 2 of this volume):

6. @Ra____: @CCriadoPerez GOD… All you FEMINAZIS need a good dick up your arse…… so uptight……you need to get FUCKED UNTIL YOU DIE.

Feminazi, with its connotations of evil, dictatorship, and an unrelenting drive to subjugate and destroy a perceived enemy (presumably all males), serves not just to denigrate Criado-Perez personally. It additionally colours the feminist movement that she was campaigning for in the first place with the connotations of the Second World War, Hitler, unthinking obedience to extremist ideology, and ethnic cleansing. It therefore subverts a positive and progressive concept – the equality of women and men – with an extremely negative, emotionally charged concept. By these means, it attempts to corrupt the liberal and positive strides towards equality with a roundly condemned and abhorrent ideology.

Others figurative patterns in the data operate beyond the level of the word, drawing metonymically on (often questionable) socio-cultural scenarios, and increase their significance in interaction and recycling between participants. For instance, in the examples below, the figurative expressions refer to particular 'characters' either from TV shows, making them intertextual references, or draw on cultural stereotypes, representing the traits of the types of individuals they denote (i.e. there is a metonymic motivation to these metaphors):

7. @Ka____: @____ @____ @____ @CCriadoPerez .. and quite proud. But you're just a *cat lady* with a twitter account.
8. @pi____: @____ @CCriadoPerez Don't be jealous because no one looking for your *ass, crypt keeper*.
9. @pi____: '@____: @____ @CCriadoPerez @____ clearly someone has *mommy issues*.' Idc about your *mommy issues*, but I'll be your *daddy*.

Cat lady has connotations of an elderly, lonely, socially awkward women, whilst *crypt keeper* – arguably a reference to the HBO TV series *Tales from the Crypt* – has connotations of an unkempt, living corpse. These are related to a pattern noted by Kövecses (2006, p. 162) where '[a]ssumed qualities that women and men have and that are part of the stereotype can be used to create further names for women and men'. However, perhaps closest to Kövecses' (2006) examples of social stereotype metaphors were the following:

10. @n1____: @____ @____ @____ @CCriadoPerez @____ why arent these cunts *making sandwiches* right now?
11. @pi____: @CCriadoPerez Wouldn't mind *tying this bitch to my stove*. Hey sweetheart, give me a shout when you're ready to be *put in your place*.
12. @ga____: @[well-known British Asian journalist] @CCriadoPerez Wow, fuck off you paki cunt. Shouldnt your brother be busy raping your *stinkhole* atm? *Go finish your curry* 1st.

References to the *stove, your place, sandwiches,* and *curry* metonymically stand for a stereotypical activity (cooking) and the supposed lower social standing of women. Such figurative expressions are also open to creative elaboration. For instance, in example 12, rather than sandwiches, the women are told to make or eat curry. This culturally specific elaboration (G. Lakoff & Turner, 1989) is likely linked to one of the targets being a British Asian journalist.

The same types of references also occur in tweets that cannot be categorised as 'aggressive trolling':

13. @Dw____: @_____ CBD's cure cancer dipshit. No more excuses. <u>Sandwich</u>. NOW! @_____ @CCriadoPerez @_____ @_____ @_____ @_____
14. @ga____: @*[well-known British Asian journalist]* @CCriadoPerez So when will I be arrested? So bored waiting here for nothing to happen. Go and <u>make me a sandwich</u> while I wait.

Both of these examples are similar to 10 above, but the absence of crude invectives such as *cunt* makes them more ambiguous as insults. The key lexical item, 'sandwich', becomes a kind of shorthand, with practical advantages when the communicative space is restricted to 140 characters at a time. 'Making sandwiches', and variations thereof, take on a discourse community-specific meaning and become the metonymic equivalent of a 'metaphoreme' (Cameron & Deignan, 2006). They resemble examples in Kövecses' (2006) data, but draw on more specific sociocultural stereotypes, than typical traits such as, frailty or beauty for women.

The use of these figurative expressions indirectly, but effectively signals that, as far as the attackers are concerned, the women in these interactions on Twitter are not legitimate participants in a forum of discussion, particularly about equality, rights, and socially circumscribed gender roles, and that they should instead concern themselves with more menial chores, such as making sandwiches and/or cooking – presumably for males. These examples are demeaning in the same way as *cunt* and highlight the patriarchal view that a woman's place should be confined to the domestic arena. This implied subjugation and domination becomes explicit in the Force metaphors in example 11 (*tie, put in your place*). Indeed, this links to the historic invisibility of women in public discourse, and particularly in those arenas of power where social roles, rights, and privileges have been negotiated.

Overall, we found it particularly useful to look at metaphor as a strategy for causing offence since impoliteness-via-metaphor can pack a particularly rich semantic punch – it compactly, efficiently, and vividly conveys a large amount of information (Ortony, 1975). With very few words, a user can invoke a wealth of negative attitudes and associations, and this is particularly useful on a medium with a highly restricted character-count.

Future directions

The study we presented here is qualitative in nature and focused on a small and very specific dataset. Though the types of examples we discussed parallel the results of studies conducted on larger and more general corpora (e.g. Baider & Gesuato, 2003), as we have pointed out repeatedly, there is a real need for more research on this topic. We hope that future research will focus specifically on the following:

- the connection between metaphor and offence in different contexts and media: given the very specific data that we discussed, it will be important to investigate whether similar patterns of metaphor use in offending utterances are found among different age groups, in different social contexts as well as modes of communication;
- the links between metaphor, offence, and gender in large corpora of everyday communication: There already are some studies suggesting that metaphorical references to men and women display somewhat different patterns, e.g. derogatory Animal metaphors tend to be more frequent and more varied and have worse connotations for women (cf. R. T. Lakoff, 1973; Hines, 1999; Baider & Gesuato, 2003), but further studies are needed to go beyond individual conceptual domains;
- the role of metaphor in different types of aggression: Less obvious and direct forms of aggression and insult may draw on metaphor more or in different ways to what we were able to discuss in this chapter.

Acknowledgement

The study described in the Current Research section was supported by the Economic and Social Research Council (grant number ES/L008874/1).

Notes

1 Whilst linguistic interest in impoliteness is just blossoming, law, anthropology, business, psychology, and politics have long been researching this phenomenon, usually at the macro-level and under terms such as 'conflict', 'negotiation', and 'crisis'.
2 Throughout this chapter, linguistic examples are in italics with figurative expressions underlined where appropriate.
3 Animal metaphors are also used in terms of endearment (e.g. 'monkey' for toddlers) and can, in culturally specific ways, simply stand for certain human traits ('lion' = bravery; 'mouse' = timidity; 'owl' = wisdom) (Haslam et al., 2011).
4 This is assuming that one considers humans and other animals different enough to warrant the label of metaphor (cf. Goatly, 2007; Pragglejaz Group, 2007).
5 It is worth noting that there is an overlap between these categories and the insult variants in Culpeper's (2011, p. 135) work. However, due to issues of space it is not possible to discuss this further here.
6 In the examples throughout, all usernames, aside from Criado-Perez, have been anonymised or redacted to protect the identity of potentially innocent contributors. Metaphors are underlined and metonymy is marked by dashed underline. Additionally, for the sake of clarity, we have not highlighted every instance of metaphor and metonymy in our examples, but only those which are relevant to the point that is being made.

Further reading

Culpeper, J. (2011). *Impoliteness: Using language to cause offence*. Cambridge, UK: Cambridge University Press.
Deignan, A. (2010). The evaluative properties of metaphors. In G. Low, Z. Todd, A. Deignan, & L. Cameron (Eds.), *Researching and applying metaphor in the real world*. Amsterdam, The Netherlands: John Benjamins.
Hardaker, C. (2013). "Uh.....not to be nitpicky,,,,,but...the past tense of drag is dragged, not drug": An overview of trolling strategies. *Journal of Language Aggression and Conflict*, 1(1), 57–85.
Littlemore, J. (2015). *Metonymy: Hidden shortcuts in language, thought and communication*. Cambridge, UK: Cambridge University Press.

References

Andersson, L., & Pearson, C. (1999). Tit for tat? The spiraling effect of incivility in the workplace. *Academy of Management Review, 24*(3), 452–471.

Austin, J. P. M. (1987). *The dark side of politeness: A pragmatic analysis of non-cooperative communication.* Christchurch, New Zealand: University of Canterbury.

Baider, F., & Gesuato, S. (2003). Masculinist metaphors, feminist research. *Metaphorik.de, 05,* 6–35.

Bandura, A. (1973). *Aggression: A social learning analysis.* Englewood Cliffs, NJ: Prentice Hall.

Beebe, L. M. (1995). Polite fictions: Instrumental rudeness as pragmatic competence. In J. E. E. Alatis, C. A. Straehle, B. Gallenberger, & M. Ronkin (Eds.), *Linguistics and the education of language teachers: Ethnolinguistic, psycholinguistic and sociolinguistic aspects. Georgetown University Round Table on Languages and Linguistics* (pp. 154–168). Georgetown, WA: Georgetown University Press.

Bocij, P. (2004). *Cyberstalking: Harassment in the Internet Age and how to protect your family.* Westport, CT: Praeger.

Bousfield, D. (2008). *Impoliteness in interaction.* Amsterdam/Philadelphia: John Benjamins.

—— (2010). Researching impoliteness and rudeness: Issues and definitions. In M. A. Locher & S. L. Graham (Eds.), *Interpersonal pragmatics: Vol. 6. Handbook of pragmatics* (pp. 101–134). Berlin, Germany: Mouton de Gruyter.

Cameron, L., & Deignan, A. (2006). The emergence of metaphor in discourse. *Applied Linguistics, 27*(4), 671–690.

Cameron, L., Maslen, R., & Low, G. (2010). Finding systematicity in metaphor use. In L. Cameron & R. Maslen (Eds.), *Metaphor analysis* (pp. 116–146). London: Equinox.

Chan, A. S.-l., & Yap, F. H. (2015). "Please continue to be an anime lover": The use of defamation metaphors in Hong Kong electoral discourse. *Journal of Pragmatics, 87,* 31–53. doi: 10.1016/j.pragma.2015.07.001.

Charteris-Black, J. (2003). Speaking with forked tongue: A comparative study of metaphor and metonymy in English and Malay phraseology. *Metaphor and Symbol, 18*(4), 289–310. doi: 10.1207/s15327868ms1804_5.

Culpeper, J. (2005a, March). *Creativity and impoliteness in literature and real life conversation.* Plenary paper given at the conference Politeness: Multidisciplinary Perspectives on Language and Culture, Nottingham, UK.

—— (2005b). Impoliteness and entertainment in the television quiz show: *The Weakest Link. Journal of Politeness Research: Language, Behaviour, Culture, 1*(1), 35–72.

—— (2010). Conventionalized impoliteness formulae. *Journal of Pragmatics, 42*(3), 232–233, 245.

—— (2011). *Impoliteness: Using language to cause offence.* Cambridge, UK: Cambridge University Press.

Culpeper, J., Bousfield, D., & Wichmann, A. (2003). Impoliteness revisited: With special reference to dynamic and prosodic aspects. *Journal of Pragmatics, 35,* 1545–1579.

Deignan, A. (2005). *Metaphor and corpus linguistics.* Amsterdam, The Netherlands: John Benjamins.

—— (2010). The evaluative properties of metaphors. In Z. Todd, A. Deignan, & L. Cameron (Eds.), *Researching and applying metaphor in use* (pp. 357–373). Amsterdam/Philadelphia: John Benjamins.

Eelen, G. (2001). *A critique of politeness theories.* Manchester, UK: St. Jerome.

Gibbs, R. W., Jr. (1994). *The poetics of mind: Figurative thought, language, and understanding.* Cambridge, UK: Cambridge University Press.

Goatly, A. (1997). *The language of metaphors.* London/New York: Routledge.

—— (2007). *Washing the brain: Metapor and hidden ideology.* Amsterdam, The Netherlands: John Benjamins.

Goffman, E. (1967). *Interactional ritual: Essays on face-to-face behavior.* London: Penguin Press.

Graham, S. L. (2007). Disagreeing to agree: Conflict, (im)politeness and identity in a computer-mediated community. *Journal of Pragmatics, 39,* 742–759.

Hardaker, C. (2010). Trolling in asynchronous computer-mediated communication: From user discussions to academic definitions. *Journal of Politeness Research: Language, Behaviour, Culture*, 6(2), 215–242. doi: 10.1515/jplr.2010.011.
—— (2013). "Uh.....not to be nitpicky,,,,,but...the past tense of drag is dragged, not drug": An overview of trolling strategies. *Journal of Language Aggression and Conflict*, 1(1), 57–85.
—— (2015). "I refuse to respond to this obvious troll": An overview of responses to (perceived) trolling. *Corpora*, 10(2), 201–229.
Haslam, N., Loughnan, S., & Sun, P. (2011). Beastly: What makes animal metaphors offensive? *Journal of Language and Social Psychology*, 30(3), 311–325.
Haugh, M. (2010). When is an email really offensive? Argumentativity and variability in evaluations of impoliteness. *Journal of Politeness Research*, 6, 7–31.
Herring, S. C. (1999). The rhetorical dynamics of gender harassment on-line. *The Information Society*, 15(3), 151–167.
—— (2003). Computer-mediated discourse. In D. Schiffrin, D. Tannen, & H. E. Hamilton (Eds.), *The Handbook of Discourse Analysis*. Oxford, UK: Blackwell.
Herring, S. C., Job-Sluder, K., Scheckler, R., & Barab, S. (2002). Searching for safety online: Managing "trolling" in a feminist forum. *The Information Society*, 18, 371–384.
Hines, C. (1999). Foxy chicks and Playboy bunnies: A case study in metaphorical lexicalization. In M. K. Hiraga, C. Sinha, & S. Wilcox (Eds.), *Cultural, typological and psychological perspectives in cognitive linguistics* (pp. 9–24). Amsterdam, The Netherlands: Benjamins.
Holmes, J., Marra, M., & Schnurr, S. (2008). Impoliteness and ethnicity: Māori and Pākehā discourse in New Zealand workplaces. *Journal of Politeness Research: Language, Behaviour, Culture*, 4(2), 193–219.
Honeycutt, C. (2005). Hazing as a process of boundary maintenance in an online community. *Journal of Computer-Mediated Communication*, 10(2). Retrieved from http://jcmc.indiana.edu/vol10/issue12/honeycutt.html 12/12/10.
Hutchby, I. (1992). Confrontation talk: Aspects of "interruption" in argument sequences on talk radio. *Text*, 12(3), 343–371.
—— (1996). *Confrontation talk: Arguments, asymmetries, and power on talk radio*. New Jersey/London: Lawrence Erlbaum.
Kochman, T. (1981). *Black and white styles in conflict*. Chicago, IL: University of Chicago Press.
Koller, V. (2011). Analyzing metaphor and gender in discourse. In F. Manzano (Ed.), *Unité et diversité de la linguistique* (pp. 125–158). Lyon, France: Atelier intégré de publication de l'Université Jean Moulin – Lyon 3.
Kövecses, Z. (2005). *Metaphor in culture: Universality and variation*. Cambridge, UK: Cambridge University Press.
—— (2006). Metaphor and ideology in slang: The case of WOMAN and MAN. *Revue d'Études Françaises*, 11, 151–166.
—— (2010). *Metaphor: A practical introduction* (2nd ed.). New York: Oxford University Press.
Lakoff, G. (2002). *Moral politics: How liberals and conservatives think* (2nd ed.). Chicago, IL: University of Chicago Press.
Lakoff, G., & Johnson, M. (1980). *Metaphors we live by*, Chicago, IL: University of Chicago Press.
Lakoff, G., & Turner, M. (1989). *More than cool reason: A field guide to poetic metaphor*. Chicago, IL: University of Chicago Press.
Lakoff, R. T. (1973). Language and a woman's place. *Language in Society*, 2(1), 45–80.
—— (1989). The limits of politeness: Therapeutic and courtroom discourse. *Multilingua*, 8(2–3), 101–129.
Lea, M., & Spears, R. (1991). Computer-mediated communication, deindividuation and group decision-making. *International Journal of Man-Machine Studies*, 34, 283–301.
Leach, E. (1964). Anthropological aspects of language: Animal categories and verbal abuse. In E. Lenneberg (Ed.), *New directions in the study of language* (pp. 23–63). Cambridge, MA: MIT Press.

Leech, G. N. (1983). *Principles of pragmatics*. London: Longman.

Levin, M., & Lindquist, H. (2007). Sticking one's nose in the data: Evaluation in phraseological sequences with 'nose'. *ICAME Journal*, *31*, 87–110.

Littlemore, J. (2015). *Metonymy: Hidden shortcuts in language, thought and communication*. Cambridge, UK: Cambridge University Press.

López Rodríguez, I. (2009). Of women, bitches, chickens and vixens: Animal metaphors for women in English and Spanish. *Cultura, Lenguaje y Representación / Culture, Language and Representation*, *7*, 77–100.

Maalej, Z. (2007). Doing CDA with the Contemporary Theory of Metaphor: Towards a discourse model of metaphor. In C. Hart & D. Lukes (Eds.), *Cognitive linguistics in critical discourse analysis: Application and theory* (pp. 132–158). Newcastle, UK: Cambridge Scholars Publishing.

Musolff, A. (2004). *Metaphor and political discourse: Analogical reasoning in debates about Europe*. Basingstoke, UK: Palgrave Macmillan.

—— (2006). Metaphor scenarios in public discourse. *Metaphor & Symbol*, *21*(1), 23–38.

Obeng, S. G. (1997). Language and politics: Indirectness in political discourse. *Discourse & Society*, *8*, 49–83.

Office of National Statistics. (2015). *Internet access – households and individuals 2015*. Retrieved from http://www.ons.gov.uk/peoplepopulationandcommunity/householdcharacteristics/homeinter-netandsocialmediausage/bulletins/internetaccesshouseholdsandindividuals/2015-08-06.

Ortony, A. (1975). Why metaphors are necessary and not just nice. *Educational Theory*, *25*(1), 45–53.

Partington, A. (2006). Metaphors, motifs and similes across discourse types: Corpus-assisted Discourse Studies (CADS) at work. In A. Stefanowitsch & S. T. Gries (Eds.), *Corpus-based approaches to metaphor and metonymy* (pp. 267–304). Berlin, Germany: Mouton de Gruyter.

Pragglejaz Group. (2007). MIP: A method for identifying metaphorically used words in discourse. *Metaphor and Symbol*, *22*(1), 1–39.

Reicher, S., Spears, R., & Postmes, T. (1995). A social identity model of deindividuation phenomena. *European Review of Social Psychology*, *6*, 161–197.

Semino, E. (2008). *Metaphor in discourse*. Cambridge, UK: Cambridge University Press.

Semino, E., Demjén, Z., & Koller, V. (2014). 'Good' and 'bad' deaths: Narratives and professional identities in interviews with hospice managers. *Discourse Studies*. doi: 10.1177/1461445614538566.

Shin, J. (2008). Morality and Internet behavior: A study of the Internet troll and its relation with morality on the Internet. In K. McFerrin, R. Weber, R. Carlsen, & D. A. Willis (Eds.), *Proceedings of Society for Information Technology and Teacher Education International Conference 2008* (pp. 2834–2840). Chesapeake, VA: AACE.

Spencer-Oatey, H. D. M. (2007). Theories of identity and the analysis of face. *Journal of Pragmatics*, *39*(4), 639–656.

Topçu, Ç., Erdur-Baker, Ö., & Çapa-Aydin, Y. (2008). Examination of cyberbullying experiences among Turkish students from different school types. *CyberPsychology & Behavior*, *11*(6), 643–648.

Willard, N. E. (2007). *Cyberbullying and cyberthreats: Responding to the challenge of online social aggression, threats, and distress*. Champaign, IL: Research Press.

Part V
Applications and interventions
Using metaphor for problem solving

25

Using metaphor in healthcare
Mental health

Dennis Tay

Introduction

Psychological counselling, or psychotherapy, is a key component of intervention for many mental health conditions including mood (e.g. bi-polar), anxiety (e.g. obsessive-compulsive), and adjustment disorders. The many different types of psychotherapy (Prochaska & Norcross, 2009) share the nickname 'the talking cure' since treatment occurs in a conversational setting where the therapist attempts to understand and help modify feelings, values, attitudes, and behaviours which are thought to underlie the client's condition (Meltzoff & Kornreich, 1970). The typically abstract nature of these matters suggests the potential therapeutic utility of metaphors, which may be used to conceptualize and express the abstract in terms of the concrete (Lakoff & Johnson, 1980, 1999). As McMullen remarks (1996, p. 251), therapists and clients often 'struggle to find words' to convey 'difficult-to-describe sensations, emotions, psychological states, and views of self'. Metaphors used in this type of situation may also provide fascinating material for language and discourse analysts interested in the complexities of figurative speech and thought in social interaction (McMullen, 2008; Tay, 2014b). Consider the following exchange between client and therapist. Stretches of language which are metaphorical according to the criterion of contrast and comparison between basic and contextual meanings (Cameron & Maslen, 2010; Pragglejaz Group, 2007; Steen, Krennmayr, Dorst, & Herrmann, 2010) are underlined.

1. Client: I'm super, super sensitive the last four or five days. I haven't been around people much, and it's kind of purposeful, I think. I just don't want to be around them, because I don't really feel like talking and because, well, they are something other than – it's fun to talk to them when I've <u>got my act together</u>, but when I don't, it's like it <u>takes my mind away</u> from what I'm doing. And I've had enough trouble, I don't want to <u>lose track</u> of it anymore. But I was noticing on the way home that, <u>from</u> one song on the radio <u>to</u> the next, my mood <u>shifts</u>, sometimes almost <u>180 degrees</u>. And it's like, <u>the way</u> I am right now, just the slightest little thing can change my emotions. It's like a <u>feather in a rapid stream</u>, which I don't like. I hate

the instability of it. And yet, there doesn't seem to be any way I can solidify my emotions. Because the more I concentrate on them, the more likely I am to force them to move rapidly in one direction or another.
2. Therapist: Now there's something frightening about being so vulnerable to being affected by outside things. Like talking to somebody else, or a song shifting you.

This exchange illustrates the kinds of metaphor-related issues likely to interest mental health professionals and discourse analysts alike. The former might observe the particular metaphoric creativity of the client, question the extent to which his/her metaphors provide insights into his/her mental state, and wonder how they should best respond. The latter might be struck by the interplay between diverse source and target domains, the mixture of novel and conventional metaphors, and how the therapist subsequently picks up on these.

Metaphor in mental health interventions has indeed been examined from both therapeutic and discourse analytic viewpoints, which have advanced in their own ways our understanding of its therapeutic relevance and application. In this chapter, I provide an overview of these viewpoints and summarize how they have shed light on the forms, functions, and effects of metaphor use. I also note some critical debates and controversies, which point towards the need for closer integration between therapeutic and discourse analytic perspectives in current and prospective research. I then introduce some ongoing work, and suggest future directions aimed at integrating these complementary perspectives.

Overview of relevant research and applications

The study of metaphor as a linguistic, conceptual, and interactional phenomenon in psychotherapy has been differently guided in the mental health and discourse analytic literatures. Broadly speaking, mental health researchers adopt a more functional approach and attempt to connect metaphor use with therapeutic processes (Stott, Mansell, Salkovskis, Lavender, & Cartwright-Hatton, 2010), while discourse analysts focus on the characteristics of metaphor in therapist–client talk without necessarily confronting questions of efficacy and effectiveness (McMullen, 2008; Tay, 2013).

An important objective in mental health research is to clarify the relationship(s) between the process and outcome of treatment (Orlinsky, Michael, & Willutzki, 2004), linking what happens during the course of therapy to its eventual result. Therapeutic research on metaphor has aligned with this objective by theorizing and demonstrating how metaphors may be integrated into therapy sessions to bring about positive change. In terms of theoretical foundation, many contemporary researchers have drawn from, or expressed ideas similar to the cognitive linguistic understanding of metaphor as a way to construct realities in subjective yet psychologically powerful ways (Goncalves & Craine, 1990; Lankton, 1987; Siegelman, 1990; Wickman, Daniels, White, & Fesmire, 1999). The general consensus is that aspects of clients' issues, experiences, and feelings tend to constitute abstract 'targets', with an open-ended array of conceptual materials constituting potential 'sources' which provide insight into the former. This cognitive orientation, which broadens the traditional definition of metaphor, has also allowed therapists to theorize about the relevance of metaphor in nonverbal therapeutic resources such as art, film, and dance (Samaritter, 2009; Sharp, Smith, & Cole, 2002).

Moving beyond their global function as a conceptualization tool, therapists have further suggested how metaphors can play more nuanced and localized functions such as making a point more vivid, introducing new insights, making the therapeutic encounter less intimidating, and facilitating recall of previously discussed content (Barlow, Pollio, & Fine, 1977; Cirillo & Crider, 1995; Lyddon, Clay, & Sparks, 2001; Witztum, van der Hart, & Friedman, 1988). Specific interventions related to metaphor have also been designed by therapists. Therapists who advocate the value of client-generated metaphors have formulated step-by-step protocols to identify, affirm, and elaborate clients' metaphorical expressions into fuller conceptual representations of target topic(s) of interest. Examples include Kopp and Craw's (1998) seven-step protocol and Sims' (2003) six-step model, which guide therapists to use specific prompts such as "What does the metaphor look like?" and "What connections do you see between [the metaphoric image] and the original situation?" Alternatively, those who focus on therapist-generated metaphors have proposed inventories of 'stock metaphors', or readymade analogies such as 'living with anorexia is driving a car without petrol' which could be used with relevant clients (Blenkiron, 2010; Stott et al., 2010).

Metaphor is furthermore seen as relevant to another major piece of the process-outcome puzzle – the 'therapeutic alliance', or collaborative and affective relationship between therapist and client (Bordin, 1979), which is known to be a good predictor of treatment outcomes (Horvath & Luborsky, 1993; Mead & Bower, 2000). The relevance of metaphor shifts here from the cognitive to the cultural and interpersonal dimensions. It has been argued that sensitivity towards culturally specific and salient metaphors is a way for therapists to demonstrate empathy towards clients' worldviews and values. For example, metaphors from the Qur'an and metaphorical *dichos* (folk sayings) from Latino culture have been shown to evoke positive responses in Muslim (Ahammed, 2010; Dwairy, 2009) and Latino clients (Zuñiga, 1992) respectively. Some therapists discuss the interpersonal dimension of metaphor in terms of whether therapists and clients collaboratively develop metaphorical themes (Angus & Rennie, 1988).

Last but not least, some studies relate patterns of metaphor use with aspects of therapeutic process and change. Levitt, Korman, and Angus (2000) compared clients' use of 'burden' metaphors between dyads with good and poor outcomes, and found that only the former involved a gradual transformation from metaphors of 'being burdened' to metaphors of 'unloading the burden'. Likewise, Sarpavaara and Koski-Jännes (2013) examined clients' use of the CHANGE AS A JOURNEY metaphor, and found that those who construed themselves in a more active role of reaching the destination (e.g. 'the direction is correct, but still there's a need to continue the journey, to keep going in the same direction') tended to recover better than those who did not (e.g. 'why try to change something so hard. When the time comes, one sort of finds his own path'). Focusing on therapeutic processes rather than outcomes, Gelo and Mergenthaler (2012) discovered that client metaphors tended to be associated with moments of therapeutic engagement, while therapist metaphors were associated with moments of reflection. On the whole, the body of research summarized above has considerably advanced knowledge of the forms, processes, and effects of metaphor use and management in psychotherapy.

Psychotherapy has also interested linguists whose primary focus is not on therapeutic process and outcome, but how it provides an exemplary context to study language and communication (Ferrara, 1994; Labov & Fanshel, 1977; Peräkylä, Antaki, Vehviläinen, & Leudar, 2011). Tay (2013) identifies key contextual dimensions which characterize psychotherapy and provide useful entry points for metaphor research: the *individual* (i.e. unique characteristics of therapists and/or clients), *interactional* (interactional dynamics between therapist and client), *topical* (nature of topic being discussed by therapist and client), *discoursal* (different genres or theoretical paradigms of therapy), and *socio-cultural* (different linguistic and cultural contexts of therapy), which may individually or collectively 'induce' (Kövecses, 2009) the characteristics of metaphors used. Some of these characteristics, which have been analysed with respect to one or more of the above dimensions, include the nature of source and target domains used by specific patient groups (Charteris-Black, 2012; McMullen & Conway, 2002), the rhetorical development of metaphorical mappings (Needham-Didsbury, 2014; Tay, 2010), the co-textual elements of psychotherapeutic metaphors (Tay, 2011a, 2014a), and the resonance of conventional metaphors (e.g. THERAPY AS JOURNEY) across different levels of psychotherapeutic discourse such as psychological theories, therapist training models, and therapist–client talk (Tay, 2011b).

Common across these studies is a shared emphasis on articulating the contextually modulated nature of metaphor, rather than its therapeutic functions and effects. Despite this, they are often able to highlight noteworthy implications for clinical practice due to their characteristically deeper engagement with nuanced aspects of metaphor theory less often seen in therapeutic research. Tay (2013), for instance, analyses an extended period of metaphor co-construction in terms of how the source concepts supplied by therapist and client are derived from across the three levels often discussed in metaphor research – embodied, cultural, and idiosyncratic (Lakoff & Johnson, 1999; Quinn, 1991; Ritchie, 2006), and offers recommendations on how therapists can use and manage metaphors with these levels in mind. Another example is Ferrara's (1994) analysis of what she calls 'ratification', the process by which therapists bring metaphors previously mentioned by clients back into focus, which she suggests is a strategy for affirming client agency and developing therapeutic insight. From an analysis of metaphor repetition and mixing in interviews with clinically depressed individuals, Charteris-Black (2012, p. 215) comes to a similar conclusion that 'therapists – rather than trying to change the metaphors used by their clients – should engage with clients' metaphors through strategies such as priming and repetition'. These examples reflect a general coherence underlying discourse analytic research, where the main objective has been to describe the contextual richness of metaphors in psychotherapy, followed by some attempt to highlight useful implications for practice.

Critical issues and controversies

The two approaches summarized above have been confronted with their share of critical issues and controversies. Researchers who regard the therapeutic process as a contextual backdrop rather than focus of inquiry face critical issues common among metaphor research in other discourse domains such as how best to identify, analyse, and interpret figurative language (Cameron & Maslen, 2010). The data collection process in this specific context may also present unique challenges such as explaining the rationale and value of metaphor research to prospective therapist collaborators, and justifying to clients why sensitive conversations should be shared. Issues such as data ownership and preservation of anonymity in the dissemination of findings are also sources of potential controversy (Ferrara, 1994).

On the other hand, as detailed in McMullen (1996, 2008), researchers who have a more direct stake in the therapeutic role of metaphor face a broader range of conceptual, methodological, and empirical issues and controversies. One concern lies with the somewhat limited engagement of therapeutic research with developments in contemporary metaphor theory, despite early promising attempts to contextualize key aspects to therapeutic research agendas (Kopp, 1995; Wickman et al., 1999). For example, psycholinguistic models of metaphor processing (Bowdle & Gentner, 2005; Giora, 1997; Glucksberg, 2003), discourse models of metaphor production (Cameron et al., 2009; Wee, 2005), and parameters of socio-cultural variation in metaphor use (Kövecses, 2005) may all have underexplored relevance to therapeutic concerns, insofar as they inform us about cognitive, discursive, and socio-cultural tendencies and preferences of metaphor use. Many studies of metaphor from the therapeutic perspective have not adequately considered the connections these aspects may have with therapeutic variables and processes. In this regard, Teasdale's (1993, p. 342) warning that mental health practice 'may appear to thrive without bothering too much about its isolation from basic cognitive science until the point is reached where, deprived of new input, progress grinds to a halt', seems particularly apt.

Another fundamental concern which may cast doubt on the applicability of existing therapeutic research is that, despite the plethora of studies which suggest how metaphors are useful, or how patterns of metaphor use are associated with indicators of positive change, it is still unclear whether and how metaphor exerts a direct causal effect on change. The existence of so many different therapeutic paradigms (Prochaska & Norcross, 2009) makes it difficult to compare findings across studies, and raises the question of whether metaphor use, like any other therapeutic element, should be regarded as a 'common factor' across these paradigms (Wampold, 2001), or theorized as paradigm-specific. Consider the case of empirical studies on the relationship between metaphor use and 'client experiencing'; i.e. the extent to which clients consciously and willingly explore their inner thoughts and feelings (Klein, Mathieu-Coughlan, & Kiesler, 1986). While positive correlations were identified from 'process-experiential' therapy sessions, which focus on helping clients express and explore emotions (Levitt et al., 2000), no significant relationship was found in sessions where a more generic therapeutic approach was used (Rowat, De Stefano, & Drapeau, 2008). Paradigmatic differences aside, McMullen (1996, 2008) explains the general conceptual and practical difficulties involved with trying to establish causal links between metaphor and change. Experimental manipulation and control of a naturalistic discourse feature like metaphor in spontaneous therapy talk is unlike the typical randomized control trial, since factors such as interest and intensity of participation might co-vary with metaphor use and confound the causal picture, leading one to wonder if the efficacy of metaphor can ever be separated from such contextual characteristics.

Reflecting on these issues, some researchers have called for what I describe as a 'contextual turn' in the study of metaphor in psychotherapeutic counselling (Gelo, 2008; McMullen, 2008; Tay, 2013). Therapists are increasingly urged to recognize the limitations of an approach which assumes global mechanisms linking metaphor use and therapeutic change, and to focus on how metaphors do therapeutic work in particular contexts and circumstances even if this comes at the expense of generalizability. Discourse analysts who may already adopt a contextual approach must also demonstrate more clearly how this can yield findings of therapeutic interest, where therapeutically oriented questions may be engaged at the primary level of analysis rather than the secondary level of 'implications'. In other words, the onus is to analyse metaphor use with respect to both discourse analytic and therapeutic constructs and categories, as well as the significant interfaces and relationship(s) between them. This is necessary in order to demonstrate more convincingly how contemporary metaphor research can address 'real world' concerns in substantial ways (Low, Todd, Deignan, & Cameron, 2010).

The next section introduces specific examples of current research which are taking steps toward this integration of discourse analytic and therapeutic interests. This will be followed by a summary of implications and recommendations for research and practice, and a discussion of concrete future directions for this research area.

Examples of current research: counselling

The contextual nature of metaphor in psychotherapy can be investigated with complementary qualitative and quantitative methods (Nicaise, 2010; Zhang, Speelman, & Geeraerts, 2011). With a qualitative approach, one identifies specific aspect(s) of metaphor theory and the therapeutic process, and explores the interfaces between them on the basis of detailed examination of a limited set of examples. On the other hand, a quantitative approach aims to characterize larger amounts of data with pre-determined variables of discourse analytic and therapeutic interest, and investigate statistically significant relationships between these variables as noteworthy patterns of metaphor use. The following examples of recent and ongoing research demonstrate both approaches in realizing the contextual turn in psychotherapeutic metaphor research.

The relevance of 'metaphor types' to counselling protocols

A recent attempt to engage the interface between metaphor theory and therapeutic process is Tay (2012), which demonstrates how the discourse analytic notion of 'metaphor types' (Wee, 2005) could be applied to enhance counselling protocols designed by therapists to develop clients' metaphoric conceptualizations (Kopp & Craw, 1998; Sims, 2003). Inspired by psycholinguistic models of metaphor processing, Wee (2005) had identified two major metaphor types, or patterns of metaphor elaboration in discourse. The 'correspondence' metaphor type is where discourse producers spell out mappings between source and target in a fairly exhaustive and isomorphic way, while the 'class inclusion' metaphor type is where discourse producers construct the relationship between source and target on the basis of some overarching similarity between the two. Figure 25.1 shows a condensed form of one such counselling protocol (Kopp & Craw, 1998) and the proposed enhancements at step 6 detailed in Tay (2012).

Steps 1 to 5 of this protocol require therapists to draw attention to spontaneous metaphors which supposedly reflect how clients conceptualize their situation, and prompt them to elaborate and perhaps change the attendant 'metaphoric images' (i.e. source domains). For example, a HIV carrier who spontaneously describes his condition as a 'large dark cloud hanging over me' was invited to elaborate details about the cloud, and eventually expressed his wish that the cloud would 'clear up and sun would shine' (Kopp & Craw, 1998, p. 308). Step 6 crucially invites clients to 'connect' between these source domain(s) and the original situation (i.e. target domain), to help them appreciate how changes made to the source domain might translate into actual change. However, no advice is provided on how therapists could guide clients to perform this connection, and here is where metaphor types, which are essentially different strategic ways to construct source–target relations in discourse, could be meaningfully applied.

Tay (2012) shows how particular ways of constructing source–target relations are more suited for particular objectives in therapeutic talk, depending on whether the focus is to explore previously unconsidered elements, relations, or attributes in the client's life circumstances. This more nuanced consideration directly translates into an expansion of the protocol at step 6, where the original notion of 'connection' is problematized, and more specific guidelines are provided to therapists.

The mechanism of metaphor in trauma talk

Another recent qualitative study which is grounded in metaphor theory but explicitly related to therapeutic models is Tay and Jordan's (2015) account of metaphors used by clients with post-traumatic stress disorder (PTSD). According to the American Psychiatric Association's

> **Seven-step interview protocol**
> 1. Notice metaphors
> 2. What does the metaphor look like?
> 3. Explore metaphor as sensory image
> 4. What is it like to be/what are you feeling as you [the metaphoric image]?
> 5. If you could change the image in any way, how would you change it?
> 6. What connections do you see between [the metaphoric image] and the original situation?
>
> **Enhancement**
>
> If the focus is to discover previously unconsidered elements/relations in the client's life circumstances, *use correspondence metaphor type*:
>
> - expand the source domain to elicit different entities, focusing on the relations between them;
> - transfer these entities and relations to corresponding ones in the target domain.
>
> If the focus is to discover previously unconsidered attributes that characterize the client's life circumstances, *use class inclusion metaphor type*:
>
> - focus on attributes of source domain entities which could be applied to the target domain;
> - transfer these attributes and emphasize their applicability to both source and target.
>
> 7. How might the way you changed the image apply to the current situation?

Figure 25.1 Enhancing therapeutic protocols which use metaphor.

Source: Adapted from Tay (2012).

(2013) *Diagnostic and Statistical Manual of Mental Disorders* (DSM-V), PTSD develops from exposure to one or more traumatic events such as sexual assault, serious injury, or the threat of death to self and others – most of which involve vivid and concrete bodily experiences. Tay and Jordan observe that, under the conventional wisdom of therapeutic metaphor use which frames clients' issues as target domains and incorporates conceptual materials external to the therapeutic setting as source domains (Blenkiron, 2010; Stott et al., 2010), these concrete bodily experiences would be regarded as target topics. Yet according to conventional theoretical understanding of metaphor, experiences which are already concrete would not require metaphoric conceptualization. This raises the question whether and how metaphors are still strategically relevant in the context of PTSD. Analyses of interviews with PTSD-diagnosed earthquake victims suggests that, although earthquake-related experiences were indeed mostly literally described, these ostensible target domain experiences could be used as source concepts upon which further abstract topics were initiated and discussed – akin to what Koller (2004) calls 'topic-triggered metaphors'. Consider the following example where the subject is discussing her experience with an aftershock. Her literal descriptions of the situation, 'the ground was still moving' (Line 1), 'we were in the dark' (Line 3), and 'that unknown in the dark' (Line 3) are possible sources due to their concrete bodily nature, and could present useful inferential structures for transiting into discussion of more abstract issues. This possibility appears to be realized in Line 5 as the near-literal experience of being 'kicked in the butt by Mother Nature' transits into a metaphorical description of being 'kicked in the guts by the authorities', who were perceived to be slow to offer assistance.

1. Subject: It was probably the worst, even almost as bad as the earthquake was that night. Um, the ground was still moving.
2. Interviewer: Right.

3. Subject: Um, and we were in the dark, we didn't know what the future was going to, we didn't know whether there was going to be a really bad one, we were aware that there could be, we were aware that something perhaps even worse could happen. I don't know, we didn't know. It was that unknown in the dark.
4. Interviewer: So that first night.
5. Subject: It was very frightening. We were lying in bed and [partner] said, but we're pretty practical people, and he said, we've just been <u>kicked in the butt</u> by Mother Nature, now we're going to get <u>kicked in the guts</u> by the authorities . . .

The therapeutic utility of metaphors in PTSD is thus affirmed by such illustrative analysis, and the idea that therapeutic topics can themselves function as sources critically interrogates the received wisdom that source domains of therapeutic metaphors are always 'borrowed' from something external to the therapeutic setting.

Metaphor usage patterns from the interaction of contextual factors

Analysis of metaphor and metonymy based on quantitative methods complement rich qualitative descriptions by revealing otherwise invisible usage patterns across larger amounts of discourse data (Nicaise, 2010; Zhang et al., 2011). Quantitative approaches to psychotherapeutic metaphor research are furthermore motivated by the aforementioned need to analyse metaphor use with respect to both discourse analytic and therapeutic constructs, which in turn motivates correlational methods to investigate the presence and strength of associations between discourse analytic and therapeutic variables. The former may involve formal and structural aspects such as source and target while the latter may include 'therapeutic function of metaphor' (Cirillo & Crider, 1995; Lyddon et al., 2001), 'degree of client experiencing' (Gelo & Mergenthaler, 2012; Klein et al., 1986), 'phase of therapy', and so on. One example is Tay's (2015a) analysis of metaphors in a corpus of 'case study articles', a popular mental healthcare communication genre on Chinese university counselling service websites. Each case study article has distinct sections which highlight aspects such as the client's background, the therapy process, the therapist's analysis, and general psychology knowledge relevant to the case at hand. Part of the study investigated whether source and target categories correlate with the sections under which the metaphors appeared, thereby shedding light on the systematicity of metaphor as a conceptual and rhetorical device of mental healthcare communication. A significant and strong association was found for targets ($\chi^2(12, N = 1287) = 586.35, p < .0001$, Cramer's V = 0.3897) but not sources ($\chi^2(4, N = 1448) = 8.17, p = 0.086$, Cramer's V = 0.0751), suggesting that there is a tendency to use certain targets when focusing on certain aspects of the client's case, while the distribution of sources is far less patterned.

Another example is an ongoing study by the author which attempts to model interactions between multiple variables such as target, therapeutic function, phase of therapy (beginning, middle, or end), speaker (therapist or client), and client identity (different individual clients) according to their frequency of occurrence in a corpus of Chinese psychotherapy talk. A log-linear analysis of more than 2,000 metaphor vehicle terms across 15 hours of talk has revealed higher-order interactions which may interest metaphor researchers and therapists alike. For example, a significant interaction was found between target, speaker, and function, suggesting that while therapists and clients expectedly use metaphors for different functions, this varies according to what the metaphors are actually about. Therapists are much more likely to perform an 'expert-like' expository role when the metaphors relate to objective situations faced by clients, but less likely to do so when the metaphors relate to subjective aspects of the client's self. Consider an example:

1. Therapist: 所以女儿有能力的时候,所以赶紧干吧！让她赶紧,摧着快马加鞭。是不是一直像那个赶马车,使劲的甩鞭子,让她继续干,赶紧干？ So when the daughter is still able to, let her do more work! <u>Whip the galloping horse</u>. Is it like <u>being on a wagon</u>, <u>whipping the horse</u>, and letting her do as much work as possible?
2. Client: 对 Correct
3. Therapist: 你看所以她觉得这就像工具。她就觉得在你眼里面她就是工具。她产生这样的感觉。您可以理解了吗？ You see, so she thinks that in your eyes, she is just <u>a tool</u>. She has these feelings, can you understand?

In Line 1, the therapist's metaphor describes an intimate, subjective aspect of the client's familial relationship. It is tentative and exploratory, requiring the patient's confirmation that it is appropriate. It is only upon this confirmation (Line 2) that he reverts to the characteristically explanatory use of metaphor in Line 3, where the target is now a more objective evaluation of the client's situation. Such findings continue to reveal the contextual nuances and intricacies which underline psychotherapeutic metaphor use.

Implications and recommendations for practice

The major trend highlighted in the discussion above is that metaphor-related research and practice has begun to move away from global mechanisms of metaphor and therapeutic change, towards specific functions and settings of metaphor use. The examples of current research summarized above, which examine metaphor characteristics under various contextual conditions such as localized discourse objectives, specific client populations, and emerging non-verbal forms of therapy, reflect the growing recognition of metaphor as a 'multi-faceted phenomenon' which itself 'encompasses multiple phenomena' (Cameron & Maslen, 2010, p. 7). What this all means for clinical practice is that the use of structured interventions such as protocols (Kopp & Craw, 1998) and stock metaphors (Stott et al., 2010) may well benefit from greater sensitivity towards the spontaneous, creative, and emergent qualities of metaphor as they unfold in therapist–patient interaction. A therapist who selects from her prepared inventory a metaphor to describe and explain anorexia as 'driving a car without petrol' (Stott et al., 2010) should recognize that its source(s), target(s), mapping(s), entailments, and/or potential discursive elaborations are flexible rather than fixed. Anderson and Goolishian's (1988, p. 372) metaphorical descriptions of therapy as a 'two-way exchange, a crisscrossing of ideas' and the therapist as a master conversational artist – an architect of dialogue – whose expertise is in creating a space for and facilitating a dialogical conversation, are particularly apt in this regard.

The issues raised concerning the integration of discourse analytic and therapeutic interests in metaphor research also lead to a call for closer communication between discourse analysts and therapists. While there will always be distinct foci in their different literatures, more concrete steps could be taken by collaborative research teams to exchange information and share expertise. Besides the aforementioned data collection, aspects across the research process such as the conceptualization of research gaps, filtering of data, analysis, and discussion of implications can all be strengthened with cross-checks and discussion. It is especially important for discourse analysts to understand how to frame their proposed implications in ways which appeal to, and could be tested in actual therapeutic practice (Tay, 2015b).

My ongoing exploration of the relationship between metaphor and the phenomenon of psychological transference (i.e. the tendency for clients to re-experience and map past experiences onto present ones) illustrates how even trained metaphor researchers are sometimes unable to accomplish the basic task of metaphor identification without input from therapists, since metaphor use is in this context closely interwoven with the expression of a particular psychological dynamic. On the flip side, it is encouraging to know of growing initiatives among therapists such as training workshops and publications which aim to apply discourse analytic insights to therapeutic work, and raise awareness of discourse analysis within the therapeutic community (Mathieson, Jordan, Carter, & Stubbe, 2015).

Future directions

While this chapter has discussed recent and ongoing work from the perspective of the contextual turn in psychotherapeutic metaphor research, I would like to end by suggesting other themes and directions which could constitute independent strands in their own right. An obvious theme which occupies not only a central place in metaphor scholarship (Kövecses, 2005) but also cross-cultural psychotherapy research (Tseng, Chang, & Nishizono, 2005) is the nature of metaphors in therapy across different cultural and linguistic contexts (Dwairy, 2009; Liu et al., 2013; Zuñiga, 1992). Since cross-cultural situations easily arise from variation in any of the four elements of therapist, patient, locale, and therapeutic method (Wohl, 1989), psychotherapy talk provides an intriguing context for descriptions of metaphor across cultures and languages. Such work would also be especially exigent in cultures where professional psychotherapy has only recently begun to gain widespread acceptance (Zhong, 2011). Furthermore, the interactional nature of metaphor in psychotherapy (Ferrara, 1994) would provide an additional perspective on metaphor variation research, which has tended to focus on more stable and conventional semantic differences.

Another underexplored aspect is how the form and function of metaphors vary across different levels of therapeutic discourse – from the 'small d' of face-to-face interaction to the 'big D' (Gee, 2005) of metaphorically framed therapy models, theories, and ideologies. Broadening the description of metaphors beyond face-to-face interaction may also raise interesting implications for their clinical use. Tay (2011b), for instance, examined how the process of therapy itself is conceptualized as a journey at the different levels of face-to-face talk, therapist training models, and psychotherapeutic theories, and how the respective mappings and discourse functions differ accordingly. While therapists who are explaining the process of therapy may be expected to simply inherit metaphors from the 'higher' level of psychotherapeutic theories, Tay (2011b) suggests that metaphors in face-to-face talk could provide useful 'feedback' material for theorists looking to frame processes of therapy in metaphorical ways. An exigent area of investigation would be metaphors in the fast growing domain of e-health discourse; i.e. internet supported therapeutic interventions such as self-help blogs and discussion forums (Barak, Klein, & Proudfoot, 2009), and their similarities and differences with metaphors in face-to-face interaction.

Notwithstanding the general optimism about the therapeutic value of metaphors, it is also important to critically examine when and how they could be non-helpful or even harmful for clients. Rhodes and Jakes (2004) have, for instance, suggested, based on semi-structured interviews with delusional patients, that delusional beliefs result from a gradual 'fusion' of two conceptual domains, where an originally figurative statement (e.g. *I am like someone possessed*) gradually comes to be perceived as literal (*I am possessed by the devil*). The possibility that client-generated metaphors contribute to the onset of delusional thinking provides a counterpoint to the general sentiment that they are always positive opportunities for creative exploration and meaning-making. As for therapist-generated metaphors, Blenkiron cautions therapists against 'pushing (metaphoric) comparisons too far' (2005, p. 56) since too much explicit metaphorical reasoning may be perceived as trivial, unscientific, or even offensive, especially if clients cannot relate with the source concept(s) involved (cf. Tay, 2014a). One client I know unflatteringly described metaphor use in psychotherapy as 'psychobabble'. On that note, demographic differences in attitudes and receptiveness towards metaphor use in psychotherapy remains a virtually unexplored research area, and may help to clarify important issues such as disparities between 'folk' and 'expert' understanding of what metaphor is, and how much metaphor use is appropriate (cf. Stiles & Shapiro, 1994).

Acknowledgement

This work is partly supported by the General Research Fund (Project no. 25600515) of the University Grants Committee, Hong Kong Special Administrative Region.

Further reading

McMullen, L. M. (2008). Putting it in context: Metaphor and psychotherapy. In R. W. Gibbs, Jr. (Ed.), *The Cambridge handbook of metaphor and thought* (pp. 397–411). Cambridge, UK: Cambridge University Press.

Stott, R., Mansell, W., Salkovskis, P., Lavender, A. & Cartwright-Hatton, S. (2010). *Oxford guide to metaphors in CBT: Building cognitive bridges*. Oxford and New York: Oxford University Press.

Tay, D. (2014). Metaphor theory for counselling professionals. In J. Littlemore & J. R. Taylor (Eds.), *Bloomsbury companion to cognitive linguistics* (pp. 352–367). London: Bloomsbury.

References

Ahammed, S. (2010). Applying Qur'anic metaphors in counseling. *International Journal for the Advancement of Counselling*, 32(4), 248–255.

American Psychiatric Association. (2013). *Diagnostic and statistical manual of mental health disorders* (5th ed.). Arlington, VA: American Psychiatric Publishing.

Anderson, H., & Goolishian, H. (1988). Human systems as linguistic systems: Preliminary and evolving ideas about the implications for clinical theory. *Family Process*, 27(4), 371–393.

Angus, L. E., & Rennie, D. L. (1988). Therapist participation in metaphor generation: Collaborative and non-collaborative styles. *Psychotherapy*, 25(4), 552–560.

Barak, A., Klein, B., & Proudfoot, J. G. (2009). Defining Internet-supported therapeutic interventions. *Annals of Behavioral Medicine: A Publication of the Society of Behavioral Medicine*, 38(1), 4–17. doi: 10.1007/s12160-009-9130-7

Barlow, J., Pollio, H., & Fine, H. (1977). Insight and figurative language in psychotherapy. *Psychotherapy: Theory, Research and Practice*, 14(3), 212–222.

Blenkiron, P. (2005). Stories and analogies in cognitive behaviour therapy: A clinical review. *Behavioral and Cognitive Psychotherapy*, 33, 45–59.

—— (2010). *Stories and analogies in cognitive behaviour therapy*. West Sussex, UK: John Wiley & Sons.

Bordin, E. S. (1979). The generalizability of the psychoanalytic concept of the working alliance. *Psychotherapy: Theory, Research and Practice*, 16(3), 252–260.

Bowdle, B. F., & Gentner, D. (2005). The career of metaphor. *Psychological Review*, 112(1), 193–216.

Cameron, L., & Maslen, R. (Eds.). (2010). *Metaphor analysis*. London: Equinox.
Cameron, L., Maslen, R., Todd, Z., Maule, J., Stratton, P., & Stanley, N. (2009). The discourse dynamics approach to metaphor and metaphor-led discourse analysis. *Metaphor and Symbol, 24*(2), 63–89. doi: 10.1080/10926480902830821.
Charteris-Black, J. (2012). Shattering the bell jar: Metaphor, gender, and depression. *Metaphor and Symbol, 27*(3), 199–216. Retrieved from http://www.scopus.com/inward/record.url?eid=2-s2.0-84863889208&partnerID=40&md5=e44b3186d7ead78e4c97168991e41bde.
Cirillo, L., & Crider, C. (1995). Distinctive therapeutic uses of metaphor. *Psychotherapy, 32*, 511–519.
Dwairy, M. (2009). Culture analysis and metaphor psychotherapy with Arab-Muslim clients. *Journal of Clinical Psychology, 65*(2), 199–209. doi:10.1002/jclp.20568.
Ferrara, K. W. (1994). *Therapeutic ways with words: Oxford studies in sociolinguistics*. New York: Oxford University Press.
Gee, J. P. (2005). *An introduction to discourse analysis: Theory and method* (2nd ed.). New York: Routledge.
Gelo, O. C. G. (2008). *Metaphor and emotional-cognitive regulation in psychotherapy: A single case study*. Ulm: Ulmer Textbank.
Gelo, O. C. G., & Mergenthaler, E. (2012). Unconventional metaphors and emotional-cognitive regulation in a metacognitive interpersonal therapy. *Psychotherapy Research, 22*(2), 159–175.
Giora, R. (1997). Understanding figurative and literal language: The graded salience hypothesis. *Cognitive Linguistics, 8*, 183–206.
Glucksberg, S. (2003). The psycholinguistics of metaphor. *Trends in Cognitive Sciences, 7*(2), 92–96. doi: 10.1016/S1364-6613(02)00040-2.
Goncalves, O. F., & Craine, M. H. (1990). The use of metaphors in cognitive therapy. *Journal of Cognitive Psychotherapy: An International Quarterly, 4*(2), 135–149.
Horvath, A. O., & Luborsky, L. (1993). The role of the therapeutic alliance in psychotherapy. *Journal of Consulting and Clinical Psychology, 61*(4), 561–573. Retrieved from http://www.scopus.com/inward/record.url?eid=2-s2.0-0027250382&partnerID=40&md5=521a94241fd4e9f50131962cc836f78a.
Klein, M., Mathieu-Coughlan, P., & Kiesler, D. (1986). The experiencing scales. In W. Pinsof & L. Greenberg (Eds.), *The psychotherapeutic process: A research handbook* (pp. 21–72). New York: Guilford Press.
Koller, V. (2004). Businesswomen and war metaphors: "Possessive, jealous and pugnacious"?, *Journal of Sociolinguistics, 8*(1), 3–22. doi:10.1111/j.1467-9841.2004.00249.x.
Kopp, R. R. (1995). *Metaphor therapy: Using client-generated metaphors in psychotherapy*. New York: Brunnel/Mazel.
Kopp, R. R., & Craw, M. J. (1998). Metaphoric language, metaphoric cognition, and cognitive therapy. *Psychotherapy, 35*(3), 306–311. doi: 10.1037/0033-3204.35.3.306.
Kövecses, Z. (2005). *Metaphor in culture: Universality and variation*. Cambridge, UK: Cambridge University Press.
—— (2009). The effect of context on the use of metaphor in discourse. *Iberica, 17*, 11–23.
Labov, W., & Fanshel, D. (1977). *Therapeutic discourse*. New York: Academic Press.
Lakoff, G., & Johnson, M. (1980). *Metaphors we live by*. Chicago, IL: University of Chicago Press.
—— (1999). *Philosophy in the flesh: The embodied mind and its challenges to Western thought*. New York: Basic Books.
Lankton, S. (1987). Central themes and principles of Ericksonian therapy. *Ericksonian Monographs*. New York: Brunner/Mazel.
Levitt, H., Korman, Y., & Angus, L. (2000). A metaphor analysis in treatments of depression: Metaphor as a marker of change. *Counselling Psychology Quarterly, 13*(1), 23–35. doi: 10.1080/09515070050011042.
Liu, L., Miller, J. K., Zhao, X., Ma, X., Wang, J., & Li, W. (2013). Systemic family psychotherapy in China: A qualitative analysis of therapy process. *Psychology and Psychotherapy: Theory, Research*

and Practice, 86(4), 447–465. Retrieved from http://www.scopus.com/inward/record.url?eid=2-s2.0-84887810755&partnerID=40&md5=0227acabd8e588684d25630f4accdfca.

Low, G., Todd, Z., Deignan, A., & Cameron, L. (2010). *Researching and applying metaphor in the real world.* Amsterdam and Philadelphia: John Benjamins.

Lyddon, W. J., Clay, A. L., & Sparks, C. L. (2001). Metaphor and change in counselling. *Journal of Counseling & Development, 79*(3), 269–274.

Mathieson, F., Jordan, J., Carter, J., & Stubbe, M. (2015). Nailing down metaphors in CBT: Definition, identification and frequency. *Behavioural and Cognitive Psychotherapy,* 1–13.

McMullen, L. M. (1996). Studying the use of figurative language in psychotherapy: The search for researchable questions. *Metaphor and Symbolic Activity, 11*(4), 241–255. doi: 10.1207/s15327868ms1104_1.

—— (2008). Putting it in context: Metaphor and psychotherapy. In R. W. Gibbs, Jr. (Ed.), *The Cambridge handbook of metaphor and thought* (pp. 397–411). Cambridge, UK: Cambridge University Press.

McMullen, L. M., & Conway, J. B. (2002). Conventional metaphors for depression. In S. R. Fussell (Ed.), *The verbal communication of emotions: Interdisciplinary perspectives* (pp. 167–181). Mahwah, NJ: Lawrence Erlbaum.

Mead, N., & Bower, P. (2000). Patient-centredness: A conceptual framework and review of the empirical literature. *Social Science and Medicine, 51*(7), 1087–1110. Retrieved from http://www.scopus.com/inward/record.url?eid=2-s2.0-0034309873&partnerID=40&md5=ba790fc0aab295cb9ced1e7fa6534dec.

Meltzoff, J., & Kornreich, M. (1970). *Research in psychotherapy.* New York: Atherton Press.

Needham-Didsbury, I. (2014). Metaphor in psychotherapeutic discourse: Implications for utterance interpretation. *Poznan Studies in Contemporary Linguistics, 50*(1), 75–97. doi: 10.1515/psicl-2014-0005.

Nicaise, L. (2010). Metaphor and the context of use: A multidimensional approach. *Metaphor and Symbol, 25*(2), 63–73. doi: 10.1080/10926481003715978.

Orlinsky, D., Michael, R., & Willutzki, U. (2004). Fifty years of psychotherapy process-outcome research: Continuity and change. In *Bergin and Garfield's handbook of psychotherapy and behavior change* (pp. 307–389). Hoboken, NJ: Wiley.

Peräkylä, A., Antaki, C., Vehviläinen, S., & Leudar, I. (Eds.). (2011). *Conversation analysis and psychotherapy.* Cambridge and New York: Cambridge University Press.

Pragglejaz Group. (2007). MIP: A method for identifying metaphorically used words in discourse. *Metaphor and Symbol, 22*(1), 1–39. doi: 10.1207/s15327868ms2201_1.

Prochaska, J. O., & Norcross, J. C. (2009). *Systems of psychotherapy: A transtheoretical analysis* (7th ed.). Belmont, CA: Brooks/Cole.

Quinn, N. (1991). The cultural basis of metaphor. In J. Fernandez (Ed.), *Beyond metaphor: The theory of tropes in anthropology* (pp. 56–93). Stanford, CA: Stanford University Press.

Rhodes, J. E., & Jakes, S. (2004). The contribution of metaphor and metonymy to delusions. *Psychology and Psychotherapy: Theory, Research and Practice, 77*(1), 1–17. doi: 10.1348/147608304322874227.

Ritchie, D. (2006). *Context and connection in metaphor.* Basingstoke and New York: Palgrave Macmillan.

Rowat, R., De Stefano, J., & Drapeau, M. (2008). The role of patient-generated metaphors on in-session therapeutic processes. *Archives of Psychiatry and Psychotherapy, 1*, 21–27.

Samaritter, R. (2009). The use of metaphors in dance movement therapy. *Body, Movement and Dance in Psychotherapy, 4*(1), 33–43. Retrieved from http://www.scopus.com/inward/record.url?eid=2-s2.0-67651093951&partnerID=40.

Sarpavaara, H., & Koski-Jännes, A. (2013). Change as a journey: Clients' metaphoric change talk as an outcome predictor in initial motivational sessions with probationers. *Qualitative Research in Psychology, 10*(1), 86–101. doi: 10.1080/14780887.2011.586256.

Sharp, C., Smith, J. V, & Cole, A. (2002). Cinematherapy: Metaphorically promoting therapeutic change. *Counselling Psychology Quarterly, 15*(3), 269–276. doi: 10.1080/09515070210140221.

Siegelman, E. Y. (1990). *Metaphor and meaning in psychotherapy*. New York: Guilford Press.
Sims, P. A. (2003). Working with metaphor. *American Journal of Psychotherapy, 57*(4), 528–536.
Steen, G., Krennmayr, T., Dorst, A. G., & Herrmann, J. B. (2010). *A method for linguistic metaphor identification: From MIP to MIPVU*. Amsterdam and Philadelphia: John Benjamins.
Stiles, W. B., & Shapiro, D. A. (1994). Disabuse of the drug metaphor: Psychotherapy process-outcome correlations. *Journal of Consulting and Clinical Psychology, 62*(5), 942–948.
Stott, R., Mansell, W., Salkovskis, P., Lavender, A., & Cartwright-Hatton, S. (2010). *Oxford guide to metaphors in CBT: Building cognitive bridges*. Oxford and New York: Oxford University Press.
Tay, D. (2010). Revisiting metaphor types as discourse strategies: The case of psychotherapeutic discourse. *Text & Talk, 30*(4), 445–463. doi: 10.1515/TEXT.2010.022.
—— (2011a). Discourse markers as metaphor signalling devices in psychotherapeutic talk. *Language & Communication, 31*(4), 310–317. doi: 10.1016/j.langcom.2011.02.001.
—— (2011b). THERAPY IS A JOURNEY as a discourse metaphor. *Discourse Studies, 13*(1), 47–68. doi: 10.1177/1461445610387736.
—— (2012). Applying the notion of metaphor types to enhance counseling protocols. *Journal of Counseling & Development, 90*(2), 142–149.
—— (2013). *Metaphor in psychotherapy: A descriptive and prescriptive analysis*. Amsterdam and Philadelphia: John Benjamins.
—— (2014a). An analysis of metaphor hedging in psychotherapeutic talk. In M. Yamaguchi, D. Tay, & B. Blount (Eds.), *Approaches to language, culture, and cognition* (pp. 251–267). Basingstoke, UK: Palgrave Macmillan.
—— (2014b). At the heart of cognition, communication, and language: The value of psychotherapy to metaphor study. *Metaphor and the Social World, 4*(1), 48–64.
—— (2015a). Metaphor in case study articles on Chinese university counseling service websites. *Chinese Language and Discourse, 6*(1), 28–56.
—— (2015b). Pesquisa aplicada à metáfora: Tendências, questões, metodologicas e ferramentas de software. In A. G. Vieira, W. R. Silva, & M. L. de S. Góis (Eds.), *Visibilizar a linguística aplicada: Abordagens teóricas e metodológicas* (pp. 111–130). Pontes.
Tay, D., & Jordan, J. (2015). Metaphor and the notion of control in trauma talk. *Text & Talk, 35*(4), 553–573.
Teasdale, J. D. (1993). Emotion and two kinds of meaning: Cognitive therapy and applied cognitive science. *Behaviour Research and Therapy, 31*(4), 339–354.
Tseng, W.-S., Chang, S. C., & Nishizono, M. (2005). *Asian culture and psychotherapy: Implications for East and West*. Honolulu, Hawaii: University of Hawaii Press.
Wampold, B. E. (2001). *The great psychotherapy debate: Models, methods, and findings*. Mahwah, NJ: Lawrence Erlbaum.
Wee, L. (2005). Class-inclusion and correspondence models as discourse types: A framework for approaching metaphorical discourse. *Language in Society, 34*(2), 219–238. doi: 10.1017/S0047404 505050098.
Wickman, S. A., Daniels, M. H., White, L. J., & Fesmire, S. A. (1999). A "primer" in conceptual metaphor for counselors. *Journal of Counseling & Development, 77*, 389–394.
Witztum, E., van der Hart, O., & Friedman, B. (1988). The use of metaphors in psychotherapy. *Journal of Contemporary Psychotherapy, 18*(4), 270–290. doi: 10.1007/BF00946010.
Wohl, J. (1989). Integration of cultural awareness into psychotherapy. *American Journal of Psychotherapy, 43*, 343–355.
Zhang, W., Speelman, D., & Geeraerts, D. (2011). Variation in the (non)metonymic capital names in Mainland Chinese and Taiwan Chinese. *Metaphor and the Social World, 1*(1), 90–112. doi: 10.1075/msw.1.1.09zha.
Zhong, J. (2011). Working with Chinese patients: Are there conflicts between Chinese culture and psychoanalysis? *International Journal of Applied Psychoanalytic Studies, 8*(3), 218–226.
Zuñiga, M. E. (1992). Using metaphors in therapy: Dichos and Latino clients. *Social Work, 37*(1), 55–60.

26

Using metaphor in healthcare
Physical health

Zsófia Demjén and Elena Semino

Introduction

As shown throughout this volume, metaphors are regularly used to talk and think about experiences that are subjective, complex and sensitive in terms of experiences that are less subjective, simpler and more concrete. Health and illness, and the emotions associated with them, are among the experiences that we often talk about through metaphors. As is the case more generally, these metaphors tend to rely on perceived similarities between different kinds of experiences. For example, the metaphorical use of 'battle' in 'she died after a long battle with cancer' relies on the perception of a similarity between being ill with cancer and fighting in a war: both experiences are difficult and potentially life-threatening, both require perseverance, and so on. However, as our use of the term 'perceived' similarity suggests, metaphors do not reflect objectively given similarities, but can create similarities between unlike things: they can reflect, convey and reinforce different ways of seeing and experiencing different aspects of our lives. In the terms used in Conceptual Metaphor Theory (see Chapter 1), the choice of different source domains 'frames' the target domain in different ways, highlighting some aspects and backgrounding others (Lakoff and Johnson 1980; Ritchie 2013).

The 'framing' power of metaphor is particularly important when metaphors are used in relation to illness, and specifically physical illness, the topic of this chapter (see Chapter 25 for metaphor and mental health). Physical illness tends to be an unwelcome and unpleasant experience, during which we are vulnerable and in need of support. While metaphors may help us express ourselves and make sense of what is happening to us, they may also contribute to negative feelings, such as anxiety and shame. The extracts below, from an online forum for people with cancer (see Current Research section), involve contrasting metaphorical framings of the experience of the disease:

Example 1

'I have kind of prepared myself for a battle with cancer'

'we are on the Bowel cancer journey'

The use of 'battle' places the illness in the role of an opponent that the patient has to beat individually. The use of 'journey', in contrast, potentially constructs cancer as a path that can be travelled along collectively. These different framings have potential consequences for how the patient might perceive and make sense of their own experience and also for how the illness and the patient may be approached by others, including family, friends and healthcare professionals. For example, the Journey[1] metaphor might more easily lead to eventual acceptance, while the Battle metaphor, like violence-related metaphors more generally, invites an attitude of resistance and a seeking out of further invasive treatments, and may suggest that not recovering is a personal defeat. It is for these reasons that War metaphors for cancer have been widely criticised (e.g. Sontag 1979/1991; Miller 2010; Granger 2014).

In the next section, we discuss the main trends in previous research on metaphor and physical illness, with a particular focus on practical applications in healthcare. We then present some of the debates and controversies in this area, followed by a current research project on metaphors for cancer, and a planned practical application of the project's findings. In the final section we provide some reflections on practical implications and future research and applications.

Overview of research on metaphor and illness, and its practical applications

Discussions of metaphor and the experience of illness often begin with references to Susan Sontag's classic treatises on the metaphors for cancer and tuberculosis (Sontag 1979/1991) and AIDS (Sontag 1989/1991). To Sontag, metaphors obscure the experience of illnesses and create mythologies that perpetuate fear and shame. More specifically, Sontag (1979/1991) argued that Military metaphors around cancer (e.g. 'invasive', 'aggressive', 'colonisation') encourage a punitive view of the illness, constructing the patient as a victim and the disease as the culprit. At the same time, the patient may also become culpable if they are 'beaten' by the disease and 'fail' to get better. According to Sontag (1989/1991), Military metaphors around AIDS have a similar effect, but tend to focus on infectious agents 'invading' from the outside, which 'immobilise' certain 'defences', thereby allowing other opportunistic diseases to 'attack' (Sontag 1989/1991). Sontag's proposed solution to the shortcomings of these metaphors is the elimination of metaphors from communication around health and illness altogether, in favour of literal language only.

Sontag's work raises at least three main issues which have been extensively dealt with in subsequent work and which will also be central to this chapter: (a) the nature of dominant metaphors for different illnesses in different contexts; (b) the implications of dominant metaphors for public perceptions and for the experience of patients in particular; and (c) how the problems associated with dominant metaphors should be addressed.

There is now a large and varied scholarly literature on metaphor use in relation to physical illness (cf. Gibbs and Franks 2002). Broadly speaking, research on metaphor in physical health(care) contexts falls into four main types:

- metaphor and public communication about illness, as in news reports (e.g. Koteyko et al. 2008) and pharmaceutical advertising (e.g. Reisfield and Wilson 2004);
- metaphor and the 'lived experience' of illness and health(care), focusing on:
    - different illnesses, such as cancer (e.g. Gibbs and Franks 2002) and motor-neuron disease (e.g. Locock et al. 2012);

- o   different aspects of the experience of illness, including physical symptoms such as pain (e.g. Loftus 2011), other experiences such as emotions (e.g. Locock et al. 2012) and the patients' views of themselves and their lives (e.g. Appleton and Flynn 2014);
- metaphors used by different stakeholder groups, such as patients and General Practitioners (e.g. Skelton et al. 2002), or patients, family carers and healthcare professionals (e.g. Demmen et al. 2015);
- metaphor as a practical tool in communication about health and illness, for example, in order to improve general well-being (e.g. Taylor and McLaughlin 2011) or to increase understanding of the illness itself and of management regimes (e.g. Aanand et al. 2011).

Different studies focus on different types of data, including doctor–patient interactions (e.g. Skelton et al. 2011), interviews (e.g. Gibbs and Franks 2002), focus groups (e.g. Appleton and Flynn 2014) and online writing (e.g. Semino et al. 2015). Depending on the choice of data and research questions, some studies take a qualitative approach (e.g. Appleton and Flynn 2014), while others involve quantitative analyses, including the computer-aided methods of Corpus Linguistics (e.g. Crawford et al. 2008; Demmen et al. 2015). While most studies focus on English-language data, some involve other languages, such as Stibbe's (1996) study of metaphors for illness in Chinese, Lascaratou's (2007) work on metaphors and metonymies for pain in Greek, and Schwabe et al.'s (2008) study of patient descriptions of seizures in German.

In the rest of this section, we introduce some representative studies from each of the main research directions mentioned above.

Metaphor and illness in public communication

A number of studies have considered the metaphors used in the media for different kinds of illnesses, and their potential implications for the public's views and behaviour. Studies of metaphors in the press coverage of infectious diseases such as methicillin-resistant Staphylococcus Aureus (MRSA) (e.g. Crawford et al. 2008) or avian flu (e.g. Koteyko et al. 2008) often revolve around the explanatory function of metaphors[2] and connections between metaphor and 'framing'. Framing in this sense is 'to select some aspects of a perceived reality and make them more salient in a communicating text, in such a way as to promote a particular problem definition, causal interpretation, moral evaluation, and/or treatment recommendation for the item described' (Entman 1993: 52).

Crawford et al. (2008) and Nerlich and Koteyko (2009) traced how metaphor scenarios in the press coverage of MRSA changed over time, from when the disease was relatively unknown and a remote threat, to when it became a political issue because of a dramatic increase in the number of infections. Initially, the risk of MRSA was communicated through the personification of bacteria and the attribution of evil intent to them. However, as the number of cases increased, the responsibility was shifted from the personified bacteria to doctors and hospitals, who became guilty through what Nerlich and Koteyko called a 'crime of omission', for example by not paying enough attention to hand-washing in hospitals (2009: 156). These different framings facilitated different courses of action: while action initially focused on a battle between doctors and the bacteria, the second framing led to a focus on cleanliness, with consequences for policy decisions. Koteyko et al. (2008) make a similar point after examining the use of 'journey', 'war' and 'house' metaphors in the UK press coverage of avian influenza (H5N1) between 2005 and 2006.

Expanding the range of illnesses, Hanne and Hawken (2007) compared the metaphors used in the *New York Times* over a nine-month period for five different diseases: avian flu, cancer, diabetes, heart disease, and HIV/AIDS. They reported some overall quantitative differences, with diabetes and avian flu attracting the highest frequencies of metaphor use, and heart disease the lowest. They also noted differences in the frequencies of particular metaphors for different diseases: war-related metaphors for the effects of disease were highest for avian flu, for example, and lowest for heart disease, while mechanistic metaphors to do with plumbing (e.g. 'flow deficit' and 'blockages') were most frequent for heart disease. The authors noted that the war-related metaphors used in reporting on cancer and HIV/AIDS appeared to be less emotive than observed by Sontag a few decades earlier; in contrast, the mechanical 'plumbing' metaphors that are prevalent in reporting on heart disease may downplay the seriousness of the disease itself. Overall, the authors emphasise the consequences of different metaphors for both individual behaviour and public policy, and suggest that greater awareness of these consequences is needed on the part of medical professionals, educators and journalists. They also propose a new 'car driving' metaphor to explain to the general public the interaction of lifestyle choices and other factors (e.g. genetic inheritance, chance infections) in health and longevity. Most people are familiar with how our safety when driving a car depends on a combination of factors under our own control (e.g. not speeding) and factors outside our control (e.g. other motorists). A metaphor exploiting this type of knowledge, Hanne and Hawken suggest, could be more effective in encouraging healthy behaviours than existing conventional metaphors for major conditions such as diabetes and heart disease.

Several recent studies document the persistent widespread use of war-related metaphors for cancer in the media. Camus (2009) reports that CANCER IS WAR is the most frequently used metaphor in a corpus of articles about cancer from the UK *Guardian* newspaper. Reisfield and Wilson (2004) note how what they call the 'martial metaphor' for cancer is not just generally dominant, but is also exploited by pharmaceutical companies to promote chemotherapy drugs. On a patient information site for a particular type of medication, for example, women are encouraged to 'FIGHT HARD and FIGHT BACK in your battle against advanced breast cancer' (Reisfield and Wilson 2004: 4025). While recognising the potential negative consequences of these metaphors, Reisfield and Wilson also point out that they may have positive effects for some patients. We will return to this point in relation to these and other metaphors in the course of the chapter.

Metaphor and patients' 'lived experience' of illness

A number of studies have investigated the use of metaphor on the part of patients, and particularly people who have been treated for cancer. Gibbs and Franks (2002) and Appleton and Flynn (2014) take different approaches to metaphors in patients' lives after cancer treatment. Gibbs and Frank studied the metaphors used in interviews with six women who had survived cancer, while Appleton and Flynn analysed focus group discussions with 18 people who had recently been treated for cancer. Both studies emphasise the multiple functions that metaphors can have in the experience of illness, including: expressing emotions, making sense of the illness as part of one's life, managing a new sense of self, and planning for the future. Gibbs and Franks (2002) note how all interviewees use highly conventional metaphors that are based in ordinary embodied experiences. These include, for example, CANCER IS AN OBSTACLE ON LIFE'S JOURNEY ('it brought me to the kind of... the edge of the abyss'), CANCER IS A FLUID WITHIN THE SELF CONTAINER ('it was like the plug had just been pulled in me and I was empty'), CANCER AND ITS TREATMENT IS A GAME ('One option was to do nothing and just live with the odds') and CANCER CLEARS VISION AND ALLOWS FOR NEW UNDERSTANDING ('It allowed me to see life in a different way'). These metaphors allow the cancer experience to be integrated into people's lives, giving it meaning and highlighting the experience's potential to stimulate intellectual and emotional growth. Appleton and Flynn point out how participants had different responses to common metaphorical expressions such as cancer 'journey' or cancer 'survivor', but also emphasise that metaphors appeared to be consistently central to how participants managed their emotions and identities during and after cancer treatment. They conclude that careful attention to patients' metaphor use 'may assist nurses and other health professionals to achieve clearer and more meaningful exchanges when planning care interventions' (Appleton and Flynn 2014: 381).

Metaphor has also been shown to play an important role in conveying the experience of physical symptoms, and particularly pain, for patients. More specifically, pain sensations are often expressed in terms of references to causes of damage to the body, as in 'a stabbing pain' and 'a splitting headache' (e.g. Schott 2004). This results in metonymy when the pain is in fact caused by that particular type of damage to the body (e.g. a 'burning pain' caused by contact with a flame), or in metaphor when that particular cause of physical damage does not apply (e.g. a 'burning pain' felt in the stomach without contact with any flames) (Lascaratou 2007; Kövecses 2008; Semino 2010). Loftus (2011) discusses metaphors not simply as a way of expressing what one's pain feels like, but also as a way of understanding one's pain and dealing with it. He discusses particularly the metaphor THE BODY IS A MACHINE, which, he argues, is central in Western healthcare. When applied to acute pain, Loftus argues, this metaphor could be seen as adequate: a toothache involves a 'fault' that can be 'fixed' by a dentist, resulting in the disappearance of the pain. However, this metaphor does not account adequately for chronic pain, where nothing can realistically be described as 'broken' and so cannot be 'fixed'. By framing their experience in this way, however, chronic pain patients may 'be easily drawn into the downward spiral of searching for a technical fix that they believe must exist and that they must have' (Loftus 2011: 220), resulting in frustration and disappointment. In such cases, Loftus argues, there is evidence that patients benefit from being encouraged to see their pain in terms of different metaphors, such as LIFE IS A JOURNEY or PAIN IS A NUISANCE, which make it easier to accept the pain as part of one's life and to find ways of living with it (see also Gallagher et al. 2013).

Metaphor and different stakeholder groups in healthcare

Several studies have investigated differences in the use of metaphor by members of different stakeholder groups in healthcare. Skelton et al. (2002) constructed a corpus of 373 UK general practice consultations and identified instances of metaphor use by searching for a variety of what Goatly (1997) calls 'signalling expressions', including comparators (e.g. 'like', 'as if') and selected verbs (e.g. 'feel', 'look', 'resemble'). Both doctors and patients were found to speak about illnesses using war-related metaphors (e.g. 'battle' and 'attack'). However, doctors tended to use more machinery-related metaphors as explanatory tools, and spoke of themselves as 'problem-solvers' and 'controllers of disease'. In contrast, patients primarily used metaphors to describe their symptoms and emotional/psychological states. The authors suggest that this difference may not be a bad thing, as it reflects how doctors reinterpret the patients' individual descriptions as accounts of something familiar and comprehensible. This allows doctors to present themselves as authoritative, which patients might find reassuring.

Demmen et al. (2015) made use of the semantic annotation tool in the software Wmatrix (Rayson 2008) to study the use of violence-related metaphors in a 1.5-million-word corpus consisting of interviews with and online forum posts by members of three stakeholder groups in cancer care and end-of-life care: people with advanced cancer, family carers looking after a loved one with cancer, and healthcare professionals (see ucrel.lancs.ac.uk/melc/). Metaphor use among the three groups was found to vary both in terms of the selection and function of Violence metaphors and in frequency of use. Healthcare professionals use Violence metaphors less frequently than the other two groups, possibly reflecting an awareness of the shortcomings of these metaphors. In addition, the members of each group use these metaphors to express their different perspectives in the experience of cancer and end of life. For example, patients use the verb 'hit' metaphorically to describe the effects of cancer treatment (e.g. 'They hit me with radiation for 10 days'), while carers use it to describe their experience of grieving after their loved one has died ('Now grief is hitting me every day'). These findings suggest differences in views, challenges and needs, which need to be taken into account in the context of healthcare.

Metaphor-based interventions in healthcare

Most studies of metaphor in the context of physical illness reflect on the implications of their findings for the experience of patients, and for training and practice in healthcare communication. In particular, healthcare professionals emphasise the need for doctors and nurses to be sensitive to their own and their patients' uses of metaphor, in order to avoid potentially harmful metaphors and, more positively, to use metaphors as tools to contribute to well-being and mutual understanding (e.g. Czechmeister 1994; Skott 2002; Reisfield and Wilson 2004; Appleton and Flynn 2014). Some of the studies we have discussed above also make specific suggestions for changes in metaphor use that would benefit patients, as in the case of Hanne and Hawken's (2007) 'car-driving' metaphor and Loftus's (2011) discussion of experiments involving the introduction of new metaphors for chronic pain for the benefit of sufferers.

A study by Hauser and Schwartz (2015) has confirmed more specifically how metaphors may affect people's behaviour in relation to health and illness. In a series of experiments, the metaphorical framing of cancer as an enemy was shown to reduce people's intention to engage in self-limiting prevention behaviours (e.g. not smoking) while not increasing the intention to engage in self-bolstering prevention behaviours (e.g. taking regular exercise). This confirms that metaphors can potentially be used to explain and encourage behaviours that may have positive effects on people's health and life expectancy. The studies we discuss in the rest of this section provide further concrete examples of how metaphors can be or have been used in healthcare settings for a variety of different purposes.

Krieger et al. (2010) explored how the metaphors physicians use to explain the idea of randomisation in clinical trials might influence patients' decisions to participate in such trials. They considered two metaphors for explaining the role of chance in clinical trials: the standard metaphor that compares the person's chances of being allocated to the clinical or control group to the flipping of a coin, and a 'culturally derived' metaphor that compares the role of chance in trials to having a boy or a girl when pregnant. They found that when randomisation was explained using the 'the sex of the baby' metaphor in conditions of low attention, more people were willing to sign up for clinical trials than if randomisation was simply defined or explained using standard metaphors for chance, such as the 'flip of a coin' metaphor. For older women with a cultural background of strong family values (the target group), the 'sex of the baby' metaphor was more effective because both outcomes are perceived to be not just equally likely, but also equally welcome, in the communities that participants belonged to. However, the standard 'flip of a coin' metaphor might suggest there is an equal chance that the treatment itself will be un/helpful. Aanand et al. (2011) similarly compared two educational interventions aimed at explaining to diabetes patients the importance of three metabolic markers: sugar level, blood pressure and cholesterol. An intervention that included the use of a 'weather forecast' metaphor was found to substantially increase understanding and later recall of information about the three markers and their significance.

The potential relevance of patients' metaphor use in diagnostics is shown by Schwabe et al.'s (2008) discussion of a series of interdisciplinary studies of doctor–patient consultations involving seizures, conducted in Germany. The distinction between seizures that are epileptic in origin and ones that are not is crucial, as it has implications for treatment: epileptic seizures are treated with drugs, while non-epileptic seizures often respond to psychotherapeutic interventions. However, the two conditions tend to have similar physical manifestations and can only be distinguished from patients' own descriptions of their history and experience. Schwabe et al. found that, among other things, patients with epileptic seizures tended to use consistent metaphoric descriptions of their experiences, 'following a single metaphoric concept throughout the whole consultation' (Schwabe et al. 2008: 65), such as 'seizure as an aggressive entity with its own volition'. In contrast, patients with non-epileptic seizures were less consistent in their metaphor use.

A final promising kind of metaphor-based intervention in physical healthcare aims to foster well-being in patients and their families, and to facilitate communication with healthcare professionals. Gallagher et al. (2013), for example, found that the provision of educational materials based on metaphor helped people with chronic pain reconceptualise their pain in ways that reduced 'catastrophic thought processes', which are linked with increases in pain experience, preoccupation with symptoms, use of analgesics and so on (see also Stewart 2015). In the context of end-of-life care, Taylor and McLaughlin (2011) discuss the use of metaphors as one of a set of 'tools of engagement' in establishing what the most important concerns of patients and families are, which is particularly important where time is short. In their discussions of serious illness, death and end-of-life care with patients and their relatives, Taylor and McLaughlin use a 'river of life with waterfall' metaphor. This scenario to some extent relies on the conventional LIFE IS A JOURNEY metaphor, but is somewhat more specific to account for what happens when someone receives a terminal diagnosis:

> A serious diagnosis or recurrence tips you over the edge of a waterfall into a whirlpool. You fall out of the boat and lose your oars and nearly drown. However you do get back into your boat and you find your oars and perhaps different people are now in your boat with you. Others are watching with interest on the towpath. Inevitably another crisis will happen and the boat will go over another waterfall and the cycle is repeated.
> *Taylor and McLaughlin 2011: 14*

Taylor and McLaughlin point out that the scenario has a number of positive potential entailments (e.g. the scenery in the new stretch of river may be different, but just as beautiful as before), which can help people come to terms with serious illness and their own mortality.

Critical issues, debates and controversies

The main areas of controversy in relation to metaphor and physical illness are: (i) a mostly historical debate as to whether metaphors for illness should be used at all and (ii) a very current debate over whether some metaphors should be eliminated and others promoted.

In her 1979 essay, Sontag famously advocated and hoped for a future in which communication around illness could be entirely non-metaphorical. She saw metaphor as a means for obfuscation and vagueness in cases where the medical profession was still unclear about a particular illness, and emphasised the negative consequences of dominant metaphors for patients in particular. This position has now come to be seen as both unrealistic and unnecessarily negative. First, it is now widely accepted, including among medical and healthcare researchers and practitioners, that metaphor is a ubiquitous and important aspect of language and thought, which cannot be eradicated. Second, Sontag focuses on the potential for metaphors to have negative consequences, but ignores the multiple ways in which metaphors can have positive functions and effects in health communication, as demonstrated in the course of this chapter (e.g. Czechmeister 1994; Reisfield and Wilson 2004; Hanne and Hawken 2007; Loftus 2011). Czechmeister (1994), in particular, describes metaphor as a 'two-edged sword', which can be a 'rich resource' or a 'potential burden', depending on how it is used (1231). This shifts attention to how to ensure that metaphors do indeed constitute a 'rich resource' for all involved in healthcare.

Indeed, when Sontag revisited her original argument, she acknowledged that metaphor cannot be completely avoided, but added: 'that does not mean there aren't some metaphors we might well abstain from or try to retire' (1989/1991: 93). She also reiterates her thesis that 'Military metaphors contribute to the stigmatizing of certain illnesses and, by extension, of those who are ill' (99). This observation relates to the second area of debate: whether some metaphors, such as Military metaphors, have overwhelmingly negative consequences, especially for patients, and should therefore be avoided.

Violence-related metaphors for illness have been regularly and systematically criticised in the decades since the publication of Sontag's essays. After disagreeing with Sontag's overall approach to metaphor, Gwyn (1999), for example, concurs with the indictment of the Military metaphor:

> In its wrongful overstatement, the military metaphor provides us all (and the mass media in particular thrive on this) with an identifiable evil that is all too easily transferred onto the persons who are subject to the illnesses themselves.
>
> *Gwyn 1999: 207*

Miller (2010) criticises the word 'aggressive' as a term used in oncology, suggesting that, although it is a technical term for healthcare professionals, it can be unnecessarily frightening for patients. He similarly suggests that Military metaphors more broadly are an aspect of cancer-related language that some patients dislike. Kate Granger, a UK medical consultant who died of cancer in 2016, repeatedly wrote in the media against the use of metaphors such as 'fight' and 'battle' for the experience of people in her position:

> "She lost her brave fight." If anyone mutters those words after my death, wherever I am, I will curse them. I would like to be remembered for the positive impact I have made on the world, for fun times and for my relationships with others, not as a loser. When I do die, I will have defied the prognosis for my type of cancer and achieved a great deal

with my life. I do not want to feel a failure about something beyond my control. I refuse to believe my death will be because I didn't battle hard enough.

*http://www.theguardian.com/society/2014/apr/25/
having-cancer-not-fight-or-battle*

Semino et al. (2014) found that UK hospice managers use 'fight' and 'battle' metaphorically to describe a way of approaching the terminal phase of illness that leads to a 'bad' death. Lisa Bonchek-Adams, who regularly wrote online about her experience of progressive breast cancer, was similarly criticised in the UK *Guardian* newspaper and the *New York Times* for an approach to her illness that was described as excessively and inappropriately war-like (https://www.theguardian.com/commentisfree/2014/jan/08/lisa-adams-tweeting-cancer-ethics [page subsequently removed]; http://www.nytimes.com/2014/01/13/opinion/keller-heroic-measures.html?_r=0). While war-related metaphors for cancer in particular appear to still be commonly used in the UK media and charity campaigns, an awareness of the shortcomings of these metaphors has influenced the drafting of recent policy documents in the UK's National Health System. The *NHS Cancer Reform Strategy* (2007), for example, does not contain any instances of the expressions 'battle' and 'war', and talks instead of a metaphorical cancer 'journey', with clinical 'pathways' of care (see also Reisfield and Wilson 2004).

The main danger of these critical voices, however, is that they can marginalise and potentially silence those who find war-related metaphors motivating or helpful. Reisfield and Wilson (2004: 4025) discuss the case of a World War II historian for whom it was 'enabling' to approach the experience of metastatic prostate cancer as a personal war. Similarly, in a 2013 TED talk entitled 'We need a heroic narrative for death', US journalist Amanda Bennett proudly claims the right to have interpreted her husband's cancer as a joint and exhilarating fight, right up to his eventual death (https://www.ted.com/talks/amanda_bennett_a_heroic_narrative_for_letting_go). Indeed, there is an emerging consensus in the literature on metaphor and illness that individual variation needs to be recognised in responding to and introducing metaphors when interacting with patients (e.g. Czechmeister 1994; Reisfield and Wilson 2004; Loftus 2011; Appleton and Flynn 2014). Gwyn (1999) more specifically emphasises the need to give patients with chronic illnesses the opportunity to use metaphors that draw from areas of life that are meaningful to them. Writing in the *Times* in 2014, journalist Melanie Reid makes this point particularly strongly while discussing her experience as a tetraplegic: 'We must be allowed to regard our affliction any damn way we want: to control it with our own words. It is, after all, uniquely ours' (http://www.thetimes.co.uk/tto/magazine/article4264246.ece).

In the next section we introduce a project that addresses some of these complex issues, and a practical application of the project's findings.

An example of current research: violence and journey metaphors for cancer

The academic and media controversies around Military/War/Violence metaphors as described above were part of the context for the ESRC-funded Metaphor in End-of-Life Care (MELC) project at Lancaster University[3] (see also Demmen et al. 2015). The MELC project broadly investigated how health professionals, cancer patients and unpaid family carers used metaphor to talk about their experiences, attitudes and expectations of end-of-life care (e.g. terminal illness, palliative treatment, preparations for dying) (see http://ucrel.lancs.ac.uk/melc/). The research team collected a corpus of 1.5 million words comprised of semi-structured interviews and online forum contribution by members of all three groups mentioned above, as shown in Table 26.1.

Table 26.1 MELC corpus composition

Number of words	Patients	Carers	Healthcare professionals	Total
Semi-structured interviews	100,859	81,564	89,943	272,366
Online forum posts	500,134	500,256	253,168	1,253,558
Total	600,993	581,820	343,111	**1,525,924**

The overall methodology combined a manual intensive analysis of a 90,000-word data sample, with a systematic computer-aided exploration of particular semantic fields in the whole corpus by means of the USAS semantic annotation tool included within the online software Wmatrix (Rayson 2008). These semantic fields were identified as potentially containing relevant metaphorical expressions during the manual analysis of the sample data, which was based on the Metaphor Identification Procedure proposed in Pragglejaz Group (2007). For example, 'veteran' in 'a chemo veteran' was identified as a metaphorical expression in the sample analysis and was then allocated to the semantic field of 'War'. The USAS semantic field 'G3: Warfare' was then explored in the entire corpus to identify further metaphorical expressions of the same kind (cf. Koller et al. 2008).

Among the semantic fields explored as part of the project were those related to Journeys (including a variety of movement-related metaphors) and Violence (including a range of metaphors to do with Physical Aggression as well as War/Battle metaphors). In particular, the research team investigated the use of these metaphors by cancer patients in the corpus, in order to determine whether some metaphors (in this case, Journey metaphors) were really 'better' than others (in this case, Violence metaphors) and if so, what 'better' meant, at least from the patient's perspective (cf. Semino et al. 2015).

The following examples were typical of the ways in which patients used Journey and Violence metaphors (in the examples below, we underline the most relevant metaphorical expressions; original spellings from online forum posts have been retained):

Example 2: Patients' Journey metaphors

'you are not alone, I have walked the same pathway as you for the last three years'

'the best people to help you are the ones who've been there before or are heading there with you'

'My journey may not be smooth but it certainly makes me look up and take notice of the scenery!'

Example 3: Patients' Violence metaphors

'I feel such a failure that I am not winning this battle.'

'I am a walking time bomb.'

'what did i think all my normal little cells were doing after being hit by a sledgehammer of both toxic chemicals and radiation'

These metaphors seemed to support the notion that cancer patients' Journey metaphors express and reinforce more positive attitudes and emotions than Violence metaphors. However, the following examples were also typical of patients' metaphor use:

Example 4: Patients' Journey metaphors

'Well, I have not done so well with my own "cancer journey" through the wilderness of my own local hospitals.'

'How the hell am I supposed to know how to navigate this road I do not even want to be on'

Example 5: Patients' Violence metaphors

'my consultants recognised that I was a born fighter'

'I don't intend to give up; I don't intend to give in. No I want to fight it. I don't want it to beat me, I want to beat it.'

'Your words though have given me a bit more of my fighting spirit back. I am ready to kick some cancer butt!'

'you are such a fighter'

Here the pattern seemed to be reversed: the Violence metaphors are used in a much more positive way than the Journey metaphors. In order to make sense of this, the team investigated the framings provided by different uses of these metaphors, specifically in terms of the patient's empowerment and disempowerment in the context of the illness. Empowerment and disempowerment, were defined as an increase or decrease in the degree of agency that the patient has, or perceives him/herself to have, as manifest in the metaphors and their co-text. This involves the (perceived) ability to control or react to events for one's own benefit, where this ability is desired by the patient and not externally imposed.

The team found that patients can and do use Violence metaphors in disempowering ways, as shown in Example 3. In such extracts, the patient is often unsuccessfully fighting the disease or the disease is presented as an aggressive opponent, while the patient is in a vulnerable passive position, unable to predict or control the situation. As expected, patients also can and do use Journey metaphors in ways that are empowering, as in Example 2. These metaphors convey a sense of purpose, control and companionship and point out some positive aspects of being ill.

However, Violence metaphors can also have positive and empowering functions, as in Example 5, and Journey metaphors can also be used in disempowering ways (Example 4). Some patients use Violence metaphors when they are successfully and proudly trying to recover from the disease, or when they want to motivate themselves or each other. Equally, Journey metaphors can also disempower patients, when they express a lack of acceptance of or control over their situation, emphasising the overwhelming difficulties these people face as cancer sufferers.

Overall then, the difference between helpful (or 'better') and unhelpful metaphors is not in the Violence vs. Journey contrast. The key distinction is between metaphors that empower and those that disempower the patient (cf. Appleton and Flynn 2014, and Reisfield and Wilson's 2004 'enabling' function of metaphor). This is a more nuanced view of the contrasts between different metaphors for cancer. Violence and Journey metaphors may indeed facilitate different ways of framing the patient's experience, but their precise functions vary depending on who uses them and how. Violence metaphors are not always negative, while Journey metaphors are not always a better alternative, at least when it comes to patient empowerment. Different metaphors work differently for different people at different times in different contexts.

A 'Metaphor Menu' for cancer patients

The MELC project clearly shows that no particular metaphor should be either censored or imposed on anyone. Rather, patients should ideally be encouraged and enabled to use the metaphors that work best for them. To help achieve this, the project team have created a 'Metaphor Menu' for cancer patients – a collection of quotes from patients in the project data and other sources, accompanied by images, that might be helpful as a resource for people with new diagnoses.

The Menu includes not just various examples of Violence and Journey metaphors, but also metaphors drawing from music, nature, games, fairground rides and the experience of dealing with unwanted guests, such as the following:

> Cancer is part of me, the cure for cancer is the acceptance of it, to heal is to meet the rogue cells within and convince them to sing in tune with the rest of the body.
> *http://www.theguardian.com/society/2014/apr/25/having-cancer-not-fight-or-battle*
>
> For me, cancer arrived as an unwelcome lodger, parking itself in the back room and demanding attention. For three years I tried to be a courteous if unwilling host. Eventually the time came to invite my cancer to leave. She has left the place in a bit of a mess, and I'm conscious that she has kept the key. Still I'm hopeful that in due course all I will be left with is the rich memory of time spent with a stranger I never expected to meet.
> *Andrew Graystone: http://www.bbc.co.uk/news/magazine-24985184*

The intention is that, as in a restaurant, the Menu provides a variety of options: different people will find different metaphors more or less appealing, but there is no judgement involved in preferring one option over another. Ideally, each person will find something that may validate a feeling or view they already have, articulate something they have not been able to express before, or provide a new and helpful perspective.

Recommendations for practice and future directions

The literature we have reviewed and the specific research we have reported suggest that metaphors can do both harm and good in communication around physical illness. Therefore, members of all stakeholder groups in healthcare should focus on how to harness metaphor as a useful resource, rather than striving for its eradication or attempting to censor some metaphors and impose others. Achieving this goal involves a keen awareness of metaphorical language and thinking, especially on the part of healthcare professionals, and attention to the implications of different metaphors, both for the general public and for individual patients. As individuals may relate and react to metaphors differently, a variety of strategies may be needed depending on the context of communication. For example, the decision to avoid war-related metaphors in policy documents is clearly justified, and healthcare professionals would be ill-advised to introduce these metaphors in interactions with patients. On the other hand, where such metaphors are used positively by patients, they should be accepted as one of the many ways in which individuals may decide to approach their illness. Overall, what is required is: attention to one's own and others' language use; responsiveness to the feelings and views expressed by different linguistic choices; acceptance and tolerance of individual variation; and creativity in devising ways of harnessing the potential of metaphor as a resource for individual expression, explanation, sense-making and so on.

Future studies and applications could usefully include:

- further systematic research on metaphors used for different kinds of illnesses, in different countries and languages, by different stakeholder groups, and in different types of communication, such as: studies of metaphors in policy documents and charity campaigns, and comparative studies of metaphors used by patients who have the same illness but differ in age, gender and stage of disease;
- greater use of research findings and authentic examples in the training of healthcare professionals;
- creation of resources that make a range of different metaphors available for patients and members of different stakeholder groups, such as the Metaphor Menu described above.

The research and applications we have discussed in this chapter have provided the foundations for these and other positive developments in the study and exploitation of metaphor in physical healthcare.

Notes

1 We use initial capitals to describe a group of metaphors consisting of various linguistic expressions drawing from the same a semantic field. We do not wish to call these conceptual or systematic metaphors so use a non-theory-specific notation.
2 For additional examples on the educational and explanatory power of metaphor (also applicable to healthcare contexts), see Chapters 20 and 26, respectively, on education and science.
3 The project, which ran from 2012 to 2014, was conducted by an interdisciplinary team of linguists, computer scientists and healthcare professionals at Lancaster University and the Open University in the UK. It was funded by the Economic and Social Research Council (ES/J007927/1). See: http://ucrel.lancs.ac.uk/melc/index.php.

Further reading

Gibbs, R.W., Jr. and Franks, H. (2002) 'Embodied metaphor in women's narratives about their experiences with cancer', *Health Communication*, 14(2): 139–165.
Harvey, K. and Koteyko, N. (2013) *Exploring Health Communication: Language in Action*, London: Routledge.
Reisfield, G.M. and Wilson, G.R. (2004) 'Use of metaphor in the discourse on cancer', *Journal of Clinical Oncology*, 22(19): 4024–4027.
Semino, E. (2008) *Metaphor in Discourse*, Cambridge, UK: Cambridge University Press (pp. 175–190).

References

Aanand, D.N., Teal, C.R., Rodriguez, E. and Haidet, P. (2011) 'Knowing the ABCs: A comparative effectiveness study of two methods of diabetes education', *Patient Education and Counseling*, 85: 383–389.
Appleton, L. and Flynn, M. (2014) 'Searching for the new normal: Exploring the role of language and metaphors in becoming a cancer survivor', *European Journal of Oncology Nursing*, 18: 378–384.
Camus, J.T.W. (2009) 'Metaphors of cancer in scientific popularization articles in the British press', *Discourse Studies*, 11: 465–495.
Crawford, P., Brown, B., Nerlich, B. and Koteyko, N. (2008) 'The "moral careers" of microbes and the rise of the matrons: An analysis of UK national press coverage of methicillin-resistant Staphylococcus aureus (MRSA)', *Health, Risk and Society*, 17: 331–347.

Czechmeister, C.A. (1994) 'Metaphor in illness and nursing: A two-edged sword. A discussion of the social use of metaphor in everyday language, and implications of nursing and nursing education', *Journal of Advanced Nursing*, 19: 1226–1233.

Demmen, J., Semino, E., Demjén, Z., Koller, V., Payne, S., Hardie, H. and Rayson, P. (2015) 'A computer-assisted study of the use of Violence metaphors for cancer and end of life by patients, family carers and health professionals', *International Journal of Corpus Linguistics*, 22: 205–231.

Entman, R.M. (1993) 'Framing: Towards clarification of a fractured paradigm', *Journal of Communication*, 43: 51–58.

Gallagher, L., McAuley, J. and Moseley, G.L. (2013) 'A randomized-controlled trial of using a Book of Metaphors to reconceptualize pain and decrease catastrophizing in people with chronic pain', *Clinical Journal of Pain*, 29(1): 20–25.

Gibbs, R.W., Jr. and Franks, H. (2002) 'Embodied metaphor in women's narratives about their experiences with cancer', *Health Communication*, 14(2): 139–165.

Goatly, A. (1997) *The Language of Metaphors*, London: Routledge.

Granger, K. (2014) 'Having cancer is not a fight or a battle', *The Guardian* (http://www.theguardian.com/society/2014/apr/25/having-cancer-not-fight-or-battle, accessed June 2015).

Gwyn R. (1999) '"Captain of my own ship": Metaphor and the discourse of chronic illness', in L. Cameron and G. Low (eds) *Researching and Applying Metaphor*, Cambridge, UK: Cambridge University Press.

Hanne, M. and Hawken, S.J. (2007) 'Metaphors for illness in contemporary media', *Medical Humanities*, 33: 93–99.

Hauser, D.J. and Schwartz, N. (2015) 'The war on prevention: Bellicose cancer metaphors hurt (some) prevention intentions', *Personality and Social Psychology Bulletin*, 41: 66–77.

Koller, V., Hardie, A., Rayson, P. and Semino, E. (2008) 'Using a semantic annotation tool for the analysis of metaphor in discourse', *Metaphorik.de*, 15: 1241–1260.

Koteyko, N., Brown, B. and Crawford, P. (2008) 'The dead parrot and the dying swan: The role of metaphor scenarios in UK press coverage of avian flu in the UK in 2005–2006', *Metaphor and Symbol*, 23: 242–261.

Kövecses, Z. (2008) 'The conceptual structure of happiness and pain', in C. Lascaratou, A. Despotopoulou and E. Ifantidou (eds) *Reconstructing Pain and Joy: Linguistic, Literary and Cultural Perspectives*, Cambridge, UK: Cambridge Scholars Publishing.

Krieger, J.L., Parrott, R.L. and Nussbaum, J.F. (2010) 'Metaphor use and health literacy: A pilot study of strategies to explain randomization in cancer clinical trials', *Journal of Health Communication: International Perspectives*, 16: 3–16.

Lakoff, G. and Johnson, M. (1980) *Metaphors We Live By*, Chicago, IL: University of Chicago Press.

Lascaratou, C. (2007) *The Language of Pain: Expression or Description*, Amsterdam, The Netherlands: John Benjamins.

Locock, L., Mazanderani, F. and Powell, J. (2012) 'Metaphoric language and the articulation of emotions by people affected by motor neuron disease', *Chronic Illness*, 8: 201–215.

Loftus, S. (2011) 'Pain and its metaphors: A dialogical approach', *Journal of Medical Humanities*, 32: 213–230.

Miller, R.S. (2010) '8 words and phrases to ban in oncology!', *Oncology Times*, 32: 20.

Nerlich, B. and Koteyko, N. (2009) 'MRSA – portrait of a superbug: A media drama in three acts', in A. Musolff and J. Zinken (eds) *Metaphor and Discourse*, Basingstoke, UK: Palgrave Macmillan.

Pragglejaz Group. (2007). 'MIP: A method for identifying metaphorically used words in discourse', *Metaphor and Symbol*, 22(1), 1–39. doi:10.1207/s15327868ms2201_1.

Rayson, P. (2008). 'From key words to key semantic domains', *International Journal of Corpus Linguistics*, 13: 519–549.

Reisfield, G.M. and Wilson, G.R. (2004) 'Use of metaphor in the discourse on cancer', *Journal of Clinical Oncology*, 22: 4024–4027.

Ritchie, D. (2013) *Metaphor*, Cambridge, UK: Cambridge University Press.

Schott, G.D. (2004) 'Communicating the experience of pain: The role of analogy', *Pain*, 108: 209–212.

Schwabe, M., Reuber, M., Schöndienst, M. and Gülich, E. (2008) 'Listening to people with seizures: How can linguistic analysis help in the differential diagnosis of seizure disorders?', *Communication & Medicine*, 5: 59–72.

Semino, E. (2010) 'Descriptions of pain, metaphor and embodied simulation', *Metaphor and Symbol*, 25: 205–226.

Semino, E., Demjén, Z., Demmen, J., Koller, V., Payne, S., Hardie, H. and Rayson, P. (2015) 'The online use of "Violence" and "Journey" metaphors by cancer patients, as compared with health professionals: A mixed methods study', *BMJ Supportive and Palliative Care*, doi:10.1136/bmjspcare-2014-000785.

Semino, E., Demjén, Z. and Koller, V. (2014) '"Good" and "bad" deaths: Narratives and professional identities in interviews with hospice managers', *Discourse Studies*, 16: 667–685.

Skelton, J.R., Wearn, A.M. and Hobbs, F.D.R. (2002) 'A concordance-based study of metaphoric expressions used by general practitioners and patients in consultation', *British Journal of General Practice*, 52: 114–118.

Skott, C. (2002) 'Expressive metaphors in cancer narratives', *Cancer Nursing*, 25: 230–235.

Sontag, S. (1979/1991) 'Illness as metaphor', in *Illness as Metaphor and AIDS and Its Metaphors*, London, New York: Penguin Modern Classics.

—— (1989/1991) 'AIDS and its Metaphors', in *Illness as Metaphor and AIDS and Its Metaphors*, London, New York: Penguin Modern Classics.

Stibbe, A. (1996) 'The metaphorical construction of illness in Chinese culture', *Journal of Asian Pacific Communication*, 7: 177–188.

Stewart, M. (2015) 'The hidden influence of metaphor within rehabilitation', *In Touch*, 153: 8–13.

Taylor R. and McLaughlin, K. (2011) 'Terror and intimacy: Unlocking secrets at the end of life', *Journal of Holistic Healthcare*, 8: 12–17.

27
Using metaphor as a management tool

Linda Greve

Introduction

Gareth Morgan – who has made considerable contributions to understanding organisations and change through metaphor (e.g. Morgan 1988, 2006) – said in an interview in Copenhagen in 2009:

> It is a fundamental insight to all leaders that everything is "just" a metaphor, and that the metaphor is a way of shaping the world.
>
> *Greve and Hildebrandt 2011: 8*

As suggested by the title of this chapter, in a managerial context metaphor is itself often seen metaphorically as a tool. Tools are related to craftsmanship; they are useful but also detached from the user, and thus something one needs to learn to master. Viewing metaphor as a tool is the most common approach to the use of metaphor in management. Managers might use metaphors as part of a communication strategy or to better understand an organisation. In recent years the focus has shifted specifically towards metaphor as a meaning-making tool. Metaphors are increasingly being used as a means to better understand employees, and to establish a common understanding of a given situation or change in the organisation.

This chapter provides insights into how metaphor has been and could be used as a managerial tool. The chapter will begin with a historical overview of metaphors in managerial contexts from different perspectives, before moving on to critical issues and debates that add nuance to views of metaphor as a management tool. A section on current research then showcases the potential of metaphor as a creative meaning-making tool. This is followed by practical recommendations for managers wanting to make use of metaphors in their professional lives and by suggestions for further directions for research and practice. Thus, the aim of this chapter is to both provide insight into metaphor use in management and to showcase some very concrete ways in which it can be used, and without the need for detailed linguistic or cognitive scientific training.

Before going on to the historical overview, consider the following example of metaphor use in management:

A large Danish public institution is being re-organised. It is going from having regional offices and regional IT systems to being a large centralised organisation. The tasks are the same, but for reasons of efficiency and quality, a new IT system is being implemented. The employees are unhappy with the changes. Their everyday routine is being tampered with and all the well-established procedures and working practices will be changed due to the new IT system.

Management choose to respond to criticisms with the strategic use of a metaphor. The specific metaphor chosen is culturally founded in Danish society. It is: IT SYSTEMS ARE CLOTHES.

The old IT systems, the manager tells his employees, were the Confirmation clothes (almost all Danes are confirmed at the age of 14). Maybe the first grown-up and expensive outfit you had. It was tailored just for you. It made you feel good and grown up.

The new system, on the other hand, is off-the-peg. It comes in small, medium and large, and you know the feeling of being between sizes. Small is too small and medium is a little too big. But the quality is fine. And it saves you money and time. It is not the great, bespoke quality of the Confirmation clothes. But let's be honest – even that great outfit lost its shape and became unfashionable over time. The new style is more adaptable to fashion trends and developments.

This example is from my own work as a consultant. The metaphor helped the employees understand the necessity of the change and made reference to something which they have embodied experience of. It also allowed the employees to maintain continuity with the old system while embracing the new. These are all important aspects of using metaphor as a tool, as I will discuss later.

Overview of relevant research and applications

Although early studies by management scholars tended to present metaphors and other tropes as forms of linguistic adornment (e.g. Pinder and Bourgeois 1982), most recent studies of managerial metaphors acknowledge the fundamentally different understanding of metaphors put forward by Lakoff and Johnson in 1980 (see Chapter 1). Nevertheless, as outlined above, managerial research still tends to see metaphor as a tool – something you can learn to master, rather than primarily a characteristic of cognition (e.g. Abel and Sementelli 2005; Nonaka 1994; Vince and Broussine 1996). Thus, even though scholars emphasise that metaphors are more than just icing on the cake (Hogler et al. 2008), the analysis and presentation of metaphor is in many cases much more applied and intuitive than in empirical or theoretical linguistic research (as demonstrated throughout this volume).

Definitions of metaphor in this field are nonetheless inspired by Lakoff and Johnson's understanding that 'the essence of metaphor is understanding and experiencing one kind of thing in terms of another' (1980: 5). Morgan, as one of the founders of metaphor theory in management, defines metaphor as 'Constructive falsehood' (2006: 4). Nonaka describes the phenomenon as 'a creative, cognitive process which relates concepts that are far apart in an individual's memory' (Nonaka 1994: 21) and further:

> When two concepts are presented in a metaphor, it is possible not only to think of their similarity, but also to make comparisons that discern the degree of imbalance, contradiction or inconsistency involved in their association.
>
> *Nonaka 1994: 21*

These definitions thus share a focus on comparing unlike concepts, and adding to the understanding of one concept by the use of another. In more recent research, the definitions emphasise the creative potential of metaphor as in: '[Metaphor] is, rather, the generation and creation of new meaning beyond a previously existing similarity' (Cornelissen 2005: 751).

As already suggested, the managerial approach to metaphor is, however, different from the linguistic approaches represented in various chapters of this book. The definitions above, for example, make no distinction between the conceptual and linguistic dimensions of metaphor. In linguistics, some forms of metaphor use are seen as deliberate by some researchers – for example, metaphoric expressions in a meticulously planned speech (Steen 2008; Steen 2011) whereas other uses are seen as part of everyday talk, with speakers not necessarily aware of the metaphoric nature of their language use. In linguistic research these distinctions are much debated (e.g. Gibbs 2011), but these debates do not appear to have crossed over into the managerial approach to metaphor yet. The managerial literature is also very focused on verbal metaphors, and not on the use of metaphor in other modes such as gesture or images.

Metaphors and reasoning about organisations

As is well known, metaphor is frequently used as a vehicle for describing something abstract, subjective or sensitive. This holds for all sorts of different phenomena, but, in the following, I will discuss research on metaphors for *takeovers*, *organisations* and *knowledge* in managerial contexts in particular.

Using 'imagery' as a synonym for metaphor, Hirsch and Andrews (1983) describe how using different types of metaphors evokes different interpretations of and reactions to takeover processes. They investigated the language around company mergers and acquisitions and found a number of source domains indicating the level of hostility, or the nature of relations, between the involved parties. A takeover could be either a 'courtship' or a 'western' (as in the film genre), a 'game' or 'warfare'. They outlined four functions of imagery in takeovers. It can be:

1. a way of creating distance between the organisation and events by describing them as a fictional scenario;
2. a way to assign roles to the instigators of the takeover;
3. a way to evaluate what has taken place; or
4. a way of appealing to values that might be under pressure due to the change.

Hirsch and Andrews conclude that the use of language and imagery during takeovers reveals the attitudes that underlie participants' actions. The authors made no reference to the, at the time, new book by Lakoff and Johnson (1980), but their argument runs along similar lines, stating that language and what they call imagery is important in understanding business relations.

A few years later, in 1986, Gareth Morgan published an influential contribution to organisational theory: *Images of Organization* (the third edition appeared in 2006). Unlike Hirsch and Andrews, Morgan very clearly drew on Lakoff and Johnson (1980) and used the term 'metaphor'. He described eight main metaphors which are used to describe contemporary organisations:

1. Machines
2. Organisms
3. Brains
4. Cultures
5. Political Systems
6. Psychic Prisons
7. Flux and Transformation
8. Instruments of Domination.

Whether the organisation is a machine or a brain, an organism or a psychic prison, Morgan – just like Hirsch and Andrews – claimed that the metaphor shapes the understanding of reality and to a large extent shapes organisational life.

The way in which metaphors shape reasoning and understanding around organisations is also central to Andriessen's work in knowledge management[1] and intellectual capital (Andriessen 2006, 2008). Andriessen states that it is important to understand the consequences of different metaphors as they 'determine what we diagnose as KM [knowledge management] problems in organisations and what we develop as KM solutions' (Andriessen 2008: 5). In his study of western and eastern management literature, he finds two dominant metaphors: KNOWLEDGE IS STUFF (e.g. it can be externalised, acquired, held, invested in) and KNOWLEDGE IS LOVE (e.g. it can be articulated, verbalised or elicited). However, the reification of knowledge in knowledge management activities makes employees in his study opposed to the KNOWLEDGE IS STUFF metaphors. They prefer the KNOWLEDGE IS LOVE metaphor since it emphasises the human side of knowledge and downplays its connotations of being potentially measurable. On the basis of this study of metaphors for knowledge in management literature, metaphors are described as something that an organisation can negotiate and change.

Metaphors of organisational change

Understanding the roles metaphor can play in takeovers, organisations or knowledge management proves very useful, because it opens up avenues for managing change. For example, Abel and Sementelli (2005) emphasise the advantages of using 'endogenous evolution' metaphors instead of, for example, mechanical metaphors for change. The message for the employees involved in organisational change shifts from 'we are changing the software' or 'improving some gears in the engine' to 'the organisation is growing and developing in new directions'. Abel and Sementelli argue that the latter kind of metaphor leads to less resistance to the change. The clothing example from the introduction also involved a non-mechanical metaphor for organisational change. The manager described both the old scenario and the new scenario in terms of variants of the same overall metaphor IT SYSTEMS ARE CLOTHES (i.e. bespoke Confirmation clothes vs. off-the-peg clothes). Using the same overarching metaphor gives meaning to the ongoing process, helps to integrate the future with the past and provides an understanding of what is to come for employees unable to imagine a workday with different routines.

In the following sections, I continue to focus on metaphor-based approaches to change. The particular studies were selected to give a sense of diversity in terms of claims, time of origin and views on the value of metaphor as a tool.

Myths, metaphors and cultural change

Myth and storytelling are central elements in creating culture (Schein 2010), and based on what is known from, for example, the study of religion (Theissen 1999), myth, rituals and ethics can create strong cultures and identities for both organisations and the individuals in them (Greve and Hildebrandt 2011). In exploring myth and metaphor, Pondy (1983) claims that a company is just another form of social structure and should be investigated as such. Myths and metaphors work by the same rules in a corporation as in every other social setting.

Pondy defines myth as 'things which never happened but always are' (Pondy 1983: 159) and also uses the concept of 'extended metaphor': two different categories being identified with each other, repeated, and referred back to over time. In this sense myth is a type of extended metaphor (note that this term is used differently here than in linguistic and cognitive approaches to metaphor). According to Pondy, the function of extended metaphor is twofold:

- placing the metaphorical explanation beyond doubt and critique;
- bridging the gap between the familiar and the strange.

This approach to metaphors in knowledge management and change management is rather narrative in nature. Metaphors are being used as a way of constructing a narrative (see also Chapter 23).

Making the implicit explicit by use of metaphors

A different use of metaphor in organisational change focuses on how to make implicit knowledge explicit. Implicit or tacit knowledge (Polanyi 2012) is the things that we know but that are part of routines and integrated into everyday practice, like riding a bicycle or texting on a phone. Explicit knowledge is what we know we know and that which we are able to put into words. Making implicit knowledge explicit is essential for managing and developing knowledge in a company. This is what makes knowledge shareable and transferable. Nonaka and Takeuchi's influential book *The Knowledge-Creating Company* (Nonaka and Takeuchi 1995), and the article that preceded it (Nonaka 1994), emphasise the use of metaphor and analogy in revealing knowledge that we are unaware we have, but which is fundamental to the co-creation of new knowledge. Nonaka writes:

> Metaphor is not merely the first step in transforming tacit knowledge into explicit knowledge; it constitutes an important method of creating a network of concepts which can help to generate knowledge about the future by using existing knowledge.
> *Nonaka 1994: 21*

Thus, employees should talk about, or in other ways represent, what they implicitly know by use of metaphors known by the rest of the group in order to make it explicit to themselves as well as others. This process not only provides insights for others but can also lead to a network of metaphors expanding knowledge for oneself. Nonaka and Takeuchi's (1995) book greatly contributed to popularising metaphor as a managerial tool for innovation.

Understanding emotions through metaphors

Vince and Broussine (1996) developed another use for metaphor in the context of organisational change: understanding the emotions around change in a given group of affected individuals. They too acknowledge that metaphors can create the opportunity for organisations to change, but argue that the main challenge for managers wanting to change their organisations is that change per se is regarded as a problem. Metaphors can thus be used to 'diagnose' the emotions regarding change and as an invitation to discussion. Vince and Broussine quote Barrett and Cooperrider's (1990) four roles for metaphors in change processes:

- Transformative
- Facilitative
- Providing a steering function
- Inviting active experimentation.

An important element in this process is the interaction across different levels of the organisation. Making emotions and feelings explicit is essential in order for the change process to succeed. Metaphors are seen as a window into the 'soul' of a social system (Vince and Broussine 1996: 59) and a way of 'reaching into the subjective terrain of unconscious experience' (Vince and Broussine 1996: 60) and accessing what is implicit. This is in line with Nonaka's method, but, rather than focusing on how metaphors can be used to access and create knowledge, Vince and Broussine focus on understanding emotions. Their method involves drawing out emotions and turning abstract emotions into something more concrete through metaphors that can be shared between employees and managers. This in turn helps to create imagery around emotions in connection with change.

From the overview of how metaphors are or have been used in management practice, I now turn to some of the critical issues and debates on the topic.

Critical issues, debates and controversies

The above-mentioned approaches to metaphor use in organisations have each in their own way triggered debate and critique. It is therefore important to touch upon at least some of the potential problems of applying metaphors in managerial research and theory. Here I raise the issues of whether metaphors are 'contaminating' management research and the consequences of variation in the interpretation of metaphors.

Pinder and Bourgeois are strong opponents of the use of tropes in general and especially metaphors (1982). Writing after the publication of Lakoff and Johnson's (1980) *Metaphors We Live By*, the authors recognise that metaphors are important in everyday language, but their critique is directed towards the use of metaphor in administrative science (covering all organisational sciences, psychology, sociology, economics and anthropology). Their argument is that the unconstrained use of metaphor in the presentation and dissemination of formal theory can lead to the misinterpretation of facts and reality. This echoes the critique levelled at the use of metaphor in the context of illness by Susan Sontag (1979/1991) (see Chapter 26). Pinder and Bourgeois's aim was to remove as many tropes from scientific language as possible because 'it is worthwhile to strive to minimise the dysfunctional effects of metaphorical language in [scientific] activities' (1982: 651). This view would not necessarily preclude the use of metaphor as a management tool in the practice of organisational change, but would discourage their use for theorising about organisations as exemplified by Morgan's (1988, 2006) work above.

A second controversial issue concerns the extent to which it is possible to generalise on how a metaphor might be intended or interpreted in a particular organisational context. Argaman (2008), for example, agrees with Pondy (1983) and Abel and Sementelli (2005) on the importance of metaphor's ability to shed light on underlying assumptions which affect behaviour within organisations. However, he argues that there is nevertheless no guarantee that different individuals mean the same things with any given metaphor. Seeing the process of change as sailing a boat, for example, still leaves room for interpretation and therefore misunderstanding. Is sailing a boat safe or unsafe? Exciting or life-threatening? These are possible entailments that the manager needs to be aware of in order to successfully produce and use metaphors for management. Introducing a metaphor and then investigating how it is perceived by the parties involved reveals that, even though a metaphor can provide a common understanding and vision for, say, a process of change, individuals also perceive and understand metaphors through different filters and preconceptions, which makes it difficult to predict how a manager-introduced metaphor will be understood.

An example of current research

Recent research on metaphor as a management tool has laid further emphasis on its externalising function as described by Nonaka, as well as by Vince and Broussine. The dominant trend in current research seems to be less concerned with revealing existing metaphors and more preoccupied with producing external metaphorical landscapes as a means of negotiation, and as a way of making differences in individuals' understandings more evident. This most recent development in the field of metaphor in management involves what Heracleous and Jacobs (2008: 319) describe as 'crafting symbolic artefacts'. In this section, I will present my own research in this area. I begin by establishing the theoretical context with two key studies, the first concerning multimodal metaphor and creativity, the second concerning metaphor and strategy. I then discuss my own work on metaphor crafting for knowledge in knowledge-intensive groups. I also address more generally how divergences in understanding can be uncovered by the use of simple toys.

A key study underpinning my own research is El Refaie's (2013) work on how creativity can be boosted by multimodal metaphors and the new associations they facilitate. El Refaie writes:

> [. . .] the term 'multimodal resonances' [is used] to describe the way creative multimodal metaphors are often grasped intuitively and imaginatively, through a process that involves a sort of sympathetic vibration, both between the source and target domain and between the distinct semiotic modes that are used to represent a metaphor.
>
> *El Refaie 2013: 242*

El Refaie expands the modes of analysis to include gesture and preverbal intuitions, thus performing a cross-modal analysis of the creative process. This in turn might hold the key to letting us move beyond the '"concept prison" of our old, established patterns of thinking' (El Refaie 2013: 247). From a management perspective, the relevance of El Refaie's study is that it stresses the importance of using different modes; e.g. pictures and gestures as well as language in 'allowing unexpected connections to emerge' (El Refaie 2013: 246). These kinds of new connections can be used to create a common vocabulary or a more nuanced understanding of a new product or process. This is in line with the benefits of using metaphors in what Pinder and Bourgeois (1982) called heuristic speculation.

The push beyond established thinking is also a feature of the study by Heracleous and Jacobs (2008). They build on the metaphor of Strategy as Craftsmanship introduced by Mintzberg (1987), but put the metaphor into action in a novel way. They use toy animals and building bricks as a means for creating strategies. The rationale behind this is to make use of the embodied dimension of metaphors via the use and manipulation of physical objects. Much like war strategists made 3D maps of territories during warfare, Heracleous and Jacobs propose a method allowing employees to craft strategy in 3D. Their case study is a European telecom organisation involved in a merger. The method proposed is a three-step approach, paraphrased below (Heracleous and Jacobs 2008: 314):

1. Individuals construct and interpret a physical object relating to the goal of the workshop.
2. In groups, the individual constructions are integrated into a collective construction including contradictions and differences. This stage serves to make evident consonance and dissonance in understandings between the group members. This step is repeated in different group settings involving e.g. stakeholders, managers, etc.
3. The final constructions are discussed and subjected to 'what-if' scenarios by the participants.

The result of such a process is to facilitate negotiations and to make differences explicit. The metaphors developed in the course of the study were divided into one overarching metaphor and a number of constituent metaphors. The overarching metaphor is: The strategy development process is a journey of disoriented animals moving towards a common space. The constituent metaphors were:

1. Organisation members are disoriented animals.
2. Strategy-making is a combustion engine transforming fuel into kinesthetic energy.
3. The renewed strategy process is a set of gearing wheels transmitting energy between entities.
4. The relation between strategist and organisation is that of a safari park with its inhabitants, in which each kind of animal is allotted different degrees of freedom.

These metaphors are obviously influenced by the material with which they were crafted. Had there not been animals among the building bricks, the metaphors might have been different all together. This is not a problem according to Heracleous and Jacobs, as the purpose of crafting shared metaphors is not to reveal already existing metaphors but rather to create a common model as a common point of reference and as a basis for negotiation.

My own work is very much influenced by the two studies above. It too deals with externalising metaphors in groups as a means of understanding how groups co-create and negotiate understandings of abstract phenomena. The topic of investigation is knowledge, but the approach can also easily be applied to innovation, strategy, cooperation, change or any other relevant concept (Greve 2016).

To investigate how groups co-create and negotiate understandings of knowledge, employees from six creative startups were provided with toy building bricks, just as in Heracleous and Jacobs's (2008) study. The brand was LEGO Serious Play, which has been used in a number of other research projects (Bjørndahl et al. 2014; Frick et al. 2013). Each group consisted of three to five persons and the interventions took place in their own office space. Each session lasted one hour and all sessions were video recorded, transcribed and coded afterwards. The groups were asked to do the following:

1. Build three buildings: each building session lasted five minutes. The first topic served the purpose of familiarising the group with the bricks, and was 'Build your dream office'. The second building task was 'Experience'. The third building task was 'Knowledge' (cf. the method developed by Bjørndahl et al. (2014) in an experimental setup).
2. Explain the final building.
3. Put the building away and take part in a semi-structured discussion about knowledge.

The discussion was moderated by myself as the researcher but primarily took place between the participants. When the researcher asked questions, only metaphors about knowledge initiated or proposed by the one or more participants were used, in order to avoid influencing the results.

The general idea of the study was to combine language analysis and analysis of joint epistemic action. Epistemic action refers to actions which could be performed by the mind alone, and which benefit from being made external: e.g. using a calculator instead of performing the calculation mentally, or writing ideas down in a brainstorm rather than remembering them all. Joint epistemic actions are epistemic actions conducted by more than one individual (Bjørndahl et al. 2014; Kirsh and Maglio 1994; Roepstorff 2008). The purpose of combining these two approaches was to make it possible for the groups to co-create metaphors for knowledge and to investigate how this was done. In the analysis, I focused specifically on the following:

- How did the group approach the building task?
- Which metaphors for knowledge were used?

The method for analysing how the buildings were built follows Bjørndahl et al. (2014). They proposed a taxonomy of three approaches to such a building task:

1. Illustration: One participant presents how the topic can be physically represented and executes this with little or no help from the rest of the group.
2. Elaboration: As with illustration, a plan is presented, but once building begins, the group deviates from the original idea.
3. Exploration: The group members co-construct a building without an initial plan, taking inspiration from just the bricks or materials themselves.

The groups from the creative start-ups tended to favour the second building approach – elaboration, but there are some traces of all three in the dataset. The groups tended to stick with the approach they had used in the first and second building tasks when 'building knowledge' in the last task. Two of the six groups clearly used a shared mode to co-create a metaphor for knowledge with the bricks, which influenced the conversation afterwards. Specifically, they referred back to the buildings using gesture and pointing towards where the building had been. They made use of what El Refaie (2013) calls cross-modal resonance. The study makes it evident that it is not enough to make a shared mode available to a group for its members to engage in a joint epistemic action. The shared mode does not always become a common point of reference and thus the dynamics of the group need to be investigated in order to determine if indeed the group has co-created a concept.

Using metaphor as a management tool

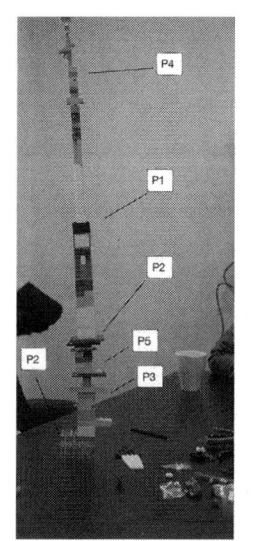

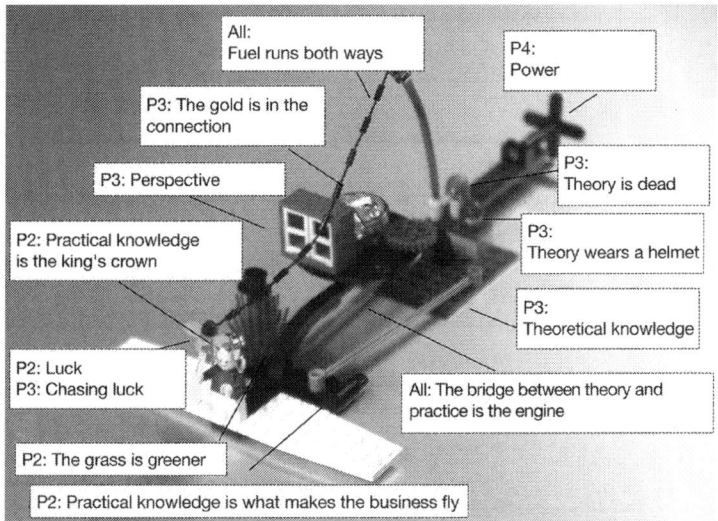

Figure 27.1 Two buildings from the dataset, showing two different representations of knowledge. To the left: Knowledge is a tower; to the right: Knowledge is a vessel. P# indicates which participant contributed which element.

Two groups were especially successful in co-creating a concept for knowledge in bricks, which they referred back to and used for negotiation afterwards. The success could not be attributed to the finished products themselves, since the two groups built two very different buildings. Figure 27.1 shows the two buildings produced by the groups, representing the overarching metaphors: Knowledge is a tower, and Knowledge is a vessel.

Both buildings were used to make inferences about the concept of knowledge and to reason about the nature of knowledge, as suggested by Cornelissen (2005). In the case of Knowledge is a tower, during the discussion phase one participant stated that each assignment in the company demands a combination of different skills and competencies. This implies that it is not appropriate to build individuals' knowledge separately. Instead, as in a tower, one can combine the knowledge of all the employees inside the company. As can be seen, the structure of the building influenced the verbal discussion of what knowledge is. Even after the building was put away, it remained a common point of reference for the group.

In the case of Knowledge is a vessel, the group engaged in a vivid discussion about the differences between theoretical and practical knowledge, which were discussed as elements in the vessel. In talking about this, participants pointed to the places on the table where the elements had been placed in the building. Again it was evident that the metaphor created in bricks became part of a shared understanding.

It emerged from the study that, although the groups used very different concepts to explain knowledge and approached the building task in very different ways, the more they worked together on building the concepts in bricks, the more they used the building as a shared point of reference. The approach has been applied to a group of change consultants in a Danish food production company which led to a change in the company's knowledge sharing strategy (Greve 2015).

To conclude this section on three examples of current research, there is evidence of the value of externalisation and of the importance of using diverse and contradictory metaphors more as a way of creating new meanings than as a source of problems (Cornelissen 2005).

Recommendations for practice

On the basis of the above-mentioned theories and examples, in this section, I summarise a few recommendations for anyone wishing to make use of metaphor in the context of management.

When a manager wants to understand the status quo or change the current (metaphorical) understandings of a group, the following elements should be taken into consideration:

(1) The first recommendation is to state the purpose of the investigation and decide which is more important – understanding how the organisation narrates itself in terms of metaphors or how individuals or groups understand the organisation. There is a big difference between analysing material produced for official communications and facilitating a conversation or interviews with individuals.
(2) Especially with groups, it is important to draw attention to how metaphors emerge. Some may only be mentioned once. Some might be repeated over time and in different modes. Some might be developed by an individual or by the group. To understand a concept, such as knowledge or strategy, and the emotions connected to it, it is essential to be aware of both when co-creation happens and when it does not happen. If no co-creation or development or sharing of metaphors between users occurs, that might suggest a very top-down process or that the participants are unable to build on and use each other's ideas and thoughts.
(3) As has been mentioned above, drawing, building or in other ways externally representing a concept in question can help to create metaphorical understandings, both for individuals and groups. Of course, there are limitations to every material. Nevertheless, providing a group or an individual with a range of modes for metaphorical expression will increase their ability to express metaphors and to let the modes support each other in explaining a complex or abstract phenomenon.

Future directions

For future research and development of the field to progress, further studies of the use and effects of metaphors in organisations will be needed, perhaps with an increased focus on managers themselves and their use of metaphor. Even though organisations are social systems like any other, as stated by Vince and Broussine (1996), managers hold a special role in these social systems and thus should be subjected to more investigation. Returning to the opening example, a number of questions arise: are clothes a good metaphor to describe a change in IT systems in that setting, and, if so, why? How was the metaphor proposed by managers understood or taken up, and what effect did it have on the managers' implementation of the change process? Answering these and many more questions on metaphors in usage will be relevant to both public- and private-sector managers in the future.

Note

1 Wiig (1997: 1) defines knowledge management as: '(1) to make the enterprise act as intelligently as possible to secure its viability and overall success and (2) to otherwise realise the best value of its knowledge assets'.

Further reading

Andriessen, D. (2008) 'Stuff or love? How metaphors direct our efforts to manage knowledge in organisations', *Knowledge Management Research and Practice*, 6(1), 5–12.

Cornelissen, J. P. (2005) 'Beyond compare: Metaphor in organization theory', *Academy of Management Review*, 30(4), 751–764.

Heracleous, L. and Jacobs, C. D. (2008) 'Crafting strategy: The role of embodied metaphors', *Long Range Planning*, 41(3), 309–325.

References

Abel, C. F. and Sementelli, A. J. (2005) 'Evolutionary critical theory, metaphor, and organizational change', *Journal of Management Development*, 24(5), 443–458.

Andriessen, D. (2006) 'On the metaphorical nature of intellectual capital: A textual analysis', *Journal of Intellectual Capital*, 7(1), 93–110.

—— (2008) 'Stuff or love? How metaphors direct our efforts to manage knowledge in organisations', *Knowledge Management Research and Practice*, 6(1), 5–12.

Argaman, E. (2008) 'In the same boat? On metaphor variation as mediating the individual voice in organizational change', *Applied Linguistics*, 29(3), 483–502.

Barrett, F. J. and Cooperrider, D. L. (1990) 'Generative metaphor intervention: A new approach for working with systems divided by conflict and caught in defensive perception', *Journal of Applied Behavioral Science*, 26(2), 219–239.

Bjørndahl, J. S., Fusaroli, R., Østergaard, S. and Tylén, K. (2014) 'Thinking together with material representations: Joint epistemic actions in creative problem solving', *Cognitive Semiotics*, 7(1), 103–123.

Cornelissen, J. P. (2005) 'Beyond compare: Metaphor in organization theory', *Academy of Management Review*, 30(4), 751–764.

El Refaie, E. (2013) 'Cross-modal resonances in creative multimodal metaphors: Breaking out of conceptual prisons', *Review of Cognitive Linguistics*, 11(2), 236–249.

Frick, E., Tardini, S. and Cantoni, L. (2013) *White Paper on LEGO (R) SERIOUS PLAY – A State of the Art of Its Applications in Europe*, Universitá della Svizzera Italiana Lugano, Switzerland: European Commision. Online. Available at: http://s-play.eu/en/news/70-s-play-white-paper-published (accessed 4 January 2016).

Gibbs, R. W., Jr. (2011) 'Are "deliberate" metaphors really deliberate? A question of human consciousness and action', *Metaphor and the Social World*, 1(1), 26–52.

Greve, L. (2015) 'Knowledge sharing is knowledge creation: An action research study of metaphors for knowledge', *Journal of Organizational Knowledge Communication*, 2(1), 66–80.

—— (2016) *Metaphors for Knowledge in Knowledge Intensive Groups. An Inductive Investigation of How and Which Metaphors Emerge in Conversations*, PhD dissertation, Aarhus University. Online. Available HTTP: http://pure.au.dk/portal/files/96255917/LG_Thesis.pdf (accessed 9 September 2016).

Greve, L. and Hildebrandt, S. (2011) *Forandrende Ledelseskommunikation*, København: Samfundslitteratur.

Heracleous, L. and Jacobs, C. D. (2008) 'Crafting strategy: The role of embodied metaphors', *Long Range Planning*, 41(3), 309–325.

Hirsch, P. M., and Andrews, J. A. Y. (1983) 'Ambushed, shootout, and Knights of the Roundtable: The language of corporate takeovers', in *Organizational Symbolism*, Greenwich, CT: JAI Press.

Hogler, R., Gross, M. A., Hartman, J. L. and Cunliffe, A. L. (2008) 'Meaning in organizational communication: Why metaphor is the cake, not the icing', *Management Communication Quarterly*, 21(3), 393–412.

Kirsh, D. and Maglio, P. (1994) 'On distinguishing epistemic from pragmatic action', *Cognitive Science*, 18(4), 513–549.

Lakoff, G. and Johnson, M. (1980) *Metaphors We Live By*, Chicago, IL: University of Chicago Press.

Mintzberg, H. (1987, July–August) 'Crafting Strategy', *Harvard Business Review*. Online. Available at https://hbr.org/1987/07/crafting-strategy (accessed 4 January 2016).

Morgan, G. (1988) *Riding the Waves of Change: Developing Managerial Competencies for a Turbulent World* (Vol. xvii), San Francisco, CA: Jossey-Bass.

—— (2006) *Images of Organization*, Thousand Oaks, CA: SAGE.

Nonaka, I. (1994) 'A dynamic theory of organizational knowledge creation', *Organization Science*, 5(1), 14–37.

Nonaka, I., and Takeuchi, H. (1995) *The Knowledge-Creating Company: How Japanese Companies Create the Dynamics of Innovation*, New York: Oxford University Press.

Pinder, C. C. and Bourgeois, V. W. (1982) 'Controlling tropes in administrative science', *Administrative Science Quarterly*, 27(4), 641–652.

Polanyi, M. (2012) *Personal Knowledge: Towards a Post-Critical Philosophy*, Chicago, IL: University of Chicago Press.

Pondy, L. R. (1983) 'The role of metaphor and myth in organization and in the facilitation', in *Organizational Symbolism* (pp. 157–166), Greenwich, CT: JAI Press.

Roepstorff, A. (2008) 'Things to think with: Words and objects as material symbols', *Philosophical Transactions of the Royal Society B: Biological Sciences*, 363(1499), 2049–2054.

Schein, E. H. (2010) *Organizational Culture and Leadership* (4th edition), San Francisco, CA: Jossey-Bass.

Sontag, S. (1979/1991) 'Illness as metaphor', in *Illness as Metaphor and AIDS and Its Metaphors*, London, New York: Penguin Modern Classics.

Steen, G. (2008) 'The paradox of metaphor: Why we need a three-dimensional model of metaphor', *Metaphor and Symbol*, 23(4), 213–241.

Steen, G. J. (2011) 'The contemporary theory of metaphor – now new and improved!', *Review of Cognitive Linguistics*, 9(1), 26–64.

Theissen, G. (1999) *The Religion of the Earliest Churches: Creating a Symbolic World*, Minneapolis, MN: Fortress Press.

Vince, R. and Broussine, M. (1996) 'Paradox, defense and attachment: Accessing and working with emotions and relations underlying organizational change', *Organization Studies*, 17(1), 1–21.

Wiig, K. M. (1997) 'Knowledge management: Where did it come from and where will it go?', *Expert Systems with Applications*, 13(1), 1–14.

28
Using metaphor in the teaching of second/foreign languages

Fiona MacArthur

Introduction and definitions

As all of the chapters in this volume make clear, metaphor is far from an unimportant aspect of human communication, or the product of extraordinary people who possess a special 'way with words', such as poets, novelists or great orators. Rather, it is used – to a greater or lesser extent – by all humans to express themselves when talking about topics ranging from their feelings (emotions such as anger or sadness) to the football match they are watching on TV. And since it is such an important part of everyday language use, one would expect that attention to metaphor would be an integral part of every language course designed for learners of a second or foreign language (S/FL). However, the simple truth is that it seldom, if ever, is. One of the main objectives of this chapter is to explore why this might be so.

Other chapters in this volume explore the difficulties that learners of English experience with metaphor-related words and phrases (see Chapters 19 and 34); here, I turn to the foreign or second language classroom, focusing on how research has contributed to showing how learners may be helped (or hindered) in their efforts to get to grips with this aspect of the target language. As in other chapters, attention will be paid solely to *English* as a second/foreign language, as this is where research has been most prolific to date. Furthermore, I will limit my discussion to *conventional* English metaphors, that is, those metaphors which are so entrenched in the language that their use will mostly likely pass unnoticed by expert speakers of the language. For the learner of a S/FL, such conventional metaphorical extensions of target language words may appear quite novel, because the polysemous senses of the equivalent word in the first language may be quite different. For example, the verb 'strike' is more or less equivalent to the Spanish verb *golpear* when it is used in its basic sense ('he struck the edge of the table with his knee' can be rendered as *golpeó el borde de la mesa con la rodilla*). However, while for English speakers it is quite usual to say such things as 'Louise was struck down with leukaemia' or 'another possibility that strikes me', neither of these senses of 'strike' are possible for Spanish *golpear*.

Polysemy can be defined as 'the phenomenon whereby a single linguistic form is associated with a number of related but distinct meanings or senses' (Tyler and Evans 2001: 1). The most obvious examples of general principles governing polysemy or meaning extension are metaphor and metonymy. The systematicity of such figurative projections or mappings has been the subject of numerous studies (e.g. Dirven 1985; Nerlich et al. 2003) in order to explain the motivation of multiple senses of the same linguistic form. This makes metaphor – in this respect at least – relevant to S/FL learning, for while a learner's increasing command of the target language will be reflected in the *breadth* of vocabulary knowledge gained, it will also be accompanied by a corresponding *depth* of knowledge of the semantic potential of the target language words and phrases s/he knows (McCarthy 2007; Meara 1996).

Although conventional metaphors may be realised by single lexical items (for example, 'it struck me that . . . ' or 'it's sheer unbridled greed'), it seems that most often they are realised by fixed and semi-fixed phrases (Deignan 2005; Cameron and Deignan 2006). In turn, these metaphorical phrases – or metaphoremes, as Cameron and Deignan (2006) refer to them – tend to be associated with a cluster of very specific linguistic, conceptual and pragmatic features. Conventional metaphors are rarely neutral, but evaluate the situation or event being talked about. Furthermore, they may fulfil particular discourse functions (summarising or signalling topic closure or transition, for example [Drew and Holt 1998]) and therefore may be somewhat restricted in terms of when and where they can be used appropriately. It can be seen, then, that learning to use conventional metaphors in the target language can pose a considerable challenge for the learner.

When considering the place that metaphor might have in the description of a speaker's overall communicative competence, Littlemore and Low (2006) conclude that the ability to use and understand metaphor has an important role to play in every area of communicative competence. That is, metaphorical competence can contribute to grammatical competence, textual competence, illocutionary competence, sociolinguistic competence, and strategic competence. However, Littlemore and Low's insightful discussion of the role of metaphor in all these areas, and the difficulties that may be experienced by learners, finds virtually no echo in current models for language teaching and assessment, and is conspicuously absent from the guidelines laid down in the Common European Framework of Reference for Languages (CEFR).

In the next section, I describe some of the research that has been carried out into metaphor in the learning of English, which is largely based on the cognitive linguistics (CL) notion of *motivation*. Then I discuss some of the issues raised by this research when considered in relation to S/FL syllabi and teaching materials, followed by the main research methods that have been used in this field, drawing attention to some weaknesses that may partly explain why CL-inspired research has not had a greater impact on syllabus design and language teaching materials. I then provide an example of a somewhat different type of research recently carried out and suggest some directions that could usefully be taken in relation to metaphor and S/FL teaching. Finally, I describe some of the pedagogical implications of this research for S/FL teachers.

Overview of relevant research to date

In this section I give an overview of research into metaphor and S/FL learning, describing first some studies which have used the CL notion of *motivation* to enhance learners' understanding and recall of conventional metaphors in English. Because of the constraints on a summary of this kind, this overview will inevitably omit mention of some research that has been carried out, focusing instead on the main trends in this field and the major research findings.

CL-inspired research into S/FL learning has mostly focused on the teaching of vocabulary, seeking to propose and validate instructional activities that exploit the motivation for the sense of target language lexis, examining the effect of fostering learners' deep engagement with metaphorical language uses through the use of verbal explanation, physical enactment or visual illustrations.

One early – informal – study in this line (Kövecses and Szabó 1996) used conceptual metaphor theory (CMT) (see Chapter 1) to discover whether explanations of the orientational metaphors motivating phrasal verbs with 'up' and 'down' (e.g. 'look up' or 'break down') would enhance learning. Two groups of Hungarian students were taught 20 different phrasal verbs; one group was presented simply with translations and explanations of the meanings of the phrasal verbs, and were asked to memorise them. The other group, however, were additionally provided with a motivated explanation for these meanings of these phrasal verbs. In a follow-up sentence completion task, Kövecses and Szabó tested students not only on the 20 phrasal verbs that had already been memorised but on a further 10 phrasal verbs which had not been explained or memorised. Interestingly, while the results for the targeted items were very similar for both groups, the learners who had received the explanation of the orientational metaphors motivating the uses of 'up' and 'down' in the targeted phrasal verbs outperformed the other group when tested on previously unencountered – but similarly motivated – phrasal verbs. Other researchers have carried out similar studies. For example, Boers (2000) conducted an experiment to explore this kind of instructional approach to a wider range of conceptual metaphors (CM) realised by phrasal verbs (for example, VISIBLE IS OUT or VISIBLE IS UP, as instantiated in phrasal verbs like 'find out' or 'show up', respectively). In this case, the participants were 39 French-speaking students; otherwise the approach was very similar. As in the Kövecses and Szabó experiment, the control and experimental groups were taught the same phrasal verbs in the same way, except that the experimental group was provided with a list of the 26 phrasal verbs grouped under various conceptual metaphors, while the control group was provided with a list of the same verbs arranged in alphabetical order. In an immediate follow-up test (a gap-fill exercise testing 10 of the items) the experimental group significantly outperformed the control group, suggesting that using CMs to present phrasal verbs was beneficial, at least in relation to short-term recall. However, neither study provided robust evidence that this was due to the promotion of any figurative thinking on the learners' part: the results could equally well have been the result of presenting the phrasal verbs in organised groups rather than in simple lists. Likewise, it may be that the kind of conceptual metaphors motivating these phrasal verbs (orientational metaphors or the relatively concrete extensions of 'out' in the Boers experiment) lent themselves particularly well to this kind of treatment. In other cases, involving relatively concrete and relatively abstract phrasal verbs (as reported in Condon and Kelly 2002), CMs motivating phrasal verbs that could only be explained verbally (as opposed to being illustrated by a drawing) did not prove helpful in recall.

Boers and his colleagues have carried out a number of experiments into idiom learning in English as S/FL (e.g. Boers 2001; Boers et al. 2004; Boers et al. 2006). In these studies, the hypothesis guiding the research programme is that the deep engagement with target language words and phrases that is brought about by semantic or etymological elaboration is likely to foster better understanding and recall of otherwise opaque language uses, such as is found in idioms like 'to be par for the course' or 'to show someone the ropes'. If a learner engages deeply with target language forms and meanings – that is, makes some kind of mental effort – this is likely to result in the information being committed to long term memory. The results of this research have largely confirmed the initial hypothesis. When learners are asked to think about the source domains or scenarios that underlie different idioms in English (for example, by choosing between three possible origins for a particular idiom), the extra effort required leads to gains in understanding and recall, both in the short and the long term.

As has already been mentioned, fewer studies have focused on the metaphorically motivated polysemy of content words. One important exception to this is reported in Verspoor and Lowie (2003), a study which found exactly the same kind of benefits for engaging with the metaphorically motivated senses of individual words through semantic elaboration as that found by Boers and his colleagues for idioms or phrasal verbs. Using 18 different words of different classes (e.g. verbs like 'sprawl' or 'spawn', nouns such as 'cog' or 'nugget' or an adjective like 'perennial'), Verspoor and Lowie showed that providing the core sense of a figuratively used word as a cue to its figurative meaning in context was very effective in fostering long-term retention of this meaning. When contrasted with other means of working out the meaning of a word in context, they concluded that:

> guessing the meaning of a figurative sense through a core sense provides the second language learner with an opportunity for a precise elaboration, enabling the learner to incorporate the figurative sense into a semantic network more effectively and recall it later.
>
> *Verspoor and Lowie 2003: 569*

Another study into polysemy was carried out by Boers (2000). Here, the research focused on verbs of motion ('soar', 'plunge', 'dive' or 'slide', among others). Boers asked two groups of French-speaking students to categorise the verbs in different ways. The experimental group were asked to group the verbs according to source domains (aircraft, diving and mountaineering), while the control group were asked to categorise the verbs according to a cline describing speed and direction of change. That is, both groups had to engage in a similar cognitive effort (and hence deep processing), the only difference being that the students in the experimental group were explicitly using imagery. Interestingly, in a follow-up essay (based on graphs about unemployment rates), the experimental group used a far greater range of the verbs than their control peers. However, the immediate gains of this group of students were cancelled out a year later, as, when given a similar task, there was no difference in the performance of the two groups.

It is perhaps unsurprising, given that cognitive linguistics has provided exhaustive descriptions of the embodied nature of human thought, that researchers should have turned their attention to enactment and mime-based instruction in fostering learners' ability to interpret the metaphorical extensions of manner of motion verbs in English, like 'stumble' or 'dodge'. Lindstromberg and Boers (2005) carried out three experiments with Dutch-speaking learners of English that showed the mnemonic benefits of engaging the learners in simulations of the movements referred to by verbs like those mentioned above, not only in fostering learning of the basic or literal senses of these verbs but also in using this understanding to interpret their metaphorical senses (for example, 'dodge' with the sense of 'avoid' a question or similar, or 'stumble' ['on'/'across'] in the sense of 'accidentally encounter' something). This research is particularly interesting because it relates to another kind of teaching/learning activity that S/FL professionals are likely to be familiar with: Total Physical Response (TPR) (Asher 1969). TPR is a language teaching method that is based on the coordination of language input with physical movement on the part of learners (for example, learners respond with physical movement to instructions such as 'stand up' or 'raise your hand') and has been used in many S/FL classrooms, particularly with beginners. Thus, it may well be that many a teacher is unknowingly or unconsciously laying the groundwork for developing metaphor competence in S/FL classrooms when s/he uses the method (occasionally or consistently) to ensure learning of those elements of the language that lend themselves to such treatment.

A somewhat different approach to exploring the sense relations between different uses of the same word is reported in MacArthur and Littlemore (2008). In this study, two groups of learners (university students in Spain and England learning English and Spanish respectively) were invited to explore the uses of 14 denominal verbs using animal names ('to dog' or *torear*, for example), body part terms ('to shoulder' or *codearse*, for example) or the names of other familiar objects ('to chair' or *caldear*, among others) in two large corpora (the BNC for the English verbs and the CREA for the Spanish ones). Before beginning the activity (which was done in pairs or groups of three), the students were asked to say what they thought these words might mean when used as verbs. Their answers showed that they had little idea of how words such as these could extend their meanings figuratively and, if they were able to come up with a possible meaning for the verbal forms, it was found that they tended to base this sense on an A is B metaphor in their first language (L1). In their exploration of single sentences illustrating the uses of these verbs in the two corpora, the students displayed certain patterns of behaviour that were constant across both groups; they all noticed and remembered particular examples of the metaphorical uses of these verbs in the two corpora for similar reasons. The content of the corpus examples, the ease with which the items lent themselves to the use of gesture when their meaning was being discussed, and phraseology and alliteration appeared to influence the salience of certain items the learners came across in the corpus and their ability to remember them. In this study, MacArthur and Littlemore (2008) found that learners needed a substantial amount of help and guidance from their teachers in their collaborative quest for meaning, mainly because of the richness and rawness of the data with which they were confronted. This means that such a data-driven approach to metaphorically motivated word senses is not something that learners could undertake autonomously. On the other hand, the findings suggested that more empirical research of this kind would be useful for the design of teaching materials: the frequency of a figurative sense of a word did not correlate with its transparency for these particular students, which may mean that teachers and/or materials designers run the risk of missing the 'best example' from the learner's perspective if priority is given to the most highly frequent metaphorical sense of verbs in teaching materials.

As has been seen, pedagogy-oriented cognitive linguists have found that informing second language learners of the motivation behind the figurative meaning of idioms can be helpful in the sense that this helps to make that meaning more memorable. This finding is commonly attributed to the advantages of mental imagery and concreteness of meaning (cf. Paivio's [1986] 'Dual Coding' theory). That is, the positive results derive from fostering the creation of appropriate mental images of the metaphors in question. Not surprisingly, then, this research has suggested useful roles in fostering metaphor awareness for another kind of teaching aid frequently employed in S/FL teaching: visual aids. Visuals have been used as integral elements of metaphor-related learning activities, such as when pictures appear as adjuncts to explanations of idiom meanings (e.g. Kövecses et al. 1996–1998), favouring the visual representation of the idiom using humorous cartoon-style pictures. Line drawings have also been used in form-focused follow-up activities in English as S/FL teaching materials to prompt recall of a previously learnt idiom (e.g. Gude and Duckworth 1998; McCarthy and O'Dell 2002). However, a number of studies (Boers et al. 2008; Boers et al. 2009; MacArthur 2006) have shown that pictures are not particularly effective when it comes to prompting recall of the exact wording of an idiom (for example, a line drawing designed to prompt the idiom 'play ball with someone' elicited instead a calque of the Spanish idiom *pasar la pelota* ['pass the ball'] among a group of Spanish university students). According to the data reported by Boers et al. (2009), students' retention of the precise wording in idioms can even be hampered by learning the meaning of the idiom in conjunction with a picture: students are likely to remember the picture but not the words if the latter are not already familiar to them. In the case of already familiar word forms, on the other hand, an association with pictures does appear mnemonically effective (Szczepaniak and Lew 2011), because recall of the picture can then prompt recall of its corresponding word.

Critical issues, debates and controversies

As has already been mentioned, one of the problems facing metaphor researchers who wish their research to lead to pedagogical applications is the fact that the whole concept of metaphor and metaphorical competence is not reflected in any of the major models currently guiding syllabus design, such as the CEFR. This means that it is difficult to see how metaphor-related activities of the type described in the previous section could be contemplated, let alone built into S/FL instructional programmes. It is true that some recent course books show a certain awareness of the need for attention to metaphor use (e.g. Clandfield et al. 2011) and the presentation and practice of phrasal verbs in recently published text books may reflect cognitive linguistic views for the motivation of these linguistic items: these are nowadays more likely to be grouped around a specific particle (e.g. 'up' or 'out'), which can be associated with a stable meaning, as opposed to being grouped around the lexical verb (e.g. 'put' or 'turn') as was the case in the past. Nevertheless, a focus on metaphor is most often found in works of reference, such as dictionaries (for example, the *Collins COBUILD English Guides: Metaphor* [Deignan 1995] or the *Macmillan English Dictionary for Advanced Learners* [2007]), metaphor-led exercise books (Rudzka-Ostyn 2003 or Lazar 2003) or works providing incidental exercises for the language classroom (e.g. Boers and Lindstromberg 2008) rather than the course books used regularly in teaching sessions. That is, metaphor is still regarded as somewhat marginal in the materials published for English as S/FL.

Indeed, the approach to metaphorically motivated polysemy continues to be quite unsystematic in mainstream course books (see Amaya-Chávez [2010] for the treatment of 'hand', 'cool' and 'run' in the textbooks used in two primary and two secondary school classrooms in Spain). In general, authors fail to notice – or draw learners' attention to – meaningful links between the different senses of words.

It might be argued, however, that metaphor does not need any special attention in S/FL, because learners might be able to develop metaphoric competence quite independently of any interventions on the part of their teachers or course books. Two examples cited in MacArthur (2010) of proficient learners of English seem to suggest that, even without specific attention to metaphor, some learners do develop the ability to use figurative language in remarkably effective and creative ways. In a similar vein, Littlemore et al.'s (2014) study of the use of metaphor in learner writing at different levels of proficiency signals that German and Greek learners of English were using metaphor at all stages of proficiency, and Nacey's (2014) study of Norwegian learners' use of prepositions showed a good command overall of the metaphorical uses of spatial prepositions. None of these results could be directly attributed to specific attention to metaphor in the classrooms where English was learned – or at least, not to the published materials used there. It may of course be that experienced teachers do use metaphor-driven explanations or activities to help learners to understand and remember conventional metaphors in their target language, but at present there is no empirical evidence to show that this is so.

A further problem is that it is not clear to what extent the results of the controlled experiments carried out can actually be transferred to language classrooms. Most of these studies have focused on university students, and on particular aspects of English (idioms or phrasal verbs). Yet second/foreign languages are included in the curriculum of many countries at much earlier ages than this, and age impacts not only on *how* metaphor can be taught but also on *what* should be taught. Learners need to become familiar with different types of metaphor at different ages, and will also bring to bear different types of knowledge in interpreting novel metaphors in the target language (MacArthur and Piquer-Píriz 2007). Apart from the question of how the metaphorical senses of target language words should be introduced at different stages of the language-learning process, there is the all-important notion of topic, and what learners need to be able to understand and express at different stages. In their examination of 200 written exam scripts of Greek and German learners, Littlemore et al. (2014) found that the number of metaphors involving open class items increased significantly at B2 or upper-intermediate level, in response to the communicative demands made of learners at this stage. This radical qualitative and quantitative change in metaphor use suggests that, in response to tasks requiring that they state their personal opinions on certain issues or highlight their personal significance, learners needed to use metaphorical language. Before this, metaphor use mostly involved function words like prepositions.

In addition, the issue of the cognitive effort required for the deep processing of metaphors described above is not a negligible factor in the question of transferring results to S/FL classrooms. The willingness or ability of learners to engage deeply with this aspect English has proved to be quite variable. For example, the corpus-based approach to discovering the figurative extensions of target language words reported in MacArthur and Littlemore (2008) was much more successful with the group of English majors at a Spanish university than it was with a group of students from an English university who were taking Spanish as a module outside their main discipline. Similarly, Condon (2008) found that the *timetable* of classes could affect learning outcomes. Of the two groups submitted to the same cognitive-linguistic approach to learning phrasal verbs, one was actually outperformed by their control group peers – a result she attributed to the fact that for this group the class hour chosen for the presentation and practice was their last class hour of the day, and the students were too tired to dedicate the necessary cognitive effort to assimilating the CL explanations (Condon 2008: 149).

Last but not least, semantic elaboration of the kind fostered in much research has proved beneficial in understanding and recall of the target metaphors when tested in gap-fill exercises but, as Boers et al. (2009) showed, the experimental groups outperformed control groups only when a very generous scoring method was used. If the learners' production of the idioms or phrasal verbs was strictly controlled for the exact *form* of a metaphor, results were much less encouraging. Semantic elaboration leads to understanding and recall of the *sense* of a metaphor, but not necessarily to the exact way it is realised in English. And of course control of the form is a very important aspect of S/FL learning.

Main research methods

The research carried out into CL-inspired instructional methods has, in general, returned positive results. However, when the research methodology used in these experimental studies is scrutinised and compared with the research methods used in applied linguistics generally, the results are not so robust. In his overview of a number of quasi-experimental studies carried out between 1996 and 2010, Boers (2013, 2014) points to various problems with the nature of the research evidence provided. For example, of the 17 studies considered by Boers (2014), 6 lacked precise testing of what the learners already knew before being exposed to this type of instruction; in 3 the CL approach involved *more* learning activities rather than different ones (thus introducing a confounding variable).

Boers also draws attention to the questionable ecological validity of the comparison treatment, which makes the CL-inspired approach look much superior simply because the activities carried out with the control group in some studies were quite unlike those done with the experimental group. The control group treatment is often described as a 'traditional' approach, using word lists which the learners simply have to memorise with no teacher guidance on meanings – something which is difficult to imagine happening in a 'real' language classroom. Thus, when the learning gains for the control groups were measured between pre- and post-tests, in one case the control group did not gain at all, and in another it actually regressed. This suggests that the control group condition was unpedagogical, making the treatments impossible to compare in any meaningful way.

Evidently, the deficiencies pointed out by Boers in his overviews may go some way to explaining why CL-inspired research has had little impact on actual language teaching. More robust and rigorous research methods would need to be applied in order to ensure their validity. However, apart from these issues, a number of problems remain. One of these is that research of this kind is *forms-focused*, in other words, it suggests that metaphor can best be taught or learned through treatment in separate lessons or sessions devoted to metaphors as discrete points of language learning (as advocated by, for example, DeKeyser [1998] for teaching grammar). However, an alternative view would be to adopt a focus-on-form approach which would consist in 'drawing students' attention to linguistic elements as they arise in lessons whose overriding focus is on meaning or communication' (Long 1991: 45–46). This was the approach advocated by Low (1988) in an early publication on the topic of how to teach metaphor. Nevertheless, as Boers (2013: 217) puts it, 'there is still a dearth of research into the effects of distributed ("as the opportunity presents itself") CL-style interventions'.

An example of current research

A common problem experienced by S/FL learners in their use of idioms and conventional metaphors is knowing when they can be used appropriately. For example, although learners might understand that 'birdbrain' can be used to describe someone who is not very intelligent, unless they are given explicit guidance on how the phrase is used, they may use the word to describe themselves –'Sometimes I must admit that I am a little birdbrain'– or in direct address – 'Don't you be a birdbrain person' (BBC World Service), showing that they have not fully understood the usage restrictions on this kind of metaphor, which is derogative, and hence most likely to be used to describe a person not present (unless the intention is to be deliberately insulting and provoke some kind of confrontation). A study carried out by MacArthur and Boers (forthcoming) has sought to explore the ability of learners to judge when it is appropriate to use a conventional metaphor or idiom in context by asking them to choose between using a previously learnt metaphorical expression (for example, 'let the cat out of the bag') or its literal counterpart ('reveal a secret') in a given discourse context, comparing the effectiveness of a verbal explanation or a visual illustration in teaching this aspect of usage. The study, carried out with 32 students from a Spanish university and 18 from a Belgian one, specifically aimed to discover whether the use of an appropriate visual prompt could act as a short cut to understanding usage restrictions on idioms in discourse, in comparison with a verbal explanation. The learners were provided either with a verbal explanation of the meaning and connotations of twenty idioms or with a (static) visual illustration that was fully congruent with its motivation (for example, a photograph of a snake half hidden in grassland to illustrate 'be a snake in the grass'). Overall, it was found that verbal explanations were more effective than the visual prompts in guiding learners' appropriate choices of a metaphor rather than a literal expression in the discourse context provided. However, the poor post-test performance of all the students (whether they had been provided with a verbal or visual cue to the usage restrictions of the idioms) confirms how difficult this aspect of metaphor use is for learners. This draws attention to the need for further research in this area, for while advances have certainly been made in terms of how to better foster understanding and recall of the *meaning* of English metaphors, little has been done to tackle the question of how learners can be helped to come to grips with usage: the evaluative stance implied by many, if not most, idioms and conventional metaphors must be well understood if learners are to be able to interpret them accurately and produce them appropriately (i.e. 'idiomatically').

Future directions

CL-inspired research into how metaphor can be taught effectively has certainly contributed to understanding how verbal explanation, physical enactment or visuals may contribute to helping learners to understand and memorise such difficult aspects of English as phrasal verbs or idioms. However, as the overview of the research methods used makes clear, it is necessary for researchers interested in carrying out pedagogically oriented research of this kind to ensure that the weaknesses in design of many of the experiments carried out to date be avoided.

Furthermore, although this type of research tells us something about how well learners are able to recall the form and meaning of target language metaphors when they are asked to complete a gap-fill exercise, for example, it tells us nothing about whether they are also able to use them appropriately in context or interpret their use when used by an expert speaker of English. To date, there has been little metaphor-driven research examining what kind of instructional methods can foster understanding of their pragmatic functions, focusing instead on activities that consider solely the form and sense of metaphorical phrases, rather than their use in discourse.

In my view, it would also be worth devoting effort to bridging the gap between the quasi-experimental methods mostly used so far in this type of research and actual classroom practice. S/FL teachers are not experts in metaphor and may not be equipped to notice (identify) or discuss metaphorical language uses, as they might be for explaining elements of grammar, for example, so it is difficult to see how the results of the empirical research carried out to date can be transferred to classrooms. That is, if *learners* are to benefit from metaphor-focused pedagogical activities, the *mediators* in the process – the teachers themselves – must be provided with the skills and metalanguage necessary to discuss metaphor. Examining how this might be achieved could enrich current approaches to researching metaphor in S/FL learning (see MacArthur [2010] for fuller discussion). In terms of learners themselves, there is a need for longitudinal studies that focus on the development of metaphor use in relation to the language learning programmes and activities that students are exposed to (cf. Larsen-Freeman and Cameron 2008). As has already been noted, some learners develop the ability to use metaphor – sometimes extremely well – in their L2. However, the evidence for this competence is either somewhat anecdotal (e.g. MacArthur 2010) or based on examination results that only show what students who have actually passed internationally recognised exams such as the TESOL Cambridge ones can achieve (e.g. Littlemore et al. 2014). Likewise, we do not know if this competence is a result of attention to metaphor in the classes they have attended or to something else entirely, and whether the metaphorical competence displayed by these learners is replicated by the whole of the learner group or depends on variables such as the amount of natural language input learners may be exposed to outside the classroom or cognitive style variables, to mention just two possibilities.

Implications and recommendations for practice

As far as practising S/FL teachers are concerned, a crucial implication of the research carried out to date is the importance of learners' deep engagement with the metaphorical senses of the words and phrases they encounter and the ability to relate these to the core senses motivating their metaphorical uses. This is because the ability to establish meaningful relations between the metaphorical use of a word and its basic sense in the target language has been found in numerous studies to foster comprehension and recall. In this regard, it may be vital that learners gain *complete* knowledge of the core sense of words they will later encounter used metaphorically in different contexts. Establishing meaningful links between chains of meaning depends crucially on the learner's grasp of what that core sense of a given word is. This means that, particularly in early stages of language learning, caution should be exercised when using translation as a means of elucidating the meaning of highly polysemous words such as prepositions, because there may be little genuine correspondence between the core senses of such words in the L1 and the L2, and translation shortcuts may hinder learning of such important components of the English lexicon as phrasal verbs at later stages. As has been seen, visuals and enactment in the form of TPR activities may be very helpful in this regard and can indeed be used to revise and consolidate knowledge of the core senses of L2 words at different stages of the language learning process. Likewise, helping learners to correctly interpret an unfamiliar (metaphorical) use of a lexical item as it is encountered in a text can be done through providing a cue to the literal sense of the word or phrase through enactment, a visual illustration or verbal explanation.

On the other hand, it should be acknowledged that a great deal of possibly unnecessary encyclopaedic knowledge might have to be stored by learners if this 'core-sense first' approach is adopted to words that do not denote everyday concrete entities or actions. For example, lexical items such as 'watershed' (most commonly used to denote an event or time when important changes happen) or 'odds' (most usually employed to express how likely it is that something will happen) illustrate this issue. Metaphorical uses of words such as these are much more frequent than their basic ones in discourse and understanding the motivation for their metaphorical senses (originating in physical geography and gambling, respectively) might require lengthy explanations that will hardly merit the time this would take in class. In other words, establishing the core meaning of a word that motivates its metaphorical senses is not appropriate in all cases.

Conclusion

The overview of metaphor research in the field of S/FL learning offered in this chapter has inevitably omitted mention of some of the studies that have been carried out in this field in recent years. Yet, as can be seen even from those that have been mentioned, this is a productive area of applied metaphor research, which will – we hope – contribute to improving existing instructional methods and syllabus design in order to take account of this very important aspect of human communication.

Further reading

Boers, F. and Lindstromberg, S. (eds) (2008) *Cognitive Linguistic Approaches to Teaching Vocabulary and Phraseology*, Amsterdam, The Netherlands: Mouton de Gruyter.

Littlemore, J. and Juchem-Grundmann, C. (eds) (2010) 'Applied cognitive linguistics in second language learning and teaching', *AILA Review*, 23: 1–6.

Robinson, P. and Ellis, N. C. (eds) (2008) *Handbook of Cognitive Linguistics and Second Language Acquisition*, New York and London: Routledge.

References

Amaya-Chávez, E. (2010) 'The gaps to be filled: The (mis)treatment of the polysemous senses of *hand, cool* and *run* in EFL text books', in G. Low, Z. Todd, A. Deignan & L. Cameron (eds), *Researching and Applying Metaphor in the Real World*, Amsterdam and Philadelphia: John Benjamins (pp. 81–104).

Asher, J. J. (1969) 'The total physical response: Theory and practice', *Annals of the New York Academy of Sciences*, 379: 324–331.

BBC World Service (n.d.). 'Learning English. Video English 3', http://www.bbc.co.uk/worldservice/learningenglish/radio/specials/1559_videoenglish_3/ (accessed 30 July 2015).

Boers, F. (2000) 'Metaphor awareness and vocabulary retention', *Applied Linguistics*, 21: 553–571.

—— (2001) 'Remembering figurative idioms by hypothesising about their origin', *Prospect*, 16: 35–43.

—— (2013) 'Cognitive linguistic approaches to teaching vocabulary: Assessment and integration', *Language Teaching*, 46(2): 208–224.

—— (2014) '*Cognitive linguistics and language pedagogy: Finding ways forward*', plenary lecture delivered at the IX International SCOLA Conference, Universidad de Extremadura, Spain, 15–17 October.

Boers, F., Demecheleer, M. and Eyckmans, J. (2004) 'Etymological elaboration as a strategy for learning figurative idioms', in P. Bogaards and B. Laufer (eds), *Vocabulary in a Second Language: Selection, Acquisition and Testing*, Amsterdam, The Netherlands: John Benjamins (pp. 53–78).

Boers, F., Eyckmans, J. and Stengers, H. (2006) 'Motivating multiword units: Rationale, mnemonic benefits, and cognitive style variables', in S. H. Foster-Cohen, M. M. Krajnovic and J. M. Djigunovic (eds), *EUROSLA Yearbook*, vol. 6, Amsterdam, The Netherlands: John Benjamins (pp. 169–190).

Boers, F. and Lindstromberg, S. (2008) *Teaching Chunks of Language*, Cambridge, UK: Cambridge University Press.

Boers, F., Lindstromberg, S., Littlemore, J., Stengers, H. and Eyckmans, J. (2008) 'Variables in the mnemonic effectiveness of pictorial elucidation', in F. Boers and S. Lindstromberg (eds), *Cognitive Linguistic Approaches to Teaching Vocabulary and Phraseology*, Berlin, Germany: Mouton de Gruyter (pp. 189–116).

Boers, F., Piquer, A., Stengers, H. and Eyckmans, J. (2009) 'Does pictorial elucidation foster recollection of figurative idioms?', *Language Teaching Research*, 13(4): 367–388.

Cameron, L. and Deignan, A. (2006) 'The emergence of metaphor in discourse', *Applied Linguistics*, 24(1): 671–690.

Clandfield, L., Benn, R. B. and Jeffries, A. (2011) *Global Upper-Intermediate Student's Book*, Oxford, UK: Macmillan.

Condon, N. (2008). 'How cognitive linguistic motivations influence the learning of phrasal verbs', in F. Boers and S. Lindstromberg (eds), *Cognitive Linguistic Approaches to Teaching Vocabulary and Phraseology*, Berlin, Germany: Mouton de Gruyter (pp. 133–158).

Condon, N. and Kelly, P. (2002) 'Does cognitive linguistics have anything to offer English language learners in their efforts to master phrasal verbs?', *I.T.L. (Institut voor Togepaste Linguistik)*, 137–138: 205–231.

Deignan, A. (1995). *Collins COBUILD English Guides: Metaphor*, London: HarperCollins.

—— (2005). *Metaphor and Corpus Linguistics*. Amsterdam, The Netherlands: John Benjamins.

DeKeyser, R. (1998) 'Beyond focus on form: Cognitive perspectives on learning and practicing second language grammar', in C. Doughty and J. Williams (eds), *Focus on Form in Classroom Second Language Acquisition*, New York: Cambridge University Press (pp. 42–63).

Dirven, R. (1985) 'Metaphor as a basic means for extending the lexicon', in W. Paprotté and R. Dirven (eds), *The Ubiquity of Metaphor: Metaphor in Language and Thought*, Amsterdam, The Netherlands: John Benjamins (pp. 85–119).

Drew, P. and Holt, E. (1998) 'Figures of speech: Figurative expressions and the management of topic transition in conversation', *Language in Society*, 4: 495–522.

Gude, K. and Duckworth, M. (1998) *Proficiency Masterclass: Workbook*, Oxford, UK: Oxford University Press.

Kövecses, Z. and Szabó, P. (1996) 'Idioms: A view from cognitive semantics', *Applied linguistics*, 17(3): 326–355.

Kövecses, Z., Tóth, M. and Babarci, M. (1996–1998) *A Picture Dictionary of English Idioms* (four volumes), Budapest, Hungary: Eötvös Loránd University Press.

Larsen-Freeman, D. and Cameron, L. (2008) *Complex Systems and Applied Linguistics*, Oxford, UK: Oxford University Press.

Lazar, G. (2003) *Meanings and Metaphors: Activities to Practise Figurative Language*, Cambridge, UK: Cambridge University Press.

Lindstromberg, S. and Boers, F. (2005) 'From movement to metaphor with manner-of-movement verbs', *Applied Linguistics*, 26(2): 241–261.

Littlemore, J., Krennmayr, T., Turner, J. and Turner, S. (2014) 'Investigating figurative proficiency at different levels of second language writing', *Applied Linguistics*, 35(2): 117–144.

Littlemore, J. and Low, G.D. (2006) 'Metaphoric competence and communicative language ability', *Applied Linguistics*, 27(2): 268–294.

Long, M. H. (1991) 'Focus on form: A design feature in language teaching methodology', in K. de Bot, R. B. Ginsberg and C. Kramsch (eds), *Foreign Language Research in Cross-Cultural Perspective*, Amsterdam, The Netherlands: John Benjamins (pp. 39–52).

Low, G. D. (1988) 'On teaching metaphor', *Applied Linguistics*, 9(2): 125–147.

MacArthur, F. (2006) 'The effects of pictorial representations on the learning of imageable idioms in EFL', paper presented at the 6th International Conference on Researching and Applying Metaphor (RaAM6), Leeds, 10–12 April.

—— (2010) 'Metaphorical competence in EFL: Where are we and where should we be going? A view from the language classroom', *AILA Review*, 23: 155–173.

MacArthur, F. and Boers, F. (forthcoming) 'Using visuals to illustrate the source domains of idioms: Can they help learners appreciate usage restrictions too?', in C. Jurchem and S. Nieimier (eds), *KNOWING IS SEEING: Metaphor and Language Pedagogy*, Berlin, Germany: Mouton de Gruyter.

MacArthur, F. and Littlemore, J. (2008) 'A discovery approach using corpora in the foreign language classroom', in F. Boers and S. Lindstromberg (eds), *Cognitive Linguistic Approaches to Teaching Vocabulary and Phraseology,* Amsterdam, The Netherlands: Mouton de Gruyter (159–188).

MacArthur, F. and Piquer-Píriz, A. (2007) 'Staging the introduction of figurative extensions of familiar vocabulary items in EFL: Some preliminary considerations', *Ilha do Desterro*, 53: 123–134.

McCarthy, M. (2007) 'Assessing development of advanced proficiency through learner corpora. Position paper', http://calper.la.psu.edu/downloads/pdfs/CALPER_ALP_Corpus.pdf (accessed 30 July 2015).

McCarthy, M. and O'Dell, F. (2002) *English Idioms in Use*, Cambridge, UK: Cambridge University Press.

Macmillan English Dictionary for Advanced Learners (2007) 2nd edn, Oxford, UK: Macmillan Education.

Meara, P. (1996) 'The dimensions of lexical competence', in G. Brown, K. Malmkjaer and J. Williams (eds), *Performance and Competence in Second Language Acquisition*, Cambridge, UK: Cambridge University Press (pp. 35–53).

Nacey, S. (2014) 'Metaphoricity in English L2 learners' prepositions', paper presented at the 10th Conference of the Association for Researching and Applying Metaphor, Metaphor in Communication, Science and Education, University of Cagliari, Italy, June 20–23.

Nerlich, B., Todd, Z., Herman, V. and Clarke, D. D. (eds) (2003) *Polysemy: Flexible Patterns of Meaning in Mind and Language*, Berlin, Germany: Mouton de Gruyter.

Paivio, A. (1986) *Mental Representations: A Dual-Coding Approach*, New York: Oxford University Press.

Rudzka-Ostyn, B. (2003) *Word Power: Phrasal Verbs and Compounds: A Cognitive Approach*, Berlin and New York: Walter de Gruyter.

Szczepaniak, R. and Lew, R. (2011) 'The role of imagery in dictionaries of idioms', *Applied Linguistics*, 32(3): 323–347.

Tyler, A. and Evans, V. (2001) 'Reconsidering prepositional polysemy networks: The case of over', *Language*, 77(4): 724–765.

Verspoor, M. and Lowie, W. (2003) 'Making sense of polysemous words', *Language Learning*, 53(3): 547–586.

29
Using metaphor for peace-building, empathy, and reconciliation

Lynne Cameron

Introduction

In situations of conflict and violence, harmonious human relations are disrupted; the 'otherness' of people is foregrounded as shared humanity retreats into the background. The complexity of individual lives fades as people are lumped together into groups that threaten territory or integrity. Differences between groups are heightened and similarities are downplayed in this process of other-ing. The dehumanised Other becomes a faceless enemy, all empathy denied.

Repairing a society ruptured by conflict requires the renewed possibility of empathy as part of re-humanising and beginning to see others as neighbours again. Empathy is about one person connecting with another, reaching across gaps between Self and Other to understand how 'the Other' feels and thinks, lives their life, and sees their world (Cameron 2013: 3). In this chapter, I demonstrate how metaphor can contribute to dialogic processes of peace-building and reconciliation, and how metaphor became integral to a dynamic model that sees empathy as something we *do*, rather than something we 'have' (Cameron 2013).

Extract 1 gives an example of metaphor used in talk to show empathy. The speaker is a British Jewish woman participating in a focus group discussion on terrorism in the UK. Vehicle terms of verbal metaphors[1] are underlined.

Extract 1

1732 I think,
1733 the Palestinians actually,
1734 have a .. good cause to be angry.
1735 and,
1736 erm,
1737 they've been persecuted,
1738 for a <u>long long</u> time,
1739 .. and,
1740 nobody <u>took</u> any notice,
1741 .. of their .. <u>cry</u>.

```
1742    and,
1743    .. what happens,
1744    when you put somebody in a corner,
1745    they start to fight.
1746    and they're fighting dirty.
```
Focus group of women, London

The verbal metaphors in the last three lines create a small metaphorical story-scenario (Cameron, Low and Maslen 2010) as the speaker tries to explain Palestinian anger: 'fighting dirty' as a result of being 'put in a corner'. As the speaker imagines the perspective and emotions of Palestinians, and actions that might result, the metaphorical story-scenario helps her engage in an act of empathy. Metaphor supports an 'imaginative connecting' with a distant other that can underpin empathy.

Metaphor in dialogue may also function to encourage empathy in other participants. As often happens when people discuss difficult topics, metaphors open up an alternative space in dialogue; this shared dialogic space affords the possibility of coming together in a new perspective on the topic to speakers who may have come to the talk with disparate views. In this alternative space, metaphors can support speakers in 'imaginative connecting' with each other. I suggest that metaphor is important in creating affordances for imaginative connecting in peace-building, reconciliation, and empathy.

The term 'peace-building' is itself metaphorical, suggesting that peace is some kind of object or material that develops through a process of deliberate construction. As a metaphor, 'building' both hides and highlights (Lakoff and Johnson 1980). It highlights peace as open to change, and the intentional nature of processes designed to develop peace. Among possibilities backgrounded by the building metaphor is that of understanding peace as more organic, as something to be grown and nurtured. Later, I demonstrate how metaphors were deliberately chosen to highlight most relevant aspects of the concept of empathy, and to open up productive ways of thinking and understanding.

Situations of conflict and violence involve simplifications and intensification around who is 'Other' in relation to 'Self', and an amalgamating of individuals into groups to be defended or attacked. Conflict and violence often involve dehumanisation of the enemy, rendering people less than human, in a process that justifies changing or abandoning moral codes that would otherwise inhibit violence and killing. In Bakhtinian terms, the 'other-ing' that takes place in conflict can be described as creating an extreme alterity (Cameron 2013; Clark and Holquist 1986).

Peace-building and reconciliation act to close the gap of enhanced alterity constructed through violence and conflict. Empathy helps in reaching across alterity to understand how another person feels and thinks, lives their life, and sees their world.

> The work of empathy is precisely trying to imagine a view of the world that one does not share, and in fact may find it quite difficult to share.
>
> *Halpern and Weinstein 2004: 581*

Note that empathy is more than simply 'putting oneself in the other's shoes'. This kind of 'self-focused empathy' does only part of the work needed to imagine another's life. Each individual is the product of their unique embodied experience in the world, and thus it is never possible to fully understand how someone else feels. 'Other-focused empathy' requires a leap of imagination to try to enter the world of the other and feel how it is for *them* in *their* shoes.

The imaginative connecting of empathy happens in how people think about each other, the labels they assign to each other, the stories they tell about each other, the attitudes they hold about each other and that they perform in dialogue. All these ways of connecting may draw on metaphor. Cognitive and affective connecting may be accompanied by more concrete connecting. For example, to mark progress towards peace, former enemies may engage in symbolic handshakes or sit next to each other in signing ceremonies. Such symbolic physical acts work as metonymies for the re-humanising and re-connecting processes of peace-building and reconciliation.

The difficulty referred to by Halpern and Weinstein above is a result of the extremes of conflict. Finding empathy for someone who may have inflicted violence on you or your family can be difficult and uncomfortable; entering into their perspective may require dealing with moral reasoning quite different from, and alien to, your own. Somehow, the other's moral reasoning has to be understood, while not endorsed, so that the actions generated by that reasoning can be understood.

Through the dialogue and interaction of peace-building, re-humanising can take place. People need once again to be seen and known as individuals with shades of characters, rather than being all painted with the same brush. In extract 1, metaphor shifts the Other from the social group 'Palestinians' (1733) to an individual, if generic, 'somebody' (1744).

Dehumanising and re-humanising are not symmetric processes; dehumanising is the work of a moment and always possible even after reconciliation and peace agreements. As Halpern and Weinstein (2004) report, drawing on their studies in the former Yugoslavia and the work of Gobodo-Madikizela (2002) in South Africa, re-humanising happens much more slowly and requires hard work; and it can be undone very quickly. Because strong group mentalities rule during conflict, reconciliation often needs strong leadership, to support people in thinking beyond a 'them and us' perspective.

The Overview section that follows highlights key issues from three areas relating to conflict: metaphor in the dialogue of reconciliation, in framing conflict issues, and in labelling the Other. The Issues, Debates and Controversies section highlights issues around working with metaphors in discourse data, around choosing how to label these metaphors, and the importance of non-metaphorical language and physical action. The following section describes Current Research into metaphor and the development of empathy through talk, reporting the discovery of a 'negativity bias' in metaphor use. As a practical application, I describe how metaphor was employed in developing a practitioner-oriented model of empathy dynamics. The chapter closes with some indications for the use of metaphor in mediation and suggestions for further research.

Overview of metaphor and language around conflict

Levels of metaphor in reconciliation dialogue

Peace-building and reconciliation bring former enemies into dialogue, often mediated by a third party. For example, conflict transformation in northern Kenya was facilitated by a church-based peace-building team who brought together people from different communities in various activities that afforded opportunities for interaction (Cameron and Weatherbed 2014); in the reconciliation conversations used in extracts below, Jo Berry talks face-to-face with former IRA bomber, Patrick Magee, who had killed her father (Cameron 2007, 2011).

Such talk and interaction across the extreme alterity generated by conflict is a dynamic process in which people listen, make sense of what they hear, and speak. They may describe how they have been affected and try to explain their motivations for engaging in violence. As they talk, connections, memories, images and emotions are activated, and may be offered into the talk.

Metaphor can occur at various levels in these discourse dynamics. The most 'visible' is verbal metaphor, in which some kind of incongruous or alien term occurs in the flow of the discourse. In extract 2, verbal metaphor vehicles in the talk of Patrick Magee are underlined, following the method of Metaphor-Led Discourse Analysis (Cameron et al. 2009; Cameron and Maslen 2010).

Extract 2

I am the person that caused your <u>pain</u>.
Even though it was the Irish Republican Army,
it was the republican <u>movement</u>,
it was the republican <u>struggle</u> that caused your <u>pain</u>.
But I can't <u>walk away from</u> the fact that it was..
I was <u>directly</u> responsible to that.
I can't <u>hide behind</u> the sort of..
<u>the bigger picture</u>

Across a stretch of talk, connected metaphor vehicles may be used, allowing the analyst to propose a 'systematic metaphor'. It should be emphasised that a systematic metaphor is an analytic construct, derived from the specific data and context; it may not necessarily have any 'conceptual' validity (and different kind of evidence would be needed to claim so). Chapter 6 of this volume offers more detail on this idea. In this particular conversation, the speaker denies the possibility of metaphorically <u>walking away from</u> responsibility or <u>hiding behind</u> group membership, and instead accepts being <u>directly</u> responsible for the killing. These metaphors combine to produce a scenario in which the perpetrator must confront the human consequences of violence; perpetrator and victim come face-to-face and thus become visible to each other. Other metaphors in the conversations use terms connected to SEEING to talk about knowing and understanding the other person, leading to the systematic metaphor DEHUMANISING IS NOT SEEING THE OTHER AS A WHOLE HUMAN BEING – REHUMANISING IS SEEING THE OTHER AS A WHOLE HUMAN BEING. Other verbal metaphors include the following:

it's so easy to <u>lose sight</u> of the enemy's humanity

it's never <u>the whole picture</u> . . . sometimes you get <u>a glimpse</u>

until we do <u>see each other in our true light</u> . . . we're always going to be <u>dealing with</u> some <u>reduction</u> or <u>caricature</u>

Non-metaphorical language and physical action also contribute to the idea that reconciliation involves acknowledging the full complex humanity of the other. There is talk of 'coming face to face with' the other and there is actual sitting side by side on a sofa.

In the messiness of talk, the analyst hunts for patterns in how people use metaphor. Such patterns can be semantic, distributional, and functional. Systematic metaphors mark a semantic pattern, with multiple, semantically connected vehicles related to a topic across a discourse event. 'Metaphor clusters' show distributional patterns, of places in the talk with a particularly high density of metaphors (see Cameron and Stelma 2004 for methods of finding clusters; also Koller 2003). Functional patterns occur when metaphors show a tendency to be used for particular functions rather than others. For example, in primary classrooms, teachers were found to use metaphors particularly when controlling behaviour and at the beginnings of lessons when presenting an overview of content (Cameron 2003). A further pattern, identified empirically, is 'the negativity bias' and this is explained later in the chapter.

Metaphor in framing, evaluating and distancing the Other

Verbal metaphors work locally and across a conversation. Metaphor also works at the larger discourse level of the 'frame' (Bateson 1972; Goffman 1974; Ritchie and Cameron 2014). A *frame* can be thought of as a set of expectations that participants bring to an occasion (Tracy 1997), be that a social or political event, a conversation, or media content. Metaphorical framing occurs when an issue or idea is framed with metaphorical language, and recent research shows that framing influences reasoning around an issue or idea.

For example, Schön (1993) argued that framing in public policy debates often involves metaphors. He analysed debates over urban renewal policy in the 1950s, in which deteriorating neighbourhoods were framed either as 'blighted areas' or as 'natural communities'. The first frame implied the need to cure or remove the 'blight' as something decayed and diseased; the alternative frame suggested something organic that must be supported and strengthened. Similar contradictory frames are apparent in many other policy debates; contemporary examples include 'right to life' vs. 'right to choose' and 'estate tax' vs. 'death tax' (Coleman and Ritchie 2011). Schön argues that the way an issue is framed can powerfully affect not only how the issue is understood but also what sort of solutions can be considered.

More recent work by Thibodeau and Boroditsky (2011) has shown that metaphorical framing influences people's reasoning. They tested the capacity of familiar idiomatic metaphors to achieve framing effects through a series of experiments built around the metaphorical phrases 'crime is a wild beast' and 'crime is an infectious virus'. Participants were asked to read a short paragraph describing an increase in the frequency of crimes in a fictitious city that included one or the other of these metaphors along with crime rate statistics, which were identical in the two conditions. Participants were significantly more likely to search for more information and advocate solutions to the crime problem that were consistent with the metaphorical frame to which they had been exposed than solutions consistent with the frame to which they had not been exposed. Those exposed to the phrase 'crime is a wild beast' tended to advocate solutions consistent with capture and imprisonment; those exposed to the phrase 'crime is an infectious virus' tended to advocate solutions consistent with treating and applying preventative measures. Equally significant, when asked why they advocated these particular solutions, almost all participants referred to the statistics; in fact, participants in both conditions were given the same statistics and so these could not account for differences. These results support Gibbs's (2006) claim that metaphor vehicles, even when highly conventional, can influence responses, despite readers or hearers not being consciously aware of them.

Conflict and social group identity

If we add to this framing effect what we know about how conflict relates to group identity and categorisation, we can see how powerful metaphor can be in dehumanising processes. Work on inter-group relations and self-identity (Brown and Hewstone 2005; Pettigrew 2008;

Pettigrew and Tropp 2008; Staub 2001; Tajfel 1981) has shown how prejudice, conflict or tension heighten differences between groups, and how simplifying categorisations of the Other contribute to strengthening self-identity. The neuroscience of empathy also demonstrates bias towards in-group members (Lamm, Batson and Decety 2007; Xu, Zuo, Wang and Han 2009). Conversely, it has long been known that inter-group contact can lead to reduction in prejudice (Allport 1979), and more recently that contact contributes to allowing the Other multiple identities (Brown and Hewstone 2005) and to increased perception of outgroup complexity (Swart, Hewstone, Christ, and Voci 2010).

Haslam's (2006) review suggests that two kinds of dehumanising processes prevail in relation to social groups: 'animalistic dehumanization' that denies people uniquely human characteristics, instead seeing them as somehow animal-like; and 'mechanistic dehumanization' that denies people human nature, seeing them instead as some kind of objects or automata. Haslam does not mention metaphor explicitly, but his two-way categorisation of dehumanisation has a clear link to metaphor. The use of ANIMAL metaphors for dehumanised groups has been studied by, among others, Santa Ana (1999) and Musolff (2007) (see also Chapter 24 in this volume); activation of animal narratives and scenarios prompt emotions of revulsion and disgust, and carry dangerous entailments such as the need to metaphorically cleanse an area or prevent spread and contagion. An UP/DOWN orientation places the dehumanised Other lower than the Self, making them sub-human and open to humiliation and control (cf. the Great Chain of Being metaphor in Chapter 1). Mechanistic dehumanising metaphors represent 'the other as cold, robotic, passive, and lacking in depth ... implies indifference rather than disgust' (Haslam 2006: 153).

Metaphor thus seems to be deeply entangled with the dehumanising and distancing of the Other that accompanies conflict and violence, through the framing of conflict issues and by contributing to the simplification of social identities and groupings.

Critical issues, debates and controversies

Metaphor is an instrument that can be employed for good or bad. It can intensify hatred between groups through labelling, through dehumanising, and through suggesting narratives of threat and danger. Metaphor can also contribute to attempts to grow empathy, build peace, and support reconciliation. It can facilitate the imaginative connecting required for re-humanising, by offering new spaces in dialogue where participants can move beyond the simplifying assumptions of conflict and reconnect with the Other.

In contexts of peace-building and reconciliation, we are dealing with the micro-dynamics of discourse – metaphor is being used in the flow of talk and response 'in the moment'. I have long argued that the Discourse Dynamics approach and its associated method of Metaphor-Led Discourse Analysis are appropriate theoretically and practically for researching such events and processes (e.g. Cameron et al. 2009; Cameron and Maslen 2010).

> The 'discourse dynamic commitment' seeks to understand how actual people use language resources in the shifts and flow of dialogue and interaction.
>
> *Cameron, in press*

Conceptual metaphor theory (CMT), because of its commitment to generalise away from individual instances of use (Lakoff 1993), may be misleading if applied to particular instances of dialogue and interaction. In this section, I discuss two particular issues that arise.

The naming issue in metaphor research: risks in generalising upwards from discourse examples

While metaphor can contribute to dehumanising other social groups, a study of Arab collective identities in post 9/11 USA (Witteborn 2007) and another of college students (Moskalenko, McCauley and Rozin 2006) suggest that identity labels and groupings are themselves subject to change in circumstances of conflict. They are not necessarily fixed ways of seeing the other. Research into the metaphors that people use should investigate these dynamics, tracking their changing nature rather than assuming fixed beliefs or attitudes.

Likewise, although negative metaphors are undoubtedly used in the media about minority groups in US and UK society (Charteris-Black 2006; Santa Ana 1999; O'Brien 2003; Van Teeflen 1994), researchers have an ethical responsibility when they choose formulations for the metaphors not to exacerbate negative attitudes towards the Other. It can be risky to generalise too far away from the actual metaphor vehicles found in data. For example, Deignan (2005) re-analyses data from the study by Santa Ana (1999) and shows that the evaluative function of the metaphors is not as clear-cut as suggested in the original study.

Vehicle terms of verbal metaphors used in dialogue are often verbs and verbal nouns rather than concrete nouns, e.g. flooding, swarms, galloping rather than water, locusts or horses. There is now substantial corpus evidence that this grammatical difference matters. Different forms work differently as metaphors (e.g. Deignan 2005), and as Semino et al. (2004) remind us, talk of 'galloping cancer' does not necessarily imply that people imagine horses in their bodies (see also Chapter 7). Care must therefore be taken when generalising upwards to select labels for vehicle groupings and metaphors: a neutral label like UNSTOPPABLE MOVEMENT may more accurately reflect what people say than an excessively negative label such as PESTS.

Not using metaphors at all

We saw above how metaphorical and non-metaphorical language occur in combination, and the same phenomenon can be observed in extract 1, where being 'put in a corner' (metaphorically) gives rise to 'fighting' (non-metaphorical). This point is important – metaphor contributes to the construction and development of ideas in talk but, in my experience, speakers are seldom totally reliant on metaphor. In fact, people can think-and-talk without using metaphors at all. Examining stretches of metaphor-free reconciliation talk revealed an interesting pattern, in which 'metaphor absences' seem to work as a challenge to the other person. Metaphor creates a certain distance from emotional pain that may make it easier to talk about. When metaphor is absent, highly painful events are narrated in a way that refuses mitigation. Such 'bald narratives', direct talk without metaphor, seem to have a role in pushing participants in reconciliation to come to terms with responsibility and reality (Cameron 2011).

Current research: metaphor and empathy in reconciliation conversations

In my study of metaphor in conversations between Jo Berry and Patrick Magee (Cameron 2007, 2011),[2] I examine how victim and perpetrator use, negotiate and resist metaphors, and how reconciliation is marked by convergence over time towards shared metaphors.

The Other, who had been distanced and dehumanised through conflict, violence and loss, comes to be known through and with metaphor in the discourse activity of the conversations. The study found that metaphor contributes to the reconciliation process and supports the development of empathy in the following ways:

- Metaphor motivates and guides participation in reconciliation.
- Metaphor enables discourse encounters, as speakers adopt, adapt or challenge each other's metaphors.
- Metaphor allows access to the emotions of the Other, while being affectively protective.

The study made use of the construct of 'empathy' to describe changes in attitudes to the Other arising out of the process of reconciliation, and introduced the notion of verbal and nonverbal 'gestures of empathy' to describe stretches of interaction that actively contribute to participants connecting across the gap of alterity generated by violence and conflict (Cameron 2011). Three types of gestures of empathy were found:

(1) *Allowing connection.* These gestures of empathy offer the Other access to the speaker's thinking and feelings about the past, the present and the future. They include:

- offering the Other an explanation of feelings about events and situations;
- attempting to explain events and emotions to the Other;
- being willing to open oneself up to relive memories;
- being willing to try to explain reasons for choices and behaviours;
- opening oneself to critical reflection on past choices and actions, and sharing that with the Other.

(2) *Entering into the other's perspective.* These gestures of empathy attempt to understand the world view of the other through what is known about their experiences and emotions. They include:

- anticipating the effect of one's words on the Other, and mitigating them: 'there's that cruel word . . . ';
- acknowledging the Other's feelings, through choice of word or phrase: 'you who've lost your father . . . ';
- offering the Other a summary of what has been heard: 'I suppose that's because you carried your grief in isolation . . . ';
- adding to the Other's explanation or argument with one's own supporting contribution;
- speaking as if from the Other's perspective to contextualise an utterance such as a request for further information: 'this may be difficult for you but could you tell me . . . '.

(3) *Shifting the perceived relation with the Other.* These gestures of empathy mark a shift in the relations between self and other. They include:

- repositioning the Other: 'your father . . . was a legitimate target (for the IRA). Meeting you though, I'm reminded of the fact that he was also . . . your father . . . ';
- repositioning the Self, e.g. from being a victim to taking some responsibility through social group affiliation: 'even though I'm the victim, I can also see I'm part of the people that oppressed you';
- discovering or acknowledging what is shared by both Self and Other, such as grief at lost comrades or being part of a family: 'the pain on every side'.

A possible negativity bias in metaphor use

Across multiple studies of discourse in contexts of violence and conflict, I have found an intriguing pattern that I call 'the negativity bias' of metaphor. I have found two types of discourse 'negativity' at work: (1) in relation to affect, i.e. making people feel physically or emotionally uncomfortable in some way, and (2) grammatically, i.e. the negative particle 'not' used with the verb.

The negativity bias appears as a functional pattern at the level of metaphor clusters, in which people use metaphor to express what they fear, dislike, or do not want in 'negative alternative hypothetical' (n-a-h) scenarios. Extract 3 shows an example of an n-a-h scenario as Pat Magee explains how his motivation for participating in IRA violence was political rather than personal 'hatred':

Extract 3

Pat: [it's] not enough to sustain,
during a struggle like this.
Jo: hmh
Pat: I don't think so.
you –
you couldn't keep up with it,
if it was just driven by that sort of –
(1.0) hatred that gnaws away at you.
Jo: [hmh]
Pat: [you would] soon be a casualty of it.

The metaphors cluster in the short period of talk as Pat describes and highlights what it would be like to be motivated by hatred, i.e. the opposite of his actual situation. It is as if he first sets out his 'reality', and then presents the contrasting scenario in order to justify his choice to the other dialogue participant. We can note the affective strength of the 'alternative' metaphors that make up this contrasting scenario and their negative evaluative force. Several are extreme case formulations: driven; gnaws away at; casualty. The hypothetical nature of this contrasting scenario is signalled by conditional tenses ('would', 'could'), by the conditional clause marker 'if', and by the negative forms 'it's not enough' and 'you couldn't keep up with it' that indicate the contrasting scenario did *not* happen.

Extract 4 shows another, very short, n-a-h scenario in which Jo Berry speaks of feeling connected to other victims through her grief at her father's death, and then contrasts this with metaphors of *SEPARATION*.

Extract 4

Jo: and it felt like my heart was broken,
through the conflict.
(1.0) and,
the suffering was .. my suffering.
I couldn't separate it.
I couldn't be detached anymore.

The emphatic metaphors in the last two lines create and deny an alternative, contrasting scenario in which Jo's suffering would be individual, unconnected with others'.

In summary, negative alternative hypothetical (n-a-h) scenarios in talk are characterised by the following features:

- They relate to, and elaborate, a position taken by one of the speakers by focusing on the alternative or opposite; a contrasting scenario or narrative is evoked.
- The hypothetical nature of this contrasting scenario is made clear through the use of conditional tenses and clauses, often with negative polarity, signalled by words such as *if, couldn't* . . .
- Strong verbal metaphors combine to exaggerate the alternative, hypothetical scenario, emphasising its high negative affect.
- The n-a-h scenario thus serves to demonstrate and support the speaker's motivations and choices to the listener.

Similar effects can be created by single metaphors, as well as by clusters of metaphors. For example, when Jo asks:

can I <u>open</u> my heart enough to hear Pat's story?

she implies and rejects the negative alternative hypothetical scenario of a '<u>closed</u> heart', unable to do empathy.

Metaphors used in this way help people to express and highlight what they reject, fear, or do not want.

Data collected in the Living with Uncertainty project[3] (LwU), from situations of violence and conflict in the UK, Brazil, the USA and Kenya, also shows a clear negativity bias around many of the verbal metaphors. A negativity bias also appears in other data I have worked with, from more peaceful situations, so that, although the bias may be foregrounded in talk about negative topics such as crime and violence, it seems to be more widespread. The very vivid metaphors that feature when the negativity bias is active would seem to have a role in increasing the possibility of empathic understanding through talk. They attract a listener's attention, while demonstrating and supporting the speaker's explanation of motivations and choices.

Using metaphor in developing a practitioner-oriented model of empathy

An aim of the Living with Uncertainty project (LwU), and its follow-up project Empathy Dynamics in Conflict Transformation,[4] was the development of a dynamic model of empathy in dialogue and interaction. To develop a model that would be usable by practitioners, the researchers worked with a conflict transformation NGO, deriving the model from project data collected together and choosing terminology in collaborative workshops. Metaphor was employed deliberately and reflectively in developing the model of empathy, exploiting three features that have emerged from my analyses of metaphor in use:

- Metaphor has a negativity bias.
- Making meaning from multiple, mixed, partial, overlapping metaphors is generally unproblematic (Cameron, in press).
- Metaphors have a particular facility for engaging emotional memory Cameron and Seu (2012).

Selecting the most appropriate metaphors to include in a model is a recursive process, moving between published literature, empirical findings, and systematic verbal metaphors across the data. A commitment to the complex dynamics of discourse systems (Larsen-Freeman and Cameron 2008) required generalised metaphors to be in the grammatical form of verbs.

The reflections of Jo Berry and Patrick Magee on their processes and their dialogic 'journeys' towards understanding each other offered metaphors for the model. In extract 5, Pat reflects on Jo's metaphor for reconciliation as building bridges,[5] and turns it around to apply to the political situation in Ireland that, he felt, motivated IRA violence. He produces a chain of three verbal metaphors as antonyms of building bridges: creating distances, barriers, exclusions.

Extract 5

```
1633   Pat   there's an <X adverse / inverse X>,
1634         to that er,
1635         ... (1.0) you know,
1636         er,
1637         ... (2.0) figure of speech
1638         you know,
1639         bridges.
1640         ... bridges can be built.
1641         ... and that is if you,
1642         .. actively –
1643         er,
1644         .. create,
1645         er,
1646         .. distances.
1647         ... barriers.
1648         ... or what are they?
1649         they are exclusions
1650         ... (1.0) and er,
1651         .. a thing I believe absolutely fundamentally,
1652         is that er,
1653         ... (1.0) if you exclude anybody's voice,
1654         ... (1.0) you know,
1655         ... you're se- –
1656         you're sowing the seed for later violence.
```

For the positive process of coming to know the Other in the model, CONNECTING was selected as the key systematic metaphor (Cameron 2007, 2011). Building bridges was one type of CONNECTING used in the data, alongside others such as shared, closeness. EMPATHY AS CONNECTING was also implied through metaphorical ways of describing lack of empathy – detached, shut out, locked out – and by metaphorical descriptions of actions that create empathy, such as breaking down barriers. While the individual verbal metaphors were too specific to use in a model, the label given to their systematic metaphor worked well as part of the model: EMPATHY IN DIALOGUE IS CONNECTING.

The CONNECTING metaphor was developed in line with empirical findings from the full set of LwU studies, and with published studies in other disciplines, to provide a further layer to the model that describes <u>how</u> people do empathy in talk. Close discourse analysis of how Jo and Pat managed their CONNECTING produced this descriptive part of the model, including the three types of gestures of empathy described above, two of which were given labels linked to CONNECTING: '<u>Allowing</u> connection' and '<u>Entering into</u> the Other's world'.

Antonyms or contrasts of CONNECTING were needed to describe how empathy is negotiated and resisted (Cameron 2012). I added the theoretical construct of 'dyspathy' to describe processes that work to prevent empathy (Cameron 2012). Three metaphorically labelled types of dyspathy emerged as ways of resisting empathy with labels suggested by data such as extract 5: DISTANCING, BLOCKING and LUMPING (Cameron et al. 2013). DISTANCING describes people avoiding empathy by positioning the Other as inaccessible through being far away and thus beyond consideration; BLOCKING describes people avoiding empathy by putting in place some kind of affective barrier, such as stereotyping or prejudice, that removes the need to think of others as individual and complex human beings. The third metaphorical antonym for CONNECTING that Pat produces in extract 5, exclusions, was covered by BLOCKING, along with other verbal metaphors such as '<u>lock</u> me <u>in</u> there' and '<u>closed down</u>'. LUMPING was chosen as a label for the mechanism by which empathy is avoided when other people are 'lumped together' in a group or mass, rather than being seen as individuals. These metaphors of CONNECTING, DISTANCING, BLOCKING and LUMPING form the core of the new discourse dynamics model of empathy–dyspathy (Figure 29.1). The development process ensured that the three together have ecological and construct validity for describing, at a carefully constructed superordinate level, the human dialogic, psychological and neurological processes of empathy.

An online manual was collaboratively produced to introduce the model of empathy dynamics and is now being used in Kenya and Nepal (Cameron and Weatherbed 2014).

Implications and recommendations for practice in reconciliation and conflict transformation

By listening for how conflicted parties (individuals and groups) respond to each other's metaphors, mediators can gain insights into the processes of reconciliation and conflict transformation. Indicators of potential and progress towards understanding the Other include:

- the same or similar metaphor adopted by both parties to reconciliation or conflict transformation;
- a metaphor not only adopted, but also extended, adjusted or challenged – this will offer clues to differences in perceptions;
- appropriation, when one party 'allows' another to use a particularly emotive metaphor to refer to their own feelings or experiences.

The potential of extending and shifting metaphors is available for mediators to use in intervening in talk:

- to explore ideas in more detail by extending and elaborating a metaphorical scenario;
- to encourage the sharing of metaphors;
- to explicitly encourage the challenging of metaphors.

When speakers connect metaphors to the real world e.g. physical actions like walking connected to JOURNEY metaphors, they may indicate powerful images and actions that mediators

empathy

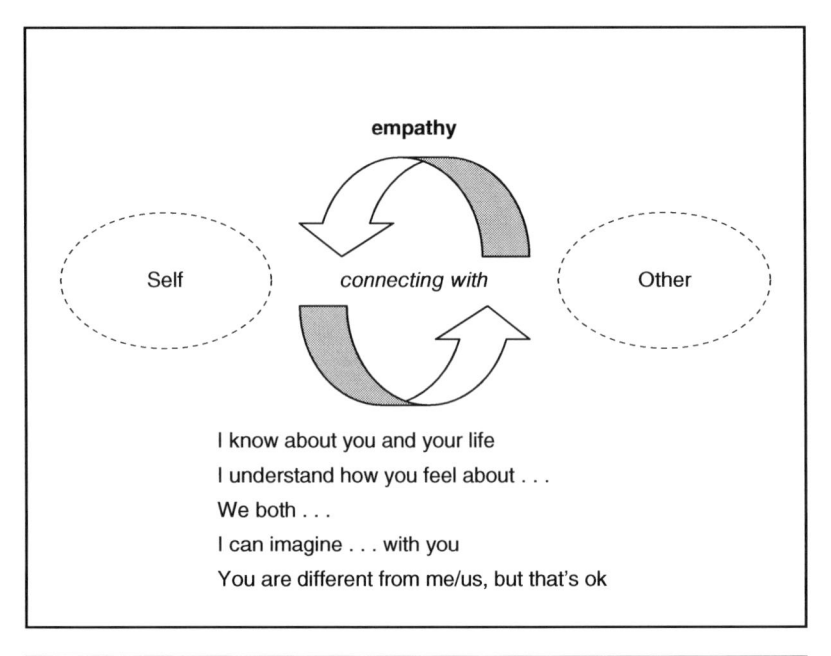

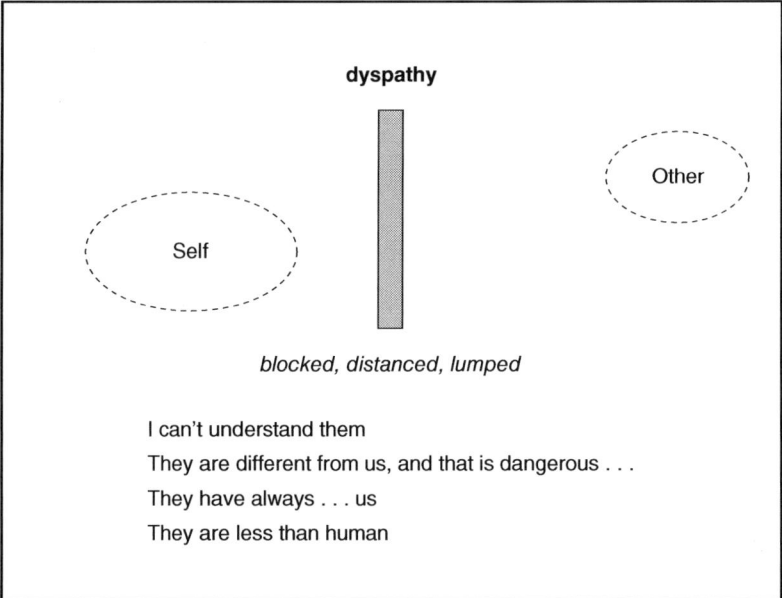

Self — connecting with — Other

I know about you and your life
I understand how you feel about . . .
We both . . .
I can imagine . . . with you
You are different from me/us, but that's ok

dyspathy

Self   Other

blocked, distanced, lumped

I can't understand them
They are different from us, and that is dangerous . . .
They have always . . . us
They are less than human

Figure 29.1 Discourse dynamics model of empathy–dyspathy.

can explore and that may prompt symbolic actions: e.g. a shared walk might carry meaning far beyond its simple physical activity.

Parties to reconciliation or peace-building may come with competing (metaphorical) frames for stories, topics and memories, and are likely to experience encounters with contradictory frames (Ritchie and Cameron 2014). Frame conflict is often only implicit, and parties may remain unaware that they are framing differently. In other instances, parties may deliberately choose language to frame issues in a way favourable to their own position. In more complex cases, parties may be aware and intentional about some aspects of the framing but quite unaware of other aspects. Bringing implicit frames to the surface and making them explicit may be of benefit, both for understanding what went wrong in past interchanges and for improving the outcome of future dialogue.

Future directions

Further investigation into the negativity bias of metaphor in dialogue

The 'negativity bias of metaphor' merits further investigation, using corpus techniques and a range of data types, particularly from positive contexts. If the negativity bias can be confirmed, it would upturn accepted views of how we 'live by' metaphors, to use a famous phrase (Lakoff and Johnson 1980). If metaphor does indeed serve to highlight the negative, painful, angry side of human life, often in order to move us away from it, then metaphor is not a neutral indicator of how we think. Instead, metaphor would work as an indicator of what we reject, fear, or dislike. Metaphors do not simply construct concepts but point towards meaning and affect via their opposites or negatives. Rather than 'living by' metaphors, i.e. constructing our world through metaphorical concepts, it may be that we use metaphors to make the quiet shade we wish to live in.

More holistic research

This chapter has shown how various levels of metaphor can support the imaginative connecting with other people that is involved in doing empathy, peace-building and reconciliation. Metaphor can also contribute to conflict and dehumanisation. Moreover, metaphorical language is often integrated with non-metaphorical language and with physical, sometimes symbolic, actions in the world. And people sometimes do not use metaphor at all. I close with a call for more holistic research and methods that help understand more fully how metaphor operates within the vital human processes of moving away from conflict towards peace-building and reconciliation.

Notes

1 'Verbal metaphor' is the term used in the discourse dynamics approach (Cameron et al. 2009) to refer to stretches of talk or written text where words or phrases are used metaphorically; no assumption of underlying conceptual metaphorising is made. It is similar to, but not the same as 'linguistic metaphor', which is held to be an instantiation of conceptual metaphor.
2 Research funded by the UK Arts and Humanities Research Board (now Council).
3 The Living with Uncertainty project (LwU) was funded by the UK Economic and Social Research Council under its Global Uncertainties programme. Details and publications can be found on the project website: http://www.open.ac.uk/researchprojects/livingwithuncertainty/.
4 This work was funded by the UK Economic and Social Research Council as a Knowledge Exchange project. Details and publications can be found on the project website: http://www.open.ac.uk/edict.
5 Pat's reference to Jo's 'figure of speech' is one of very few instances where the discourse provides explicit evidence of metaphoricity.

Further reading

Cameron L. (2007) 'Patterns of metaphor use in reconciliation talk', *Discourse and Society*, 18: 197–222.

Cameron, L. and Seu, I. B. (2012) 'Landscapes of empathic understanding: Spatial metaphors and metonymies in responses to distant suffering', *Text & Talk*, 32(3): 285–305.

Schön, D. A. (1993) 'Generative metaphor: A perspective on problem-setting in social policy', in A. Orton (ed.) *Metaphor and Thought*, Cambridge, UK: Cambridge University Press.

See also

Living with Uncertainty project: http://www.open.ac.uk/researchprojects/livingwithuncertainty/.
Empathy Dynamics in Conflict Transformation project: http://www.open.ac.uk/edict.

References

Allport, G. W. (1979) *The Nature of Prejudice*, New York: Basic Books.

Bateson, G. (1972) *Steps to an Ecology of Mind*, New York: Ballantine.

Brown, R. and Hewstone, M. (2005) 'An integrative theory of intergroup contact', *Advances in Experimental Social Psychology*, 37: 255–343.

Cameron, L. (2003) *Metaphor in Educational Discourse*, London: Continuum.

—— (2007) 'Patterns of metaphor use in reconciliation talk', *Discourse and Society*, 18: 197–222.

—— (2011) *Metaphor and Reconciliation*, New York: Routledge.

—— (2012) 'Dyspathy: The dynamic complement of empathy', Living with Uncertainty Working Paper 5. Online. Available at: http://www.open.ac.uk/researchprojects/livingwithuncertainty/node/4 (accessed 7 August 2015).

—— (2013) 'A dynamic model of empathy and dyspathy', Living with Uncertainty Working Paper 6. Online. Available at: http://www.open.ac.uk/researchprojects/livingwithuncertainty/node/4 (accessed 7 August 2015).

—— (in press) 'Mixed metaphors from a discourse dynamics perspective: A non-issue?', in R.W. Gibbs, Jr. (ed.) *Mixing Metaphor*, Cambridge, UK: Cambridge University Press.

Cameron, L., Low, G. and Maslen, R. (2010) 'Finding systematicity in metaphor use', in L. Cameron and R. Maslen (eds) *Metaphor Analysis: Research Practice in Applied Linguistics, Social Sciences, and the Humanities*, pp. 116–146, London: Equinox.

Cameron, L. and Maslen, R. (eds) (2010) *Metaphor Analysis: Research Practice in Applied Linguistics, Social Sciences, and the Humanities*, London: Equinox.

Cameron, L., Maslen, R. and Todd, Z. (2013) 'Dialogic construction of Self and Other in response to terrorism', *Journal of Peace and Conflict*, 19(1): 3–22.

Cameron, L., Maslen, R., Todd, Z., Maule, J., Stratton, P. and Stanley, N. (2009) 'The discourse dynamics approach to metaphor and metaphor-led discourse analysis', *Metaphor & Symbol*, 24(2): 63–89.

Cameron, L. and Stelma, J. (2004) 'Metaphor clusters in discourse', *Journal of Applied Linguistics*, 1(2): 107–136.

Cameron, L. and Seu, I. B. (2012) 'Landscapes of empathic understanding: Spatial metaphors and metonymies in responses to distant suffering', *Text & Talk*, 32(3): 285–305.

Cameron, L. and Weatherbed, S. (2014) *The Empathy Manual*. e-book, available from iBooks Store. Online. Available at: http://www.open.ac.uk/edict (accessed 7 August 2015).

Charteris-Black, J. (2006) 'Britain as a container: Immigration metaphors in the 2005 election campaign', *Discourse & Society*, 17(5): 563–581.

Clark, K. and Holquist, M. (1986) *Mikhail Bakhtin*, Cambridge, MA: Harvard University Press.

Coleman, C.-L. and Ritchie, L. D. (2011) 'Examining metaphors in bio-political discourse', *Lodz Papers in Pragmatics*, 7: 29–59.

Deignan, A. (2005) *Metaphor and Corpus Linguistics*, Amsterdam, The Netherlands: John Benjamins.
Gibbs, R. W., Jr. (2006) 'Metaphor interpretation as embodied simulation', *Mind and Language*, 21: 434–458.
Gobodo-Madikizela, P. (2002) 'Remorse, forgiveness and re-humanization: Stories from South Africa', *Journal of Humanistic Psychology*, 42(1): 7–32.
Goffman, E. (1974) *Frame Analysis*, New York: Harper & Row.
Halpern, J. and Weinstein H. M. (2004) 'Rehumanizing the Other: Empathy and reconciliation', *Human Rights Quarterly*, 26: 561–583.
Haslam, N. (2006) 'Dehumanization: An integrative review', *Personality and Social Psychology Review*, 10: 252–264.
Koller, V. (2003) 'Metaphor clusters, metaphor chains: Analyzing the multifunctionality of metaphor in text', *Metaphorik.de*, 5: 115–134. Online. Available at: http://www.metaphorik.de/sites/www.metaphorik.de/files/journal-pdf/05_2003_koller.pdf (accessed 7 August 2015).
Lakoff, G. (1993) 'The contemporary theory of metaphor', in A. Ortony (ed.) *Metaphor and Thought*, New York: Cambridge University Press.
Lakoff, G. and Johnson, M. (1980) *Metaphors We Live By*, Chicago, IL: University of Chicago Press.
Lamm, C., Batson, C. D. and Decety, J. (2007) 'The neural substrate of human empathy: Effects of perspectives-taking and cognitive appraisal', *Journal of Cognitive Neuroscience*, 19: 42–58.
Larsen-Freeman, D. and Cameron, L. (2008) *Complexity Theory and Applied Linguistics*, Oxford, UK: Oxford University Press.
Moskalenko, S., McCauley, C. and Rozin, P. (2006) 'Group identification under conditions of threat: College students' attachment to country, family, ethnicity, religion, and university before and after September 11, 2001', *Political Psychology*, 27: 77–97.
Musolff A. (2007) 'What role do metaphors play in racial prejudice? The function of antisemitic imagery in Hitler's *Mein Kampf*', *Patterns of Prejudice*, 41: 21–43.
O'Brien, G. V. (2003) 'Indigestible food, conquering hordes, and waste materials: Metaphors of immigrants and the early immigration restriction debate in the United States', *Metaphor and Symbol*, 18(1): 33–47.
Pettigrew, T. F. (2008) 'Future directions for intergroup contact theory and research', *International Journal of Intercultural Relations*, 32: 187–199.
Pettigrew, T. F. and Tropp, L. R. (2006) 'A meta-analytic test of intergroup contact theory', *Journal of Personality and Social Psychology*, 90: 751–783.
Ritchie, L. D. and Cameron, L. (2014) 'Open hearts or smoke and mirrors: Metaphorical framing and frame conflicts in a public meeting', *Metaphor & Symbol*, 29: 204–223.
Santa Ana, O. (1999) '"Like an animal I was treated": Anti-immigrant metaphor in US public discourse', *Discourse and Society*, 10: 191–224.
Schön, D. A. (1993) 'Generative metaphor: A perspective on problem-setting in social policy', in A. Orton (ed.) *Metaphor and Thought*, Cambridge, UK: Cambridge University Press.
Semino, E., Heywood, J. and Short, M. (2004) 'Methodological problems in the analysis of a corpus of conversations about cancer', *Journal of Pragmatics*, 36: 1271–1294.
Staub, E. (2001) 'Individual and group identities in genocide and mass killing', in R. Ashmore, L. Jussim and D. Wilder (eds) *Social Identity, Intergroup Conflict, and Conflict Reduction*, New York: Oxford University Press.
Swart, H., Hewstone, M., Christ, O. and Voci, A. (2010) 'The impact of crossgroup friendships in South Africa: Affective mediators and multigroup comparisons', *Journal of Social Issues*, 66: 309–333.
Tajfel, H. (1981) *Human Groups and Social Categories*, Cambridge, UK: Cambridge University Press.
Thibodeau, P. H. and Boroditsky, L. (2011, Feb.) 'Metaphors we think with: The role of metaphor in reasoning', *PLoS ONE*, 6(2), e16782.
Tracy, K. (1997) 'Interactional trouble in emergency service requests: A problem of frames', *Research on Language and Social Interaction*, 30: 315–343.

Van Teeflen, T. (1994) 'Racism and metaphor: The Palestinian–Israeli conflict in popular literature', *Discourse & Society*, 5(3): 381–405.

Witteborn, S. (2007) 'The situated expression of Arab collective identities in the United States', *Journal of Communication*, 57: 556–575.

Xu, X., Zuo, X., Wang, X. and Han, S. (2009) 'Do you feel my pain? Racial group membership modulates empathic neural responses', *Journal of Neuroscience*, 29: 8525–8529.

30
Using metaphor to influence public perceptions and policy
How metaphors can save the world

Joseph Grady

Introduction

While the subtitle of this chapter is somewhat facetious, it is based on a serious idea: that metaphor may play an indispensable role in helping people and societies deal with critical challenges. Far from being merely a rhetorical or literary device, metaphor may constitute one of our species' fundamental survival tools.

In this chapter I will explore ways in which metaphor plays a role in public discussions of important issues, as well as approaches to identifying metaphors that can help make these discussions more constructive.

Some of the insights and much of the material for discussion – including examples of metaphors that have been empirically shown to be more or less effective for helping people talk and reason about particular topics – arise from collaborative work with anthropologist Axel Aubrun, co-founder of Cultural Logic and the Topos Partnership, communications research and strategy firms working with nonprofit organizations, primarily at the national level in the US.

The work of the firms focuses on helping these advocacy groups to engage public support on a wide range of issues. Topics we have worked on include everything from global warming to nuclear weapons, health equity, labour unions, (illegal) immigration, the value of the arts, early child development and the role of government in society.

Typical projects focus on central research questions such as the following:

- How does 'the public' (i.e. a diverse sample of non-experts) currently think about the issue?
- How do non-experts currently respond to messages about the topic, such as statements from advocates?
- What are the cognitive and cultural models that shape people's thinking on the issue?
- What are the messages that can help change their perspectives, engage their interest and support?
- And frequently: What metaphor(s) help with the goal above?

For reasons discussed in the remainder of the chapter, metaphors often play an important role both in current thinking about a given issue, and in discourse approaches that show empirical signs of helping non-experts take a more engaged and constructive stance.

The remainder of the chapter will first establish the widespread nature of metaphor in discourse about public-interest issues, and then explore the potential benefits of such metaphors. It will introduce several specific examples from our issue-related work, and reflect on some lessons learned regarding the identification of metaphors that can be beneficial to communication.

Overview: metaphor in talking and thinking about public-interest issues

A glance at virtually any media related to public-interest topics quickly yields examples of important subjects being discussed in metaphorical ways. Consider the following references to national security (emphasis added in each case):

> [Egyptians must] abide by their treaty with Israel. That is a *red line* for us, because not only is Israel's security at stake, but our security is at stake if that *unravels*.
>
> *President Barack Obama,*
> *in debate with candidate Mitt Romney, 22 October 2012*

> States do not acquire nuclear arsenals in order to annihilate their enemies. On the other hand, states are desperate to create a strong *nuclear shield* in order to avert wars by deterring 'would-be' aggressors once and for all.
>
> *Kamran Shahid, 16 June 2010,*
> Express Tribune, *Pakistan*

In the first case, a limit on acceptable action is metaphorically characterized as a (red) demarcation in physical space – consistent with broader patterns of conceptualization in which actions are seen as physical motion, different possible actions are motion in different directions, categories are conceived as bounded physical areas and so forth. (See discussions of related 'event-structure' metaphors in Lakoff 1993.) President Obama then goes on to characterize a treaty between Egypt and Israel as a physical object that can 'unravel' – consistent with a common pattern in which complex abstract arrangements and structures are conceived of as woven material. (See Grady 1997 for discussion of ways in which complex abstract entities are conceived as diverse types of structured physical objects.)

In the next example, the writer uses the common metaphor of anything that protects us from harm, physical or otherwise, as a 'shield' or other physical protection. (The common expression 'nuclear shield' is, of course, an instance of this much broader pattern.)

Are such metaphors specifically characteristic of expert discourse or political rhetoric? An abundance of evidence suggests that they are not discourse specific, but are instead typical of thought and language in general. The following excerpt is drawn from 2009 interview conducted by Cultural Logic with an American non-expert on the topic of US national security (emphasis added):

> You can only *sit on top of the heap* so long before somebody comes and *pushes you down* and I think the longer you *sit*, the *harder the push is* – as the resentment builds and builds and builds.

The highlighted expressions are immediately recognizable as instances of a common metaphorical pattern in which dominance is understood as location on top of a hill, and struggles for dominance are physical struggles for that spatial position. This pattern reflects the much broader pattern, noted in *Metaphors We Live By* (Lakoff and Johnson 1980; Chapter 1), in which social dominance is a higher position. (This pattern is one of many that are so basic as to be observed in languages and cultures around the world and from different periods in history. See Grady 1999.)

The topic of national security is anything but an isolated case. Rather, the common use of metaphors to speak and write about national security is repeated across issue after issue. We could quickly collect similar examples from both elite and non-expert sources, either oral or written, on topics such as environmental and economic issues, and others from the list mentioned above.

Furthermore, there is significant evidence that such metaphors *matter*, in the sense that they may reflect or even cause particular ways of thinking about important topics, where different stances, actions and choices may result.

In an influential 1979 article (reprinted as Schön 1993), philosopher Donald Schön explored what he considered the critical role of metaphorical language and thought in the arena of social policy.

> When we examine the problem-setting stories told by the analysts and practitioners of social policy, it becomes apparent that the framing of problems often depends upon metaphors underlying the stories which generate problem setting and set the directions of problem solving.
>
> *Schön 1993: 138*

In other words, the very definitions of social problems ('problem-setting') are often based on metaphorical conceptualizations of situations. In the same passage, Schön goes on to offer an example: The various social services offered by a town or state may be viewed as 'fragmented' from one metaphorical point of view (i.e. 'something like a vase that was once whole and now is broken'), even though these same services 'might be seen, alternatively, as autonomous'. 'Under the spell of the metaphor,' he observes, 'it appears obvious that fragmentation is bad and coordination, good'. As this example illustrates, the ultimate significance of the metaphors used to reason about a given issue is that they have the power to guide thinkers to particular conclusions about appropriate *action*.

A second example offered by Schön concerns the issue of housing: Squatter settlements in various countries are described and understood as 'blight' on urban landscapes, a metaphorical conceptualization related to visual aesthetics and/or health. Given this metaphorical conceptualization, the most natural solution may be eradication of the settlements, even if these are serving community needs relatively well when looked at through a different lens.

In short, Schön argued that the metaphors we use to talk about a given public-interest topic both reflect and promote a particular perspective, and that, in doing so, they may have implications for the public policies that are considered and agreed upon.

Experimental evidence has confirmed the principle that metaphors for public-interest topics matter, in the sense that they lead to particular inferences, with likely implications for action. Thibodeau and Boroditsky (2011) conducted experiments showing that subjects may reason differently about crime based on a single-word metaphorical cue, even when they are not conscious of having read the metaphor. Subjects who read nearly identical paragraphs about crime responded differently to questions about appropriate policy, based on whether a single word appeared as 'virus' or 'beast' – presumably because these words triggered different patterns of conceptualization and reasoning. Actions and policies related to viruses may have to do with prevention, making communities 'healthier', etc., while actions related to beasts are more likely to involve force. And the experimenters found these differences with respect to policy preference were significant: differences were greater between subjects who saw 'virus' and 'beast' than between Republicans and Democrats, for instance.

In short, both analysis and empirical, scientific study confirm that the metaphors used to talk and think about a given public-interest issue can lead to significantly different perspectives about action on that issue.

The studies by Thibodeau and Boroditsky follow up on analyses such as Schön's, as well as a great deal of subsequent work on how issues are metaphorically 'framed' in thought and discourse. In several influential publications (e.g. Lakoff 1996, 2004), George Lakoff has explored the significance of metaphorical framing in discussions of public-interest issues. For instance, he (Lakoff 2004) argues that the metaphorical pattern 'a nation is a person' played an important role in justifying bombing raids on Iraq that were destined to kill many civilians:

> Ordinary American citizens are using this metaphor when they say things like 'Saddam is a tyrant. He must be stopped.' What the metaphor hides, of course, is that the three thousand bombs to be dropped in the first two days [of a US-led assault on Iraq] will not be dropped on that one person. They will kill many thousands of people hidden by the metaphor, people that we are, according to the metaphor, *not* going to war against.
> *Lakoff 2004: 69*

This example, from a chapter entitled 'Metaphors that Kill', asserts the real-world implications of metaphor in the strongest possible terms.

More recent works have continued to examine the significance of metaphorical framing in public-interest contexts, including the contexts of infectious diseases (e.g. Brown et al. 2009) and conflict mediation (e.g. Ritchie and Cameron 2014). For instance, Ritchie and Cameron (2014) study the transcripts of a public meeting in Portland, Oregon, in which city officials and African-American community members discussed the 2003 shooting of a young, unarmed African-American woman during a confrontation with police. In this case, the authors do not focus on the central role of a single metaphor in framing the issue in question, but rather discuss how the use of various metaphors in the course of the interaction reflect and possibly exacerbate tensions created by very different perspectives on the incident. While city officials use metaphors about 'openness' and 'connection' to describe their hope of rebuilding trust among the participants, community members use metaphorical language like 'smoke and mirrors' and 'double talk' to convey their frustration at officials' unwillingness to address systemic problems with racial profiling and police violence. The metaphors here, targeted at the process of public discussion itself, offer further illustration of how figurative language can shape public-interest outcomes: Ritchie and Cameron argue that the metaphors serve to both reflect and establish distinct agendas for the two sets of participants, and to make resolution more difficult to achieve.

Benefits of metaphor

Even if people do tend to use metaphors when talking and thinking about public-interest topics, and it is shown that metaphors can affect their beliefs about action, this does not necessarily mean that metaphors are helpful. In principle, any attempt to create constructive dialogue and action on a given issue might benefit from clearer, less figurative language, for instance. Our experience, on the other hand, suggests that this is not the case.

Consider a basic question that advocates ask themselves regularly: Why does the public fail to take responsibility on a given issue – whether that issue has to do with the environment, infrastructure, children's wellbeing or any number of other topics advocates devote their professional lives to? One obvious possibility is that advocates are confronted with a *moral failure* on the part of the public. People are simply too self-interested, narrow or uncaring to worry about a given topic. While moral qualities are certainly relevant, our work suggests that it is often far more fruitful to focus on a different explanation for public indifference: a *cognitive failure*. This is the idea that people simply do not understand or 'see' a given topic in a way that allows them to appreciate it fully. They may have no clear grasp of the causal dynamics at work, who is affected, what the stakes are more broadly, or how intervention can make a difference. Put briefly, they may simply see no role for themselves on the issue.

In Schön's terms, this difficulty might be laid at the feet of those who have done the 'problem-setting'. But in fact, we conclude that there is a broader challenge that is not necessarily the fault of previous communicators. Rather, many of the forces, phenomena and systems that humanity or a given society must now manage and contend with are poor targets for human cognition. Climate dynamics, the development of a child's neural system, ocean ecosystems, economic cause-and-effect, and even the role of government or labour unions in society, are all examples of topics that are a poor fit with basic modes of human reasoning. We can hypothesize an 'Everyday Action' mode of thinking that concerns our interactions with our immediate physical and social environment, and that seems naturally to match the contexts in which people lived and evolved over most of our history and prehistory. Such 'everyday actions' would take place at a particular physical scale, e.g. they might involve objects we can manipulate with our hands; would take place at a particular temporal scale, e.g. seconds or minutes; would involve concrete objects or forces, and/or other people (or animals) around us; and so forth. (The psychological principles behind the definition of such 'everyday actions' would presumably be related to those associated with 'basic level objects' – see e.g. Rosch et al. 1976 – and would presumably be facilitated by the richly developed sensori-motor and social-cognition structures in the brain, each of which has been the subject of interesting and intense study.)

Clearly, topics like global warming or economic policy are a poor fit with the thinking that allows us to handle these types of basic interactions. Yet public support on these issues is often necessary for progress or even for meaningful discussion – among voters, decision-makers, experts, the public and so forth. Metaphor offers the possibility of a bridge from 'everyday action' thinking to topics that societies must find a way to deal with despite their complexity or abstractness. The role of analogies and metaphors in science pedagogy has, of course, been well studied (e.g. see Duit 1991; Cameron 2003). Metaphors and analogies are known to help people apply their understanding of familiar and/or concrete topics to new or more abstract ones. For instance, the flow of blood through a blood vessel can be thought of as the flow of water in a pipe (see Pontiga and Gaytán 2005). Pipes and water are familiar, concrete entities that can be interacted with at typical human scales of space and time, and whose behaviours (at least at the relevant scales and levels of specificity) we understand well. Clearly, if we are hoping for a significant percentage of lay people to participate in discussion, reasoning and decision-making regarding a complex issue, it should 'feel' cognitively more like water and pipes than the unseen and less well-understood system of capillaries and other blood vessels.

Besides rendering topics 'easier to think' in various ways, our experience suggests that metaphors can have other advantages more related to discourse dynamics and expectations. In particular, metaphors can sometimes have the advantage of being more *novel* than literal references to a topic (though certain metaphors are commonplace and anything but novel, of course), and may also be aids to memorability of a given communication, an effect perhaps related to novelty. There is a wealth of research indicating that novelty is a factor that aids memory (see e.g. Kishiyama and Yonelinas 2003), and novel metaphors may also aid memory by virtue of being concrete and aiding understanding. Novelty is probably also helpful in another way: Many public-interest topics have been discussed innumerable times in public forums, so that it can be difficult to attract attention to what seems to be a familiar or even clichéd topic, such as the environment. A metaphor that suggests a new conceptualization may have a better chance of 'breaking through the noise' of chaotic public discourse. In sum, metaphors, and in particular novel metaphors may be indispensable tools for informed public discussion and collective decision-making.

The next sections offer a number of examples and continue the discussion of the various qualities that can make a metaphor effective as a tool for creating more useful public dialogue.

Examples of current research: metaphors that can change perceptions of public-interest issues

As mentioned earlier, the work of Cultural Logic and Topos has entailed exploration of a wide range of public-interest topics, and in many of these cases, particular metaphors have been found to have helpful effects on lay people's attention to, interest in and understanding of a given issue. This section briefly discusses several of those examples, leading to discussions in the following sections, respectively, of the challenges associated with identifying such metaphors, and some of the qualities they are likely to possess.

'Carbon dioxide blanket'

Despite decades of coverage in media, many Americans continue to be confused or indifferent about the topic of global warming. In research exploring their attitudes and what might make them more engaged, Cultural Logic found that a metaphorical description of the thickening 'blanket' of carbon dioxide that is collecting in the atmosphere and trapping heat created noticeably more attention to the topic and interest in addressing it. This metaphor helps explain a simple causal dynamic that most Americans are unaware of, and does so with reference to a simple, concrete and familiar scenario they understand well and can easily map onto the global climate context. Understanding of a simple causal mechanism creates greater interest and a greater sense of responsibility for the issue.

Interestingly, the most common misperception about the cause of global warming is that a 'hole in the ozone layer' is to blame. Presumably this misunderstanding has taken hold partly because of its simple, concrete nature – localized depletion of atmospheric ozone is understood as something like a 'hole in the roof'. (For further discussion of the 'blanket' metaphor associated with global warming, see the next section.)

'Brain architecture'

In research on Americans' attitudes towards various interventions relating to children and their lives and outcomes, we found that a focus on how experience affects the development of 'brain architecture' promoted more engaged and constructive discussion. By default, Americans' interest in public policy interventions to help children is diminished by at least three cognitive/cultural factors:

- an often unstated assumption that everything that matters in a child's life has to do with family rather than the broader community or society (a perspective that can be called the 'family bubble');
- a focus on the 'mental' (as opposed to physical) dimension of development, having to do with learning, remembering, forgetting, values, etc.;
- and an assumption that development follows its own course over time regardless of circumstances.

The first factor limits the apparent relevance of government or public interventions, the second makes various kinds of intervention appear less important because bad experiences can always be 'forgotten', new lessons can always be 'learned' etc., and the third makes intervention an even lower priority.

But when interview subjects are asked to think about early childhood experience in terms of positive or negative effects on the development of 'brain architecture' they tend to take a different stance, assume that stakes are higher and public responsibility and potential for helpful intervention is greater. Presumably, the more concrete nature of the causality in question (i.e. having to do with brains and/or metaphorical buildings) is at least partly responsible for these different attitudes.

'Arts ripple effect'

In research on how to best convey the significance and value of the arts, we found that a particularly helpful metaphorical idea is the image of the 'ripple effect' of community benefits from arts establishments in a neighbourhood. For instance, theatres, galleries, and so forth create greater vitality, making communities more attractive and ultimately more prosperous.

Part of the effectiveness of this idea comes from the simple, 'imageable' nature of the *ripple* metaphor: The effects of a new gallery, for instance – including greater vibrancy – may radiate outward throughout the surrounding neighbourhood, just as ripples spread outward across the surface of a pond.

Policies as 'pipes'

In research on how to talk constructively about the complex relationship between the economy and public policy, we found that one helpful metaphor frames policies and policy decisions as metaphorical 'pipes' that end up directing the flow of money in one direction or another. For instance, different regulatory choices regarding the credit industry (e.g. requirements for declaring bankruptcy, limits on interest rates) can end up directing more or less money to lenders and away from borrowers.

Several aspects of this explanation are helpful to lay people, but one factor that aids comprehension and interest is the simple, concrete nature of the metaphorical framing, which builds in a broad sense on the 'event structure' metaphor referred to earlier. (Note that the 'pipes' metaphor also draws on a common metaphorical conceptualization of money as a liquid resource – as in usages like 'cash flow' and 'liquidity'.)

Recommendations for practice: finding the 'right' metaphor

While metaphors have potential to create clearer, more accurate and better-remembered understandings of a given topic, identifying a metaphor that actually has these qualities can be very challenging. In an experiment seeking to replicate the effects found by Thibodeau and Boroditsky (2011) (discussed above), Shinohara et al. (2012) tested the effects of two different metaphorical terms on beliefs about genetically modified organisms, more specifically food containing GMOs. In this instance, the researchers found no significant results – demonstrating that we cannot simply assume that a given metaphor will have effects on reasoning.

A second example concerns the topic of global warming. In conversations with hundreds of Americans, Cultural Logic found that only a small fraction spontaneously mention the idea of a 'greenhouse' – the predominant metaphor that has been used in media coverage and other public discourse on the topic over the past several decades (see also Chapter 20). In principle, greenhouses offer a superb analogy for the heat-trapping mechanism that is causing climate change: they are relatively simple concrete objects. Yet for some reason this analogy has failed to significantly affect public understanding of the issue. One possibility is that the predominant *mis*understanding – the ozone hole perspective referred to earlier – has simply 'blocked out' the more accurate one. Certainly this 'ozone confusion' would seem to be a factor. Another likely factor is that many Americans simply have no immediate grasp of the *mechanism* of greenhouses themselves. Since relatively few people use or interact with these structures, associations are vague rather than having clear causal dynamics, for instance: greenhouses are simply pleasant places where plants grow and are protected from the elements. In short, one of the ways a particular metaphor can fail is that it is not understood and therefore not adopted.

A second way a metaphor might fail is that it leads to misunderstandings – i.e. people draw the wrong inferences from the metaphor. For instance, there has been some significant criticism of Richard Dawkins' famous metaphor of the 'selfish gene'; Denis Noble (2006), for one, has observed that the metaphor, while helpful in some ways, obscures important relationships between genes and other levels of biological structure and behaviour, as well as the functional relationships among different genes themselves. Metaphors intended to help lay people understand an important topic in a new way can fail even more fundamentally, when people take away the wrong inferences and *not* any of the right ones. For instance, in research on the topic of child development, we found that the discussion of the role of neural 'connections' was easily misunderstood or misremembered as a reference to important *social* 'connections' in the life of a child – most participants did not pick up inferences about brain development in this context.

Finally, it is easy for metaphors to fail because they are often essentially dismissed as ornamental language. In research on a variety of topics, we have found that candidate metaphors for introducing new understandings are simply ignored in favour of more literal expressions of the same basic point. For instance, 'wage stagnation' is translated to the simple idea that wages have not increased.

To find out whether metaphors already in use in public discourse have 'succeeded' – i.e. whether they have stuck with people, lead to the right reasoning and so forth – it is possible to gather information through media reviews, interviews with members of the public, and so forth. But to know whether a 'new' metaphor – or one that is currently not well known – is worth promoting, testing is required. There are a number of tools one might use to test the qualities of a metaphor, but one that has proven particularly helpful is an adaptation of experiments described by Bartlett (1932), the essential idea of which is that 'chains' of participants pass along a brief statement to each other, doing the best they can to remember and reproduce what they heard – as in the children's whispering game variously known as Telephone, Gossip, Secret Message, Grapevine, Chinese Whispers, etc. Following Bartlett, other researchers have used this same basic 'transmission chain' approach to study the various cultural factors that can interfere with comprehension or transmission of a given narrative or set of ideas (see, for instance, Bangerter 2000; Kashima 2000; Mesoudi and Whiten 2004; Mesoudi et al. 2006; Mesoudi 2007).

The following are excerpts from such a transmission chain conducted by Cultural Logic. In this case, the first participant (A) viewed a brief video that used a 'blanket' metaphor to explain the heat-trapping mechanism by which increasing atmospheric carbon dioxide causes global warming. A then did her best to pass the content along to a new participant (B) (who did not see the video). A then left the room and B attempted to pass the information along to new participant C.

A: The carbon dioxide that's given off by the cars and everything else basically creates almost like a blanket around the Earth and traps in all that heat, melting ice caps and causing other problems.
B: One of the ways global warming is a problem is that ... carbon dioxide covers the earth almost like a blanket, trapping the heat. And that's one of the problems.
C: CO_2 [carbon dioxide] is blanketing the earth, or trapping, and CO_2 is causing the global warming. And in this web site it talks about solutions and how to reduce or minimize the blanketing or the trapping of CO_2.

These excerpts illustrate several important facts. First, the blanket explanation is easy to understand and to repeat or paraphrase. Just as importantly, it is perceived as *helpful* for conveying the relevant content. Many metaphors disappear in the course of such chains – or are even dropped by the first participant, for reasons alluded to above: participants may fail to understand the metaphor, may not regard it as a central aspect of the communication, may implicitly treat it as an unnecessary linguistic 'ornament', and so forth. In short, the core idea of *blanket*, in this case, is 'sticky' – presumably due to factors discussed above such as clarity, concreteness and novelty. (For an interesting discussion of the 'stickiness' of ideas, see Heath and Heath 2007.) Unless an idea is sticky in this way it is unlikely to have the capacity to change either individual thinking or public discussion and ultimately the culture. The following statement from Sperber (1985: 86) refers to oral cultures, but applies well to any culture (including the US) where important ideas spread broadly through personal discussion or the media.

> In an oral tradition, all cultural representations are *easily remembered ones*; hard to remember representations are forgotten, or transformed into more easily remembered ones, before reaching a cultural level of distribution.

In addition to the clarity and memorability of the idea, the testing excerpts above hint at other important qualities of the 'blanket' metaphor – in particular, its effectiveness at leading to the right inferences and conclusions, regarding the causes of global warming and what actions would mitigate it.

Conclusion: qualities of effective metaphors

The experience of assessing metaphors for particular kinds of effectiveness leads to a number of considerations that may be of interest to scholars studying metaphor as a linguistic, psychological or social phenomenon – as well as to those who are interested in creating more compelling advocacy approaches on public-interest issues.

Some of these considerations are very straightforward. For instance, does the metaphor involve a readily accessible 'mapping' – i.e. a set of correspondences between source and target that people can readily grasp – even without much explanation? As we have seen, the 'greenhouse' metaphor seems largely to have failed as an explanatory approach at least for the American public, seemingly in part because the mapping is not immediately grasped. Due to a lack of familiarity with a key aspect of the conceptual source – namely the heat-trapping mechanism of greenhouses – people do not easily see the mapping that communicators intend.

Another obvious question is whether a given metaphor has the proper 'entailments', in Lakoff and Johnson's sense. Once grasped, does the metaphor lead people to the intended inferences? For example, a metaphor which frames various public institutions and systems as 'public structures' (i.e. likening school systems, library systems and so forth to *physical* structures) is helpful in part because it leads people to the inference that such institutions should be *maintained* – even if this requires effort and cost.

Other considerations are subtler, such as the following:

> *Reification*: Metaphors appear to be more effective (clear, memorable, likely to be the focus of discussion) when they involve what we can call 'reification' – i.e. treating a phenomenon as though it were a (relatively) concrete, definable *thing*, and focusing discussion on this object (see Langacker 1987: 183–213 for discussion of *things* as a cognitive class). Examples discussed earlier include the idea of brain architecture, public structures and the blanket of carbon dioxide. In each case the metaphorical framing offers audiences a new object (or class of objects) to contemplate, in addition to various predications about this object – e.g. the explanation of how the blanket traps heat. We hypothesize that objects have a special type of tangibility that makes them natural focuses of attention, and that this is a reason that reification helps people focus on, understand and retain a new perspective on a given topic.
>
> *Imageability*: Related to reification is the idea of imageability (see e.g. Swaab et al. 2002) – the degree to which a given concept can be pictured in the mind, i.e. through simulation of vision or other perception. Given considerations already discussed, it is obvious that sensory vividness should in principle be a helpful factor for a metaphor. On the other hand, our experience suggests that there can be interesting trade-offs associated with this quality. Consider the three example metaphors mentioned just above: brain architecture, public structures and the blanket of carbon dioxide. The idea of a blanket is probably more vivid and easier to picture than the more generic idea of 'architecture' (see discussions of *basic level objects*, such as Rosch et al. 1976), which in turn is certainly associated with richer and more specific images than the idea of 'structures'. While 'structures' is generic enough to stretch the bounds of metaphoricity, it proves effective in all the ways discussed earlier in the chapter, and seems appropriately generic to the broad class of systems and institutions it is intended to refer to. Experience even suggests that such a relatively generic (and not very imageable) term can have the advantage of *not* striking listeners as an obvious metaphor. As we have seen, metaphors are sometimes

ignored as ornamental language, something other than the basic expression of a given point. In this sense a metaphor with low imageability can sometimes 'fly under the radar' in a helpful way.

Terms of art: A final consideration is that metaphors may have particular impact when presented as 'terms of art', established language used by experts. Many of the examples already cited – 'public structures', 'arts ripple effect', 'carbon dioxide blanket', 'brain architecture' and so forth – were presented in this way in testing, because there appear to be several advantages to this treatment of metaphorical terms. Most basically, messages framed as explanations of new terms of art have the advantage of clearly focusing attention on the new concept to be learned (e.g. 'Early experience is important because of its effects on the development of what experts call "brain architecture"'). More interesting is that, unlike explicit similes or analogies, which call attention to the fact that a given term is *not* to be literally confused with the target concept, a term-of-art presentation suggests that a given metaphor has been institutionalized as an established conceptualization (see Bowdle and Gentner's 2005 discussion of the 'shift from comparison to categorization' as metaphors become more conventionalized). That is, there is a significant difference between saying that 'atmospheric concentration of carbon dioxide acts *like* a blanket' and simply referring to the 'carbon dioxide blanket': The latter implies a much closer semantic relationship (polysemy) between two conceptual senses of the term *blanket*. Finally, a new term offers listeners a brief way of summarizing, referring to and remembering the new concept: essentially, a new term of art, when effective, functions as a mnemonic for a rich new way of conceptualizing a topic.

Of course, the bottom line for real-world communicators is the demonstrable effectiveness of a given metaphor. The above considerations offer theorists material for further speculation or research, and may offer advocates some guidance in selecting metaphors for their communications, but whether a metaphor actually has the power to help save the world can only be determined empirically, by testing its effectiveness with real people.

Further reading

Lakoff, G. (2004) *Don't Think of an Elephant! Know Your Values and Frame the Debate: The Essential Guide for Progressives*, White River Junction, VT: Chelsea Green Publishing.
Schön, D. (1993) 'Generative metaphor: A perspective on problem-setting in social policy', in A. Ortony (ed.), *Metaphor and Thought*, 2nd edn, Cambridge, UK: Cambridge University Press, pp. 137–163.
Thibodeau, P.H. and Boroditsky, L. (2011) 'Metaphors we think with: The role of metaphor in reasoning', *PLoS ONE*, 6(2): e16782. doi: 10.1371/journal.pone.0016782.

References

Bangerter, A. (2000) 'Transformation between scientific and social representations of conception: The method of serial reproduction', *British Journal of Social Psychology*, 39: 521–535.
Bartlett, F.C. (1932) *Remembering*, Oxford, UK: Macmillan.
Bowdle, B.F. and Gentner, D. (2005) 'The career of metaphor', *Psychological Review*, 112(1): 93–216.
Brown, B., Nerlich, B., Crawford, P., Koteyko, N. and Carter, R. (2009) 'Hygiene and biosecurity: The language and politics of risk in an era of emerging infectious diseases', *Sociology Compass*, 3: 811–823.
Cameron, L. (2003) *Metaphor in Educational Discourse*, London, UK: Continuum.

Duit, R. (1991) 'On the role of analogies and metaphors in learning science', *Science Education*, 75(6): 649–672.

Grady, J. (1997) '"Theories are Buildings" revisited', *Cognitive Linguistics*, 8(4): 267–290.

—— (1999) 'Crosslinguistic regularities in metaphorical extension'. Talk presented at the Annual Meeting of the Linguistics Society of America, Los Angeles, CA.

Heath, C. and Heath, D. (2007) *Made to Stick: Why Some Ideas Survive and Others Die*, New York: Random House.

Kashima, Y. (2000) 'Maintaining cultural stereotypes in the serial reproduction of narratives', *Personality and Social Psychology Bulletin*, 26: 594–604.

Kishiyama, M. and Yonelinas, A. (2003) 'Novelty effects on recollection and familiarity in recognition memory', *Memory and Cognition*, 31(7): 1045–1051.

Lakoff, G. (1993) 'The contemporary theory of metaphor', in A. Ortony (ed.), *Metaphor and Thought*, 2nd edn, Cambridge, UK: Cambridge University Press, pp. 202–251.

—— (1996) *Moral Politics: What Conservatives Know and Liberals Don't*, Chicago, IL: University of Chicago Press.

—— (2004) *Don't Think of an Elephant! Know Your Values and Frame the Debate: The Essential Guide for Progressives*, White River Junction, VT: Chelsea Green Publishing.

Lakoff, G. and Johnson, M. (1980) *Metaphors We Live By*, Chicago, IL: University of Chicago Press.

Langacker, R.W. (1987) *Foundations of Cognitive Grammar, Vol. I: Theoretical Prerequisites*, Stanford, CA: Stanford University Press.

Mesoudi, A. (2007) 'Using the methods of experimental social psychology to study cultural evolution', *Journal of Social, Evolutionary, and Cultural Psychology*, 1(2): 35–58.

Mesoudi, A. and Whiten, A. (2004) 'The hierarchical transformation of event knowledge in human cultural transmission', *Journal of Cognition and Culture*, 4: 1–24.

Mesoudi, A., Whiten, A. and Dunbar, R. (2006) 'A bias for social information in human cultural transmission', *British Journal of Psychology*, 97: 405–423.

Noble, D. (2006) *The Music of Life: Biology Beyond Genes*, Oxford, UK: Oxford University Press.

Pontiga, F. and Gaytán, S.P. (2005) 'An experimental approach to the fundamental principles of hemodynamics', *Advances in Physiology Education*, 29: 165–171.

Ritchie, L.D. and Cameron, L. (2014) 'Open hearts or smoke and mirrors: Metaphorical framing and frame conflicts in a public meeting', *Metaphor and Symbol*, 29(3): 204–223.

Rosch, E., Mervis, C.B., Gray, W., Johnson, D. and Boyes-Braem, P. (1976) 'Basic objects in natural categories', *Cognitive Psychology*, 8: 382–439.

Schön, D. (1993) 'Generative metaphor: A perspective on problem-setting in social policy', in A. Ortony (ed.), *Metaphor and Thought*, 2nd edn, Cambridge, UK: Cambridge University Press, pp. 137–163.

Shinohara, K., Matsunaka, Y. and Mitsuishi, S. (2012) 'The influence of conceptual metaphor on reasoning and attitude'. Talk given at the 9th International Conference on Researching and Applying Metaphor, Lancaster University, UK.

Sperber, D. (1985) 'Anthropology and psychology: Towards an epidemiology of representations', *Man*, 20(1): 73–89.

Swaab, T.Y., Baynes, K. and Knight, R.T. (2002) 'Separable effects of priming and imageability on word processing: An ERP study', *Cognitive Brain Research*, 15(1): 99–103.

Thibodeau, P.H. and Boroditsky, L. (2011) 'Metaphors we think with: The role of metaphor in reasoning', *PLoS ONE*, 6(2): e16782. doi: 10.1371/journal.pone.0016782.

Part VI
Language, metaphor, and cognitive development

31
Metaphor processing

Herbert L. Colston and Raymond W. Gibbs, Jr.

Introduction

Imagine you are a linguist looking for a job. You search the internet and come across one ad posted by a private company in California that is 'seeking native linguists with strong language skills and in tune with their culture.' The ad goes on to list various requirements for the position, including educational background, previous work experience, and different personal attributes, explicitly stating, 'The ability to juggle chainsaws (nice to have) with a good sense of humor will be ideal.' Do you understand what is meant by 'the ability to juggle chainsaws'? Of course, this phrase is not meant literally, but refers metaphorically to the idea of being able to deal with many difficult tasks at the same time. How do people come to a metaphorical understanding of the 'juggle chainsaws' phrase exactly when they read it? Our aim in this chapter is to explore some of the complexities associated with people's processing of metaphorical language.

The varieties of metaphorical language

Scholars often note the ubiquity of verbal metaphors, in part to overcome lay beliefs that metaphor resides in only special, creative, and unusual discourses (e.g., poetry). Cognitive linguistic studies have done much to advance the idea that many conventional expressions both reflect enduring metaphorical thoughts (i.e., conceptual metaphors) and convey metaphorical messages (Kövecses, 2010; Chapter 1). Still, arguments persist over what constitutes metaphor and how best to measure its prevalence in speech and writing (see Colston, 2015, for a review). But one can safely acknowledge that metaphor is incredibly varied in both its forms and functions. Consider a few examples that illustrate some of the diversity of metaphorical language.

> 'A is B' or resemblance metaphors ('My job is a jail')
> Conventional metaphors ('My marriage is on the rocks')
> Novel metaphors motivated by conceptual metaphors ('The sunlit path of racial justice')
> Novel metaphors not motivated by conceptual metaphors ('Time is an arrow')

> Polysemy (e.g., the verb 'see' in 'I can't see the point of your argument')
> Grammatical metaphors ('The cast drew great applause from the audience')
> Proverbs ('Don't let the cat out of the bag')
> Idioms ('John blew his stack')
> XYZ metaphors ('Art is the sex of the imagination')

Metaphor also blends with other figures of speech as seen in the following examples.

> Metaphor with metonymy ('U.S. slowdown punctures Michelin's profits')
> Metaphor with irony ('You are the cream of my coffee')

In addition to these individual verbal metaphors, metaphorical language extends across discourse in the form of extended and mixed metaphors (see Chapter 12).

The presence of these varying forms of metaphor immediately raises an important question: Do people process all these metaphors in the same way? Although most scholars believe some version of the idea that understanding metaphor involves recognition of some cross-domain mappings, it is not clear that a single 'metaphor processing' system exists which readily handles the diversity of verbal metaphors found in naturalistic discourse. This conclusion greatly complicates our telling a simple story about how metaphor processing actually works.

Critical issues: the diversity of methods and processing experiences

Metaphor scholars within psycholinguistics and cognitive neuroscience have created a myriad of methods for studying metaphor processing. Among the most widely used experimental techniques within metaphor studies are: full-sentence reading times, word-by-word reading times (including both moving window and eye-movement measures), paraphrase judgment response times, priming methods, free recall, cued recall, mental imagery studies, summarization and paraphrase of meaning tasks, question answering, different bodily enactment tasks, and various brain scanning measures such as event-related potentials (ERPs) and functional magnetic resonance imaging (fMRI).

Each of these varied experimental techniques may tap into different aspects of metaphor processing. For example, full-phrase or -sentence reading-time studies offer the best evidence on the total cognitive effort required to interpret a complete verbal metaphor. This method has been successfully applied to address various theoretical debates over the difficulty in processing different kinds of linguistic metaphors. Methods examining the time it takes people to read individual words in verbal metaphors, via moving-window or eye-movement techniques, are useful for exploring local processing of specific metaphorically used words in context. These online techniques, along with brain scanning measures such as ERPs, provide insights into the interaction of linguistic, social/pragmatic, and cognitive knowledge during real-time metaphor processing. Asking people to paraphrase, or rapidly judge suggested paraphrases of, verbal metaphors allows researchers to study the meaning products understood when people process metaphor. Similarly, imagery tasks provide another method for exploring the contents of what people have understood after quickly reading or hearing a metaphorical phrase. Bodily engagement tasks, where people are asked to perform specific gestures or adopt different postures, are critical for investigating the role of embodied experience and action in creating metaphorical understandings of words, phrases, and longer stretches of discourse.

In general, no single method is capable of examining all facets of metaphor processing, but each technique may reveal different aspects of verbal metaphorical experience.

It is really surprising to see how little scholars explicitly discuss why their preferred method necessarily is best for examining some feature of metaphor understanding. For the most part, researchers employ those methods and technologies that are most appropriate for their own research interests and disciplinary backgrounds. Some claims are occasionally made for the presumed benefits of one method (e.g., eye-movement measures) compared to another (e.g., full-sentence or -phrase reading time). At the same time, many psycholinguists and cognitive neuroscientists argue that only certain methods (e.g., eye-movements as opposed to mental imagery tasks) are relevant to studying immediate, online processing of metaphor. Yet these simple claims ignore the more complex problem that not all metaphor processing is the same, especially given that the full meanings of metaphors are rarely inferred within a few seconds on a first-time reading.

One problem for any account of metaphor processing is that 'processing' or 'understanding' metaphorical meaning is not a singular activity that all listeners/readers engage in in the same way. People's experience of metaphorical meaning can be crudely distinguished along a temporal continuum of processing that includes, at the very least, comprehension, recognition, interpretation, and appreciation (Gibbs, 1994; Gibbs & Colston, 2012):

- Comprehension refers to the immediate moment-by-moment process of creating meanings for utterances.
- Recognition refers to the products of comprehension as types (i.e., determining whether an utterance conveys a particular type of meaning such as metaphorical).
- Interpretation refers to the products of comprehension as tokens (i.e., determining the specific content of the meaning type).
- Appreciation refers to some esthetic judgment given to a product either as a type or token.

These different facets of processing or understanding are not completely separate but overlap in complex ways. For instance, people can ordinarily comprehend metaphors without any conscious or tacit recognition that they have encountered a metaphor. At the same time, people may recognize that a word string is a metaphor without necessarily understanding any of its metaphorical meanings. People may also gradually appreciate metaphors as they are processed in an incremental manner over time. These different temporal moments of processing have complex relations with one another that are not easily disentangled. Still, it is important not to assume that the experimental study of one aspect (e.g., appreciation) necessarily informs the theoretical analysis of another part (e.g., comprehension). For example, our conscious intuitions about metaphorical meaning may not be directly relevant to understanding the fast-acting cognitive processes which produce those interpretations.

As noted earlier, most of the experimental literature concentrates on fast, crude comprehension of metaphors, although a literature on people's slower interpretations of metaphor, especially when seen in literary texts, is emerging. The numerous experimental methods available provide different kinds of information that are relevant to a variety of research questions, ranging through, for example, the study of how much mental effort is required to understand a metaphor, the role that individual word meanings play in the process of assembling an overall metaphorical understanding of some phrase, and what brain areas are most active during the processing of different kinds of metaphor (see also Chapter 32). Finally, the recent experimental research on metaphor processing explores different types of people, including university students, children, elderly adults, native and non-native speakers, and individuals who are schizophrenic, depressed, brain damaged, or autistic (see also Chapter 33).

This brief overview illustrates the important point that the ways people process metaphors depends on a host of personal, linguistic, and contextual factors. Gibbs and Colston (2012) reviewed the vast literature on metaphor understanding and showed that the data one obtains in psycholinguistic and cognitive neuroscience experiments can be influenced by four broad, interacting factors: (1) the people, (2) the specific language and utterance encountered in context, (3) the specific understanding task, and (4) the method by which the data are analyzed to assess language comprehension. It is simply impossible to control for all these factors to create a 'neutral' or 'normative' theory of metaphor processing that directly applies to all people in all contexts. Our claim is that attempting to create a single theory by which all people understand metaphor makes little sense. Nonetheless, psycholinguists and others can still test several broad ideas about how metaphors are understood and investigate more specific claims about the details of metaphor processing that may significantly constrain theories of metaphorical language use.

How difficult is it to process verbal metaphors?

One of the most enduring debates in the metaphor literature concerns how difficult it is to process a verbal metaphor in context. A classic view holds that metaphors convey meanings that are more complex than those conveyed with literal language. The 'standard pragmatic view' suggests that people infer metaphorical messages by first analyzing what an utterance literally means, then finding that meaning inappropriate in context, and finally using pragmatic knowledge to interpret what people imply by their use of metaphors (Grice, 1975). However, many processing-time experiments investigating the cognitive effort needed to process metaphorical discourse found that listeners/readers can often understand the meanings of metaphors quite quickly without having to first analyze and reject their literal meanings, especially when such expressions are encountered in realistic social contexts (Gibbs, 1994; Gibbs & Colston, 2012). This conclusion applies not only to familiar, conventional metaphors (e.g., 'John blew his stack'), but, at least in some cases, to novel metaphors as well (e.g., 'The troops slowly approached the babysitter,' where 'troops' refers to a small group of children). Of course, some metaphors may take additional effort to understand because of their novelty or the context in which they appear. For example, adults spend more effort processing referential metaphors (e.g., 'The butcher was sued for malpractice' stated in the context of talking about a surgeon) than synonymous literal expressions (e.g., 'The surgeon was sued for malpractice') (Gibbs, 1990; Noveck, Bianco, & Castry, 2001).

Certain theories of figurative language interpretation still maintain, despite the evidence presented above, that literal meanings are analyzed during metaphor processing. Earlier behavioral research suggested that individual word meanings appear to be momentarily activated during metaphor understanding, even if these meanings are contextually irrelevant. One cross-modal priming study (i.e., people hear a metaphor and then quickly make lexical decisions to visually presented letter strings) showed, for example, that the literal meanings of words (e.g., 'plant' and 'spike') in metaphors (e.g., 'John is a cactus') remain active until at least 400 milliseconds after the entire verbal metaphor has been interpreted (Rubio-Fernandez, 2007). More recent neurophysiological studies demonstrate that hearing metaphors (e.g., 'Those lawyers are hyenas') gives rise to particular brain waves (e.g., N400) which are associated with additional cognitive effort. Processing literal statements (e.g., 'Those carnivores are hyenas') does not, however, show the same degree of N400 activation (Weiland, Bambini, & Schumacher, 2014).

Another hypothesis, called the 'graded salience view,' claims that salient word or phrase meanings are automatically retrieved during figurative language processing regardless of the context (Giora, 2003). For instance, processing familiar metaphors (e.g., 'step on someone's toes') should activate both of their literal (e.g., foot) and metaphorical (e.g., offend) meanings, even when these metaphors are seen in discourse contexts supportive of their metaphorical meanings. Processing unfamiliar metaphors (e.g., 'Their bone density is not like ours') should initially activate only their literal meanings, as these are most salient. Different empirical studies, ranging from reading-time to word-fragment completion experiments, support this general idea for how people interpret different kinds of metaphorical language (Giora, 2012).

Metaphor processing may still demand greater processing costs at the lexical level than do many literal utterances. Still, it remains unclear whether these costs at the lexical level necessarily result in more difficult processing of metaphorical statements as a whole. In fact, some utterances may be interpreted metaphorically by default, especially when these expressions are negative, unfamiliar, free of semantic anomaly, and ambiguous between literal and metaphorical interpretations. For example, statements such as 'You're not my boss' are rated as being more metaphorical in isolation (meaning 'You should stop acting as if you are literally my boss'), and are easier to read in metaphorical contexts than in literal ones (Giora et al., 2013). These findings demonstrate that some linguistic expressions may directly convey metaphorical meaning by default, even if they are novel.

One model of metaphor processing embraces the notion of constraint satisfaction (Katz & Ferretti, 2003; Katz, 2005). Under this view, understanding any utterance requires people to simultaneously consider different linguistic and nonlinguistic information that best fit together to make sense of what a speaker or writer is saying. Constraint satisfaction models do not posit any obligatory analysis of context-free or literal meanings. One test of the constraint satisfaction view examined people's immediate understanding of expressions like 'Children are precious gems' as having metaphorical (children are valuable) or ironic (children are burdens) meaning (Pexman, Ferretti, & Katz, 2000). Several sources of information could induce either the metaphorical or ironic meaning, including the occupation of the speaker, whether the statement was counterfactual to information in the previous discourse, and the familiarity of the expression. Results from an online reading task (i.e., moving window) demonstrated that the 'A is B' statements were initially read as metaphors, but that the speaker's occupation and counterfactuality of the statement given in the previous context play an early role in processing. Furthermore, knowing that a speaker is often associated with irony slows down reading of the first word in the following statement if the context leads one to expect a metaphorical reading. Yet if listeners know that the speaker is often ironic, this immediately acts to speed up processing right after the target statement if the context induces an ironic meaning. The complex interaction between the three sources of information is consistent with the idea that understanding whether an expression is meant metaphorically or ironically depends, similar to other aspects of language, on multiple sources of information being examined and interpreted continuously during online reading (see also Chapter 32).

One advantage of a constraint satisfaction model is its tremendous flexibility. Metaphor processing is neither always easy nor always difficult, but varies depending on the interaction of many factors present in each situation, including, again, who the people are, the specific type of metaphors involved, the context, and the specific processing task.

How do the topic and vehicle interact during metaphor processing?

A great deal of attention has been given to how people process 'A is B' and 'A is like B' metaphors and similes. Even though these appear to be infrequent uses of metaphor, 'A is B' metaphors have been the major focus of scholarship since ancient times. Understanding a metaphor such as 'My job is a jail,' for example, is thought to depend on how listeners figure out the properties that jobs and jails share. Psychological studies demonstrate, however, that the novel features emerging from metaphor comprehension are not simply those shared by one's separate understandings of the topic (e.g., 'my job') and vehicle (e.g., 'is a jail') (Gineste, Indurkhya, & Scart, 2000; Utsumi, 2005). Instead, similarity in meaning is created as an emergent property of metaphor understanding, and not just those meanings that are shared by the topic and vehicle terms. Several theoretical proposals have been advanced to describe the process by which emergent metaphorical meanings are inferred.

The 'structure-mapping' theory of metaphor claims that people begin processing a metaphor by first aligning the representations of the source and target domain concepts (e.g., respectively, the concepts corresponding to 'jail' and 'job') (Gentner, Bowdle, Wolff, & Boronat, 2001). Once these two domains are aligned, further inferences are directionally projected from the source to the target domain. These inferences reflect relational, and not just feature-specific, aspects of the metaphor comprehension processes. For instance, when people read, 'Plant stems are drinking straws,' they infer that both plants and straws convey liquid to nourish living things (a relational meaning) and not just that both plants and straws are long and thin (i.e., feature commonalities). Metaphors expressing relational information (e.g., 'Plant stems are drinking straws') are judged to be far more apt than those that only map object features ('Her arms are twin swans') (Tourangeau & Rips, 1991). People also prefer topic–vehicle pairings expressed as similes (e.g., 'The sun is like an orange') when they involve feature mappings (e.g., 'sun-orange'), but not when they involve relational mappings (e.g., 'eyeball-curtains' in the form of 'Eyeballs are curtains') (Aisenman, 1999).

An alternative view claims that 'A is B' metaphors are better understood via categorization processes as class-inclusion (i.e., one example of an ad-hoc category), and not comparison, statements (Glucksberg, 2001; see also Chapter 3). For example, the word 'snake' evokes different meanings in the phrases 'My lawyer is a snake' (i.e., the folk-attributed personality of a snake) and 'The road was a snake' (i.e., how a snake moves). Thus, in the context of talking about lawyers, 'snake' best exemplifies the abstract category of 'unsavory personality attributes' while it reflects something about the abstract category of 'physical shapes of things' in the context of roads. Experimental studies show, in fact, that people do not always consider the literal referents of metaphor vehicles (e.g., real sharks) when reading metaphorical statements (e.g., 'Lawyers are sharks'), because this irrelevant information is suppressed during comprehension. These findings are most consistent with the claim that metaphor understanding involves creating a new, ad-hoc category that includes both the topic and the vehicle and not merely comparing one's knowledge about topic and vehicle domains (Glucksberg, 2001; also see Chapter 3).

A different proposal, titled the 'career of metaphor theory,' combines aspects of both the comparison and categorization views (Gentner & Bowdle, 2008). This theory claims that a shift occurs in the mode of understanding from comparison to categorization processes as metaphors become conventionalized. People preferred 'A is B' metaphors (e.g., 'Faith is an anchor') to similes (e.g., 'Faith is like an anchor') when these statements shifted from being novel to conventional. Novel similes (e.g., 'Friendship is like wine') were read more quickly than the corresponding metaphors, while the metaphors (e.g., 'Alcohol is a crutch') were read more quickly than the corresponding similes when these statements were conventional. Finally, giving people repeated exposures to novel similes using the same base term over time provoked individuals to shift to using the metaphor form in subsequent statements, indicating a shift from comparison to categorization processes of metaphor understanding within the course of a single study (see Goldstein, Arzouan, & Faust, 2012, for neurophysiological evidence related to this process).

Still, novel metaphors may not always be interpreted as comparisons, or in terms of their simile counterparts, contrary to the career of metaphor view (Glucksberg & Haught, 2006). For example, one study asked participants to read very novel metaphorical statements, such as 'A newspaper is (like) a daily telescope,' in either categorical or comparison form (i.e., 'A is B' vs. 'A is like B'), and found that the categorization versions were read much faster than were the similes. The career of metaphor view is unable to deal with the idea that novel apt metaphors can be understood via categorization, and not comparison, processes. Really good metaphors sound best as categorizations, and sometimes work only as categorical assertions, such as 'My lawyer is a well-paid shark' (compared to 'My lawyer is like a well-paid shark'). One possibility is that comparison and categorization models may reflect different processing strategies for understanding metaphor, with each being better suited depending on the aptness of the metaphor. When a metaphor is apt, it is typically understood via a categorization process. Less apt metaphors and similes are interpreted via comparison processes (Haught, 2013).

Several other models of metaphor processing that focus on 'A is B' structures also deserve mention, although these have not produced the same kind of experimental evidence to support their claims as have the earlier reviewed proposals. Relevance theory maintains that metaphor is a form of 'loose talk' and can be understood through various pragmatic processes of narrowing and broadening, all of which are guided by the presumption of optimal relevance (Sperber & Wilson, 2008; Wilson & Sperber, 2012; see Chapter 3). For this reason, metaphor understanding works more along the lines of a categorization process than a comparison one. Conceptual blending theory claims that metaphors, similar to many other forms of language, are interpreted via the projection of information from various input spaces to create a separate blended space which yields a new emergent meaning structure (Fauconnier & Turner, 2008; see also Chapter 2). In this way, metaphor processing is not simply explained in terms of the projection of information from the source domain to the target domain, as is typically assumed by conceptual metaphor theory. Certain cognitive neuroscience research demonstrates additional brain activations in places where the blending processing is presumed to be especially prominent (Yang et al., 2013).

Conceptual metaphor in verbal metaphor processing

A major finding from cognitive linguistics is that conventional expressions with similar metaphorical meanings are sometimes motivated by different conceptual metaphors (Lakoff & Johnson, 1980). For instance, the American conventional phrase 'blow your top' expresses anger in terms of a pressurized container whose top blows off under high pressure (ANGER IS HEAT IN A PRESSURIZED CONTAINER), while 'jump down your throat' reflects the metaphoric mapping ANGRY BEHAVIOR IS AGGRESSIVE ANIMAL BEHAVIOR by expressing anger in terms of an angry animal that attacks by jumping at someone's throat.

Do people tacitly understand that conventional metaphorical phrases referring to the same topic can be motivated by different conceptual metaphors? Participants in one study were quite good at linking idioms (e.g., 'blow your stack') with their underlying conceptual metaphors (e.g., ANGER IS HEATED FLUID IN THE BODILY CONTAINER), suggesting that they have tacit beliefs of conceptual metaphors that motivate their understanding of some idioms (Nayak & Gibbs, 1990). Furthermore, people recognize that some idioms, but not others, are appropriate in certain contexts because of the congruence between these phrases' motivating conceptual metaphors and how a context metaphorically describes some topic. These findings showed that people use their conceptual metaphor knowledge to make sense of why some idioms and conventional metaphors convey specific metaphorical meanings.

Psycholinguistic studies have also demonstrated that people access conceptual metaphors during online processing of verbal metaphors. For example, people's reading of conventional metaphorical phrases (e.g., 'John blew his stack') primed their subsequent lexical decision judgments for word strings related to the conceptual metaphors motivating the figurative meanings of the idioms (e.g., 'heat' for ANGER IS HEATED FLUID IN THE BODILY CONTAINER) (Gibbs et al., 1997). Furthermore, people took less time to make lexical decisions for a word like 'heat' after reading 'John blew his stack' than after 'John jumped down his throat' which was motivated by a different conceptual metaphor. Although these studies show that conceptual metaphors immediately shape even conventional metaphor understanding, it is unclear whether people compute the conceptual metaphor mappings or simply retrieve them en bloc from memory.

Experimental studies show that switching metaphors in discourse can be cognitively difficult if these are motivated by different conceptual metaphors. In one study, people at an airport (Chicago O'Hare) were presented a priming question about time in either the ego-moving form (e.g., 'Is Boston ahead or behind in time?') or the time-moving form (e.g., 'Is it earlier or later in Boston than it is here?') (Gentner, Imai, & Boroditsky, 2002). After answering, the participants were asked the target question 'So should I turn my watch forward or back?' that was consistent with the ego-moving form. The experimenter measured response times to the target question with a stopwatch disguised as a wristwatch. Response times for consistently primed questions were shorter than for inconsistently primed questions. Switching metaphorical schemas caused an increase in processing time. People took less time to interpret verbal metaphors when these were all related to a single conceptual metaphor in discourse than when they were not (Thibodeau & Durgin, 2008).

Many metaphor studies have explored people's understanding of temporal events using the 'ambiguous time question.' Thus, if told that 'the meeting originally scheduled for next Wednesday has been moved forward two days,' should people respond that the meeting is now on Monday or Friday? One set of studies examined people's understanding of the TIME IS MOTION conceptual metaphor by first asking people to read a 'fictive' motion sentence (e.g., 'The tattoo runs along his spine') or a sentence that did not imply fictive motion (e.g., 'The tattoo is next to the spine') and then answer the 'move forward' question (Matlock, Ramscar, & Boroditsky, 2005). People gave significantly more Friday than Monday responses after reading the fictive motion expressions, but not the non-fictive motion statements. These results imply that people inferred the TIME IS MOTION conceptual metaphor when reading the fictive motion expressions. Thus, by inferring TIME IS MOTION when reading 'The tattoo runs along his spine,' people are primed to understand the ambiguous 'move forward' question in a future (e.g., Friday) as opposed to a backward (e.g., Monday) direction (also see Matlock et al., 2011).

Some studies have gone on to show that important individual differences exist in how people respond to ambiguous time questions. One study first asked people to fill out a survey that assessed their personality trait of anger. Later on, when responding to the ambiguous time question, participants with higher trait anger were more likely to adopt the ego-moving perspective (e.g., 'Friday') than the time-moving view (e.g., 'Monday') (Hauser, Carter, & Meier, 2009). A different set of experiments demonstrated that people who were high on the personality dimension of procrastination adopted the time-moving perspective, while those with angry personalities were more likely to use the ego-moving viewpoint. These studies highlight the relevance of personality factors, one of many possible individual differences, in theories of metaphor processing.

Many psycholinguistic studies have investigated cognitive linguistic ideas on the role of embodied experience and, more specifically, embodied simulations in verbal metaphor understanding (Bergen, 2012; Gibbs, 2006). We understand language as if we imagine ourselves engaging in actions relevant to the words spoken or read. Simulation processes, under this view, are not purely mental or neural, but involve and effect many full-bodied sensations. For instance, in one series of studies on metaphorical talk about time, students waiting in line at a café were given the statement 'Next Wednesday's meeting has been moved forward two days' and then asked 'What day is the meeting that has been rescheduled?' (Borodistky & Ramscar, 2002). Students who were farther along in the line (i.e., who had thus very recently experienced more forward spatial motion) were more likely to say that the meeting had been moved to Friday rather than to Monday.

Other studies show that people's speeded comprehension of metaphorical phrases like 'grasp the concept' were facilitated when they first made, or imagined making in this case, a grasping movement (Wilson & Gibbs, 2007). Finally, yet another test of the embodied simulation hypothesis asked people to read sentences conveying literal meanings (e.g., 'She climbed up the hill'), metaphorical meanings (e.g., 'She climbed up in the company'), and abstract (e.g., 'She succeeded in the company') meanings (Santana & de Vega, 2011). As they read the sentences, participants made single hand movements, up or down, which matched or mismatched the sentence meanings. Analysis of the hand movement times showed that people performed them faster when they matched the meanings for all three types of sentences. These findings suggest that both metaphorical and abstract sentence meanings recruit embodied representations related to, in this case, vertical spatial movements.

Most generally, there is good evidence that relevant bodily movement does not interfere with people's comprehension of abstract metaphorical meaning. Instead, moving in certain ways enhances the embodied simulations people ordinarily construct during their interpretation of metaphorical language. Neuroscience work has also shown activation in the motor system of participants' brains when they read both literal statements (e.g., 'grasped the stick') and metaphorical statements (e.g., 'grasped the idea') (Desai et al., 2011). This offers additional evidence that embodied simulations may underlie our understanding of metaphorical meanings.

One implication of the psycholinguistic and neuroscience research is that people do not just access passively encoded conceptual metaphors from long-term memory during online metaphor understanding, but simulate what these actions may be like to create detailed understandings of speakers' metaphorical messages. Gibbs and Santa Cruz (2012; also see Chapter 4) argue that people's inferences about conceptual metaphors are emergent properties of self-organization processes which are created in the moment of thinking, speaking, and understanding. Under this view, various levels of metaphorical experience, ranging from culture to neural processes, dynamically operate along different time-scales to 'soft-assemble' conceptual metaphors that are finely adaptive to specific contexts.

Individual differences in metaphor processing

As mentioned earlier, it is critical to recognize that the major findings of different experimental studies do not imply that virtually all people participating in these studies necessarily behave in the same manner, nor does a single person behave the same way throughout the course of a single experiment. For example, various experimental studies have demonstrated that individuals with higher working memory spans and higher IQ scores are better able to draw divergent cross-domain mappings during verbal metaphor processing than are people with more limited working memory spans and lower IQ scores (Chiappe & Chiappe, 2007; Iskandar & Baird, 2014). Similarly, differences in people's executive control also influence the speed with which they read both literal and metaphorical uses of verbs in sentences (Columbus et al., 2015). Individual differences in cognitive capacity give rise to varying results on standard measures of metaphor processing abilities (see also Chapters 32 and 33).

Perhaps the most complex literature in the study of metaphor processing is seen in research on metaphor and the brain. One long-standing belief is that the most critical language areas in the brain are found in the left cerebral hemisphere (LH). But a variety of evidence suggests that damage to the right hemisphere (RH) impairs significant aspects of metaphorical language comprehension (Federmeier, Wlotko, & Meyer, 2008). For example, individuals with left-hemisphere brain lesions can readily match metaphors with appropriate pictures, while right-hemisphere patients were less able to correctly see the correspondence between specific verbal metaphors and pictures that expressed their meanings (MacKenzie et al., 1997). Individuals with unilateral RH damage do not show typical semantic priming effects for targets associated with the metaphorical meanings of words in context (e.g., 'chicken-scared') although LH-damaged patients exhibit these speeded facilitation effects (Klepousniotou & Baum, 2007). The RH is critical to processing novel metaphors in sentential contexts, and when people make semantic relatedness judgments for verbal metaphors (Yang, 2014). Having an intact RH may be necessary for understanding some aspects of metaphorical word meanings.

One proposal, called the 'fine-coarse semantic coding theory,' suggests that the left hemisphere engages in fine semantic coding, which is critical to most linguistic processing (Jung-Beeman, 2005). On the other hand, the right hemisphere engages in coarse semantic coding when more than one plausible meaning is considered or when there is sustained attention given to a wide range of meanings, as in the case of metaphor. Individuals with RH damage are less able to draw connections between diverse concepts, which hinders their ability to quickly interpret metaphor (Faust, 2012).

But other studies indicate that both hemispheres play a role in interpreting unfamiliar metaphorical sentences (Ahrens et al., 2007), and that right-hemisphere-damaged patients can give adequate paraphrases of many conventional metaphorical phrases (e.g., 'hand over' or 'broken heart') (Giora et al., 2000). Moreover having more exposure to a novel metaphor (e.g., 'burning lie,' 'processed smile') changes the patterns of hemisphere activity from right lateralization to an equal involvement of both hemispheres (Mashal et al., 2013). Another study demonstrated no differences in the activation of the two hemispheres when people interpreted metaphorical word meanings in sentence contexts (Coulson & Van Petten, 2007). In general, it is unclear whether an intact RH is essential for metaphor processing, although this depends, perhaps, on the people studied, the types of metaphors examined, and the specific experimental task.

Various neurological disorders also hamper metaphorical language understanding. Traumatically brain-injured patients show weaker abilities to make judgments about the valence of novel metaphors than do controls (Yang et al., 2013). Patients with schizophrenia and Alzheimer's disease sometimes experience difficulty explaining the meanings of proverbs and novel metaphors, but not conventional metaphors and idioms (Roncero & deAlmeida, 2014). Explaining what metaphors mean is a more difficult task than fast processing of metaphorical meaning. But the challenge faced by certain populations of people in describing what metaphors mean suggests that cognitive and physiological impairments make metaphor processing more difficult (also see Chapter 33). Neuroscience studies, most generally, suggest that many factors contribute to schizophrenics' difficulties in interpreting metaphorical meaning, notably: deficiencies in abstract thought, difficulties with personal associations to words in verbal metaphors, the inability to suppress literal readings of statements, integrating statement meanings with context, and the impairment of theory of mind abilities.

Autistic adults also sometimes suffer from different figurative language deficits, with one popular proposal suggesting that this is due to reduced Theory of Mind abilities. For example, one classic study asked both autistic and typically developing children, along with a group of adults, to answer different questions regarding their understandings of both metaphor and irony in context (Happe, 1993). Autistic individuals were somewhat impaired in their understanding of the metaphors, but were especially poor at irony understanding. Irony is widely recognized as being more complex in terms of the inferences needed to infer what speakers actually believe and intend (e.g., related to people's Theory of Mind abilities), which partly explains autistics' difficulties with irony. But other studies show that some individuals diagnosed with autism spectrum disorders, especially those with Asperger syndrome, are as good at automatically processing metaphor as typically developing individuals (Giora et al., 2012; Herman et al., 2013). Once again, different understanding tasks (e.g., answering questions vs. speeded sensibility judgments) will sometimes provide different empirical findings regarding individuals' abilities to process metaphor.

Conclusions and future directions

The empirical research on metaphor processing is enormously complex. This fact stands in stark contrast with the wide variety of theories within linguistics, psychology, and philosophy that aim to explain how metaphors are ordinarily produced and interpreted. Our review of some of the highlights of the empirical literature again leads us to conclude that there is no single theory that readily explains metaphor understanding as done by all people in all discourse situations. We maintain that scholars should explicitly create theories that are sensitive to the real complexities of metaphor use. This move will require that scholars properly acknowledge variations in the people who use metaphor, the different kinds of metaphor, the contexts in which metaphor is used, the rhetorical goals in using metaphor, and the wide variety of understanding tasks. Embracing this perspective also demands that metaphor processing not be seen as an isolated linguistic ability and that metaphor use be properly recognized as being always contextual, communicative, multimodal, and thoroughly embodied.

A second task metaphor scholars need to tackle is to explore the ways that metaphorical language accomplishes different pragmatic goals in both speech and writing. People rarely use verbal metaphors to simply express particular, or even vague, metaphorical meanings. Instead, they speak and write using different metaphors to accomplish a variety of rhetorical goals and induce many pragmatic effects. When psychologists measure the time it takes to process a metaphorical utterance, for example, they are implicitly examining the pragmatic inferences that people draw when interpreting some statement in context. However, the pragmatic effects of metaphorical language, which guides what metaphorical meanings are actually processed, needs to be included in any theoretical account of metaphor understanding.

For example, studies show that people take different amounts of time, and draw different pragmatic inferences, when processing a metaphor, such as 'Lawyers are also sharks,' depending on whether the speaker wishes to affirm an existing belief about lawyers, to introduce a new idea about lawyers, or to contradict a previously stated belief about lawyers (e.g., 'Lawyers are saints') (Gibbs, Tendahl, & Okonski, 2011). The rhetorical functions that a metaphor has in some specific discourse influence both its processing and what other pragmatic meanings may be understood. To give another example, people spend less time processing a metaphor (e.g., 'My marriage is an icebox') when it answers a yes-no question (e.g., 'Are you happy in your marriage?'), compared to when the same expression is stated as part of one person's description of her marriage (Gibbs, 2010). People also typically draw fewer metaphorical meanings when hearing 'My marriage is an icebox' after a yes-no question than when the statement is seen in a context where a single speaker is simply describing her marriage. Thus, people interpret a metaphor only to the extent that it offers enough meanings to draw a relevant contextual message.

Pragmatic effects may arguably be more pronounced in some aspects of verbal metaphor use, given the multitude of complex processes available in metaphorical language interpretation, and patent in mere exposure to some kinds of metaphorical language. Even though scholars have long been interested in metaphor processing, almost all of the attention is given to how people determine the metaphorical meaning alone, with little consideration given to what other affective and pragmatic inferences are derived. Simply put, we need to study the pragmatic effects that people infer as part of their processing of metaphor and see these not as secondary by-products of metaphorical meaning, but as an essential reason for why metaphor is used in the first place.

Further reading

Gibbs, R. W., Jr. (2015). *Metaphor wars: Conceptual metaphor in human life*. New York: Cambridge University Press.

Bowes, A., & Katz, A. (2015). Metaphor creates intimacy and enhances one's ability to infer the internal states of others. *Memory and Cognition, 43*, 953–963.

Kovesces, Z. (2015). *Where metaphors come from: Reconsidering context in metaphor*. New York: Oxford University Press.

References

Ahrens, K., Liu, H.-L., Lee, C.-Y., Gong, S.-P., Fang, S.-Y., & Hsu., Y.-Y. (2007). Functional MRI of conventional and anomalous metaphors in Mandarin Chinese. *Brain and Language, 100*, 163–171.

Aisenman, R. (1999). Structure-mapping and the simile-metaphor preference. *Metaphor and Symbol, 14*, 45–52.

Bergen, B. (2012). *Louder than words: The new science of how the mind makes meaning*. New York: Basic Books.

Boroditsky, L., & Ramscar, M. (2002). The roles of body and mind in abstract thought. *Psychological Science, 13*, 185–189.

Chiappe, D., & Chiappe, P. (2007). The role of working memory in metaphor production and comprehension. *Journal of Memory and Language, 56*, 172–188.

Columbus, G., Sheikh, N., Cote-Lecaldare, M., Hauser, K., Baum, S., & Titone, D. (2015). Individual differences in executive control relate to metaphor processing: An eye movement study of sentence reading. *Frontiers in Human Neuroscience*. doi: 10.3389/fnhum.2014.01057.

Colston, H. (2015). *Using figurative language*. New York: Cambridge University Press.

Coulson, S., & Van Petten, C. (2007). A special role for the right hemisphere in metaphor comprehension? ERP evidence from hemifield presentation. *Brain Research, 1146*, 128–145.

Desai, R., Binder, J., Conant, L., Mano, Q., & Seidenberg, M. (2011). The neural career of sensory-motor metaphors. *Journal of Cognitive Neuroscience, 23*, 2376–2386.

Fauconnier, G., & Turner, M. (2008). Rethinking metaphor. In R. W. Gibbs, Jr. (Ed.), *The Cambridge handbook of metaphor and thought* (pp. 53–66). New York: Cambridge University Press.

Faust, M. (2012). Thinking outside the left box: The role of the right hemisphere in novel metaphor comprehension. In M. Faust (Ed.), *The handbook of the neuropsychology of language. Language processing in the brain: Basic science* (pp. 425–448). Malden, MA: Wiley-Blackwell.

Federmeier, K. D., Wlotko, E. W., & Meyer, A. M. (2008). What's 'right' in language comprehension: Event-related potentials reveal right hemisphere language capabilities. *Language and Linguistics Compass, 2*(1), 1–17.

Gentner, D., & Bowdle, B. (2008). Metaphor as structure-mapping. In R. W. Gibbs, Jr. (Ed.), *The Cambridge handbook of metaphor and thought* (pp. 109–128). New York: Cambridge University Press.

Gentner, D., Bowdle, B., Wolff, P., & Boronat, C. (2001). Metaphor is like analogy. In D. Gentner, K. Holyoak, & B. Kokinov (Eds.), *The analogical mind: Perspectives from cognitive science* (pp. 199–253). Cambridge, MA: MIT Press.

Gentner, D., Imai, M., & Boroditsky, L. (2002). As time goes by: Understanding time as spatial metaphor. *Language and Cognitive Processes, 17*, 537–565.

Gibbs, R. W., Jr. (1990). Comprehending figurative referential descriptions. *Journal of Experimental Psychology: Learning, Memory, and Cognition, 16*, 56–66.

—— (1994). *The poetics of mind: Figurative thought, language, and understanding*. New York: Cambridge University Press.

—— (2006). *Embodiment and cognitive science*. New York: Cambridge University Press.

—— (2010). The wonderful, chaotic, creative, heroic, challenging world of researching and applying metaphor: A celebration of the past and some peeks into the future. In G. Low, Z. Todd, A. Deignan, & L. Cameron (Eds.), *Researching and applying metaphor in the real world* (pp. 11–33). Amsterdam, The Netherlands: Benjamins.

Gibbs, R. W., Jr., Bogdonovich, J., Sykes, J., & Barr, D. (1997). Metaphor in idiom comprehension. *Journal of Memory and Language, 37*, 141–154.

Gibbs, R. W., Jr., & Colston, H. (2012). *Interpreting figurative meaning*. New York: Cambridge University Press.

Gibbs, R. W., Jr., & Santa Cruz, M. (2012). Temporal unfolding of conceptual metaphoric experience. *Metaphor and Symbol, 27*, 299–311.

Gibbs, R. W., Jr., Tendahl, M., & Okonski, L. (2011). Inferring pragmatic messages from metaphor. *Lodz Papers in Pragmatics, 7*, 3–28.

Gineste, M.-D., Indurkhya, B., & Scart, V. (2000). Emergence of features in metaphor comprehension. *Metaphor and Symbol, 15*, 117–135.

Giora, R. (2003). *On our mind: Salience, context and figurative language*. New York: Oxford University Press.

—— (2012). Happy New War: The role of salient meanings and salience-based interpretations in processing utterances. In H.-J. Schmid (Ed.), *Cognitive pragmatics* (Handbook of Pragmatics, Vol. 4, pp. 233–260). Berlin, Germany: Mouton de Gruyter.

Giora, R., Gazal, O., Goldstein, I., Fein, O., & Stringaris, A. (2012). Salience and context: Interpretation of metaphorical and literal language by young adults diagnosed with Asperger's syndrome. *Metaphor and Symbol, 27*, 22–54.

Giora, R., Livnat, E., Fein, O., Barnea, A., Zeiman, R., & Berger, I. (2013). Negation generates nonliteral interpretations by default. *Metaphor and Symbol, 28*(2), 89–115.

Giora, R., Zaidel, E., Soroker, N., Batori, G., & Kasher, A. (2000). Differential effects of right- and left-hemisphere damage on understanding sarcasm and metaphor. *Metaphor and Symbol, 15*, 63–83.

Glucksberg, S. (2001). *Understanding figurative language: From metaphor to idioms*. New York: Oxford University Press.

Glucksberg, S., & Haught, C. (2006). On the relation between metaphor and simile: When comparison fails. *Mind and Language, 21*, 360–378.

Goldstein, A., Arzouan, Y., & Faust, M. (2012). Killing a novel metaphor and reviving a dead one: ERP correlates of metaphor conventionalization. *Brain and Language, 123*, 137–142.

Grice, H. P. (1975). Logic and conversation. In P. Cole and J. Morgan (Eds.), *Syntax and semantics: Vol 3. Speech acts* (pp. 41–58). New York: Academic Press.

Happe, F. (1993). Communicative competence and theory of mind in autism: A test of relevance theory. *Cognition, 48*, 101–119.

Haught, C. (2013). A tale of two tropes: How metaphor and simile differ. *Metaphor and Symbol, 28*(4): 254–274.

Hauser, D. J., Carter, M. S., & Meier, B. P. (2009). Mellow Monday and furious Friday: The approach-related link between anger and time representation. *Cognition and Emotion, 23*, 1166–1180.

Herman, I., Haser, V., van Elst, L. T., Ebert, D., Müller-Feldmeth, D., Riedel, A., & Konieczny, L. (2013). Automatic metaphor processing in adults with Asperger syndrome: A metaphor interference effect task. *European Archive of Psychiatry and Clinical Neuroscience, 268*, S177–S187.

Iskandar, S., & Baird, A. (2014). The role of working memory and divided attention in metaphor interpretation. *Journal of Psycholinguistic Research, 43*, 555–568.

Jung-Beeman, M. (2005). Bilateral brain processes for comprehending natural language. *Trends in Cognitive Sciences, 9*, 512–518.

Katz, A. N. (2005). Discourse and social-cultural factors in understanding nonliteral language. In H. Colston & A. Katz (Eds.), *Figurative language comprehension: Social and cultural influences* (pp. 183–207). Mahwah, NJ: Erlbaum.

Katz, A. N., & Ferretti, T. R. (2003). Reading proverbs in context: The role of explicit markers. *Discourse Processes, 36*(1), 19–46.

Klepousniotou, E., & Baum, S. (2007). Disambiguating the ambiguity advantage effect in word recognition: An advantage for polysemous but not homonymous words. *Journal of Neurolinguistics, 20*, 1–24.

Kövecses, Z. (2010). *Metaphor: A practical introduction* (2nd ed.). New York: Oxford University Press.

Lakoff, G., & Johnson, M. (1980). *Metaphors we live by*. Chicago, IL: University of Chicago Press.

Mackenzie, C., Begg, T., Brady, M., & Lees, K. (1997). The effects on verbal communication skills of right hemisphere stroke in middle age. *Aphasiology, 11*, 929–945.

Mashal, N., Vishne, T., Laor, N., & Titone, D. (2013). Enhanced left frontal involvement during novel metaphor comprehension in schizophrenia: Evidence from functional neuroimaging. *Brain and Language, 124*, 66–74.

Matlock, T., Holmes, K., Srinivasan, M., & Ramscar, M. (2011). Even abstract motion influences the understanding of time. *Metaphor and Symbol, 26*(4), 260–271.

Matlock, T., Ramscar, M., & Boroditsky, L. (2005). The experiential link between spatial and temporal language. *Cognitive Science, 29*, 655–664.

Nayak, N., & Gibbs, R. W., Jr. (1990). Conceptual knowledge in the interpretation of idioms. *Journal of Experimental Psychology: General, 119*, 315–330.

Noveck, I., Bianco, M., & Castry, A. (2001). The costs and benefits of metaphor. *Metaphor and Symbol, 16*, 109–121.

Pexman, P., Ferretti, T., & Katz, A. (2000). Discourse factors that influence the online reading of metaphor and irony. *Discourse Processes, 29*, 201–222.

Roncero, C., & deAlmeida, R. (2014). The importance of being apt: Metaphor comprehension in Alzheimer's disease. *Frontiers in Human Neuroscience, 8*(973), 1–14.

Rubio-Fernandez, P. (2007). Suppression in metaphor interpretation: Differences between meaning selection and meaning construction. *Journal of Semantics, 24*, 345–371.

Santana, E., & de Vega, M. (2011). Metaphors are embodied, and so are their literal counterparts. *Frontiers in Psychology, 2,* 1–12.

Sperber, D., & Wilson, D. (2008). A deflationary account of metaphors. In R. W., Jr. Gibbs (Ed.), *Cambridge handbook of metaphor and thought* (pp. 84–105). New York: Cambridge University Press.

Utsumi, A. (2005). The role of feature emergence in metaphor appreciation. *Metaphor and Symbol, 20,* 151–172.

Thibodeau, P., & Durgin, F. (2008). Productive figurative communication: Conventional metaphors facilitate the comprehension of related novel metaphors. *Journal of Memory and Language, 58,* 521–540.

Tourangeau, R., & Rips, L. (1991). Interpreting and evaluating metaphors. *Journal of Memory and Language, 30,* 452–472.

Weiland, H., Bambini, V., & Schumacher, P. B. (2014). The role of literal meaning in figurative language comprehension: Evidence from masked priming ERP. *Frontiers in Human Neuroscience, 8,* ArtID 583.

Wilson, D., & Sperber, D. (2012). *Meaning and relevance.* New York: Cambridge University Press.

Wilson, N., & Gibbs, R. W., Jr. (2007). Real and imagined body movement primes metaphor comprehension. *Cognitive Science, 31,* 721–731.

Yang, F.-P., Bradley, K., Huq, M., Wu, D.-L., & Krawcyk, D. (2013). Contextual effects on conceptual blending in metaphors: An event-related potential study. *Journal of Neurolinguistics, 26,* 312–326.

Yang, J. (2014). The role of the right hemisphere in metaphor comprehension: A meta-analysis of functional magnetic resonance imaging studies. *Human Brain Mapping, 35,* 107–122.

32
Psycholinguistic approaches to metaphor acquisition and use

Albert N. Katz

Introduction

Much of our thinking about metaphor can be traced to the writings of Aristotle in *The Poetics* and in *The Rhetoric*. In the former he defines metaphor as the act of giving a thing a name that belongs to something else. From the examples he provides we can understand the cognitive work in producing and comprehending metaphor as involving the replacement of one term with another in a meaning hierarchy (from 'species' to 'genus') or by reasoning through analogy. In *The Rhetoric* the emphasis is on the aesthetic force of metaphor. Aristotle claims in part that lively or good metaphors (a) convey information rapidly, (b) are especially apt if the information is not already cognitively represented and (c) involve an eye for seeing resemblances between otherwise unlike things. The emphasis here then is on novelty, the emergence of new ways of understanding and the creation of pleasurable communication. Aristotelian thought has influenced subsequent study of metaphor, and here I examine two of the emphases that arise from the Aristotelian tradition: the cognitive work involved in comprehending and constructing metaphor, and second, its aesthetic force and novelty. I do this unabashedly, from the perspective of a cognitive psychologist and experimental psycholinguist. As such, the extensive literature that arises from the cognitive linguistic tradition, or some other traditions, such as Relevance Theory, only makes an appearance now and then and only as it has been adapted by experimentalists.

Overview of main trends in psycholinguistic approaches to metaphor

Psycholinguistics is a multidisciplinary approach to understanding the relation between linguistic behaviour and psychological processes. Lying mainly at the intersection of experimental psychology and linguistic theory, the field borrows heavily also from the study of philosophy, sociolinguistics and both computer science and neuroscience. Psycholinguists are interested in using behavioural linguistic output, what people actually say or write, to make inferences about the mental structures and processes that permit the comprehension and production of language. Psycholinguists make use of many of the methods discussed elsewhere in this book but, in addition, make use of tasks derived from experimental psychology, such as examining errors in reproducing previously seen or heard texts or manipulating a given theoretically interesting variable (e.g. the concreteness of the words in the metaphoric expression) and measuring the impact of the manipulation (to see, for instance, whether the manipulation led to the text being read more rapidly or perceived as less apt).

Increasingly, psycholinguists derive their theoretical models from online tasks (tasks that monitor linguistic behaviour moment by moment during the act of comprehension or production) (see Spivey, McRae, & Joanisse, 2012). For instance, during reading, psycholinguists can measure how long a person spends focused on each word in a text or, on reading a given word embedded in a longer text, and whether their eyes move to reconsider a word already examined. In some studies, Event-Related Potential (ERP) technology is employed wherein brain waves are measured that are tied to each word in a text a person is reading. For instance, if a person is reading a metaphorical expression (e.g. 'The doctor is a butcher'), electrodes situated on the scalp will pick up the electrical signals of neurons activated with, let's say, the word 'butcher'. One can examine the electronic pattern associated with that word over time. By now, there is a set of well-known patterns related to the comprehension of language. One such neural pattern is a negative deflection from baseline that peaks at around 400 milliseconds after a word is presented (the so-called N400) and is taken as a measure of a momentary difficulty in comprehension.

Psycholinguistics and metaphor

An important aspect of psycholinguistic research has been understanding basic issues in ambiguity resolution. For instance, consider a sentence such as 'The policeman saw the thief on the mountain with binoculars'. There is a syntactic ambiguity in which comprehension depends on resolving whether the policeman was using the binoculars or whether the thief had with him a pair of binoculars. Or consider a sentence such as the 'The man threw the rock at the bank'. Here there is an ambiguity because the word 'bank' could refer to a river bank or a financial institution. Research in this tradition has tried to resolve whether both meanings of the word are initially activated, even when the context is biased towards one of the meanings (see Katz, 1998, for a review of this literature).

One could argue that metaphor is another instance of ambiguity in which a word or phrase is not being used in its literal or potentially most common manner. Consider the metaphor 'that lawyer is a shark' where clearly the person is not a fish. Nonetheless, one concept (the so-called vehicle or source, 'shark') is being used to provide information about the other concept (the so-called topic, 'lawyer'). Roughly starting in the 1970s, it was assumed that the basic 'problem' in metaphor comprehension is in describing mechanisms wherein one could find 'similarity' between seemingly unlike words (see Ortony, 1979) or in classifying a word as a member of an implied category (e.g. 'animate entities that are vicious, aggressive and merciless', which would include both sharks and some lawyers) (see Glucksberg & Keysar, 1990). In this latter word-based tradition (discussed in more detail later), metaphor, especially of the A is B variety, is treated as a class assertion statement, no different than the phrase 'that dog is a collie'. With metaphoric expressions, such as 'that butcher is a surgeon', one also attempts to classify 'butcher' into a superordinate category. However, because 'butcher' is not a category label like 'collie', comprehension requires that 'butcher' takes on a secondary meaning to stand for a category, such as a 'class of people that does delicate, difficult and expert work'.

In contrast to the emphasis on the linguistic basis for metaphors above, there are those who shifted the narrative to the conceptual aspects involved. In an early version of this shift, Lehrer (1978) and Kittay and Lehrer (1981) proposed and tested the implications that one has to consider of the semantic fields of the words being juxtaposed when considering metaphor comprehension and the growth of metaphors in a population. That is, metaphor is considered as a juxtaposition not merely of topic and vehicle words, but rather of the complex of words associated with each. Although at one level one can understand this set as based on concepts, Lehrer (1978) often uses the term 'semantic field' as synonymous with 'lexical set'. As such, I would argue that still the main focus here is on the structure of the lexicon and on understanding metaphor as the transfer of meaning from a vehicle to a topic.

A complete rupture between linguistic usage and conceptual underpinnings was introduced by Lakoff and Johnson (1980; see also Lakoff, 1993), who radically shifted the emphasis from the expressed metaphoric utterance to an implied cognitive basis. As discussed in Chapter 1, the basic argument is that multiple metaphoric expressions are better understood as deriving from a deeper cognitive structure in which concepts from different domains are mapped onto one another. As such, Lakoff and Johnson claim, the identification of cross-domain conceptual mappings (such as LIFE IS A JOURNEY) motivates the use and understanding of a set of seemingly unrelated expressions (e.g. 'I am near the end of my life'; 'I am stuck at the crossroads of where I want to go'). It is argued further that the basis for the conceptual mapping is rooted in experience with the world and its embodiment. Conceptual metaphors structure how we perceive and understand the world and motivate our thinking; some are also considered primary (Grady, 1997) and as being automatically aroused. Many of the chapters in this book have assumed and embraced this position. In contrast, bar a few exceptions, this model has not been adopted by most experimental psychologists for reasons discussed at the end of this chapter. Consequently, the research described presently will be based on more traditional psychological approaches to metaphor understanding.

A question related to how one processes metaphor is why metaphor (or other tropes) is even necessary, given that in many cases an acceptable 'literal' alternative is available. From the cognitive linguistic perspective, the metaphoric mapping of concepts is a natural consequence of an underlying cognitive system and, by default, requires no additional layer of explanation. Indirect evidence for the embodiment of metaphor as part of our genetic inheritance can be found in recent primate research. For example, Dahl and Adachi (2013) found evidence that our closest evolutionary relative, the chimpanzee, systematically maps an abstract social dimension, dominance hierarchy, as a metaphor wherein UP IS DOMINANT. In contrast, the typical experimentalist response is that metaphor serves some pragmatic functions, in addition to communicative ones (see Katz, 1996a), and from this perspective understanding how metaphors are acquired and developed in the general population is particularly interesting.

The acquisition of metaphor

Two aspects of the acquisition of metaphor will be described: developments over the course of (a neuro-typical) childhood and, second, developments due to repeated usage of particular metaphors over time.

Developmental aspects of metaphor acquisition

Experimental psychologists turned their attention to the study of metaphor, in part as a question in cognitive development (see Billow, 1975; Winner, 1988). Given the schism between linguistic and cognitive conceptions of metaphor, it is unsurprising that different emphases are given to developmental questions of metaphor from these two perspectives. For instance, if metaphor is mainly a matter of language, then metaphor acquisition should parallel the acquisition and use of language. In contrast, if metaphor is mainly a matter of conception, then its acquisition should parallel what is known about cognitive development. The interpretive problem is exacerbated by the fact that language and conceptual growth both show rapid development in early life.

Despite difficulties such as disentangling linguistic from cognitive development, it is clear that metaphoric abstraction, or at least some forms of abstraction that are metaphor-like, emerge with early language production and comprehension (see Billow, 1981; Gentner, 1977; Malgady, 1977; the review by Winner, 1988). It is widely recognized that by age 5, children are exhibiting relatively sophisticated metaphor acquisition and usage, with ever-increasing complexity in usage occurring well into adolescence. In an influential early study, Billow (1975) studied children ranging in age from 5 to 13 years old. Harkening back to distinctions made by Aristotle, Billow distinguished between two kinds of metaphors, single attribute 'similarity' metaphors, where two objects share a feature (A is similar to B, e.g. 'his hair is spaghetti'), and 'proportional' or 'analogical' metaphors, involving the coordination of four elements: A is to B as C is to D, e.g. 'my head is an apple without any core', where head is to apple as brain is to core. Billow presented examples of each type of metaphor and asked the children to give their interpretation of them. With metaphors based on single attribute similarity a clear developmental trend was found: 5-year-olds could explain the basis of the metaphor about 30 per cent of the time, 7-year-olds almost 75 per cent of the time and performance was close to 100 per cent for the 11-year-olds. Understanding proportional metaphor was overall more difficult but also demonstrated a developmental trend: 9-year-olds performed at about 40 per cent competence, and the ability to give a correct explanation of a metaphoric relation reached about 80 per cent for the 13-year-olds.

Other work has emphasized the development of cognitive knowledge. For instance, recall the suggestion made earlier, that metaphors cannot be considered simply as combinations of two dissimilar terms but, rather, as juxtapositions of two entire semantic fields. Keil (1986), adopting this position, argued that metaphoric competency should become apparent with the growth of knowledge about different conceptual domains. For instance, Keil (1979) found that children acquire knowledge about the semantic fields associated with 'animals' much earlier than they do about the semantic field associated with 'personality traits'. Consequently one might expect that, for a young child, a fairly novel metaphor, such as 'the boy was a bear', would be easier to understand than 'the man was a smooth character'. Keil (1986) presented metaphors based on the juxtaposition of items from different semantic fields to children from between 5 to 10 years of age, and asked them to explain what the sentence meant. He focused on whether metaphoric linkages would be given (e.g. given 'the boy was a bear', would characteristics of bears, such as 'scary' or 'wild', be used to describe the boy?) and observed that these metaphoric links increased with age. More importantly, he found that correct metaphoric explanations of different pairings from semantic fields emerged at roughly the same age. However, there was a difference in the age at which this emergence occurred, as a function of the knowledge held about a domain. In other words, metaphoric understanding of instances of people–personality trait comparisons (girl-outgoing; boy-reserved) that required more knowledge about the personality trait domain all emerged together but at an older age. This supports the notion that metaphor abilities (in both acquisition and use) develop on a domain-by-domain basis and as a function of the semantic knowledge held in the two domains juxtaposed in metaphor.

The approach taken by Keil is compatible with notions developed in Gentner's (1983) structure-mapping theory, wherein analogical reasoning involves a mapping of knowledge from one domain (which in her terminology is the *base*, analogous to use by others of the terms *source* or *vehicle*) into another (the *target* or *topic*), such that a system of relations that holds among the base objects also holds among the target objects. As extended to metaphor, this means that the recognition of metaphor as a set of relations found with both source and topic would show a developmental trajectory: earlier life metaphoric usage and understanding would be based on attribute similarities, while older children's usage would be based on systematic relations. This hypothesis is empirically supported (Gentner, 1988).

More recent work has taken two main directions. The first approach has been in trying to disentangle the role played by language development from that played by conceptual knowledge development, while the second involves examining the role of embodiment in metaphor acquisition. In an example of the former, Stites and Özçalişkan (2013a) distinguished the development of linguistic ability from conceptual knowledge for metaphors that link time to motion through space. Four groups of children (between the ages of 3 to 7) and an adult group were presented with metaphoric expressions such as 'the trip to the zoo is coming up soon', where time is described as an object in motion in space (in contrast with the literal, 'the dog is coming up to you'). Children were tested with the use of puppets and were introduced to the context with a short story; such as the experimenter stating: '*This is Patrick* (pointing to a picture of a child character). *This is Patrick's mom* (pointing to picture of an adult character). *Patrick's mom tells him that his trip to the zoo is coming up. Patrick is excited. He shouts 'YEAH!'* The testing then followed. The participant was asked '*Why is Patrick excited?*' and had to choose between two puppets giving different answers: Elmo stating '*His trip to the zoo is soon*' (correct choice), and Grover stating '*His trip to the zoo is now*' (incorrect choice). Comprehension was established based on the number of scenarios in which the correct option was chosen and understanding was based on follow-up questioning of the choice the children had made. In addition to the metaphor task, linguistic ability was assessed using a standardized test of verbal ability, the Peabody Picture Vocabulary Test (Dunn & Dunn, 2007). Performance increased with age, with the 6-year-olds performing near, or at, adult levels. More importantly from a theoretical perspective, Stites and Özçalişkan found that linguistic and cognitive factors selectively predict changes in children's metaphorical abilities. Explanation of metaphors – which requires use of oral language – was related to increasing verbal ability. Comprehension of metaphors – which did not require language production – was associated with the children's understanding of the conceptual domains that constitute the metaphor. It seems likely that more studies along these lines will continue to find nuanced relations between conceptual and linguistic growth throughout development.

The second direction that more recent research has taken involves examining the role played by embodiment in metaphor acquisition. In many ways, this literature is still at the promissory note level: rich in promise but yet to be widely studied empirically. The logic for these studies follows from both the developmental sequencing discussed above and embodied notions of cognition. From the former is the notion that mapping occurs initially at an attribute level, usually from physical to more abstract domains of experience. Embodied cognition holds that complex cognitive abilities are rooted in the bodily experiences we have with our environments, wherein, for instance, time is related to the bodily experience of the number of steps taken, and the manner, in which one moves through space. With adults, three spatial metaphors are used frequently: (a) time moves but an observer is stationary (e.g. 'winter is coming'), (b) time is stationary but the observer is moving (e.g. 'we are approaching the winter months') and (c) events move relative to one another independent of the observer ('spring follows winter').

Using procedures and age groups similar to the previous study, Stites and Özçalişkan (2013b) examined children's comprehension of the three different forms of metaphorically structuring time described above. Performance both in understanding and explaining spatial metaphors where events move independently of the observer was poorer than for the other two spatial metaphors for time. The authors speculate that this may be due to the fact that this metaphor is less embodied, not involving the child interacting with his or her environment directly. As noted above, the research literature on the developmental use of concepts structured by embodied metaphors is not extensive. Nonetheless, it is expected that more studies will be forthcoming, and already there are emerging literatures looking at the role played by embodiment in learning music and motor interactions (e.g. Bakker, Antle, & Van Den Hodden, 2012) and, at least with adults, metaphor and gestures (e.g. Casasanto, 2008).

The 'career' of metaphor over time

Recall the developmental literature discussed above in which younger children understand metaphors as a shared attribute linking two words or concepts, and older children see metaphor as a systematic mapping of relations. Gentner and her colleagues have elaborated on this observation and proposed that novel metaphor is processed and understood as comparison, whereas, with increasing experience and conventionalization, the metaphor shifts to categorical processing (see Gentner & Bowdle, 2001; Bowdle & Gentner, 2005). This proposal is incorporated into a model that considers familiarity, grammatical class, and different forms of processing. This model has in part been implemented in a computer program (Falkenhainer, Forbus, & Gentner, 1989; see Gentner, 1983) (a related model is described in Chapter 3).

Consider a novel metaphor such as 'Love is a rocket ship'. Without going into the complexities of Gentner's model, or its computer instantiation, the model works by seeing whether the source (rocket ship) has a secondary meaning different from its canonical sense of 'a ship that goes into space'. With novel metaphors there should be no such secondary meanings and the model proposes that people initially try to find ways in which love is <u>like</u> rocket ships via a comparison process involving the alignment of elements. If the source continues to be used in the same way and becomes conventional, then 'rocket ship' in addition to its canonical meaning obtains a secondary figurative meaning 'things that are both exciting and scary'. Accordingly, another metaphor, for instance, 'dinner with my boss is a rocket ship', would now be processed as a class inclusion statement wherein dinner with one's boss is an instance of the category: 'exciting but scary'.

The model can explain additional aspects of metaphor, such as the distinction between when metaphor is preferred and when simile is preferred. Given that novel metaphors are assumed to be processed as comparisons, one can expect that novel metaphor is in many ways analogous to a simile. As predicted, Bowdle and Gentner (2005) found that novel metaphors are more strongly preferred, and processed more rapidly, in simile form (X is like Y) than in metaphor form (X is Y). In contrast, conventional metaphors are equally acceptable in either the metaphor or the simile form, arguably because conventional metaphor statements can be processed either through comparison, by mapping the target onto the primary, literal meaning of the base, or through categorization, by mapping the target onto the secondary, figurative meaning of the base.

This model has invigorated research in a number of domains. Acknowledging the theoretical distinctions and the evidence that metaphor comprehension can be either via categorization or comparison, alternatives to the career theory have been suggested and tested, including emphases on factors other than conventionality, such as aptness (Glucksberg & Haught, 2006) and interpretive diversity (Utsumi, 2007). The theory has also renewed experimental investigations into the use and differences between metaphor and simile (e.g. Aisenman, 1999), alternate roles played by novelty and conventionality (see, for instance, Giora, 2003), aspects of the alignment principles in structure-mapping (e.g. Estes & Hassan, 2004) and attempts at mapping changes in neural processing as metaphor becomes conventionalized (e.g. Cardillo, Watson, Schmidt, Kranjec, & Chatterjee, 2012; Subramaniam, Faust, Beeman, & Mashal, 2012), amongst others.

The use of metaphor

There are many chapters in this book that look at how metaphor is used and applied within specific domains. Given the experimental psycholinguistic thrust of this chapter, here I will emphasize the literature more specific to psychological experiments. Moreover, Gibbs's (2013) reminder notwithstanding, there is a limited literature that uses the tools of the experimental psycholinguist to look at the role that social factors play in metaphor use.

Metaphor used to conceptualize and communicate difficult or novel concepts

The conceptualization and communication of novel concepts is especially marked in the sciences, especially when based on mathematics. There are numerous cases of the use of proportional or analogical metaphor, of the logical form A is to B as C is to D to explain scientific discovery (some common examples would be conceptualizing electrons as planets spinning around a nuclear sun or talking of 'black holes' or the mind as a computer) (see also Chapter 20). Dunbar's (2000) research program, for example, included the investigation of analogy and proportional metaphor to see how frequently they were used by physical scientists working in their laboratories and with their research groups. He found that analogies and metaphors were very frequently used in all aspects of the scientific process. Moreover he found differences in metaphoric use in different phases of a research project. When scientists communicated their findings to other members of the lab, or to the general public, they mapped across distant concepts (for instance, comparing the HIV virus to a pearl necklace). However, Dunbar rarely observed the use of distant concept mappings in the formulation of novel hypotheses or in conceptualizing experiments. Thus, as with the developmental studies mentioned above, metaphor operates differently in conceptualizing a relation and in communicating it.

Metaphor use as aesthetic expression

As noted earlier, the aesthetic aspect of metaphor has a long history, tracing back to the writings of Aristotle. Experimental psychologists tackling this issue have examined metaphor aptness as a proxy for aesthetic effectiveness. In general, the argument is that apt or pleasing metaphors are those that are mapped between sufficiently unlike concepts to be unusual or creative, but are at the same time sufficiently similar on some dimensions to make them comprehensible and not anomalous. That is, the pleasure is found in seeing the similarity in otherwise dissimilar concepts. As noted in the section above, Dunbar (2000) observed a similar pattern when scientists communicated their findings.

There is another experimental tradition that finds analogous results. Trick and Katz (1986) examined proportional (analogic) metaphors of the form 'The Ayatollah Khomeini is a praying mantis'. They employed mathematical scaling procedures to determine the similarity between source and target domains (e.g. World Leaders and Insects). Using these techniques, they then determined the similarity on relevant dimensions for the expressed item (e.g. Khomeini) within the domain of world leaders compared to that of praying mantises within the field of insects. Trick and Katz (1986) found that the most pleasing analogic metaphors were those in which the dimensions associated with the source and target domains were dissimilar but the relationships within each domain were somewhat similar.

In the same tradition, Haught (2014), in a recent experiment, shows that even when the similarity between source and target domains remains constant (to use the example above, between world leaders and insects), one can manipulate the nature of the shared dimensions on which the mappings are based in order to produce more apt metaphors. Katz (1989) developed a metaphor production task in which participants were provided metaphor frames of the form 'x is the _____ of Category X' (e.g. 'Chemistry is the _____ of the Sciences') and a list of 24 concepts, previously scaled for similarity to the topic (e.g. chemistry). From this list they were asked to 'choose an alternative that would complete the sentence so as to form a metaphor that a reader would be able to understand and would think is an especially good or aesthetically apt comparison'. Katz observed that the most aesthetically pleasing metaphors were those with a vehicle only moderately dissimilar from the topic and for which there are instance-specific concepts within each domain that are neither too obvious nor too marginal. These findings implicate two sources of semantic information used in metaphor production and comprehension: first, finding an appropriate source domain sufficiently distant from the topic domain and second, finding points of similarity within both domains. Results consistent with the two-source model are found in Katz (1996b), who used tasks seldom employed in the cognitive linguistic tradition: feature listing, recognition memory and a vehicle choice task.

Examples of current research in psycholinguistics

Current research into metaphor in the psycholinguistic tradition continues to focus on the use of metaphor and the interpretation of what different usage patterns might mean. In contrast with discourse approaches to metaphor usage for example, the focus in psycholinguistic approaches is very much on the individuals using and/or interpreting the metaphors, rather than on the entailments of specific metaphors with relation to the topics or targets they describe. In this section I describe how experimentalists are examining the use of metaphor in identity expression, and in creating a sense of intimacy.

Metaphor use as a means of asserting identity

There is evidence that use of metaphor serves as a social identity marker. Katz and Pexman (1997) showed that undergraduate Canadian students have a stereotype of the type of language used by people in different occupations, with some associated with high metaphor usage (e.g. priests) and others associated with high irony/sarcasm usage (e.g. comedians). When a different group of participants were given an ambiguous sentence in a text (e.g. 'children are precious jewels') they tended to interpret it as metaphoric assertion when it is stated by a priest but as a metaphor being used ironically when stated by a comedian. In subsequent work, Pexman, Ferretti, and Katz (2000) monitored word-by-word processing of text and found that the interpretation of the statements as metaphor occurred at a very early stage of processing, indicating that merely reading that the statement was made by a priest activated stereotypic knowledge about the type of speech (metaphor) that might be forthcoming.

There is also evidence that metaphor use by Canadian undergraduate students is associated with male language production. Hussey and Katz (2006) asked same-gender undergraduate dyads to take part in conversations online. The protocols produced were analyzed for different categories of metaphor. For each category, more metaphor was produced by the male participants. Metaphor production differed by gender as a function of friendship status: men produced the same amount of metaphor when chatting with a friend or a stranger, whereas women produced more metaphor when talking to friends. Indeed, virtually no metaphor was produced in the female-female stranger dyads. Examination of the male usage indicated metaphor use was very often employed as a form of one-upmanship. In a subsequent study Hussey and Katz (2009) found strong support for the notion that the use of metaphor is an indication of male identification. In a set of four studies, participants were presented snippets of actual conversations. However, with no gender identification provided, the text was changed by either adding or deleting metaphor to the conversations of one of the interlocutors. Participants perceived the 'metaphor users' as males (irrespective of their actual gender). Moreover, when gender information was manipulated, interlocutors denigrated the speaker on subsequent rating forms when the supposed interlocutor spoke in 'gender-inappropriate' ways (i.e. when 'females' frequently used metaphor or 'males' frequently used literal language counterparts).

Metaphor use in creating interlocutor intimacy

Metaphor usage also seems to indicate how well interlocutors know each other. Horton (2007; see Cohen 1978) presented participants with texts containing conversations between two characters whose relationship was ambiguous. In each narrative, one character replied either metaphorically or literally to some personal information provided by the other character. Horton found that his readers judged the characters as 'closer' (i.e. knowing each other better) when one of the characters responded with a metaphorical expression. In subsequent research, Horton (2013) manipulated the degree of intimacy between characters presented in short written stories. Critical utterances contained either a literal or metaphoric expression that commented on an aspect of information previously given in the discourse. Horton found that, especially with more novel metaphor usage, readers read metaphoric utterances as fast as literal utterances in the context of close, familiar relationships, but were slower to read metaphoric utterances in the context of unfamiliar relationships. This pattern indicates that the level of intimacy established between characters appears to shape the ease with which readers integrate meanings expressed via metaphor into their understanding of the narrative situation.

Bowes and Katz (2015) replicated the effect observed in Horton (2007), but made some notable elaborations. In each of three studies, participants read metaphorical or literal sentences in different contexts and afterwards completed an ostensibly unrelated task, the Reading the Mind in the Eyes Test (RMET). The RMET consists of a series of pictures of people's eyes. For each picture participants are required to identify the emotion being expressed. In the first study participants were presented metaphorical or literal sentences in short pre-constructed discourse contexts (such as those employed in Horton, 2007) and were asked questions about the characters in the stories. In the second study participants were presented with either a literal sentence or its metaphoric counterpart and asked to write a short passage incorporating the sentence. In study 3, participants were presented with either metaphors or their literal counterparts without any discourse context, and speed of reading was measured. In all three studies, better identification of the emotions in the RMET test was observed after participants had processed metaphorical sentences, rather than literal counterparts. Additional analyses across the three studies revealed that metaphors but not literal counterparts were: first, associated with fictive contexts which contain references to mental states; and second, on a post-task, when participants are asked to provide the first word that came to mind given a cue (e.g. the word 'hand'), those participants who had read metaphors produced words that implicated a human agent (e.g. 'mother') whereas those who had read literal counterparts produced a non-human object (e.g. 'fork'). This was the finding even when no context was given and the task was merely to read a list of metaphors or literal sentences. These results indicate that metaphor not only creates a sense of intimacy between interlocutors, but that this social bond impacts on how we pay attention to the states of knowledge held by other people.

Current debates and future directions

Conceptual metaphor theory and experimental psycholinguistics

One cannot underestimate the impact of conceptual metaphor theory (see Chapter 1 and many other chapters in this book) on metaphor studies. The seminal book by Lakoff and Johnson (1980) has been cited about 40,000 times in a wide range of academic fields. And yet, as reviewed here, the theory has not attracted much support from experimental psycholinguists and has been roundly criticized by some who have questioned the primacy and psychological reality of tenets of the theory. For instance, McGlone (2007) argues that there is very little experimental evidence that conceptual metaphors are evoked online (i.e. during the act of comprehension), though they may come into play later as rationalizations. In a later paper (2011), McGlone elaborated on what he saw as additional problems including what he claimed were ambiguities and circularity of logic. I would argue that some of these misgivings arise from the paucity of experimental studies that are directed at the questions that drive cognitive psychology or the failure to use methodology common in experimental psycholinguistics. There are a few such studies in the literature (e.g. Katz & Law, 2010; Katz & Taylor, 2008). Nonetheless, there is a need to take concepts from conceptual metaphor theory and translate them into hypotheses testable in the laboratory using measures sensitive to rapid responding, gathered during the act of comprehension (online) and testing assumptions through computational simulations and brain imaging studies. On the other hand, experimental psycholinguists have to be more aware of the limitations of their approach. For instance, most of the experimental studies described above have employed artificial or truncated nominal metaphors of the form A is a B. From an experimental perspective this choice has been dictated by the necessities of obtaining good control over extraneous variables. Nonetheless, the types of metaphoric expressions used in everyday situations have not been subjected to the same experimental scrutiny as found in those studies that have employed such impoverished stimulus sets. Clearly, experiments that are more ecologically valid are dearly needed.

On issues of metaphor development

One could argue that most of the work related to the age when metaphoric cognition emerges was completed decades ago. But it should be recognized that the bulk of this work was done from the perspective of metaphor as an issue in linguistic transference. Given evidence of metaphoric mapping in chimps and the ever-increasing support for embodied aspects of language, it seems appropriate to re-examine the development of metaphoric cognition employing the tools used in embodiment studies. A logical extension would be to see if there are developmental trajectories based on our increasing experiences with the physical world. I am not aware of any longitudinal study of this nature and, even using cross-section methodology, the study of embodiment in children still is (dare I say it?) in its infancy. Similarly, experimental research in parent–child verbal (and non-verbal) interaction would be an important adjunct to understanding the emergence of metaphor as a social phenomenon. Where, for instance, are the studies examining parent–child interactions and the role they play in the emergence of metaphoric language? Where are the studies that look at the role(s) which different environments play in the acquisition and use of metaphor for native language speakers, or studies that examine socio-economic effects or that of gender?

On the use of metaphor in everyday social situations

There is an already established literature examining the role of metaphor in different social environments, well-documented in other chapters in this volume. Nonetheless, there is a need to experimentally examine further how and when metaphor is used as a form of identity construction or to create a sense of intimacy. I assume that identity will be most salient when expressed in interactive social situations (rather than, let us say, in descriptive connected discourse). However, given the finding from Hussey and Katz (2009) that male identity was interpreted/deduced from written texts containing metaphor, this remains an empirical question, (though in that study the texts consisted of transcripts of interactive communication and may not generalize to less interactive situations). One can envision studies employing both experimental and corpus based methodology. Similarly, there is a need to test more fully the notion that metaphor creates intimacy amongst interlocutors within the context of real-life interactive communication, as well as testing whether these effects are embodied (for instance, through brain and cognitive/perceptual mechanisms that mediate 'closeness' decisions).

The correspondence between the mere act of reading metaphor and the increased ability to infer the emotional state of others is consistent with an explanation that metaphor engages bodily emotions in the reader that sensitize him/her to their impact on potential interlocutors. Experiments to test this hypothesis are currently being conducted.

On metaphor use as a vehicle for persuasion

There are various chapters in this book in which metaphor has been used to change attitudes or otherwise be persuasive; as such, they have not been discussed here, even though there is an experimental literature that describes when metaphor can be an effective persuasive tool (see Sopory & Dillard, 2002). There is no agreement however on why this may be so. Ottatti and Renstrom (2010) proposed the following three testable hypotheses arising from the social psychological literature on why metaphor might be an effective medium for persuasion: directly influencing attitudes towards the communication topic, affecting impressions of the person using metaphor, and, finally, via the manner in which the receiver processes literal statements contained in the communication. Direct tests of all three hypotheses are wanting.

Concluding remarks

I hope that my unabashed advocacy has demonstrated how experimentalist approaches can provide cross-pollination of ideas and tests of issues in metaphor theories emerging from other disciplines and approaches. Given the focus of this chapter, it should be emphasized that there are literatures within the experimental tradition that have not been addressed, or addressed only in passing, such as cross-cultural cognition, second language learning, the increasing use of imaging studies to map behaviour onto brain areas, and individual differences, to name just some areas that could have found a place in this already lengthy chapter.

Further reading

Gibbs, R. W., Jr. (1994). *The poetics of mind*. Cambridge, UK: Cambridge University Press.
—— (2005). *Embodiment and cognitive science*. Cambridge, UK: Cambridge University Press.
Glucksberg, S. (2001). *Understanding figurative language: From metaphors to idioms*. New York: Oxford University Press.
Spivey. M. J., McRae, K., & Joanisse, M. (Eds.) (2012). *Cambridge handbook of psycholinguistics*. Cambridge, UK: Cambridge University Press.

Acknowledgement

The writing of this chapter was supported by a grant from the Natural Sciences and Engineering Research Council of Canada to AK.

References

Aisenman, R. A. (1999). Structure-mapping and the simile-metaphor preference. *Metaphor & Symbol, 14*, 45–51.
Bakker, S., Antle, A., & Van Den Hoven, E. (2012). Embodied metaphors in tangible interaction design. *Personal and Ubiquitous Computing, 16*, 433–449.
Billow, R. (1975). A cognitive-developmental study of metaphor comprehension. *Developmental Psychology, 11*, 415–423.
—— (1981). Observing spontaneous metaphor in children. *Journal of Experimental Child Psychology, 3*, 430–445.
Bowdle, B. F., & Gentner, D. (2005). The career of metaphor. *Psychological Review, 112*, 193–216.
Bowes, A., & Katz, A. (2015). Metaphor creates intimacy and enhances one's ability to infer the internal states of others. *Memory & Cognition*. [online 12 March 2015] available from DOI 10.3758/s13421-015-0508-4.
Cardillo, E., Watson, C., Schmidt, G., Kranjec, A., & Chatterjee, A. (2012). From novel to familiar: Tuning the brain for metaphors. *NeuroImage, 59*, 3212–3221.
Casasanto, D. (2008). Similarity and proximity: When does close in space mean close in mind? *Memory & Cognition, 36*, 1047–1056.
Cohen, T. (1978). Metaphor and the cultivation of intimacy. *Critical inquiry, 5*, 3–12.
Dahl, C., & Adachi, I. (2013) Conceptual metaphorical mapping in chimpanzees (Pan troglodytes). [online] available from *elife* 2:e00932 10.7554/eLife.00932.
Dunbar, K. (2000). How scientists think in the real world: Implications for science education. *Journal of Applied Developmental Psychology, 21*, 49–58.
Dunn, L. M., & Dunn D. M. (2007). *Peabody picture vocabulary test*, 4th ed. (PPVT-4). Minneapolis, MN: Pearson.

Estes, Z., & Hassan, U. (2004). The importance of being nonalignable: A critical test of the structural alignment theory of similarity. *Journal of Experimental Psychology: Learning, Memory, & Cognition, 30*, 1082–1092.

Falkenhainer, B., Forbus, K., & Gentner, D. (1989). The structure-mapping engine: Algorithm and examples. *Artificial Intelligence, 41*, 1–63.

Gentner, D. (1977). If a tree had a knee, where would it be? Children's performance on simple spatial metaphors. *Papers and Reports on Child Language Development, 13*, 157–164.

—— (1983). Structure-mapping: A theoretical framework for analogy. *Cognitive Science, 7*, 155–170.

—— (1988). Metaphor as structure mapping: The relational shift. *Child Development, 59*, 47–59.

Gentner, D., & Bowdle, B. (2001). Convention, form, and figurative language processing. *Metaphor & Symbol, 16*, 223–247.

Gibbs, R. W., Jr. (2013). Metaphoric cognition as social activity: Dissolving the divide between metaphor in thought and communication. *Metaphor and the Social World, 3*, 54–76.

Giora, R. (2003). *On our mind: Salience, context and figurative language.* New York: Oxford University Press.

Glucksberg, S., & Haught, C. (2006). On the relation between metaphor and simile: When comparison fails. *Mind & Language, 21*, 360–378.

Glucksberg, S., & Keysar, B. (1990). Understanding metaphorical comparisons: Beyond similarity. *Psychological Review, 97*, 3–18.

Grady, J. (1997). *Foundations of meaning: Primary metaphors and primary scenes.* Ph.D. dissertation, University of California, Berkeley.

Haught, C. (2014). Spain is not Greece: How metaphors are understood. *Journal of Psycholinguistic Research, 43*, 351–356.

Horton, W. S. (2007). Metaphor and readers' attributions of intimacy. *Memory & Cognition, 35*, 87–94.

—— (2013). Character intimacy influences the processing of metaphoric utterances during narrative comprehension. *Metaphor & Symbol, 28*, 148–166.

Hussey, K., & Katz, A. (2006). Metaphor production in online conversation: Gender and friendship status. *Discourse Processes, 42*, 75–98.

—— (2009). Perception of the use of metaphor by an interlocutor in discourse. *Metaphor & Symbol, 24*, 203–236.

Katz, A. (1989). On choosing the vehicles of metaphors: Referential concreteness, semantic distances, and individual differences. *Journal of Memory and Language, 28*, 486–499.

—— (1996a). On interpreting statements as metaphor or irony: Contextual heuristics and cognitive consequences. In J. Mio & A. Katz (Eds.), *Metaphor: Implications and applications.* Mahwah, NJ: Lawrence Erlbaum.

—— (1996b). Pragmatics and the processing of metaphors: Category dissimilarity in topic and vehicle asymmetry. *Pragmatics & Cognition, 4*, 265–304.

—— (1998) Figurative language and figurative thought: A review. In A. Katz, C. Cacciari, R. W. Gibbs, Jr., & M. Turner (Eds.), *Figurative language and thought.* New York: Oxford University Press.

Katz, A., & Law, A. (2010). Experimental support for conceptual metaphors with an episodic memory task. *Metaphor & Symbol, 25*, 263–270.

Katz, A., & Pexman, P. (1997) Interpreting figurative statements: Speaker occupation can change metaphor to irony. *Metaphor & Symbol, 12*, 19–41.

Katz, A., & Taylor, T. (2008). The journeys of life: Examining a conceptual metaphor with semantic and episodic recall. *Metaphor & Symbol, 23*, 148–173.

Keil, F. (1979). *Semantic and conceptual development: An ontological perspective.* Cambridge, MA: Harvard University Press.

—— (1986). Conceptual domains and the acquisition of metaphor. *Cognitive Development, 1*, 73–96.

Kittay, E., & Lehrer, A. (1981). Semantic fields and the structure of metaphor. *Studies in Language, 5*, 31–63.

Lakoff, G. (1993). The contemporary theory of metaphor. In A. Ortony (Ed.), *Metaphor and thought*, 2nd ed. Cambridge, MA: Cambridge University Press.

Lakoff, G., & Johnson, M. (1980). *Metaphors we live by*. New York: University of Chicago Press.

Lehrer, A. (1978). Structures of the lexicon and transfer of meaning. *Lingua, 45*, 95–123.

Malgady, R. (1977) Children's interpretation and appreciation of similes. *Child Development, 48*, 1734–1738.

McGlone, M. (2007). What is the explanatory value of a conceptual metaphor? *Language & Communication, 27*, 109–126.

—— (2011). Hyperbole, homunculi, and hindsight bias: An alternative evaluation of conceptual metaphor theory. *Discourse Processes, 48*, 563–574.

Ortony, A. (1979). Beyond literal similarity. *Psychological Review, 86*, 161–180.

Ottati, V., & Renstrom, R. (2010). Metaphor and persuasive communication: A multifunctional approach. *Social and Personality Psychology Compass, 4*, 783–794.

Pexman, P., Ferretti, T., & Katz, A. (2000). Discourse factors that influence online reading of metaphor and irony. *Discourse Processes, 29*, 201–222.

Sopory, P., & Dillard, J. (2002). The persuasive effects of metaphor: A meta-analysis. *Human Communication Research, 28*, 382–419.

Spivey, M. J., McRae, K., & Joanisse, M. (Eds.) (2012). *Cambridge handbook of psycholinguistics*. Cambridge, UK: Cambridge University Press.

Stites, L., & Özçalişkan, S. (2013a). Teasing apart the role of cognitive and verbal factors in children's early metaphorical abilities. *Metaphor & Symbol, 28*, 116–129.

—— (2013b). Developmental changes in children's comprehension and explanation of spatial metaphors for time. *Journal of Child Language, 40*, 1123–1137.

Subramaniam, K., Faust, M., Beeman, M., & Mashal, N. (2012). The repetition paradigm: Enhancement of novel metaphors and suppression of conventional metaphors in the left inferior parietal lobe. *Neuropsychologia, 50*, 705–2719.

Trick, L., & Katz, A. (1986). The domain interaction approach to metaphor processing: Relating individual differences and metaphor characteristics. *Metaphor & Symbolic Activity, 1*, 185–213.

Utsumi, A. (2007). Interpretive diversity explains metaphor–simile distinction. *Metaphor & Symbol, 22*, 291–312.

Winner, E. (1988). *The point of words: Children's understanding of metaphor and irony*. Cambridge, MA: Harvard University Press.

33
Metaphor acquisition and use in individuals with neurodevelopmental disorders

Gabriella Rundblad

Introduction

As previous chapters in this volume have already demonstrated, metaphor is an inherent part of human life, not just in terms of how we communicate with others, but also in how we perceive and learn about the world and people around us. Utilisation of metaphors in educational contexts is well established (Cameron, 2003), and is in no way limited to language learning and literacy. In fact, it is almost impossible to learn about science without the use of metaphors (Jakobson & Wickman, 2007; Niebert, Marsch, & Treagust, 2012; see also Chapter 20). Metaphor is also crucial in establishing, expressing and negotiating our own identity with others. In everyday life, metaphor is seldom a one-way communication tool; rather it is essential that both speaker and hearer utilise metaphor in a similar fashion. But what happens if a person cannot or struggle to learn to understand and appropriately use metaphors?

This chapter will discuss to what extent individuals with neurodevelopmental disorders, such as autism spectrum disorder, find metaphor acquisition difficult. By studying metaphor in atypically developing individuals, we can better grasp what most likely underpins normal metaphor acquisition and use, and by contrasting disorders, we can attain insight into how difficulties with metaphors can (potentially) be overcome. We will also address which types of metaphors have been investigated and how these types relate to cognitive linguistic theory. Although there are numerous neurodevelopmental disorders, metaphor studies have to date been limited to five disorders: specific language impairment (SLI), autism spectrum disorder (ASD), Down's syndrome (DS), Williams syndrome (WS), and schizophrenia.[1] Before outlining how the term *metaphor* has been applied in studies of atypical language development and what these studies have found, we first need to briefly introduce the neurodevelopmental disorders that this chapter will focus on.

Neurodevelopmental disorders

The development of the human brain and nervous system starts already in the early prenatal stage. When this growth is impaired, we can often discern an impact on the child's behaviour, emotion, memory, intelligence, and/or language. The causes of neurodevelopmental disorders are typically genetic. New genetic disorders are continuously discovered, but whether these disorders include abnormal language development remains to be established. At the same time, well-researched, genetically complex language disorders such as SLI and ASD are still under active investigation (Carter & Scherer, 2013; Simpson et al., 2015). In the case of SLI, data from behavioural studies targeting language performance are well established, while investigations into the cause and origin of the disorder remain (at least in part) inconclusive. For ASD, we find a great need for more detailed subtyping according to language (Rice, Warren, & Betz, 2005).

Specific language impairment (SLI)

SLI is the standard diagnosis applied to children who report with (moderate to severe) atypical language development in the absence of another diagnosis. In other words, the language impairment cannot be ascribed to a physical handicap, environmental deprivation or a lower than average cognitive ability (American Psychiatric Association, 2013). The exact definition of this disorder has been debated for decades (Bishop, 1997). In practice, this means that some children who are later diagnosed with another neurodevelopmental disorder might have first been given the diagnosis of SLI. Although SLI is commonly thought of as a language-only disorder, studies have shown co-morbidity with poor motor skills (Hill, 2001; Richtsmeier & Goffman, in press), poor auditory perception (Bishop & McArthur, 2004), and most recently a correlation between linguistic and cognitive ability (Liao et al., 2015).

Autism spectrum disorder (ASD)

Individuals with ASD are commonly divided into three main subgroups: Asperger syndrome, high-functioning ASD, and low-functioning ASD. However, in DSM-5, Asperger's was eliminated and collapsed under ASD (Kent et al., 2013). In contrast to individuals with low-functioning ASD, some of whom use five or fewer words per day,[2] individuals with high-functioning ASD present with 'relatively and selectively preserved language and cognitive abilities' (Felder, McPartland, Klin, & Volkmar, 2014, p. 1). Some studies prefer to distinguish between ASD with normal language and with language impairment. Similar to the distinction between high-functioning and low-functioning ASD, ASD individuals with normal language and with language impairment typically differ significantly on tests measuring verbal IQ and non-verbal IQ. Nevertheless, characteristics common for both groups (regardless of label) include difficulties with social communication, social interaction, and social imagination – all of which are often paired with challenging behaviour.

Down's syndrome (DS)

DS is caused by a partial or full trisomy of chromosome 21, which can often be identified prenatally by a nuchal translucency scan, alternatively through an amniocentesis test. Individuals with DS have distinct facial appearances, but also suffer from heart conditions among other physical conditions. They typically present with non-verbal IQ ranging from 35 to 70 (Chapman & Hesketh, 2000). Children with DS are delayed in their language development. However, it is important to note that it is predominantly syntax acquisition that is affected, thus they 'show an incongruence between nonverbal cognition and grammatical development but a congruence between vocabulary and nonverbal cognitive skills' (Rice et al., 2005, p. 20).

Williams syndrome (WS)

WS is a rare genetic disorder that is caused by a micro-deletion on the long arm of chromosome 7q11.23. Individuals with WS are recognisable by their dysmorphic facial characteristics, hoarse voice, and overfriendly behaviour, and in addition they tend to suffer from a range of health conditions (e.g. kidney problems and joint abnormalities). WS is also associated with impaired cognitive ability, with non-verbal IQ ranging between 40 and 100 (Pober, 2010). Similar to children with DS, children with WS show strength in their vocabulary acquisition, but struggle with grammar.

Schizophrenia

Unlike the previous four disorders, which without a doubt are neurodevelopmental in origin, schizophrenia displays a much greater variability in age of onset,[3] as well as a greater number of candidate genes. This heterogeneity has called into question whether schizophrenia is a neurodevelopmental disorder or a degenerative brain process (Gross & Huber, 2008). It has recently been argued that its 'illness-related cognitive impairment is neurodevelopmental in origin and characterized by slower gain (developmental lag) but not cognitive decline' and that 'the severity of underlying neurodevelopmental abnormality determines the age that cognitive deficits first become apparent' (Bora, 2015, p. 1). Although schizophrenia is typically classified after psychosis sets in, the declining cognitive profile of those who will go on to be diagnosed with schizophrenia has been said to be striking enough that individuals could be identified (and potentially treated) much earlier (Kahn & Keefe, 2013).

These five neurodevelopmental disorders overlap to various degrees in several respects. Similar to schizophrenia, some individuals with ASD experience paranoid ideations (Jänsch & Hare, 2014; Unenge Hallerbäck, Lugnegård, & Gillberg, 2012). DS, WS and low-functioning ASD share a below average cognitive ability, but only DS and WS feature distinct physiology. Although SLI is defined as language impairment without cognitive impairment and high-functioning ASD (or ASD with normal language) is thought of as normal language ability without cognitive impairment, the social communication impairment of ASD can generate a linguistic representation almost indistinguishable to that of a child with SLI. In other words, clinical linguists and educational psychologists are often faced with the task of dissecting whether a child's language is abnormal due to a neurodevelopmental language impairment or is the by-product of 'awkward' language in an overwhelming social situation that is often further impaired by inappropriate behaviour.

We will return to the five disorders shortly, but first we will briefly outline a few points about methodology and terminology, since, as shall become apparent, many of the inconsistent results in this field stem from the methodological approach and terminology applied.

Methodology, terminology and critical issues

Studies of developmental disorders have commonly compared performance (e.g. on a language task) in a disorder group with both a typically developing (TD) group matched for chronological age, and a second TD group matched on mental age, where mental age can be linked to verbal ability or non-verbal ability. In matching approaches, significant differences in performance between the disorder group and both control groups are interpreted as impairment. An absence of difference between the disorder group and the mental age control group (i.e. both these groups differ significantly from the chronological age control group), on the other hand, is indicative of delay rather than impairment. More recent approaches, such as developmental trajectories or growth models employ a wide age range[4] to be able to gauge performance development (Thomas et al., 2009). Statistical analysis using a linear regression model plots performance against chronological age as well as mental age. Developmental trajectories allow comparison between groups for onset and rate of development, which in turn enables clear discrimination between delay due to late onset, delay due to slow rate of development and impairment.[5] Both approaches have been utilised in studies of metaphor in neurodevelopmental disorders.

One of the primary issues in psycholinguistic and clinical linguistic studies of figurative language is the lack of consensus around the term *metaphor*. At best, the term is applied in accordance with the definitions outlined in earlier chapters of this volume. Thus, we find that some studies have targeted clearly defined types of metaphors; for example, sensory metaphors (Van Herwegen, Dimitriou, & Rundblad, 2013) and primary metaphors (Olofson et al., 2014; Özçalişkan, 2005). But at the opposite end, we find studies of so-called 'child metaphors', which have been extensively questioned (Gentner, 1988). In one of his early papers, Kanner (1946, p. 242) described instances where a child with ASD would use 'metaphorical language' or 'irrelevant phrases', such as 'Peter eater' for saucepans because the child's mother had once said 'Peter, Peter, pumpkin eater' while dropping a saucepan. There is, thus, also a tendency to overextend *metaphor* for other linguistic devices. In addition, we find metaphors grouped under umbrella terms such as *pragmatics, inference, analogy, figure of speech, figurative language, lexical ambiguity* and *polysemy*, usually together with other devices that are not metaphors (e.g. idioms, irony, similes, metonymy, hyperbole and litotes) (Rundblad & Annaz, 2010a). In this chapter, we will exclusively look at studies where the test materials included metaphors, notably linguistic realisations of conventional conceptual metaphors (e.g. exploding for 'very angry'), sensory metaphors (e.g. smooth for 'charming') and perceptual metaphors (e.g. flying for 'running fast').

In the context of neurodevelopmental disorders involving language, it is imperative that we investigate the full time course of an individual's language development. This means that we need to include age as an independent variable, in some way; preferably by means of longitudinal studies. We need to be able to distinguish whether the individuals' atypical language is delayed or potentially irrevocably impaired. Further, to get a clear picture of what areas of language are affected and in what way, it is essential that clear and delineated terminology, based on current linguistic theory, is employed. The relation between language and cognition can be very complex. Each type of figurative language has most likely its own course of development, and it has also been argued that some types of figurative language function as a stepping stone or scaffold for more complex types (Rundblad & Annaz, 2010a). Theory-specific and age-sensitive studies are crucial.

In the next section, we will look at the extent to which the different types of metaphors identified and described in cognitive linguistic theory have been investigated in atypical language populations. To this end, we will briefly review studies of metaphor comprehension, processing and production for each of the five disorders outlined above.

Overview of literature on metaphor acquisition and use

There are three main components to the study of acquisition and use of metaphors: comprehension, production, and processing. Studies focusing on the acquisition of metaphor commonly look at either comprehension or production. Production also overlaps with processing, in its focus on metaphor use. However, the greatest overlap is between processing and comprehension. An important feature of processing studies is the need to test novel metaphors as opposed to lexicalised ones. When participants are tested on lexicalised metaphors, they retrieve the meaning directly from the mental lexicon. In child language studies, it can at times be impossible to ensure that a lexicalised metaphor is not unfamiliar, and thus novel, to individual children. Novel metaphors, on the other hand, require the language user to create meaning, and it is that process of creation that processing studies target. Each of these three areas tend to be associated with specific research techniques; brain scans are nowadays increasingly utilised in processing studies, while stories form a significant part of many comprehension studies.

There are sadly only a few metaphor studies in DS, and some of these are actually studies where DS participants function as a control group, rather than being the focus of the study. It is possible that this shortcoming is at least partially due to the general assumption that language in DS is 'merely' delayed. In short, we should expect to find the same patterns, whether for comprehension, processing or production, in DS as for TDs, except that onset is later and possibly the rate of development is slower (Tager-Flusberg et al., 1990).

Comprehension

In comprehension tasks, participants need to communicate what they understand the target metaphor to mean, unlike processing studies where they typically select 'yes' or 'no' to signal whether a test sentence is meaningful or not. This can be achieved by the participant selecting an option, which could be a picture, synonym or definition. Comprehension tasks where the participant is required to verbalise their understanding can, on the other hand, affect performance in disorder groups and very young TD children negatively; yet, data from such tasks can be very informative and should not be discouraged.

One thing that can complicate metaphor comprehension is difference in executive function. Executive function includes 'a variety of higher order strategic/organizational cognitive functions including inhibition, working memory, attentional flexibility and planning' (Rhodes, Riby, Park, Fraser, & Campbell, 2010, p. 1217). Both DS and WS are associated with impaired executive function (Rhodes et al., 2010; Rowe, Lavender, & Turk, 2006). In a rare DS case study, an adult Italian woman was required to verbally explain what each target metaphor means (Papagno & Vallar, 2001). The study concluded that metaphor comprehension was impaired, and suggested that the poor performance could be linked to the participant's impaired visuo-spatial ability and executive function. Similarly, 11 WS individuals were required to explain the meaning of two statements in a story: one metaphoric and one sarcastic (Karmiloff-Smith, Klima, Bellugi, Grant, & Baron-Cohen, 1995). The authors found a very strong positive correlation between metaphor and sarcasm ability. Importantly, only half of the participants succeeded on the task. More recently, comprehension on lexicalised metaphor was tested in 30 WS individuals between the age of 7;01[6] and 39;10 years old (Rundblad, Dimitriou, & Van Herwegen, in press). The task utilised pictures in order to reduce executive function demand. Using a developmental trajectories approach, the study found that onset of metaphor comprehension in the WS population is around 6 years old and comprehension does improve with chronological age as well as verbal ability – a result which is attributed to the fact that the test sample included middle aged WS adults. In order to determine whether performance truly is delayed or impaired, it is necessary to test a much larger age range than what is normal in TD language studies.

Results from an early study with children with SLI suggested that metaphor comprehension in this disorder is intact (Vance & Wells, 1994). The test materials included idioms, dead metaphors as well as perceptual metaphors, and a forced choice out of three pictures was used to indicate comprehension. In forced-choice designs, participants must indicate their understanding by selecting one answer from three (or more) options provided, which are usually in picture format. Generally, these depict the intended metaphorical meaning, a possible but less likely literal meaning, and one or more distractors. However, the TD children were matched on verbal ability rather than chronological age, and were thus significantly younger (6;4–7;8 years old) than the SLI children (7;10–13;1 years old). Contrasting verbal and visual metaphor comprehension, Highnam and colleagues (1999, p. 27) tested 12 children who were 'language disordered' but with a performance IQ score above 80 on WISC-R and 12 age-matched TD controls. The study used the Metaphoric Triads Task (Kogan, Connor, Gross, & Fava, 1980), which includes sensory metaphors, perceptual metaphors and conceptual metaphors (Kogan & Chadrow, 1986).[7] Results showed better comprehension in the TD group for both visual and verbal metaphors, and both groups performed better on visual metaphors. Highnam and colleagues (1999, p. 30) suggest that 'the iconicity of metaphors in visual form renders them less abstract than the more highly arbitrary medium of verbal coding', but also that visual metaphor tasks are mediated by language and thus are affected to a greater degree in individuals with language impairments. There are no recent studies that specifically target metaphor comprehension in SLI (but see the discussion of sentence completion tasks in the metaphor production section below).

There are numerous metaphor comprehension studies in ASD, most of which have looked at children and adolescents with high-functioning ASD or Asperger's. Two studies using the same metaphor comprehension task, one with high-functioning ASD children (Dennis, Lazenby, & Lockyer, 2001) and one with high-functioning ASD adolescents (Minshew, Goldstein, & Siegel, 1995), found significantly worse performance compared to TD controls matched on chronological age and non-verbal ability. One of the reasons put forth as underlying the impaired performance, but which was not tested for, was a lower ability to detect the intentionality behind the metaphorical utterance (Dennis et al., 2001). More recently, a small sample of ASD children (age range 5;4–11;4) were compared to age-matched TD controls on comprehension of lexicalised metaphors incorporated into short stories, where participants were required to express their understanding (Rundblad & Annaz, 2010b). Onset of comprehension in the ASD children was found to be around age 7.5 years. Using developmental trajectories, the study found that metaphor comprehension was severely impaired in the ASD group as it did not improve reliably with chronological age, nor with increasing verbal ability. The authors also looked at the effect of Theory of Mind (ToM) on comprehension (Baron-Cohen, 2001; Baron-Cohen, Leslie, & Frith, 1985). ToM refers to the ability to mind read or infer other people's feelings, intentions and thoughts. A crucial distinction is made between first-order ToM (i.e. 'I think person X thinks Y') and second-order ToM (i.e. 'I think person X thinks person Y thinks Z'), where second-order ToM is more complex and therefore typically develops later than first-order ToM. Although the authors had presumed a correlation between first-order ToM abilities based on results for metaphor production in this population (Happé, 1993), no such link could be found.

In a study of pragmatic comprehension in 25 adults with schizophrenia, metaphor comprehension was measured using a computerised story task where participants were required to select 'yes' or 'no' to indicate whether an utterance made sense (Langdon, Coltheart, Ward, & Catts, 2002). Results showed impaired metaphor understanding as well as poor first-order ToM abilities and executive function deficits; however, no causal link between first-order ToM and metaphor comprehension could be established, unlike irony comprehension which did show an association with first-order ToM. In contrast, Mo and colleagues

(2008) did find a correlation between metaphor comprehension and second-order ToM abilities, while irony showed no correlation, when testing 29 participants with schizophrenia. These results are interesting and potentially conflicting, given the common assumption that irony is harder to comprehend than metaphor, and thus should require second-order ToM abilities (Happé, 1993).

Recent years have seen metaphor comprehension studies extend towards novel metaphors, testing whether lexicalised metaphors are understood earlier and better. Thus, Hebrew-speaking children with ASD tested on visual metaphors (i.e. the Metaphoric Triads Task), lexicalised metaphors and novel metaphors, proved to perform better on visual metaphors, though they performed worse on all metaphor tasks compared to age-matched TDs (Mashal & Kasirer, 2012). Interestingly, the study also found a relative weakness in suppressing irrelevant contextual information in the ASD group, but no difference between novel and lexicalised metaphors.

An investigation using a forced-choice picture design of 34 children and adults with WS tested performance on novel sensory metaphors (e.g. marshmallow meaning 'a soft pillow') and non-sensory metaphors (e.g. turtle referring to 'a slow car') (Van Herwegen et al., 2013). The study found that onset of novel metaphor comprehension is around the age of 8 in WS and comprehension did not improve with chronological age or with verbal ability; instead a significant impairment, compared to age-matched TDs controls, was established. Although the stories and pictures were specifically designed to be suited to WS participants with poor working memory, it is still possible that poor comprehension was due to impaired executive function, which was not included in analysis.

Olofson and colleagues tested comprehension of novel and lexicalised primary conceptual metaphors in children and adolescents with ASD (age range 7;03–22;03) and age-matched TD controls (Olofson et al., 2014). The ASD group was partly recruited from a mainstream school and partly from a private ASD centre, which could indicate a division between high-functioning and low-functioning ASD. Conceptual Metaphor Theory (CMT) (Lakoff & Johnson, 1980) and Grady's theory of primary conceptual metaphors (Grady, 1999) hold that primary metaphors are acquired through embodied experiences very early in childhood. Thus, we should expect no improvement in performance with increasing chronological age and no difference in performance due to lexicalisation. The study found that ASD participants understood novel and lexicalised primary metaphors equally well, albeit not as well as the TD controls. Further, it was found that chronological age did not impact performance at all, but that verbal ability was a marginally significant predictor for novel metaphor comprehension for both ASDs and TDs. There was also an indication of better performance on lexicalised metaphors in the mainstream ASD group, but with a sample size of 13, replication is necessary before firm conclusions can be drawn.

Processing

Online processing tasks typically involve error rates, reaction time or eye tracking measures. Reaction time studies commonly combine with some form of neurological technique, such as fMRI, ERP and TMS.[8] Studies of metaphor processing have thus far been limited to schizophrenia and ASD (to date, ASD studies have predominantly been limited to Asperger's).

A key focus in metaphor processing has been on lexicalised versus novel metaphors, often under the auspices of Giora's (1997) Graded Salience Hypothesis (GSH). Although

GSH originated in the context of idioms, it has been extended to metaphors. GSH argues that whether a word is used in its literal or figurative meaning is far less relevant than whether that word and its intended meaning is familiar/lexicalised and salient in the context that it occurs in. Therefore, GSH predicts that performance on lexicalised metaphors will be better than on novel ones. Based on two experiments in Hebrew measuring error rates and reaction time with young adult TD controls and young adults with Asperger's, Giora and colleagues (2012) found consistent evidence that both test groups performed better on familiar metaphors. While controls did not struggle to process novel metaphor, the Asperger's participants needed a supportive (i.e. salient) context to be able to judge them as meaningful.

Like neurological TD studies, neurodevelopmental disorder studies have also sought to address whether metaphor resolution is linked to a right hemisphere or a left hemisphere superiority. An fMRI study on German adults with schizophrenia tracked the signal changes caused by novel metaphor processing to the left inferior frontal gyrus (BA 45) alone (Kircher, Leube, Erb, Grodd, & Rapp, 2007), while healthy individuals displayed signal changes in the left lateral inferior frontal gyrus (BA 45/47) and the right superior/middle temporal gyrus (BA 39) (Rapp, Leube, Erb, Grodd, & Kircher, 2004). In a parallel Hebrew study, Mashal and colleagues (2013) tested both lexicalised and novel metaphors. The healthy controls displayed the same pattern for novel metaphors as the previous study, namely that both hemispheres are recruited. The clinical group, on the other hand, exhibited a failure to recruit the right hemisphere and a consequent compensatory recruitment of the left middle frontal gyrus (BA 46) and the left precuneus (BA 7). In a study featuring Asperger's individuals and TD controls, a visual field paradigm[9] was used that required participants to make semantic judgements about word pairs, including perceptual lexicalised and novel metaphors (Gold & Faust, 2010). As for schizophrenia, the right hemisphere contributed less to novel metaphor processing in the Asperger's participants, negatively affecting their performance. Right hemisphere processing is specific for novel metaphors only (Bohrn, Altmann, & Jacobs, 2012), in line with GSH.

ERP studies of semantic processing in schizophrenia have generally found greater N400 amplitudes. N400 is a downward spike detectable around 400 milliseconds after the stimulus is presented and is typical when processing words and meanings. The greater N400 amplitudes mean the semantic processing 'cost' in schizophrenia is generally greater than in the general population. In a French study of individuals with schizophrenia versus healthy controls, participants were tested on 160 highly lexicalised metaphors (Iakimova, Passerieux, Laurent, & Hardy-Bayle, 2005). Results showed longer reaction time latencies and greater N400 amplitudes for the clinical group. However, greater amplitudes were found for all test conditions. Thus, the study concluded that there was no evidence of a specific metaphor processing deficit, but instead individuals with schizophrenia display a general reduced efficiency in integrating and making sense of the semantic context.

Gold and colleagues (2010) tested 17 adults with Asperger's and 16 controls (all Hebrew speakers) on 60 lexicalised metaphors and 60 novel metaphors elicited from poetry. The Asperger's group elicited greater N400 amplitudes for metaphors, with differences between lexicalised and novel stimuli being clearly discernible. Thus, a similar inability to integrate semantic information is found for Asperger's, as we saw for schizophrenia. In a follow-up paper, Gold and Faust put forth the argument that individuals with Asperger's experience difficulties with novel metaphors because these 'violate semantic rules, in a non-systemized manner' (2012, p. 67). It is, thus, the well-established ToM inabilities in ASD that underlie their poor performance.

Production

There are significantly fewer production studies compared to comprehension and processing, most likely due to many neurodevelopmental disorders affecting speech and fluency, making production studies more challenging. We can discern two types of production designs: (a) the participant produces coherent speech which can vary in length from a short sentence to a story or retelling, and (b) the participant responds verbally with an answer, which usually is less than a sentence long, but which crucially includes the sought metaphor. It should be noted that some studies prefer to classify sentence completion tasks as comprehension tasks rather than production tasks.

Comparing performance between individuals with ASD with a control group of individuals with moderate learning difficulties (matched on verbal ability), Happé (1993) utilised a sentence completion task where participants were required to select a simile, metaphor, or a synonym from a list of target words that also included one distractor item. Although the author does not discuss metaphor types tested, the targets listed suggest that they were lexicalised perceptual metaphors (e.g. 'The dancer ... was a swan'). Heavily influenced by Relevance Theory (Sperber & Wilson, 1995; see Chapter 3), Happé opted to sub-divide the ASD group by performance on a battery of ToM tasks. The battery consisted of first-order and second-order ToM tasks, and ASD participants were divided into three groups: failed both types of tasks, passed only first-order tasks, and passed both types of tasks. Both individuals with ASD and with moderate learning difficulties performed equally well on synonyms and similes, but for the metaphor condition, the ASD participants who had failed both ToM tasks performed significantly worse. The use of a verbal ability matched control group suggests that the difference in performance is not due to general verbal ability, instead Happé suggested the main contributor to metaphor ability is ToM ability. However, this study did not control for age (i.e. there was a wide age range (10–28 years old)) and there was no TD control group.

Happé's study was replicated by Norbury (2005), who included a TD group (matched on chronological age and non-verbal ability) as well as additional background measures for verbal ability. The age range in Norbury's study was 8–15 years old. Unlike Happé's study, this study included several disorder groups: SLI, pragmatic language impairment, and Asperger's/high-functioning ASD/ASD. In contrast to Happé's results, Norbury found that verbal ability contributed significantly more than ToM ability to metaphor performance. However, one of the verbal ability tasks actually contained metaphors, which could explain the discrepancy compared to Happé's results for ToM ability. Nevertheless, these two studies show a clear impairment in metaphor production in ASD and quite likely in SLI as well, as the disorder groups were combined in Norbury's analysis.

Neither Norbury nor Happé sought to determine when metaphor production first starts to develop in ASD and SLI, but Norbury's results showed that performance improves with age. A recent study testing Hebrew-speaking adults with high-functioning ASD and TD controls found that the high-functioning ASD group was not only more prolific at producing metaphors for common emotions, but they also created more novel metaphors (Kasirer & Mashal, 2014). This study used a sentence completion task, and participants were particularly encouraged to be creative. It might seem as if this result is at odds when compared to the previous studies. However, metaphor as a tool to describe one's disorder and perception of self is well documented in the adult ASD community (Blackman, 2014; Williams, 1998). In fact, Williams sees life with ASD as living a metaphor. Blackman, who is non-verbal and communicates by typing, describes herself as wordless, with language inside her, but when she writes poetry she needs to stand outside herself to look at who she is. It seems that a pronounced focus on self is typical for poets with ASD (Roth, 2008). Many of the metaphors used by individuals with ASD are sensory in nature; they are generally understandable, yet strikingly different. These novel sensory metaphors could perhaps be explained by Baron-Cohen and colleagues' (2013, p. 40) finding that synaesthesia, which is 'a neurodevelopmental condition in which a sensation in one modality triggers a perception in a second modality', is three times as common in adults with ASD than in TDs. This study included predominantly individuals with high-functioning ASD/Asperger's. If indeed the metaphors generated in Kasirer and Mashal's study are due to their participants being synaesthets, it is debatable whether we should treat them as metaphors at all.

Using a wordless picture book that participants needed to tell a story about, Naylor and Van Herwegen (2012) looked at production of metaphors along with several other figurative language devices in individuals with WS (age range: 7–18 years) and age-matched TD controls. Unfortunately for our purpose, the different figurative language devices were not separated in the analysis, nor were types of metaphors distinguished. The study found no reliable developmental trajectory for either group when plotting results against chronological age. The authors concluded therefore that since there was also no significant difference in frequency of metaphors produced, there is no delay or impairment in metaphor production in WS. However, closer scrutiny of the study show that performance improved significantly with better non-verbal ability and verbal ability[10] in the WS group alone. This difference between the two groups could be indicative of a delay in early metaphor production in the WS group that had disappeared by the time they participated in the study.

Schizophrenia is associated with increasingly atypical language, especially in areas such as semantics and pragmatics (Salavera, Puyuelo, Antonanzas, & Teruel, 2013), with similarities often being drawn with the language of ASD. The earliest studies of metaphor production in schizophrenia did not distinguish metaphor from similes, but interestingly found frequent use of figurative language (Billow, Rossman, Lewis, Goldman, & Raps, 1997). In a recent study, Dutch speaking adults diagnosed with schizophrenia (all with average non-verbal IQ) and age-matched controls were asked to describe an emotional event in their personal life (Elvevåg, Helsen, De Hert, Sweers, & Storms, 2011). Coding for 'spontaneous metaphors' (which we equate with linguistic realisations of 'conceptual metaphors'), surprisingly few metaphors were found and there was no statistically significant difference in production between the schizophrenia group and the control group. The authors suggest that this low incidence could be due to anhedonia in the clinical group, which was not measured; however, that would not explain the comparatively low rate in the control group.

Short summary

As this section has shown, studies of metaphor acquisition and use have made great progress investigating neurodevelopmental disorders, though less so in DS and SLI. Consistently, individuals with SLI, ASD, DS, WS and schizophrenia perform below TD/healthy controls, with child studies suggesting a delayed onset of metaphor acquisition or slower rate of development of metaphor abilities. In the case of WS, DS and SLI, there is some indication that performance will improve with time, while ASD and schizophrenia show severe impairment that persists into (early) adulthood, especially with regards to novel metaphors. The next section will discuss how these results tie in with theories and models, and whether there is scope and reason for intervention.

Implications for theory and intervention

There is generally a strong focus in neurodevelopmental studies on theoretical accounts that seek to explain why non-neurotypical individuals differ in their performance compared to controls. The three main theories, which are not at all metaphor or language specific, are ToM, executive function, and weak central coherence (WCC). There is some overlap between WCC and GSH in their emphasis on salience and context, but unlike WCC, GSH is specific to figurative language.

Although it seems clear that executive function easily impacts performance in various disorders, especially those associated with below average non-verbal ability (i.e. WS and DS), the role it plays in metaphor acquisition and use is more to do with its effect on language overall. In particular, intact executive function is needed to process the sentences and stories that make up the test materials. Therefore, executive dysfunction is only a partial explanation, and should preferably be controlled for experimentally.

This chapter has outlined great variability in results with regard to ToM. Some studies have found very clear links between metaphor performance and first-order ToM, while others found no correlations at all. ToM can, like WCC, be tested in a great many ways and it is possible that the choice of ToM task contributes to whether a relation is found or not. However, there is increasing suggestion that while ToM and metaphor acquisition and use are impaired in many individuals with one of our five disorders, ToM need not be a prerequisite to using and understanding some or all aspects of metaphoric language (Tendahl & Gibbs, 2008). Importantly, there is evidence suggesting that the development of language skills precedes the development of ToM, thus reducing the likelihood of causal link (Hale & Tager Flusberg, 2003). The question we ask is whether ToM is needed for some metaphors.

GSH stresses the importance of context for metaphor resolution; however, context reliance is abated in the case of familiar (i.e. lexicalised) metaphors. There is compelling evidence that novel metaphors are harder to comprehend and process, and that they are more reliant on salience. The conspicuously more demanding nature of novel metaphors is also visible in hemisphere/hemifield studies that show a clear connection between metaphor failure and failure to sufficiently activate the right hemisphere. Putting all the evidence in favour of GSH aside, we also need to address instances where the predicted difference between lexicalised and novel metaphors fails to realise.

Cognitive linguistics assumes that early metaphor development is grounded in embodied experience (Gibbs, Lima, & Francozo, 2004). Studies that have tested young children on primary metaphors have found that once acquired, performance on novel primary metaphors are as good as for lexicalised metaphors. This raises the issue as to what types of metaphors have been tested. Generally, mixed types of metaphors have been selected, and very few disorder studies have exclusively focused on conceptual metaphors, preferring more traditional types such as perceptual metaphors. It is very likely that the conflicting results in the studies discussed in this chapter are the product of non-conceptual metaphors actually relying on ToM and salience, while conceptual and primary metaphors do not.

Turning to the question of practical applications, we quickly note that there are few intervention studies, yet ASD authors such as Williams and Blackman describe how they have 'retrained' their thinking, suggesting intervention as a viable and desirable avenue. Mashal and Kasirer (2011) specifically focussed on novel metaphors. They used 'thinking maps' to teach ASD children the semantic relations between words that the children might not even have noticed are related. The outcome of the study showed an improvement in novel metaphor comprehension, as well as a correlation with semantic knowledge.

It is clear that further studies of metaphor acquisition and use are greatly needed, and in addition to cross-sectional studies, we need longitudinal studies with and without interventions. These needs are addressed in the next section.

Future directions

The most apparent and acute need is that we devise more systematic ways of testing metaphors that highlight the patterns that different sub-types of metaphor may give rise to. Even primary metaphors, which for a long time seem to have been one homogeneous group, are susceptible to differences between subgroups (Siqueira & Gibbs, 2007), and TD results for complex conceptual metaphors (Lachaud, 2013) need to be replicated and extended to atypical populations. Further, a wider range of potential underlying abilities need to consistently be tested for, to determine the extent to which they can predict metaphor performance. Thereafter, theory driven intervention studies should be designed to address whether targeting established underlying abilities (e.g. sense relations or ToM) can improve performance of different types of metaphors, or whether utilising the differences and links between metaphorical sub-types or other figurative language devices (e.g. metonymy) could have an even greater impact.

Delayed or impaired metaphor acquisition is not specific to neurodevelopmental disorders, e.g. individuals with unilateral cochlear implants struggle with metaphors despite normal discourse inference comprehension (Nicastri et al., 2014). We thus need to extend the atypical populations we study in order to get a more comprehensive overview of performance, underlying factors and obstacles. In addition, language investigations of siblings to individuals with neurodevelopmental disorders (Jones & Conti-Ramsden, 1997; Yirmiya et al., 2006) forces the question as to how wide the disorder spectrum might be and where the 'true' boundaries for abnormal language may lie.

Finally, one of the 'default' problems with any area of psycholinguistic research is the relative abundance of studies on English. A related issue is publication language; for example, there is increasing research in Korean on executive function and metaphor comprehension in SLI (Hong & Yim, 2014) and metaphor/simile production in attention deficit hyperactivity disorder (Lim, 2010), but these publications are only available in Korean. Access to published studies should whenever possible, include translation options.

Notes

1 A substantial number of people have one of these five neurodevelopmental disorders. In the UK, the combined prevalence rate is estimated to approximately 9%, with SLI contributing 7% and ASD 1% of that figure (Baird et al., 2006; Nation, 2008).
2 Approximately 20% of children with ASD are nonverbal (Rice et al., 2005).
3 Earliest age of onset is 13 years.
4 In matching approaches, it is essential that the age range within the disorder and TD groups is comparatively narrow. Matching studies can of course include age as an additional, well-defined independent ordinal variable (i.e. the study would include two or more age samples per group).
5 While it is very hard to imagine some form of 'catching up' for the last two, it is possible that a child with delayed onset carries on developing when typical peers have reached mature performance.
6 7;01 stands for 7 years and 1 month.
7 Note that Kogan and colleagues label the first two types of metaphors *physiognomic* and *configural*.
8 While structural MRI can detect brain size differences (e.g. ASD is associated with overall larger brain areas, except for the corpus callosum which is smaller [Stanfield et al., 2008]), fMRI

(i.e. functional magnetic resonance imaging), ERPs (i.e. event-related [brain] potentials), and TMS (i.e. transcranial magnetic stimulation) can determine areas of brain activation (Friederici, Pfeifer, & Hahne, 1993; Gabrieli et al., 1996; George, Wassermann, & Post, 1995). Note that although TMS has been used in both ASD and schizophrenia, metaphor studies using TMS are still lacking in disorder populations. Similarly, fMRI studies in ASD have targeted irony.

9 This experimental technique presents visual stimuli either on the left (causing signals to go to the right hemisphere) or the right (transmitted to the left hemisphere) visual field. If the participant performs better on items displayed on the left, the conclusion that the right hemisphere has a functional advantage can be drawn, and vice versa for right field presentations.

10 Notably, synonym ability yielded the strongest trajectory.

Further reading

Eddy, C. M., Mitchell, I. J., Beck, S. R., Cavanna, A. E., & Rickards, H. E. (2010). Impaired comprehension of nonliteral language in Tourette syndrome. *Cognitive and Behavioral Neurology, 23*(3), 178–184.

Elvevåg, B., Helsen, K., De Hert, M., Sweers, K., & Storms, G. (2011). Metaphor interpretation and use: A window into semantics in schizophrenia. *Schizophrenia Research, 133*(1–3), 205–211.

Giora, R., Gazal, O., Goldstein, I., Fein, O., & Stringaris, A. (2012). Salience and context: Interpretation of metaphorical and literal language by young adults diagnosed with Asperger's syndrome. *Metaphor and Symbol, 27*, 22–54.

Kircher, T. T. J., Leube, D. T., Erb, M., Grodd, W., & Rapp, A. M. (2007). Neural correlates of metaphor processing in schizophrenia. *NeuroImage, 34*(1), 281–289.

Olofson, E. L., Casey, D., Oluyedun, O. A., Van Herwegen, J., Becerra, A., & Rundblad, G. (2014). Youth with autism spectrum disorder comprehend lexicalized and novel primary conceptual metaphors. *Journal of Autism and Developmental Disorders, 44*(10), 2568–2583.

References

American Psychiatric Association. (2013). *Diagnostic and statistical manual of mental disorders* (5th ed.). Washington, DC: Author.

Baird, G., Simonoff, E., Pickles, A., Chandler, S., Loucas, T., Meldrum, D., & Charman, T. (2006). Prevalence of disorders of the autism spectrum in a population cohort of children in South Thames: The Special Needs and Autism Project (SNAP). *Lancet, 368*(9531), 210–215.

Baron-Cohen, S. (2001). Theory of mind in normal development and autism. *Prisme, 34*, 174–183.

Baron-Cohen, S., Johnson, D., Asher, J., Wheelwright, S., Fisher, S. E., Gregersen, P. K., & Allison, C. (2013). Is synaesthesia more common in autism? *Molecular Autism, 4*, 40.

Baron-Cohen, S., Leslie, A. M., & Frith, U. (1985). Does the autistic child have a 'theory of mind'? *Cognition, 21*, 37–46. doi: 10.1016/0010-0277(85)90022-8.

Billow, R. M., Rossman, J., Lewis, N., Goldman, D., & Raps, C. (1997). Observing expressive and deviant language in schizophrenia. *Metaphor and Symbol, 12*(3), 205–216.

Bishop, D. V. M. (1997). *Uncommon understanding: Development and disorders of language comprehension in children*. New York: Psychology Press.

Bishop, D. V. M., & McArthur, G. M. (2004). Immature cortical responses to auditory stimuli in specific language impairment: Evidence from ERPs to rapid tone sequences. *Developmental Science, 7*(4), F11–F18. doi: 10.1111/j.1467-7687.2004.00356.x.

Blackman, L. (2014). *Carrying autism, feeling language: Beyond Lucy's story*. Brisbane, Australia: Book in Hand.

Bohrn, I. C., Altmann, U., & Jacobs, A. M. (2012). Looking at the brains behind figurative language: A quantitative meta-analysis of neuroimaging studies on metaphor, idiom, and irony processing. *Neuropsychologia, 50*(11), 2669–2683.

Bora, E. (2015). Neurodevelopmental origin of cognitive impairment in schizophrenia. *Psychological Medicine*, *45*(1), 1–9.

Cameron, L. (2003). *Metaphor in educational discourse*. Bloomsbury.

Carter, M., & Scherer, S. (2013). Autism spectrum disorder in the genetics clinic: A review. *Clinical Genetics*, *83*(5), 399–407.

Chapman, R. S., & Hesketh, L. J. (2000). Behavioral phenotype of individuals with Down syndrome. *Mental Retardation and Developmental Disabilities Research Reviews*, *6*(2), 84–95.

Dennis, M., Lazenby, A., & Lockyer, L. (2001). Inferential language in high-function children with autism. *Journal of Autism and Developmental Disorders*, *31*(1), 47–54.

Elvevåg, B., Helsen, K., De Hert, M., Sweers, K., & Storms, G. (2011). Metaphor interpretation and use: A window into semantics in schizophrenia. *Schizophrenia Research*, *133*(1–3), 205–211. doi: http://dx.doi.org/10.1016/j.schres.2011.07.009.

Felder, M. A., McPartland, J. C., Klin, A., & Volkmar, F. R. (2014). *Asperger syndrome: Assessing and treating high-functioning autism spectrum disorders*. Guilford Press.

Friederici, A. D., Pfeifer, E., & Hahne, A. (1993). Event-related brain potentials during natural speech processing: Effects of semantic, morphological and syntactic violations. *Cognitive Brain Research*, *1*(3), 183–192.

Gabrieli, J. D., Desmond, J. E., Demb, J. B., Wagner, A. D., Stone, M. V., Vaidya, C. J., & Glover, G. H. (1996). Functional magnetic resonance imaging of semantic memory processes in the frontal lobes. *Psychological Science*, *7*(5), 278–283.

Gentner, D. (1988). Metaphor as structure mapping: The relational shift. *Child Development*, 47–59.

George, M. S., Wassermann, E. M., & Post, R. M. (1995). Transcranial magnetic stimulation: A neuropsychiatric tool for the 21st century. *Journal of Neuropsychiatry and Clinical Neurosciences*, *8*(4), 373–382.

Gibbs, R. W., Jr., Lima, P. L. C., & Francozo, E. (2004). Metaphor is grounded in embodied experience. *Journal of Pragmatics*, *36*(7), 1189–1210.

Giora, R. (1997). Understanding figurative and literal language: The graded salience hypothesis. *Cognitive Linguistics*, *8*, 183–206.

Giora, R., Gazal, O., Goldstein, I., Fein, O., & Stringaris, A. (2012). Salience and context: Interpretation of metaphorical and literal language by young adults diagnosed with Asperger's syndrome. *Metaphor and Symbol*, *27*, 22–54. doi: 10.1080/10926488.2012.638823.

Gold, R., & Faust, M. (2010). Right hemisphere dysfunction and metaphor comprehension in young adults with Asperger syndrome. *Journal of Autism and Developmental Disorders*, *40*(7), 800–811.

—— (2012). Metaphor comprehension in persons with Asperger's syndrome: Systemized versus non-systemized semantic processing. *Metaphor and Symbol*, *27*(1), 55–69. doi: 10.1080/10926488.2012.638826.

Gold, R., Faust, M., & Goldstein, A. (2010). Semantic integration during metaphor comprehension in Asperger syndrome. *Brain and Language*, *113*(3), 124–134. doi: http://dx.doi.org/10.1016/j.bandl.2010.03.002.

Grady, J. (1999). A typology of motivation for conceptual metaphor: Correlation vs. resemblance. *Amsterdam Studies in the Theory and History of Linguistic Science*, Series 4, 79–100.

Gross, G., & Huber, G. (2008). [Schizophrenia: Neurodevelopmental disorder or degenerative brain process?]. *Fortschritte der Neurologie-Psychiatrie*, *76*, S57–62.

Hale, C. M., & Tager Flusberg, H. (2003). The influence of language on theory of mind: A training study. *Developmental Science*, *6*, 346–359.

Happé, F. G. E. (1993). Communicative competence and theory of mind in autism: A test of relevance theory. *Cognition*, *48*(2), 101–119.

Highnam, C., Wegmann, J., & Woods, J. (1999). Visual and verbal metaphors among children with typical language and language disorders. *Journal of Communication Disorders*, *32*(1), 25–35. doi: 10.1016/s0021-9924(98)00027-6.

Hill, E. L. (2001). Non-specific nature of specific language impairment: A review of the literature with regard to concomitant motor impairments. *International Journal of Language & Communication Disorders, 36*(2), 149–171.

Hong, Y., & Yim, D. (2014). The relationship between working memory and metaphor comprehension in school-age children with specific language impairments. *Communication Sciences and Disorders, 19*(2), 191–198. doi: 10.12963/csd.14115.

Iakimova, G., Passerieux, C., Laurent, J.-P., & Hardy-Bayle, M.-C. (2005). ERPs of metaphoric, literal, and incongruous semantic processing in schizophrenia. *Psychophysiology, 42*(4), 380–390. doi: 10.1111/j.1469-8986.2005.00303.x.

Jakobson, B., & Wickman, P.-O. (2007). Transformation through language use: Children's spontaneous metaphors in elementary school science. *Science Education, 16*(3), 267–289. doi: 10.1007/s11191-006-9018-x.

Jänsch, C., & Hare, D. (2014). An investigation of the 'jumping to conclusions' data-gathering bias and paranoid thoughts in Asperger syndrome. *Journal of Autism and Developmental Disorders, 44*(1), 111–119. doi: 10.1007/s10803-013-1855-2.

Jones, M., & Conti-Ramsden, G. (1997). A comparison of verb use in children with SLI and their younger siblings. *First Language, 17*(51), 165–184.

Kahn, R. S., & Keefe, R. S. (2013). Schizophrenia is a cognitive illness: Time for a change in focus. *JAMA Psychiatry, 70*(10), 1107–1112.

Kanner, L. (1946). Irrelevant and metaphorical language in early infantile autism. *American Journal of Psychiatry, 103*, 242–246.

Karmiloff-Smith, A., Klima, E., Bellugi, U., Grant, J., & Baron-Cohen, S. (1995). Is there a social module? Language, face processing, and theory of mind in individuals with Williams syndrome. *Journal of Cognitive Neuroscience, 7*(2), 196–208.

Kasirer, A., & Mashal, N. (2014). Verbal creativity in autism: Comprehension and generation of metaphoric language in high-functioning autism spectrum disorder and typical development. *Frontiers in Human Neuroscience, 8*.

Kent, R. G., Carrington, S. J., Couteur, A., Gould, J., Wing, L., Maljaars, J., . . . Leekam, S. R. (2013). Diagnosing autism spectrum disorder: Who will get a DSM-5 diagnosis? *Journal of Child Psychology and Psychiatry, 54*(11), 1242–1250.

Kircher, T. T. J., Leube, D. T., Erb, M., Grodd, W., & Rapp, A. M. (2007). Neural correlates of metaphor processing in schizophrenia. *NeuroImage, 34*(1), 281–289. doi: http://dx.doi.org/10.1016/j.neuroimage.2006.08.044.

Kogan, N., & Chadrow, M. (1986). Children's comprehension of metaphor in the pictorial and verbal modality. *International Journal of Behavioral Development, 9*(3), 285–295.

Kogan, N., Connor, K., Gross, A., & Fava, D. (1980). Understanding visual metaphor: Developmental and individual differences. *Monographs of the Society for Research in Child Development*, 1–78.

Lachaud, C. M. (2013). Conceptual metaphors and embodied cognition: EEG coherence reveals brain activity differences between primary and complex conceptual metaphors during comprehension. *Cognitive Systems Research, 22–23*, 12–26. doi: http://dx.doi.org/10.1016/j.cogsys.2012.08.003.

Lakoff, G., & Johnson, M. (1980). *Metaphors we live by*. Chicago, IL: University of Chicago Press.

Langdon, R., Coltheart, M., Ward, P. B., & Catts, S. V. (2002). Disturbed communication in schizophrenia: The role of poor pragmatics and poor mind-reading. *Psychological Medicine, 32*(7), 1273–1284.

Liao, S.-F., Liu, J.-C., Hsu, C.-L., Chang, M.-Y., Chang, T.-M., & Cheng, H. (2015). Cognitive development in children with language impairment, and correlation between language and intelligence development in kindergarten children with developmental delay. *Journal of Child Neurology, 30*(1), 42–47.

Lim, J. (2010). The comprehension of figurative meaning in ADHD children with and without language impairment. *Communication Sciences & Disorders, 15*(3), 307–320.

Mashal, N., & Kasirer, A. (2011). Thinking maps enhance metaphoric competence in children with autism and learning disabilities. *Research in Developmental Disabilities, 32*(6), 2045–2054. doi: http://dx.doi.org/10.1016/j.ridd.2011.08.012.

—— (2012). Principal component analysis study of visual and verbal metaphoric comprehension in children with autism and learning disabilities. *Research in Developmental Disabilities, 33*(1), 274–282. doi: http://dx.doi.org/10.1016/j.ridd.2011.09.010.

Mashal, N., Vishne, T., Laor, N., & Titone, D. (2013). Enhanced left frontal involvement during novel metaphor comprehension in schizophrenia: Evidence from functional neuroimaging. *Brain and Language, 124*(1), 66–74. doi: http://dx.doi.org/10.1016/j.bandl.2012.11.012.

Minshew, N. J., Goldstein, G., & Siegel, D. J. (1995). Speech and language in high-functioning autistic individuals. *Neuropsychology, 9*(2), 255–261.

Mo, S., Su, Y., Chan, R. C., & Liu, J. (2008). Comprehension of metaphor and irony in schizophrenia during remission: The role of theory of mind and IQ. *Psychiatry Research, 157*(1), 21–29.

Nation, K. (2008). Developmental language disorders. *Psychiatry, 7*(6), 266–269. doi: 10.1016/j.mppsy.2008.04.003.

Naylor, L., & Van Herwegen, J. (2012). The production of figurative language in typically developing children and Williams syndrome. *Research in Developmental Disabilities, 33*, 711–716. doi: http://dx.doi.org/10.1016/j.ridd.2011.11.013.

Nicastri, M., Filipo, R., Ruoppolo, G., Viccaro, M., Dincer, H., Guerzoni, L., . . . Mancini, P. (2014). Inferences and metaphoric comprehension in unilaterally implanted children with adequate formal oral language performance. *International Journal of Pediatric Otorhinolaryngology, 78*(5), 821–827. doi: http://dx.doi.org/10.1016/j.ijporl.2014.02.022.

Niebert, K., Marsch, S., & Treagust, D. F. (2012). Understanding needs embodiment: A theory-guided reanalysis of the role of metaphors and analogies in understanding science. *Science Education, 96*(5), 849–877. doi: 10.1002/sce.21026.

Norbury, C. F. (2005). The relationship between theory of mind and metaphor: Evidence from children with language impairment and autistic spectrum disorder. *British Journal of Developmental Psychology, 23*, 383–399. doi: 10.1348/026151005x26732.

Olofson, E. L., Casey, D., Oluyedun, O. A., Van Herwegen, J., Becerra, A., & Rundblad, G. (2014). Youth with autism spectrum disorder comprehend lexicalized and novel primary conceptual metaphors. *Journal of Autism and Developmental Disorders, 44*(10), 2568–2583. doi: 10.1007/s10803-014-2129-3.

Özçalişkan, S. (2005). On learning to draw the distinction between physical and metaphorical motion: Is metaphor an early emerging cognitive and linguistic capacity? *Journal of Child Language, 32*(2), 291–318.

Papagno, C., & Vallar, G. (2001). Understanding metaphors and idioms: A single-case neuropsychological study in a person with Down syndrome. *Journal of the International Neuropsychological Society, 7*(4), 516–527.

Pober, B. R. (2010). Williams-Beuren syndrome. *New England Journal of Medicine, 362*(3), 239–252.

Rapp, A. M., Leube, D. T., Erb, M., Grodd, W., & Kircher, T. T. J. (2004). Neural correlates of metaphor processing. *Cognitive Brain Research, 20*(3), 395–402. doi: http://dx.doi.org/10.1016/j.cogbrainres.2004.03.017.

Rhodes, S. M., Riby, D. M., Park, J., Fraser, E., & Campbell, L. E. (2010). Executive neuropsychological functioning in individuals with Williams syndrome. *Neuropsychologia, 48*(5), 1216–1226. doi: http://dx.doi.org/10.1016/j.neuropsychologia.2009.12.021.

Rice, M. L., Warren, S. F., & Betz, S. K. (2005). Language symptoms of developmental language disorders: An overview of autism, Down syndrome, fragile X, specific language impairment, and Williams syndrome. *Applied Psycholinguistics, 26*(1), 7–27.

Richtsmeier, P. T., & Goffman, L. (in press). Learning trajectories for speech motor performance in children with specific language impairment. *Journal of Communication Disorders.* doi: http://dx.doi.org/10.1016/j.jcomdis.2015.02.001.

Roth, I. (2008). Imagination and the awareness of self in autistic spectrum poets. *Autism and Representation, 12*, 145.

Rowe, J., Lavender, A., & Turk, V. (2006). Cognitive executive function in Down's syndrome. *British Journal of Clinical Psychology, 45*(1), 5–17. doi: 10.1348/014466505X29594.

Rundblad, G., & Annaz, D. (2010a). Development of metaphor and metonymy comprehension: Receptive vocabulary and conceptual knowledge. *British Journal of Developmental Psychology, 28*, 547–563. doi: 10.1348/026151009X454373.

—— (2010b). The atypical development of metaphor and metonymy comprehension in children with autism. *Autism, 14*, 29.

Rundblad, G., Dimitriou, D., & Van Herwegen, J. (in press). From impairment to cognitive delay: A study of figurative language in Williams syndrome highlighting methodological issues. *International Journal of Disability, Development and Education.* doi: http://dx.doi.org/10.1016/S0140-6736(13)62436-8.

Salavera, C., Puyuelo, M., Antonanzas, J. L., & Teruel, P. (2013). Semantics, pragmatics, and formal thought disorders in people with schizophrenia. *Neuropsychiatric Disease and Treatment, 9*, 177–183.

Simpson, N. H., Ceroni, F., Reader, R. H., Covill, L. E., Knight, J. C., Nudel, R., ... Pickles, A. (2015). Genome-wide analysis identifies a role for common copy number variants in specific language impairment. *European Journal of Human Genetics, 23*, 1370–1377.

Siqueira, M., & Gibbs, R. W., Jr. (2007). Children's acquisition of primary metaphors: A crosslinguistic study. *Organon, 21*(43), 161–179.

Sperber, D., & Wilson, D. (1995). *Relevance: Communication and cognition* (2nd ed.). Oxford, UK: Blackwell.

Stanfield, A. C., McIntosh, A. M., Spencer, M. D., Philip, R., Gaur, S., & Lawrie, S. M. (2008). Towards a neuroanatomy of autism: A systematic review and meta-analysis of structural magnetic resonance imaging studies. *European Psychiatry, 23*(4), 289–299. doi: http://dx.doi.org/10.1016/j.eurpsy.2007.05.006.

Tager-Flusberg, H., Calkins, S., Nolin, T., Baumberger, T., Anderson, M., & Chadwick-Dias, A. (1990). A longitudinal study of language acquisition in autistic and Down syndrome children. *Journal of Autism and Developmental Disorders, 20*(1), 1–21.

Tendahl, M., & Gibbs, R. W., Jr. (2008). Complementary perspectives on metaphor: Cognitive linguistics and relevance theory. *Journal of Pragmatics, 40*(11), 1823–1864.

Thomas, M. S., Annaz, D., Ansari, D., Scerif, G., Jarrold, C., & Karmiloff-Smith, A. (2009). Using developmental trajectories to understand developmental disorders. *Journal of Speech, Language, and Hearing Research, 52*(2), 336–358.

Unenge Hallerbäck, M., Lugnegård, T., & Gillberg, C. (2012). Is autism spectrum disorder common in schizophrenia? *Psychiatry Research, 198*(1), 12–17. doi: 10.1016/j.psychres.2012.01.016.

Van Herwegen, J., Dimitriou, D., & Rundblad, G. (2013). Development of novel metaphor and metonymy comprehension in typically developing children and Williams syndrome. *Research in Developmental Disabilities, 34*(4), 1300–1311. doi: http://dx.doi.org/10.1016/j.ridd.2013.01.017.

Vance, M., & Wells, B. (1994). The wrong end of the stick: Language-impaired children's understanding of non-literal language. *Child Language Teaching and Therapy, 10*(1), 23–46.

Williams, D. (1998). *Autism and sensing: The unlost instinct*. London, Philadelphia: Jessica Kingsley.

Yirmiya, N., Gamliel, I., Pilowsky, T., Feldman, R., Baron-Cohen, S., & Sigman, M. (2006). The development of siblings of children with autism at 4 and 14 months: Social engagement, communication, and cognition. *Journal of Child Psychology and Psychiatry, 47*(5), 511–523.

34

Metaphor comprehension and production in a second language

Susan Nacey

Introduction

The 1980 publication of Lakoff and Johnson's *Metaphors We Live By* on Conceptual Metaphor Theory (CMT) marked a paradigm shift in metaphor studies, advancing the view of metaphor as a fundamental cognitive process (see Chapter 1). Rather than merely being an optional and ornamental element in discourse, the metaphors we produce in language are viewed in CMT as mirroring the way we conceive of the world around us. Metaphor operates primarily on the level of thought, through 'conceptual metaphors' that help define our understanding of reality. With the conceptual metaphor TIME IS MONEY, for instance, we map some of the properties of a 'source' domain (money) onto a 'target' domain (time); time is in some way compared to and understood in terms of money. Such conceptual metaphors are, in turn, reflected in language by the actual words and expressions we produce – so-called 'linguistic metaphors', exemplified by the lexical verb in *we're wasting time*. In brief, metaphor is intrinsic to language because metaphor is intrinsic to thought.

Studies exploring metaphor acquisition in children developing their first language (their L1) indicate that children may begin to make sense of the world through metaphorical reasoning as early as infancy, a competence which grows with age and experience (cf. Wagner *et al.*, 1981; Winner, 1988). Being inherent in human nature, it stands to reason that such 'metaphoric competence' necessarily also plays an important role in the acquisition of subsequently learned languages, not just the L1. This chapter explores various ways in which metaphor relates to second/foreign language (L2) development, along with many of the central issues and questions addressed by recent research (see also Chapter 19 about metaphor in education and Chapter 28 on teaching metaphor in an L2). The next section first elaborates upon the concept of metaphoric competence, presenting an overview of different perspectives concerning its definition and potential significance for L2 learners. The subsequent sections explore studies examining L2 metaphoric competence: the extent to which learners comprehend the metaphors of the target language, and the types of metaphors they produce in discourse. The chapter then moves on to one of the burning issues in this field – namely, the practical pedagogical implications of L2 metaphoric competence. This is followed by some preliminary analysis from ongoing research in the field. The final section rounds off the chapter by discussing possible directions for future research.

Overview of literature on metaphoric competence

More or less concurrently with the development and later expansion of CMT, applied linguists gradually began exploring the practical implications of the theory for language learning and teaching. In 1988, Low wrote what turned out to be a landmark paper, one of the first to extend the view of the centrality of metaphor to L2 language learning. He proposed a reformulation of CMT in terms of 'metaphoric competence': 'a number of skills related to metaphor which native speakers are frequently expected to be good at, and which learners need to develop to some degree if they hope to be seen as competent users of the language' (Low, 1988, p. 129). His suggested list of skills includes the ability to interpret seemingly anomalous sentences, as well as knowledge about the boundaries of conventional metaphor both with respect to what people tend to say and tend *not* to say. Learners also need to know about the interactive aspects of metaphor, including being mindful of socially sensitive metaphors (for example, 'animal' metaphors in connection with gender) or of the possibility of 'multiple layering' when an expression refers to both literal and metaphorical meaning at one and the same time (Low, 1988, pp. 133–4). Low's skills-based approach is intended as a basic framework to guide the practical application of metaphor theory in the classroom and improve learners' L2 language competence.

Littlemore (2001a) operates with an alternative definition of metaphoric competence as consisting of four separate components: '(a) originality of metaphor production, (b) fluency of metaphor interpretation, (c) ability to find meaning in metaphor, and (d) speed in finding meaning in metaphor' (Littlemore, 2001a, p. 461). She expands upon Low's contention that metaphoric competence varies from person to person, suggesting that the different aspects of metaphoric competence may develop independently and at varying rates in different learners. Specifically, Littlemore – and later Littlemore and Low (2006b) – find that a learner's degree of metaphoric competence may depend upon their cognitive learning style, i.e. 'a person's habitual way of perceiving, organizing, and processing information' (Littlemore, 2001a, p. 462). Littlemore and Low (2006a) additionally demonstrate how metaphoric competence, as part of what they term 'figurative thinking', contributes to linguistic, sociolinguistic, discourse and strategic elements of communicative competence.

An alternative perspective on metaphoric competence is offered by Danesi (1994), who maintains that it primarily relates to the level of thought rather than the surface manifestation of language: 'student-based discourse texts seem to follow a native-language conceptual flow that is "clothed" [...] in target language grammar and vocabulary' (Danesi, 1994, p. 454). Based on a few pilot studies, Danesi finds that learner 'infelicities' are caused by a mismatch between the concepts fundamental to speakers of the L1 and L2 in question. He concludes that learners need to utilize the L2 conceptual system rather than their own to sound truly native-like. By contrast, Philip (2006) maintains that learners' infelicities are linguistic rather than conceptual – that is, inappropriate L2 encoding of shared concepts. One of her examples comes from an Italian learner who writes the *escape of the brains* (a literal translation of *la fuga dei cervelli*), instead of the conventional L1 English expression *brain drain* (Philip, 2006, p. 5). Although the cultures share similar underlying conceptual metaphors here, the metaphor is realized differently in the two languages and results in the production of unconventional L2 collocations. Philip concludes therefore that sensitivity to phraseological patterns in an L2 trumps the need for conscious awareness of conceptual domains when it comes to metaphor production.

Metaphoric competence in its most encompassing sense thus concerns the ability to decode and encode metaphorically structured concepts (cf. Danesi, 1994), the practical skills and knowledge required to do so (cf. Low, 1988), and the awareness of conventional phraseological patterns and how such patterns may vary between languages (cf. Philip, 2006). In a broader sense, metaphoric competence concerns the overall 'ability to acquire, produce, and interpret metaphor' (Littlemore, 2001a, p. 459), important for all aspects of communicative competence in an L2 (cf. Littlemore & Low, 2006a). Most research concerning metaphoric competence has centred around this wider sense of the concept by using different methods to investigate comprehension and/or production of metaphor by L2 learners, as demonstrated in the following subsections.

Studies of L2 metaphor comprehension

Perhaps the most obvious way of gaining insight into learners' metaphoric competence is to measure their understanding of metaphorical language. The very concept of 'understanding' is not as straightforward as many might first suppose, however, leading Gibbs (1994, pp. 116–18), for example, to decompose it into four main components: comprehension, recognition, interpretation and appreciation. 'Comprehension' is the immediate and ongoing process of creating meaning from utterances by linking linguistic information (e.g. syntax, lexis, phonemes) and context. Psycholinguistic research indicates that this process is rapid, taking anywhere from milliseconds to a few seconds. 'Recognition' refers to the conscious identification of an utterance as a type, e.g. recognizing a metaphor *as metaphor*. 'Interpretation' involves the analysis of the products of comprehension by, for example, expanding upon the entailments of a particular metaphor. These meanings may or may not have been intended by the speaker/writer. Finally, 'appreciation' involves the aesthetic judgement of an utterance, determining its quality. Gibbs explains that much of what is involved in the understanding of figurative language is comprehension, i.e. grasping the intention of utterances. The remaining three steps are later, and optional, products of understanding.

Investigations into the understanding of metaphor have thus far not looked into all four of Gibbs' proposed components. Most research into the understanding of L2 metaphor focuses upon the comprehension or the interpretation stages (or both stages, sometimes conflated), rather than whether learners actually recognize the language as non-literal or whether they 'like' it in some way. One example of a comprehension study is Golden (2006), comparing the metaphor comprehension of Norwegian L1 15-year-old students with that of their minority-language peers (speakers of Norwegian with varying L1 language backgrounds). The metaphorical expressions Golden asked these students about had all been identified from Norwegian-language textbooks that were aimed at these students; she wanted to find whether there were any differences between different subgroups of students, as well as whether certain metaphorical expressions were more difficult to understand than others. To do so, Golden asked her informants to choose the appropriate meaning of the selected Norwegian metaphorical expressions from among a number of distractors in a multiple-choice task. She found that all her informants had difficulties comprehending the same metaphors, but to varying degrees: if a particular metaphor presented only a slight problem for some L1 speakers, it was likely to present an even greater challenge to L2 learners. These findings have important pedagogical implications, especially for textbook authors and publishers who may not necessarily realize that certain conventional metaphorical expressions may not communicate well to their target audience.

Picken (2005, pp. 73–9) investigated the degree to which L2 English learners comprehend so-called 'invisible' metaphors in literature, with the aim of exploring the extent to which metaphor poses comprehension problems. He asked 30 first-year Japanese university students of English to write explanations for the penultimate line in one of two versions of almost identical stories. In each case, the line in question called for a metaphorical interpretation, but the explicitness of metaphor in the two versions differed. In the more explicit text – *In her heart, she was drowning* – the metaphorical reasoning was triggered by a so-called 'topic domain signal' (the phrase *in her heart*), precluding the literal understand of the 'drowning'. In the less explicit version – *She was drowning* – the metaphor was 'invisible' in the sense that the metaphorical meaning had to be entirely inferred from context. Findings showed that the invisible version was significantly more often misinterpreted; students believed the topic was the literal sense of drowning. Picken's results thus indicate that metaphor comprehension may be significantly affected by linguistic form, where absence of signalling might lead L2 learners to interpret a metaphor as a literal event in the world of the text at hand, rather than a metaphorical one.

While Golden and Picken looked into metaphor comprehension in written texts, Littlemore (2001b) investigated L2 learners' comprehension of metaphor in spoken discourse. Her informants were Bangladeshi students attending a British university as part of an overseas studies programme; Littlemore wanted to investigate whether metaphor, which may rely on shared culturally specific knowledge, played any negative role in their understanding of university lectures. She first recorded and transcribed some of the students' lectures, then asked them to underline any language they perceived as difficult. Afterwards, the students were asked to explain ten metaphors that had been preselected by Littlemore from the lectures, and it was found that they were frequently unable to successfully do so; many of the students' explanations were inappropriate. What was surprising was that some of what they had clearly not understood had *not* been marked by them as difficult language – that is, they were sometimes completely unaware of any possible comprehension problems; they truly believed they had understood correctly. Such misinterpretation would not be serious if metaphor only played a minor role in lectures, but Low et al. (2008) later found that it actually has quite an important function in academic talks. Metaphor is used both to organize discourse and to convey speaker opinion; moreover, it is *never* overtly explained. Students might therefore grasp the basic content but miss out on the speaker's evaluation, thereby potentially misinterpreting the overall message. This type of research has since prompted practical advice for raising metaphoric awareness among both international students and British university lecturers (further described in the next section).

In a 2004 study, Littlemore turned toward investigating the *interpretation* rather than comprehension stage of metaphor understanding, by exploring the mental processes that L2 learners employ when deciphering metaphor. For this research, she videotaped intermediate level Japanese learners of English as they worked together in a group to decipher the meanings of previously unknown metaphorical expressions such as *pig out* and *skirt an issue*, all of which the learners had encountered in context; this type of method is known as a 'goal-directed interactive think-aloud technique' (Littlemore, 2004, pp. 2/14). Littlemore observed a range of interpretation strategies, depending upon the richness of available context. By way of example, learners faced with minimal context figured out meaning by applying potentially relevant source domain features to the context, as when they worked out the meaning of *cradle work* (referring to the suspended platforms which window cleaners use to ascend tall buildings) by identifying the possibly relevant features of a baby cradle. With richer context, learners did the opposite: they used the context as a framework to identify pertinent source domain features. An added observation was the extensive use of gesture that promoted understanding. Sometimes a single simple gesture was enough to trigger a complex interpretation, or one student's gesture would help another student come up with the meaning of the expression in question. Such observations lend support to the CMT claim that metaphor is fundamental to cognition, in that linguistic metaphor would seem to reflect 'embodied cognition' – that is, the idea that our understanding of the world around us (including abstract concepts) depends to some extent on our physical experience. On a more practical level, Littlemore's study suggests that teachers should encourage learners to use clues in both the context and in the source domain to figure out the meaning of metaphor, as well as to use gesture.

Piquer-Píriz (2008) applied a similar think-aloud protocol in her series of studies conducted with young Spanish learners of English, aged 5 to 11 years old. Her main aim was to explore the extent to which very young learners exploit the literal meaning of a lexeme when trying to decipher its metaphorical sense; she too was interested in interpretation strategies and exploring ways of promoting L2 acquisition of metaphorical lexis. Her work, however, is especially noteworthy because little research about L2 metaphor development among very young children has thus far been conducted.

Specifically, Piquer-Píriz wanted to uncover whether and how these children made sense of metaphorical semantic extensions from familiar body parts such as HEAD, as in *the head of a hammer*. To do so, the children were asked to complete various tasks such as labelling the metaphorical 'head' of objects (e.g. a hammer, a bed, a staircase) in photographs; their interaction and negotiation as they explained their interpretations were recorded and transcribed. Piquer-Píriz's findings show that semantic motivation from literal to metaphorical sense plays a significant role in interpretation, the human body being especially salient at the youngest ages. Like Littlemore's (2004) research highlighting the importance of gesture, Piquer-Píriz's work provides support for embodied cognition, given that her very young informants employ metaphorical reasoning, even in an L2. Piquer-Píriz further maintains that teachers and materials designers should foster metaphorical thinking as an aid to vocabulary enrichment, also for very young children.

Adding metaphorical production to the investigative mix

A further means of shedding light on L2 metaphoric competence is to investigate spoken or written L2 language *production*, rather than (or in addition to) L2 comprehension and interpretation strategies. An example of a relatively early study looking into both metaphorical production and comprehension at the same time is Charteris-Black's (2002) small-scale study of the second language figurative competence of Malay learners of English. He first selected 40 contemporary figurative units from Malay and English found in standard reference works, and then classified and compared them to create an analytical framework: a contrastive model with six types of figurative units. These types ranged on a scale based on how closely the metaphorical expressions in the two languages resembled each other (linguistic similarity), together with how closely the underlying metaphors in the two conceptual systems matched (conceptual similarity). For instance, Charteris-Black's 'Type 1' figurative units are judged completely equivalent because both their conceptual basis and linguistic realizations closely correspond (e.g. the English expression *a broken heart* has a similar corresponding Malay expression). At the opposite extreme, 'Type 6' figurative units have different conceptual bases in the two languages and are also linguistically encoded in culturally specific ways (e.g. Malay *makin angin* [eat wind] for English *to travel for fun*, which do not resemble each other either conceptually or linguistically even though they mean the same thing). One might assume that such expressions would be far less transparent for language learners.

After developing his six-fold taxonomy, Charteris-Black first tested a group of Malay undergraduate students of English in their comprehension of metaphor, by administering a multiple-choice exercise requiring them to select the appropriate meaning of expressions given in context. He followed this up by a production task, a 'cued completion exercise', requiring learners to fill in the appropriate expression within the presented context (helped by a short clue, to avoid the choice of alternative phrases). His main findings indicate that 'Type 1' English figurative units present the fewest difficulties for Malay students. The most challenging metaphors for learners were those with an equivalent linguistic form, but different conceptual bases. These are expressions that may look alike in the two languages, but mean very different things; he cites the example of *get the wind up*, which refers to anxiety in (British) English but to anger in Malay. On the basis of his research, Charteris-Black offers pedagogical suggestions. Specifically, in cases where L1 and L2 conceptual metaphors differ, he advises teachers to explicitly highlight the differing source and target domains in the classroom. By contrast, when L1 and L2 conceptual metaphors are shared, there is then no need to overtly focus on any underlying concept. Rather, he advises teachers to instead point out and work with any differences in the L1 and L2 *linguistic* realizations of those concepts.

Another means of investigating both L2 comprehension and production of figurative language is adopted in MacArthur and Littlemore's (2011) research into metaphor in intercultural communication. They looked at the ways in which metaphor contributes to the joint construction of meaning in *spoken* interaction between L1 and L2 speakers of English, rather than written material. To do so, they first identified all metaphors in the transcriptions of two types of oral data: one set containing elicited, semi-structured interviews between people with different first languages (L1 Polish/L1 English and L1 Spanish/L1 English), and one set containing naturally occurring conversations between an L1 Spanish speaker and her colleagues, some of whom had English as their L1. The particular focus of their subsequent analysis was on lexical repetition of metaphorical words and phrases. They conclude that, although topic and content affect metaphor density, both native speakers and non-native speakers use metaphor in spoken discourse. Indeed, the use of particular metaphorical words in back-and-forth spoken dialogue may actually indicate the degree to which an L2 speaker has become part of a particular discourse community, exemplified by when L2-speaking teachers adopt a key term such as *cover* in their professional discourse (e.g. *cover a topic*). MacArthur and Littlemore also observe that non-conventional metaphorical language produced by non-native speakers, as when an L2 speaker says *coal print* instead of the conventional English expression *carbon footprint*, does not lead to communication breakdown; misunderstandings, if any, are quickly and easily resolved. Based on such observations, MacArthur and Littlemore suggest that L2 language learners be trained in exploiting the metaphorical potential of target language vocabulary, since adapting even a limited stock of words may prove more valuable than memorizing a large number of seldom-used idioms. This type of research is important for its holistic approach, by viewing production and comprehension in real-life discourse as two parts of a whole: comprehension in spoken discourse affects production, and production affects comprehension.

Detailed investigation into L2 learner metaphor production alone is relatively rare, the first major corpus-based investigation having been conducted by Nacey (2013). This research compares the metaphorical production of Norwegian L2 learners of English from the Norwegian sub-corpus of the International Corpus of Learner English (NICLE) with that of British L1 novice writers from Louvain Corpus of Native English Essays (LOCNESS), partially to uncover any significant differences. All linguistic metaphors in roughly 20,000 words of text in both corpora were first identified following a version of the Metaphor Identification Procedure Vrije Universiteit (MIPVU), a procedure allowing for the reliable and valid identification of metaphors in discourse (for more about MIPVU see Steen *et al.*, 2010). Findings indicate that the texts in the two corpora mirror each other in many ways. For instance, metaphor is highly frequent in both sets of texts, representing 18% and 16.7% of all lexical units in NICLE and LOCNESS respectively. Moreover, both groups (even the L2 language learners) tend to express their arguments in quite conventional language. Novel metaphors – those whose contextual meanings are not codified in standard English dictionaries – are fairly rare. This observation is contrary to what one might expect given the general focus in metaphor literature on novelty, often linked with creativity (see e.g. Kövecses, 2010). Nacey (2013) proposes that a better indicator of possible metaphorical creativity may be deliberate metaphor, i.e. metaphor produced with the express intention of prompting a shift in perspective about a topic through reference to a seemingly unrelated 'alien' concept (cf. Steen, 2008). One documented example from the Norwegian L2 English texts is the simile *Working today is like being in a competition*, where a comparison between two unrelated semantic domains (flagged by *like*) may only be understood through recourse to metaphorical reasoning; otherwise, this reference to competition in a discussion about working would be incongruous. With such examples to go by, Nacey suggests that future investigations into deliberate metaphor might prove fruitful in clarifying the fuzzy boundary between creativity and error in L2 learner texts.

A concurrent study of L2 metaphor production is Littlemore *et al.* (2013). They were granted access to the Cambridge Learner Corpus, a database of anonymized Cambridge examination scripts written by EFL learners of different L1 language backgrounds. These scripts had been marked following the assessment criteria in the Common European Framework of References for Languages (CEFR), a document intended to guide 'language syllabuses, curriculum guidelines, examinations, textbooks, etc. across Europe' (Council of Europe, 2001, p. 1). From this corpus, Littlemore *et al.* selected 100 essays written by Greek learners of English and 100 essays written by German learners of English, with each group represented by 20 essays falling into each of the five CEFR proficiency levels, ranging from the 'elementary' A2 level to the 'mastery' C2 level. The overall objective of this study was to uncover how metaphor use varied across these levels in terms of amount, word class (open or closed), distribution of metaphor clusters, function, appropriateness, and L1 language background. Findings indicate, perhaps unsurprisingly, that metaphoric density in learner texts increases with proficiency level. Arguably more important is that the *type* of metaphor usage changes around the B2 level; as more content words are metaphorically used, the amount of error involving metaphor increases (and peaks), and L1 transfer of metaphorical expressions into the L2 becomes more common. In short, something happens at the B2 level: learners seem to experiment with language to a greater extent than at earlier levels, perhaps in response to the more demanding nature of their assigned writing tasks. Such research has immediate practical applications, since Littlemore *et al.* used their findings to propose CEFR descriptors for metaphor use, something that had been missing from the framework. When it comes to teaching and assessment, they suggest that teachers provide more scaffolding to help learners with their production of metaphorical language, and also propose that language assessors be more tolerant of deviation from conventional L1 language at the B2 level than they otherwise might be. Learners need an experimentation phase in order to mature linguistically.

Critical issues

When Low first offered his definition of metaphoric competence in 1988, he simultaneously called for practical measures to adapt theories about metaphor and language learning to the 'shop floor' of the classroom. This has hardly happened. An examination of the CEFR guidelines from the perspective of a metaphor scholar demonstrates that contemporary notions about metaphoric competence are almost entirely absent. Metaphor is mentioned primarily in terms of obstacles, a trope that only appears in language towards the 'proficient' C1/C2 levels. The CEFR view of metaphor is informed more by the layman's impression of metaphor being something unusual and extraordinary than by the cognitive linguist's view of metaphor being ubiquitous in both language and thought (for more about metaphor and the CEFR see Nacey, 2013, pp. 40–55). The CEFR, however, clearly states that its categories and examples are not intended to be exhaustive, but are instead suggestions that should be adjusted to suit the individual reader's own practice – hence the CEFR descriptors for metaphor use proposed by Littlemore and her colleagues (2013; described above). Unfortunately, the chances that such suggestions from a single study will have much impact on teaching practices out in the field are slim, given that far more practitioners consult the CEFR itself, rather than scholarly articles.

Boers (2014), too, notes a general lack of transfer from theory to practice, saying that findings from metaphor scholars have yet to filter down to textbooks. He attributes this absence to a general belief that cognitive linguists focus on the parts of language that do not merit prioritization, metaphorical language being thought of as an 'icing-on-the-cake' type of knowledge: useful, but not absolutely necessary. He argues that metaphor scholars need to provide more compelling evidence for the importance of metaphorical language for learners, as he finds that earlier studies simply lack rigour and, as a result, may not be persuasive enough. Given enough convincing evidence, however, the problem still remains as to how to translate theory into practice. Dissemination of 'digestible' material through easily accessible channels is essential. One good example of this is a British Council publication about the role of metaphor in academic tutorials, offering clear suggestions for British university lecturers on how to make themselves better understood by international students, both at home and abroad (Littlemore et al., 2012). This report uses examples from recorded, oral, office hour consultations between L1 and L2 speakers of English, to illustrate how and when metaphor in language and gesture is used by the different participants, highlighting moments that might lead to misunderstandings. Most importantly, practical advice is proffered to help lecturers avoid the potential pitfalls of metaphor use in tutorials.

Implementation of activities designed to stimulate metaphoric competence needs to be viewed by teachers as doable, given practical constraints such as limited time and large classes. Such implementation also needs to be as painless as possible – that is, teachers need practical activities that they may adapt to their classroom needs, rather than just theory (see van der Branden 2009 about the implementation of innovations in the classroom). The integration of activities focusing on various aspects of metaphoric competence into standard teaching aids and tools (such as textbooks) is crucial if research into metaphoric competence is to have much real impact on language teaching, learning, and assessment. Such integration needs to be carried out in a principled manner and in such a way that will better prepare pupils for any obligatory examinations they will face. At the moment, there are some excellent activity books anchored in a cognitive linguistic view of language. An example is Lindstromberg and Boers (2008), which offers numerous activities designed to make pupils aware of chunks and the cultural and/or embodied motivation behind them. However, many of the activities in such books, while valuable in and of themselves, are 'stunts', in that it is challenging to adapt them to other language areas and/or texts without a good deal of work. Ideally, activities fostering metaphoric competence should be incorporated into standard textbooks and other learning aids so that teachers, who are frequently pressed for time, need not hunt for appropriate activities elsewhere. The more (mostly metaphorical) steps that must be taken to apply insights from metaphor research to the classroom, the less likely it is that metaphor research will indeed be applied.

An example of current research

Different types of learner corpora allow for studies into metaphor and second language development from various perspectives (see Chapter 8 for corpus linguistic approaches to metaphor). My latest research in the field investigates metaphor production in multiple learner translations, looking into the ways in which advanced Norwegian learners of English translate metaphor from their L1 into English. Most previous scientific literature about metaphor in translation has either viewed metaphor as a translation problem – 'a kind of ultimate test of any theory of translation' (Toury, 1995, p. 81) – or consisted of guidelines for metaphor translation (see also Chapter 17). Perhaps the most well-known set of guidelines is that of Newmark (1988, pp. 88–91): his proposed metaphor translation procedures constitute a top-down approach, since actual translations were never consulted in their development (according to Fernández, 2011, p. 265). A growing body of research is being produced in the field of Descriptive Translation Studies, however, to explore what translations actually *are*, rather than what they should be (e.g. Rosa, 2010; Toury, 1995). Investigation into the metaphors produced by L2 language learners therefore contributes to this descriptive endeavour.

The data for my study comes from the Norwegian-English Student Translation Corpus (NEST; available at: http://clu.uni.no/humfak/nest/), a corpus of L2 learner language – more specifically, a multiple translation corpus containing translations written by language learners rather than professional translators. The investigation identifies and categorizes the translation of metaphors from 25 different Norwegian source texts (ST) in a total of 284 English translated texts (TT), thereby both describing individual translations and providing comparative descriptions of several TTs derived from the same ST. The STs range in length from 200 to 900 words and cover different topics and text types; the translations were produced as part of a university course and intended as a means for learners to improve their English language skills, through illustrating a variety of contrastive challenges for the learners to translate and later discuss. In this study, focus is placed upon the translations of three types of metaphors, identified using MIPVU: (1) metaphorical verbs, codified in Norwegian, (2) metaphorical idioms, which are often culture-specific and (3) potentially deliberate metaphorical expressions such as similes and other metaphorical analogies (cf. Nacey, 2013; Steen, 2008; see Chapter 15 for more detail on metaphorical idioms). All metaphors identified have been categorized following Newmark's classification guidelines for metaphor translation. As it turns out, however, his top-down approach does not sufficiently account for all translation solutions actually chosen by the language learners, leading to a proposed modification of Newmark's classification that more closely reflects the data under study, based on real decisions rather than theoretical options.

What follows is a sample analysis of one of the three types of metaphor under investigation: idioms. The NEST STs contain relatively few idioms, not unsurprising given Moon's (2007, p. 1050) contention that smaller corpora (< 100 million words) yield only isolated

Table 34.1 Translations of *karakteristisk for hans kjerringa-mot-strømmen-holdning*

	Translation
1	characteristic for his 'against-the-stream-attitude'
2	characteristic to his 'kjærringa mot strømmen' attitude (the Norwegian folktale about the old woman who always had to have her own way)
3	characteristic for his 'going against the grain attitude'
4	typical of his go against the stream-attitude
5	characteristic for his 'go against the grain' attitude
6	characteristic of his 'swimming upstream-nature'
7	characteristic for his go against the grain-attitude
8	characteristic for his 'swimming-against-the-currant-attitude'
9	characteristic of him to go against the current
10	characteristic for his attitude of contrariness

Source: NEST_Oppno.s38.

instances of idioms, except for 'anomalous local densities' of an idiom repeated in a single text. Nevertheless, because comprehension of unfamiliar idioms often depends upon some degree of shared cultural knowledge, they are of interest when investigating translation strategies of metaphor. Translation of idioms may pose particular problems when it comes to the balance between faithfulness to an ST and the production of a TT that is both understandable and idiomatic for the language and text type in question.

One NEST idiom is found in an ST about the life of Norwegian author Bjørnstjerne Bjørnson. He is described as being an independent individualist with a characteristic *kjerringa-mot-strømmen-holdning* [literal translation: hag-against-stream-attitude]. The phrase derives from a Norwegian folktale where a disagreeable wife argues with her husband about the best way to harvest grain. While he intends to mow the grain with a scythe, she insists that it be cut with shears; the husband finally silences his wife's nagging by drowning her in a nearby river. He later searches for her body to give her a proper funeral, only to find that she has drifted upstream, against the current. The (rather sexist) idiom thus refers to people who are both stubborn and irritating, who do what they want without listening to others. While variants of this folktale are known in other cultures, there is no traditional English equivalent. Packing so much cultural information into a comprehensible English translation is challenging for novice translators, ten of whom translated this text. Their solutions are presented in Table 34.1.

Only a single student chose an approximate literal paraphrase (Translation 10), this being the least popular translation strategy. Although all the others retained metaphor, none chose a transliteration reproducing the Norwegian metaphor with the same metaphor in English. The students have thus realized that an English readership may not have the necessary cultural background knowledge to fully understand the phrase when rendered word-for-word, and have produced alternative versions. In most cases, *kjerringa* (literal translation: hag) has been dropped in the English version. The one exception is Translation 2, where the core elements of the phrase remain in the original Norwegian (presumably evaluated as untranslatable), followed by a lengthy explanation – making this version arguably the least idiomatic of the ten translations.

Six of the nine remaining cases retain the image of resistance to flowing water, alternatively translated as *stream* (influenced by the partial false friend in the ST, Norwegian *strøm*), *current*, or *currant* (a spelling error). Two of these six add information to the metaphor by introducing the element of swimming, something unrelated to the original story because the wife had been drowned, meaning that her body floated rather than swam. Three of the students chose to substitute another TL metaphor, *go against the grain*, for the Norwegian metaphor. The two metaphors are semantically close, but the English metaphor introduces certain connotations that are absent from the original metaphor – that is, someone doing something against the grain is performing an action unexpected of them and contrary to their normal inclination. By contrast, the wife from the folktale behaves true to form.

These translations offer several indications that the informants are still very much English language learners: this may be noted by the choice of *stream* where *current* or *flow* might be more appropriate, by the spelling error *currant*, and by the apparent lack of realization of the extra connotations of the TL metaphor. In addition, most of the students demonstrate colligation problems, by not adopting the standard English colligation *is characteristic of*. The most common choice of preposition is *for*, the basic translation of Norwegian *for* that is appropriate for the SL context. Nevertheless, what is evident from these translations is that all the informants in some way acknowledged the translation challenge raised by this idiom, by attempting to unpack the Norwegian metaphor and repack it in English. Such observations demonstrate that L2 metaphor research may be contributing to additional fields of enquiry, in the present case essentially by marrying the fields of metaphor, learner corpus research and Descriptive Translation Studies.

Future directions

A great deal of research into the metaphoric competence of L2 language users has already been conducted, despite the relatively young age of the field as a whole. Findings from studies such as those outlined in this chapter have consequences not just for practical pedagogical concerns and considerations but also for theoretical issues, both related to the field of metaphor and to other fields (such as translation). Additional research about learner varieties of languages other than English is called for, as is investigation into metaphor use among more diverse learner populations than university students. Further studies into metaphor in both spoken and multimodal discourse (including gesture) would also be welcome, as would both quasi-diachronic studies of metaphor acquisition (i.e. tracking the metaphor development of different individuals across time and proficiency levels à la Littlemore et al., 2013) and longitudinal studies (tracking metaphor development in the *same* individual students). Finally, future investigation into the understanding and production of metaphor could explore the areas of bidirectional transfer (from an L2 to an L1), cross-linguistic influence across multiple languages, and the role of metaphor in code-switching. In short, there is still a great deal of work to be carried out.

Further reading

Littlemore, J., Krennmayr, T., Turner, J., & Turner, S. (2013). An investigation in metaphor use at different levels of second language writing. *Applied Linguistics*, 35, 117–44.

Littlemore, J., MacArthur, F., Cienki, A., & Holloway, J. (2012). *How to make yourself understood by international students: The role of metaphor in academic tutorials*. London: British Council; Online. Available at: http://englishagenda.britishcouncil.org/research-papers/how-make-yourself-understood-international-students-role-metaphor-academic-tutorials (accessed 26 November 2015).

MacArthur, F. (2010). Metaphoric competence in EFL: Where are we and where should we be going? A view from the classroom. *AILA Review*, 23, 155–73.

References

Boers, F. (2014). Cognitive linguistics and language pedagogy: Finding ways forward. Paper presented at the 9th AELCO International Conference: 'Applied Cognitive Linguistics: New challenges', Universidad de Extremadura, Badajoz, Spain, September.

Charteris-Black, J. (2002). Second language figurative proficiency: A comparative study of Malay and English. *Applied Linguistics*, *23*, 104–33.

Council of Europe. (2001). *Common European Framework of Reference for Languages*, Cambridge, UK: Cambridge University Press; Online. Available at: http://www.coe.int/t/dg4/linguistic/source/Framework_EN.pdf (accessed 26 November 2015).

Danesi, M. (1994). Recent research on metaphor and the teaching of Italian. *Italica: Bulletin of the American Association of Teachers of Italian*, *71*, 453–64.

Fernández, E. S. (2011). Translation studies and the cognitive theory of metaphor. *Review of Cognitive Linguistics*, *9*, 262–79.

Gibbs, R. W., Jr. (1994). *The poetics of mind: Figurative thought, language, and understanding*. Cambridge, UK: Cambridge University Press.

Golden, A. (2006). Om å gripe poenget i lærebøkene: Minoritetselever og metaforiske uttrykk i lærerbøker i samfunnsfag. *Nordand Nordisk Tidsskrift for Andrespråksforskning*, *2*, 79–101.

Kövecses, Z. (2010). A new look at metaphorical creativity in cognitive linguistics. *Cognitive Linguistics*, *21*, 663–97.

Lakoff, G., & Johnson, M. (1980). *Metaphors we live by*. Chicago, IL: University of Chicago Press.

Lindstromberg, S., & Boers, F. (2008). *Teaching chunks of language: From noticing to remembering*. Rum, Austria: Helbling Languages.

Littlemore, J. (2001a). Metaphoric competence: A language learning strength of students with a holistic cognitive style? *TESOL Quarterly*, *35*, 459–91.

—— (2001b). The use of metaphor in university lectures and the problems it causes for overseas students. *Teaching in Higher Education*, *6*, 333–49.

—— (2004). Interpreting metaphors in the EFL classroom. *Cahiers de l'APLIUT*, *23*, 57–70; Online. Available at: http://apliut.revues.org/3339?lang=en (accessed 26 November 2015).

Littlemore, J., Krennmayr, T., Turner, J., & Turner, S. (2013). An investigation in metaphor use at different levels of second language writing. *Applied Linguistics*, *35*, 117–44.

Littlemore, J., & Low, G. (2006a). *Figurative thinking and foreign language learning*. Basingstoke, UK: Palgrave Macmillan.

—— (2006b). Metaphoric competence, second language learning, and communicative language ability. *Applied Linguistics*, *27*, 268–94.

Littlemore, J., MacArthur, F., Cienki, A., & Holloway, J. (2012). *How to make yourself understood by international students: The role of metaphor in academic tutorials*. London: British Council; Online. Available at: http://englishagenda.britishcouncil.org/research-papers/how-make-yourself-understood-international-students-role-metaphor-academic-tutorials (accessed 26 November 2015).

Low, G. (1988). On teaching metaphor. *Applied Linguistics*, *9*, 125–47.

Low, G., Littlemore, J., & Koester, A. (2008). Metaphor use in three UK university lectures. *Applied Linguistics*, *29*, 428–455.

MacArthur, F., & Littlemore, J. (2011). On the repetition of words with the potential for metaphoric extension in conversations between native and non-native speakers of English. *Metaphor and the Social World*, *1*, 201–38.

Moon, R. (2007). Corpus linguistic approaches with English corpora. In H. Burger (Ed.), *Phraseologie: Ein internationales Handbuch der zeitgenössischen Forschung*, vol. Halbbd. 2 (pp. 1045–59). Berlin, Germany: Mouton de Gruyter.

Nacey, S. (2013). *Metaphors in learner English*. Amsterdam, The Netherlands: John Benjamins.

Newmark, P. (1988). *A textbook of translation*. Essex, UK: Pearson Education Limited.

Philip, G. (2006). 'Drugs, traffic, and many other dirty interests': Metaphor and the language learner. Paper presented at RaAM6 Researching and Applying Metaphor, University of Leeds, UK, April 2006; Online. Available at: http://amsacta.cib.unibo.it/archive/00002125/ (accessed 26 November 2015).

Picken, J. D. (2005). Helping foreign language learners to make sense of literature with metaphor awareness-raising. *Language Awareness*, *14*, 142–52.

Piquer-Píriz, A. M. (2008). Young learners' understanding of figurative language. In M. S. Zanotto, L. Cameron, & M. C. Calvacanti (Eds.), *Confronting metaphor in use: An applied linguistic approach* (pp. 183–98). Amsterdam, The Netherlands: John Benjamins.

Rosa, A. A. (2010). Descriptive translation studies (DTS). In Y. Gambier & L. Doorslaer (Eds.), *Handbook of translation studies* (pp. 94–104), vol. 1, Amsterdam, The Netherlands: John Benjamins.

Steen, G. J. (2008). The paradox of metaphor: Why we need a three-dimensional model of metaphor. *Metaphor & Symbol*, *23*, 213–41.

Steen, G. J., Dorst, A. G., Herrmann, J. B., Kaal, A. A., Krennmayr, T., & Pasma, T. (2010). *A method for linguistic metaphor identification: From MIP to MIPVU*. Amsterdam, The Netherlands: John Benjamins.

Toury, G. (1995). *Descriptive translation studies – and beyond*. Amsterdam, The Netherlands: John Benjamins.

van der Branden, K. (2009). Diffusion and implementation of innovations. In M. H. Long & C. Doughty (Eds.), *The handbook of language teaching* (pp. 659–72). Chichester, UK: Wiley-Blackwell.

Wagner, S. E., Winner, D., Cicchetti, H., & Gardner, H. (1981). 'Metaphorical' mapping in human infants. *Child Development*, *52*, 728–31. Online. Available at: http://www.jstor.org/stable/1129200?seq=1#page_scan_tab_contents (accessed 26 November 2015).

Winner, E. (1988). *The point of words: Children's understanding of metaphor and irony*. Cambridge, MA: Harvard University Press.

Epilogue
Metaphors for language and communication

Philip Eubanks

Introduction

As the range of chapters in this handbook demonstrates, metaphors are fundamental to how we think about a great many things. That includes language and communication—what language is, what it does, how it does it, and what qualities it can possess. In English, we have many everyday metaphors that explain how linguistic communication works. We *put our thoughts into words* or *get our ideas onto paper*. We *cram a lot of ideas into* a sentence, utter words that are *packed with emotion*, and *pour ourselves* into our words. Yet even routine metaphoric thought can inspire extravagant expressions and creative ideas.

The eighteenth-century philologist Samuel Johnson coined this famous phrase: 'Language is the dress of thought.' It relies on the same logic as *to put thoughts into words*. That is, it assumes that thoughts—or ideas—can be put into and taken out of language. Yet *language is the dress of thought* goes further. It tells us that language both contains *and* ornaments thought. Dr. Johnson exploited that metaphoric idea to its fullest. He wrote:

> As the noblest mien, or most graceful action, would be degraded and obscured by a garb appropriated to the gross employments of rustics or mechanics; so the most heroic sentiments will lose their efficacy, and the most splendid ideas drop their magnificence, if they are conveyed by words used commonly upon low and trivial occasions.
>
> *Johnson & Lonsdale, 2006, p. 230*

Johnson was a gifted user of metaphor. But it is not difficult for us to understand him because he makes use of metaphorical ideas that persist today. You may have heard someone say that obscure writing *dresses up simple ideas in fancy words*.

The examples I have mentioned so far are just the beginning of how we use metaphors to understand (and misunderstand) language and communication. In this chapter, I will try to unravel some of the major ways that people think metaphorically about linguistic communication. All of these metaphors are expressed in familiar phrases and thus go largely unnoticed. At the same time, inventive metalinguistic metaphors often bear an important relationship to metaphoric phrases we hear and use all of the time. I will begin my discussion with perhaps the most pervasive language metaphor of all, the CONDUIT METAPHOR; then I will turn to metaphors that we use to make sense of arguing, the writing process, the nature and quality of language, and finally languages.

Conduits, codes, and how we (do not) communicate: an overview

The metaphoric expressions I mentioned above form a pattern that has been described as the CONDUIT METAPHOR. It was first analyzed by Michael Reddy (1979) in a ground-breaking essay that made two important points: first, that the CONDUIT metaphor operates almost unnoticed in our everyday discourse; second, that it profoundly misleads us about how linguistic communication actually works. In challenging the CONDUIT metaphor, Reddy (and many others who agree with him) face a formidable opponent. It is used routinely by all English speakers, and it is so deeply entrenched in our language and thought that it seems to be the simple truth.

Yet it is far from simple. The CONDUIT metaphor is not just one metaphor but rather a collection of metaphoric ideas. To begin with, if we imagine we are putting thoughts into words, we must imagine—the metaphor *entails*—that words have insides and outsides. We also have to imagine that our thoughts (or ideas) exist independently, ready to be inserted into proper containers—words and texts. Naturally, if thoughts can be inserted into linguistic containers, they must be something we can handle. So the CONDUIT metaphor entails that ideas are objects. Finally, if we imagine that others can extract ideas from our words and texts, we have to imagine a way for ideas to get from us to our audience: Our idea-filled words need to be sent through an imaginary conduit that keeps them from dispersing as they travel from writer to reader or speaker to listener (Reddy, 1979; Lakoff & Johnson, 1980, pp. 10–14).

It is rather impressive how all of us make sense of this complex bundle of metaphors without pausing to think about it. But, then, we get a lot of practice. The CONDUIT metaphor is expressed in many ways and can be found in innumerable conversations and texts. Consider how we talk about books in everyday conversation. We often say that *the answer is in the book*, that a book is *full of ideas* (in fact, it may be *jam packed with good ideas*), that a book *gets its point across* well, that we *gleaned a lot from* a book, that we *found an idea in* a book, that after reading a book, we *came away with a lot of good ideas*. Taken together, these expressions establish all of the elements of the CONDUIT metaphor—packaging meaning, sending meaning, taking meaning out of its packages. And it *does* seem like common sense.

Yet the more we examine the CONDUIT metaphor, the less accurately it seems to explain linguistic communication. Reddy says that the CONDUIT metaphor fools us into thinking that linguistic communication is an effortless transaction—that all a listener or reader has to do is to retrieve the precise meanings that have been sent to them. After all, the meaning is *right there in the words*. For example, if I tell you that *your coffee cup is on the table*, it may seem as if I have simply placed my images of *your coffee cup* and *the table* into their proper linguistic containers, connected them with a *to be* verb and the preposition *on*, and *sent* them to you. All you have to do is to remove those images and relations from my words.

But linguistic communication is seldom so straightforward, maybe never. Consider an example provided by George Lakoff and Mark Johnson: *Please sit in the apple-juice seat.* Without some context, the sentence doesn't make much sense. But suppose you and some friends are sitting around a kitchen table where three places have been set with orange juice and one with apple juice. In that situation, you would easily understand which chair is the apple-juice seat. And you would continue to understand it even after someone drinks all of the apple juice and puts the empty glass in the sink. The phrase *apple-juice seat* only makes sense when it is part of human activity (Lakoff & Johnson, 1980, p. 13).

As it happens, all linguistic communication depends on human activity: The meaning is never *in the text*. Even *your coffee cup is on the table* is more complicated than it may seem. It is difficult to imagine anyone uttering that sentence without intending something that is not quite *in* the words. I might use that sentence to let you know where to pour your coffee—into *your* cup. Or I might say it because I want you to hurry up and drink your coffee so that we can go someplace. *Let's go! Your coffee cup is on the table!* Or I might leave out the word *cup* and say, *Your coffee is on the table!* I would expect you to understand that your coffee is in a cup, even though I did not bother to put that *into words*.

Some scholars find the CONDUIT metaphor so wanting that they recommend we avoid it altogether (Reddy, 1979; Bowden, 1993). My own view is that the CONDUIT metaphor is with us to stay. One reason for that is its ethical utility. True, it does not fully and accurately describe how linguistic communication works. But in many situations, it expresses an important ethical ideal. The CONDUIT metaphor describes and thus encourages direct and comprehensible linguistic communication, which can matter a great deal.

Consider, for example, a report on an accident at a military base in Port Chicago, California, during World War II. Because of negligent engineering and safety practices, two cargo ships loaded with bombs and cartridges exploded, killing 320 people and injuring many more. The report casts those in charge in a favorable light, using language that is *direct*: 'The commanding officer and his subordinates studied the various handling methods and gear in use by similar activities. They conducted experiments toward improving these methods and the gear used' (quoted in Dragga & Gong, 2014, p. 87). The statement—written in the active voice—leaves no doubt who was acting responsibly. But when it is a matter of placing blame, the language is quite *indirect*: 'Careless and some unsafe acts by individuals have occurred in the past' (quoted in Dragga & Gong, 2014, p. 87). We are left to wonder: Who are these individuals? And how did those careless acts come to pass? Of course, we do not need to hark back to obscure historical reports to understand the value of *straight talk*. Unethical communicators often use *indirections, evasions,* and *circumlocutions* to hide their meanings.

Even if we were able to stop ourselves from using ordinary conduit expressions, we might not be able to expunge all of the metaphors that derive from the CONDUIT metaphor. As I have said, the CONDUIT metaphor entails the notion that ideas are objects placed into language. One common metaphoric object is food. We *chew* on ideas because they are *food for thought*. Some speech and writing can provide *intellectual nourishment*—which is *fed* to *hungry minds*. But even if some ideas are not *morsels of wisdom*—in fact, some ideas we just cannot *stomach*—they are still objects. We *toss them around, hold onto them, cling to them,* sometimes *juggle too many of them*. Indeed, I suspect we will all be *juggling* ideas for a long time to come—and that when we *get a handle* on them, we will *put them into words*.

Before moving on to other metalinguistic metaphors, I want to mention a metaphor closely related to the CONDUIT metaphor: the CODE MODEL (Shannon & Weaver, 1949). For me, it is difficult to tell where the CONDUIT metaphor ends and the CODE MODEL begins because they are evoked by some of the same language. Yet they are different. The CODE MODEL tells us that words correspond to ideas. In that metaphoric framework, when we put ideas *into* words, we are looking up words in a mental code book to find which one is associated with the idea we want to transmit. We may put our ideas *into* a language code, but the words (or texts) do not contain meaning; they merely refer to it. In this metaphor, when we communicate, we send a coded message to a receiver, who—conveniently enough—has the same mental code book as we do. The receiver does not remove ideational objects from words but rather uses the code to reconstruct the message.

Some find the CODE MODEL a better explanation of linguistic communication than the CONDUIT metaphor (for example, Reddy). Others, however, criticize it on much the same grounds as they criticize the CONDUIT metaphor (for example, Johnson-Eilola, 2004; Sperber & Wilson, 2002). It is unlikely or impossible, they point out, for a receiver to reconstruct precisely the same message that the sender intends to transmit. Indeed, postmodern language theorists have spilled a lot of ink explaining the uncertain relationship between linguistic codes and intended meanings (for example, Derrida, 1982). According to postmodernists, everything we write and say is deeply influenced by the fine grain of each unique moment so that no message can be precisely interpreted by anyone.

But even if linguistic communication is not as surefire as the CONDUIT metaphor or the CODE MODEL would have us believe, perhaps all is not lost. Margaret Atwood, for one, finds the unreliability of codes to be an exhilarating challenge—the essence of writing, which unlike speaking is not aided by paralinguistic cues. She observes that writers can only leave 'some marks for you to decipher, much as one of John le Carré's dead spies has left a waterlogged shoe with a small packet in it for George Smiley' (Atwood, 2002, pp. 125–6). No reader cracks the writer's code in the same way as other readers—or in the way that the writer expects.

Argument is war (and more)

The CONDUIT metaphor is one of many *conceptual metaphors*—an overarching metaphor that we use to produce concrete phrases, both conventional and novel (see Chapter 1). We rely on these conceptual metaphors, day in and day out. We think of our lives as journeys (*I'm finally getting somewhere!*), love as madness (*I'm crazy about you!*), comprehension as seeing (*See what I mean?*), and much more.

So it is no surprise that we use quite a number of conceptual metaphors to make sense of linguistic communication. Think about one of the most common forms of writing and speech: argument. Imagine you are debating with someone about a controversial topic. It makes perfect sense to think that one of you would *win* the argument and the other *lose*, doesn't it? In fact, until one person *wins* and the other *loses*, it may seem that the argument is not really over. If the debate is intense, it would be quite normal for arguments to be *attacked* and *defended*, for ideas to be *shot down*, for you and your opponent to *gain* or *lose ground*, and for one or the other of you to admit *defeat* and therefore *surrender* (see Lakoff & Johnson, 1980, p. 5). We think that way because we rely on a conceptual metaphor: ARGUMENT IS WAR.

Like all conceptual metaphors, ARGUMENT IS WAR has certain entailments—things that it necessarily implies. For instance, if we think of arguments as wars or battles, we see the people involved in arguments as contending *sides*. We also accept the idea that the point of arguing is to achieve *victory* and that one side's *victory* requires the other side's *defeat*. Furthermore, and not necessarily for the best, ARGUMENT IS WAR entails that arguing is a metaphorically violent activity. Thus argumentative opponents can be *destroyed*—maybe even *decimated* or *ripped to shreds*.

ARGUMENT IS WAR is so powerful a metaphor, say Lakoff and Johnson, that without it we would not know what argument *is*. To make that point, they ask us to imagine a world in which argument is a dance (Lakoff & Johnson, 1980, p. 6). For most of us, that is an absurdity. Even if we can stretch our minds far enough to imagine argument as a ballet or a tango, seeing argument as a dance conjures up something out of the ordinary. If argument is a ballet, what do the arguers hope to achieve? Aesthetic exhilaration?

At the same time, ARGUMENT IS WAR is not the only conceptualization of argument that makes sense to us. For instance, we routinely think of arguing as construction. We *build* our arguments on strong *foundations*, *structure* them well or poorly, and think of the parts of *sound* arguments as *building blocks*. That may seem to be an alternative to ARGUMENT IS WAR. In fact, though, it can reinforce the WAR metaphor because an argument that is *built* can also be *knocked down*. In that respect, ARGUMENT IS BUILDING operates as part of a metaphor system that includes ARGUMENT IS WAR.

Some metaphors soften ARGUMENT IS WAR's harshest implications. We often think of argument as fist fighting or some other form of physical aggression—violent, yes, but not quite war (Semino, 2005). It is also commonplace for us to imagine argument as a game. True, some games are themselves metaphorical wars. But to score points in an argumentative game avoids the most violent implications of ARGUMENT IS WAR. If we claim to have won an argumentative game, it is not immediately clear what we have won—a pitched battle or a friendly game of chess (Ritchie, 2003). So it is fair to say: Even though we rely on conceptual metaphors to help us think about the world, they do not do all of our thinking for us. We can select and shape our metaphors (see also Parts IV and V of this volume).

We can also oppose them. Some experts on argumentation strongly resist ARGUMENT IS WAR. In *Everything's an Argument*, Lunsford, Ruszkiewicz, and Walters acknowledge that the predominant Western model of argument stresses disputation or verbal combat. But they point out that the conflictual model is often counterproductive because it turns our attention away from more beneficial forms of arguing (Lunsford et al., 2007, p. 5). That is surely true. We have many reasons for making claims and providing evidence that have little to do with winning. We argue in order to inform, to make better decisions, to explore. Lunsford et al. even claim that argument can be a part of meditation or prayer (Lunsford et al., 2007, p. 5).

The rhetorical scholar Sharon Crowley claims that competitive metaphors—WAR and GAME metaphors alike—do not even make much sense. She points out, for example, that arguments cannot be won the way a basketball game can be won (2006, p. 33). In a sports contest, victory is decided according to explicit rules, and the winner's victory is always coupled with the loser's defeat. But to win an argument deprives the losing 'side' of nothing except, perhaps, an abstract sense of self-worth. Just as likely, the loser of an argument *benefits* from having gained a better understanding of an idea or an issue. Of course, 'winning' an argument can bring extrinsic rewards in some situations. But Crowley's point is still a good one: Arguments are not necessarily zero-sum contests. In fact, usually they are not.

Nonetheless, despite this logical weakness, all of us are deeply influenced by the win–lose frame for argumentation. It is more than just a theoretical concern. Competitive metaphors do not just tell us what argument is; they influence the way we *go about* arguing. In the United States, for example, polarized, contentious argumentation dominates public discourse. It is used for political gain, and it shapes the way the news media frame issues large and small.

An anecdote told by former Secretary of Labor Robert Reich sums up the problem well. He describes a television appearance with an ideological opponent. During the first segment, he and his opponent found some common ground and had not engaged in acrimonious debate. Reich was gratified. But during the commercial break, the show's producer urged him to 'get angry'. 'Why should I?' Reich asked. The producer explained: 'Because you have hundreds of people—thousands, millions of people—who are surfing through hundreds of television channels, and they will only stop when they see a gladiator contest, a kind of a blood-letting, a kind of a mud wrestling' (Reich, 2014).

Metaphors of *winning* and *losing* arguments raise important questions for Reich and many others. And why not? If conceptual metaphors shape our understanding of something as fundamental as how we use language to communicate with each other, it makes a difference what form that understanding takes.

But lest we think the ramifications of ARGUMENT IS WAR—or any other metaphor—are easy to untangle, consider another example: *The Great Debaters*, a 2007 film starring Denzel Washington. The film is based on a true story from the 1930s, during the time of racially discriminatory Jim Crow laws in the southern United States. Washington plays the debating coach at Wiley College, a historically black institution in Texas. He is a demanding coach who uses a startling version of the war/game metaphor to teach and inspire his team. Washington tells his team that debate is a 'blood sport' (*The Great Debaters*, 2007). When one team member unnecessarily concedes a debating point, Washington corrects him, saying: 'Would you punch yourself in a street fight? Then don't punch yourself in a word fight' (*The Great Debaters*, 2007).

To some, that may seem a simplistic or counterproductive way to think of argumentation. But the film intersperses scenes of Wiley College's debate victories—over white institutions, including Harvard—with scenes of violent oppression of blacks by white supremacists. The contrast is striking. In that context, argument is not just metaphorical war; it is a substitute for actual violence—a remedy, not an incitement. As one of the debaters puts it after an impressive victory, 'I didn't need a gun. I didn't need a knife. My *weapons* were *words*' (*The Great Debaters*, 2007).

Writing processes: flow, block, birthing, and voice

Some of our most persistent metalinguistic metaphors relate to writing and how we go about it. On that topic, one of my favorite expressions is usually credited to the twentieth-century sports writer Red Smith: 'Writing is easy. You just open a vein and bleed.' Part metaphor and part irony, Smith's quip resonates because it evokes the conceptual metaphor FLOW. When writing is difficult, it is a painful struggle—it refuses to *flow*. But when writing *flows*, it seems there is no writing process at all. Ideas and words simply emerge—magically, inexplicably—from inside of us.

As you might expect, FLOW is expressed in many familiar ways. Sometimes words *pour* out of us, *come streaming* out of us, *spill* out of us. Sometimes we keep the *creative juices flowing*. The source of our words may be mysterious, but they come from *somewhere deep inside*. If the writing fails to flow, it may be necessary to *prime the pump*. And if *priming the pump* does not work, it may be time to lower our standards—to just, if you will pardon the expression, *vomit on the page*.

Whatever the specific FLOW expression, the aim is to avoid the writer's worst enemy: *writer's block*. When writers are *blocked*, they may have material in their head, but it is obstructed—often by an internal critic who passes judgment before words or ideas can emerge. Sometimes, the problem is just that *the well has run dry*. Even the prolific Mark Twain experienced a version of *writer's block*. Halfway through *The Adventures of Tom Sawyer*, he realized that his 'tank had run dry' (Twain & DeVoto, 1940, p. 197). Fortunately, after he'd set the book aside for two years, he returned to it only find that 'when the tank runs dry you've only to leave it alone and it will fill up again in time' (Twain & DeVoto, 1940, p. 197).

The FLOW metaphor is rooted in the CONDUIT metaphor, which tells us, in part, that words are containers for meaning and that writers and speakers are containers for words. That is, according to the FLOW metaphor, writing emerges from within you. That logic makes any number of familiar metaphors possible. For example, creative writers frequently talk about having a story *inside of them* that *must get out.* Yet even familiar metaphors can be reworked in compelling ways. Zora Neale Hurston once wrote, 'There is no agony like bearing an untold story inside you' (1969, p. 221). Somewhat less elegantly, the fantasy novelist Amber Benson says of her writing (and all artistic expression), 'It's like in *Alien*, where there's that creature, and it just has to get out. . . . If it's out your stomach, out your nose, it doesn't matter. It will not be silenced' (Piccoli, 2014).

Benson's grotesque image calls to mind a more conventional metaphor: WRITING IS GIVING BIRTH. Writers old and new, famous and obscure, refer to their books as *their children.* Louisa May Alcott, Graham Greene, and Ray Bradbury have said it. Yann Martel, Colleen McCullough, Elif Shafak, Christopher Smith, and Barbara Delinsky have said it. The self-styled writer of crime thrillers Claude Bouchard (2011) says on his blog, 'My books are my children. They were born of me. I sired them, brought them into this world.' But if writers habitually call books their children, their birthing experience varies. Sally Koslow (2014) observes: 'Writing a book is like giving birth to an elephant.'

The inside-to-out schema gives rise to another familiar metaphor—a metaphor that is indispensable to creative and literary writing: VOICE. Writers (with a capital W) can spend years trying to *find their voice.* VOICE is a more complicated metaphor than it may seem. It is tempting to say that the voice in writing duplicates the writer's speech. But we can write like we talk and still lack *voice*. As the essayist Louis Menand points out, people's speech is full of repetitions, interruptions, false starts, and other flaws. If you want to find your voice, he says, 'You have to wait, and what you are waiting for is something inside you to come up with the words. That something, for writers, is the voice' (2004, p. 102).

The metaphor of VOICE is prompted by a chain of metonymies. Metonymy, very broadly, is the figure that substitutes one thing for another based on contiguity. A typical example is *The White House announced.* That phrase cannot be taken literally because the White House is a building and cannot announce anything. But we can readily substitute the White House for the President's spokesperson because the building is contiguous with the people who work there.

Here is how VOICE works as a metonymy. Writing is contiguous with speech in the sense that we can write down what we want to say. But speech is, in turn, contiguous with thought, which is internal speech that happens in the mind. Thought is not the end of the metonymic chain because thoughts record our experiences. So the chain proceeds from writing to speech to thought to experiences. The bestselling writing guru Ann Lamott puts it this way: When you find 'your own true voice,' your writing expresses 'the truth of your experience that can only come through in your own voice' (1995, pp. 198–9).

If we go one metonymic step further, we reach the crux of the matter: the self. We *are* our experiences. To find your *voice* is, ultimately, to express your*self* (Eubanks, 2011, pp. 60–92). That metonymic logic is found in the classic American style guide, *The Elements of Style*:

> When we speak of Fitzgerald's style, we don't mean his command of the relative pronoun, we mean *the sound his words make on paper*. All writers, by the way they use the language, reveal something of their spirits, their habits, their capacities, and their biases. . . . All writing is communication; creative writing is communication through revelation—*it is the Self escaping into the open.*
>
> Strunk & White, 1999, pp. 66–67, emphasis added

From a slightly different perspective, William Zinsser discusses the difficulties of allowing the self to escape onto paper. In *On Writing Well*, now in its thirtieth edition, he observes, '[T]he self who emerges on paper is far stiffer than the person who sat down to write. The problem is to find the real man or woman behind the tension' (2011, p. 5).

Yet VOICE is more than just a chain of metonymies. It becomes a metaphor along the way—because it both relies on a series of metonymies and, at the same time, erases the metonymies' most literal implications. To return to Louis Menand's (2004) explanation, writers may be admired for the voice that comes through on their written pages, their literal voice has nothing to do with their metaphorical *voice*. Indeed, they seldom exhibit that same manner of expression in person. That is why, for Menand, the writer's voice is distinct from speech—closer to a *singing voice*.

Writing is, of course, multifaceted and so are its processes. The metaphors I have discussed in this section relate chiefly to literary writing. Most of us do not worry about *finding our voice* when we compose an e-mail or write an academic paper. Still, we may want our writing to *flow*, and we sometimes pass through a period of *incubation* before we put our fingers on the keyboard, even if we do not ultimately call our term papers *children*.

Power, passion, and incendiary language

Metaphors also shape the way we think about our written products—both the words we speak and the words we put onto the page. We want our texts to *flow smoothly*—a complementary application of the conceptual metaphor FLOW. We certainly do not want what we say and write to be *choppy* or *disjointed*. In fact—depending on the genre—we can desire all kinds of metaphoric things from spoken or written texts. Metaphors help us make sense of linguistic style.

Chief among the 'good style' metaphors is *clarity*. The rhetorical scholar Carolyn Miller explains that *clarity* is a manifestation of the WINDOWPANE theory of language—'the notion that language provides a view out onto the real world' (1979, pp. 611–12). According to the WINDOWPANE theory, if our language is *clear*, we see reality accurately. If our language is overly decorated or obscure, we have difficulty seeing the reality to which language refers. If our language is *opaque*, we may not see it at all. On the face of it, the WINDOWPANE theory seems to make sense. We should speak and write clearly, shouldn't we?

However, Miller is highly suspicious of the WINDOWPANE theory. She associates it with a positivist view of science—a philosophy that seeks an 'observational language' that represents reality with complete accuracy (1979, pp. 611–13). Miller (and many others) point out that the WINDOWPANE theory greatly underestimates the role of human interaction—rhetoric—in constructing our understanding of the world. The truth is, Miller argues, language cannot provide us unfiltered access to objective reality. Rather it shapes the world for us. Language creates what we, by common agreement, treat as reality. As a matter of theory, I have to agree with her.

But the WINDOWPANE theory has staying power for a good reason. No one makes the case better than the language scholar Stephen Pinker. He advocates a version of clear writing called the 'classic style', an approach to style he borrows from Francis-Noël Thomas and Mark Turner. The key to the classic style, Pinker explains, is *showing* readers what you want them to see. Even if the aim is to explain something that is difficult or abstract, a classic writer helps readers to *visualize* it. Indeed, when writing succeeds, 'Prose is a window onto the world' (Pinker, 2014, p. 29).

Pinker is far from naïve about the way linguistic representation really works though. He acknowledges 'that the world doesn't just reveal itself to us, that we understand the world through our theories and constructs,' but adds 'it's just that good writers don't flaunt this anxiety in every passage they write; they conceal it for clarity's sake' (2014, p. 37). That makes sound metaphorical sense because the guiding metaphor for the classic style is 'seeing the world' (2014, p. 29). That is, clarity is rooted in an inescapable conceptual metaphor: KNOWING IS SEEING. In English, to understand is *to see*; to explain is *to show*; to learn is *to discover*; to explain something well is to make *plain as day*. No wonder experts on style perennially recommend *clear* writing.

Yet the CLARITY metaphor is seldom enough to describe good style in full. Consider what classic style guides have to say. In *The Elements of Style*, Strunk and White advocate clarity of expression, though they concede that there is 'no assurance that a person who thinks *clearly* will be able to write *clearly*' (Strunk and White, 1999, pp. 66–67, emphasis added). But they also describe well-styled prose with an array of complementary metaphors:

> Who can confidently say what ignites a certain combination of words, causing them to explode in the mind? Who knows why certain notes in music are capable of stirring the listener deeply, though the same notes slightly rearranged are impotent?
>
> *Strunk & White, 1999, p. 66*

Good style is *clear*, yes. But well-styled writing also *ignites*, *explodes*, and *stirs* a reader the way *music stirs* a listener. Without those qualities writing is *impotent*. Or consider William Zinsser's array of metaphors. For him good writing is characterized not just by *clarity* but also by *strength*, *humanity*, *warmth*, and *aliveness* (2011, p. 5). What all of these additional style metaphors have in common is this: They describe an effect that linguistic communication can have on its audience. They tell us that LANGUAGE IS POWER. (See Chapters 20, 21, 22, and 24.)

We should note that LANGUAGE IS POWER can be configured in more than one way. For example, it is often said that *English is the language of power*. In that configuration, LANGUAGE IS POWER is not, strictly speaking, a metaphor. That is, *English is the language of power* does not mean that language has the qualities of power. Rather it is a metonymy that recognizes English's contiguity with political, economic, social, and military power.

As a metaphor, however, LANGUAGE IS POWER projects the qualities of power onto language. That version of LANGUAGE IS POWER is expressed aptly by the novelist Diane Setterfield:

> There is something about words. In expert hands, manipulated deftly, they take you prisoner. Wind themselves around your limbs like spider silk, and when you are so enthralled you cannot move, they pierce your skin, enter your blood, numb your thoughts. Inside you they work their magic.
>
> *2006, pp. 8–9*

Metaphorically speaking, language can exercise all sorts of power over a reader or listener. It can *capture* us, *entangle* us, *enthrall* us, *pierce* us, *numb* us, and *cast a magic spell over us*.

Frequently, these linguistic exercises of metaphorical power are expressed as adjectives. Thus what linguistic communication does becomes what it is. If writing *explodes* in the reader's mind, it is *explosive*; if it *stirs* passion in a reader, it is *stirring*; if a reader feels its *warmth* and *humanity*, it is *warm* and *human*; if it *seduces* us, it is *seductive*; if it inspires *heat* in us or if it inspires people to set real or metaphorical fires, it is *incendiary*; if it *soothes* us, it is *gentle*.

A final word: metaphors and languages

In this chapter, I have reviewed some of the major ways we routinely talk and think about language and communication, but only some of them. I have said nothing, for example, about composing and reading as a *journey*. I have said nothing about *flowery* language or *cluttered* prose. But rather than inventory all that I have left out, I want to close by briefly mentioning some ways we think metaphorically not about language but about language*s*.

Metaphors are often used to express linguistic pride. I am reminded of the French singer Yves Duteil's 'The Language of Our Home'.[1] In Duteil's song, the French language carries its story in its accents, it evokes music and the aroma of herbs, goat cheese, and wheat bread, it sings of its sorrows and hopes. And when French is spoken it is as if the wind is caught in a harp, composing a symphony. Languages are a gift, and what better linguistic gift than metaphor to arouse our admiration of them.

But even that has its metaphoric complications. Consider the Académie Française—the French lexicographers who try to *purify* their language by decrying such Anglicisms as '*updater, customiser*, and *être blacklisté*' (Rubery, 2014). The Académie's stated mission is, in part, to defend the French language against the English language, which is insidiously *devouring* French from the inside (Rubery, 2014).[2] To many in the English-speaking world, not least in the United States, the Académie's work sounds laughable. Yet in the US we have our own language anxieties, and we also talk about those anxieties metaphorically.

A so-called 'English only' movement has been afoot in the United States for the past decade or more. The US has no official language. It is only by tradition an English-speaking country. So federal and state communication is sometimes translated into Spanish to accommodate a significant Spanish-speaking population. Some lawmakers and activists now want to require that all government business be conducted in English. The proposed legislation is called 'The English Unity Act.'

LINGUISTIC UNITY is a powerful metaphor. Proponents of English only legislation argue that a common language *brings us together*—that it creates a *bond* which makes us *stronger* as a nation. Opponents point out that immigrants to the United States need no inducement to learn English. The children of immigrants almost always become proficient in English, and overwhelmingly the grandchildren of immigrants have English as their native tongue. But multilingualists do not reject the unity metaphor *per se*. Rather they use it for their own purposes.

For example, NCTE (National Council of Teachers of English) (2011) argues that when students incorporate their home languages into school writing, this '*reduces the distance* between home and school.' That is, the proximity of two languages *unifies* home and school. For NCTE, the consequences of denying students access to their home languages implicates a metaphor we considered earlier in this chapter: 'When students' home languages—spoken or written—are denied, their *voices* become muted and *they* become *invisible* in the larger society' (NCTE, 2011). To take away someone's home language is to take away their *voice*—which is, ultimately, to *erase them*.

Metaphors about language*s* encompass the same rhetorical uncertainties as other major metaphors. As we have seen in this chapter, even well-established metaphors—such as the CONDUIT metaphor or ARGUMENT IS WAR—can have more than one implication, depending on the situation in which they are evoked and on the point of view of the speaker or audience. But that does not subtract from the importance of these metaphors. Indeed, these complications make it all the more important that we notice our metaphors and that we exercise care when we interpret them.

I often hear the phrase *it's just a metaphor*. But it is always a mistake to dismiss metaphors as mere decoration or whimsy. It matters what we think about linguistic *unity* and linguistic *invisibility*. It matters whether we think language acts a *conduit* for conveying unfiltered thoughts, whether *argument is war*, whether our *voices* express our *selves*. All of this matters because language is *powerful*, and its most potent turns of phrase rest on deeply entrenched, largely unconscious metaphoric concepts. If we want to understand the world and how we live in it, we could do worse than to follow our metaphors.

Notes

1 'La langue de chez nous.'
2 Rubery quotes the Académie's website: 'la langue anglaise qui insidieusement *la dévore de l'intérieur*.'

Further reading

Elbow, P. (2007). Voice in writing again: Embracing contraries. *College English, 70*(2), 168–88.
Hart, G. (2011). Writing is like playing a sport: Letting go of gendered assumptions and using metaphor successfully in the writing classroom. *Journal of Teaching Writing, 26*(1), 21–38.
Tobin, L. (1989). Bridging gaps: Analyzing our students' metaphors for composing. *College Composition and Communication, 40*(4), 444–58.

References

Atwood, M. (2002). *Negotiating with the dead: A writer on writing.* Cambridge, UK: Cambridge University Press.
Bouchard, C. (2011). 'My books are my children.' Claudeboudardbooks.com. Online posting. Available at: http://www.claudebouchardbooks.com/apps/blog/show/7657734-my-books-are-my-children (accessed 21 November 2014).
Bowden, D. (1993). The limits of containment: Text-as-container in composition studies. *College Composition and Communication, 44*, 364–79.
Crowley, S. (2006). *Toward a civil discourse: Rhetoric and fundamentalism.* Pittsburgh, PA: University of Pittsburgh Press.
Derrida, J. (1982). 'Différance,' in *Margins of philosophy*, trans. Alan Bass. Chicago (pp. 1–27). Chicago, IL: University of Chicago Press..
Dragga, S. & Gong, G. (2014). Dangerous neighbors: Erasive rhetoric and communities at risk. *Technical Communication, 61*, 76–94.
Duteil, Y. (1985). La langue de chez nous [song]. Meaux, France: Editions de L'ecritoire.
Eubanks, P. (2011). *Metaphor and writing: Figurative thought in the discourse of written communication.* Cambridge, UK: Cambridge University Press.
Great debaters, The [motion picture]. (2007). Chicago, IL: Harpo Productions.
Hurston, Z. N. (1969). *Dust tracks on a road.* New York: Arno Press and the *New York Times*.
Johnson, S. & Lonsdale, R. H. (2006). *The lives of the most eminent English poets: With critical observations on their works.* Oxford, UK: Clarendon Press.
Johnson-Eilola, J. (2004). The database and the essay: Understanding composition as articulation, in A. F. Wysocki, J. Johnson Eilola, C. L. Selfe & G. Sirc (Eds.) *Writing new media: Theory and applications for expanding the teaching of composition.* Logan, UT: Utah State University Press.
Koslow, S. (2014, 1 August). Writing a book is like giving birth to an elephant. *More magazine.* Online magazine. Available at: http://www.more.com/reinvention-money/second-acts/writing-book-giving-birth-elephant (accessed 9 November 2014).

Lakoff, G. & Johnson, M. (1980). *Metaphors we live by*. Chicago, IL: University of Chicago Press.

Lamott, A. (1995). *Bird by bird: Some instructions on writing and life*. New York: Anchor Books.

Lunsford, A. A., Ruszkiewicz, J. J. & Walters, K. (2007). *Everything's an argument: With readings*. Boston, MA: Bedford/St. Martin's.

Menand, L. (2004, 28 June). Bad comma: Lynne Truss's strange grammar. *The New Yorker*, 102–104.

Miller, C. R. (1979). A humanistic rationale for technical writing. *College English, 40*, 610–17.

NCTE. (2011). Resolution on the student's right to incorporate heritage and home languages in writing. Ncte.org. Online posting. Available at: http://www.ncte.org/positions/statements/homelanguages (accessed 21 November 2014).

Piccoli, D. (2014, 13 October). Amber Benson on her iconic 'Buffy' role and brand new novel, *The witches of echo park*. *AfterEllen.com*. Online magazine. Available at: http://www.afterellen.com/amber-benson-on-her-iconic-buffy-role-and-brand-new-novel/10/2014/ (accessed 9 November 2014).

Pinker, S. (2014). *The sense of style: The thinking person's guide to writing in the 21st century*. New York: Viking.

Reddy, M. (1979). The CONDUIT METAPHOR: A case of frame conflict in our language about language, in A. Ortony (Ed.) *Metaphor and thought* (pp. 284–324). Cambridge, UK: Cambridge University Press.

Reich, R. (2014). Aspen lecture: The politics and economics of inequality. *Aspenideas.com*. Website. Available at: http://www.aspenideas.org/session/politics-and-economics-inequality (accessed 19 November 2014).

Ritchie, D. (2003). 'ARGUMENT IS WAR'—or is it a game of chess? Multiple meanings in the analysis of implicit metaphors. *Metaphor and Symbol, 18*(2), 125–46.

Rubery, J. (2014, 20 March). Can the Académie française stop the rise of Anglicisms in French? *OxfordWords Blog*. Online. Available at: http://blog.oxforddictionaries.com/2014/03/academie-francaise/ (accessed 10 June 2015).

Semino, E. (2005). The metaphorical construction of complex domains: The case of speech activity in English. *Metaphor and Symbol, 20*(1), 35–69.

Setterfield, D. (2006). *The thirteenth tale: A novel*. New York: Atria Books.

Shannon, C. E. & Weaver, W. (1949). *The mathematical theory of communication*. Urbana, IL: University of Illinois.

Sperber D. & Wilson D. (2002). Pragmatics, modularity and mind-reading. *Mind and Language, 17*, 3–33.

Strunk, W. & White E. B. (1999). *The elements of style*, 4th ed. London: Longman.

Twain, M. & DeVoto, B. (1940). *Mark Twain in eruption: Hitherto unpublished pages about men and events*. New York: Harper & Brothers.

Zinsser, W. K. (2011). *On writing well: The classic guide to writing nonfiction*, 35th ed. New York: HarperCollins.

Index

Abel, C. F. 403, 406
academic discourse 286–7, 291–2; climate change 290; incidence of metaphor in 84; parts-of-speech 173–4, 175; second language learners 506; textual patterning 185, 188
ACMC *see* asynchronous computer-mediated communication
active metaphors 210
ad hoc concepts 48–9, 51, 53
adaptive behaviour 57, 59
adjectival metaphors 38, 166, 169, 172, 173–4, 180, 348
adult education 286–7
advertising 6, 323–36; active metaphors 210; nonverbal metaphor 149; overview of research 325–8; pharmaceutical 386; reality construction 17; television 160; visual metaphors 35, 148, 150, 154–5
Advertising Standards Authority (ASA) 329–31
aesthetic expression 478–9
aggression 224, 315, 353, 354–5, 359, 364, 521
Allan, K. 236, 238, 239
allegory 339–41, 342–3
alterity 427, 428, 433
Alzheimer's disease 467
ambiguity 473
American Sign Language (ASL) 267, 268, 269, 270, 271–2
analogical metaphors 475, 478–9
analogy: five-step method 104, 105, 106; second language learners 511
anchorage 151
Animal Farm (Orwell) 341, 343
animal metaphors 356–7, 360, 361, 364, 407, 431
antisocial online behaviour 358–63
applied linguistics 73, 103
appreciation 459, 505
Arabic 9, 248–9, 251, 252
architectural discourse 194, 195, 198–203, 292–3
Aristotle 1, 3, 8, 28, 326, 475; aesthetic expression 478; definition of metaphor 207–8, 472; literary metaphor 209; politics 309, 310, 318
artificial intelligence (AI) 229–30
ASA *see* Advertising Standards Authority
ASD *see* autism spectrum disorder
ASL *see* American Sign Language
Asperger syndrome 467, 487, 492, 493, 494
Asplund, M. 299, 301, 302, 305–6
asynchronous computer-mediated communication (ACMC) 354
audiences 154–5
autism spectrum disorder (ASD) 486, 487, 488, 495; 'child metaphors' 489; comprehension 491, 492, 496; metaphor processing 467, 492, 493; nonverbal children 497n2; prevalence 497n1; production studies 494–5
autobiographical comics 156–9

backwards projection 31
BASE *see* British Academic Spoken English corpus
Benjamins Translation Studies Bibliography 247–8
Berber Sardinha, T. 121, 174
Berry, Jo 344, 428, 432–7
Bible 251
Black, Max 13, 226, 230
Blackman, L. 494–5, 496
Blair, Tony 184, 343, 348
blending 4, 28–41, 150, 342, 345, 463
blogs 297, 314–16, 380
BNC *see* British National Corpus
Boers, F. 289, 415, 416, 418, 419–20, 510
Boroditsky, L. 289, 303, 312, 430, 445–6, 450
Bourgeois, V. W. 405, 407
Bowdle, B. F. 236–7, 477
brain: 'brain architecture' 448–9, 452, 453; coordination during conversation 64; embodied simulation hypothesis 465; Event-Related Potential technology 473; interpersonal interaction 62; metaphor processing 460–1, 463, 466–7, 490; metaphor understanding 53; neural connections 450;

neural theory of metaphor 18–19, 25–6; neurodevelopmental disorders 493, 497n8; right and left hemisphere functioning 466, 493, 496, 498n9; self-organization 60
brands 323, 324, 327, 329, 331
Bressem, J. 137, 138
Brick 156
British Academic Spoken English (BASE) corpus 286
British National Corpus (BNC) 108, 110, 117–18, 123, 229; conventionality 223–4; emotions 120; identification of metaphor 74, 79, 84; parts-of-speech 172; second or foreign language learning 417
British Sign Language (BSL) 264–5, 267, 268, 269, 273
Broussine, M. 405, 406, 410
Brown Corpus 117–18
BSL *see* British Sign Language
Burgers, C. 328, 329
Burke, Kenneth 28, 132–3, 310–11
Bush, George 154, 337, 338, 340
business communication 7, 181, 197–8, 400–12

Caballero, Rosario 292–3, 328, 329
Cambridge Learner Corpus 509
Cameron, David 89, 227
Cameron, Lynne 73, 291, 362; educational contexts 284–5, 286–7; empathy 9; linguistic metaphors 103–4, 106; metaphoremes 414; parts-of-speech 166, 167–8, 169–70, 173, 176; public-interest issues 446; reconciliation 7, 182, 185, 344, 426–42; systematic metaphors 88, 89, 91, 92, 113; textual patterning 179, 182, 185; units of analysis 83; vehicle coding 93
cancer 34–5, 74, 107–9, 110, 385–6, 388–9, 390, 392–6, 432
'career of metaphor' hypothesis 236–7, 462–3, 477–8
Carroll, N. 149–50, 155
categorization 208, 462–3, 477–8
CBT *see* Conceptual Blending Theory
CDA *see* critical discourse analysis
CEFR *see* Common European Framework of References for Languages
change: organizational 401, 403, 405, 406; psychotherapy 375
Charteris-Black, J.: corpus linguistics 120; Critical Metaphor Analysis 311; genre 196; identification of metaphor 84; pragmatic perspective 326; psychotherapy 374; second language learners 507–8
child development 448–9, 450, 475, 476
Chinese 9, 249, 252
Chinese Sign Language 271
Cienki, Alan 73, 74

cinema 153–4
CL *see* cognitive linguistics
classifiers 266–7, 270, 276
climate change 6, 290, 297, 298–306, 347; 'blanket metaphor' 448, 451, 452, 453; 'greenhouse' metaphor 301, 450, 452
Clinton, Bill 344
clustering 181–2, 185, 190, 197–8, 201, 203, 429
CMA *see* Critical Metaphor Analysis
CMC *see* computer-mediated communication
CMT *see* Conceptual Metaphor Theory
COCA *see* Corpus of Contemporary American English
code model 519–20
coding 93–4, 97
cognition 7, 8, 326; Conceptual Metaphor Theory 1; embodied 53, 476–7, 507; emergence of metaphoric 481–2; language development 489; self-organization 59
cognitive development 474–5
cognitive failure 447
cognitive linguistics (CL) 50, 238, 297, 457, 472, 510; advertising 325–6; conceptual metaphors 62, 66, 220, 463; embodied experience 496; everyday language 222; identification of metaphor 73; literary metaphor 209; mapping 77, 474; metonymy 83; primary metaphors 113; quantitative turn 127; second or foreign language learning 414–15, 416, 417, 418, 419–20, 421; sign language 269, 277; stories 341–2
colligation 117, 119, 166, 513
collocation 111–12, 117, 504; corpus linguistics 119, 122; educational contexts 285
Colston, Herbert L. 65
combination of metaphors 182–3
Common European Framework of References for Languages (CEFR) 509, 510
communication: argument is war metaphor 520–2; communicative competence 414, 504, 505; computer-mediated 9, 353–4; conceptual metaphors 22; conduit metaphor 518–20; discourse-pragmatic studies 325–6; intercultural 508; metaphor and 517–28; modes of 148–9; Relevance Theory 43, 47, 54n3, 54n4; translation 248; writing processes 522–4
comparison 462–3, 477–8
complex metaphors 38, 39
complex system metaphors 22, 23
compound metaphors 18, 113
comprehension: children 476; metaphor processing 459, 462, 465; neurodevelopmental disorders 489, 490–2, 496, 497; novel metaphors 225; parts-of-speech 165; psycholinguistics 473; Relevance Theory 45; second or foreign language learning 422, 505–7, 508; stories 345; *see also* understanding

computational linguistics 85, 229–30
computer-mediated communication (CMC) 9, 353–4, 358–63
concept broadening 48
concept identification 80
Conceptual Blending Theory (CBT) 28–41, 150, 342, 345, 463
Conceptual Metaphor Theory (CMT) 1–2, 3, 8, 13–27, 91, 114–15, 208; advertising 325; Blending Theory compared with 4, 28–9, 33–4, 35, 39; corpus linguistics 118–19, 120; critiques of 24–5, 61; diachronic variation 234; embodied cognition 507; framing 385; future directions 25–6; gendered metaphors 357–8; interlocking metaphor hierarchies 19–24, 26; linguistic metaphors 102; literary metaphor 342; mapping 112, 272; metaphoric competence 504; multimodal metaphors 148, 153; political discourse 311–12, 313, 314, 318; primary metaphors 492; psycholinguistics 481; second or foreign language learning 415; symbols 160; textual patterning 178; thought processes 219; Translation Studies 249, 251
conceptual metaphors 1–2, 5, 16–17, 133, 220, 503; blending 28, 29–34, 35–6, 39; cognitive mappings 50, 112–13; concrete and abstract domains 16; corpus linguistics 109–12, 118–19, 120; correspondences 14–15; cultural context 19; diachronic variation 233, 234, 236; dynamical perspective 66–7; embodied thoughts 61; evidence for 102; grounded nature of 17–19; Gulf war 102–3; impoliteness 358; interlocking hierarchies 19–24, 26; language change 235; literary texts 209; metaphor processing 463–5; neurodevelopmental disorders 489, 491, 495; novel 226–7, 457; pervasiveness 14; psycholinguistics 473–4; second or foreign language learning 415, 507–8; sign language 263, 271–2, 274, 276; textual patterning 180; translation 252, 253, 256
conceptualization 76, 84, 144, 325, 478
conduit metaphor 136–7, 263, 518–20, 522, 527
conflict 426, 427, 428, 430–1, 433, 435, 439
consciousness 214
context: conceptual metaphors 19; corpus linguistics 127; dynamical perspective 62; gestures 136; interpretation of metaphor 65; lexical pragmatics 49; literary metaphor 210; metaphorical understanding 67; novel metaphors 227–8, 230; political discourse 89; psychotherapy 375, 378–9; sign language 275; stories 348; translation 254
conventionality 5, 57, 220–1, 222–4, 228, 230, 457; advertising 325, 327; 'career of metaphor' hypothesis 237, 478; gestures 134; parts-of-speech 167, 176; textual patterning 182, 186, 187
conversation: active metaphors 210; incidence of metaphor in 84; parts-of-speech 174–5, 176; production and comprehension 508; sign language 274; stories 337; textual patterning 185, 188, 190
coordination 57, 63–4
Cornelissen, J. P. 402, 403, 409
corpus linguistics 5, 8, 117–30, 221–2, 229; conceptual metaphors 104, 108, 109–12, 113; conventionality 223–4; identification of metaphor 73, 84, 85; linguistic metaphors 103; novel metaphors 226; parts-of-speech 165, 168–70, 174, 176; second or foreign language learning 417, 419, 508–9, 511–13; translation 252–3
Corpus of Contemporary American English (COCA) 117, 221
Corpus of Early English Correspondence Sampler (CEECS) 117, 122–6
correlation metaphors 153–4, 155, 157
correspondences 14–15
Corts, D. P. 179, 181–2, 286
counselling 6, 375, 376–9
creativity: advertising 325; lexical 220; multimodal metaphors 155–6, 406; novelty linked with 509; Relevance Theory 43; stories 345; textual patterning 181
crime 303, 311–12, 430, 445–6
Crisp, Peter 73, 74, 340–1, 342, 343
critical discourse analysis (CDA) 8, 196, 311, 313, 318, 326–7
Critical Metaphor Analysis (CMA) 311, 313, 314
cross-cultural research 380
cross-language research 119, 176, 193–4, 220
Crowley, Sharon 521
Culpeper, J. 355, 364n5
Cultural Logic 443, 444, 448, 450
culture: conceptual metaphors 19; cultural context 62; gestures 133; metaphor variation 193–4; organizational 404; psychotherapy 380; systematic metaphors 91; translation 248, 252–3
Cunningham, Darryl 156
Czechmeister, C. A. 392

Dagut, M. 249, 252
Dahl, C. 474
Dale, R. 59
Dancygier, Barbara: blending 4, 28–41; domains 239; literary metaphor 112, 114; usage of metaphor 234
Danesi, M. 504
Darian, S. 181
Dasher, R. B. 235

Index

data collection 92–3, 374; *see also* methodological issues
data mining 128
Davidson, D. 51–2
Dawkins, Richard 296, 450
'dead metaphors' 237–8, 244, 490–1
deductive approach 76, 78
dehumanization 428, 429, 431, 433, 439
Deignan, Alice 73, 222, 244n10, 253; corpus linguistics 119, 120, 165; evaluation 356, 432; genre 196, 197, 198, 290; metaphoremes 414; parts-of-speech 166, 168–9, 171, 176
deliberateness 61, 210, 313, 509
denotation 44–5
depression 156–9
Descriptive Translation Studies 511, 513
diachronic variation 233–46, 312, 333
dialogue 427, 428–30, 439
Dickinson, Emily 112, 114
dictionaries 110, 114, 122, 222; conventionality 223; identification of metaphor 81, 84, 85; second or foreign language learning 418
directionality 238–9
discourse 34, 36, 61, 68; data 103, 104; genre and 194, 195–203; gestures 140; parts-of-speech 169, 171, 173; psychotherapy 374–5, 380; systematic metaphors 88–9, 90, 92; telic 349; textual patterning 179; *see also* political discourse
discourse analysis: advertising 325, 326–7; corpus linguistics 127; critical 8, 196, 311, 313, 318, 326–7; educational contexts 284; identification of metaphor 73; Metaphor-Led Discourse Analysis 8, 429, 431; peace-building and reconciliation 437; psychotherapy 371, 372, 374, 375, 376, 378, 379–80
Discourse Dynamics approach 88, 431, 437, 438, 439n1
'discourse metaphors' 179, 185, 297, 312
discourse-pragmatic studies 325–6
domains 74, 133, 268; abstract and concrete 239; aesthetic expression 479; blending 32; Conceptual Metaphor Theory 14–18, 19–21, 23, 24, 28–30, 503; corpus linguistics 112, 118–19, 120, 121, 122, 127; cross-domain mapping in thought 75–6; deductive approach 78; diachronic variation 238, 244; discourse 34; framing 385; gestures 136, 137, 142, 143; identification of metaphor 77; inductive approach 78; metaphor processing 462; metaphorical pattern analysis 123; metonymy 353; multimodal metaphors 148–9; primary metaphors 113; propositional analysis 105; psychotherapy 372, 374, 376, 377; structure-mapping theory 476; textual patterning 181, 182, 183, 186; visual metaphors 150, 151, 152, 155

Dorst, Aletta G. 93, 114, 166, 176
double-mapping model 271, 272
double-scope blends 31, 40n6
Down's syndrome (DS) 486, 487, 488, 490, 495, 496
DS *see* Down's syndrome
dynamical systems perspective 4, 8, 57, 58–68
dyspathy 437, 438

EAP *see* English for Academic Purposes
Early Modern English 120, 122–6
The Economist 290
educational contexts 6, 283–95, 486; adult education 286–7; advertising 334
El Refaie, Elisabeth 347, 406, 408
ELAN 137
emblems 133, 134, 135
embodiment 61, 66–7, 68, 91, 482; advertising 333; bodily engagement tasks 458; cognitive linguistics 496; embodied cognition 53, 476–7, 507; embodied simulation hypothesis 465; literary metaphor 212, 213, 214; metaphor acquisition 476–7
emergent properties 50–1
emotions 20, 22, 23, 326; blending 34; corpus linguistics 103, 119–20; hope 122, 126–7; organizational change 405; psycholinguistics 482; reconciliation 433
empathy 9, 213–14, 426–8, 431, 433, 435–8
English 6, 236, 264, 526; corpus linguistics 119, 120, 122–6; identification of metaphor 84; metaphor variation 194; parts-of-speech 169; second or foreign language learning 413, 414–15, 418–19, 421, 511–13; translation 254–6
English for Academic Purposes (EAP) 287, 288, 290
entity classifiers 266–7, 270, 276
Entman, R. 298
ERPs *see* Event-Related Potentials
ethics, in advertising 329–30
ethos 324
etymology 80–1
evaluation 356, 432
evaluative metaphors 284–5
Event-Related Potentials (ERPs) 458, 473, 493, 498n8
events 20–1, 57
executive function 490, 491, 492, 496, 497
explicatures 43–4, 49
extended metaphors 53n1, 326; advertising 333; allegory 339, 340–1; definition of 340; identification of metaphor 75; myth 404; paranarratives 211; Relevance Theory 52; textual patterning 186–7, 190–1
extension 182, 185–7, 189, 190, 269
eye-tracking 257

Faber, Michael 206–7, 210, 211–14
Fabiszak, M. 120, 122, 126
familiarity 43, 223, 327, 461
Fauconnier, G. 4, 33, 40n6, 225, 342, 344
fiction: active metaphors 210; incidence of metaphor in 84; parts-of-speech 173–4; textual patterning 185, 187–90; translation of crime fiction 253–4; *see also* literary metaphor; stories
figurative language 28, 37–8, 39, 224; computer algorithms 229; genre and register 290; impoliteness 354, 355, 356, 358; language development 489; literary metaphor 206, 207; metaphor processing 460, 461; neurodevelopmental disorders 495; political discourse 311; *see also* metaphor; metonymy; simile
films 153–4, 155, 160
five-step method 104–9
FLOB *see Freiburg–LOB Corpus of British English*
Fludernik, Monika 209, 341–2
Forceville, Charles 148–9, 150–1, 152, 154, 155, 159
foregrounding 207, 208
Forney, Ellen 156–8, 160n1
framing 9, 289; climate change 298; peace-building and reconciliation 430, 438–9; physical health 385, 386, 387; policy 430, 445, 449; public-interest issues 446
Francis, Pope 37–9, 96, 97, 98
Freiburg-Brown Corpus of American English (FROWN) 122–5
Freiburg-LOB Corpus of British English (FLOB) 122–5
French 6, 133, 236, 254–6, 526
FROWN *see Freiburg–Brown Corpus of American English*

Geeraerts, D. 235, 238
gender: advertising 327; gendered metaphors 357–8; impoliteness and offence 362–3, 364; translation metaphors 248
generative metaphors 297
generic space 30, 32, 33, 150
genre 5, 8, 153, 193–205, 254; advertising as a 323–4; educational contexts 290; linguistic metaphors 114; literary metaphor 210; political discourse 318
Gentner, D. 236–7, 476, 477
German 6, 251, 255, 259
gestures 5, 8, 64, 67, 131–47, 160, 406; analyzing metaphor in 134–6; conceptual metaphors 17; critical issues 143; embodied simulation hypothesis 465; of empathy 433, 437; guidelines for the identification of metaphor in 137–42; interpretation of metaphor 506–7; nonverbal metaphor 149; sign language and 277; study of 133–4
Gesuato, S. 358
Gibbs, Raymond W., Jr. 74, 478; allegory 343; cancer metaphors 388; comprehension 505; conceptual metaphors 24; frequency of metaphors 14; influence of metaphors 430; literary metaphor 342; stories 346
Giora, R. 228, 492–3
Gkiouzepas, L. 150, 152, 154
Goatly, Andrew: active metaphors 210; genre 196; parts-of-speech 165, 166–7; signalling 184, 389; textual patterning 179, 180, 181, 182, 184
Gombrich, E. H. 149, 150
Graded Salience Hypothesis (GSH) 461, 492–3, 496
Grady, Joseph 73; cognitive mappings 112–13; primary metaphors 15, 18, 492; public-interest issues 7, 443–54
grammatical metaphors 253, 458
Great Chain of Being 23, 318, 361
The Great Debaters (film) 522
Green, M. C. 345, 348
ground 208, 259n1
groups: evolutionary forces in 62; group identity 430–1; self-organization 60
GSH *see* Graded Salience Hypothesis

Halliday, M. 196, 253
Halpern, J. 427, 428
Hanks, P. 225, 226
Hanne, M. 388, 390
'hard-sell' advertising techniques 324
Harris, R. A. 340, 341
Haslam, N. 357, 431
Hawken, S. J. 388, 390
HCE *see Helsinki Corpus of English Texts*
healthcare 6–7; mental health 156–9; physical health 385–99
Hebda, A. 120, 122, 126
Hellsten, I. 297, 301, 303
Helsinki Corpus of English Texts (HCE) 122–6
Heracleous, L. 406, 407
Herrmann, J. B. 93, 166, 176
Heywood, J. 104, 107, 108–9, 110
Hightower, Jim 337, 338, 340
Historical Thesaurus of English 236, 238, 239–43, 244n6, 244n9
Hitler, Adolf 310–11, 318, 362
HIV/AIDS 386, 388
Hobbes, Thomas 309, 310
Hogg, M. K. 150, 152, 154
humour 178, 183, 324, 325
Hussey, K. 480, 482
hybrid metaphors 150, 152
hyperboles 53

533

iconicity: gestures 131–2, 139, 144; sign language 264, 265, 267–8, 269, 271, 272–4; visual metaphors 491
identification of metaphor 4–5, 8, 73–87, 505; academic exchanges 291; five-step method 104, 106, 107; genre 196; gestures 136–42; parts-of-speech 165, 170–3; political discourse 313; translation 252–3
identity 430–1, 432, 479–80, 482
ideology 102, 178–9, 183–4
idioms 119, 346, 458; conceptual metaphors 463–4; neurodevelopmental/neurological disorders 467, 490–1; second or foreign language learning 415, 417–18, 419, 420–1, 511–13
image schemas 18, 36–7, 38–9
image theory of metaphor 51–2
imageability 452–3
images 35, 149, 152–3; advertising 326; architectural metaphors 200–1, 203; iconic 132; managerial metaphors 402; 'one-shot' metaphors 107–8; second or foreign language learning 417; stories and 347; verbal 152; *see also* visual metaphors
immigration 313–17
implicatures 45–6, 47–8, 49
impoliteness 6, 9, 353–67; antisocial online behaviour 358–63; definition of 353–4
incongruity 77, 82, 83
indirectness 77, 83
inductive approach 76, 78
inference 15, 50; interpretation of metaphor 65; metaphor processing 462; scenarios 312
insults *see* impoliteness
interaction metaphors 22, 23
interaction theory of metaphor 251
interactional approach 355
intercultural communication 508
international students 287, 290–2, 506
interpretation 65, 67; gestures 136; metaphor processing 459, 460; metaphoric competence 504, 505; multimodal metaphors 154; parts-of-speech 165, 166–7; political cartoons 347; Relevance Theory 45; second language learners 506–7; sign language 275
intertextual relations 184–5
intimacy 480–1, 482
intonation units 93
invariance hypothesis 15
irony 28, 458, 479; advertising 329; autistic individuals' understanding of 467; metaphor processing 461

Jaspal, R. 299–300, 301, 302, 305, 306
Johnson, Mark: argument is war metaphor 76, 78, 520; cognitive linguistics 73; conceptual mapping 28–9, 133, 474; Conceptual Metaphor Theory 1–2, 3, 13, 14, 61, 118, 208, 325, 481, 503; conduit metaphor 136; criticism of 24; definition of metaphor 338; 'entailments' 452; Grady's work 112; happy/good metaphors 125; linguistic communication 518; managerial metaphors 401, 402; political discourse 311; primary metaphors 18; structural metaphors 270; terminology 234; translation 254; types of metaphors 269; war metaphors 102, 109
Johnson, Samuel 517
Jordan, J. 376–7
journey metaphors 57, 114, 268; advertising 331–3; architectural discourse 194, 195, 199; blending 34; cancer 385–6, 389, 394–5; Conceptual Metaphor Theory 1, 16–17, 18, 21, 112; embodiment 66; love 221, 222, 270; peace-building and reconciliation 436, 437; physical health 387, 389, 391; political discourse 183, 184; psychotherapy 373, 380; Relevance Theory 42, 50; sign language 270, 274–5, 277n5; systematic metaphors 97–8

Kaal, A. A. 166, 176
Kamler, B. 287–8
Kanner, L. 489
Kant, Immanuel 3
Kasirer, A. 495, 496
Kay, C. 235, 236, 238
Kendon, A. 134, 138
Kesey, Ken 119, 212, 342
Kia 328
Kimmel, M. 183, 215
knowledge 407–9; implicit and explicit 404; knowledge management 403, 410n1; recontextualization of 198; second or foreign language learning 414
Koller, V.: advertising 327; business communication 181, 197–8; corpus linguistics 118, 119, 120; topic-triggered metaphors 183, 377
Koteyko, Nelya 387
Kövecses, Zoltan 13–27, 73; emotions 119–20, 126; gendered metaphors 357–8, 362, 363; linguistic expressions 252; metaphor variation 193–4; novelty 224–5; second or foreign language learning 415
Krennmayr, Tina: identification of metaphor 93; influence of metaphor on reader 289–90; linguistic metaphors 107; textual patterning 182, 183, 186–7
Kress, G. 149, 153, 157

Lakoff, George: argument is war metaphor 76, 78, 520; cognitive linguistics 73; conceptual mapping 28–9, 133, 474; Conceptual

Metaphor Theory 1–2, 3, 13, 14, 61, 118, 208, 325, 481, 503; conduit metaphor 136; criticism of 24; 'dead metaphors' 237–8, 244; definition of metaphor 338; emotions 119–20; 'entailments' 452; framing 298; Gulf war 102–3; invariance hypothesis 15; literary metaphor 155, 209–10; managerial metaphors 401, 402; Master Metaphor List 126; metaphor as communication tool 99; neural theory of metaphor 25; 'one-shot' metaphors 107–8; political discourse 311; primary metaphors 18; public-interest issues 446; science communication 303; structural metaphors 270; terminology 234; translation 254; types of metaphors 269; variation 225; war metaphors 102, 109

language 2–3, 7, 517; acquisition 8, 90, 220, 475; change in 233, 234–7; Conceptual Metaphor Theory 25, 61; conventionality and novelty 219–20; everyday 222; gesture and 64; identification of metaphors in 73–87; linguistic unity 526, 527; neurodevelopmental disorders 489; as power 525, 527; Relevance Theory 43; specific language impairment 486, 487, 488, 490–1, 494, 495, 497; translation 247–62; units of analysis 83; varieties of metaphorical 457–8; windowpane theory of 524; *see also* communication; figurative language; linguistics

Late Middle English 120, 125
Lehrer, A. 239, 473–4
levels of schematicity 36, 38, 39
lexical patterning 222, 223
lexical pragmatics 43, 48–50
lexical units 79–80, 81–2, 83, 85, 170–2, 274
lexicalization 220, 230
lexicon 14, 25
Lindstromberg, S. 416, 510
linguistic metaphors 14, 16–17, 24, 61, 102–16, 503; conventionality 224; corpus data 109–12; current research 114; future directions 85, 114; methodological issues 103–9; neural theory of metaphor 25–6; novel 226–7; parts-of-speech 173; processing 65; Relevance Theory 50; systematic metaphors 88; textual patterning 178, 179, 185, 186; translation 253; understanding 66
linguistics: applied 73, 103; computational 85, 229–30; contrastive 220; deliberate and everyday metaphors 402; discourse 195; Systemic Functional Linguistics 197; *see also* cognitive linguistics; corpus linguistics; language; psycholinguistics
literalization 183–4
literary metaphor 5, 112, 114, 155, 178, 206–18, 342; creativity 345; definition of literature 207; metaphor paranarratives 211–14; textual patterning 179, 180–1, 184, 186

Littlemore, Jeannette 104; communicative competence 414; evaluation 356; identification of metaphor 84, 171; linguistic metaphors 114; metaphoric competence 504, 505; parts-of-speech 169; second or foreign language learning 417, 418, 419, 506–7, 508, 509, 510
Locke, John 309, 310
LOCNESS *see* Louvain Corpus of Native English Essays
Loftus, S. 389, 390
logos 324, 326
Louvain Corpus of Native English Essays (LOCNESS) 509
Low, G. D.: academic discourse 286, 287, 506; applied linguistics 73; communicative competence 414; second or foreign language learning 420, 504; textual patterning 185
Luokkanen, M. 299, 301–2
LwU *see* Living with Uncertainty project

MacArthur, Fiona 114, 169, 291–2, 413–25, 508
McMullen, L. M. 371, 374, 375
McNeill, D. 131, 134, 136, 138
Magee, Patrick 344, 428, 429, 432–7
management 7, 400–12
mapping 50, 75–6, 112–13, 133, 474; blending 32; Conceptual Metaphor Theory 14–15, 28–9, 30; deductive approach 78; double-mapping model 271, 272; extended metaphors 187; five-step method 104, 105, 106, 107; gestures 136, 142; identification of metaphor 75, 77; linguistic metaphors 109, 114; 'metaphor types' 376; metonymy 83; 'one-shot' metaphors 108; primary metaphors 36–7; psychotherapy 374; public understanding 452; sign language 273; stories 348; structure-mapping theory 462, 476, 478
Mapping Metaphor project 128, 239–43, 244n9, 244n10
Martin, J. H. 121, 127
Mashal, N. 493, 495, 496
Maslen, Robert 83, 88–101, 113
meaning: basic 80; contextual 80; coordination during conversation 63–4; dynamical perspective 65; gestures 134, 135, 465; ideational 104; lexical pragmatics 48; literal 52, 53, 183–4, 356, 460–1, 507; metaphor processing 460, 461, 462, 467–8; metaphoric competence 504; novel metaphors 225; parts-of-speech 172; second or foreign language learning 416, 417, 422; sign language 276; *see also* comprehension; polysemy
media 305
medicine 345–6

Index

megametaphor 326
Meir, I. 272, 275
Menand, Louis 523, 524
mental health 371–84
mental imagery 52, 54n9
mental simulations 144
Mergenthaler, E. 373
Merkel, Angela 256
metaphor 1–9, 56–7; acquisition of 474–7, 489, 496–7, 513; architectural discourse 198–203; Aristotle on 310; benefits of 446–8; boundaries of 237–8; conventionality and novelty 219–32; corpus linguistic approaches 117–30; definitions of 193, 207–8, 251, 338, 353, 401–2, 489; directionality of 238–9; in educational contexts 283–95, 413–25; language and communication 517–28; as 'loose use' of language 43, 45–8, 463; 'metaphor types' 376, 377; multimodal texts 131–47, 323–36; negativity bias 430, 434–5, 439; neurodevelopmental disorders 486, 489–97; use of 75, 478–81, 482; variation 193–4; *see also* conceptual metaphors; identification of metaphor; linguistic metaphors; literary metaphor; multimodal metaphors; systematic metaphors
Metaphor Identification Procedure (MIP) 4–5, 8, 74, 79–82, 83, 84–5, 133; parts-of-speech 170–1; *see also* identification of metaphor
Metaphor Identification Procedure Vrije Universiteit (MIPVU) 74, 79–82, 83, 84–5; coding 93; parts-of-speech 170–1; second language learners 509
Metaphor-Led Discourse Analysis 8, 429, 431
metaphor processing 7, 8, 65, 457–71, 474; conceptual metaphor 463–5; difficulty in 460–2; diversity of methods and experiences 458–60; individual differences 466–7; neurodevelopmental disorders 489–90, 492–3; parts-of-speech 167–8, 176; psychotherapy 374–5; Relevance Theory 45, 52, 328; second or foreign language learning 419; stories 345; textual patterning 186; topic and vehicle interaction 462–3; translation 258
metaphoremes 414
metaphoric competence 7, 503–13
metaphorical pattern analysis (MPA) 123–4
metaphoricity: gestures 133, 141, 142, 143; parts-of-speech 165, 167, 168, 170–1
methodological issues 8; Conceptual Metaphor Theory 24; educational contexts 284; gesture 136–42; identification of metaphor 76–82; impoliteness 358; linguistic metaphors 103–9; multimodal metaphors 149–55; neurodevelopmental disorders 488–9; parts-of-speech 170–3; second or foreign language learning 419–20; systematic metaphors 92–6, 97–8; textual patterning 185–6; translation 258
metonymy 8, 28, 160, 235, 353, 458; advertising 329, 333; antisocial online behaviour 359–60, 361, 364n5; evaluation 356; gestures 140, 142; images 35; second or foreign language learning 413–14; sign language 268, 277; voice 523–4
Metropolis (film) 149–50
MIG-G *see* Metaphor Identification Guidelines for Gesture
Miliband, Ed 304
Miller, Carolyn 524
Miller, R. S. 392
'mind styles' 212, 213
MIP *see* Metaphor Identification Procedure
MIPVU *see* Metaphor Identification Procedure Vrije Universiteit
misogyny 359–63
mixing of metaphors 182–3, 374
Mo, S. 491–2
modes: of communication 148–9; of representation 137, 141–2
Moon, R. 224, 225, 511–12
Morgan, Gareth 400, 401, 402–3, 406
motivation 414, 418
MPA *see* metaphorical pattern analysis
MRSA 387
Müller, C. 133, 137, 141, 143
multilingual translation 254–6, 258–9
multimodal metaphors 5, 148–62, 406–7; advertising 334; architectural 200–1; audience responses 154–5; autobiographical comics 156–9; categorization of nonverbal and multimodal metaphors 149–54
Musolff, Andreas 8, 9; animal metaphors 431; linguistic metaphors 113; scenarios 339, 344
myth 404

Nacey, Susan 84, 418
narratives: definition of 337–8; systematic metaphors 96
national security 444–5
negativity bias 430, 434–5, 439
Nerlich, B. 299–300, 301, 302, 303–5, 306, 387
neural theory of metaphor 18–19, 25–6
neurological disorders 466–7
neuroscience 66, 458–60, 463, 465, 467; *see also* brain
New Criticism 208
Newmark, P. 250, 511
news texts: active metaphors 210; illness 386; incidence of metaphor in 84; parts-of-speech 173–6; source identification 305; textual patterning 178–9, 180, 183, 185, 186–7, 188, 190; translation 259

newspapers: climate change 298, 299–300, 301, 304, 305, 306; corpus linguistics 120, 122; immigration discourse 314–15, 316; parts-of-speech 174–5; textual patterning 183; topic-triggered metaphor 183
Newton, Isaac 296
Nietzsche, Friedrich 13
Noble, Denis 450
nominal metaphors 166, 167–8, 169, 285, 481
Nonaka, I. 401, 404, 406
nonverbal metaphors 149–54
nouns 38, 167, 168, 170–5, 176, 348
novelty 5, 57, 220–1, 224–7, 230, 457; advertising 325, 327–8; Aristotle on 472; 'career of metaphor' model 477, 478; comprehension 490; conceptual metaphors 102; conceptualization of novel concepts 478; context 227–8; Graded Salience Hypothesis 496; lexical patterns 22; metaphor processing 460, 462–3; neurodevelopmental/neurological disorders 467, 492, 493, 495, 496; parts-of-speech 167; public-interest issues 448; second language learners 509; textual patterning 181, 182, 187

Obama, Barack 347, 444
offence 6, 353–67; antisocial online behaviour 358–63
Old English 120, 122, 242
online tasks 473
One Flew Over the Cuckoo's Nest (Kesey) 119, 212, 342
'one-shot' metaphors 107–8, 109
online communication 390, 394, 480; immigration discourse 314–16; impoliteness and offence 353–4, 358–63
onomasiological approach 239
onomatopoeia 131–2, 134–5, 267
ontological metaphors 263, 270, 276
'optimal innovation' 228, 230
oral cultures 451
organizational culture 404
orientational metaphors 263, 269–70, 276
Ortiz, M. J. 153
Ortony, Andrew 1, 2, 3, 9
Oshlag, R. S. 286
Ottati, V. 327, 482
Oxford English Corpus 108, 110–12
Oxford English Dictionary (OED) 81, 122, 233–4, 236, 239, 240–1, 244n1
Özçalişkan, S. 476, 477

pain 389, 390, 391
Palestinians 183–4, 426–7, 428
parables 339
paranarratives 211–14, 215
parasite metaphor 314–17

paratelic discourse 349
parsing 140
parts-of-speech 5, 165–77, 241; corpus linguistic approaches 168–70; metaphor recognition and processing 167–8
Pasma, T. 93, 166, 176
pathos 324, 326
patterns 123–4, 178–92, 212, 429–30
Pauwels, E. 296
peace-building 7, 427, 428, 431, 438–9; *see also* reconciliation
Pedroso de Moraes Feltes, H. 113
Pelosi, A. 113
perceptual metaphors 489, 490–1, 496
perceptual resemblance 152, 153
perceptual simulation 348
Perry, Rick 337, 339, 348, 349n1
personality factors 465
personification: advertising 327, 328, 329, 330, 331; architectural discourse 202; parts-of-speech 172–3, 175
perspective-changing 210–11
persuasion: advertising 323–36; gestures 144; political discourse 6, 309, 313, 314, 317; psycholinguistics 482; self-organization 60; textual patterning 186; visual metaphors 148
pervasiveness of metaphors 14
phenomenology 51
Philip, Gill 119, 504
Philip, R. 5, 8, 9
phraseology 222, 223, 504, 505
pictorial metaphors 150–1, 154, 155
Pinder, C. C. 405, 407
Pinker, Stephen 524–5
Plato 310
poetics 207
poetry 210, 211, 215, 342–3
policy framing 430, 445, 449
Polish 254
political discourse 6, 309–22; Arabic speeches 251; argument in 521; Conceptual Metaphor Theory 311–13; corpus linguistics 120; immigration 313–17; political cartoons 153, 154, 342, 347; stories 337, 338, 339, 343, 346, 348; systematic metaphors 89–90, 99; textual patterning 183, 184; translation 255–6, 259
Pollio, H. 179, 181–2, 286
polysemy 14, 28, 77, 240, 458; conceptual metaphors 25, 102; multimodal metaphors 154; second or foreign language learning 413–14, 416, 418, 422; synchronic 234–5; translation 248; *see also* meaning
Pondy, L. R. 404, 406
postmodern approaches 355, 520
post-traumatic stress disorder (PTSD) 376–8
Pound, Ezra 82, 83
power, language as 525, 527

Index

Pragglejaz Group 4, 8, 74, 91, 133; coding 93; translation 252–3
pragmatics 8, 42; advertising 328; discourse-pragmatic studies 325–6; metaphor processing 460, 467–8; Relevance Theory 43, 44, 45, 48–50, 53
prejudice 90, 437
prepositions 172, 419, 422
primary metaphors 15, 18–19, 21, 113, 489; advertising 333; blending 36–7, 38–9; children 496; domains 239; neurodevelopmental disorders 492, 497
process, metaphor as a 133
processing 7, 8, 65, 457–71, 474; advertising 327; conceptual metaphor 463–5; difficulty in 460–2; diversity of methods and experiences 458–60; individual differences 466–7; neurodevelopmental disorders 489–90, 492–3; parts-of-speech 167–8, 176; psychotherapy 374–5; Relevance Theory 45, 52, 328; second or foreign language learning 419; stories 345; textual patterning 186; topic and vehicle interaction 462–3; translation 258
production: neurodevelopmental disorders 489, 494–5; second language learners 507–9
proportional metaphors 475, 478–9
propositional analysis 104–5
propositions 46, 51–2, 54n2, 54n3
proverbs 228–9, 339, 458, 467
psycholinguistics 8, 73, 311, 472–85; cognitive and behavioural processes 92; comprehension 505; conceptual metaphors 464; conventionality 223; diachronic variation 244; dynamical perspective 67; embodied experience 465; interpretation of metaphor 65; metaphor processing 458–60; novel metaphors 225; parts-of-speech 176; political discourse 318; psychotherapy 374–5
PTSD *see* post-traumatic stress disorder
public communication: illness 386, 387–8; public-interest issues 7, 443–54; systematic metaphors 99

qualitative research 376, 387
quantitative research 127, 128, 376, 378, 387
Qur'an 252, 373

racism 316–17
reality construction 17
reception studies 327–8, 333
recognition: metaphor processing 459; metaphoric competence 505; parts-of-speech 165, 167–8; textual patterning 186; *see also* identification of metaphor
reconciliation 7, 179, 182, 344, 426–42; practitioner-oriented model of empathy 435–7
recontextualization 198, 297, 331, 333

recurrence 181, 185, 189, 190
Reddy, Michael 136–7, 518
referential function of gestures 137, 139–40, 143
register 5, 84, 290; genre and 197; linguistic metaphors 114; parts-of-speech 166, 170, 173; political discourse 318; science 296–7; textual patterning 187–90
Reich, Robert 521
Reid, Melanie 393
Reisfield, G. M. 388, 393
Relevance Theory 4, 42–55, 328, 463, 472, 494; lexical pragmatics 48–50; linguistic underspecification 43–5; metaphor as 'loose use' 45–8
reliability 82, 84, 91–2
religion: allegory 339; Antonio Federici advertising controversy 330–1; climate change metaphors 300–1
repetition 179–81, 185, 189, 190, 226, 374
resemblance metaphors 457
rhetoric 61, 207, 297; advertising 324; Aristotle 326; climate change 297; political discourse 310–11; science 296
Ricoeur, Paul 207, 208, 211
'ripple effect' 449
Ritchie, L. David 6, 109–10, 337–52, 446
Romaine, S. 299, 300
Romanian 254–5
Romney, Mitt 337, 339, 348
Russian 134, 254
Russill, C. 297, 302

Santa Ana, O. 431, 432
Santa Cruz, M. 465
sarcasm 490
Sarpavaara, H. 373
scenarios 113, 339, 356; political discourse 312, 314; stories 344; systematic metaphors 96
'schema refreshment' 211
schematicity, levels of 36, 38, 39
schizophrenia 467, 486, 488, 491–2, 493, 495
Schön, Donald 297, 430, 445, 447
Schwabe, M. 387, 391
science 6, 196, 197, 210, 296–308, 486; adult education 286, 287; 'carbon' language 303–5; contextual model 296, 303; deficit model 296–7; novel concepts 478; positivist view of 524; translation metaphor 198
second or foreign language (S/FL) learning 3, 7, 8–9, 413–25; metaphoric competence 503–15; parts-of-speech 169, 176; research methods 419–20
selective projection 30
self-organization 58–60, 62–3, 64, 67, 465
'selfish gene' 450
semantic change 5–6, 233, 234–5

semantic coding 466
semantic elaboration 419
semantic fields 474, 475
Sementelli, A. J. 403, 406
Semino, Elena 73, 104, 432; advertising 324–5; corpus linguistics 122, 127; definition of metaphor 338; 'discourse metaphors' 185; evaluation 356; genre 196, 198; linguistic metaphors 107, 108–9, 110, 114; recontextualization 331; signalling 184; textual patterning 178, 179–80, 181, 182, 185–6, 212
semiotics 134
sensory metaphors 489, 491, 492, 495
Shakespeare, William 17, 43, 52–3, 63, 75, 233, 234, 264, 342
Short, Mick 104, 107, 108–9, 110, 208
Shuttleworth, M. 254, 258
sign language 6, 8, 9, 263–79; critical issues and debates 272–5; current research 275–6; form-meaning pairings 135; formational features of 264–8; future directions 276–7; overview of research 268–72
signalling 184, 186–7, 188–90, 289–90, 389, 506
signs 75
similarity 17–18, 28, 247, 385, 473, 475, 479
simile 8, 37, 75; Aristotle on 310; blending 40n7; 'career of metaphor' model 477; literary metaphor 207, 215; pictorial 150; processing 462–3; second language learners 511; textual patterning 181, 182
simultaneous cueing 152
single-scope blends 32, 33, 40n6
Sjørup, A. C. 257, 258
Sketchengine 110–11
Skorczynska, H. 198
SL *see* source language
SLI *see* specific language impairment
Smith, Red 522
Snaevarr, S. 337, 338, 339
social context 62
social media 297, 358–63
social psychology 355, 482
social semiotic theory 149
soft-assembly 58, 63
'soft-sell' advertising techniques 324, 329, 334
Sontag, Susan 386, 388, 392, 405
source domains 74, 133, 268; aesthetic expression 479; blending 32; cognitive linguistics 66; Conceptual Metaphor Theory 14–18, 19–21, 23, 29–30, 503; corpus linguistics 103, 112, 118–19, 120, 122; deductive approach 78; discourse 34; five-step method 107; framing 385; gestures 137, 142, 143; identification of metaphor 77; Mapping Metaphor project 241; metaphor processing 462; metaphorical pattern analysis 123; multimodal metaphors 148–9; parts-of-speech 168; primary metaphors 113; propositional analysis 105; psychotherapy 372, 374, 376, 377, 378; second or foreign language learning 415–16; structure-mapping theory 476; textual patterning 181, 183, 186; visual metaphors 150, 151, 152, 155
source language (SL) 249, 250–1, 252
Spanish 102, 119, 194, 254–5, 413, 417–18
specific language impairment (SLI) 486, 487, 495, 497; ASD comparison 488; comprehension 490–1; prevalence 497n1; production studies 494
speech 134–5
Spenser, E. 341
Sperber, D. 45, 48, 50, 51, 54n4, 54n8, 451
sports 120, 327, 521
state metaphors 22
Steen, Gerald J.: expressions 187; five-step method 103, 104–8; identification of metaphor 4, 8, 73–87, 93; literary metaphor 209, 210, 342; methods 115; parts-of-speech 166, 167, 172, 173; textual patterning 185, 187–8
Stefanowitsch, A. 103, 120, 123, 124, 126–7
Stelma, J. 179, 182, 185
stereotypes 327, 334, 357, 362–3, 437
Stites, L. 476, 477
stories 6, 337–52; comprehension studies 490; definition of 338; organizational culture 404; systematic metaphors 96
strategy development 407
structural metaphors 270, 274
structure-mapping theory 462, 476, 478
Strunk, W. 523, 525
style, writing 524–5
stylistics 73, 208, 215
Susskind, Patrick 342
Swedish 253
Sweetser, E. 39n1, 40n7, 112; domains 239, 240; levels of schematicity 36; literary metaphor 114; semantic change 235; usage of metaphor 234
Swindlehurst, K. 119, 212
symbolism 186
symbols 159–60
synaesthesia 495
systematic metaphors 5, 88–101, 113; peace-building and reconciliation 429; research methods 92–6; textual patterning 179
Systemic Functional Linguistics 197
systems perspective *see* dynamical systems perspective

tacit knowledge 404
takeovers 402
target domains 74, 133; aesthetic expression 479; blending 32; Conceptual Metaphor

Theory 14–18, 19–21, 23, 29–30, 503; corpus linguistics 118–19, 120, 122, 127; deductive approach 78; framing 385; gestures 137, 142; identification of metaphor 77; linguistic metaphors 114; metaphor processing 462; metaphorical pattern analysis 123; multimodal metaphors 148–9; primary metaphors 113; propositional analysis 105; psychotherapy 372, 374, 376, 377, 378; structure-mapping theory 476; visual metaphors 150, 151, 152, 155
target language (TL) 249, 250–1, 252, 258
Taub, S. 267, 271–2
Tcaciuc, L. S. M. 254–5
teachers: children's education 284–5; second or foreign language learning 421, 422, 510; teacher training 288–9
television 328
telic discourse 349
tenor 208, 259n1
terrorism, perceptions of 91, 92–6
textbooks 510–11
texts: literary metaphor 211; multimodal 5, 148–62; response to 289–90; written 135, 149, 226
textual patterning 178–92, 212
Theory of Mind (ToM) 467, 491–2, 493, 494, 496
Thibodeau, P. H. 289, 303, 312, 430, 445–6, 450
Thomas, Francis-Noël 524
thought 16–17, 50, 61, 73–4, 76, 219–20, 222; *see also* cognitive linguistics; conceptual metaphors
time 476–7; ambiguous 464–5; time-scales 62, 63, 67, 465
TL *see* target language
Tolmie, S. 340, 341
ToM *see* Theory of Mind
topics 94–6, 97–8, 259n1, 474; discourse 195; educational contexts 285; genres 203; gestures 142, 143; 'invisible' metaphors 506; metaphor processing 462; structure-mapping theory 476; textual patterning 178; topic-triggered metaphors 183, 377
transcription 93
transfer 44
translation 9, 247–62; multilingual 254–6, 258–9; procedures/methods 249–51; second language learners 511–13; translatability of metaphor 249; translation metaphor in science 198
trauma 376–8
Trim, R. 236, 237, 243
trolling 355, 358
tropes 6, 29, 39, 405
tuning devices 120
Turner, Mark: blending 4, 33, 40n6, 342; literary metaphor 155, 209–10; parables 339; scenarios 344; variation 225; writing style 524
Twitter 297, 359–63

Under the Skin (Faber) 206–7, 210, 211–14, 215
understanding 7, 43, 53, 460, 463; communicative competence 505; dynamical perspective 65; embodied nature of 66–7; neurodevelopmental disorders 490–2; *see also* comprehension
units of analysis 83, 138, 170–1, 179; *see also* lexical units
usage approach 75

validity 82, 84, 92, 420
values 284–5, 297, 326, 333
Van Leeuwen, T. 153, 157
Van Mulken, M. 154–5, 160
variation 5, 193–4, 225; across languages 6; diachronic 233–46, 312, 333; intra- and cross-cultural 312, 318; news texts 175; psychotherapy 375
Veale, Tony 229, 230
vehicles 96, 97, 208, 259n1, 345; coding 93–4; educational contexts 285; influence of 430; labels 432; metaphor processing 462; stories 348; structure-mapping theory 476; vehicle construction 166
verbal images 152
verbo-pictorial metaphors 151–2
verbs: metaphor processing 466; parts-of-speech 166, 167–71, 173–4, 175–6; peace-building and reconciliation 436; second or foreign language learning 415, 416–17, 419, 511; stories 348; vehicle labels 432
Vereza, S. 109, 110
Vince, R. 405, 406, 410
VisMet project 159
visual aids 417–18, 420–1, 422
visual metaphors 17, 35, 148; architectural texts 200–1, 202–3; audience responses 154–5; autobiographical comics 156–9; categorization of 149–54; neurodevelopmental disorders 491, 492; sign language 269
visual salience 143
visualization 51
vital relations 31
voice 523–4, 527
VU Amsterdam Metaphor Corpus 127, 169, 173, 174

war metaphors: advertising 17, 331–3; argument is war metaphor 30, 32–3, 50, 104–7, 520–2, 527; business communication 198; cancer 34, 74, 385–6, 388, 392–6; climate change 298–300; Conceptual Metaphor Theory 29–30, 102, 112; corpus linguistics 109–10, 120;

identification of metaphor 73, 76–9; PCTR project 94; physical health 387, 388, 392, 396; Relevance Theory 42; textual patterning 181
Wearing, C. 51, 53
web data 229–30
Wee, L. 198, 376
Weinstein H. M. 427, 428
White E. B. 523, 525
Wilcox, P. P. 269–70, 277n5
Williams, D. 494, 496
William's syndrome (WS) 486, 488, 490, 492, 495, 496
Wilson, D. 45, 48, 50, 51, 54n4, 54n8
Wilson, G. R. 388, 393
Wmatrix 74, 122, 390
women 357–8, 359–63, 364
word classes *see* parts-of-speech
WordNet database 121
writing processes 522–4
writing style 524–5
written texts 135, 149, 226
WS *see* William's syndrome

Zinsser, William 524, 525

Taylor & Francis eBooks

Helping you to choose the right eBooks for your Library

Add Routledge titles to your library's digital collection today. Taylor and Francis ebooks contains over 50,000 titles in the Humanities, Social Sciences, Behavioural Sciences, Built Environment and Law.

Choose from a range of subject packages or create your own!

Benefits for you
- Free MARC records
- COUNTER-compliant usage statistics
- Flexible purchase and pricing options
- All titles DRM-free.

Benefits for your user
- Off-site, anytime access via Athens or referring URL
- Print or copy pages or chapters
- Full content search
- Bookmark, highlight and annotate text
- Access to thousands of pages of quality research at the click of a button.

REQUEST YOUR FREE INSTITUTIONAL TRIAL TODAY

Free Trials Available
We offer free trials to qualifying academic, corporate and government customers.

eCollections – Choose from over 30 subject eCollections, including:

Archaeology	Language Learning
Architecture	Law
Asian Studies	Literature
Business & Management	Media & Communication
Classical Studies	Middle East Studies
Construction	Music
Creative & Media Arts	Philosophy
Criminology & Criminal Justice	Planning
Economics	Politics
Education	Psychology & Mental Health
Energy	Religion
Engineering	Security
English Language & Linguistics	Social Work
Environment & Sustainability	Sociology
Geography	Sport
Health Studies	Theatre & Performance
History	Tourism, Hospitality & Events

For more information, pricing enquiries or to order a free trial, please contact your local sales team:
www.tandfebooks.com/page/sales

Routledge — Taylor & Francis Group
The home of Routledge books

www.tandfebooks.com

Printed in Great Britain
by Amazon